The Merovingian Kingdoms
450–751

Ian Wood

LONGMAN
London and New York

Longman Group UK Limited
Longman House, Burnt Mill,
Harlow, Essex CM20 2JE, England
and Associated Companies throughout the world.

Published in the United States of America
by Longman Publishing, New York

© Longman Group UK Limited 1994

First published 1994

ISBN 0 582 218780 CSD
ISBN 0 582 49372 2 PPR

British Library Cataloguing-in-Publication Data

A catalogue record for this book is
available from the British Library

Library of Congress Cataloging in Publication Data
Wood, I. N. (Ian N.), 1950–
The Merovingian Kingdoms, 450–751 / Ian Wood.
p.   cm.
Includes bibliographical references and index.
ISBN 0-582-21878-0. -- ISBN 0-582-49372-2 (pbk.)
1. Merovingians. 2. France--History--To 987. 3. France--Church
history--To 987. 4. France--Kings and rulers--History. I. Title.
DC65.W48 1993
940'. 013--dc20   92-46027
                                                                                          CIP

Set by 7 in 10/12 Bembo
Produced by Longman Singapore Publishers (Pte) Ltd.
Printed in Singapore

Contents

List of Abbreviations

AASS	*Acta Sanctorum.*
CSEL	*Corpus Scriptorum Ecclesiasticorum Latinorum* (Vienna).
MGH	*Monumenta Germaniae Historica*
AA	*Auctores Antiquissimi* (Berlin, 1877–1919).
Epistolae	(Berlin, 1887–).
Formulae	*Formulae Merowingici et Karolini Aevi* (Hannover, 1886).
Leges	*Leges Nationum Germanicarum* (Hannover/Leipzig, 1892–).
SRG in usum scholarum	*Scriptores Rerum Germanicarum in usum scholarum seperatim* editi (Hannover/Leipzig, 1871–).
SRM	*Scriptores Rerum Merowingicarum* (Hannover/Leipzig, 1885–1951).
SS	*Scriptores* (Hannover/Leipzig, 1826–1934).
Pardessus, *Diplomata*	J.M. Pardessus, *Diplomata Chartae, Epistolae, Leges ad res Gallo-Francicas spectantia* (Paris, 1843–9).
Pertz, *Diplomata*	G.H. Pertz, *Diplomata regum Francorum e stirpe Merowingica, MGH, Diplomatum Imperii 1* (Hannover, 1872).
Pertz, *Diplomata Spuria*	G.H. Pertz, *Diplomata regum Francorum e stirpe Merowingica, MGH, Diplomatum Imperii 1* (Hannover, 1872).
Pertz, *Diplomata Arnulforum*	G.H. Perz, *Diplomata maiorum, domus e stirpe Arnulforum, MGH, Diplomatum Imperii 1* (Hannover, 1872) *Patrologia Latina.*

Preface

This book has been a very long time in the making. That it should have taken so long to write has much to do with the pressure placed on British universities in the 1980s. This background has doubtless also had its impact on the emphasis placed here on the political power of women.

There have, however, been other gains from the long delays in this book's completion. I have benefited from the advice of European and American friends whom I knew scarcely, if at all, ten years ago. In particular I have learnt much from Hartmut Atsma, Evangelos Chrysos, Alain Dierkens, Martin Heinzelmann, Stephane Lebecq, Patrick Périn and Herwig Wolfram on this side of the Atlantic, and from Dick Gerberding, Kathleen Mitchell, Tom Noble, Barbara Rosenwein and Walter Goffart in the United States and Canada. Dick, Tom and Barbara read the whole text in draft, and generously offered advice on how to improve what I had written. I have been equally fortunate in my friends in Britain. All who have worked at the weekends arranged by Wendy Davies at her house in Bucknell have helped in one way or another. Most especially, Patrick Wormald offered generous and searching criticism of my views of Merovingian law, while Paul Fouracre and Jinty Nelson scrutinized every chapter, improving the whole immeasurably. So thorough were Jinty's comments that her daughter once concluded that I was a student having an essay returned!

Inevitably there are more general debts, to friends, colleagues and teachers who have influenced my work; among them Peter Brown, Thomas Charles-Edwards, David Farmer, Edward James, John Le Patourel, Robert Markus, John Matthews, Sabine McCormack, Peter Sawyer and Michael Wallace-Hadrill; to students who have asked awkward questions; also to numerous librarians, in Oxford, London, especially at the Institute of Historical Research, and the Brotherton Library, Leeds, who have made the task of research easier than it might have been.

Finally, in the long course of working on Merovingian history I have incurred many personal debts; especially to Romaine and Timmy, who thought I would be better off working on a different kind of Burgundy than that of Avitus of Vienne, and above all to my parents. As a child, every summer holiday included a trip to the south of France, and on the drive down and back each year my mother had the task of reading a child's history of France from cover to cover. The origins of this book go back to those journeys.

INW
26 October 1992

Introduction: Constructing Merovingian History

In the history of Europe the period between the end of the Roman Empire in the fifth century and the cessation of Viking raids in the eleventh is one of particular importance. It was a time of transition, or rather transitions, from a Mediterranean-based empire to a world of states which were to develop into those of modern Europe. Within these six centuries of transition, the earliest saw the greatest changes: the collapse of the Empire and the first emergence of what might be called the Nation State. It was the fifth century that saw the origins of France and the sixth that saw those of England. And if the lines of development from Visigothic Spain and from Ostrogothic and Lombard Italy to their modern counterparts were not to be so direct, they nevertheless marked major developments in the transformation of the Roman World.

Within the first three centuries which followed the end of Roman rule the kingdom which emerged in France, Belgium, the Rhineland and Switzerland holds a preeminent place. Of the states which succeeded the Roman Empire it was the longest lasting. It was also, for much of the time, the most powerful. Nevertheless it has had a bad press. The reasons for this are complex, but two stand out. First the dynasty which ruled the Frankish kingdom from 481 to 751, the Merovingian dynasty, was subject to a *damnatio memoriae* by the family which usurped its power, the Carolingians. Nor was this *damnatio memoriae* difficult to effect. Despite their achievements the Merovingians themselves had been the subject of hostile comment from the late sixth century onwards. The historian Gregory of Tours thought that the Merovingians failed for the most part to live up to the example of their great forebear Clovis I (481–511). The next major historian to write about the Franks, the seventh-century chronicler Fredegar, implicitly compared Clovis's sons to bears and wolves and his grandsons to dogs.[1] The second reason for the bad press which has greeted the Merovingian Age is its lack of great cultural figures. The kingdom of the Franks produced no equivalent to

---

1. Fredegar, III 12.

pope Gregory the Great, to the Visigothic writer Isidore of Seville, or to the English theologian and historian Bede. For this reason the development of European culture is usually seen as running from the Mediterranean to Northumbria, returning to the kingdom of the Franks only in the eighth century when English missionaries crossed the Channel to work on the continent.[2] At the most schematic of levels this reading may have some sense, but it is so much of a simplification of the cultural history of the period that it amounts to no more than a travesty. The Merovingian kingdom was not the cultural backwater it is often represented as having been; nor is its failure to produce a scholar of the stature of Gregory I, Isidore and Bede enough to eclipse its importance as the greatest state in western Europe.

Yet, although the kingdom of the Franks was important, its history, like all early medieval history, is difficult to reconstruct. And here lies a further reason for the comparative underestimation of its importance. For the reconstruction of the narrative history of early medieval Europe we are never lavishly equipped. There are historical narratives, including those of Isidore for the Visigoths, Paul the Deacon for the Lombards and Bede for the Anglo-Saxons. To some extent the kingdom of the Franks is well served, with Gregory of Tours, Fredegar and his continuators, the early-eighth-century *Liber Historiae Francorum* and the Carolingian *Annales Mettenses Priores*. None of these, however, provide a detailed account of the later seventh century. There is, therefore, a crucial lacuna in the narrative of Merovingian history which is not easily filled.

There is a further problem. Although the seventh century poses particular difficulties of reconstruction, it is an act of delusion to think that Gregory of Tours, any more than the other early medieval historians, is an accurate witness. Certainly he is not as obviously biased and suspect as the *Annales Mettenses Priores*. Nevertheless he has his own axes to grind, and at times this unquestionably led him to falsify evidence.[3] Our sources have the limitations of any source: even allowing for their inadequate knowledge, they each present an incomplete account of events, by means of interpretation, falsification and omission, depending on their form and intentions. For periods where the documentation is extensive it is possible to some extent to counteract the problems posed by suspect evidence by comparing accounts of the same event, and by overlaying the information so as to limit, though never to remove entirely, the danger of being hoodwinked by a rogue document. There is rarely enough contiguous evidence in the early medieval period to make this possible. It is often impossible to be absolutely certain of what took place or when it happened.

One result of this is that a valid narrative of the Frankish, or any early medieval kingdom, is scarcely possible. At the same time, given the established traditions of historical writing, a non-narrative history of the

2. e.g. C. Dawson, *The Making of Europe*.
3. e.g. I.N. Wood, 'Gregory of Tours and Clovis', *Revue Belge de Philologie et d'Histoire* 63 (1985), p. 257.

Merovingians would not make easy reading for anyone unfamiliar with the range of documentation. For this reason I have attempted to offer a narrative of sorts within this book, while at the same time trying to indicate the difficulties in constructing that narrative. In order to do so I have tended to set out in each chapter an account of events as provided by one or more sources, and also to analyse the account and the events.

This book is a narrative history only in so far as narrative is an aid to comprehension. Each chapter is more concerned with a theme or issue than with a reconstruction of what happened. The themes have, however, been set out in a roughly chronological order. Thus the sixth century has been divided up into chapters on the creation of the Merovingian State, its structure, the power of the Church, the problem of civil war, the position of the queen and the importance of legislation. This order is intended to reflect the coming to the fore of certain problems in the development of the kingdom. Almost every chapter, therefore, is intended both to move the narrative forward as well as to analyse an issue.

The issues I have chosen to analyse have most often been determined by the sources. My approach has not been determined by established historical debates. This is a natural concomitant of my emphasis on the problems of narrative and documentation. For many of the historical debates which have raged about the early Middle Ages there is simply not the evidence to solve them one way or the other, however vital we may think the issue in question. In time new ways may be found to approach the problems of the Frankish aristocracy, of Merovingian and early Carolingian armies, or that of royal land. As yet, however, there are many questions which can be answered, but which have not received due attention. By concentrating on some of these it may be possible to construct some foundations for a future, more adventurous, and problem-based reading of Merovingian history.

As it stands this book is primarily an account of the politics, in the widest sense of the word, of the Merovingian period. This may seem odd in the light of problems of accuracy posed by the sources. It is, however, precisely these problems which have prompted the political nature of my reconstruction. The sources may not provide an accurate account of political events. On the other hand no early medieval writer set pen to papyrus or parchment without good reason: the reasons usually involved power or land. More often than not, therefore, an understanding of our sources involves an understanding of the politics of the early Middle Ages, even if that understanding is sometimes limited to an appreciation of the aims of the author, rather than an acceptance of his or her information.

If, in certain respects, a largely political history of the Merovingian period may seem limited, it has a particular value. Although the Merovingian kingdom in the seventh century had no historian to compare with Bede, it produced a comparatively large amount of other evidence, including a number of early saints' *Lives* and also charters. As a result, despite the difficulties of providing a coherent narrative, it is possible to reconstruct the political structures of the Merovingian kingdom in more detail than is possible for those of other contemporary states. In this way the Merovingian kingdom may provide a model for understanding the politics of the Visigothic, Lombard and Anglo-Saxon kingdoms. Indeed there are a number of ways in which Merovingian political history sheds light on and is linked to that of its neighbours. A history of the kingdom of the Franks is thus more than an account of one successor state; it is more even than the account of the greatest of those states, with all the implications that that may have for the first three centuries following the collapse of Roman in the west. It is also an analysis of early medieval politics.

Chapter One

The Barbarians in Gaul

In 476 the west Roman Empire came to an end with the deposition of Romulus Augustulus. It was replaced by a number of states ruled by barbarian kings. By the early sixth century Italy was in the hands of the Ostrogoths; France was divided between the Franks, the Burgundians and the Visigoths, who also controlled Spain; what had been the Roman province of Africa had been transformed into the Vandal kingdom. A century later the map had been slightly redrawn, with the Lombards controlling northern Italy, the Franks unchallenged in France, and peoples known variously as Angles and Saxons dominant in much of the old diocese of *Britannia*. It was the kingdom of the Franks which was to exercise most influence for the longest period of time. For the first three centuries of its existence, until 751, it was ruled over by a single family, that of the Merovingians. Merovingian history deserves detailed study in its own right, but it also needs to be understood in the broader context of Late Antique and early medieval history. This broader context is particularly important for an understanding of the earliest stages of the creation of the Frankish kingdom, for the Franks and the Merovingians were relatively late participants in the crisis which saw the collapse of the western Empire and the establishment of the successor states. The collapse of imperial power in Gaul and Germany, and the activities of the Visigoths and Burgundians provide a necessary background for early Merovingian history.

The coming of the barbarians

The Roman dioceses of Gaul and the Seven Provinces, which were to constitute most of the Frankish kingdom, essentially covered what is now France, Belgium, Germany west of the Rhine, and most of Switzerland. Geographically this territory is extremely varied, including Mediterranean, Atlantic and Channel coasts, the river valleys of northern France, of western Germany and of Burgundy, together with the western Alps and the mountains of central France. Culturally it was equally diverse. To a large extent the areas nearest to the Mediterranean were the most civilized, but there were cities further north with important cultural traditions, including Lyons, Bordeaux and Autun, and there were other cities, including Trier and Paris, which had at times been the residences of emperors. Taken as a whole, by the late fourth century the two dioceses had gained much from four centuries of Roman rule. Not that those centuries had been times of uninterrupted peace. There had been civil wars in plenty, and major barbarian incursions, particularly in the north-eastern provinces of Germany and *Belgica*. Even in times of peace it required constant vigilance to keep the peoples across the Rhine in check. But for the most part the frontier troops had succeeded in their task of keeping the barbarians at bay.

Then, on the last night of the year 406, or so one of our sources claims,[1] the frozen Rhine was crossed by a number of barbarian groups, including Vandals, Alans and Sueves. As a result the German frontier was broken, and for the next two years the provinces of Germany and Gaul were plundered by the invaders. Although the majority of these barbarians moved on to Spain in 409, some stayed behind: there were Alans active in Gaul under their leader Goar for the next thirty years; they were to be settled in *Gallia Ulterior*, that is on land to the north of the Loire, in the 440s.[2] Elsewhere, any respite that was felt in 409 was short lived; in 412 another barbarian people, the Visigoths, crossed to Gaul from Italy, where they had sacked the city of Rome in 410. They established themselves in the south-west, and their king, Athaulf, held court in Narbonne.[3]

The Visigoths

The Visigoths had been a sedentary people living north of the Danube. In the sixth century they were said to have come originally from the island of Scandza, to have migrated to the Black Sea, and thence to have come into contact with the Roman Empire. The historical value of their origin legend is open to question; a national migration from the Baltic is unlikely, but the story may have been built out of traditions relating to specific groups which had played a part in the formation of the Gothic nation at various stages in its history.[4] From the mid-third century the Goths certainly impinged on the Empire, launching raids against the Balkans and Asia Minor. Subsequently relations between the Romans and Visigoths improved and the latter were relatively peaceful. In 376, however, the Visigoths found themselves under extreme pressure from the Huns, an Asiatic people from the steppes. The majority of them negotiated entry into the Roman Empire under the

1. Prosper, *Chronicle*, 1230
2. *Chronicle of 452*, 127; Constantius, *Vita Germani* VI 28.
3. H. Wolfram, *History of the Goths*, pp. 161–3.
4. Wolfram, *History of the Goths*, p. 12.

leadership of Fritigern. Harsh treatment by the Romans over the next two years transformed the refugees into a people fighting for survival, and in 378 they defeated and killed the Roman Emperor, Valens, at the battle of Adrianople. Thereafter they moved around the Balkans, sometimes in open war with the Romans, sometimes bound by treaty. In 401 they entered the western part of the Empire, under the leadership of Alaric I. Once again they oscillated between friendship with the Romans and outright hostility, depending on the possibility of imperial recognition and acceptance. The sack of Rome in 410 marked the most hostile period in the relations between Alaric and the imperial court. Within a year of the sack Alaric died and in 412 his brother-in-law, Athaulf, led his people out of Italy and into Gaul.[5]

At first Athaulf joined a confederacy of Burgundians and Alans, which had established the usurping emperor Jovinus in power, but he soon abandoned the usurper and his brother for an alliance with the legitimate emperor, Honorius. What he wanted was a position within the Empire – according to the historian Orosius, he wished to support Rome with barbarian arms.[6] When negotiations with Honorius failed to bring rewards Athaulf showed both his anger and his desire to be associated with the Empire by marrying the emperor's sister, Galla Placidia, who had been a captive since 410. Then, in 415, he moved to Spain, where he was murdered. His successor but one, Wallia, made an attempt to lead his people across to Africa, but failed, and instead came to terms with the Roman leader Constantius, for whom he campaigned against the Vandals and Alans in Spain. Subsequently, perhaps in 418, perhaps in 419, a new treaty brought the Visigoths back to Aquitaine.[7]

After they had been settled in Aquitaine the Visigoths were relatively loyal to the Roman state, although in 422 they deserted the Romans during a campaign against the Vandals in Spain. At the same time, the conflict between competing factions among the Romans themselves meant that the Visigoths could intervene against one or other party, or try to exploit the situation for their own gain. Thus, they took advantage of the confusion surrounding the usurpation of the emperor Joannes in 423, and the subsequent establishment of Valentinian III, to attack Arles in 425. They did the same in 430 when trouble was brewing between the two Roman generals, Aëtius and Boniface, and in 433 they supported Galla Placidia against Aëtius. In 436 the Visigothic king Theoderid tried to expand his territory towards the Rhône valley, but was checked by Aëtius and his general Litorius. In 438, however, Litorius was captured and killed when he attacked the Visigoths at Toulouse. Nevertheless, Theoderid did fight for the Romans against the Sueves in Spain in 446, and in 451 he provided the most substantial portion of the confederacy which

5. Wolfram, *History of the Goths* pp. 161–2; P. Heather, *Goths and Romans 332–489*, pp. 219–20.

6. Orosius, *Historia adversos Paganos*, VII 43, 4–7.

7. Wolfram, *History of Goths*, pp. 170–4; Heather, *Goths and Romans*, pp. 220–1; I. N. Wood, 'Continuity or calamity?: the constraints of literary models', in J. Drinkwater and H. Elton, eds, *Fifth-Century Gaul: A Crisis of Identity*, p. 15.

faced Attila and the Huns at the battle of the Catalaunian Plains. The battle saw the defeat of Attila, and the end of his invasion of Gaul. It also saw the death of Theoderid.[8]

The causes of Attila's decision to attack Gaul in 451 are obscure, although legends explaining it circulated from very early on. Some thought that he had been paid to attack the Visigoths by Gaiseric, king of the Vandals, who were now settled in North Africa; others that he was making good a claim to be the husband of princess Honoria, daughter of Valentinian III, or that he was intervening in a dispute over the succession to the kingship of the Franks.[9] What is certain is that Attila's decision to invade Gaul marked the failure of Aëtius's policies, which had depended on using the Huns to further his own career in Italy, and to keep the barbarians in check in Gaul. Having been a hostage among the Huns himself, he had called in Hunnic troops to support the usurper Joannes in 425; he fled to them after his defeat at the hands of Boniface in 432; and he was probably behind their destruction of the Burgundian kingdom in the mid-430s.[10] Granted this set of policies, Aëtius can scarcely have been well placed to gather the confederacy which kept Attila in check at the Catalaunian Plains. A man better placed to gain the support of the Visigoths was Avitus, praetorian prefect of Gaul from 439. In 455 the Goths were to be the prime movers in his elevation to imperial office.[11]

The Burgundians

The Visigoths were the first of the barbarian peoples to be formally settled within Gaul. The Alans, who were given land around Valence in *c.* 440, and in *Gallia Ulterior* two years later, were the second.[12] The third major group to be settled were the Burgundians, who were apparently given *Sapaudia* a year after the grant of *Gallia Ulterior* to the Alans. Although the name Savoy later developed out of *Sapaudia*, the area in question seems to have lain to the north of Geneva.[13]

By the ninth century the Burgundians were thought to have come from Scandinavia. This legend was probably developed in emulation of those relating to the early years of the Goths. In reality, like the Visigoths, they had long been neighbours of the Romans. Pliny knew of the Burgundians, and

8. Wolfram, *History of the Goths*, pp. 173–8.

9. John of Antioch, fr. 199 (2); Priscus, fr. 15, 16; cited in C.D. Gordon, *The Age of Attila*, pp. 104–6.

10. Gordon, *The Age of Attila*, pp. 45–50.

11. Wolfram, *History of the Goths*, p. 179.

12. *Chronicle of 452*, 124, 127.

13. *Chronicle of 452*, 128; on the difficulties of this entry, see Wood, 'Continuity or calamity?: the constraints of literary models', p. 15; on the region, see P. Duparc, 'La Sapaudia', *Comptes rendus de l'Academie des Inscriptions et Belles-Lettres* (1958), pp. 371–83.

Orosius thought that they had reached the Rhineland in the days of the emperor Tiberius, receiving their name because they lived in settlements called *burgi*. His account of their arrival and his etymology for their name cannot be trusted. The Burgundians first come fully into view in the pages of Ammianus Marcellinus, where they are to be found to the east of the Rhine. The emperor Valentinian I enlisted their support against the Alamans in 369. Ammianus also thought that they were descended from the Romans. Biologically this cannot be true, but it may be an assertion of political friendship and thus relate to Valentinian's diplomacy.[14]

Burgundians may have been involved in the crossing of the Rhine in 406. Six years later their ruler Guntiarius joined Goar, ruler of the Alans, to set up Jovinus as emperor.[15] Guntiarius appears again as ruler of a Burgundian kingdom in the Rhineland which was destroyed by the Huns in *c.* 435.[16] Shortly after, at a date given both as 443 and 447 by the same chronicle source, they were settled in *Sapaudia*.[17] The seventh-century chronicler Fredegar thought that they were given lands by the Gallo-Roman aristocracy, who thereby gained tax exemption in the days of Valentinian I.[18] It may be that this information actually relates to the reign of Valentinian III, and therefore that it is the same as the grant of *Sapaudia*, but this is by no means certain. More than one treaty is known to have been made with the Burgundians, although some may not have had imperial approval. Thus, Marius of Avenches records a land division made with Gallo-Roman senators, under the year 456, that is at the time of the fall of the emperor Avitus.[19] His successor, Majorian, apparently overthrew this arrangement, pushing the Burgundians out of the environs of Lyons in 458.[20]

The behaviour of those Burgundians who settled within the Empire is similar to that of the Visigoths. They campaigned for the Romans, for instance at the battle of the Catalaunian Plains.[21] At the same time they also exploited the current political situation for their own ends. In 455, the year after Aëtius's murder, and the year in which Valentinian III was assassinated, they were clearly extending their territory, since they are recorded as being driven back by the Gepids.[22] The expansion recorded by Marius under the following year was probably made with the connivance of Avitus, or in the aftermath of his deposition. For the most part, from the reign of Valentinian I through to the early fifth century, the Burgundians were among the most

14. I. N. Wood, 'Ethnicity and the ethnogenesis of the Burgundians', in H. Wolfram and W. Pohl, eds, *Typen der Ethnogenese unter besonderer Berücksichtigung der Bayern*, 1, p. 58.

15. Olympiodorus, fr, 17, cited in Gordon, *The Age of Attila*, p. 39.

16. Prosper, *Chronicle* 1322; Hydatius, *Chronicle*, 108; *Chronicle of 452*, 118.

17. *Chronicle of 452*, 128.

18. Fredegar, II 46.

19. Marius of Avenches, *Chronicle*, s.a. 456; *Auctarium Havniense*, s.a. 457, 2.

20. Sidonius Apollinaris, carm, V, ll. 564–7.

21. Jordanes, *Getica* XXXVI 191.

22. *Auctarium Havniense*, s.a. 455, 5.

loyal federates of the Empire, and they were proud of their connections with the Romans. The conflict with Majorian was caused by his reversal of the policies of Avitus, rather than any hostility towards the Empire held by the Burgundians themselves.

The settlement of the barbarians

An outline of the settlement of the barbarians in Gaul up until the 450s is necessarily made up of fragments from a variety of sources, not all of which are in agreement. Thus, according to the Spanish chronicler Hydatius the settlement of the Visigoths in Aquitaine took place in 418; according to the Gallo-Roman Prosper, it happened a year later.[23] The difference may seem slight, but it could affect interpretation of the event, since the most important assembly of the Gallic provinces, the Council of the Gauls, was re-established in the former year.[24] The Council may have played a major role in planning the transfer of the Visigoths to Aquitaine. A third source, the *Chronicle of 452*, gives a date of 415, which is plainly wrong, although the error may result from confusion of Athaulf's period of rule in Narbonne with the later settlement.[25] Subsequently, however, the *Chronicle of 452* complicates matters more seriously, not only by being in conflict with other sources over the dating of events, but also by itself providing two alternative dating systems, wrongly correlated. This would be of little significance if the Chronicle in question were not the only source to record some important episodes. The grants of Valence and *Gallia Ulterior* to the Alans, and that of *Sapaudia* to the Burgundians are not attested elsewhere. Any narrative of the settlements in Gaul, therefore, is inevitably tentative.[26]

So too is any interpretation of the nature of the settlements. It used to be assumed that the barbarians were settled according to the Roman practice of billeting, whereby a soldier was given one-third of a house. Recently this has been challenged, and it has been suggested that the third which was allocated was one-third of the taxation due on a property.[27] The evidence is not detailed enough to sustain either argument. The chronicles, which provide our only evidence on the first phases of the settlements, speak about grants of land to live in, of seats of habitation, and about the division of territory. Visigothic and Burgundian law-codes are more precise, but they date from later generations. Thus the Burgundian Code, or *Liber Constitutionum*, was issued in 517. It contains an important law on settlement, which is likely to predate the promulgation of the code itself, although by how much is

23. Hydatius, *Chronicle*, 69; Prosper, *Chronicle*, 1271.
24. Wolfram, *History of the Goths*, p. 173.
25. *Chronicle of 452*, 73; see Wood, 'Continuity or calamity?: the constraints of literary models', p. 15.
26. Wood, 'Continuity or calamity?: the constraints of literary models', p. 15.
27. esp. W. Goffart, *Barbarians and Romans: Techniques of Accommodation*, passim.

unclear. The law itself envisages a number of phases in the settlement of the Burgundians. Some barbarians had already received land from the king who issued the law, others had been endowed by his predecessors; those who had not benefited in this way were to receive two-thirds of a property, one-third of the slaves and half the woodland. This implies grants stretching over at least two generations. A later law dealing with landless newcomers, specifies that they should receive half the property, and not two-thirds.[28] Although the references to property could imply tax yield rather than real estate, related laws which deal with land clearance make this unlikely. The Burgundian legal evidence, therefore, suggests that land rather than tax revenue was granted. At the same time, it reveals a succession of different grants, none of which can be shown to be associated with the original concession of Sapaudia.

Just as the barbarians themselves seem to have changed their policies about settlement, so too the Romans are unlikely to have had a monolithic system for settling the barbarians within the Roman Empire. At times taxation may have been a significant factor, either because the barbarians were simply allocated revenue, or, as in the case misrecorded by Fredegar, because Romans gained tax exemption as a result of conceding land to the barbarians. In addition the practice of billeting was used on occasion; it is described plainly in a poem written by a Gallo-Roman landowner, Paulinus of Pella, who originally thought himself lucky not to have had Visigoths billeted on him, but afterwards regretted not having them to protect his estates.[29] Later, another Gallic aristocrat, Sidonius Apollinaris, objected to the smell and the noise of a group of Burgundians who were established on his estate.[30] The settlement of the barbarians was plainly varied, and our sources provide only a hint of its complexities.

The same holds true when it comes to a consideration of the reasons for the individual grants made by the Romans. The Visigothic settlement in Aquitaine is usually seen as proof of the success of the Roman general Constantius, in blockading Wallia and his people when they were in Spain. The choice of Aquitaine is then linked variously to the ability of the people of that part of Gaul to pay, the possibility that they may have backed the wrong side in the recent usurpations against the emperor Honorius, and the threat from separatist groups north of the Loire, who were known as *Bacaudae*.[31] The evidence is not good enough to support any one of these interpretations to the total exclusion of either of the others. Moreover, it is possible that they underestimate the position of the Visigoths at the time of the transfer. Although Wallia had come to terms with Constantius in 416, he

28. *Liber Constitutionum*, 54, 55, *constitutio extravagans* 21; Wood, 'Ethnicity and the ethnogenesis of the Burgundians', pp. 66–7.

29. Paulinus, *Eucharisticon*, 11. 281–90.

30. Sidonius Apollinaris, carm. XII.

31. E.A. Thompson, 'The settlement of the barbarians in southern Gaul', *Journal of Roman Studies* 46 (1956), pp. 65–75; see also E.A. Thompson, *Romans and Barbarians*, pp. 251–5; J.M. Wallace-Hadrill, 'Gothia and Romania', in Wallace-Hadrill, *The Long-Haired Kings*, pp. 25–48.

had subsequently campaigned on the emperor's behalf, against other barbarian groups in Spain. The settlement, therefore, was not the direct result of any capitulation. Further, when the Visigoths did return to Gaul, it was to an area where Athaulf had once established his court. Wallia may have had some say in the grant made to his people.

In the case of the Alans, the extent of the deserted countryside round Valence is unknown; so too are the circumstances of the concession. The fact that the land was deserted, however, may have been significant. The settlement of the Alans near Valence may have more in common with imperial attempts to solve the problem of abandoned land, *agri deserti*, than with other grants to the barbarians. It is possible to reconstruct the circumstances of the second concession to the Alans, of land in *Gallia Ulterior*, with rather greater certainty. Here the *Bacaudae* were unquestionably a factor. At about the time of the settlement of the Visigoths in Aquitaine there had been unrest north of the Loire, which had been suppressed. This unrest is sometimes seen in terms of the class war, but strictly speaking this is unlikely to have been the case, since the rebels appear to have included dispossessed aristocrats. Problems flared up again in the 430s, when the *Bacaudae* gained a leader called Tibatto. Aëtius sent the Alans under Goar against Tibatto and his followers. This mission was briefly halted by Germanus, bishop of Auxerre, but Tibatto was subsequently captured and the *Bacaudae* suppressed.[32] The area of *Gallia Ulterior* conceded to the Alans may well have been that area which had supported Tibatto, and the grant may well have been a means of punishing the rebels and keeping them under surveillance, as well as being a reward for the followers of Goar. The Alans certainly treated the inhabitants of the region ruthlessly. Although the land was meant to be divided between Romans and barbarians, many of the former were forcibly ejected, and there was a further uprising, led by a doctor called Eudoxius.[33]

The settlement of Sapaudia is less easy to understand. A Burgundian kingdom on the Rhine ruled by Guntiarius had been destroyed by the Huns not long before.[34] The survivors can scarcely have been in a strong position to demand territory from the Romans. Nor can they have been substantial enough to have provided defence against further attacks from the Huns or from the Alamans. Nevertheless, Sapaudia was divided up between the Burgundians and the native population. Moreover, a few years later, the Burgundians did provide troops to fight against Attila at the Catalaunian Plains. Aëtius certainly gained manpower through his grants to the Visigoths, Burgundians and Alans.

32. *Chronicle of 452*, 117, 119, 127; Constantius, *Vita Germani* VI 28.
33. *Chronicle of 452*, 133.
34. Prosper, *Chronicle*, 1322; Hydatius, *Chronicle*, 108; *Chronicle of 452*, 118.

Imperial weakness

Manpower may hold a key to many of the policies adopted by the Romans in dealing with the barbarians. The successes first of Constantius and then of Aëtius in dealing with the Germanic invaders obscure the real weakness of the Roman position. Had they been stronger, the Romans would doubtless have dealt more forcefully with the barbarian threat. In fact the western Empire was probably in a much weaker position after 406 than the sources suggest. From 395 onwards the rivalry between the advisers of Honorius in the west and Arcadius in the east had ensured a lack of cooperation, if not downright hostility, between the two halves of the Roman Empire. It was in this context that the Visigoths moved from the Balkans into Italy. The subsequent breaking of the Rhine further exacerbated matters. When Honorius failed to respond to the new problem, a usurper, Constantine III, decided to deal with the defence of Gaul himself. In this way the barbarians encouraged usurpation, and the usurpers drew attention away from the barbarians.[35] Indeed, the *Ravenna Annals* seem to suggest that the court did not recognize the barbarians as a significant problem; they concentrate on recording and depicting the failures and executions of usurpers.[36] To some extent the priorities of Honorius and his advisers may have been justified. However, the result of the civil wars caused by the usurpations of the first two decades of the fifth century appears to have led to a considerable decline in the Roman, as opposed to a federate, army. Roman troops as such scarcely appear after the first decade of the fifth century in any source, except the *Notitia Dignitatum*, which appears to be an idealized list drawn up in the 420s, and not a statement of the reality of the imperial fighting forces.[37] Writing in the sixth century the Gothic historian Jordanes knew of only one Roman squadron at the battle of the Catalaunian Plains.[38] In the light of this Constantius is perhaps unlikely to have been in a position to destroy Wallia completely in 416: Stilicho, who had been in a position at least as strong, had failed to destroy Alaric. Besides, there was the possibility that the Visigoths could be used to shore up the Empire. The same was true of the Alans and the Burgundians in the 430s and 440s. To survive, the western Empire depended on federates, and the early barbarian settlements were a way of ensuring a supply of federate forces. Athaulf's wish, to support the Empire with Visigothic troops, had effectively been granted.

35. J.F. Matthews, *Western Aristocracies and Imperial Court A.D. 364–425*, pp. 308–10.

36. *Ravenna Annals*, ed. B. Bischoff and W. Koehler, 'Eine illustrierte Ausgabe der spätantiken Ravennater Annalen', in W.R.W. Koehler, ed., *Studies in Memory of A. Kingsley Porter*, pp. 125–38.

37. P. Salway, *Roman Britain*, p. 476, n. 2.

38. Jordanes, *Getica*, XXXVI 191.

The last emperors

The battle of the Catalaunian Plains was proof that the imperial policy could work, if only for a limited period of time. The events of the next decade were to show just how weak was the western Empire. In 454 Valentinian killed Aëtius, supposedly with his own hand, accusing the general of treachery.[39] Although this has been seen as a crucial error on the emperor's part, he may not have been wrong in his assessment of his *magister militum*. Besides, it was not the general's assassination so much as that of the emperor a year later which was vital. Some of the barbarian federates are known to have understood their loyalty as being to Valentinian; his death, therefore, absolved them from any treaty with the Empire.[40] Further, with the murder of Valentinian the house of Theodosius came to an end in the West; as a result there was no clear heir to the imperial throne, which was open to competition. Inevitably the confusion that followed tested even the most loyal barbarians, who could suddenly discover that the emperor they supported had been overthrown by a palace coup, and that there was a hostile ruler in his place.

Valentinian's immediate successor, Petronius Maximus, was killed in the commotion preceding the Vandal sack of Rome in 455. In response the Visigoths raised the Gallic aristocrat Avitus to the imperial office. He, however, was unpopular in Italy, and was soon opposed by his own general, Ricimer, who sided instead with Majorian.[41] Ricimer more than anyone else dominated the politics of the last twenty years of the Roman Empire in the west. A soldier of mixed Visigothic and Suevic extraction, he came to power under Avitus, was responsible for his fall, and was effectively involved in the appointment of all the western emperors to hold office between 457 and his own death in 472.[42]

Avitus's fall alienated the Visigoths. His successor, Majorian, is unlikely to have gained the support of the Burgundians in 458, when he drove them out of the lands which they had received with the approval of the Gallo-Roman senators. Nor was he immediately popular with large sections of the Gallic aristocracy from whom Avitus himself had come. Nevertheless he managed to establish his authority over Gaul and its barbarian settlers, until he fell foul of Ricimer, who had him executed in 461.[43] The emperor's death in its turn alienated his supporters, most notably the Gallo-Roman Aegidius,[44] who

39. John of Antioch, fr. 200 (1), 201 (1, 2), cited in Gordon, *The Age of Attila*, pp. 50–2.

40. John of Antioch, fr. 201 (6), cited in Gordon, *The Age of Attila*, pp. 113–14.

41. John of Antioch, fr. 201 (6), 202, cited in Gordon, *The Age of Attila*, pp. 113–16.

42. *Fasti Vindobonenses Priores*, s.a. 461; Cassiodorus, *Chronicle* s.a. 461; *Chronicle of 511*, 635–6; John of Antioch, fr. 202, 207, 209 (1, 2), cited in Gordon, *The Age of Attila*, pp. 116–17, 120, 122–3.

43. John of Antioch, fr. 203, cited in Gordon, *The Age of Attila* p. 117.

44. Priscus, fr. 30, cited in Gordon, *The Age of Attila*, pp. 118–19.

began an independent career in Soissons, in the north of Gaul, which was to hold some significance for the early history of the Franks.

After the execution of Majorian, Ricimer appointed Severus as emperor; four years later he agreed to the elevation of Anthemius, but in 472 he had Anthemius executed and replaced him with Olybrius. The appointment and overthrow of individual emperors were largely matters of Italian politics, but they had significant repercussions in Gaul, not least because of the close personal connections between Ricimer and the Burgundian royal family, the Gibichungs. One of Ricimer's brothers-in-law, Gundioc, appears as the leading military official, the *magister militum*, in Gaul during the reign of Severus (461–5).[45] The family connection was enhanced when Gundioc's son, Gundobad, became Ricimer's right-hand man, and as such he was responsible for the execution of Anthemius. Gundobad's importance was further enhanced when Ricimer died, for he took over his mentor's position at court. After Olybrius's death in 472 it was he who appointed Glycerius as emperor. Meanwhile other members of the family benefited from his position. During Glycerius's reign Gundobad's uncle, Chilperic I, became *magister militum*, and was to be found exercising authority in Lyons and Geneva.[46] When Glycerius died in 474, however, Gundobad seems to have returned to Gaul. The move may have been connected with the fact that the new emperor, Julius Nepos, was an eastern appointment. Certainly his authority was not recognized by Gundobad's uncle, Chilperic, who appears to have regarded support for him as treasonable.[47]

Chilperic's rule in the Rhône valley and the region to the east provides a rare insight into the complexities of provincial government in the 470s. Although his authority was undoubtedly derived from the Roman office which he held, the area over which he exercised control seems not to have been determined by any Roman administrative division, but rather by the presence of the Visigoths to the west and by other smaller groups, including Aegidius and his followers, to the north. The Roman poet and letter-writer Sidonius Apollinaris coined the phrase *Lugdunensis Germania* to describe it.[48] In some respects Chilperic seems to have been well regarded. Relations between him, his wife and bishop Patiens of Lyons were particularly cordial, according to Sidonius in a letter which provides the only depiction of the Burgundian ruler's cultural and religious connections: Chilperic admired the banquets provided by Patiens and his wife admired the bishop's fasts.[49] Nevertheless, Sidonius did fear for the safety of his own family in the aftermath of the accession of Nepos.[50] And there were others who saw Chilperic's rule as something new. According to the early-sixth-century *Life of*

45. John of Antioch, fr. 209, cited in Gordon, *The Age of Attila*, pp. 122–3.
46. Sidonius Apollinaris, epp. V 6; V 7; VI 12, 3; *Vita Patrum Iurensium*, II 10 (92), II 11 (96).
47. Sidonius Apollinaris, epp. V 6; V 7.
48. Sidonius Apollinaris, ep. V 7, 7.
49. Sidonius Apollinaris, ep. VI 12, 3.
50. Sidonius Apollinaris, epp. V 6; V7.

the Jura Fathers, abbot Lupicinus attacked Chilperic's power as being a type of kingship (*condicio regia*) rather than an exercise of public justice (*ius publicum*).[51] That it was something new is further indicated by Sidonius's extraordinary description of Syagrius as 'a new Solon of the Burgundians in interpreting law', implying that a Roman aristocrat had devoted himself to drafting edicts for Chilperic and his Burgundians.[52] Nevertheless, the Gibichung family remained attached to the idea of the Roman Empire. Gundobad and his son Sigismund both wanted the title of *magister militum* in the sixth century, long after the last emperor in the west had been deposed.[53]

The creation of the Visigothic kingdom

By 476 the Visigothic position was very different. The immediate result of the battle of the Catalaunian Plains in 451 had been the succession of Theoderid's eldest son, Thorismund. His policies looked back to the more aggressive activities of his father; he fought the Alans, and he attacked Arles.[54] His reign, however, was short-lived, and his brother and successor, Theodoric II, cooperated rather more closely with the Empire, sending a third brother Frideric against the Spanish *Bacaudae* in 454 and appointing Avitus emperor in the following year.[55] Sidonius describes the Visigothic court in a letter of this period. He paints a picture of the king's day, starting with his religious observance, and running through his holding court, surrounded by barbarian troops and approached by foreign legates, his tour of the royal stables, his restrained lunch, followed by a game of dice, his hearing of litigants, and dinner.[56] Sidonius, perhaps for political reasons, is concerned to portray a restrained and civilized man, with a good deal of power and authority.

After the overthrow of Avitus in 456 Majorian had to use force to bring the Visigoths into line, but thereafter they fought for him against the Sueves in Spain. In the confusion following Majorian's death in 461, however, they found themselves fighting against one of his closest supporters, Aegidius, first in the south, and subsequently in the Loire valley, where Frideric was killed in 463.[57] Two years later Aegidius himself died, providing opportunity for Visigothic expansion in the Loire valley.[58] Despite this territorial expansion Theodoric was still technically a federate of the Roman Empire, working in the service first of Severus and then of Anthemius. This relationship between the Visigoths and the Romans was broken by Euric, who murdered his brother Theodoric in 466 and seized the Visigothic throne.[59]

51. *Vita Patrum Iurensium*, 92 (II, 10).
52. Sidonius Apollinaris, ep. V 5, 3.
53. Avitus, epp. 78, 93, 94.
54. Wolfram, *History of the Goths*, p. 178.
55. Wolfram, *History of the Goths*, pp. 178–9.
56. Sidonius Apollinaris, ep. I 2.
57. Wolfram, *History of the Goths*, p. 180.
58. Wolfram, *History of the Goths*, p. 181.
59. Wolfram, *History of the Goths*, p. 181.

The first clear indication of a real shift in attitude towards the Roman Empire comes not from evidence relating to Euric himself, but rather from a letter of Sidonius discussing the accusations levelled against the prefect of Gaul, Arvandus, in 468. The latter was accused of treason on account of a letter he had sent to Euric, advising him not to make peace with the Greek emperor, that is Anthemius, but rather to attack the Britons who were stationed on the Loire, and to divide Gaul with the Burgundians. Sidonius depicts the scheme as madness; nevertheless he maintained his friendship for Arvandus, and he may even have given up his office of prefect of the City of Rome in order not to be involved in sentencing his friend.[60] Arvandus's scheme was premature. But Euric did take some of the advice offered. He attacked and defeated the British forces which Riothamus had brought to the Loire in support of the emperor.

The events of the next few years are recorded in considerable detail by Sidonius. Having returned from Rome at the end of 468, he was suddenly consecrated bishop of Clermont in 470. Since the Auvergne was central to Euric's strategy between 469 and 475, Sidonius is a well-informed, and involved, witness. Already at the start of the period Euric moved to isolate the Auvergne, by annexing the territories to the south and west. In so doing he seems to have been acting in concert with a Roman official called Seronatus. Despite his determination to maintain his friendship with Arvandus, Sidonius shows nothing but hostility towards Seronatus, whose plans impinged too closely on his own life.[61] In 471 Euric launched his first onslaught against Clermont. Military resistance was organized by Sidonius's brother-in-law, Ecdicius, son of the emperor Avitus. In response, Anthemius sent an army from Italy under the command of his son, but Euric's forces crossed the Rhône, destroying it and killing its general. The Burgundians then intervened, pushing the Visigoths back across the river.[62]

The following year Euric attacked Clermont again; once more Ecdicius organized the defence, probably using Burgundian troops. Anthemius intended to acknowledge his achievements by giving him the title of *patricius*, but the emperor was himself killed by Gundobad. Under his successor, Olybrius, the Burgundians seem to have continued to defend the Auvergne against the Visigoths. Sidonius, suspected by the Burgundians, and threatened by the Visigoths, thought the situation intolerable; but worse was to follow. With the death of Olybrius and the appointment of Julius Nepos the Burgundians under Chilperic found themselves in opposition to the emperor; presumably they withdrew from any involvement in the defence of the

---

60. Sidonius Apollinaries, ep. I 7; on this see J.D. Harries, 'Sidonius Apollinaris, Rome and the barbarians: a climate of treason?', in Drinkwater and Elton, eds, *Fifth-Century Gaul*, pp. 298–308; H.C. Teitler, 'Un-Roman activities in late antique Gaul: the cases of Arvandus and Seronatus', ibid. pp. 309–17.

61. Sidonius Apollinaris, epp. II 1; V 13; VII 7, 2; Teitler, 'Un-Roman activities in late antique Gaul'.

62. Wolfram, *History of the Goths*, pp. 181–4.

Auvergne. Nepos at first delighted Sidonius by conferring on Ecdicius the patriciate which Anthemius had promised. Shortly afterwards, however, in 475 the emperor conceded the Auvergne to Euric in return for Provence, which the Visigoths had apparently overrun two years previously. Clermont was taken over by the *dux* Victorius, a Gallo-Roman whom Euric had appointed as governor of *Aquitania Prima*; Sidonius was sent into exile. The treaty agreed between Euric and Julius Nepos was one of the last imperial acts to affect Gaul. The deposition of Nepos and then that of Romulus Augustulus in 476 saw the end of the line of western Roman emperors. Euric moved to reconquer Provence, which he did, despite the opposition of the Burgundians.[63]

In the immediate aftermath of annexation or conquest Euric's rule was far from pleasant. Laymen who had opposed the Visigoths are likely to have suffered; so too did ecclesiatics. Here there was an additional complication in that Euric and his people were arian Christians, who believed that the Holy Trinity was a hierarchy, in which the Father, Son and Holy Ghost were not equal, while the majority of the Gallo-Romans, including Sidonius, were catholics, and insisted on the equality of the three persons in the Godhead. Euric, therefore, was able to combine politics and religion, in persecuting the catholic Church. Just before his own exile Sidonius described to bishop Basil of Aix-en-Provence the state of the Church in the areas under Visigothic rule: Bordeaux, Perigueux, Rodez, Limoges, Javols, Eauze, Bazas, Comminges and Auch were all without bishops, and it was impossible to enter basilicas because their doorways were overgrown with brambles.[64] A century later Gregory of Tours treated this description as representing the normal state of the catholic Church under Euric.[65] In fact there is plenty of evidence to suggest that the oppression was merely temporary, being imposed while the king established his grip on the country.[66] Thereafter the sees were filled; Sidonius himself returned to Clermont, where the chief opposition to him came from his own clergy.[67]

The kingdom which Euric created was substantial. It occupied most of the land of France south of the Loire and west of the Rhône. In addition, regular campaigns within Spain had brought much of the area to the south of the Pyrenees under Visigothic control, even if as yet there were few Gothic settlements in the region. Further, Euric's court was clearly a place of far-reaching importance. In a somewhat panegyrical poem Sidonius described some of those in attendance on the king; Saxons, a Frank, a Herule and a Burgundian; Ostrogoths seeking help and Roman protection.[68] Elsewhere he refers to a treaty imposed by the king on the peoples who lived on the river

63. Wolfram, *History of the Goths*, pp. 184–9.
64. Sidonius Apollinaris, ep. VII 6.
65. Gregory, *Decem Libri Historiarum*, II 25.
66. Wolfram, *History of the Goths*, pp. 199–200.
67. Gregory, *Decem Libri Historiarum*, II 22–3.
68. Sidonius Apollinaris, ep. VIII 9, 5.

Wahal, that is the Franks.[69] Whether Euric really could enforce a settlement so far away is open to question, but clearly he tried to exert influence considerably to the north-east of his own territories.

The Gallo-Romans quickly reached accommodation with the new rulers, despite differences in culture and religion. Some like Seronatus and Victorius moved to do so even before 476. Numerous others must have done so as well. Sidonius wrote to a number of Romans who achieved eminent positions under Euric, including Leo, who became one of the king's leading advisers. In a letter addressed to him in 476 or 477, Sidonius talks of Euric restraining weapons with laws.[70] If the laws in question were the great legal compilation known as the *Codex Euricianus*, then the king must have had the support of numerous Roman lawyers from relatively early in his reign.[71] Syagrius likewise collaborated with the Burgundians in legal matters before 469.[72] Within a mere twenty years of the murder of Valentinian III the Romans had accustomed themselves to new political circumstances, and the barbarian rulers had taken over many of the duties which had formerly been exercised by provincial governors as well as military leaders. The new establishment was to be more durable than the experiment envisaged by Athaulf and attempted by Constantius and Aëtius, where a traditional Roman government was supported by barbarian arms.

69. Sidonius Apollinaris, ep. VIII 3, 3.
70. Sidonius Apollinaris, ep. VIII 3, 3.
71. On the *Codex Euricianus*, see Wolfram, *History of the Goths*, pp. 194–5.
72. Sidonius Apollinaris, ep. V 5, 3.

Chapter Two

Literary Continuity and Discontinuity: Late-Fifth- and Sixth-Century Culture

The impact of the barbarian invasions and settlements in Gaul can be seen in the substantial literary output of the fifth century. This literature, however, presents considerable problems for the historian. First, it is geographically confined: it almost all comes from southern and central Gaul. Very little of it relates to the north and north-east, although Salvian does describe the sack of Trier.[1] It is also the product of a single class. Indeed the majority of fifth- and early-sixth-century writers whose works have survived were related to each other.[2] Despite these limitations the surviving evidence for the fifth century depicts the period in two radically different ways. Most of the works produced in the first half of the century portray a period of social and religious cataclysm, which is arguably compatible with the archaeology of the north-eastern provinces, where evidence for decline in the cities, towns and villas, and dramatic changes in burial practices, gives a picture of disruption. By contrast Sidonius Apollinaris, the most prolific writer of the second half of the century, implies almost total continuity with the imperial past. This discrepancy makes any assessment of the extent of dislocation caused by the barbarian invasions extremely difficult. It also points to a third limitation within the sources; that of genre. To a very large extent the sources of the first part of the period which suggest calamity are moralizing tracts intended to prompt spiritual and social reform. Sidonius's writings are verse panegyrics addressed to emperors, and letters: both literary forms which tend to emphasize the traditional values of the senatorial aristocracy and imperial court.[3]

Although this poses a very particular problem for understanding the history of Gaul in the fifth century, similar evidential difficulties continue into the Merovingian period. The contemporary evidence for the generation after Sidonius, that is the last decades of fifth- and the first of sixth-century Gaul, is

---

1. Salvian, *De Gubernatione Dei* VI 39, 72–7, 82, 85–9.
2. Wood, 'Continuity or calamity?: the constraints of literary models', pp. 10–11.
3. Wood, 'Continuity or calamity?: the constraints of literary models'.

largely made up of letter collections. These again imply considerable social and cultural continuity at a senatorial level. They impose a particular perspective on the period, albeit one that is often ignored, because it does not provide a narrative framework for understanding late Roman and early Merovingian history. Such a framework is provided only by sources written towards the end of the sixth century, by the short chronicle of Marius of Avenches and, above all, by the *Decem Libri Historiarum,* or *Ten Books of Histories,* of Gregory of Tours.

The *Ten Books of Histories* have determined the outlines of early Merovingian history. They are, nevertheless, unique. Indeed in the preface to his work Gregory appears to proclaim their uniqueness. Inevitably there is a danger of relying too much on Gregory. Despite their importance, for much of the period for which they provide the chief narrative, the *Decem Libri Historiarum* are not strictly speaking contemporary. Moreover, they are not representative of the culture of early Merovingian Gaul. It is, therefore, important to be aware of the changing nature of the evidence for the period, before turning to the narrative of early Merovingian history. At the same time the cultural history of the late fifth and sixth centuries is worthy of attention in its own right.

Sidonius Apollinaris and the last days of the Empire

Sidonius Apollinaris was born into one of the leading senatorial families in Gaul in the early 430s. He was well educated at Lyons and Arles. He married the daughter of Avitus, then praetorian prefect of the Gauls. When in 455 his father-in-law became emperor, Sidonius accompanied him to Italy and delivered a panegyric in his honour in 456. Shortly afterwards Avitus was overthrown, and Sidonius, back in Lyons, had the problem of welcoming the new emperor Majorian, again with a verse panegyric. Subsequently Sidonius seems to have retired from the limelight until the fall of Majorian, and the elevation of Anthemius, for whose first consulship in 468 he also delivered a panegyric. In recompense Anthemius created Sidonius prefect of the city of Rome. Within a year, however, the latter had returned to Gaul, and in somewhat mysterious circumstances he became bishop of Clermont in 471. Thereafter he was one of the prime figures in the resistance to Euric, until Nepos conceded the Auvergne to the Visigoths. For Sidonius the immediate result was exile, but after one or two years he did return, and lived out his life as bishop, albeit harassed by his own clergy, until the late 480s.[4]

Granted his education and career it is not surprising that Sidonius, both in his panegyrics and also in his letter-collection, was able to see the last days of the imperial court within a traditional perspective. It is difficult, nevertheless, to assess the extent to which this perspective is actually appropriate to the reigns of Avitus, Majorian and Anthemius. The confused events of the 450s

---

4. For the narrative of Sidonius's life, see C.E. Stevens, *Sidonius Apollinaris.*

and 460s are not easily squared with the literary image of the period purveyed by Sidonius. Equally problematic is the validity of Sidonius's very cultured presentation of the barbarian courts of Theodoric II, Euric and Chilperic I.[5] Here, the author might have had political reasons to present the barbarians in as positive a light as possible. Except in very specific cases Sidonius's attitudes and style encourage the reader to see continuity where there may have been disruption. Thus his writings give the opposite impression to those of the earlier moralists like Salvian, and even of that conveyed by Paulinus of Pella, a member of the senatorial aristocracy who collaborated with the Visigoths in the early years of their settlement in Aquitaine, but eventually lost the majority of his property, as he relates in his autobiographical poem, the *Eucharisticon*.[6]

Asceticism and culture in the fifth and sixth centuries

The question of the dislocation in the literary evidence for the fifth century can be approached from a different angle. Paulinus of Pella provides an unusual example of a member of the senatorial aristocracy known to have been bankrupted by the barbarian invasions. A number of his contemporaries, however, willingly gave up their wealth during the opening decades of the fifth century. One of the most notable features of the first years of the invasions was the development of monasticism in southern Gaul. The patrons of this monastic movement were largely members of the Gallo–Roman aristocracy. Of these the most influential was Honoratus, the founder of the island monastery of Lérins, just off the southern coast of Gaul. Lérins itself was important in two ways; first it played a major part in the promotion of monastic ideals in Gaul, and second it trained a succession of bishops who made a substantial impact on the Gallo–Roman, and later Frankish, Church.[7] It was not the only important monastic centre in Gaul; already Martin, bishop of Tours at the end of the fourth century, had established an ascetic tradition in the Touraine and Poitou,[8] and in Marseilles John Cassian, an easterner with first-hand knowledge of Egyptian asceticism, wrote two of the classics of monastic literature, the *Institutes* and the *Conferences*.[9] Cassian, however, was associated with Lérins, as was Salvian, himself a priest of Marseilles.[10]

5. Sidonius Apollinaris, epp. I 2; VI 12, 3; VIII 9, 5.
6. Paulinus, *Eucharisticon*, ll. 291–405.
7. The classic account is to be found in F. Prinz, *Frühes Mönchtum im Frankenreich*, pp. 47–87; on the position of Lérins in the ecclesiastical politics, see R.W. Mathisen, *Ecclesiastical Factionalism and Religious Controversy in Fifth-Century Gaul*, pp. 69–205.
8. C. Stancliffe, *St Martin and his Hagiographer*, passim; P. Rousseau, *Ascetics, Authority and the Church*, pp. 143–65.
9. O. Chadwick, *John Cassian*, passim; Rousseau, *Ascetics, Authority and the Church*, pp. 169–234.
10. R. Markus, *The End of Ancient Christianity*, pp. 164, 168.

This tradition of aristocratic asceticism spread through Gaul largely as a result of the episcopal careers of certain Lérinian monks. One of the most influential of these was the Briton Faustus, bishop of Riez. Among those who regarded Faustus as their spiritual master was Sidonius, whose brother had been in some way saved by the bishop.[11] The religious culture of Lérins and of Faustus in particular seem at first sight to be at odds with the rhetorical culture of Sidonius's own writings. Even when the latter does raise religious matters, he seems to deal with them from a different perspective than that of the ascetic theology of Faustus or the spiritual philosophy of another great writer and friend, Claudianus Mamertus. Again, however, the problem is a matter of style as much as one of substance. On the one hand the theologians of the fifth century were also experts in rhetoric, even if the style they chose as being appropriate to their religious works was different from that used by Sidonius in his letters and poems; on the other, Sidonius is known to have composed some ecclesiastical works including an epitaph for the ascetic Abraham, poems for various churches, as well as a version of the Mass which appears not to have survived.[12]

Sidonius's letters and poems portray a world in which imperial values and late Roman rhetorical culture flourish. The relationship of this picture with that provided by Salvian and his fellow moralists, who saw the early fifth century as a period of destruction, is not immediately apparent. Yet Sidonius belonged to the same aristocratic class as Salvian and the early ascetics of Lérins, although he belonged to a younger generation. He was also closely connected with some of those bishops who had spent time in the island monastery. Taken together, this evidence indicates some of the complexity of cultural responses to the developments of the fifth century, even though it relates to only one particular section of society.

The ascetic culture of Lérins was to continue to be of significance. One of the island's greatest pupils was Caesarius, bishop of Arles from 503 to 543. Born of noble family in territory controlled by the Burgundians, he left his parents and went to Lérins, where his asceticism was too severe for his health. As a result he was sent to Arles, where he came into contact with the rhetorician Julianus Pomerius. Meanwhile he attracted the attention of bishop Aeonius of Arles, who negotiated his release from the community of Lérins, and ordained him. Thereafter he became abbot of one of the city's suburban monasteries, and then bishop. In that office he had to deal first with the Visigothic king Alaric II and then with the Ostrogoth Theodoric I. He was twice accused of treason, but was exonerated on both occasions. Subsequently he witnessed the transfer of Provence to the Franks. His writings include two monastic rules and a large number of sermons, notable for the simplicity of their style as well as their message. Despite his connections with Julianus Pomerius, whom he influenced greatly, Caesarius was able to disregard the

11. Sidonius Apollinaris, epp. VI 3; VI 9; carm. XVI.
12. Sidonius Apollinaris, epp. II 10, 4; VII 17, 2; Gregory, *Decem Libri Historiarum* II 22.

rhetorical traditions of his own class. As a preacher who cultivated an accessible style of preaching, as a monastic legislator, and as the convenor of a number of major church councils, he was perhaps the most influential product of Lérins.[13]

Letter-writing in the sixth century

In the literature to have survived from the sixth century, however, the legacy of Sidonius is as significant as that of Lérins. Indeed, Caesarius apart, the major writers of the next generation looked back to Sidonius as their model. In so doing they extended the problem of determining the relationship between rhetoric and reality into the early barbarian period. Two writers whose letter-collections survive, Ruricius of Limoges and Avitus of Vienne, openly revered the style of Sidonius,[14] and a third, Ferreolus of Uzès, is known to have modelled his own writings on those of the bishop of Clermont.[15] Ennodius of Pavia, whose career took him to Italy, but whose family came from Provence, wrote in a similar style. Among the writings of Ruricius, Avitus and Ennodius are numerous letters of friendship, or *amicitia*, which were one of the traditional means of cultivating and maintaining contact with one's peer group. Sidonius, like the Late Antique authors on whom he modelled himself, had written such letters to ensure the existence of a pool of friends on whom he could count in times of need. The writers of the next generation did the same.[16]

Both Ruricius and Avitus were close relatives of Sidonius, as well as literary followers.[17] Avitus was also related, if only as godson, to bishop Mamertus, brother of the theologian Claudianus.[18] He succeeded his father, Hesychius, as bishop of Vienne, in or about 490.[19] His cathedral city was one of the favourite centres of the Burgundian kings, and he therefore had much to do with both Gundobad and his son Sigismund. With the former, who like Euric was an arian, he corresponded at length over questions of doctrine.[20] Sigismund converted to catholicism before becoming king in 516. The bishop of Vienne was probably not responsible for his conversion, but he undoubtedly exercised considerable influence at the start of the new reign. He even seems to have been responsible for Sigismund's most formal letters, those

13. J.M. Wallace-Hadrill, *The Frankish Church.*, pp. 13–16, 55–7, 97–9.
14. Ruricius, ep. II 26; Avitus, epp. 43, 51.
15. Gregory, *Decem Libri Historiarum*, VI 7.
16. I. N. Wood, 'Administration, law and culture in Merovingian Gaul', in R. McKitterick, ed., *The Uses of Literacy in Early Medieval Europe*, pp. 67–71.
17. On the family connections of this group, see R.W. Mathisen, 'Epistolography, literary circles and family ties in Late Roman Gaul', *Transactions of the American Philological Association* 111 (1981), pp. 95–109.
18. Avitus, hom. 6.
19. Avitus, hom. 6.
20. e.g. Avitus, epp. 1–4, 21–2, 30.

addressed to the eastern emperor.[21] He was not, however, simply a political figure. In his letters to Gundobad, in some of his sermons, and in his versification of the first two books of the Bible, he showed himself to be a reasonable theologian. And in his lengthy poem on virginity, the *Consolatoria de castitatis laude*, he revealed the commitment of himself and his family to the ascetic life.

A comparison of Sidonius and Avitus reveals something of the continuities and discontinuities of the late fifth and early sixth centuries, and thus of the period which saw the transformation of the barbarian settlements into fully fledged kingdoms. Avitus, like Sidonius, was a master of rhetoric; if anything his style is more complex than that of his model, although his grammar is less classical. Also like Sidonius he found a career in the Church, although this seems to have been a matter of choice at a relatively early age, whereas Sidonius became bishop after a major secular career, without any obvious preparation. Avitus's father, who was perhaps a tribune in 456, experienced the same shift from secular to ecclesiastical office as Sidonius.[22] A generation later the political opportunities which had been available in the middle of the fifth century were closed, but equally the restrictions of the 470s had lifted. As bishop of a major city Avitus was involved in court politics to an extent that Sidonius, cut off from the centre of Visigothic power in Clermont, was not. He was also more adept at using his rhetorical skills in the service of theology and asceticism. In so doing he combined the religious culture of Lérins and the rhetorical culture of Late Antiquity more successfully than had Sidonius.

Avitus's generation is the last for which a full Roman education in the schools of Gaul can be assumed. Nevertheless the culture of Sidonius and his followers was preserved among the surviving Gallo-Roman aristocracy. Ferreolus of Uzès, who died in 581, was the author of a letter-collection in the manner of Sidonius.[23] His name suggests that he was the scion of one of the great families of fifth-century Gaul, a family, indeed, which Sidonius held in great esteem.[24] Like Avitus, he appears to have combined rhetoric and asceticism. Although his letters have not survived, a monastic Rule which he composed is still extant. In addition, Parthenius, nephew of Ennodius of Pavia, and husband of a granddaughter of Ruricius, was highly regarded by his contemporaries for his skill in rhetoric. How he obtained this skill is not recorded, but it may be significant that he visited Ravenna, where he befriended the poet Arator.[25] He was to become one of the leading advisers of the Merovingian king Theudebert I, and was lynched after the king's death as being responsible for taxing the Franks.[26] Another family to boast a continuing literary tradition was that of the late-sixth-century patrician,

21. Avitus, epp. 78, 93–4.
22. Mathisen, 'Epistolography, literary circles and family ties', p. 100.
23. Gregory, *Decem Libri Historiarum*, VI 7.
24. Sidonius Apollinaris, ep. VII 12.
25. Mathisen, 'Epistolography, literary circles and family ties', p. 103.
26. Gregory, *Decem Libri Historiarum*, III 36.

Dynamius, who numbered Venantius Fortunatus, the greatest poet of the period, and pope Gregory the Great among his correspondents.[27]

The esteem in which the literary ability of these men was held can be seen in a collection known as the *Epistulae Austrasiacae*, which contains two of Dynamius's letters and also a passing reference to the skills of Parthenius.[28] The *Epistulae Austrasiacae* is made up of forty-eight letters, the earliest of which is a verse epistle of the 460s, and the latest is to be dated to *c.* 590. It is thought to have been put together shortly thereafter, perhaps at the Austrasian, that is the east Frankish, court, hence the title by which the collection is known.[29] A number of the letters relate to diplomatic missions between Austrasia and Byzantium, but the collection cannot have had a purely political purpose. Some letters might have been regarded even in the late sixth century as being historically important; the first two, which are among the earliest in the collection, are letters from Remigius, bishop of Rheims, to Clovis, the first Christian king of the Franks. But several of the *Epistulae Austrasiacae* have no such importance, being expressions of friendship, like the *amicitia* letters of Sidonius and his followers, sent from one member of the court to another. The compilation, therefore, might be seen as a collection of model letters, appropriate to all sorts of circumstances, formal and informal. If this is the case, it is testimony to the continuing importance of a literary tradition within the Frankish court in the late sixth century. Moreover, since letters had a considerable social function in creating and maintaining bonds of friendship, which could be exploited for political ends, the continuity of this literary tradition may also imply the continuity of patterns of political influence.[30]

That the exchange of letters continued to be significant into the seventh century is clear from the collection of Desiderius of Cahors. Desiderius was an aristocrat from Aquitaine, where he seems to have been educated. He joined the court of Chlothar II after 614, and there he formed a number of close friendships. However, when one brother who was governor of Marseilles died, he was sent to replace him, and he was later elected bishop of Cahors in place of another brother, who had been killed.[31] As bishop, Desiderius had occasion to write about numerous specific issues, but he also took time to maintain the friendships he had made at court. In so doing he was continuing a tradition which looked back to Sidonius, and to the social traditions of the late Roman aristocracy.[32]

The greatest collection of letters to have survived from post-Roman Gaul, however, is made up of the poems of Venantius Fortunatus, many of which are verse epistles. Fortunatus was not a Gallo-Roman, but an Italian. Having

27. Venantius Fortunatus, carm. VI 9–10; Gregory I, *Register*, III 33; VII 33; see also IV 37.

28. *Epistulae Austrasiacae*, 12, 16, 17.

29. P. Goubert, *Byzance avant l'Islam*, 2, *Byzance et l'Occident*, pp. 95–6.

30. Wood, 'Administration, law and culture in Merovingian Gaul', pp. 67–9.

31. For his life, see *Vita Desiderii Cadurcensis*.

32. Wood, 'Administration, law and culture in Merovingian Gaul', pp. 70–1.

been cured of an eye infection through the agency of St Martin, in 565 he decided to visit the saint's shrine at Tours. His journey took him through Austrasia, where he was hospitably received by members of the aristocracy. In return he composed short poems of thanks.[33] Throughout his career he continued to write occasional pieces for friends and patrons, among them Leontius bishop of Bordeaux, the husband of one of Sidonius's descendants.[34] He also composed more formal poems, including an *epithalamium* on the marriage of king Sigibert and the Visigothic princess Brunhild as well as panegyrics and poems for the courts of Charibert and Chilperic I. These public poems provide what is perhaps the best evidence for the ideology of the Merovingian court in the second half of the sixth century.[35] After Fortunatus left the Austrasian kingdom he travelled to Tours and ultimately to Poitiers, where he became bishop in the last years of his life. Once he reached Poitiers his literary output became increasingly religious, and included a number of prose saints' *Lives*. During his early days in Poitiers a substantial number of his poems were written for Radegund, sometime wife of the Merovingian king Chlothar I, and founder and inmate of the abbey of the Holy Cross in Poitiers. For her he composed his most important devotional works, including several hymns and a poem in praise of virginity.[36] Comparison between this last work, with its highly charged and colourful imagery, and Avitus of Vienne's work on chastity, which approaches the same subject through an examination of his own family, reveals a vast difference in the imagination of the two writers, and does suggest that despite the continuities, there had been a sharp change of taste in the first half of the sixth century. On the one hand chastity is understood as an aspect of the piety of a senatorial family, while on the other it becomes the centre of a vision of the kingdom of heaven and its saintly inhabitants.

Although Fortunatus was an Italian, and although there is nothing comparable to his books of poetry in the sixth-century west, in many respects his writings can be placed in the same tradition as those of Sidonius and Avitus. While the latter left no verse epistles, Sidonius did, as did other writers whose works are preserved in the *Epistulae Austrasiacae*. As for the content of the verse epistles of Fortunatus, like that of many fifth- and sixth-century letters, it is often concerned simply with expressions of friendship, here called *dulcedo* rather than *amicitia*, and thanks. In addition, Fortunatus's panegyrics are a revival, if not a continuation, of the form in which Sidonius had excelled. His career is further proof of the esteem in which the sixth-century aristocracy and the courts of the Merovingian kings continued to hold literary skill.

---

33. For his career, see J. George, *Venantius Fortunatus: A Latin Poet in Merovingian Gaul*, pp. 18–34.

34. George, *Venantius Fortunatus: A Latin Poet in Merovingian Gaul*, pp. 70–4.

35. George, *Venantius Fortunatus: A Latin Poet in Merovingian Gaul*, pp. 35–61; M. Reydellet, *La Royauté dans la littérature latine de Sidoine Apollinaire à Isidore de Seville*, pp. 297–344.

36. George, *Venantius Fortunatus: A Latin Poet in Merovingian Gaul*, pp. 32–4, 161–77.

Gregory of Tours and the decline of culture

It is against this background that the writings of Fortunatus's friend, Gregory of Tours, need to be considered. All too often Gregory's greatest work, the *Ten Books of Histories*, which are unquestionably the most substantial and important single source for the history of sixth-century Gaul, are considered in isolation. Despite their significance, it is necessary to place them within their historical and literary context, in order to appreciate the complexity of Gregory's achievement, and so as to avoid being hoodwinked into taking his work at face value.

Gregory was born in 538 or 539.[37] His family as he depicts it was one of the greatest senatorial families in Gaul. It was certainly of considerable importance in the sixth-century Gallic Church. Among his close relatives, Gregory numbered bishops of Lyons, Clermont and Langres, and he claimed that all except for five bishops of Tours were related to him.[38] Moreover, the family was also said to have included Vettius Epagathus, one of the Lyons martyrs of 177.[39] Gregory's father died when he was still a boy, and he was brought up first by his great-uncle, Nicetius, then a priest in Chalon-sur-Saône, but later bishop of Lyons, and afterwards by Avitus, archdeacon of Clermont, where his uncle Gallus was bishop. Avitus was later to become bishop of the same see. Gallus died in 551, and by 552 Gregory was a deacon in Lyons, where Nicetius was then bishop. Subsequently he seems to have served the martyrial church of St Julian at Brioude, in the Auvergne. In 573, however, he was elected bishop of Tours. He died in 594 or perhaps a year later.

Gregory records that he wrote ten books of histories, seven of miracles and one of the *Life of the Fathers*, together with a commentary on the Psalter, and a work on the offices of the Church, each in one book. He also mentions a preface to the Masses of Sidonius.[40] All of these survive, except for the commentary on the Psalter and the preface. The seven books of miracles are made up of one on the *Glory of the Martyrs*, another on the passion and miracles of St Julian of Brioude, four on the miracles of St Martin, and one on the *Glory of the Confessors*. In addition an account of the miracles of St Andrew and a version of the *Passion of the Seven Sleepers of Ephesus* have been attributed to Gregory. The composition of these works stretched over a considerable period of time. The *Histories* were begun in the mid-570s and not completed until shortly before Gregory's death; the four books on the miracles of St Martin were started slightly earlier and the last of them was still

---

37. For a narrative of Gregory's life, see J. Verdon, *Grégoire de Tours*.
38. Gregory, *Decem Libri Historiarum*, V 49; R.W. Mathisen, 'The family of Georgius Florentius Gregorius and the Bishops of Tours', *Medievalia et Humanistica* 12 (1984), pp. 83–95.
39. Gregory, *Decem Libri Historiarum*, I 29, 31; Gregory, *Liber Vitae Patrum*, 6, 1.
40. Gregory, *Decem Libri Historiarium*, X 31.

being extended in 593. The works on Julian, the *Glory of the Martyrs* and of the confessors seem to belong largely to the 580s, as does the legend of the Seven Sleepers. The *Life of the Fathers* was not completed until 592 at the earliest. In other words, throughout the period of his episcopate Gregory was compiling and writing his *Histories* and his hagiographical works.[41]

Gregory came from the same aristocratic milieu as Sidonius and his followers. Much of his youth was spent in Clermont, a city where the latter had been bishop, and his mentor there was Avitus, whose name indicates that he came from the same family as Sidonius's father-in-law. Some of his early ecclesiastical career was spent in Lyons, which was Sidonius's own home town. Since Gregory belonged to the senatorial aristocracy, it might have been assumed that he would accept its literary traditions. His great-grandfather, Gregory of Langres, had been a correspondent of Avitus of Vienne,[42] and the bishop of Tours himself wrote a preface to the Masses of Sidonius.[43] Nevertheless, Gregory's surviving writings do not belong to the rhetorical traditions which had been so fashionable in Late Roman and Merovingian Gaul. Indeed, at first sight he appears to deny that they existed in his own day.

Gregory prefaced his great work, the *Decem Libri Historiarum*, with the following statement:

> The cultivation of liberal letters is declining or rather dying in the cities of Gaul, since some things that are good and some that are wicked are taking place, and the savagery of the barbarians is on the loose; the anger of the kings is sharp; the churches are under threat from the heretics, and are protected by the catholics; the faith of Christ burns in some and is cold in others; those same churches are enriched by the devout and empoverished by the perfidious; nor can any grammarian skillful in the art of dialectic be found to depict this in prose or verse. Many groan frequently, saying, 'Woe to our days, because the zeal for letters has died among us, nor is it to be found in those people who can set present events down in writing'. Knowing that these and similar things are being said, in order to commemorate past deeds, so that they may come to the notice of future generations, I have not been able to hide the struggles of the wicked or the lives of those who have lived righteously, even in much uncultivated speech. And I have been particularly inspired by this: I was impressed that many of us say that 'Few understand a philosophical rhetor, and many understand rustic speech'.

---

41. For a chronology of Gregory's writings see Verdon, *Grégoire de Tours*, pp. 77–85.
42. Avitus, ep. 64.
43. Gregory, *Decem Libri Historiarum*, II 22.

In many ways this seems to contradict what is known of the culture of the senatorial aristocracy and the Merovingian court in the sixth century. Yet, on the one hand this contradiction has been hidden by privileging Gregory's comments and neglecting the importance of the *Epistulae Austrasiacae* and the writings of Venantius Fortunatus; on the other, it has been explained by the apparent lack of educational opportunities available to Gregory in the households of Nicetius and Avitus. In answer to this second argument it can be said that the education available to Desiderius of Cahors in the following century is not likely to have been any better,[44] and yet he did write in the manner of earlier letter-writers.

Gregory's account needs to be read carefully. At first sight it is rather a confused juxtaposition of two themes; literary decline and political crisis. The literary decline in question, however, is not a general one; it relates to a lack of grammarians, in other words to the absence of great schools. That is not to say that there was no literary skill around. Indeed, Gregory almost admitted as much at the end of the *Histories* when he asked his successors in the bishopric of Tours to preserve his works intact, allowing no alteration to them, except their versification.[45] This may seem a curious exception, but it is as well to remember that Gregory would have known of the versification of Sulpicius Severus's *Life of St Martin* by Paulinus of Périgueux, and that he counted among his friends the poet Venantius Fortunatus, himself the author of a poetic work on the miracles of St Martin.

Besides, Gregory's preface is in itself something of a rhetorical display, leading to a defence of his use of rustic speech. Nor is the use of rustic speech necessarily the product of a decline in literacy. Gregory might have made a deliberate choice. The standard of the bishop of Tours's Latin used to be seen as ruling out this possibility. Recently, however, scholars have become aware that there are considerable difficulties in assessing Gregory's linguistic skills. In part this change of attitude has been caused by an awareness that the earliest manuscript of the *Histories*, which contains only an abridged version of the first six books, does not reflect Gregory's own intentions. It is, therefore, dangerous to take the poor quality of the Latin in that manuscript as an indication of what Gregory wrote.[46] His own grammar and spelling may have been rather more classical than is often supposed.

Arguments about language, in any case, need to be separated from arguments about style, particularly in a period of fast linguistic change, such as the Merovingian Age. Gregory knew he was writing in a rustic style, and he thought that this had certain advantages in terms of its accessibility to the intended audience. Caesarius of Arles seems to have held a similar opinion.[47]

44. On education in the seventh century, see Wood, 'Administration, law and culture', pp. 76–7.

45. Gregory, *Decem Libri Historiarum*, X 31.

46. W. Goffart, 'From *Historiae* to *Historia Francorum* and back again: aspects of the textual history of Gregory of Tours', in Goffart, *Rome's Fall and After.*, pp. 255–74.

47. M.-J. Delage, *Césaire d'Arles: sermons au peuple*, Sources Chrétiennes 175, pp. 180–208.

Like Caesarius, Gregory was, nevertheless, able to employ rhetorical devices when he wanted to, as in the prefaces to the *Histories*. Also to be detached from the question of grammar is that of narrative skill. That Gregory was a masterful storyteller has long been recognized.[48] That there is more to his writing than an ability to recount individual anecdotes is increasingly being acknowledged. The bishop of Tours was capable of ordering his narrative for particular effect. He used juxtaposition to emphasize his moral interpretation of events, and also to imply political comments, when it would have been dangerous to speak openly.[49]

The dislocation between the culture of Sidonius and that of Gregory of Tours is not, therefore, as extreme as a reading of the preface to the *Decem Libri Historiarum* might imply. Despite the absence of great schools of rhetoric, something of the literary culture of Sidonius had survived in the continuing tradition of letter-writing. Although Gregory himself left no works within this tradition, he was able to employ tricks of style when it suited him.

In one respect, however, Gregory does appear to have broken new ground. By deciding to write history he embarked on a task which other Gallo-Romans had avoided, it seems, for over a century.[50] Admittedly two Gallic chronicles survive from the fifth century,[51] and the *Chronicle* of Gregory's own contemporary Marius of Avenches is a text of utmost importance with regard to the territories once ruled by the Burgundian kings.[52] Nevertheless chronicles, with their short annalistic entries, are scarcely to be compared with a work of history on the scale of Gregory's *Ten Books*. Closer to such history in terms of the narrative skill required is hagiography. In the century and a half prior to Gregory numerous saints' *Lives* had been written, most notably those concerned with the Lérinian saints, Honoratus, Hilary of Arles and Caesarius, as well as those devoted to Germanus of Auxerre, the Jura Fathers, and Genovefa, the virgin saint of Paris.[53] But no Gallic history survives from this period, and Sidonius had explicitly refused to write one, when asked to provide an account of Attila's invasion of 451.[54] For the end of the fourth and early fifth centuries Gregory was able to use the Spanish historian Orosius, and the works of two otherwise unknown authors, Sulpicius Alexander and Renatus Profuturus Frigeridus, but thereafter he had

48. See the surveys by W. Goffart, *The Narrators of Barbarian History*, pp. 112–19, and G. de Nie, *Views from a Many-Windowed Tower*, pp. 1–26.

49. I.N. Wood, 'The secret histories of Gregory of Tours', *Revue Belge de Philologie et d'Histoire* (forthcoming)

50. For Sidonius's refusal to write history, see ep. IV 22. The commission may have been taken up by a Goth, if Peter Heather's suggestions about Ablabius are correct: *Goths and Romans 332–489*, pp. 64–5. Earlier in the fifth century Renatus Profuturus Frigeridus and Sulpicius Alexander had written histories: Gregory, *Decem Libri Historiarum*, I 8–9.

51. S. Muhlberger, *The Fifth-Century Chroniclers*.

52. J. Favrod, *La Chronique de Marius d'Avenches (455–581)*.

53. For the date of the *Vita Genovefae*, M. Heinzelmann and J.-C. Poulin, *Les Vies anciennes de sainte Geneviève de Paris: Étude critique*.

54. Sidonius Apollinaris, ep. IV 22.

no historian to follow. Apparently, within Gaul the writing of history had no appeal from the early fifth century until Gregory determined to write an account which would put his own times on record and set them in perspective.

It is not clear what induced Gregory to resort to the writing of history. His mother did encourage him in other of his writings,[55] and certainly there is a good deal of family tradition in the ten books, which might reflect her influence, but she is not mentioned in the preface to the *Decem Libri Historiarum*. Nor is there anything to suggest that Gregory was attempting to create a new genre of national historiography, although his *History* is often, misleadingly, described as a history of the Franks.[56] He himself emphasized his concern to record the good and bad that was being done in his own day, especially in so far as it concerned the Church, and he noted among the principal actors, kings, catholics and heretics. His concerns are moral and religious, and in certain respects, therefore, although they appear to be out of line with the literary culture of Sidonius and his sixth–century followers, they do look back to the moral response which met the first wave of the barbarian invasions.

Gregory's moral and religious concerns were unquestionably a significant factor in leading him to write history.[57] Arguably they are more apparent in the early books of *Histories* than in the later ones, where his commentary on events was constrained by political circumstances. In dealing with the difficult topics of his own day he resorted to silence and ambiguity.[58] For the late fifth and early sixth centuries, however, he was less constrained.[59] His moral reading of events was given free rein. As a result, although he is our major narrative source for the period, he is not a reliable guide to the opening decades of the Merovingian kingdom.

55. Gregory, *Liber de Virtutibus sancti Martini* I, *praef.*
56. See the comments of Goffart, 'From *Historiae* to *Historia Francorum* and back again'.
57. W. Goffart, *The Narrators of Barbarian History*, pp. 112–234; G. de Nie, *Views from a Many-Windowed Tower*, pp. 68–9, 128–32, 287–93.
58. Wood, 'The secret histories of Gregory of Tours'.
59. Wood, 'Gregory of Tours and Clovis', pp. 249–72.

Chapter Three

The Establishment of Merovingian Power: the Franks before 537

The Franks were the last of the invaders of Gaul, although ultimately they were the most successful. Already under Clovis (481–511) they could boast a leader of considerable stature. Then in 534 they overthrew the kingdom of the Burgundians, and two years later they were ceded the majority of the territory held by the Goths in Provence. Despite their importance, the emergence of the Franks as a power to be reckoned with is remarkably obscure. Clovis's father, Childeric I, is the first member of the Merovingian dynasty to be well attested in the sources, but even he remains a shadowy figure. Before him most of the evidence for the royal dynasty is legendary. And although the Frankish nation was reasonably well known to the Roman emperors in the fourth century, its origins are equally hidden in myth. Nevertheless the myths and legends associated with the Franks may hold some clues to their early history: certainly these legends were important to the developing political ideologies of the Merovingian kingdom. They deserve examination before any investigation of the more obviously historical evidence which survives for the reigns of Childeric and Clovis.

The Trojan legend of the Franks

Writing in the mid-seventh century, probably in Burgundy,[1] the chronicler known as Fredegar recorded the tradition that Priam was the first king of the Franks. Friga succeeded him. The people then split up, some remaining in Macedonia, others following Friga to the Danube and the Ocean. There a further division took place. Some stayed and, ruled by Torcoth, they became known as Turks, while others followed Francio to the Rhine, where they

---

1. W. Goffart, 'The Fredegar problem reconsidered', in Goffart, *Rome's Fall and After*, pp. 319–54.

became known as Franks. Thereafter, under the leadership of military leaders, *duces*, they remained undefeated.[2]

Another version of this Trojan origin legend was written down in 727 by the author of the *Liber Historiae Francorum*. According to him or her, after the fall of Troy Priam and Antenor led twelve thousand men to the river Tanais, and then to the Maeotic swamps. From there they moved to Pannonia, where they built a city called Sicambria. Meanwhile the emperor Valentinian offered remission of tribute for ten years to any people who could drive the Alans out of the Maeotic swamps. This the Trojans did, and as a result they were called *Franci*, which the author thought was the Attic for 'fierce'. When the ten years were over the Romans tried to reimpose tribute on the Franks, but the latter killed the tax collectors. As a result Valentinian sent troops against them, but they fought back. In the battle Priam was killed. The Franks left Sicambria, and moved to the Rhine. There Sunno, Antenor's son, died, and on the recommendation of Priam's son, Marchomir, the Franks elected Faramund as their *rex crinitus*, or long-haired king.[3]

These tales are obviously no more than legend, but they contain within them some interesting elements. Common to both are Trojan and migration traditions. The Trojan story is first recorded in Fredegar, and it seems to have had some vogue in seventh- and eighth-century Francia, where other Trojan legends were preserved.[4] Its origins can only be guessed at. Of relevance may be the tradition recorded by Ammianus Marcellinus, that the Burgundians were brothers of the Romans.[5] Although he does not say so explicitly, this could mean that they were thought of as Trojans. The claim is biologically nonsensical, but it seems to have had political significance since it is first recorded in the context of a diplomatic initiative of the emperor Valentinian I, intended to secure Burgundian support against Macrianus, king of the Alamans. Interestingly Macrianus was later to die at the hands of the Franks.[6] Perhaps the Franks and the Burgundians both gained the epithet 'Trojan' at this time. It may not be chance that the *Liber Historiae Francorum* names the emperor who called the followers of Priam Franks as Valentinian.[7]

With the evidence of Ammianus in mind, it is likely that the Franks, like the Burgundians, received the epithet 'Trojan' within the context of imperial diplomacy.[8] This would not have been the only occasion on which the notion of brotherhood was used to imply a special relationship with Rome; the people of Autun, for instance, regarded themselves as being brothers of the Romans,[9] as did the men of the Auvergne.[10] Subsequently what had

2. Fredegar, III 2.
3. *Liber Historiae Francorum*, 1–4.
4. J.M. Wallace-Hadrill, *The Long-Haired Kings*, p. 80.
5. Ammianus Marcellinus, XXVIII 5, 11.
6. Ammianus Marcellinus, XXX 3, 7.
7. *Liber Historiae Francorum*, 2.
8. Wood, 'Ethnicity and the ethnogenesis of the Burgundians', pp. 57–8.
9. *Panegyrici Latini*, V 2, 4.
10. Sidonius Apollinaris, ep. VII 7, 2.

been no more than a name implying a certain diplomatic affiliation between the Franks and Valentinian must have been interpreted as providing a genuine indication of the origins of the Franks. The idea will have been elaborated through contact with what was still known of the Trojan legend. Ultimately the story, originating partly in imperial politics and partly in a literary vogue, was recorded in one version by Fredegar and in another by the author of the *Liber Historiae Francorum*. By this time, of course, the diplomatic origins of the epithet had been forgotten.

Gregory of Tours seems not to have known about the Trojan origin of the Franks, but he did know an undeveloped version of their migration legend. He thought that the Franks came from Pannonia, and that they crossed the Rhine, and marched through Thuringia, when they set up long-haired kings in every region.[11] The peculiar geography involved has disturbed many, who have wanted to emend Thuringia to Tongres, an emendation already made by a scribe of one manuscript of Gregory's *Histories*. To do so suggests that Gregory's narrative at this point is genuine history rather than legend, which may have some basis other than a purely factual one. The migration from Pannonia, for instance, could have a symbolic significance, in that St Martin of Tours also came from there.[12] As for the fuller versions of the migration, as preserved in Fredegar's *Chronicle* and in the *Liber Historiae Francorum*, they may have been written in response to the origin legends of the Goths, which had been developed by Cassiodorus and preserved by Jordanes. In fact there is no reason to believe that the Franks were involved in any long-distance migration: archaeology and history suggest that they originated in the lands immediately to the east of the Rhine.[13]

The early Franks

The Franks first appear in historical sources relating to the barbarian invasions of the third century. There they are already established in the region of the lower Rhine. In fifth-century sources their territory is described as stretching as far east as the Elbe. It is generally thought that they were a new people only in name, and that they were made up of tribes such as the *Amsivarii*, *Chattuarii* and *Chatti*, who are mentioned in earlier sources, but rarely, if at all, in later ones.[14] At the end of the century the Franks appear in the Latin panegyrics as a maritime people, causing trouble in the Channel. As such, they were the precursors of the Saxons, who came to be more and more associated with attacks on the coasts of northern Gaul and Britain. By the late fourth century, in fact, the Saxons were said to have been involved in raids

---

11. Gregory, *Decem Libri Historiarum*, II 9.
12. Gregory, *Decem Libri Historiarum*, I 36.
13. E. James, *The Franks*, pp. 35–8.
14. James, *The Franks*, pp. 35–6; the fullest discussion of this period of Frankish history is E. Zöllner, *Geschichte der Franken*.

which had previously been ascribed to the Franks. As a result, it is not always easy to distinguish between the two peoples in the context of attacks on northern Gaul.[15] Nevertheless, in the fourth century the Franks were also in close contact with the Romans, as allies and as recruits for the imperial forces. Their involvement in Valentinian's wars with the Alamans was not unique. Moreover some individual Franks did extremely well for themselves in imperial service, and one or two even gained the consulship. Their significance in the 350s is recorded by Ammianus Marcellinus.[16] Two other sources provide crucial information on this stage of Frankish development. Although the histories of Sulpicius Alexander and Renatus Profuturus Frigeridus no longer survive, Gregory of Tours had access to their works, and excerpted them. Sulpicius Alexander recorded conflict in 389 between Arbogast, a Frank who held high military office in the empire, and two *regales*, or petty kings, of the Franks, Sunno and Marcomer, and he revealed that the latter was the warleader of the *Amsivarii* and the *Chatti*.[17] The *History* of Frigeridus covered events of a slightly later period. From it Gregory learnt about the activities of the Franks in the first decades of the fifth century, including their involvement in the civil wars which followed the usurpation by Constantine III.[18]

The long-haired kings

How the information of Frigeridus related to what followed, Gregory could not understand. The Franks of the late fourth and early fifth centuries could not be squared with those led by the Merovingians in the late fifth and sixth. What particularly distressed Gregory was the failure of Sulpicius Alexander, Renatus Profuturus Frigeridus and Orosius to talk about the kings of the Franks. For the most part, Sulpicius Alexander referred to petty kings, *regales*, rather than kings, *reges*. To make matters worse, when he did refer to a *rex* he failed to name him. Since Gregory's account of the Franks in the late fifth century revolves around kings, there is a dislocation between his summary of the evidence provided by earlier Roman historians, and his account of the establishment of long-haired kings after the migration from Pannonia. Had Gregory read Ammianus Marcellinus, who does talk of a Frankish king called Mallobaudes,[19] he would have been less troubled by the apparent absence of kings in the sources. Nevertheless the dislocation in his narrative may well be historically significant.

15. I.N. Wood, 'The Channel from the fourth to the seventh centuries AD', in S. McGrail, ed., *Maritime Celts, Frisians and Saxons*, pp. 93–6.

16. Ammianus Marcellinus, XV 5, 11; see J.H.W.G. Liebeschuetz, *Barbarians and Bishops: Army, Church and State in the Age of Arcadius and Chrysostom*, pp. 8–10.

17. Gregory, *Decem Libri Historiarum*, II 9.

18. Gregory, *Decem Libri Historiarum*, II 9.

19. Ammianus Marcellinus, XXX 3, 7; XXXI 10, 6.

After excerpting Sulpicius Alexander and Renatus Profuturus Frigeridus, Gregory placed the emergence of the Merovingians at the conclusion of his version of the Frankish migration.[20] The *Liber Historiae Francorum* went some way towards connecting the evidence of Sulpicius Alexander with the Trojan migration legend by making the supposed father of Chlodio, Faramund, the son of Sunno, thus uniting the Trojan and Merovingian families.[21] Fredegar's solution to the problem is more illuminating. Having provided the Franks with a Trojan origin, he stated that after the death of Francio they were ruled by *duces*, thus providing an explanation for the lack of a royal family, which so troubled Gregory, and creating space for a new dynasty of long-haired kings. But he also provided an account of Merovech's birth, which may cast light both on the origins of the Merovingians and also on some of the peculiarities of the account provided by the bishop of Tours.[22]

According to Fredegar, Merovech was conceived when Chlodio's wife went swimming, and encountered a Quinotaur. Although it is not explicitly stated that this sea-monster was the father of eponymous founder of the Merovingian dynasty, that is clearly the impression which Fredegar intended to give. The royal dynasty, thus, was thought to have had a supernatural origin. Gregory may well have known of these claims, and have thought of them as pagan. Whereas Fredegar relates the tale of the encounter with the Quinotaur, in the corresponding section of his *Histories* the bishop of Tours has an outburst against idolatry.[23]

The origin legend of the Merovingians as recorded by Fredegar is important not only for its suggestion that the family claimed to be descended from a supernatural ancestor, but also for the implications it has for the rise of the dynasty. In his panegyric on Majorian, Sidonius Apollinaris records the defeat of Chlodio, who was supposed to be the father of Merovech, at the *vicus Helena* in Artois.[24] This episode is thought to have taken place around 448. As Chlodio's son, Merovech must therefore be a figure of the second half of the fifth century. This suggests that the emergence of the Merovingian dynasty should be dated to the same period. Faramund, who is later said to have been Chlodio's father, is not attested in any early source. The dislocation apparent in Gregory's account of the early history of the Franks may be a direct reflection of the fact that the Merovingians were not a significant dynasty before the mid-fifth century. Their origins were separate and later than those of their people.

It also may be that Gregory's references to Thuringia have more relevance to the Merovingian family than to the Franks. According to the bishop of Tours, the Franks created long-haired kings in Thuringia, that is the territory

---

20. Gregory, *Decem Libri Historiarum*, II 9.
21. *Liber Historiae Francorum*, 5.
22. Fredegar, III 9.
23. Gregory, *Decem Libri Historiarum*, II 10; see H. Moisl, 'Anglo-Saxon royal genealogies and Germanic oral tradition', *Journal of Medieval History* 7 (1981), pp. 223–6.
24. Sidonius Apollinaris, carm., V, II. 210–54.

around modern Weimar. He also wrote that Chlodio, the first member of the dynasty about whose existence we can be certain, originally ruled in *Dispargum*, which he placed in Thuringia.[25] Again historians have questioned the geography, preferring to place *Dispargum* in modern Belgium, but given that Merovech's son, Childeric, had close associations with Thuringia, where he sought asylum, and found a wife,[26] it is possible that the Merovingian family did originate in the east of Frankish territory.

Taking the early references to the Franks together with their origin legends, it seems that we are dealing with a confederacy of peoples long settled in the region of the lower Rhine, and in the river valleys to the east, as far as the Elbe and the Main. In the third and fourth centuries these peoples were responsible for riverine and maritime raids against the north-eastern provinces of Gaul and Germany. At the same time, there were elements within the confederacy which became increasingly associated with the Roman Empire. The fifth century, however, saw a change among the Franks, when the Merovingian family came to dominance. This family seems to have ascribed to itself a peculiar supernatural origin, which probably had pagan overtones. It is quite unlike the Trojan origin which may already have been attributed to the Franks as a result of imperial diplomacy, and suggests that the Merovingian dynasty did not come to the fore as a result of its connections with Rome. It is possible that it came from the east of the Frankish confederacy, rather than the Rhineland.

Childeric I

Gregory learnt from his Roman sources that Chlodio captured Cambrai, and occupied territory as far as the Somme.[27] Of Merovech he records nothing other than his supposed descent from Chlodio and that he was the father of Childeric. For the latter, however, he was able to draw on a set of annals which seems to have been written in Angers, to judge from the use of the Latin verb *venire* (to come) with reference to that city.[28] Gregory records a battle fought by Childeric at Orléans, and the arrival of Odovacer and the Saxons at Angers. This was followed by plague and the death of Majorian's sometime general, Aegidius, who left a son called Syagrius. After Aegidius's death, Odovacer took hostages from Angers. Meanwhile the Goths drove the Britons from Bourges, but the *comes* (count or more precisely companion) Paul, who led a force of Romans and Franks, attacked the Goths and took their booty. Odovacer then reached Angers, where he was followed a day later by Childeric. *Comes* Paul was killed and Childeric took the city. The annals also recorded a war between the Romans and the Saxons. The Franks

25. Gregory, *Decem Libri Historiarum*, II 9.
26. Gregory, *Decem Libri Historiarum*, II 12.
27. Gregory, *Decem Libri Historiarum*, II 9.
28. Gregory, *Decem Libri Historiarum*, II 18.

took advantage of this by seizing some islands which the Saxons had held. Then Odovacer and Childeric made a treaty, and turned against the Alamans who had invaded Italy.[29]

These incidents scarcely add up to a coherent narrative, and the chronology is uncertain. If the Britons who were defeated by the Goths were the followers of Riothamus, they provide a date of 469. The Angers annals then cast a little, albeit crucial, light on events in the Loire valley in the reign of Anthemius, but it is not clear whose side Childeric was operating on. Indeed he appears as a somewhat independent figure. As for Odovacer, he has sometimes been identified with the warleader who was to be responsible for the deposition of the last emperor, Romulus Augustulus, in 476. Yet there is nothing to support or to disprove the identification. In so far as the general picture is intelligible, it appears that we are dealing with a group of warlords in the north, some of whom could claim to be upholding Roman jurisdiction. As regards the armies of these leaders, they were heterogeneous warbands rather than ethnic groups. Some Franks were prepared to fight under the Roman Paul, just as Childeric's men had once followed Aegidius according to a rather more legendary story which Gregory of Tours knew, but which Fredegar related at greater length.[30]

In Fredegar's narrative Childeric was exiled from the Franks for his sexual profligacy, but he arranged with his faithful follower, Wiomad, that he would return when the latter had sent him half a coin which they had divided between them. Wiomad cunningly stirred the Franks up against their new ruler, the Roman Aegidius, and then equally cunningly tricked the emperor Maurice into giving Childeric a vast treasure for his return to Francia. Re-established in power, Childeric was approached by the wife of his one-time host, Bisinus, king of the Thuringians. She had followed him because of his prowess and became his queen. On their wedding night she sent him to look outside and he saw, as a symbol of their future descendants, lions, unicorns and leopards; bears and wolves; and finally dogs.[31] As it stands in Fredegar, the story is part of a complex literary construction which includes parallel tales of friendship and marriage relating to the Ostrogothic king Theodoric and to the emperor Justinian, as well as to Childeric. As for the vision of the animals, which is absent from Gregory's version of events, it has become crucial to modern interpretations of Merovingian history as a tale of steady degeneration. Nevertheless, in its emphases on Aegidius and on the Thuringians, the story of Childeric's exile does seem to be drawing on real events. The death of Aegidius was recorded within the account of the Loire wars in the Angers chronicle, and his son Syagrius later appears as the first of the opponents and victims of Childeric's son Clovis.[32] Although there is no independent evidence for the behaviour of Basina, the name Basena is known

---

29. Gregory, *Decem Libri Historiarum*, II 19.
30. Gregory, *Decem Libri Historiarum*, II 12; Fredegar, III 11.
31. Fredegar, III 11–12.
32. Gregory, *Decem Libri Historiarum*, II 27.

from a silver ladle, dating perhaps to the sixth century, found at Weimar.[33] As recorded by Fredegar, the Byzantine link, with the emperor Maurice, is chronologically impossible, but the presence of vast quantities of Byzantine coin in Childeric's grave goes some way to supporting the idea that he did have support from the eastern Empire.

Childeric's grave at Tournai, discovered originally in 1653, is perhaps the richest royal burial known from the early medieval period; the quantity of goods found was astonishing. Fortunately, they were well published soon after their discovery; unfortunately, most of them were stolen from the Cabinet des Medailles in Paris in the nineteenth century.[34] They included weapons, jewellery, and objects which may have had some symbolic significance, whether religious or royal. Most notable among the latter were numerous gold bees or cicadas, which appear once to have adorned a cloak, a small bull's head, also made of gold, and a signet-ring, which identified the occupant of the tomb. What the finds show most certainly are the wealth, resources and contacts of the dead king. Most individual objects from the grave can be paralleled on a lesser scale by finds from other Frankish burials of the period. The garnet-work on the sword, however, may indicate Gothic influence, although the use of garnets was soon to become something of a speciality of the Franks. The finds also indicate the importance of Roman tradition. Childeric's brooch was in the style of that of a high-standing imperial official. And the Byzantine coins imply some connection with Constantinople.

The burial itself is neither entirely barbarian, nor entirely Roman. It is not possible to say whether the apparently symbolic objects had any sacral meaning, although the story of Merovech's birth provides some reason to think that the authority of the Merovingian kings in this period may have been bolstered by pagan tradition. The recent discoveries of horse burials around the site of the original find of 1653, and probably to be associated with it, have, however, provided further indications of paganism.[35] But the same discoveries have drawn attention to the proximity of the grave to a Roman cemetry, beside a Roman road, on the outskirts of the city. This mixture of Roman and barbarian in terms of the burial and of the grave goods needs to be seen in the contexts of Childeric's career as recorded by Gregory, following the annals of Angers. Childeric's tomb is the archaeological counterpart to the delicate problem of the relationship of his authority with that of Aegidius, and later with that of Paul.

For Childeric's authority at the end of his life there is one further piece of information, a letter of bishop Remigius of Rheims to the king's son, Clovis,

---

33. Pauly-Wissowa, *Real-Encyclopädie der classischen Altertumswissenschaft*, s.v. *Thuringi*.

34. James, *The Franks*, pp. 58–64.

35. R. Brulet, M.-J. Ghenne-Dubois and G. Coulon, 'Le quartier Saint-Brice de Tournai à l'époque mérovingienne', *Revue du Nord* 69 (1986), pp. 361–9.

preserved in the *Epistulae Austrasiacae*.[36] In the letter the bishop congratulates Clovis on taking over his father's position in *Belgica Secunda*, the province which included the cities of Rheims, Soissons, Châlons-sur-Marne, Noyon, Arras, Cambrai, Tournai, Senlis, Beauvais, Amiens, Thérouanne, Boulogne and Laon. In addition, he insists that he should listen to clerical advice, even though the new ruler was as yet a pagan, as his father had been. The date of the letter is disputed. Some have assigned it to 481, the probable date of Childeric's death, others to 486, when Clovis is said to have defeated Aegidius's son, Syagrius, and taken over the city of Soissons which he ruled. Since Soissons was part of *Belgica Secunda* it is argued that Clovis could not have been in a position to claim his father's authority over that province until Syagrius and his kingdom had been destroyed. It is scarcely possible to make a choice between the two dates. One relevant factor concerns the extent of Syagrius's power. It has been assumed that this was considerable. If this were the case, then one of two points must follow; either Childeric himself never ruled over the whole of *Belgica Secunda*, or Syagrius established his kingdom after Childeric's death. On the other hand, there is no reason for thinking that Syagrius's power ever extended beyond Soissons.[37] Whatever date one ascribes to the letter, Remigius conceived of Childeric's power in terms of Roman provincial rule, and he also thought that the clergy had a right to advise, even though the ruler might be barbarian and pagan. Childeric must have been subjected to many of the influences which were to impinge on his son.

Clovis

With Clovis, Frankish history appears to come of age. Gregory of Tours could at last write a coherent narrative of a barbarian ruler and provide him with a chronology. Gregory's account runs as follows: first Clovis defeated Syagrius; he then married Chlothild, the daughter of a Burgundian king. She attempted to convert her husband to catholic Christianity, but failed. During a battle against the Alamans, however, he vowed to become Christian if he was victorious; as a result of his victory he was baptized by bishop Remigius of Rheims. Next he allied with Godegisel against the Burgundian king Gundobad, but the latter survived through the cunning of his minister Aridius. Then Clovis attacked the Visigoths because they were heretics. On his return he received consular office from the eastern emperor; he subsequently chose Paris as his capital; his last years were spent eliminating rival Frankish leaders.[38] Clovis's reign, Gregory claims, lasted thirty years; with a little difficulty we can compute the dates of his accession as 481, the defeat of Syagrius as 486, the victory over the Alamans as 496 and the king's

36. *Epistulae Austrasiacae*, 2.
37. James, *The Franks*, pp. 67–71.
38. Gregory, *Decem Libri Historiarum*, II 27–43.

death as 511. From independent sources we can add dates for the Burgundian war (500), and for the Visigothic campaign (507).[39]

All in all Clovis's reign seems to be straightforward. There is, however, some conflict between detail provided by Gregory in his *Histories* and that to be found in his other works; moreover earlier evidence is at odds both with specific points in the *Histories*, and also with their general interpretation, which sees Clovis's reign as the manifestation of divine support granted to the king after his conversion.[40] Thus, Gregory's hagiography reveals that the exile of Quintianus of Rodez, which is important for the interpretation of Clovis's anti-arian policies, is placed a decade early in the *Histories*.[41] So too, perhaps, is the king's victory over the Alamans, and by extension his conversion.[42] Gregory's account of Clovis seems to be more concerned to create the image of a catholic king against whom his successors could be assessed, than with any desire to provide an accurate account of the reign. In order to understand Clovis within the context of the late fifth and early sixth centuries it is necessary to emphasize the contemporary evidence, and to treat Gregory, as far as possible, as a secondary source.

For Clovis's accession, Remigius's letter provides the only evidence outside Gregory. Little is known about the period from 481 until the end of the century, but during this period there were a number of significant marriages uniting the ruling dynasties of barbarian Europe. For the most part, these marriages served to strengthen the position of Theodoric the Great, the Ostrogothic ruler of Italy, but since Clovis was drawn into this web of matrimonial alliances, it is as well to note their relevance to his career. Theodoric himself married Audofleda, the sister of Clovis, and there were further marriages between his family, the Amals, and the ruling dynasties of the Visigoths, the Thuringians, the Herules and the Burgundians – that of the Burgundian prince Sigismund being of particular importance for developments in the 520s.[43] Clovis's own marriage to the Burgundian princess, Chlothild, as portrayed by Gregory, is not on a par with the rest. Whereas Theodoric envisaged marriage alliances as a means of coordinating the policies of the western kingdoms, the bishop of Tours implies that Clovis's choice of a bride was calculated to cause unease.

39. For the Burgundian campaign, see Marius of Avenches; for the outbreak of hostilities with Alaric II, see *Chronicle of Saragossa*; *Chronicle of 511*, 688; Cassiodorus *Variae*, III 1–4.

40. Wood, 'Gregory of Tours and Clovis'.

41. Compare Gregory, *Liber Vitae Patrum*, IV 1, with *Decem Libri Historiarum*, II 35.

42. See especially A. van de Vyver, 'La victoire contre les Alamans et la conversion de Clovis', *Revue Belge de Philologie et d'Histoire* 15 (1936), pp. 859–914; 16 (1937), pp. 35–94; van de Vyver, 'L'unique victoire contre les Alamans et la conversion de Clovis en 506', *Revue Belge de Philologie et d'Histoire*, 17 (1938), pp. 793–813. More recently see Wood, 'Gregory of Tours and Clovis'.

43. For an overview of Theodoric's relations with neighbouring rulers see Procopius, *Wars*, V 12, 22; Wolfram, *History of the Goths*, pp. 307–15. For Theodoric's marriage to Audofleda, see *Anonymi Valesiani Pars Posterior*, 63; Gregory, *Decem Libri Historiarum*, III 31.

Chlothild was the daughter of Gundobad's brother, Chilperic II. According to Gregory, Gundobad murdered Chilperic, and exiled Chlothild; Clovis, however, learnt about the girl, and asked to marry her; Gundobad was afraid to refuse.[44] Fredegar elaborated on the story, providing interesting detail about Geneva being her place of exile. In so doing he may have had access to local traditions.[45] If Gundobad was responsible for the death of Chilperic, then Chlothild was not likely to encourage good relations between the Franks and the Burgundians. This point is picked up by both Gregory and Fredegar, who describe the later Frankish invasion of Burgundy in 523 as the prosecution of Chlothild's bloodfeud against her uncle's family.[46] There are, however, problems with this interpretation. If Chlothild waited from the 490s until 523 the feud cannot have been uppermost in her mind. Moreover, Avitus of Vienne in a letter to Gundobad describes him as weeping over the deaths of his brothers.[47] It may be that Chilperic's death came to be seen in a new light after the Burgundian wars of the 520s and 530s. There is also a curious parallel between the manner of his death, supposedly by drowning in a well, and the similar disposal of Sigismund's body after his defeat and capture in 524.[48] It seems that Gregory's account of the murder of Chilperic and the subsequent bloodfeud reflected later assumptions, rather than historical reality. The marriage of Chlothild, therefore, may not have had the ominous implications which the bishop of Tours attributed to it.

Even Gregory did not associate Clovis's campaign against Gundobad with Chlothild's desire for vengeance. He describes it as being initiated by the Burgundian king's brother, Godegisel, who made secret overtures to Clovis, persuaded him to invade Burgundy, and then joined him on the battlefield. Gundobad fled to Avignon, where he may have received Visigothic support. There he came to terms with Clovis and became tributary to him. Then, with the Frankish king out of the way, he besieged and killed his brother in the city of Vienne.[49] Although no clear account of this episode dates from the early sixth century, Gregory's evidence is confirmed by the chronicle of his own contemporary, Marius of Avenches. The latter, who was writing in Burgundy, is an important source of information for the kingdom of the Burgundians. He dated the war to 500.

If Chlothild's influence on relations between Franks and Burgundians is hard to assess, so too is her role in her husband's conversion. Gregory sees her as the prime mover in this, while allowing for the importance of divine intervention in Clovis's victory against the Alamans.[50] On the other hand, a letter, written by Avitus of Vienne, on the occasion of the king's baptism, ascribes no role either to the queen or to the outcome of a battle, but sees

44. Gregory, *Decem Libri Historiarum* II 28.
45. Fredegar, III 17–20.
46. Gregory, *Decem Libri Historiarum*, III 6; Fredegar III 19, 33.
47. Avitus, ep. 5.
48. Gregory, *Decem Libri Historiarum*, II 28; III 6.
49. Gregory, *Decem Libri Historiarum*, II 32–3.
50. Gregory, *Decem Libri Historiarum*, II 29–31.

Clovis's decision to become a catholic as the personal choice of an intelligent monarch.[51] This silence over Chlothild and the Alaman victory need not imply that they played no part in Clovis's conversion, but it is as well to consider what Avitus did choose to emphasize. First, he comments on the king's astuteness in seeing through the arguments of the heretics, though he implies that for some while Clovis had been persuaded by them. Second, he congratulates the king on breaking with the traditions of his ancestors. Finally, after conjuring up an image of the royal baptism, he exhorts the king to further the cause of catholicism, while praising his recent action of freeing an unnamed captive people.

Avitus's letter deals only briefly with Clovis's paganism, and it does so in terms of the king's abandonment of ancestral religion. The problem of a convert's attitude to his forebears was a considerable one. It was recognized in the Carolingian period by the author of the *Life of Wulfram of Sens*, who thought that the Frisian leader Radbod preferred to be with his ancestors in hell rather than alone in heaven.[52] For a Merovingian, whose dynasty originated with a sea-monster, rejection of previous beliefs must have been particularly hard. In Clovis's case the sharpness of the break seems to have been remarkable. It can be gauged by a comparison between Childeric's burial at Tournai, and his son's interment in the Church of the Holy Apostles in Paris.[53] Further, Childeric's grave was apparently forgotten about; the horse burials which surrounded it were already cut into in the sixth century by secondary inhumations. Clovis and his descendants did not protect the tombs of their pagan ancestor.

There is more to be learnt about the king's conversion from the bishop of Vienne. Although his letter does not deny that Chlothild had a part to play in Clovis's conversion, nor that the king decided to accept baptism during a battle against the Alamans, in some respects the information it contains is at odds with Gregory's account and, therefore, with the traditional interpretation of events. This sees Clovis as converting directly from paganism to catholicism, without ever being influenced by the arian heresy. In so doing Clovis is thought to have been unique among the kings of the continental successor states. Further, his total avoidance of arianism is held to have made him more acceptable to the catholic Gallo-Romans, than were the other kings of his generation, and to have helped ensure that the Franks were more successful than either the Burgundians or the Visigoths. Avitus's letter to Clovis suggests that this interpretation is unacceptable, since he implies that there was a genuine possibility that Clovis would opt for arianism. Moreover the title of one of the bishop of Vienne's sermons, now unfortunately lost, reveals that Clovis's sister Lenteild had accepted arianism.[54] Audofleda,

51. Avitus, ep. 46.

52. *Vita Vulframni*, 9; on the problems of this text, see I.N. Wood, 'Saint-Wandrille and its hagiography', in I.N. Wood and G.A. Loud, eds, *Church and Chronicle in the Middle Ages*, pp. 13–4.

53. Gregory, *Decem Libri Historiarum*, II 43.

54. Avitus, hom. 31; Gregory, *Decem Libri Historiarum*, II 31.

another sister, was probably converted to the heresy at the court of her husband Theodoric.[55] Clovis and the Franks might easily have become arian.

In assessing the significance of Clovis's conversion to catholicism it is worth noting the lack of a firm association between the Burgundians and heresy. This is apparent from Chlothild's own beliefs. Here was a princess who was catholic, although she belonged to a family which is usually thought of as arian. Nor was she alone; her sister was apparently catholic, and so was Gundobad's wife, queen Caretena.[56] In addition there is the letter of Sidonius, a generation earlier, recording the good works of Chilperic I and his wife, and the high regard in which they were held by bishop Patiens.[57] In fact, evidence from the early and mid-fifth century consistently portrays the Burgundians as being catholic. It is only in Gundobad's reign that there is clear evidence for an arian Church among the Burgundians, but Chlothild and her sister show that there were catholics in the royal family even then. Indeed it is hard to identify any individual Burgundian as being arian, except for Gundobad, who seriously considered converting to catholicism, and Sigismund, who did convert and was remembered as a martyr. It seems, therefore, that the Burgundians should be seen as a largely catholic people, but that for a brief period under Gundobad they had an arian Church. Since Gundobad may have been out of step with the majority of his people and his family, his own beliefs should perhaps be connected with those of his uncle, the arian Ricimer. Evidence for the Burgundians and for the Franks suggests that neither group can be neatly categorized as either arian or catholic.

The final section of Avitus's letter to Clovis, as it survives, exhorts the king to be active in the work of evangelization, and refers to the recent liberation of a captive people. Identification of this group opens up the problem of the date of the king's baptism, and by extension the chronology as well as the interpretation of the second half of his reign. Gregory linked Clovis's conversion with his victory over the Alamans. Traditionally this battle was dated to 496. Nevertheless the Belgian scholar van der Vyver pointed out that a panegyric addressed by Ennodius of Pavia to Theodoric the Great in 508 refers to a recent influx of Alamans into Ostrogothic territory, and he suggested that this should be linked to Clovis's victory, which he placed in 506.[58] The argument, although thought-provoking, was not watertight; panegyrics are not noted for their chronological reliability – and besides there could have been more than one battle against the Alamans. Gregory himself seems to refer to at least two: in addition to that in which he thought Clovis had been converted, he mentions a battle at Tolbiac or Zülpich where

55. Gregory, *Decem Libri Historiarum*, III 31.

56. Fredegar, III 17; *Vita Marcelli Deiensis* 9, ed. F. Dolbeau, 'La Vie en prose de saint Marcel, évêque de Die', *Francia* 11 (1983), pp. 97–130; see Wood, 'Ethnicity and the ethnogenesis of the Burgundians', pp. 58–60.

57. Sidonius Apollinaris, ep. VI 12, 3.

58. van de Vyver, 'La victoire contre les Alamans et la conversion de Clovis'; 'L'unique victoire contre les Alamans et la conversion de Clovis en 506'.

Sigibert, king of the Ripuarian Franks, was wounded.[59] Although it is often assumed that these were one and the same battle, there is no evidence that Clovis fought at Zülpich, and it is possible that they were separate events. In fact conflict between Franks and Alamans was probably endemic from at least the fourth century until Clovis's reign. Thereafter Gregory has nothing more to say about the Alamans. The migration mentioned by Ennodius probably reflects the collapse of the Alamanic kingdom, and the beginning of Frankish annexation of their territory.[60]

Although Ennodius's panegyric cannot be used as absolute proof that Gregory's chronology for Clovis's conversion is wrong, it does suggest that there was conflict between the Franks and the Alamans shortly before 508. Probably this conflict should be placed before the Visigothic war of 507. According to Gregory, Clovis attacked Alaric because of his dislike of arianism, whose evils he illustrates with a partial, and misplaced account of the exile of Quintianus from his diocese of Rodez. As he marched south Clovis was careful not to alienate the catholic Church or its saints. He encountered the Visigoths at the *campus Vogladensis*, usually identified as Vouillé, but more probably Voulon, near Poitiers.[61] There he defeated and killed Alaric II. Then he moved to Bordeaux for the winter, before returning to Orléans and Paris. His eldest son, Theuderic, marched south to Albi, Rodez and then to Clermont. For Gregory this was a catholic crusade, and he was able to depict it as such by omitting to tell us that after 'Vouillé' the Burgundians, who were still arian in his eyes, joined in the harassment of the Goths.

Evidence for Alaric II's reign does not fit easily with the picture of Visigothic arianism presented by Gregory. There is nothing to suggest outright conflict between arians and catholics in the kingdom of Toulouse, except in the years of expansion under Euric. Although some catholic bishops are known to have been exiled during the reign of Alaric II, where there is any detailed evidence of the circumstances, factors other than religious conflict appear to have been important. Thus Caesarius of Arles was accused by one of his own clergy of committing treason with the Burgundians at a time when they were ruled by the arian Gundobad. Later, he was again accused of treason; this time by the people of Arles and the Jews. On neither occasion was the original accusation made by the arian Goths.[62] Although Gregory states in his *Histories* that Quintianus of Rodez was suspected of treason by the Visigoths, in his *Life* of the bishop he reveals that the local catholics were opposed to him, because he had moved the bones of a favourite saint. He also implies that the exile should be dated to the reign of Clovis's successor, Theuderic I.[63]

59. Gregory, *Decem Libri Historiarum*, II 30, 37.
60. Ennodius, *Panegyricus*, 72; Wolfram, *History of the Goths*, pp. 313–14.
61. I accept the argument of R.A. Gerberding, *The Rise of the Carolingians and the Liber Historiae Froncorum*, p. 41. For the date, see *Chronicle of Saragossa; Chronicle of 511*, 688.
62. *Vitae Caesarii*, I 21, 29–30, 36.
63. Gregory, *Liber Vitae Patrum*, IV 1; Gregory, *Decem Libri Historiarum*, II 35; see also Wood, 'Gregory of Tours and Clovis', pp. 256–7.

Other evidence for Alaric II's reign suggests that he was concerned to establish good relations with the catholic Gallo-Romans in the years immediately before 'Vouillé'. He was responsible for the compilation of a Roman law-book, the *Breviary*.[64] He also supported a catholic Church council presided over by Caesarius of Arles at Agde in 506, and he approved the holding of another council in the following year,[65] although it did not meet because of the king's defeat and death at the hands of Clovis. The evidence from the Visigothic kingdom, therefore, does not support Gregory's image of hostility between the arians and catholics in Aquitaine. Catholicism is unlikely to have been the key to Clovis's success.

Moreover, sources contemporary with the war of 507 allow a different interpretation from that offered by Gregory. Avitus of Vienne associated the campaign with unspecified matters of finance.[66] Cassiodorus, Theodoric's spokesman, thought the causes of the conflict were minor, and tried, unsuccessfully, to prevent war breaking out by drawing attention to the ties of marriage which united the kings.[67] Since Gundobad and Theodoric were both arian, Avitus and Cassiodorus would have been ill-placed to describe Clovis's war as a crusade. Nevertheless, the economic factors mentioned by Avitus may have been significant. The 'Vouillé' campaign was not the first Frankish invasion of Visigothic Aquitaine. There is a reference among the additions to the chronicle of Prosper preserved in a Copenhagen manuscript to a Frankish attack on Bordeaux in 498.[68] It is possible that one of these earlier attacks had ended with a promise by Alaric II to pay tribute. Gregory states that a financial settlement ended the Burgundian war.[69] There was undoubtedly a mercenary side to the campaigns of this period.

Nevertheless, there are indications that Gregory had good reason to think that the war had a religious aspect. In his account of the manoeuvres preceding the battle of 'Vouillé' Gregory describes the appearance of miraculous signs, indicating divine approval for the Franks. For at least one of these anecdotes he had a written source; he was not the first to see the confrontation between Clovis and Alaric in religious terms.[70] In addition he records Clovis's concern for the property of the catholic Church, again citing earlier hagiographical texts in support of his case. For this last point, there is better evidence from 507. The first official document to survive from a Merovingian king is a letter addressed by Clovis to his bishops, explaining that *en route* for 'Vouillé' he had issued an edict protecting Church property.[71] Clearly Clovis was currying favour with the catholic clergy at the start of the Visigothic war; that is not to say that the war was a crusade, nor is

64. Wolfram, *History of the Goths*, pp. 196–7.
65. Wolfram, *History of the Goths*, pp. 200–1.
66. Avitus, ep. 87.
67. Cassiodorus, *Variae* III 1–4.
68. *Auctarium Havniense*, s.a. 498.
69. Gregory, *Decem Libri Historiarum*, II 32.
70. Gregory, *Decem Libri Historiarum*, II 37.
71. *Capitularia Merowingica*, 1.

it to say that the king had already been baptized. Avitus places Clovis's baptism in the aftermath of the liberation of a 'captive people'; the only group which can easily be described in these terms are the Gallo-Romans of Aquitaine. It is difficult to understand Avitus's comment as anything other than a hyperbolic reference to the defeat of the Visigoths, and the destruction of Gothic power.

A reasonable interpretation of the religious history of Clovis's reign could thus run as follows: from the moment of his father's death, Clovis had to deal with the catholic hierarchy; nevertheless he remained a pagan, even after his marriage to a catholic wife. Drawn into the complex political world of the 490s he showed an interest in the arianism of his fellow monarchs, as well as in the catholicism of Chlothild, and some members of his court were actually baptized as arians; he himself, although he may have already been converted to Christianity, did not commit himself firmly either to catholicism or arianism, although he certainly showed an interest in the views of the heretics. His final decision was possibly taken at the time of the war with Alaric, when he may have thought that there was propaganda value to be gained by standing as the defender of the catholic Church; he was subsequently baptised, probably in 508.

In 511 Clovis summoned a council of bishops to Orléans, largely to deal with ecclesiastical matters in newly conquered Aquitaine.[72] Whether he was a good master for the Church, however, is a moot point; there is correspondence of Remigius of Rheims dating from after Clovis's death, and again preserved in the *Epistolae Austrasiacae* which suggests that the king made some poor appointments, and that the bishop acquiesced in them, to the disgust of other members of the clergy.[73] Even more questionable is the significance of the king's conversion for his people. Some Franks had already been converted. Others will have followed their master to the font, but one need not believe the figure of three thousand given by Gregory. The majority of the Franks are unlikely to have been affected as yet by Christianity.

The 'Vouillé' campaign and the following year mark the high-point of Clovis's reign. In 508 Theuderic continued his father's onslaught on the Gothic south, in tandem with the Burgundians.[74] In the same year Clovis received some recognition from the emperor Anastasius. Gregory's claim that he was hailed as consul and Augustus at Tours must be a misunderstanding, although an honorary consulship is not out of the question.[75] The implications of the recognition, on the other hand, are clear from references

72. Council of Orléans (511); the geographical concerns of the council are indicated by the signatories.

73. *Epistolae Austrasiacae*, 3.

74. *Chronicle of 511*, 689, 690.

75. Gregory, *Decem Libri Historiarum* II 38. On the celebrations, see M. McCormick, 'Clovis at Tours, Byzantine public ritual and the origins of medieval ruler symbolism', in E.K. Chrysos and A. Schwarcz, eds, *Das Reich und die Barbaren*, pp. 155–80; M. McCormick, *Eternal Victory: Triumphal Rulership in Late Antiquity, Byzantium and the Early Medieval West*, pp. 335–7.

in eastern sources and from Cassiodorus. The year 508 marked the nadir of relations between the Byzantine empire and the Ostrogothic king Theodoric the Great, and war broke out.[76] Hitherto Theodoric had been regarded by the emperor as the senior figure in the barbarian west: now Clovis was to supplant him. This state of affairs was not to go unchallenged. After Alaric's death, Theodoric took it upon himself to defend the Visigoths, and to punish their attackers. Clovis was fortunate not to face the full brunt of the Ostrogothic counterattack; the Burgundians, who did, suffered for their involvement in the campaign of 508, and lost a substantial strip of land in the south of the kingdom.[77] The Ostrogothic presence in Provence, however, meant that the annexation of Aquitaine by Clovis's son Theuderic was not to continue, at least for the time being; the following years saw the resumption of Gothic power in Rodez, if not beyond.

Perhaps because he was blocked in the south, Clovis now turned his attention to the north. According to Gregory, at the end of his life he destroyed the kingdom of Cologne under Sigibert the Lame, then he turned against various other kings of the Franks, Chararic and Ragnachar, whose base was in Cambrai, along with the latter's brothers, Ricchar and Rignomer, who was killed in Le Mans. In addition he tried to discover any other royal figures, in order to eliminate potential rivals.[78] The chronology of these stories is surprising; Clovis ought to have eradicated Frankish opposition earlier in his reign. Nevertheless there are incidental details in Gregory's account which might be thought to suggest that some, if not all, of these atrocities are rightly placed; for instance Gregory states that Clovis had Chararic tonsured, which, if true, implies that the Merovingian himself had already been converted. If Gregory's ordering of events here is right, and there are no means of testing this part of his account, then the last years of Clovis's reign were concerned with the internal power politics of the Franks, whereas much of his earlier activity had taken place on an international stage.

Whatever the chronology, when Clovis died in 511 the Frankish kingdom was certainly the most powerful kingdom in Gaul, and he was apparently the favoured western ally of the Byzantine emperor Anastasius. That is not to say that his power and influence was actually greater than that of the Ostrogothic king Theodoric, nor that it was inevitable that the Franks would permanently eclipse the Burgundians in Gaul. There was still much to play for. Nevertheless Clovis had transformed the Franks from being an essentially northern people to one which was influential in the wider politics of Gaul and the Mediterranean. His reign was crucial, but not decisive in the development of Frankish power.

76. Marcellinus Comes, *Chronicle* s.a. 508; Cassiodorus, *Variae* II 38.
77. Procopius, *Wars*, V 12, 44–5; Cassiodorus, *Variae*, III 41; Wolfram, *History of the Goths*, pp. 309, 311–12.
78. Gregory, *Decem Libri Historiarum*, II 40–2.

Theuderic, the Danes and the Thuringians

When Clovis died he divided his kingdom into four. His eldest son Theuderic (511–33) ruled from Rheims, and the sons who had been born to Chlothild, Chlodomer (511–24), Childebert I (511–58) and Chlothar I (511–61), ruled from Orléans, Paris and Soissons respectively. This division set something of a precedent.[79] Clovis's own action, however, does not appear to have been traditional. The Byzantine historian, Priscus, records a disputed succession among the Franks before Attila's invasion of Gaul.[80] Although Gregory refers to Clovis's relative Ragnachar as *rex*, he does not call Ragnachar's brothers, Ricchar and Rignomer, kings.[81] It is clear, therefore, that the Frankish kingdom was not automatically divided between all the sons of the previous ruler. Clovis's decision that his kingdom should be so divided most probably reflects the precise political situation at the end of his reign. Chlothild must have been determined to see the succession of her sons. They were, however, still minors. Theuderic, who was Clovis's son by an earlier liaison, had already distinguished himself as a military leader: he could not be passed over. The division may have been the only way that Chlothild was able to ensure that part of Clovis's realm passed to her offspring.[82] Whatever the cause, the solution was to have major consequences in terms of the later political history of the Merovingians.

For the decade after Clovis's death we hear little about his sons. Only Theuderic, in the eastern kingdom of Rheims, attracted Gregory's attention, first when he sent his own son Theudebert to deal with a Danish invasion led by Chlochilaich, the Hygelac of Old English poetry,[83] and second when he became involved in the internal politics of the Thuringian royal family. Gregory of Tours places the original creation of the long-haired kings in Thuringia. And it was there that Childeric fled. Gregory has nothing to say about the Thuringians in Clovis's reign. But he does record that Clovis's son Theuderic was approached by Hermanfrid, king of the Thuringians, who was intent on destroying his brother and fellow ruler, Baderic. According to the bishop of Tours, Hermanfred offered Theuderic half the Thuringian kingdom for his help. After Baderic's destruction, however, he did not keep his agreement. Subsequently, probably in 531, Theuderic enlisted the support of his half-brother, Chlothar, in an invasion of Thuringia. Hermanfred was killed, his niece Radegund was taken prisoner by Chlothar, and the Thuringian kingdom was annexed.[84]

In Gregory's narrative the Thuringians appear as dupes for the more sophisticated and warlike Franks. This may well underestimate their

79. I.N. Wood, 'Kings, kingdoms and consent', in P.H. Sawyer and I.N. Wood, eds, *Early Medieval Kingship*, pp. 6–26
80. Priscus, fr. 16, cited in Gordon, *The Age of Attila*, p. 106.
81. Gregory, *Decem Libri Historiarum*, II 42.
82. Wood, 'Kings, kingdoms and consent', pp. 25–6.
83. Gregory, *Decem Libri Historiarum*, III 3; compare the Hygelac of *Beowulf.*
84. Gregory, *Decem Libri Historiarum*, III 4, 7–8.

significance. The Ostrogothic king Theodoric cultivated contacts with them, drawing them into his web of marriage alliances, and trying to use them as a check on Clovis in 507. They were included within the diplomacy of the successor states, even though they were outside the geographical bounds of the one-time Roman Empire.[85] They may even have converted to Christianity. Radegund is extensively commemorated as an abbess and a saint in the writings of Venantius Fortunatus and her second biographer Baudonivia. Nowhere is it suggested that she had to convert from paganism.

The end of the Burgundian kingdom and the Auvergne campaign

The defeats of Chlochilaich and Baderic are the only episodes involving the Franks which are recorded by Gregory for the decade after Clovis's death. They obscure a hiatus in the expansion of Merovingian power. During this period the Ostrogoths maintained a strong presence in Provence, and re-established Gothic authority in parts of southern Aquitaine.[86] They would continue to be a significant force in Gaul until the Byzantine threat led them to relinquish their holdings in Provence in 537.[87] Yet it was the Burgundians, if anyone, who were the most prestigious people in Gaul in the second decade of the sixth century.

Clovis's death must have come as a relief to Gundobad. There could be no doubt that the Burgundian was the leading ruler in Gaul between 511 and 516, and he may well have been the barbarian king most favoured by the court of Constantinople. At the end of his life he appears to have held the prestigious title of *magister militum*, an office he had probably held after Ricimer's death in 472. When he died in 516 his son Sigismund succeeded him, and negotiated with Byzantium for his father's title.[88] In Italy, Theodoric was worried by the Burgundian dealings with the emperor, and tried to cut communications.[89] The Franks may also have been uneasy.

A year after his elevation to the throne Sigismund gave proof of his statesmanship when at his Easter court he issued his law-book, the *Liber Constitutionum*, better, though less correctly, known as the *Lex Gundobada*.[90] But it is the ecclesiastical aspects of Sigismund's reign which are best recorded, by Avitus, Gregory, two Church councils, and the *Passio* of the king himself. Gundobad had contemplated conversion to catholicism, and Sigismund was already a catholic by 515, when he founded one of the most prestigious of

85. Cassiodorus, *Variae*, III 3; VI 1; Procopius, *Wars*, V 12, 22.
86. Wolfram, *History of the Goths*, pp. 244–5, 309–11.
87. Procopius, *Wars*, V 13, 14–29; Agathias, I 6, 3–6; Wolfram, *History of the Goths*, p. 315.
88. Avitus, epp. 78, 93–4.
89. Avitus, ep. 94.
90. I.N. Wood, 'Disputes in late fifth- and sixth-century Gaul: some problems', in W. Davies and P. Fouracre, eds, *The Settlement of Disputes in Early Medieval Europe*, p. 10; Wood, 'Ethnicity and the ethnogenesis of the Burgundians', p. 54.

early medieval monasteries, that of St Maurice at Agaune. It was distinguished by its peculiar liturgical arrangement, the *laus perennis* or perpetual chant. For this the monks were organized into groups to ensure that praise was offered unceasingly to God.[91] It was to be an arrangement which was thought particularly appropriate to royal monasteries.[92] A year after the foundation of Agaune Sigismund had become king, and in 517, the year in which the *Liber Constitutionum* was issued, a great council of the bishops of the kingdom was held at Epaon. It dealt largely with matters of church discipline, and with the problem of dismantling the arian Church in Burgundy.[93]

The apparent concord of Sigismund's opening years did not last long; within a short period of time the episcopate threatened to suspend the king from communion, because of his support for a royal official in a case of incest. To protect themselves they also determined to withdraw to a monastery. Sigismund was forced to accept the bishops' judgement.[94] Second, and more important, in 522, stirred up by his second wife, if we may believe Gregory, he had his son by a previous marriage, Sigistrix, strangled. He subsequently decided to do penance for the deed, and set off to his foundation at Agaune.[95] In 523, Chlodomer attacked the Burgundian kingdom. Gregory associates the attack with Chlothild's bloodfeud, but more likely it was an opportunist move prompted by the crisis following the murder of Sigistrix. The campaign was swift; Sigismund was handed over to Chlodomer and murdered, together with his wife and children; their corpses were thrown down a well. Subsequently his body was taken back to Agaune, where it became the object of a cult, the first royal saint-cult of the Middle Ages.[96] Chlodomer returned to Burgundy in 524, but was defeated and killed at Vézeronce by Sigismund's brother, Godomar.[97] The latter took over the kingship and established himself in power, until he was overthrown by Chlodomer's brothers, Childebert and Chlothar, ten years later.[98]

Thus far the events are reasonably certain, and in any case Gregory's narrative is backed up by entries in the chronicle of Marius of Avenches. Nevertheless there are problems with the evidence not only for the fall of Burgundy, but also for the related history of the Auvergne. In Gregory's account, Chlodomer, before setting off to Vézeronce, asked his half-brother, Theuderic, to accompany him, and the latter agreed; but when Childebert and Chlothar asked him to join them at the time of their later campaign

91. Avitus, hom. 25; *Vita Abbatum Acaunensium absque epitaphiis*, 3; Gregory, *Decem Libri Historiarum*, III 5.

92. F. Prinz, *Frühes Mönchtum im Frankenreich*, pp. 102–12.

93. Council of Epaon (517).

94. Council of Lyons; *Vita Apollinaris*, 2–3.

95. Gregory, *Decem Libri Historiarum*, III 5. The date is given by Marius of Avenches.

96. Gregory, *Decem Libri Historiarum*, III 5–6. Again the date comes from Marius. For the cult, see Gregory, *Liber in Gloria Martyrum*, 74; *Passio Sigismundi Regis*.

97. Gregory, *Decem Libri Historiarum*, III 6; Marius of Avenches, s.a. 524.

98. Gregory, *Decem Libri Historiarum*, III 11; Marius of Avenches, s.a. 534.

against the Burgundian kingdom, he refused. Instead, because his followers were anxious for a fight, he led them against the Auvergne, where there had recently been a conspiracy against him, which he wished to punish.[99]

The crucial difficulty revolves around the dating of the Auvergne campaign. Gregory makes this contemporary with the destruction of the Burgundian kingdom in 534, but this is chronologically impossible, since Quintianus, who was bishop of Clermont at the time of the attack, died in *c.* 524,[100] and Theuderic seems to have died in 533. If he led his followers against the Auvergne while one of his stepbrothers fought against the Burgundians, Theuderic must have done so in 523 or 524. Why then did Gregory specifically associate him with Chlodomer's invasion of 534? The answer may lie in a speech put into the mouth of Sigismund's wife by Gregory. In order to incite her husband against her stepson, Sigistrix, she claimed that the prince intended to kill his father, to take over Burgundy and subsequently Italy.[101] This last ambition may not be as absurd as it looks; Sigistrix was, after all, the grandson of Theodoric. The Ostrogothic king may well have reacted to his grandson's murder; he certainly sent an army to occupy territory between the Drôme and the Durance.[102] The forces of Theuderic which Gregory thought were present at Vézeronce may have been those of Theodoric, angered by the murder of his grandson. There is a further indication that this is the right solution; one of the few archaeological finds to have come from the battlefield at Vézeronce is a fine helmet, which has been thought to be of Ostrogothic workmanship.

Gregory seems to have confused the chronology of events in the 520s and 530s, just as he had muddied that of the two previous decades. The history of Burgundy and the Auvergne in the later period can, however, be reconstructed with some confidence. In 522 Sigismund killed Sigistrix. The following year Chlodomer invaded Burgundy and captured and killed Sigismund. In 524 he attacked Godomar, in alliance with the Ostrogoths, but he was killed at Vézeronce. As a result his own kingdom was divided among his brothers. Theuderic, meanwhile, mounted a punitive raid against the Auvergne – ostentatiously avoiding the Burgundian campaign. His behaviour at this point can be readily explained by the fact that he was Sigismund's son-in-law. After Vézeronce Godomar took power in Burgundy, which he held until his overthrow in 534.

The crucial lessons to be learnt from this go beyond a reconstruction of events. Despite the fact that he was born in the Auvergne in 539, Gregory was still unable to provide an accurate account of what took place in Clermont in the 520s and 530s; moreover he was thoroughly confused by the whole career of Quintianus, even though the latter's successor as bishop was

99. Gregory, *Decem Libri Historiarum* III 6, 11.
100. I.N. Wood, 'Clermont and Burgundy: 511–534', *Nottingham Medieval Studies* 32 (1988), p. 122.
101. Gregory, *Decem Libri Historiarum*, III 5.
102. Wolfram, *History of the Goths*, p. 312.

Gregory's uncle and mentor, Gallus.[103] At the same time, although he was mistaken about the chronology, his account of Theuderic's expedition was extremely vivid. And he returned to the event again and again in his works. That he had good cause is suggested by the fact that the raid is mentioned in the legal *formulae* of the Auvergne as being a time of great destruction.[104] The punitive expedition of a Merovingian monarch was not quickly forgotten. Frankish Kings could be as brutal as Euric had been in the days of Visigothic expansion.

With the conquest of Burgundy, the Frankish take-over of Gaul was almost complete; three years later the Ostrogoths, under enormous pressure from the Byzantine invading forces in Italy, handed over Provence to ensure peace with the Franks. The Merovingian kingdom was firmly established. It included most of modern France, with the exception of the old Roman province of Septimania, lying between the Rhône delta and the Pyrenees, which remained subject to the Visigoths until the eighth century, and Brittany, over which the Franks exercised influence rather than direct rule. To the east the Merovingians controlled the French- and German-speaking areas of Switzerland, as well as Belgium, Luxembourg and the Rhineland, at least as far north as Utrecht. The coastal areas of Frisia were effectively independent in the late seventh and early eighth centuries, but previously they may well have been under Frankish control. Between the accession of Clovis in 481 and and the acquisition of Provence in 537 the Merovingians had established one of the most powerful of the successor states to the Roman Empire. In time it was to become the greatest of all.

103. Wood, 'Clermont and Burgundy: 511–534'.
104. *Formulae Arvernenses*, 1.

Chapter Four

Kings and Kingdoms: The Structure of the Realm in the Sixth Century

With the conquest of Burgundy in 534 and the cession of Provence two years later, the main geographical outlines of the Merovingian kingdom were drawn. Inevitably there would be variation along the frontiers, and, more important, Frankish control over neighbouring peoples, including the Thuringians, was not constant; the hegemony exercised by the Merovingians to the east of the Rhine was an integral part of their empire. Nevertheless, the base of their power lay within the territory which they had acquired by the late 530's.

The vast block of land over which the Merovingians ruled was essentially treated as two different units; on the one hand there was the north and the east, that is the territories which had been controlled by the Franks before the 'Vouillé' campaign, together with the Burgundian kingdom; on the other there was Provence and the lands captured from the Visigoths. The first of these areas in the sixth century was usually divided up into a number of geographically coherent kingdoms. Aquitaine and Provence, once they came into the hands of the Franks, were also divided, but with less concern for geography, and the units were subordinated to the kingdoms of the north.

The divisions of the kingdom

The history of the divisions of the kingdom, or *Teilungen* as they are often known to modern scholars, is a complex one, and it is one that has to be reconstructed from narrative sources which are not concerned to describe those kingdoms, but which provide the relevant information only in passing. As a result our picture of the divisions, and of the resulting kingdoms, or *Teilreiche*, is not complete, and even the outline that we have was not properly understood until the middle of the twentieth century.[1]

1. Central to any understanding of this crucial issue are the two articles by E. Ewig, 'Die fränkischen Teilungen und Teilreiche (511–613)' and 'Die fränkischen Teilreiche im 7. Jahrhundert (613–714)', reprinted in Ewig, *Spätantikes und fränkisches Gallien*, 1 (Munich, 1976), pp. 114–71, 172–230.

When Clovis died his kingdom was divided equally between his four surviving sons. To a large extent we have to infer the nature of this earliest division from what we can learn of later arrangements; in particular we are told by Gregory of Tours that in 561 Clovis's grandsons took over the kingdoms of the previous generation; thus, Charibert I (561–7) received the portion of Childebert I (511–58), based on Paris; Guntram (561–92) that of Chlodomer (511–24), with its centre at Orléans; Chilperic I (561–84) was given the kingdom of Soissons, once held by Chlothar I (511–61); while Sigibert I (561–75) inherited the realm of Theuderic I (511–34) and his descendants, Theudebert I (534–47) and Theudebald (547–55), and established himself at Rheims.[2]

In addition to working back from subsequent arrangements, we can use Gregory's narrative to establish the spheres of activity of the various kings. Theuderic I, for instance, was faced with a Danish invasion in the Rhineland. The majority of Gregory's information on him, however, concerns his territory in Aquitaine and centres on his attack on Clermont and the Auvergne.[3] It may be significant that Clermont, which was one of the Aquitanian cities consigned to the east Frankish kingdom of Theuderic and his successors, was also one of the cities which he had invested in 507, in the aftermath of 'Vouillé'. The way in which Aquitaine was divided up and alloted to the northern kingdoms may owe much to the nature of the Frankish conquest of the area in the first three decades of the sixth century; but that is a topic on which we have scarcely any information.

The other evidence provided by Gregory on the *Teilreiche* in this period is concerned largely with modifications to the division of 511, and not with the original arrangements. Thus, after Chlodomer's death at Vézeronce, his sons were brought up by their grandmother, Chlothild, who clearly expected them to inherit their father's kingdom. Their uncles, Childebert I and Chlothar I, had other ideas and resolved to divide Chlodomer's kingdom between them. Chlothild was presented with the choice of either having her grandchildren tonsured or killed; she chose the latter solution, although one child, Chlodovald, escaped to become a monk and, in time, to be revered as St Cloud.[4] According to Gregory, Chlodomer's kingdom was divided equally between Childebert and Chlothar, but in so far as this division can be reconstructed it appears not to have been confined to the two brothers; there are grounds for thinking that Theuderic also may have profited from the murders.[5]

On Theuderic's death in 533 Childebert and Chlothar united once again to exclude a nephew from his inheritance. This time, however, the opposition was made of sterner stuff. Theudebert I was already an active

2. Gregory, *Decem Libri Historiarum*, IV 22.
3. Gregory, *Decem Libri Historiarum*, III 3, 11–13.
4. Gregory, *Decem Libri Historiarum*, III 18.
5. Ewig, 'Die fränkischen Teilungen und Teilreiche', pp. 128–9, following a letter of Leo of Sens, *Epistulae Aevi Merowingici Collectae*, 3.

figure in the last years of his father's reign, and he had the support of a military following, his *leudes*, with whose help he made good his claim to the throne.[6] When he died in 547 there was, apparently, no opposition to the succession of his son, Theudebald, although his subjects took advantage of his death to lynch the hated minister Parthenius.[7] Eight years later Theudebald died without an heir, and on this occasion Chlothar was, it seems, able to take over the eastern kingdom without opposition.[8] The same circumstances were repeated in 558, when Childebert died. For the last three years of his life Chlothar was thus sole king of the Merovingian kingdom; when he died in 561 the process of division could start again from scratch.[9]

According to Gregory the division of 561 was in many respects a return to that of 511; Charibert I received Paris, Guntram Orléans, Sigibert I Rheims and Chilperic I Soissons. There were, however, significant differences between the two divisions: for a start, in 511 the Franks did not control Burgundy, and what lands they held in Aquitaine can hardly have seemed secure with Clovis dead and the Ostrogothic king Theodoric intent on restoring the power of the Visigoths. For the south-east and in Burgundy, the arrangements of 511 could not have provided the sons of Chlothar with any precedent. Those of 561 were not, in any case, to last long. After a reign of only six years Charibert died.[10] As a result, his kingdom, with the exception of Paris, which was treated as neutral ground, was divided among his brothers, not that the division was universally respected. Indeed many of the disagreements of the following years seem to be associated with cities which had once been held by Charibert, and this was to hold true even after the murder of Sigibert, since lands which he had acquired in 567 became bones of contention between his son, Childebert II, and Guntram.[11]

Neither the murder of Sigibert in 575, nor that of Chilperic nine years later was to alter the political map of the Merovingian kingdoms in the way that the death of Charibert had done, since they each left a single male heir. Certainly in both cases the child was a minor, and there were problems in ensuring their succession to their fathers' territories, but there was no need for a new division of the kingdom.

The parallels, such as they are, between 511 and 561, together with the arrangements made to cope with the death of Charibert, lend a spurious uniformity to the divisions of the Merovingian kingdom, but one which is, at first sight, supported by the events of 595. Guntram had died three years earlier and, according to the seventh-century chronicler Fredegar, Sigibert's son, Childebert II (575–96) took over his kingdom,[12] thus uniting what had been the kingdom of Orléans, but which came to be known as the kingdom

6. Gregory, *Decem Libri Historiarum*, III 23.
7. Gregory, *Decem Libri Historiarum*, III 36.
8. Gregory, *Decem Libri Historiarum*, IV 9.
9. Gregory, *Decem Libri Historiarum*, IV 20, 22.
10. Gregory, *Decem Libri Historiarum*, IV 26.
11. For Paris, see Gregory, *Decem Libri Historiarum*, VII 6.
12. Fredegar, IV 14.

of Burgundy, with that of Rheims, or Austrasia. Chilperic's son, Chlothar II (584–629), was excluded from this arrangement, which had been agreed at the Treaty of Andelot in 587.[13] Three years after Guntram's death, however, Childebert himself died, leaving two sons, Theudebert II (596–612) and Theuderic II (596–613), of whom the former had already in 589 been given a sub-kingdom of the cities of Soissons and Meaux, at the request of some of the leading citizens – development pregnant with implications for the future.[14] Now in 596 Theudebert received Austrasia, and Theuderic Burgundy,[15] apparently cementing the divisions created by Charibert's death in 567. The political developments of the next eighteen years ensured that this was not so.

The first significant change to the political map of the Merovingian kingdom occurred with the campaign of Theudebert II and Theuderic II against Chlothar II in the year 600, as a result of which the latter was left only with the territories of Beauvais, Amiens and Rouen.[16] The alliance of the sons of Childebert II, however, was short-lived. In 611 Theuderic took the field against his brother, and promised to restore the duchy of the Dentelin to Chlothar, in return for his neutrality. A year later he overthrew Theudebert, and killed him and his sons, but after uniting Burgundy and Austrasia he died of dysentery. Although he left four sons, his grandmother, Brunhild, decided to elevate only one of them, Sigibert II (613), to the throne. Nevertheless this attempt to ensure the succession of at least one of her descendants failed; the aristocracy deserted to Chlothar II, and the old queen and her great-grandchildren, with the exception of one child, Merovech, were killed.[17] In 613 the kingdom was reunited, as it had been under the previous Chlothar in 558.

Merovingian succession

Although the division of the Merovingian kingdom is often held to have been been traditional, this was clearly not the case in 511. And although the arrangements made at Clovis's death certainly set a precedent, it did not ensure the succession of all Merovingian males, despite Gregory of Tours's famous dictum that 'all boys born of kings are called king's sons'.[18] Childebert I and Chlothar I ensured that Chlodomer's sons did not succeed

13. Gregory, *Decem Libri Historiarum*, IX 20.
14. Gregory, *Decem Libri Historiarum*, IX 36.
15. Fredegar, IV 16.
16. Fredegar, IV 20.
17. Fredegar, IV 37–42.
18. Gregory, *Decem Libri Historiarum*, V 20. This sentence should be taken in context: by Roman law (*Codex Theodosianus*, IV 6, 3) the children of a free-person and a slave were automatically slaves. Gregory is merely saying that any child sired by a Merovingian was to be regarded as having royal blood, even if the mother was servile.

their father, and they tried hard to exclude Theudebert I from the throne. Towards the second half of the sixth century Fredegund was determined that her husband Chilperic's sons by other women should not be in a position to succeed, and assisted in their fates.[19] One of them, Merovech, attempted to outwit his stepmother by marrying Sigibert's widow, Brunhild.[20] Not surprisingly princes were concerned to build up a position of strength during their fathers' lifetimes.

This probably accounts for the events of the closing years of the reign of Clovis's longest surviving son, Chlothar I. After Theudebald's death in 555, Chlothar sent his own son Chramn to Clermont, where he terrorized the bishop, Cautinus, and removed the *comes*, Firminus.[21] The prince then moved to Poitiers and allied with his uncle Childebert against his father.[22] The conflict between Chramn and Chlothar dragged on from 556 to 560, when the prince was finally defeated, captured and burned. Exactly a year later Chlothar himself died of fever at Compiègne. He was buried at the church of St Medard in Soissons.[23] Chramn's actions are best interpreted as those of a prince determined to have some share in the Merovingian kingdom: effectively he was creating a new kingdom in his father's lifetime.

Even at the time of Chlothar's death the issue of the succession seems to have been undecided. Venantius Fortunatus reveals that Chilperic was his father's favourite. Chlothar may have intended that he alone should succeed.[24] Gregory's account of what actually happened is laconic in the extreme. We are told that Chilperic seized his father's treasure and gained a following through bribery. He then went to Paris and occupied the throne of his uncle Charibert. His three half-brothers united against him and subsequently the kingdom was divided equally. The division finally arrived at in 561 was, then, a compromise made after Chilperic's bid for the throne of Paris.[25]

A further factor needs to be taken into consideration. Chlothar, like many of the early Merovingian monarchs, was uxorious: he had at least sixth wives. Three of his surviving sons – or at least of those whom he acknowledged as his – were the children of Ingund; the fourth, Chilperic, was the child of Ingund's sister, Aregund.[26] It is possible that Chilperic's actions immediately after his father's death were intended to ensure that he was not excluded from the succession by his half-brothers. Arguably unlike Chlothild in 511 and certainly unlike Fredegund, Aregund may have played no part in ensuring her son's succession. She is not known to have been involved in any way.

---

19. Gregory, *Decem Libri Historiarum*, V 14, 39.
20. Gregory, *Decem Libri Historiarum*, V 2.
21. Gregory, *Decem Libri Historiarum*, IV 12–13, 15.
22. Gregory, *Decem Libri Historiarum*, IV 16.
23. Gregory, *Decem Libri Historiarum*, IV 20–1.
24. See M. Reydellet, *La Royauté dans la littérature latine de Sidoine Apollinaire à Isidore de Séville*, p. 311.
25. Gregory, *Decem Libri Historiarum*, IV 22.
26. Gregory, *Decem Libri Historiarum*, IV 3.

Nevertheless the serial monogamy of kings is likely to have had its implications for the rivalries between their heirs. Chilperic was not the only son of Chlothar to be affected by his mother's position: in considering Chramn's bid for power it is important to remember that his mother was neither Ingund nor Aregund, but Chunsina.[27] Certainly the rivalries within the Merovingian family ensured that there could never been a simple pattern of succession

The government of the *Teilreiche*

The evidence for the divisions of the Merovingian kingdom is slight. The political narrative of the sixth century, however, makes it clear that they were not the result of automatic recourse to a pattern established in 511. The evidence for the working of government is equally slight, but there are recurrent features which allow some insight into the organization of the kingdoms. Time and again we are told that a kingdom was divided equally. This is recorded as being the case in 511, as in 524 and 561.[28] What constituted equality is open to question; certainly it is unlikely that there was a strict division according to acreage. This in any case would seem to be ruled out by references to some kings holding certain *civitates*, or cities with their surrounding territories, jointly.[29] More likely the intention was to give brothers portions which provided equal incomes. This was almost certainly the decisive factor in the division of Aquitaine. The basis for assessment, therefore, would have been administrative records such as tax registers, providing evidence of the value to the monarch of individual *civitates*, which had been the basic units of government in the later Roman Empire. When a city and its territory was divided between two kings we should understand that it was their revenues that were at stake, although certain cities also had a strategic importance, which may also have been a matter of concern.

The *civitas* was central to the division of the Merovingian kingdoms because, as in the Roman period, it was the basis of much of the administrative system. Its administrative importance is certainly attested for the sixth century, and it probably continued, although evidence is almost non-existent for the later period. Indeed, to be strictly accurate, the evidence is far from complete for the early Merovingian age, and, for that matter, even for the fifth century. We do not, for instance, know much about the administration of a *civitas*. From collections of legal *formulae* we know something about the local archives of a city, in which wills and other actions were registered, and we find various officials, the *defensor*, *curator*, *magister militum* and other members of the local *curia* being called upon to open the archives for the registration of new grants, but we have *Formularies* only from

27. Gregory, *Decem Libri Historiarum*, IV 3.
28. Gregory, *Decem Libri Historiarum*, III 1, 18; IV 22.
29. e.g. Gregory, *Decem Libri Historiarum*, VI 32.

a small number of *civitates*, and their contents are not often datable, except to the period before the ninth century, when most of them were written down. It is not clear that there was uniformity across the whole of the Merovingian kingdom in such matters.[30]

The senior official in the *civitas* was usually the *comes* (pl. *comites*), sometimes unhelpfully translated as 'count'; to be precise the word means 'companion'. On the whole the Merovingian *comites* have been seen as similar to the late Roman *comites civitatis*, and there is certainly a case for thinking that both could carry out the same duties, which included the hearing of law-suits and the enforcement of justice, and could involve military leadership as well.[31] The *comes* probably had as his subordinate another officer whose post was also of late Roman origin, the *centenarius*.[32] Information relating to *centenarii*, however, is scarce. Further, it is only for the kingdom of the Burgundians that there is evidence for anything like an all-embracing comital structure,[33] and while most, if not all, Merovingian *civitates* must have had their *comites*, or in the north, their *graphiones*,[34] in all probability local administration could vary according to regional tradition and to the will of an individual king, whose main concern was to ensure the loyalty of and to realize the revenues from his *civitates*.

Similar flexibility should also be envisaged when dealing with officials of rank superior to that of the *comes*. At times we hear of men with charge over more than one *civitas*; thus Nicetius, who had actually been removed from comital office in the Auvergne, resorted to bribery and became *dux* of the Auvergne, the Rutenois and Uzès.[35] There is even a list of offices which claims that a *dux* was in charge of twelve *civitates*, but although this text has been seen as a Merovingian document, it is almost certainly a school-book, originating perhaps in the British Isles.[36] In fact while we find *duces* in charge of groups of *civitates*, they also appear as leaders of royal armies, without any clear geographical base, and they were to be found engaged in a wide variety of other activites, including diplomatic missions.[37]

---

30. For the *Formulae* and their use in government, see I.N. Wood, 'Administration, law and culture in Merovingian Gaul', pp. 64–6; also Wood, 'Disputes in late fifth- and sixth-century Gaul: some problems', pp. 9, 12–14.

31. A.C. Murray, 'The position of the *grafio* in the constitutional history of Merovingian Gaul', *Speculum* 64 (1986), pp. 787–805.

32. A.C. Murray, 'From Roman to Frankish Gaul: "Centenarii" and "Centenae" in the administration of the Frankish kingdom', *Traditio* 44 (1988), pp. 59–100.

33. *Liber Constitutionum, prima constitutio*, 13.

34. Murray, 'The position of the *grafio* in the constitutional history of Merovingian Gaul'.

35. Gregory, *Decem Libri Historiarum*, VIII 18.

36. For a translation of the text see Wallace-Hadrill, *The Long-Haired Kings*, pp. 217–18: for its composition, see P. Barnwell, ' "Epistula Hieronimi de Gradus Romanorum": an English school book', *Historical Research* 64 (1991), pp. 77–86.

37. A.R. Lewis, 'The dukes of the *Regnum Francorum*, A.D. 550–751', *Speculum* 51 (1976), pp. 381–410.

Much eludes us about the government of the Merovingian *civitates*, but some aspects of their role within the administration of the kingdom are reasonably clear. The levying of taxes in particular seems to have been based on the *civitas*. Our most instructive anecdote for this is Gregory's account of the new taxes instituted by Chilperic in 579. Five gallons of wine was to be levied on every half acre of land, and there was to be an additional tax on manpower. The levels were so heavy that people left Chilperic's kingdom in order to avoid the taxes. In addition the arrival of the referendiary Mark at Limoges to collect the taxes provoked a riot.[38] How much was new about these demands is not clear; Gregory liked to portray tax as unwarranted and unjust. In origin, however, the taxation system of the Merovingians was undoubtedly based on that of the later Roman empire;[39] at Lyons an exemption supposedly granted by the Byzantine emperor Leo (457–74) was still in force in Gregory's day.[40]

It was exemptions that interested Gregory, and this means that our knowledge of Merovingian taxation is decidedly one-sided. Exemptions marked the generosity of the monarch, as with Theudebert's concessions to the churches of the Auvergne.[41] Wicked monarchs challenged tax-free status, as happened on more than one occasion to the church of Tours. Chlothar I even made the heinous suggestion that the churches of his kingdom should hand over one-third of their revenues to the crown.[42] Gregory records such plans in order to show how they were prevented, whether by a bishop, as in the case of Chlothar's request, or by God, as happened to Chilperic's tax demands. The disease visited on his sons prompted his wife, Fredegund, to burn the new tax registers.[43]

This bias of Gregory makes it very difficult to assess the regularity of tax collection, but on one occasion the bishop of Tours does allow some insight into what appears to be the norm. Because the tax registers of Poitiers were out of date, heavy burdens were falling on those unable to pay, including widows and orphans. This prompted the bishop, Maroveus, to ask that the city be reassessed, with the result that the poor were granted relief, and only fair taxes were levied. Childebert's tax inspectors then tried to institute the same reforms in Tours, but Gregory claimed that the city was exempt, and related the history of exemption since the time of Chlothar I.[44] However, if reorganization had not threatened Tours, it is doubtful whether we would have heard of the perfectly sensible arrangements at Poitiers, which suggest

38. Gregory, *Decem Libri Historiarum*, V 28.
39. W. Goffart, 'Old and new in Merovingian taxation', in Goffart, *Rome's Fall and After*, pp. 213–31.
40. Gregory, *Liber in Gloria Confessorum* 62; see the comment of the translator, R. Van Dam, *Gregory of Tours: Glory of the Confessors*, pp. 69–70, n. 70.
41. Gregory, *Decem Libri Historiarum*, III 25.
42. Gregory, *Decem Libri Historiarum*, IV 2.
43. Gregory, *Decem Libri Historiarum*, V 34.
44. Gregory, *Decem Libri Historiarum*, IX 30.

not only that taxation was normal in the Merovingian kingdom, but also that it could be organized efficiently, and so far as one can see, fairly.

Nevertheless taxation does not seem to have fallen on the whole population. While the Romans are described as being tributary, it seems that the lands which had originally been granted to free-born Franks had been exempt from tax, and that the Franks subsequently assumed that any lands which they came to hold were similarly exempt.[45] This at least is the neatest way of explaining some of the conflicts described in Gregory's *Histories* between free Franks and administrators who insisted that they were liable to taxation: Parthenius they lynched,[46] and Audo they deprived of his property.[47] The tax collectors were fighting an uphill struggle: during the seventh century 'truly free men' came to have immunity from paying dues to the royal fisc.[48]

Gregory claimed that Tours was free not only from taxation, but also from certain military obligations. In 578 Chilperic ordered the men of the Touraine, Poitou, the Bessin, Maine and Anjou to march against Brittany, but as Gregory explains, the poor and the men of the cathedral and of St Martin's did not go because they were exempt from public service.[49] This claim illuminates one of the recurrent features of the military history of the period; the frequent presence of the men of one *civitas* or another on campaign, above all during the civil wars which bedevilled the second half of the sixth century, when rivalry between cities seems to have exacerbated problems. Apparently the kings could rely not only on taxation from the *civitates*, but also on local armed forces. Presumably such militias date back to the last years of the Roman period, although there is no evidence for them in the fifth century. Nor was such military service the only obligation on which the sixth-century Merovingians could rely: they could expect the provision of hospitality, which could be an extremely costly business, as when Chilperic I's daughter, Rigunth, set out to meet her intended husband in Spain – her retinue devastated the country it passed through.[50]

How many of these obligations could still be demanded in the seventh century, we do not know, although there are references to tax concessions granted to Tours by Dagobert I (623/9–39),[51] to the city of Bourges by Clovis II (634–57),[52] and to families exposing children in order to avoid public exactions in the *Life* of his queen, Balthild.[53] Certain types of taxation also continued: the seventh century boasts plenty of evidence for tolls of various kinds, which will be considered in chapter 12.

45. Goffart, 'Old and new in Merovingian taxation', pp. 223–4.
46. Gregory, *Decem Libri Historiarum*, III 36.
47. Gregory, *Decem Libri Historiarum*, VII 15.
48. Goffart, 'Old and new in Merovingian taxation', pp. 230–1.
49. Gregory, *Decem Libri Historiarum*, V 26.
50. Gregory, *Decem Libri Historiarum*, VI 45.
51. *Vita Eligii*, I 32.
52. *Vita Sulpicii episcopi Biturgi*, 6–7.
53. *Vita Balthildis*, 6.

Royal resources

A king depended on the administrative structure of the *civitas* for tax revenue and for some of the manpower required for his armies. But he had additional sources of wealth and troops. Although the evidence for military organization in the Merovingian period is as poor as that for any other aspect of the administrative history of the period, it is possible, once again, to put together some picture from the narratives provided by Gregory of Tours and others.[54] There are references in the sources to *laeti*, who were probably descended from barbarian soldiers settled within the empire.[55] More important were the *leudes* of a king. These were military followers apparently of considerable social status and influence, though probably to be distinguished from the greatest magnates of the realm, many of whom had military followings of their own, and might be expected to fight for the king both inside and outside his kingdom.

Theudebert I was reliant on his *leudes* to survive the threat from his uncles on his accession,[56] and Chilperic I created an equivalent following through bribery in order to make his bid for the throne in 561.[57] The value placed on these men is most clearly stated in the Treaty of Andelot, where Guntram and Childebert II settled the question of the succession and dealt with various matters which had arisen during the early years of the latter's reign. Among these was the question of those *leudes* who had once followed either Guntram or Sigibert I, the father of Childebert, but had transferred their loyalty elsewhere; they were to be made to return to their original allegiance from the places where they were known to have settled. Neither king was to accept a member of the other's *leudes* in future.[58] A bond between a ruler and a military follower was clearly considered as binding, and there is some indication, in the assumption that Sigibert's *leudes* should follow Childebert, that the bond was hereditary. At the same time the actions of Theudebert and Chilperic, as well as those of the disloyal followers covered by the Treaty of Andelot, show that kings were expected to offer incentives, and we may well believe that the distribution of land and wealth was the major factor in ensuring that a king had a loyal following.

In terms of land, the early Merovingian kings were probably well endowed with estates and palaces, many of them perhaps originally part of the imperial fisc. These estates would have been run by appropriate staffs of officials, including *comites* of the palace, various agents, refendaries, notaries and so forth, although, once again, it is doubtful whether there was a genuinely regular pattern to the duties of this band of administrators; much clearly

---

54. B. Bachrach, *Merovingian Military Organisation 481–751*, gathers some of the material, but the approach is rather dominated by narrative.
55. On fourth-century *laeti*, see Heather, *Goths and Romans 332–489*, pp. 123–4; Liebeschuetz, *Barbarians and Bishops*, p. 12.
56. Gregory, *Decem Libri Historiarum*, III 23.
57. Gregory, *Decem Libri Historiarum*, IV 22.
58. Gregory, *Decem Libri Historiarum*, IX 20.

depended on who was attendant on the king at any one time. About the lands themselves we are badly informed; the evidence is, as usual, provided in passing. In narrative and hagiographic sources we sometimes learn of the king's presence at one or other of his estates, and in charters and other legal documents we see him making grants or judgements from some palace or royal villa. The problem which arises from this is that we are never given any inkling of the totality of a king's estates, and there is a particular difficulty in trying to construct a picture of crown land by listing all references to it from the whole Merovingian period; if kings rewarded their followers by conferring estates on them, even though the grant might not be hereditary, the pool of land must have changed constantly. Kings also endowed churches and, increasingly, monasteries. Meanwhile they replenished their land-holdings by conquest and by the confiscation of the estates of those who had fallen out of favour: rebels and criminals. Because of this fluidity in royal land-holding a list of all the known royal estates from the whole Merovingian period would be misleading; it would not allow for the pattern of acquisition and alienation. At the same time the poverty of our sources on this issue means that we cannot come anywhere near making an informed guess at the extent of the estates of any one king. What is almost certain is that royal land-holdings were vast, and they were probably particularly impressive in the north.

To the wealth they received from their estates and taxation, successful Merovingians could also add plunder and tribute from neighbouring peoples. Following the devastation of Thuringia by Chlothar I in 556 the Saxons paid an annual tribute of 500 cows.[59] Dagobert I (623/9–39) was probably richer than most Merovingian monarchs, not least because he helped Sisenand seize the Visigothic throne. As payment for this help Sisenand promised a gold dish, weighing five hundred pounds, which had been given by Aëtius to king Thorismund in the fifth century. The Goths, however, objected to this national treasure being handed over, and redeemed it for 200,000 *solidi*.[60] In addition diplomacy could be a source of treasure. In 581 a Frankish legation sent by Chilperic I returned from Constantinople with numerous gifts. Unfortunately they were shipwrecked and lost much of what they had been given. Among the objects salvaged were gold dishes, weighing a pound each, with the image of the emperor on them. Chilperic also showed Gregory a gold salver covered with gems, weighing fifty pounds. This Chilperic himself had commissioned to enhance the glory of the Franks.[61]

Descriptions of gold and silver objects commissioned by Merovingian kings and donated to churches are not infrequent in hagiography from the seventh century and later. They testify to the fact that a colossal amount of wealth passed through royal hands, and it is therefore not surprising that control of the royal treasury was a significant factor in Merovingian politics.[62] Oddly

59. Fredegar, IV 74.
60. Fredegar, IV 73.
61. Gregory, *Decem Libri Historiarum*, VI 2.
62. See e.g. Gregory, *Decem Libri Historiarum*, V 1; VII 4.

enough this is not to say that kings always had easy access to wealth: much to the disgust of monks of St Denis, Clovis II (634–57) removed silver from the apse of their church, to provide alms during a famine.[63]

There is, in fact, a paradox about the wealth of the Merovingians. Their resources were considerable; not only did they have vast incomes from taxation and from their own estates, but also they could expect considerable quantities of tribute from the subject peoples east of the Rhine and elsewhere. Nevertheless Chilperic I complained that his treasury was always empty because of the church,[64] while one retainer of a Merovingian prince attributed this penury to St Martial and St Martin, that is to the churches of Limoges and Tours.[65] Gregory regarded these claims as being marks of particular wickedness, and he saw the Merovingians as being, for the most part, rapacious. In fact these two opinions are not incompatible: a Merovingian may have had a large income, but he also had vast financial commitments; he had to reward his faithful retainers; he had to endow the shrines of the saints, to ensure their support, and that of the clergy who served them; he would also have to demonstrate his piety in almsgiving. In addition, gifts would be required in any negotiations with foreign powers, especially if they culminated in a marriage alliance. Nor was there any question of hoarding treasure for a rainy day: a king's status was related to his generosity and to the display of wealth; hence Chilperic's salver made to the glory of the Franks; hence also the fact that on the death of the magnate Rauching, who cannot have had an income comparable to that of a king, more treasure was found in his coffers than was held in the royal treasury.[66]

Royal ideology

Gregory was not greatly impressed by most of the sons and grandsons of Clovis, but there were exceptions. He admired Theudebert I, despite his injustices and adulteries.[67] He was particularly impressed by his treatment of Verdun: although bishop Desideratus had been exiled by Theudebert, he asked the king for financial aid to help restore his city. Not only was a loan of 7,000 gold coins made, but the repayment was subsequently remitted.[68] Gregory's picture of Theudebert as a great monarch can be supplemented by other sources. His qualities as a Christian king are extolled in a letter addressed to him by a certain Aurelian, who was once identified with the bishop of Arles of that name.[69] More extraordinary is another letter preserved

63. *Gesta Dagoberti I*, 17, 50.
64. Gregory, *Decem Libri Historiarum*, VI 46.
65. Gregory, *Decem Libri Historiarum*, IV 16.
66. Gregory, *Decem Libri Historiarum*, IX 9.
67. Gregory, *Decem Libri Historiarum*, III 25.
68. Gregory, *Decem Libri Historiarum*, III 34.
69. *Epistulae Austrasiacae* 10. On the author, see R. Collins, 'Theodebert I, "Rex Magnus Francorum"', in P. Wormald, ed., *Ideal and Reality in Frankish and Anglo-Saxon Society*, pp. 18–22; see also Wallace-Hadrill, *The Long-Haired Kings*, pp. 191–2.

in the *Epistulae Austrasiacae*, in which Theudebert describes to Justinian the extent of his hegemony, which, he said, stretched from Visigothic Spain to Thuringia, and from the North Sea to the Danube and Pannonia.[70] The claims sound far-fetched, but they show the extent of Theudebert's ambition. Essentially he was establishing himself as a figure of imperial stature, as his gold coinage reveals.[71] He appears to have worried the Byzantines, who thought that he was planning an attack on Constantinople.[72] Theudebert was certainly thought of as a great and powerful king.

War was clearly central to Theudebert's status, both at home and abroad. At the same time his status seems to have caused him to be associated with campaigns which took place after his death: the invasion of Italy by Buccelin, which rightly belongs in the reign of Theudebald, was assigned by Gregory to that of his father.[73] Most of the great Merovingians proved themselves in battle. Even Gregory admired the successes of the Merovingian kings over their neighbours, as did Venantius Fortunatus. Great victories could become legendary: Chlothar II's defeat of the Saxons in the early seventh century is known to have been commemorated in the songs of washerwomen.[74]

There are two other aspects to Theudebert's greatness as a monarch: Christian and Roman. These same elements form the basis of the royal virtues described in the panegyrical works of Venantius Fortunatus. For him Childebert I could be compared with the Old Testament monarch, Melchisedek[75] – and doubtless, having come from Ravenna, Fortunatus's image of Melchisedek would have been similar to that which was set up in San Vitale, where the patriarch provided an analogue to the emperor Justinian.[76] Other of the portraits in Fortunatus's poems are more classical; Chilperic is described in terms of his military prowess, his justice and his culture,[77] but Sigibert, especially in the *epithalamium* celebrating his marriage to Brunhild, is depicted in terms derived almost entirely derived from the Roman past.[78]

70. *Epistulae Austrasiacae* 20.

71. P. Grierson and M. Blackburn, *Medieval European Coinage*, I, *The Early Middle Ages (5th–10th Centuries)*, p. 116; McCormick, *Eternal Victory*, pp. 338–9.

72. Agathias I 4, 1–4; see A. Cameron, 'Agathias on the early Merovingians', *Annali della Scuola normale superiore di Pisa 37* (1968), pp. 97, 100–1, 107, 122–3; Collins, 'Theodebert I, "Rex Magnus Francorum"', pp. 9–10.

73. Gregory, *Decem Libri Historiarum*, III 32; for an accurate account of Theudebert's involvement in Italy, see Wolfram, *History of the Goths*, pp. 347–8, 355–6.

74. *Vita Faronis* 78.

75. Venantius Fortunatus, carm. II 10, 17–24; Reydellet, *La Royauté dans la littérature latine de Sidoine Apollinaire à Isidore de Séville*, pp. 322–30; George, *Venantius Fortunatus: A Latin Poet in Merovingian Gaul*, p. 43.

76. George, *Venantius Fortunatus: A Latin Poet in Merovingian Gaul*, p. 43.

77. Venantius Fortunatus, carm. 9, 1; George, *Venantius Fortunatus: A Latin Poet in Merovingian Gaul*, pp. 48–57; Reydellet, *La Royauté dans la littérature latine de Sidoine Apollinaire à Isidore de Séville*, pp. 330–1.

78. Venantius Fortunatus, carm. 6, 1a; George, *Venantius Fortunatus: A Latin Poet in Merovingian Gaul*, pp. 40–3; Reydellet, *La Royauté dans la littérature latine de Sidoine Apollinaire à Isidore de Séville*, pp. 321–2.

These traditions also have their echoes in Gregory of Tours, but with more than a note of hostility. Chilperic is compared with Nero and Herod.[79] The Christian and imperial past provided a language of criticism as well as one of praise. It should, nevertheless, not be dismissed as mere rhetoric. Chilperic's wish to appear as a cultivated monarch is not in question; he wrote poetry, however badly, and he showed some interest in such issues as the alphabet, to which he wished to add four letters, and in theology, where he came close to heresy, when he decided to abolish the distinctions between the persons of the Trinity.[80] In addition he was to be found building amphitheatres in Soissons and Paris to provide shows for the citizens.[81] Gregory may have laughed at Chilperic's attempts at apeing the culture of the Roman past, and despised him for them, but circuses were integral to the political culture of the later Roman Empire, and its Byzantine successor: the hippodrome was central to the court ritual of Constantinople.[82] Nor was Chilperic the only Merovingian monarch to involve himself in such building projects.[83] Doubtless they represent a thorough-going attempt to adopt the sort of Roman style envisaged by Fortunatus, and they presumably drew an admiring response from some of the more backward-looking members of the Gallo-Roman aristocracy.

The romanizing aspect of Merovingian ideology seems not to have impressed Gregory. His own ideals were ecclesiastical rather then Roman. There was a tradition of royal charity in the Merovingian kingdom, apparent in the Church councils and in the one surviving edict of Childebert I.[84] Of Childebert, however, Gregory had little to say. Among Merovingian monarchs it was Guntram who provided Gregory with his model of Christian kingship. He was pious, and Gregory even recounts a miracle worked by a thread taken from his cloak.[85] There is, however, another side to Gregory's portrait, from which the king emerges as a suspicious and not totally effectual ruler. One Sunday he begged the congregation of a Paris church not to assassinate him.[86] There is also reference to reprimands and complaints addressed by him to his subordinates; on one occasion we are told that the generals on an unsuccessful campaign justified their failure by explaining that although his piety was noted, he was not feared and this meant that his agents commanded no respect.[87] Even Gregory recognized his weaknesses: however much of a royal virtue it might be, piety alone was not enough. It is not

79. Gregory, *Decem Libri Historiarum*, VI 46.
80. Gregory, *Decem Libri Historiarum*, V 44; VI 46. A poem by Chilperic, *Ymnus in sollemnitate s. Medardi*, survives, ed. K. Strecker, *MGH Poetae* IV 2; see F. Brunhölzl, *Histoire de la littérature latine du Moyen Age*, I/1, *L'époque mérovingienne*, pp. 116–17.
81. Gregory, *Decem Libri Historiarum*, V 17.
82. S. McCormack, *Art and Ceremony in Late Antiquity*, pp. 79–81.
83. Procopius, *Wars*, VII 33, 5.
84. *Capitularia Merowingica*, 2.
85. Gregory, *Decem Libri Historiarum*, IX 21.
86. Gregory, *Decem Libri Historiarum*, VII 8; see also Wood, 'The secret histories of Gregory of Tours'.
87. Gregory, *Decem Libri Historiarum*, VIII 30.

likely to be a coincidence that Guntram's reign was marked by disagreements with his fellow rulers, and also by treason.

If anything it is the emperor Tiberius II who is Gregory's paragon. The bishop of Tours relates that when the emperor saw a flagstone engraved with a cross he ordered it to be raised. Below it was a second and then a third such stone. Beneath the third was a vast treasure which the emperor then used for charitable purposes.[88] Oddly enough a similar tale was told of Guntram by the eighth-century Lombard historian Paul the Deacon. Once when Guntram was out hunting he paused for a rest, and while he was sleeping a dragon climbed out of his mouth, crossed a neighbouring stream, vanished, returned and climbed back. On being told about this Guntram followed the dragon's route and discovered some treasure, which he originally determined to send to Jerusalem, but then decided to use for a *ciborium* for the church of St Marcel at Chalon.[89] The pious act would have delighted Gregory. But there are other aspects of the story which are just as appropriate to Merovingian royal ideology. The point that the king was out hunting is not insignificant: hunting was an appropriate pastime for kings, and Guntram is known from Gregory to have been a keen huntsman.[90] Nor is the dragon entirely inappropriate in a story relating to a king supposedly descended from a sea-monster.[91]

Despite Gregory's account, the Merovingians can be seen as a dynasty which cultivated a complex political ideology during the sixth century. To a large extent that ideology looked to the Roman past. So also did the governmental structures of the Merovingian kingdom. As a result the rule of Clovis's descendants was by no means unsophisticated: it could also be oppressive. This is particularly clear from Gregory's account of the convoy created to escort Chilperic's daughter Rigunth to Spain in 584. Families of serfs were forced by Chilperic to accompany the princess; some hanged themselves to avoid going; people of good birth were also expected to make the journey, and then to stay in Spain; as a result they made their wills, reckoning themselves to be as good as dead.[92] The image may be exaggerated, but it is certainly an indication of royal demands.

At the same time, although there were considerable powers on which a king and his administrators could draw, not every monarch could actually mobilize his resources. Gregory liked Guntram because of his benefactions to the Church and his regard for churchmen, although he does not hide his weaknesses. Chilperic he disliked, in part because of his attitude towards the Church and clergy, despite some remarkable acts of generosity to individual shrines. Yet it is likely that Chilperic was the more impressive monarch and

88. Gregory, *Decem Libri Historiarum*, V 19.
89. Paul, *Historia Langobardorum*, III 34.
90. Gregory, *Decem Libri Historiarum*, VIII 6; X 10.
91. Fredegar, III 9.
92. Gregory, *Decem Libri Historiarum*, VI 45.

inspired the greater respect. Power was not handed to the Merovingians on a plate, but a firmly established king, once he had control of his resources, could be very powerful indeed.

Chapter Five

The Limits of Ecclesiastical Power: Episcopal Jurisdiction and Politics

Alongside the complex structures of secular power there were other types of authority, associated with the Church. Not that Church and State were easily separable in the Merovingian period; on the contrary, the authority of the Church, and particularly that of the bishops, was connected with the power of the king, especially in the urban centres of the Frankish kingdom. Nevertheless it requires separate assessment, not least because it drew on certain areas of experience not directly dominated by the monarch.

Diocesan organization

The structure of the Merovingian Church was taken over directly from its Gallo-Roman predecessor. It was based on dioceses which for much of the kingdom were the ecclesiastical counterparts of the *civitates*, with which they were coterminous.[1] In the north and east, however, where the barbarian invasions had caused most disruption, dioceses had to be re-created, with the result that their extent reflected the connections and interests of the clergy involved in their re-creation, rather than the geography of the Roman *civitas*. Thus, unlike that of Clermont, for instance, the Merovingian diocese of Mainz did not correspond exactly to any earlier Roman administrative district.[2] Like Gallo-Roman *civitates*, dioceses were organized into provinces, and their bishops were subordinate to a metropolitan. Theoretically there was a further hierarchy within the metropolitan sees. What this was was much debated, particularly by the metropolitan bishops of Arles and Vienne.[3] In practice the authority of an individual metropolitan was influenced by political factors, such as the favour in which he was held at court. A king could forbid a bishop to attend a council called by his metropolitan, as

1. E. James, *The Origins of France*, pp. 45–6.
2. K. Heinemeyer, *Das Erzbistum Mainz in römischer und fränkischer Zeit*.
3. L. Duchesne, *Fastes épiscopaux de l'ancienne Gaule* I, pp. 84–144.

happened when Sigibert III (632–c. 656) prevented Desiderius of Cahors from going to Bourges at some date between 647 and 653.[4]

The Christian community

After the baptism of Clovis the kingdom of the Franks was theoretically a Christian state; that is not to say that all its members were Christian – indeed it would be a long time before the Christianization of the Merovingian kingdom was complete.[5] What was important was the fact that after 508 the catholic Church defined the Christian community which constituted the *regnum Francorum*. In many respects this was a return to the position of the very last years of the fourth century; the establishment of arian kingdoms on Gallic soil had removed from the catholic bishops sole authority over the definition of the Christian community, and it was only the conversion of Clovis and the expansion of the Frankish kingdom which gave the ecclesiastical hierarchy the authority once more to define the Christian life for all the members of the State.

In the Merovingian period, as earlier, the formal moments of an individual's life were marked by *rites de passage* laid down by the Church. Full entry into Christian society was determined by baptism, a ceremony which took place theoretically only on Easter day.[6] Having entered this Christian society the individual had to conform to its beliefs and to demonstrate conformity by attendance at Church, especially at the main feasts of the ecclesiastical year. At Christmas, Easter and Pentecost private chapels were not to be used for services; their priests had to attend the bishop in his cathedral city, where the leading citizens had also to be present.[7] In addition to regulating the chief feasts and rituals of the year, the Church canons prohibited Sunday work, in accordance with the Ten Commandments, and these canons were backed up by the dissemination of miracle stories concerning the fates of those who did work on Sundays. There are tales of hands withering, of buildings being burned, and of children conceived on Sunday being born deformed.[8] It is not difficult to depict the early medieval Church as a power-house of psychological oppression.

While baptism marked one *rite de passage*, death and burial marked another, and again the Church tried to set out appropriate actions.[9] Curiously, however, marriage was not seen as requiring an ecclesiastical ceremony before

4. Desiderius of Cahors, ep. II 17.
5. J.M. Wallace-Hadrill, *The Frankish Church*, pp. 23–36.
6. Council of Mâcon (585), 3; Council of Auxerre (post-585), 18. The date of Auxerre is from O. Pontal, *Die Synoden im Merowingerreich*, p. 167.
7. Council of Orléans (511), 25.
8. Council of Mâcon (585), 1; I.N. Wood, 'Early Merovingian devotion in town and country', in D. Baker, ed., *The Church in Town and Countryside, Studies in Church History* 16, pp. 61–5.
9. F.S. Paxton, *Christianizing Death*, pp. 47–69.

the twelfth century. Nevertheless the theological implications of marriage were not neglected. Although there is nothing in the early Merovingian period to compare with the concern shown by the eighth-century Anglo-Saxons as to what constituted the prohibited degrees of marriage,[10] there was considerable worry about uncanonical sexual relations. There was also great concern about the practice of concubinage, although here our major evidence has to be drawn from tales of confrontation between holy men and members of the Merovingian royal family. Nicetius of Trier threatened to excommunicate Theudebert I for adultery, and he frequently excommunicated Chlothar I.[11] He heads a long line of saints who dared to challenge the Merovingians on their sexual profligacy. Germanus of Paris excommunicated Charibert for marrying Marcovefa, a nun who was also the sister of the king's previous wife, Merofled, from whom he had as yet not separated.[12] In the next century Desiderius, bishop of Vienne, and the monk Columbanus would castigate Theuderic II for begetting bastards.[13] The question of prohibited degrees, within which marriage could not take place, also appears in the late seventh century, when bishop Leodegar of Autun is said to have attacked the marriage of Childeric II to his cousin Bilichild.[14] When kings were at loggerheads with their clergy, which was not their usual relationship, morality constituted the most dramatic battleground.

Bishops and saint cults

In addition to regulating the lives of the Christian subjects of the Merovingian kings – and also to circumscribing the activities of the Jews, the one recognized religious minority in the kingdom[15] – the bishops at least tried to monopolize the local centres and objects of devotion, which might have presented a focus of religious power outside their control.[16] One object which did escape episcopal control was the relic of the True Cross, secured by the ex-queen Radegund, for her nunnery of the Holy Cross at Poitiers. The bishop, Maroveus, refused to install the relic, and by doing so placed the nunnery in a difficult position with regard to the canons.[17] Maroveus was probably uncooperative because he did not like the challenge presented to his own status by Radegund's foundation and its relics. His own cathedral could

---

10. e.g. Boniface, epp. 26, 28, 33.

11. Gregory, *Liber Vitae Patrum*, 17, 2.

12. Gregory, *Decem Libri Historiarum*, IV 26.

13. *Passio sancti Desiderii episcopi et martyris*, 8; on the authenticity of this text, see I.N. Wood, 'Forgery in Merovingian hagiography', in *MGH Schriften* 33, *Fälschungen im Mittelalter* V, pp. 373–6; Jonas, *Vita Columbani*, I 18.

14. *Passio Leudegarii I*, 8.

15. Wallace-Hadrill, *The Frankish Church*, pp. 391–3.

16. P.R.L. Brown, *Relics and Social Status in the Age of Gregory of Tours*, Stenton Lecture 1976; Wood, 'Early Merovingian devotion in town and country', pp. 61–76.

17. Gregory, *Decem Libri Historiarum*, IX 40.

not boast anything to compare with a fragment of the True Cross. The bishop later absented himself from Radegund's funeral, and Gregory of Tours had to officiate.[18]

Great monasteries could achieve very considerable spiritual authority. To some extent, the Merovingian Church in the sixth century tried to obviate the problem presented by the religious influence of monastic communities with a stream of ecclesiastical legislation placing abbots under the supervision of the bishops.[19] This was to be the start of a long debate which would be continued in the seventh century with the growth of concessions of immunity from episcopal intervention to particular monastic foundations.[20]

Of more immediate importance, as far as the majority of the population was concerned, was the determination of the bishops to control non-monastic sites associated with the cult of the saints. Here it is important to realize that there was no formal process of canonization. The creation of a saint-cult depended essentially on two factors: the first was the existence of a congregation willing to recognize that a particular place, usually a tomb, was invested with special power;[21] the second was the official recognition of the site by the Church authorities, that is the local bishop. The significance of either of these factors varied from site to site; at times cults appear largely to have been promoted by the Church hierarchy, or by a small group with a precise, often family, interest in the new saint – this seems to be the norm for the development of the cults of the aristocratic saints of the seventh century. Instances where the motive force for the recognition of a cult site comes from the congregation are rare, but are particularly instructive for an understanding of the concern of the Church to control places of supposedly numinous power.

The devotion of the people of Dijon to an obscure tomb in one of the cemeteries outside the town was frowned on by the local bishop, Gregory of Langres, who regarded it as an act of pagan superstition. He may well have been right. Nevertheless on failing to extirpate this superstition, Gregory 'learned' in a vision that the tomb was that of the martyr Benignus, and he incorporated the site in a new church. Some years later, we are told, travellers brought back from Italy an account of the saint's life, about which nothing had been known previously.[22] The *Life* itself looks remarkably like a version of the *Passion* of the Byzantine 'megalomartyr' Menignos, relocated in Dijon, and the whole Benignus dossier is probably best interpreted as the response of a bishop to a non-Christian cult which he had not been able to stamp out.[23] It is also worth noting, however, that Gregory's family was closely associated with Dijon, and that he may well have relished the prospect of a major cult

18. Gregory, *Liber in Gloria Confessorum*, 104; Baudonivia, *Vita Radegundis*, 23.

19. Council of Orléans (511), 19; Council of Epaon (517), 19; Council of Orléans (538), 26; Council of Orléans (533), 21; Council of Orléans (541), 11.

20. See chapter 11.

21. Brown, *Relics and Social Status in the Age of Gregory of Tours*.

22. Gregory, *Liber in Gloria Martyrum*, 50.

23. Wood, 'Early Merovingian devotion in town and country', pp. 74–5.

close to his family estates. What is undeniable is the determination of the bishop to bring the cult of Benignus under the auspices of the Church, if it was going to exist at all.

In episcopal hands a cult was a powerful weapon, even against the king. This is apparent in the threat issued by Gregory of Tours warning Childebert II not to tax Tours,[24] and in numerous other stories concerning the power of St Martin to defend his shrine. When Ruccolen was sent by Chilperic to drive Guntram Boso from St Martin's he fell sick and died;[25] when Claudius assassinated Eberulf in the *atrium*, or forecourt, of the church, he himself was killed in the process.[26] Such cautionary tales lost nothing in the telling, and they served to elevate the power of the shrines of the saints, and also to protect and strengthen the right of asylum claimed for churches in Roman Law and in the Church canons.

Episcopal jurisdiction

A bishop's status was not only connected to his role in defining Christian society and to his monopolization of holy places and objects, but also based on legally conferred rights and obligations dating from the late Roman period. Many of these were connected ultimately with traditions of pastoral care which already existed in the Early Church. Concern for the poor, and the distribution of alms, responsibility for widows and orphans, and also the visitation of those in prison, all of which came to be recognized as being within the purview of the Church in legal texts, derived from the New Testament. The importance of these functions was enhanced by the barbarian invasions of the fifth century. Many bishops emerged as the saviours of their cities as they arranged for famine relief and secured the ransom of prisoners during the years of crisis. The great saint bishops of fifth-century Gaul were provided with an unequalled opportunity for the exercise of pastoral care, which they seized with open arms. At the same time, in some towns at least, bishops came to take over the duties of such late Roman officers as the *defensores*, who had been expected to defend the weak. How formal this take-over was is an open question; to a large extent the evidence derives from the funerary inscriptions of fifth- and sixth-century bishops, where the epithet *defensor civitatis* might refer to the dead man's achievements rather than his office.[27]

The extension of a bishop's power continued in other ways. Many bishops of the Late Roman period had earlier in their careers been notable civil servants; best-known is Ambrose of Milan, but Germanus of Auxerre provides a fine example from Gaul, so too does Gregory of Langres, whose episcopate

24. Gregory, *Decem Libri Historiarum*, IX 30.
25. Gregory, *Decem Libri Historiarum*, V 4.
26. Gregory, *Decem Libri Historiarum*, VII 29.
27. But see M. Heinzelmann, *Bischofsherrschaft in Gallien*.

extended into the sixth century.[28] As one-time administrators these men were well-placed to run the temporal aspects of their sees. They were also admirably equipped to act as judges in those cases which fell under their purview, although these were concerned largely with disputes involving churchmen. Bishops were involved in other law suits, but more often than not this was as unofficial peacemakers, following the gospel injunction, rather than as official justices.[29] Constantine the Great, it is true, gave the bishops a more substantial role in the administration of justice, but this was reduced during the fourth and fifth centuries.[30] Nevertheless, many bishops continued to possess legal expertise, and it is not surprising that they made use of their knowledge. So too did their Merovingian successors. The sixth-century bishop of Le Mans, Badegisel, who had been *maior* of the palace, did so in his own interests, seizing the property of others, including that of his relatives.[31]

All bishops had to be skilled administrators. Something of the range of skills required can be seen in the career of the seventh-century bishop, Desiderius of Cahors. Desiderius was well-educated in the law and became treasurer to Chlothar II; he succeeded one brother, Syagrius, as governor of Marseilles, and subsequently he was elected bishop of Cahors in place of his other brother, Rusticus, who had been murdered. The *Life of Desiderius* reveals a bishop who was a great benefactor of his city. Not only did he build and restore churches and monasteries, but also he repaired the city walls; he corresponded with Caesarius of Clermont about laying underground water-pipes,[32] and he was responsible for severing road-communications with the south to prevent the spread of plague.[33]

Although the evidence for Desiderius's activity as bishop is unequalled, it is possible to make some comparison with other Merovingian bishops; Nicetius of Dax had been *comes* before he became bishop;[34] Sidonius of Mainz and Felix of Nantes embarked on significant building programmes.[35] To such details may be added the evidence of an episcopal coinage which appears in the late sixth century.[36] Taken together these points have been thought to indicate a steady take-over of secular functions by the Merovingian episcopate, and thus to presage the emergence of a group of effectively

28. Gregory, *Liber Vitae Patrum*, 7.
29. E. James, 'Beati pacifici: bishops and the law in sixth-century Gaul', in J. Bossy, ed., *Disputes and Settlements: Law and Human Relations in the West*, pp. 25–46.
30. J. Gaudemet, *L'Église dans l'Empire Romain*, pp. 230–40; Heinzelmann, *Bischofsherrschaft in Gallien*, pp. 180–1.
31. Gregory, *Decem Libri Historiarum*, VI 9, VIII 39. For the legal knowledge of many bishops, Wood, 'Administration, law and culture in Merovingian Gaul', p. 67.
32. Desiderius, ep. I 13. In general on Desiderius, J. Durliat, 'Les attributions civiles des évêques mérovingiens: l'exemple de Didier, évêque de Cahors (630–655)', *Annales du Midi* 91 (1979), pp. 237–54.
33. Desiderius, ep. II 20.
34. Gregory, *Decem Libri Historiarum*, VII 31; VIII 20.
35. Venantius Fortunatus, carm. II 11–12; IX 9; III 6–7.
36. Grierson and Blackburn, *Medieval European Coinage* I, p. 98.

independent episcopal states by the early eighth century, of which that of Savaric of Auxerre is the best documented.[37]

This is, of course, to oversimplify the history of episcopal power in the Merovingian period; it involves the avoidance of problems presented by some of the evidence. Much of what has been deduced about the institutionalized authority held by bishops in the late fifth and early sixth century, over and above their canonical jurisdiction, depends on episcopal epitaphs: it is not easy to distinguish fact from *topos* in such documents.[38] The recurrent descriptions of bishops restoring their cities may be inspired more by notions of the ideal bishop than the reality of an individual's activities. The episcopal coinage from the end of the century presents equal, but different, problems of interpretation. That coins were minted in the names of bishops and churches is clear, but it is not certain that they mark an encroachment into a royal preserve. The one written reference to ecclesiastical coinage suggests that it should be interpreted in a very particular way. In a curious visionary text of the seventh century, Barontus, a monk of St Cyran, is told by St Peter not to hide his possessions, but instead to give away twelve *solidi*, each one weighed and signed by a priest, for the good of his soul.[39] From this one might interpret ecclesiastical coinage as money originally minted for pious purposes, for alms and perhaps for tithe, which then moved into general circulation in a society in which many different types of coinage were accepted.

In order to understand the workings of ecclesiastical power, it is necessary to consider it in context, or rather in two contexts; the relations of a bishop with the king and with the leading figures of the diocese. The evidence relating to these issues is not great, and it is unevenly distributed geographically. Further, the evidence for the late Merovingian period is not comparable to that for the sixth century. Gregory of Tours, in particular, provides evidence of unequalled richness; on the one hand he provides us with some of the most compelling images of the power of the Merovingian Church, on the other he allows us to see behind those images, and to look at the nuts and bolts supporting them.

Episcopal elections

One of the most surprising facts about Gregory's references to the sixth-century Church is his lack of concern to hide its canonical failings. Once or twice he seems to imply criticism of the manner in which a bishop was appointed, most notably in his account of the appointment of the layman Desiderius to the bishopric of Eauze, despite a promise that the post would go to a cleric,[40] but for the most part he is prepared to record events with

37. *Gesta episcoporum Autissiodorensium*, 26.
38. Heinzelmann, *Bischofsherrschaft in Gallien*.
39. *Visio Baronti*, 13.
40. Gregory, *Decem Libri Historiarum*, VIII 22.

apparent impartiality. A sizeable proportion of the episcopal appointments recorded by Gregory are quite clearly uncanonical. Indeed, despite the demands of the councils of Orléans (533, 538, 549), Clermont (535), Paris (561/2, 614), Clichy (626/7) and Chalon-sur-Saône (647/53) kings can be seen to have exercised considerable influence in the appointment of bishops until at least the late seventh century.[41] Even in the secular legislation of Chlothar II a king had the right only of veto.[42]

Many bishops owed their position to the king.[43] Some of these were admittedly men with a local following, but others, like Baudinus at Tours, Flavius at Chalon, Badegisel at Le Mans, Licerius at Arles and Charimer at Verdun were royal servants with no known connection with their sees.[44] That this was a problem of significance is suggested by the request of bishop Dalmatius of Rodez, that his successor should not be a stranger to the diocese.[45] According to Venantius Fortunatus, Gregory himself was appointed by Sigibert and Brunhild.[46] Although Gregory insisted that he was related to thirteen of his predecessors in the see, his family was most obviously connected with Burgundy and the Auvergne, and a local priest, Riculf, saw him as an outsider.[47] There were cases in which bishops were appointed in opposition to the will of a ruler, as when Dynamius, the patrician of Provence, appointed Marcellus as bishop of Uzès, despite royal support for Jovinus.[48] This, however, must have been a rare occurrence; most bishops will have received royal approval as canonically required. The sixth-century episcopate cannot, therefore, be seen as a body independent of royal patronage: in so far as the seventh-century evidence allows any assessment to be made, there was no dramatic change. Chlothar II (584–629) compelled Amandus to become bishop;[49] Balthild appointed Leodegar to Autun;[50] Theuderic III (673, 675–90/1) and Pippin II made Lantbert bishop of Lyons.[51] Although the lack of any source comparable to Gregory means that no satisfactory comparison can be made between the sixth and seventh centuries, it is, nevertheless, clear that central secular authority could still play a part in the appointment of bishops in the later Merovingian period.

41. Council of Orléans (533), 3, 4, 7; Council of Clermont (535), 2; Council of Orléans (538), 3; Council of Orléans (549), 10, 11; Council of Paris (561/2), 8; Council of Paris (614), 2; Council of - Clichy (626/7) 28; Council of Chalon-sur-Saône (647/53), 10. The date of the Council of Paris (561/2) is that given by O. Pontal, *Die Synoden im Merowingerreich*, pp. 122–4.

42. *Capitularia Merowingica*, 9, 1.

43. G. Scheibelreiter, *Der Bischof im merowingischer Zeit*, pp. 149–56.

44. Gregory, *Decem Libri Historiarum*, IV 3; V 45; VI 9; VIII 39; IX 23.

45. Gregory, *Decem Libri Historiarum*, V 46.

46. Venantius Fortunatus, carm., V 3, II. 15–16.

47. Gregory, *Decem Libri Historiarum*, V 49.

48. Gregory, *Decem Libri Historiarum*, VI 7.

49. *Vita Amandi*, 18.

50. *Passio Leudegarii I*, 2; *II*, 3.

51. *Vita Ansberti*, 12.

Royal involvement in episcopal appointments suggests that the kings and their bishops were likely to work together rather than in opposition. Although Gregory came into conflict with Chilperic over the immunities of Tours, the original concessions must indicate that in certain circumstances kings were happy to make grants to their bishops. Despite occasional conflicts between bishops and *comites*, and the apparent restriction of comital power in some towns, secular power and ecclesiastical authority should not be seen as being in conflict. Here the seventh-century evidence is actually more suggestive than that for the sixth. Desiderius of Cahors was extremely active in what might be seen as secular aspects of city administration. Given the bishop's close contact with the court of Dagobert I, it is inconceivable that these activities were a usurpation of secular authority. Indeed it is more than likely that Desiderius was encouraged in his actions by the royal court.[52] Further, since he is only one of a significant group of bishops who came from court in the early seventh century, if there was any general transfer of secular authority to bishops in this period, and the evidence is far from clear on this, the likelihood is that it was condoned by the king.

In many repects the bishops of the Merovingian kingdom were like secular magnates, and for the most part they were drawn from the same class. Just as a king needed the support of his magnates, so too he needed the support of his bishops. And just as most magnates needed royal patronage, in terms of land and office, so too did the leading clergy of the kingdom. Not surprisingly, effective kings worked well with their bishops, even when their morality was the subject of open criticism: weak kings are likely to have had very much less influence on their clergy, unless like Guntram they could command some ecclesiastical respect because of their piety.

Bishops and local society: the Auvergne

The relations between a bishop and his diocese could be rather more complicated, being affected by a wide variety of factors. First, there was the problem of the bishop's origins; if he were a complete outsider appointed by the king, his position within the community would be very different from that of a man with local connections. For both, however, there could be substantial difficulties. Although in some dioceses individual families came close to obtaining a monopoly over the episcopate, in others there was considerable rivalry which came to a head at the time of episcopal elections. The rival factions involved were sometimes family groups whose hostility was longstanding, but there could also be a local clerical faction: archdeacons tended to have high hopes of gaining the episcopate and could mobilize a body of support. All this could be complicated by the involvement of royal officials who might choose to aid one or other party. The manner of a

52. Durliat, 'Les attributions civiles des évêques mérovingiens: l'exemple de Didier, évêque de Cahors (630–655)', pp. 252–4.

bishop's election could itself affect the whole of his ensuing episcopate, if factions became too firmly entrenched; peace did not always follow the elevation of the successful candidate.

The evidence for the relations between a bishop and his diocese is unevenly distributed. Some saints' *Lives* shed specific light on individual episcopates, but Gregory of Tours provides unrivalled information in his references to the diocese of the Auvergne.[53] Although there are dangers in concentrating on a single see, the information provided by Gregory does allow a study of episcopal elections over the best part of a century. Gregory was closely involved with several of the protagonists. Not surprisingly his narratives are sometimes unquestionably biased. But if, as a result, his account may misrepresent the behaviour of his heroes and villains, it does provide a contemporary and informed view of the process of election and of the exercise of episcopal power. More generally, the Auvergne might reasonably be seen as representative of many Merovingian dioceses; Clermont was not a royal capital, nor was it a cult centre of major importance. At the same time it was not a minor, backwoods, *civitas*.

Gregory's account becomes exceptional in the second decade of the sixth century with the election of Quintianus, who had fled from his see at Rodez because of the Visigoths. Although he was apparently elected by the people of the Auvergne, he was approached by Alchima and Placidina, the mother and wife of Apollinaris, who asked him to step down in favour of their candidate. He agreed to do so, and Apollinaris, the son of a previous bishop, the great Sidonius Apollinaris, was sent off to king Theuderic as the candidate for the office, and was appointed. Apollinaris survived for only a few months, and on his death Theuderic had Quintianus installed as bishop, apparently on the grounds that the saint had been driven from Rodez because of his loyalty to the Frankish king.[54] Quintianus died in the mid–520s and he was succeeded by Gallus, Gregory of Tours's uncle. The manner of his election was dubious in the extreme; Gallus had spent much time at the court of Theuderic, but at the time of Quintianus's death he was in Clermont; while the citizens were trying to decide on a new candidate the Holy Spirit descended on Gallus, according to his relative Gregory, and on the advice of his uncle Inpetratus he set off and presented himself to Theuderic, who authorized his consecration.[55] Gallus himself died in 551, and at his death the local clergy put forward the name of the priest Cato; the bishops officiating at the burial of Gallus offered to consecrate Cato there and then, and to square the appointment with the king, who was only a minor, subsequently. Cato, however, wanted all to be canonical and refused their offer. He was,

53. I. N. Wood, 'The ecclesiastical politics of Merovingian Clermont', in P. Wormald, ed., *Ideal and Reality in Frankish and Anglo-Saxon Society*, pp. 34–57.

54. Gregory, *Decem Libri Historiarum*, III 2; *Liber Vitae Patrum*, IV 2; Wood, 'The ecclesiastical politics of Merovingian Clermont', p. 43; on the problems of the chronology, see Wood, 'Clermont and Burgundy 511–534', pp. 122–3.

55. Gregory, *Liber Vitae Patrum*, VI 3.

nevertheless, elected to the see of the Auvergne, and he took over the administration of the diocese. During this period of time he made the mistake of threatening the archdeacon, Cautinus, who fled to the court of king Theudebald, announced the death of Gallus, and was himself consecrated bishop on the king's orders. When Cato's supporters arrived at court they found that they had been pre-empted.[56] Cautinus's episcopate lasted until the plague of 571, and then, once again, a less than canonical election took place. The followers of Eufrasius resorted to simony, backed by the financial support of the Jews, but the clergy put forward the name of Avitus. Firminus, *comes* of the Auvergne, tried to prevent his name going forward, but Avitus reached the court of king Sigibert, and was consecrated in Metz, although according to the canons the ceremony should have taken place in Clermont. Gregory claims that it was the king who insisted that the consecration should be held at Metz, out of affection for the candidate, but this may be a euphemism for saying that consecration in Clermont was too dangerous.[57]

Although the election of Avitus is the last Auvergnat election covered by Gregory, two saints' *Lives* allow us to take up the story again a century later. The account of the martyrdom of bishop Praeiectus, the *Passio Praeiecti*, and the *Life of Bonitus* both present complicated narratives, which doubtless conceal specific political and religious biases, but they also provide contemporary accounts of ecclesiastical appointments in a late seventh-century diocese. The *Passio* records a peculiar set of appointments in the 660s. Before the death of Felix five leading churchmen of the *civitas* arranged that the archdeacon Garivald should become the next bishop, since such a succession was the norm. Praeiectus, however, although he was one of the five, began to have second thoughts, because of a vision which his mother had had, forecasting a great ecclesiastical career. He told the citizens of Clermont, and they advised him to buy the office. He refused, but Garivald, who was not unreasonably put out, resorted to simony, and became bishop for forty days. On his death the people of Clermont elected the *comes* Genesius, but he turned down the office, because, as a layman, he regarded the appointment as uncanonical. As a result Praeiectus was finally elected.[58]

The *Life of Bonitus* continues our information. This saint began his career in the court of Sigibert III (632–c. 656), and ultimately became prefect of Provence. His brother, Avitus, meanwhile was bishop of the Auvergne. When Avitus died in *c.* 690 he appointed Bonitus as his successor, and Pippin II, the *maior* and effective ruler of Austrasia and its dependencies in Aquitaine, agreed. Bonitus, nevertheless, came to the conclusion that his appointment was uncanonical, and recommended the elevation of Nordobert in his place.[59] The narratives of the *Passio Praeiecti* and of the *Vita Boniti* both have

---

56. Gregory, *Decem Libri Historiarum*, IV 6–7.
57. Gregory, *Decem Libri Historiarum*, IV 35; B. Brennan, 'The conversion of the Jews of Clermont in AD 576', *Journal of Theological Studies* 36 (1985), p. 323.
58. *Passio Praeiecti*, 12–14.
59. *Vita Boniti*, 3–4, 14.

their peculiarities, and it is possible that the appointment of Praeiectus and the retirement of Bonitus were less creditable than their hagiographers claim. Nevertheless they do illustrate the complexities of local ecclesiastical politics.

The Clermont elections, if that is the right word, provide a startling insight into the appointment of bishops in a *civitas*, which, if it can scarcely be called an insignificant see, was certainly not one in the forefront of royal policy. The patterns of appointment were rarely canonical, yet of the bishops considered, five – Quintianus, Gallus, Avitus, Praeiectus and Bonitus – were regarded as saints. Of these only one, Bonitus, who had been appointed while still a layman, is said to have had scruples about his elevation, although he can be compared with the *comes* Genesius, who turned down the see prior to the election of Praeiectus.

Once installed, a bishop could still have difficulties establishing his power. Again the best evidence is provided by Gregory of Tours. Quintianus, for instance, was at odds with numerous groups in the diocese. He was opposed by at least one cleric, Proculus, who took over the administration of the diocese, and scarcely allowed the bishop enough to eat.[60] Interestingly Gregory also records similar clerical opposition to Sidonius, during his episcopate, fifty years earlier.[61] Proculus met a suitably bloody end, killed at the altar of the church of Vollore, during Theuderic's raid on the Auvergne. In addition Quintianus faced hostility from a local official, Lytigius, and from Hortensius. The latter was cursed by Quintianus and as a result, so Gregory tells us, none of his descendants became a bishop.[62] Gregory recalled this curse in the context of Avitus's election in 571, when Hortensius's descendant, Eufrasius, was the leading challenger. Another man who may have caused difficulties for Quintianus was Arcadius, whose actions prompted Theuderic's raid on the Auvergne.[63] He was the son of Quintianus's predecessor, Apollinaris, and grandson of Sidonius. It is unlikely that he had kept his hands out of ecclesiastical politics in a diocese which could easily have become his family's see.

Gregory has little to say about problems faced by his uncle and mentor, Gallus. With Cautinus, however, we see the full impact of a disputed appointment on the subsequent episcopate. Not surprisingly Cato, having been deprived of the see to which he had been elected, was bitter about Cautinus's consecration. He and a group of clerical supporters refused to accept the outcome of events, despite the fact that Cautinus was at first conciliatory – he may even have been responsible for the proposal that Cato should be given the see of Tours. Cato's obdurate hostility and determination to take over the Auvergnat diocese, however, led to a hardening of lines, and Cautinus began to persecute Cato and his followers.[64] Subsequently matters were further complicated by the presence of Chramn, the son of Chlothar I,

60. Gregory, *Decem Libri Historiarum*, III 13; *Liber Vitae Patrum*, IV 1–2.
61. Gregory, *Decem Libri Historiarum*, II 23.
62. Gregory, *Decem Libri Historiarum*, III 13; IV 35; *Liber Vitae Patrum*, IV 3.
63. Gregory, *Decem Libri Historiarum*, III 9, 12.
64. Gregory, *Decem Libri Historiarum*, IV 7.

in Clermont.[65] As a prince keen to make his mark on the political stage of Merovingian Gaul, Chramn was a dangerous figure. It was important for him to build up a body of allies to ensure his succession on his father's death, but he overreached himself, was regarded as a rebel and was killed, after being defeated in battle by Chlothar. While in Clermont he emerged as the focus for those who were dissatisfied with the status quo – just as Childebert I had earlier appeared as an ally for Arcadius. Among his supporters was Cato, who hoped to receive the diocese of the Auvergne from him when Chlothar was dead. Not surprisingly Cautinus was terrified of Chramn, and on one occasion he abandoned the annual pilgrimage from Clermont to Brioude, because he thought that the prince's men were pursuing him.

Gregory's depiction of Cato and Cautinus is nuanced. Cato appears as arrogant in his determination to fulfil the canons, despite the offer to consecrate him made by the bishops who attended Gallus's funeral; his subsequent refusal of the see of Tours does nothing to enhance his reputation. Yet the final image of him working with plague victims transforms him into a heroic character.[66] Cautinus is very different. He should probably be seen as a cleric of some piety; in Gregory's miracle stories he is associated with the cult of Stremonius at Issoire.[67] In the *Histories*, however, he is sly, drunken and spineless, even lifting a sentence of excommunication on a man suspected of matricide. He is also cruel and rapacious when not faced with opposition: he has the priest Anastasius buried alive to extort a charter from him. In addition he is a great client of Jewish merchants.[68]

The Jews provide us with the single most illuminating incident of the episcopate of Avitus. Eufrasius, Avitus's rival for the see of the Auvergne, tried to secure the episcopate with the help of Jewish money. It is perhaps not surprising that when a Christian mob destroyed the synagogue in Clermont, in the aftermath of an outrage committed on a Jewish convert to Christianity, Avitus did nothing to protect the Jews, but used the incident to force them either to be baptized or to leave the city. The eradication of Judaism in the Auvergne attracted the interest not only of Gregory, but also of Venantius Fortunatus, who saw in the event the emergence of a unified Christian community.[69] Unlike his predecessor, Avitus was a powerful bishop who managed to harness the local forces which Cautinus had signally failed to dominate.

The Auvergnat evidence, thus, shows us bishops in context, some managing to dominate their diocese, others at odds with their clergy, or hampered by secular figures, most clearly by the outsider Chramn. Although

65. Gregory, *Decem Libri Historiarum* IV 13, 16.
66. Gregory, *Decem Libri Historiarum*, IV 6–7, 11, 15, 31.
67. Gregory, *Liber in Gloria Confessorum*, 29.
68. Gregory, *Decem Libri Historiarum*, IV 12, 31; X 8.
69. Gregory, *Decem Libri Historiarum*, V 11; Venantius Fortunatus, carm. V, 5; see Brennan, 'The conversion of the Jews of Clermont in AD 576', pp. 321–37; W. Goffart, 'The conversions of Avitus of Clermont and similar passages in Gregory of Tours', in Goffart, *Rome's Fall and After*, pp. 293–317.

relations between the bishops and the resident aristocracy are harder to piece together, the fortunes of one or two families are clear enough; in the pages of Gregory the descendants of Quintianus's opponent, Hortensius, appear consistently as failures; so too does the ill-fated family of the *comes* Firminus. After the death of Gallus, however, the family of Gregory itself ceases to be visible in the Auvergne. More complex is the question of the influence of the family of Avitus, one-time emperor and father-in-law of Sidonius. The latter's son was Quintianus's predecessor, and his grandson, Arcadius, the cause of Theuderic's attack on the Auvergne. Gregory's account suggests that the family's influence in Clermont subsequently came to an end, but the poems of Venantius Fortunatus show that the dynasty was still powerful elsewhere: Arcadius's son Leontius became bishop of Bordeaux.[70] There are also hints in later sources that it regained its influence in the Auvergne; there is the name Avitus, held both by the opponent of the Clermont Jews, and also, in the seventh century, by the brother and predecessor of bishop Bonitus.[71] If the sixth-century Avitus was related to Sidonius it is interesting that Gregory should imply that the family faded out after Arcadius's plot; Avitus was, after all, a friend of Gregory. The problem of the survival of the Aviti is a useful reminder of how little we know about the political structure of even our best evidenced sixth-century diocese; but from the evidence which we do have it is clear that the exercise of episcopal power in the Auvergne was no simple matter.

Theodore of Marseilles

In one respect the local political structure in Clermont was relatively simple: although Theuderic mounted a raid on the Auvergne, and although Chramn took up residence in the district, for the most part the *civitas* was not of great interest to the Merovingian kings. Difficulties facing bishops could escalate when central and local politics overlapped. One city where royal interests and local divisions often combined was Marseilles. This city was naturally of great strategic importance: much of the communication between Francia and the eastern Mediterranean seems to have passed through it in the sixth century. It is, therefore, not surprising that it should be a cause of dispute between kings. In fact, in the early Merovingian period it seems to have been held by the rulers of the eastern kingdom, but after Sigibert I's murder in 575 half of it was handed over to Guntram, presumably to cement an alliance between the young Childebert II and his uncle. When Childebert felt more secure, however, having made his peace with his other uncle Chilperic, he demanded the return of half the *civitas*.[72] This state of affairs provides the background for the misfortunes which were to confront bishop Theodore in the 580's.

70. See Venantius Fortunatus, carm., I 14–16, 18–20; III 24; IV 10.
71. *Vita Boniti*, 4.
72. Gregory, *Decem Libri Historiarum*, VI 33.

The first reference to Theodore in Gregory's *Histories* concerns an unexplained alliance of the clergy of Marseilles and Dynamius, the *patricius*, or governor, of Provence, against the bishop in 581. Theodore and the ex-governor, Jovinus, were arrested by Dynamius while travelling to the court of Childebert. The clergy of Marseilles were overjoyed and acted as if the bishop was already dead: they took an inventory of the church plate, as was required by the canons on the death of a bishop.[73] The charges made against Theodore, however, did not stick. He returned, apparently, with Gundulf, Childebert's *dux*. Dynamius tried to lock them out of the city, but he was tricked by Gundulf. Although the clergy were opposed to Theodore, it appears that the bishop did have supporters in the city because the bells were rung when he and Gundulf returned. Nevertheless Dynamius accused Theodore of plotting against Guntram, had him arrested and sent to the king for trial; again the accusations did not stand up to scrutiny.[74] Not surprisingly relations between Guntram and Childebert deteriorated.

The next difficulties confronting Theodore stemmed directly from Marseilles's position as a point of entry into the Frankish kingdom from the Byzantine empire, for it was there that Gundovald, supposedly a son of Chlothar I, landed in 582, to make a bid for the throne. As bishop, Theodore welcomed him, only to be arrested by the *dux* Guntram Boso, and sent to king Guntram on a charge of treason. Once again he was found to be innocent, but he was still kept under arrest.[75] When or why he was reinstated in Marseilles is not known, but Guntram continued to harass him; claiming in 585 that he was one of those responsible for the murder of Chilperic, apparently one of the wildest of many such accusations made by the king.[76] Further, although Marseilles was under the rule of Childebert by this time, the latter's governor Rathar, arrested Theodore and sent him to Guntram. He was probably one of a number of bishops whom Guntram intended to exile, but he was reinstated after the king fell ill. According to Gregory, all were delighted with this turn of events.[77]

There is a great deal that is unclear in this tale of episcopal misfortunes. Although Marseilles is known to have been shared between two kings for much of this time, details of the division are hard to establish. They might explain the behaviour of the various secular officials. Certainly, the complex set up in the city meant that the bishop, appointed in the time of Sigibert, was only too easily suspected of treason by Guntram – and the arrival of Gundovald clearly did not help matters. The conflict between Guntram and Childebert, moreover, allowed the clergy to oppose their bishop, while, at least from Gregory's account, it seems as though the laity supported him. Theodore does not emerge from this as a powerful man, indeed he is very

---

73. Gregory, *Decem Libri Historiarum*, VI 11; Council of Orléans (533), 6.
74. Gregory, *Decem Libri Historiarum*, VI 11.
75. Gregory, *Decem Libri Historiarum*, VI 24.
76. Gregory, *Decem Libri Historiarum*, VIII 5.
77. Gregory, *Decem Libri Historiarum*, VIII 12, 20.

much everybody else's pawn. At the same time he is depicted as a saint by the bishop of Tours, who may well have thought of him as a fellow victim of Merovingian politics. Theodore's career reveals that even a good bishop could be powerless in a city where there were too many other interests.

Gregory and Tours

Marseilles was perhaps not a particularly easy city for a bishop to manage. There was no major saint-cult which could be relied on to bolster episcopal power. Exactly how much could be gained from the support of a saintly patron can best be seen by turning to the position of Gregory at Tours, in particular to the events leading up to his trial, for purportedly slandering queen Fredegund, at Berny-Rivière. Gregory and others saw in certain happenings which took place at this time the workings of divine providence: on one occasion the boat carrying one of his opponents sank; on another a supporter was miraculously freed from prison; and throughout his trial the princess Rigunth fasted on his behalf.[78] Despite his account of these miraculous events, the problems facing Gregory were immediate and considerable.

Gregory's chief opponent in Tours in the late 570's was the *comes* Leudast. Gregory says he was the son of a slave and that he came to prominence in the household of king Charibert, whence he was promoted to being *comes* of Tours. After Charibert's death Leudast made the mistake of wishing to see Tours transferred to the kingdom of Chilperic. In the event it fell to Sigibert, and as a result Leudast lost his office. Only after Sigibert's murder in 575 did Chilperic gain permanent control of the city, whereupon Leudast regained his old office. Among his friends Leudast numbered a priest and subdeacon, both confusingly called Riculf. Between them these men accused Gregory of slandering Chilperic's queen, Fredegund, and Leudast arrested two of Gregory's supporters, the archdeacon Plato and his friend Gallienus. The accusations against Gregory were further supported by the *dux* Berulf and the *comes* Eunomius, who said that the bishop was intent on handing Tours over to Guntram. As a result Gregory was summoned to Berny-Rivière and tried. He was acquitted, apparently because he had support within the royal household, and because the bishops united to reject the evidence of an inferior against one of themselves. There was also, or so Gregory claims, a vociferous group outside the court, which had made known their belief in his innocence.[79] The whole affair had, however, been tense.

Subsequently the subdeacon Riculf was tortured and revealed what lay behind the attack on Gregory. According to Gregory the slanders against

78. Gregory, *Decem Libri Historiarum*, V 49; on Berny-Rivière, see J. George 'Poet as politician: Venantius Fortunatus' panegyric to King Chilperic', *Journal of Medieval History* 15 (1989), pp. 5–18.

79. Gregory, *Decem Libri Historiarum*, V 47–9.

Fredegund were intended to drive her from the court, thus facilitating the elevation of her stepson, Clovis, to the throne. The new king was then to appoint as bishop his old friend, the priest Riculf, whose namesake was to become archdeacon: Leudast was to become a *dux*. It may be significant that Clovis was murdered at about this time, apparently at Fredegund's instigation.[80] It is possible that Riculf's confession should be seen in the context of the aftermath of the murder, and that its accuracy should be regarded with some suspicion. Nevertheless, it is clear that Gregory himself was opposed by members of his clergy. It was during this crisis that Gregory was criticized as not being a local: even a bishop who belonged to the episcopal dynasty of Tours could be portrayed by his own clergy as an outsider. The episode should make us wary of placing too much emphasis on such notions as clerical dynasties.

In this whole scandal one figure is largely absent: St Martin. Gregory himself did not doubt the efficacy of the saint, but clearly Leudast and his supporters were less than impressed by the bishop's special relationship with his supernatural patron. For every miracle in which a saint punished someone flouting his authority, there was someone to do the flouting. In certain respects a major saint–cult was a liability: it usually meant the existence of a refuge to which political outcasts might flee. Any asylum seeker brought with him the possibility of retribution against the shrine and its local town or city from his enemies, as Gregory discovered on a number of occasions. Among the refugees who caused trouble for for the bishops of Tours were Austrapius, Merovech, Eberulf, Chariulf and Childeric the Saxon.[81] Moreover, although a great cult may have brought in more than enough wealth to compensate for the damage caused by those fleeing from the king's anger, that wealth could still attract the attention of would-be thieves. A major shrine was not an unequivocal blessing to its guardians.

Episcopal power was not cut and dried, although the canons, the saints' *Lives* and the epitaphs of bishops would like us to think that it was. The image presented by these sources is one of consensus, in which all was ultimately rightly ordered by divine forces. This vision is the creation of propaganda. The propaganda may have had some success; it was, nevertheless, necessary. Precisely because a bishop's hold on his diocese could be precarious, he needed to manipulate all the resources at his disposal; contacts at court, family connections, the canons and the cult of the saints. When Eligius became bishop of Noyon in 641 he set out to find the bones of the martyr Quentin. Maurinus, *cantor* in the royal palace, had effectively challenged Eligius to do so, by searching himself, although he died in the attempt.[82] The new bishop's credibility could and did gain much from the discovery. He needed to mobilize all his resources in order to control his diocese, much as kings had to do in order to rule their kingdoms.

80. Gregory, *Decem Libri Historiarum*, V 39, 49.
81. Gregory, *Decem Libri Historiarum*, IV 18; V 14, 19; VII 21, 43; VIII 18.
82. *Vita Eligii*, II 6.

Chapter Six

Stability in Disunity: the Civil Wars of the Sixth Century

Civil war was the spectre which haunted much of sixth-century Gaul, or so it seemed to Gregory of Tours as he wrote the preface to the fifth book of his *Histories*. In certain respects this preface is misleading. Book Five of the *Histories* covers the period from the murder of Sigibert in 575 until Gregory's own trial at Berny-Rivière in 580. These five years were a particularly disruptive time for the city of Tours, not least because of the presence of Chilperic's son Merovech, who sought asylum in St Martin's in 577.[1] Book Seven enhances the impression of a century of civil war, but again allowance must be made for the fact that this one book covers scarcely more than twelve months of 584/5, and that it is concerned largely with the attempt by the 'pretender' Gundovald to establish his claim to the Frankish throne. The crisis surrounding Gundovald casts a disproportionate shadow across Gregory's *Histories*. Indeed, it is difficult to estimate the scale of any civil war from Gregory's account.

Civil wars were not the only destructive forces in the Merovingian kingdoms. Urban politics could be extremely disruptive; Book Five of the *Histories* deals not only with Merovech, but also with Leudast, and his plots against Gregory.[2] Nor was conflict within Merovingian society the sole cause of destruction: the passage of an army heading for campaigns outside the Frankish kingdom could be devastating, as the Septimanian expedition of 585 revealed.[3] Just as bad was the passage of the retinue of Rigunth, as she set out to marry the Visigothic prince Reccared in 584. Gregory saw in the vandalism caused during this episode the fulfilment of a prophecy of Joel: 'that which the locust hath left hath the cankerworm eaten'.[4]

1. Gregory, *Decem Libri Historiarum*, V 14.
2. Gregory, *Decem Libri Historiarum*, V 47–9.
3. Gregory, *Decem Libri Historiarum*, VIII 30.
4. Gregory, *Decem Libri Historiarum*, VI 45.

Family politics 511–613

Despite the devastation which could be caused in peace-time, Gregory saw civil wars as being the single most important cause of disruption. They deserve close consideration. Clovis's campaigns and ruses against other Frankish rulers should perhaps be seen as power struggles within a small kin-group, and therefore as precursors of the civil wars that were to follow, but we know nothing about the connections between the petty kings of the years prior to 511. From the 520's onwards, however, the Merovingians were regularly at each other's throats; Theuderic I attempted to murder his half-brother Chlothar I;[5] Chlothar and Childebert I did kill the sons of Chlodomer;[6] Childebert and Theuderic's son Theudebert I almost fought against Chlothar, but a storm miraculously prevented a battle taking place.[7] In the 550's Chlothar himself was faced with the rebellion of his own son Chramn.[8]

After Chlothar's death in 561 a new set of conflicts arose, largely associated with the rivalry between Chlothar's sons, Charibert I, Guntram, Sigibert I and Chilperic I, over the division of their father's kingdom.[9] In 562 Chilperic took advantage of Sigibert's preoccupation with a campaign against the Avars east of the Rhine to seize some of his brother's cities. After defeating the Avars, Sigibert returned and took Chilperic's capital, Soissons, before restoring the status quo.[10] Matters were made worse when Chilperic had his wife Galswinth murdered: she was the sister of Sigibert's wife, Brunhild, and not surprisingly Chilperic's half-brothers ganged up on him.[11] In 566 it was Sigibert's turn to be the aggressor, when he sent an army against Arles, which was held by Guntram.[12] Sigibert and Guntram came to blows again in 573, and the crisis was exacerbated by Chilperic's attacking Sigibert's lands south of the Loire. Sigibert retaliated by calling in his allies from across the Rhine. Chilperic and Guntram united against him, but Sigibert forced Guntram to abandon the alliances on two occasions.[13] Finally in 575 Sigibert was at the point of eliminating Chilperic, but he was murdered, probably by agents of Fredegund.[14] It is possible that the wars of 573 to 575 marked the worst period of civil war in sixth-century Francia. Nevertheless it was the political complexities which followed which most attracted Gregory.

In the aftermath of Sigibert's murder the survival of his son Childebert II was uncertain: Chilperic took advantage of the difficulties facing the young

5. Gregory, *Decem Libri Historiarum*, III 7.
6. Gregory, *Decem Libri Historiarum*, III 18.
7. Gregory, *Decem Libri Historiarum*, III 28.
8. Gregory, *Decem Libri Historiarum*, IV 16. 17, 20.
9. Beginning in Gregory, *Decem Libri Historiarum*, IV 22.
10. Gregory, *Decem Libri Historiarum*, IV 23.
11. Gregory, *Decem Libri Historiarum*, IV 28.
12. Gregory, *Decem Libri Historiarum*, IV 30.
13. Gregory, *Decem Libri Historiarum*, IV 47, 49, 50.
14. Gregory, *Decem Libri Historiarum*, IV 51.

king to seize some of his cities.[15] Childebert survived in the first instance because of the loyalty of his father's followers, and later because of the intervention of his uncle Guntram.[16] Meanwhile Chilperic himself was faced with a challenge from Merovech, his son by Audovera. The prince was intent on establishing himself as king, and he appears to have chosen the period following Sigibert's death deliberately to make his bid for recognition. One measure he took to bolster his position was to marry Sigibert's widow, Brunhild.[17] He was right to feel insecure. Fredegund was determined that only her children should succeed Chilperic, and to this end she eliminated his sons by other women.[18] To survive, Merovech had to oppose his father, but his bid for power failed and he asked his servant to kill him.[19]

One result of Fredegund's actions, which also involved the murder of prince Clovis, was that by 581 Chilperic had no living son. Her three eldest sons had all died of disease, and the fourth had not yet been born.[20] Meanwhile relations between Childebert and Guntram had soured over the latter's treatment of lands once held by Sigibert. The way was therefore open for a rapprochement between Childebert and Chilperic, who now adopted the former as his heir.[21] The original alliance between Guntram and his nephew thus came to an end. The following three years saw a complex set of political manoeuvres, centred largely on the control of various cities of Aquitaine. Ultimately Childebert and Guntram patched up their quarrel, and Chilperic moved on to the defensive, only to be murdered at Chelles in 584.[22]

Chilperic left Fredegund's infant son, Chlothar II, as his heir. His survival depended on the support of the Neustrian aristocracy, and, once again on Guntram, now childless, playing the part of a kindly uncle, although he was suspicious about the child's parentage.[23] Meanwhile Gundovald, a supposed son of Chlothar, who had been excluded from the succession in 561, took advantage of the situation to revive his claim to the crown, which he had already asserted with Byzantine support in 582.[24] For the best part of a year he presented Guntram with a very serious challenge.[25] His death in 585 marks the end of the major military conflicts covered by Gregory of Tours, but there was still much disagreement between Childebert and his uncle, over

15. Gregory, *Decem Libri Historiarum*, V 1–4.
16. Gregory, *Decem Libri Historiarum*, V 1, 17.
17. Gregory, *Decem Libri Historiarum*, V 2.
18. Gregory, *Decem Libri Historiarum*, V 39.
19. Gregory, *Decem Libri Historiarum*, V 18.
20. Gregory, *Decem Libri Historiarum*, V 22, 34; VI 41.
21. Gregory, *Decem Libri Historiarum*, VI 1, 3, 31.
22. Gregory, *Decem Libri Historiarum*, VI 45, 46.
23. Gregory, *Decem Libri Historiarum*, VII 5, 7; VIII 9; on the possibility that Gregory thought that Guntram was right to question Chlothar's legitimacy, see Wood, 'The secret histories of Gregory of Tours'.
24. Gregory, *Decem Libri Historiarum*, VI 24.
25. Gregory, *Decem Libri Historiarum*, VII 10, 14, 26–8, 30–8.

land, over the participants in the Gundovald affair, over relations with Spain, and over the recognition of Chilperic's son, Chlothar II.[26] Mutual irritation is apparent up until the end of Gregory's narrative, in 591.

Guntram died in 592, and Childebert II took over his kingdom.[27] The latter, however, died four years later: of his sons, Theudebert II inherited Austrasia, and Theuderic II Burgundy.[28] The two brothers were at times united in their hostility to Chilperic's son Chlothar II, and at one moment they reduced the latter's kingdom to territory between the Seine, the Oise and the sea.[29] Theudebert and Theuderic, however, were soon to fall out, largely, according to Fredegar, at the instigation of their grandmother Brunhild.[30] Whereas Gregory had tended to see the malign influence of Fredegund as the origin of many of the problems of his own day, for Fredegar Brunhild was the evil genius of the period from 575 to 613. The old queen stirred up Theuderic against his brother, whom she called the son of a gardener, and Theuderic defeated and killed Theudebert in 612.[31] He then turned on Chlothar, but his own death, from dysentery, and the subsequent elimination of his family in 613, led to the reunification of the Frankish kingdom and brought to a close one period of Merovingian civil war.[32]

The causes of war

Within the history of these early civil wars there are certain recurrent features which are worthy of emphasis. First, there is the chronological association between the death, or reported death, of a king and political crisis. Childebert I's invasion of the Auvergne, prompted by Arcadius, followed inaccurate reports that Theuderic I had died;[33] Childebert was also to attack Rheims because he was told, again incorrectly, of Chlothar's death.[34] The conflict between Chilperic and his half-brothers began on the death of their father Chlothar I.[35] More interestingly, Merovech's bid for power followed his uncle's murder;[36] similarly Gundovald, who had been more or less ignored when he first returned to Gaul in 582, became a plausible candidate for the throne when Chilperic was killed.[37]

26. Gregory, *Decem Libri Historiarum*, IX 10, 11, 14, 16, 20, 32; X 28.
27. Fredegar, IV 14.
28. Fredegar, IV 16.
29. Fredegar, IV 20.
30. Fredegar, IV 27.
31. Fredegar, IV 27, 37–8.
32. Fredegar, IV 39–42.
33. Gregory, *Decem Libri Historiarum*, III 9.
34. Gregory, *Decem Libri Historiarum*, IV 17.
35. Gregory, *Decem Libri Historiarum*, IV 22.
36. Gregory, *Decem Libri Historiarum*, V 2.
37. Gregory, *Decem Libri Historiarum*, VI 24; VII 10.

All candidates for the throne had to be recognized as Merovingians. Most of them were unquestioned members of the royal family. But there were exceptions: Gregory of Tours denied the claims of one would-be king called Munderic, who was crushed by Theuderic I.[38] Chlothar I refused to acknowledge that Gundovald was his son, but there were others who thought that he was. They may well have been in the right: the tendency of some Merovingians to take and discard wives at will, that is to practise serial monogamy, meant that there was no clearly defined family tree.[39] Nor was the behaviour of all Merovingian queens above suspicion. The parentage of two kings was called into question; Fredegund gathered three bishops and three hundred leading laymen to swear that Chlothar II was the son of Chilperic when Guntram suggested that he was illegitimate;[40] Brunhild, however, was prepared to say that her grandson Theudebert was the son of a gardener.[41]

Even a prince whose parentage was known could not be certain of succeeding his father, especially if his mother had been discarded from the royal bed. As we have seen serial monogamy could put the claims of unquestionably legitimate princes at risk. None of Chilperic's sons by women other than Fredegund gained the throne, but they were all legitimate claimants, and two of them, Merovech and Clovis, made a bid for power in opposition to the will of their stepmother.[42] Nor was this a peculiarly Frankish problem: similar conflict had already been seen in the hostility between Sigistrix and Sigismund's second wife, in the kingdom of the Burgundians.[43] Not every Merovingian queen was as forceful as Fredegund, and the sons of various queens or concubines did inherit at the same time. Nevertheless, Merovingian kings with the same mother were more likely to cooperate than sons of different mothers. Theuderic I seems to have kept himself apart from the other sons of Clovis, though this could, in part, be explained by his greater age. Among those sons of Chlothar to survive and inherit from their father, Chilperic appears as an outsider: he was the son of Aregund, while Charibert, Guntram and Sigibert were the sons of Ingund.[44] It is possible that the earlier opposition of Chramn to his father, Chlothar, and to his brothers was linked to the fact that he alone was the son of Chunsina.[45] The problems faced by princes go a long way to explaining their activities during the lifetimes of their fathers, especially their hostility to their stepmothers. The history of the royal succession shows time and again that a

38. Gregory, *Decem Libri Historiarum*, III 14.
39. Gregory, *Decem Libri Historiarum*, VI 24; VII 14, 27, 32, 36, 38; VIII 2, 6; on the question of Gregory's view of Gundovald's legitimacy, see Wood, 'The secret histories of Gregory of Tours'.
40. Gregory, *Decem Libri Historiarum*, VIII 9.
41. Fredegar, IV 27.
42. Gregory, *Decem Libri Historiarum*, V 19, 39.
43. Gregory, *Decem Libri Historiarum*, III 5.
44. Gregory, *Decem Libri Historiarum*, IV 3, 22.
45. Gregory, *Decem Libri Historiarum*, IV 3, 16.

prince had to prove himself in order to be sure of inheriting a kingdom, and the process of building up a following and prestige was likely to cause some conflict.

For an established monarch the major conflicts with other rulers were almost inevitably concerned with land, and more particularly with the question of the divisions of the kingdom. This largely accounts for the hostilities following the death of Chlothar I in 561.[46] Problems were doubtless aggravated by Charibert's death six years later, which necessitated a redivision of his lands among his surviving brothers.[47] The murder of Sigibert I left his son's territories open to the military onslaughts of Chilperic and to the rather more devious guardianship undertaken by Guntram.[48] Concentration on the issue of the divisions of the kingdom, however, runs the risk of presenting the Merovingian civil wars in too exclusively royal a fashion. By no means all the conflict within the Frankish kingdom stemmed from the centre.

There were certainly occasions when an over-zealous army drove a king to war. Theuderic's Auvergne campaign of 524 was in part forced on him, according to Gregory of Tours, when he refused to attack Burgundy: his soldiers wanted a war of some sort and he had to provide one.[49] Sigibert's eastern troops were furious when he patched up a peace with Chilperic.[50] On the whole, although there is an exception in 583, when Childebert II's army refused to obey the policies of bishop Egidius of Rheims,[51] the military followers of the Merovingians liked to fight: a battle brought hope of booty. Similarly the militias of the *civitates* seem to have relished the opportunity to plunder neighbouring districts; in the wake of Chilperic's murder there was a particularly savage conflict between the men of Orléans and Blois on the one hand and the men of Châteaudun and Chartres, just to the north, on the other.[52]

The Gundovald affair

The involvement of the aristocracy in the civil wars and the disruptions of the Merovingian period is complex. Inevitably the interests of individual magnates varied. How royal conflicts could engage these various interests is best seen through a detailed investigation of one particular crisis. The most informative is undoubtedly that caused by Gundovald's claim to the throne, since Gregory of Tours not only allocates a considerable amount of space to the rebellion itself, but also provides evidence in the ensuing books of the *Histories* which

46. Gregory, *Decem Libri Historiarum*, IV 22.
47. Gregory, *Decem Libri Historiarum*, IV 26.
48. Gregory, *Decem Libri Historiarum*, V 1–4.
49. Gregory, *Decem Libri Historiarum*, III 11.
50. Gregory, *Decem Libri Historiarum*, IV 49.
51. Gregory, *Decem Libri Historiarum*, VI 31.
52. Gregory, *Decem Libri Historiarum*, VII 2.

illuminates the nature of the 'pretender's' following. Further, the way in which Gregory presents his account of Gundovald's rebellion and the subsequent related events is in itself revealing.

Gundovald claimed to be a son of Chlothar I. Chlothar denied the claim, but his brother Childebert I at first accepted it, as also did Chlothar's son Charibert I. Despite this support, Gundovald was rejected by Sigibert, another of Chlothar's sons, so he went to Italy, where he was received by the Byzantine general, Narses, and from there to Constantinople. Following the approaches of a member of the Frankish aristocracy, however, he returned to Gaul in 582/3, and was met by Theodore, bishop of Marseilles. His arrival was inopportune, and he soon withdrew to a Mediterranean island.[53] In 584, however, he was to be found with Mummolus in Avignon, where they were joined by Desiderius, *dux* of the recently murdered Chilperic. Together Mummolus and Desiderius elevated Gundovald to the kingship at Brives-la-Gaillarde.[54] As king, Gundovald proceeded to take oaths of loyalty from those *civitates* which had been held by Chilperic, as well as those still subject to Guntram.[55] During the course of 585 Gundovald's luck began to run out. He was deserted by Desiderius and retreated to St Bertrand de Comminges, where he was eventually deserted by his other leading followers; finally he was tricked into handing himself over to Guntram's generals and was killed.[56]

Gundovald's bid for the throne was based on his claim to Merovingian blood. Whether his claim was genuine or not is an open question. Given the complexities of Merovingian family politics, Chlothar's denial of paternity is not conclusive: he may have had good reason to disassociate himself from Gundovald's mother. Equally, Sigibert and Guntram may have been opposed to Gundovald because he threatened their own positions. On the other hand, Childebert may have backed Gundovald in order to inconvenience his brother Chlothar. Charibert's support, however, is less easily explained away. Yet more thought-provoking is a speech which Gregory puts into Gundovald's mouth shortly before his death. There Gundovald claims to have the support of Radegund and Ingitrude.[57] The former was one of the women most admired by Gregory, and as a sometime wife of Chlothar she may have been well informed about his children.[58] At the very least Gundovald's claim was plausible. His bid for the throne was in the first instance an aspect of Merovingian family politics.

53. Gregory, *Decem Libri Historiarum*, VI 24; on the Byzantine background to this, see W. Goffart, 'Byzantine policy in the west under Tiberius II and Maurice: the pretenders Hermenegild and Gundovald', *Traditio* 13 (1957), pp. 85–118; P. Goubert, *Byzance avant l'Islam*, 2, *Byzance et l'Occident*, pp. 29–68.

54. Gregory, *Decem Libri Historiarum*, VII 10.

55. Gregory, *Decem Libri Historiarum*, VII 26.

56. Gregory, *Decem Libri Historiarum*, VII 34–8.

57. Gregory, *Decem Libri Historiarum*, VII 36; see Wood, 'The secret histories of Gregory of Tours'.

58. Gregory, *Decem Libri Historiarum*, III 7.

What made the bid viable were two related factors: treasure and aristocratic support. When Gundovald first arrived in Gaul he apparently had an considerable quantity of treasure with him,[59] which must suggest that he initially had the backing of the Byzantine emperor, whose concerns about the Lombards in Italy may well have stretched to a desire to see a close ally established in Francia.[60] Childebert's *dux* Guntram Boso is said to have captured an immense amount of gold and silver when Gundovald fled from Avignon. Two years later, however, Gundovald was wealthy enough to bribe the leading citizens of Angoulême.[61] Subsequently the remnants of Rigunth's treasure, for which Waddo had been responsible, and which Desiderius had secured, fell into his hands.[62] Even when he was cornered at St Bertrand de Comminges Gundovald had quantities of gold and silver.[63]

With regard to Gundovald's aristocratic support, Gregory's account is less straightforward. When he first refers to the approach made to Gundovald in Constantinople he does not reveal the identity of the man involved.[64] Later he says that Guntram accused Guntram Boso of inviting Gundovald to return to Gaul.[65] Gundovald himself is said to have talked of conversations with Boso in Constantinople.[66] When Gundovald first arrived, however, Boso arrested bishop Theodore of Marseilles for receiving him and he stole Gundovald's treasure. Theodore claimed that he was acting on the instructions of Childebert's magnates.[67] Gregory's failure to make any clear statement about the author of the original invitation asking Gundovald to return to Gaul seems to be deliberate.[68]

The support which Gundovald received once in Gaul is easier to analyse. Theodore seems not to have acted of his own volition; his welcome to Gundovald can be discounted.[69] Gundovald's first major supporter was Mummolus: Gregory records Guntram Boso's accusation that Mummolus received Gundovald hospitably. The charge brought the two commanders to blows.[70] This might suggest that it was a calumny on Boso's part, but Gregory himself states directly that Mummolus received Gundovald.[71] Later Gundovald and Mummolus were joined by *dux* Desiderius, Bladast, Waddo and bishop Sagittarius of Gap.[72] In Bordeaux, Gundovald was supported by the bishop, Bertram.[73] These men can be divided into two groups; half had

59. Gregory, *Decem Libri Historiarum*, VI 24.
60. Goubert, *Byzance avant l'Islam*, 2, *Byzance et l'Occident*, p. 68.
61. Gregory, *Decem Libri Historiarum*, VII 26.
62. Gregory, *Decem Libri Historiarum*, VII 32, 35.
63. Gregory, *Decem Libri Historiarum*, VII 35.
64. Gregory, *Decem Libri Historiarum*, VI 24.
65. Gregory, *Decem Libri Historiarum*, VII 14.
66. Gregory, *Decem Libri Historiarum*, VII 36.
67. Gregory, *Decem Libri Historiarum*, VI 24.
68. Wood, 'The secret histories of Gregory of Tours'.
69. Gregory, *Decem Libri Historiarum*, VI 24.
70. Gregory, *Decem Libri Historiarum*, VI 26.
71. Gregory, *Decem Libri Historiarum*, VI 24.
72. Gregory, *Decem Libri Historiarum*, VII 10, 28.
73. Gregory, *Decem Libri Historiarum*, VII 31.

followed Guntram, the other half, Chilperic. The followers of Guntram were Mummolus, Sagittarius and Bertram. The latter was related to the king.[74] His support may have been determined by the presence of Gundovald's army in his cathedral city. Mummolus and Sagittarius, however, had both fallen out with Guntram: Sagittarius had been deposed from his bishopric as a result of adultery and murder.[75] For their point of view, if Gundovald could be established in the kingship, he would be a new patron. Similar pressures weighed on Desiderius, Waddo and Bladast, but for rather different reasons. They joined Gundovald after Chilperic's murder in 584. Probably all three of them were away from court at the time of the murder: Waddo was certainly in the retinue of Chilperic's daughter Rigunth, who was *en route* for Spain, where she was to have been married.[76] From Waddo's point of view the king's death was a disaster; too far from court to be involved in safeguarding Chilperic's heir, which was arranged by Fredegund, he was liable to be excluded from the ruling group in the early years of Chlothar II.[77] In Aquitaine, however, he, Desiderius and perhaps Bladast were well placed to transfer their allegiance to Gundovald, which is what they did.

The significance of Chilperic's murder for Gundovald's cause can be seen in the curious chronology of the whole affair. Since Childebert I is said to have acknowledged Gundovald's claim to Merovingian blood, the issue must have been raised before 558, perhaps long before. Gundovald probably left Francia in or shortly after 561. He was certainly in Italy before Narses died in 574, and he subsequently spent a long time in Constantinople.[78] He returned to Gaul in 582/3, but received little support. It was not until 584 that his bid for the throne made serious headway, and then only after the murder of Chilperic had left certain of his followers without a patron.

Gundovald and the opposition to Childebert II

Although Gundovald received open support from men who had fallen out with Guntram, or who had been left without a patron at Chilperic's death, Theodore of Marseilles claimed that he had been ordered to receive Gundovald by Childebert's magnates.[79] It is possible that Childebert and his mother, Brunhild, had some sympathy for Gundovald, who was careful not to lay claim to Childebert's territory; indeed he took oaths on Childebert's behalf.[80] Further, Guntram feared that Brunhild would contact the 'pretender',[81] and he actually wrote to Gundovald in her name, in order to

74. Gregory, *Decem Libri Historiarum*, IV 42, 45; V 20; VIII 2.
75. Gregory, *Decem Libri Historiarum*, V 20.
76. Gregory, *Decem Libri Historiarum*, VI 45; VII 27.
77. Gregory, *Decem Libri Historiarum*, VII 4–5, 7.
78. Gregory, *Decem Libri Historiarum*, VI 24.
79. Gregory, *Decem Libri Historiarum*, VI 24.
80. Gregory, *Decem Libri Historiarum*, VII 26.
81. Gregory, *Decem Libri Historiarum*, VII 33.

trick him into disbanding his troops.[82] After Gundovald's death Brunhild does seem to have been in communication with his sons.[83] Guntram even accused her of wanting to marry one of them; a suggestion which Gregory found preposterous.[84] She did, nevertheless, offer Waddo protection after he had left Gundovald.[85] Despite these hints, it is more likely that those magnates of Childebert who encouraged Gundovald in 582 were men who had strong reservations about the king and his mother. This is suggested in two ways. In Gundovald's description of his conversations with Guntram Boso, as set out by Gregory of Tours, Boso is reported to have said that Chilperic was dead (which was not the case at the time), that Guntram was childless, and that Childebert had no support.[86] Even though Gundovald can never have said some of the things which Gregory attributes to him, the bishop of Tours must have had some reason for putting the words into his mouth. Effectively Gregory indicates that a section of the aristocracy were dissatisfied with all three Merovingian kings, including Childebert in 582. There may be a further indication of this dissatisfaction in Gregory's account of the interrogation in 585 of two of Gundovald's envoys, who revealed to Guntram under torture that all the nobility of Childebert's kingdom had offered Gundovald the crown.[87] Further, with regard to the malcontents, there seem to be a number of connections between those men who had supported Gundovald, and the authors of a plot against Childebert which was uncovered in 587.

Two years after Gundovald's death, it was discovered that the *dux* Rauching was plotting with the followers of Chlothar II to assassinate Childebert; he was then to take control of Theudebert, the king's elder son, and of Champagne; two other men, Ursio and Berthefred, were to seize Theuderic and the rest of Childebert's kingdom; Brunhild was to be ousted from power. Guntram passed this information on to Childebert; Rauching was killed, as were Ursio and Berthefred.[88] In 590 it further became apparent that bishop Egidius of Rheims had been involved in Rauching's plot, and he was deposed from his see.[89]

Although no direct connection can be shown between the revolt of Gundovald and the conspiracy of 587, there are reasons for thinking that the two affairs may have been related. There is the consistent, but unexplained, emphasis placed by Gregory on support given to Gundovald by Childebert's followers. And there is Gregory's account of Guntram warning Childebert over the behaviour of Egidius, which is placed immediately before his

82. Gregory, *Decem Libri Historiarum*, VII 34.
83. Gregory, *Decem Libri Historiarum*, IX 28.
84. Gregory, *Decem Libri Historiarum*, IX 32.
85. Gregory, *Decem Libri Historiarum*, VII 43.
86. Gregory, *Decem Libri Historiarum*, VII 36.
87. Gregory, *Decem Libri Historiarum*, VII 32.
88. Gregory, *Decem Libri Historiarum*, IX 9.
89. Gregory, *Decem Libri Historiarum*, X 19.

description of the last days of Gundovald.[90] Gregory often uses juxtaposition deliberately. Egidius certainly operated in association with Guntram Boso. The two of them were implicated in the hounding to death of Chilperic's son Merovech in 577.[91] Since on that occasion they were working with the approval of Fredegund they are likely to have been opposed to Brunhild. Egidius was certainly hostile to the *dux* Lupus, who was Brunhild's favourite.[92] His connection with Boso may suggest that he was one of the magnates of Childebert who was involved in bringing Gundovald to Gaul. Was it merely a coincidence that the fall of Boso took place at the same time as the discovery of the Rauching plot, in which Egidius was involved?[93]

There are, however, significant differences between the political affiliations of 585 and 587. Gundovald was not only, as it seems, supported by members of the Austrasian aristocracy, but also publicly upholding Childebert's authority in Aquitaine, while challenging that of Guntram and of Chlothar. By contrast, in 587 Rauching was in alliance with Chlothar's followers and hostile to Childebert: Guntram was to be kept neutral. This switch by an important faction of Austrasian magnates may be related to developments at court. Shortly before Gundovald's death Guntram had recognized Childebert as reaching his majority:[94] he was therefore fit to rule on his own. Throughout Childebert's minority the power structure at the Austrasian court may well have favoured the likes of Boso, Rauching and Egidius. By 587, however, Brunhild seems to have become the most influential figure at Childebert's court,[95] even though Guntram, when recognizing his nephew's coming of age, had advised him not to visit his mother. From Rauching's point of view, under Brunhild's influence, Childebert was no longer a satisfactory master; he was, therefore, to be removed and his sons elevated to the kingship in his place, in the hope that they would be more amenable. Despite this difference, the plot of 587 does help illuminate the crisis of two years before. It sheds some light on those members of the Austrasian aristocracy whose loyalty was questionable. Further, if Rauching and Egidius were involved in inviting Gundovald to Gaul, the fact that their influence was unaffected by his defeat may explain why Gregory fails to name those members of Childebert's court who were responsible for the invitation. At this point in time the bishop of Tours was apparently too scared to state the truth openly.

90. Gregory, *Decem Libri Historiarum*, VII 33.
91. Gregory, *Decem Libri Historiarum*, V 18.
92. Gregory, *Decem Libri Historiarum*, VI 4.
93. Gregory, *Decem Libri Historiarum*, IX 8–10.
94. Gregory, *Decem Libri Historiarum*, VII 33.
95. Gregory, *Decem Libri Historiarum*, VIII 22; J.L. Nelson, 'Queens as Jezebels: Brunhild and Balthild in Merovingian history', in Nelson, *Politics and Ritual in Early Medieval Europe*, pp. 12–14.

Kings and magnates

If the preceding analysis is correct, then Gundovald's support can be seen to depend on three different groups: there were members of Childebert's court, seemingly anxious to keep their options open until the king was recognized as being of an age to rule; there were men who had been followers of Guntram, but whose positions had been compromised; and finally there were military leaders who had been in the service of Chilperic, but who had been too far from court at the time of his murder to ensure their survival under Chlothar II, whose own succession could scarcely be taken for granted. Thus, the Gundovald affair highlights the dangers posed by magnates caught in three different situations: by those who were unsure of their position at court, those who had already fallen from royal favour, and those whose royal patron had been killed. Despite Gregory's constant emphasis on the involvement of Childebert's men in Gundovald's cause, it seems from the chronological coincidence of Chilperic's murder and the elevation of the 'pretender' to the kingship, that it was the support of this third group, that is of Desiderius and Waddo, which suddenly made rebellion viable. Essentially those who felt themselves to be excluded from power decided to support a perfectly plausible claimant to the throne who had been waiting on the sidelines for such a following to materialize. The Gundovald crisis can thus be seen as a classic illustration of the difficulties raised at the time of the transfer of power from one monarch to another: the dispossessed and those who thought that their status was in question set about making contact with a new lord.

Looked at from this point of view Gundovald's revolt illustrates perfectly a major aspect of sixth- and indeed seventh-century politics, that is the tendency for those lacking royal support, either because of accidents of death or because they were in opposition to a particular monarch, to search out the favour of another king. There were plenty of rebels opposed to individual Merovingians, but the family's right to rule was not questioned. As a plausible candidate for the throne Gundovald could attract to himself those whose careers were under threat. There is a long history of members of the aristocracy seeking an alternative Merovingian lord; effectively it begins with Arcadius calling Childebert into the Auvergne.[96] It was not only the aristocracy who could hope for promotion from a change of regime: for instance Riculf hoped that the see of Tours would be granted to him by Chilperic's son, Clovis, as a result of the Leudast affair and Gregory's anticipated deposition.[97] After Gundovald's uprising the same search for a new Merovingian lord can be seen in Rauching's plot. The problem of the transfer of loyalty by members of the aristocracy from one Merovingian to another attracted the attention of Guntram and Childebert shortly after Rauching's death, when they met at Andelot. The treaty which they drew up dealt specifically with those *leudes* who had transferred from one king to the

96. Gregory, *Decem Libri Historiarum*, III 9.
97. Gregory, *Decem Libri Historiarum*, V 49.

other.[98] In the seventh century the decision of the aristocracy of Austrasia to abandon Brunhild and her great-grandson, and to transfer their loyalty to Chlothar II, is one of the few examples of a successful rebellion against a member of the Merovingian dynasty.[99] It succeeded because Sigibert II was extremely young, while Chlothar II was well established. Later in the century political factions still depended on association with particular claimants to the throne. The crises surrounding Ebroin, Pippin II, Charles Martel, and even Pippin III and Carloman were all concerned in part with loyalty to or control of individual members of the royal family.[100]

The search for an acceptable Merovingian lord affected local as well as court politics. It is not known why Arcadius was opposed to Theuderic's regime, but Riculf quite clearly hoped that changes at the centre would improve his prospects in his own *civitas*. Equally Leudast's position in Tours was closely connected with changing royal control of the city. Numerous conflicts within the kingdom were thus centred upon the royal court. Thus the civil wars, so decried by Gregory, actually held the kingdom together, because the struggles between members of the Merovingian family provided a focus around which other conflicts could cluster. The Merovingian civil wars, at least in the sixth century, were centripetal, rather than centrifugal.

Politics in Aquitaine

The position of Aquitaine needs to be considered in this light. In certain crucial respects Aquitaine was different from the northern heartlands of the Merovingians. Kings themselves rarely travelled south of the Loire. Their favoured residences and, therefore, their itineraries were centred in the north. Royal business in Aquitaine was conducted largely through agents. Sometimes princes acted on their fathers' behalf. On occasion, however, a prince might oppose his father. In so doing he could still ensure loyalty to the Merovingian dynasty, even if not to the individual king. Chramn used his position in Aquitaine to set himself up in opposition to his father, Chlothar I, who sent his half-brothers to destroy him.[101] Aquitaine was also the setting for Gundovald's bid for the throne. It was at Brives-la-Gaillarde that he was elevated to the kingship, and it was from the cities of Aquitaine that he received the oaths of loyalty, which most kings must have taken by proxy.[102] The south-west was far enough from the established centres of power for those who felt excluded from the throne to use it as a launching pad for rebellion. Nevertheless it was not opposed to the Merovingian dynasty.

98. Gregory, *Decem Libri Historiarum*, IX 20.
99. Fredegar, IV 40–2.
100. See chapters 13, 15 and 16.
101. Gregory, *Decem Libri Historiarum*, IV 16, 20.
102. Gregory, *Decem Libri Historiarum*, VII 10, 26.

Certainly there were Gallo-Romans of an independent turn of mind in the south. The patrician Dynamius provides perhaps the best illustration of this. He was the scion of a noble and highly educated family, and correspondent of Gregory the Great.[103] In 581, as governor of Provence, he backed the aristocrat Marcellus, to become bishop of Uzès, in opposition to Guntram's nominee, Jovinus, the then ex-governor.[104] And in the same year he tried to prevent Guntram's general, Gundulf, from entering Marseilles.[105] But he was prepared to act as Guntram's agent in his dealings with bishop Theodore of Marseilles.[106] This, however, was precisely the time that Guntram and Childebert were in dispute over Marseilles. Dynamius was making the most of the opportunities provided by the conflict to strengthen his own position. When the two kings had resolved their differences, Dynamius sided firmly with Childebert.[107] He is best seen, therefore, as a southern aristocrat who exploited the rifts within the Merovingian family for his own ends, but he never rejected Merovingian rule, and his son Evantius was even killed while on a diplomatic mission from Childebert II to the Byzantine court.[108] The relationship between centre and periphery in the Merovingian kingdom was thus extremely complex, because the connections between the two regions were exploited both by the Gallo-Roman aristocracy and by the northern rulers for their own ends up until the eighth century.

There was, therefore, a balance between court and country, and the civil wars helped to maintain this balance, by providing a central focus for local conflict. Certainly the civil wars were destructive. Moreover luck sometimes prevented the family conflicts of the Merovingians from getting out of hand: accident of survival meant that the kingdom was united in 558, when Chlothar I was left as the only surviving son of Clovis, and was able to unite the *regnum Francorum* for the first time in forty-seven years. Nevertheless the Merovingian civil wars did not pose a threat to the survival of the kingdom. Indeed, in a sense, they were a unifying part of the structure of the Frankish state in the sixth century and for much of the seventh.

103. K.F. Stroheker, *Der senatorische Adel im spätantiken Gallien*, p. 164, no. 108.
104. Gregory, *Decem Libri Historiarum*, VI 7.
105. Gregory, *Decem Libri Historiarum*, VI 11.
106. Gregory, *Decem Libri Historiarum*, VI 11.
107. Gregory, *Decem Libri Historiarum*, IX 11.
108. Gregory, *Decem Libri Historiarum*, X 2.

Chapter Seven

Laws and Law–Codes: Merovingian Legislation

The preface to Book Five of Gregory's *Histories* suggests that civil war was one of the great threats to the legacy of Clovis. In fact civil wars may not have endangered the Merovingian state to the extent that Gregory implies. In a sense they were integral to the structure of Frankish politics, serving to strengthen the bond between the Merovingian family and the aristocracy. At the same time Gregory's emphasis on the civil wars tends to divert attention from the very real achievements made by the Merovingians in keeping the peace. One of the chief functions of an early medieval king was the enforcement of justice. Einhard's criticism that the late Merovingians travelled around in ox-carts ignored the fact that in so doing they were copying late Roman provincial governors, who used this means of transport to ensure that they were accessible to petitioners.[1] Many of the petitions would have been concerned with justice. Fortunately a considerable quantity of Merovingian legal material survives to offset the negative images left by Gregory and Einhard. Some of it belongs to the years directly after 591, when Gregory's narrative comes to an end, and has the additional significance of casting some light on the later years of the reign of Childebert II (575–96), which are otherwise poorly represented in the sources. At the same time, the reign of Childebert itself provides a clear point of access to the history of Merovingian law, which all too easily can be swamped in the problems of origins, chronology and manuscript transmission.

Childebert II

The first nine years of Childebert II's reign are dominated by the problems of the young king's survival, sometimes with the help of Guntram, sometimes with the help of Chilperic, and always with the involvement of his

---

1. Einhard, *Vita Caroli Magni*, 1; J.M. Wallace-Hadrill, review of A.H.M. Jones, *The Later Roman Empire*, *English Historical Review* 80 (1965), p. 789.

aristocracy.[2] After the death of Chilperic and the revolt of Gundovald in 584, Guntram recognized his nephew as being fit to rule in his own name,[3] but even this did not ensure consistently good relations between the two kings, not least because of differences of opinion over control of certain cities, and because of the ramifications of the Gundovald affair. In order to solve the first of these differences the two kings signed the Treaty of Andelot in 587,[4] but Guntram remained suspicious of his nephew. In particular he found opportunity to complain about Childebert's policies towards the Visigoths, with whom he cultivated more cordial relations than his uncle felt was proper.[5] Despite Guntram's qualms, Childebert had extensive dealings with foreign powers: the Visigoths, the Lombards and the Byzantines. In these dealings, which are represented both in Gregory's *Histories* and in the *Epistulae Austrasiacae*, as well as the later narrative of Paul the Deacon, Childebert appears as a formidable figure.[6]

Childebert had yet to reach the height of his power in 591, when Gregory's narrative ends. Fredegar records the death of Guntram, apparently in 592, and Childebert's succession to the kingdom of Burgundy, thus uniting it to the east Frankish realm, and establishing a political axis which was to last until 613.[7] For 594 Fredegar notes a war between the Franks and the Bretons,[8] and under the following year he mentions a victory over the *Warni*, who are probably to be equated with the Thuringians.[9] In the early 590s Childebert was clearly a successful monarch. Writing in the eighth century the Lombard historian Paul the Deacon provides some additional information relating to the involvement of Childebert in the elevation of Tassilo as 'king' of the Bavarians, confirming his influence outside Francia itself.[10] Finally, he states that Childebert and his wife were poisoned.[11] From Fredegar's chronicle it is possible to date the king's death to 596,[12] but Paul is the only author to record unequivocally that Childebert was murdered.

Childebert's reign over the combined kingdoms of Sigibert and Guntram was short, and it is very poorly recorded. Nevertheless, three edicts of Childebert survive, the first issued at Andernach in 594, the second at Maastricht in 595, and the third at Cologne in 596.[13] Each was issued on

2. Gregory, *Decem Libri Historiarum*, V 1, 3. 17; VI 1, etc.
3. Gregory, *Decem Libri Historiarum*, VII 33.
4. Gregory, *Decem Libri Historiarum*, IX 11, 20.
5. Gregory, *Decem Libri Historiarum*, IX 1, 20.
6. Gregory, *Decem Libri Historiarum*, VIII 18; IX 1, 16, 25, 29; X 2–4; *Epistulae Austrasiacae* 25–48; see also Paul, *Historia Langobardorum*, III 17, 21, 22, 28, 29, 31, 34; IV 7, 11. In general (albeit with reservations) on Frankish foreign relations in this period, see Goubert, *Byzance avant l'Islam*, 2, *Byzance et l'Occident*, pp. 71–85.
7. Fredegar, IV 14.
8. Fredegar, IV 15.
9. Fredegar, IV 15.
10. Paul, *Historia Langobardorum*, IV 7.
11. Paul, *Historia Langobardorum*, IV 11.
12. Fredegar, IV 16.
13. *Decretio Childeberti*, *Capitularia Merowingica*, 7.

1 March, presumably at an annual gathering, after consultation with the king's magnates, his *obtimates*. In order to bring the edicts to the notice of all they were combined into a single law, referred to as the *Decretio Childeberti*. As such they are included as an addendum in some manuscripts of the earliest Frankish law-book, known as the *Pactus Legis Salicae*. Since Childebert was also one of the two kings involved in the Treaty of Andelot, his reign is a significant one in the history of royal legislation.

Merovingian legislation

In his edition of the Capitularies of the Frankish kings Alfred Boretius included nine pieces of legislation issued by the Merovingians. They form a heterogeneous collection of one letter, two precepts, three edicts, a decree and two 'pacts'. Three of these texts, the *Pactus pro tenore pacis*, the *Edictum Chilperici* and the *Decretio Childeberti*, are preserved in manuscripts of the *Pactus Legis Salicae*.[14] Three more, the letter of Clovis addressed to his bishops, Guntram's edict of 585 and Chlothar II's decree of 614, are associated with ecclesiastical legislation.[15] The text of the Treaty of Andelot is included in the *Histories* of Gregory of Tours.[16] Separately preserved and more difficult to date than these are the precepts of Childebert I and Chlothar II. The first is preserved only in one manuscript, and the second in two.[17] The context in which these last two laws were first issued is unknown; indeed the identification of which Childebert and which Chlothar was responsible for these laws depends on attribution by modern editors.

The variety of contexts in which the laws are preserved and the chance survival of the precepts of Childebert I and Chlothar II show that the great law-books of the Merovingian kingdom, the *Pactus Legis Salicae* and the *Lex Ribuaria*, were only one part of the legal output of the period, and they suggest that the Merovingian kings legislated often. Indicative of the lowest level of Merovingian legislation is the first book of the *Formulary* compiled by Marculf around the year 700.[18] It is largely a compendium of model royal commands and charters, with some appropriate responses. As such it is indicative of the daily involvement of the king in legal matters.

More significantly, the fact that the edicts of Guntram in 585 and of Chlothar in 614 were issued in the aftermath of Church councils raises the possibility that other royal legislation was attached to such councils, but that it

---

14. *Capitularia Merowingica*, 3; 4; 7; *Pactus Legis Salicae*, 79–93; 106–16.
15. *Capitularia Merowingica*, 1; 5; 9.
16. Gregory, *Decem Libri Historiarum*, IX 20.
17. *Capitularia Merowingica*, 2; 8.
18. P. Fouracre, '"Placita" and the settlement of disputes in later Merovingian Francia', in W. Davies and P. Fouracre, eds, *The Settlement of Disputes in Early Medieval Europe*, p. 24; Wood, 'Administration, law and culture in Merovingian Gaul', pp. 65–6.

has not been preserved.[19] The canons themselves provide an indication of royal involvement in ecclesiastical legislation. Certainly kings were responsible for summoning councils. That of Orléans in 533 was held by royal order, *ex praeceptione gloriosissimorum regum*.[20] Theudebert I authorized the meeting of the Council of Clermont in 535: the council started with prayers for the king, and it addressed a petition to him.[21] The Council of Orléans in 549 was summoned by Childebert I, and it confirmed the creation in Lyons of a *xenodochium*, or hostel, which the king and his queen Ultrogotha had founded.[22] In 551/2 Childebert called a council in Paris to judge bishop Saffaracus.[23] Among the kings of the next generation Charibert I authorized a council in Tours in 567.[24] Guntram's bishops dealt with a disagreement between their king and his brother Sigibert in 573,[25] and Guntram himself summoned two councils to Mâcon between 581 and 585,[26] and another to Valence in the same period.[27] In 614 Chlothar held a council at Paris,[28] and one at Clichy in 626/7.[29] His grandson, Clovis II, summoned his bishops to Chalon-sur-Saône between 647 and 653,[30] and Clovis's son Childeric II ordered the holding of councils at St-Pierre-de-Granon (Bordeaux) and St-Jean-de-Losne between 673 and 675.[31] For all of these the canons survive, recording royal involvement or approval.[32]

To this ecclesiastical evidence can be added information in the narrative sources. Gregory records conciliar involvement in judicial matters on a number of occasions. The cases of the troublesome bishops Salonius of Embrun and Sagittarius of Gap were dealt with on Guntram's orders at the Church councils of Lyons (567/73) and Chalon-sur-Saône (579).[33] Praetextatus of Rouen was tried at Paris in 577,[34] and Gregory himself at a gathering of bishops at the royal palace of Berny-Rivière in 580:[35] both these last trials were held under the aegis of Chilperic I. A year later the flight of Mummolus was discussed at Lyons.[36] Bishops met under royal command at

19. *Capitularia Merowingica* 5; 9.
20. Council of Orléans (533), *praef.*
21. Council of Clermont (535), *praef.*
22. Council of Orléans (549), *praef.*; 15.
23. Council of Paris (551/2); Gregory, *Decem Libri Historiarum*, IV 36.
24. Council of Tours (567), *praef.*
25. Council of Paris (573), *epistola synodi ad Sigisbertum regem*.
26. Council of Mâcon (581/3), *praef.*; (585), *praef.*
27. Council of Valence (585).
28. Council of Paris (614), *praef.*
29. Council of Clichy (626/7), *praef.*
30. Council of Chalon-sur-Saône (647/653), *praef.*
31. Council of St-Pierre-de-Granon (673/5), *praef.*; St-Jean-de-Losne (673/5), *praef.*
32. For a full assessment of royal involvement in Church councils, based on a detailed reading of all the evidence, and not just the canons themselves, see O. Pontal, *Die Synoden im Merowingerreich*.
33. Council of Lyons (567/70); Gregory, *Decem Libri Historiarum*, V 20, 27.
34. Gregory, *Decem Libri Historiarum*, V 18; VII 16.
35. Gregory, *Decem Libri Historiarum*, V 49.
36. Gregory, *Decem Libri Historiarum*, VI 1.

Poitiers in 589 and 590 to suppress the rebellion of the nuns of the Holy Cross monastery against their abbess.[37] The same year Egidius of Rheims was tried in council at Metz.[38] Fredegar reveals that Theuderic II and Brunhild used the Council of Chalon in 602/3 to depose Desiderius of Vienne.[39]

The mixture of narrative and conciliar evidence is important, for Gregory and Fredegar sometimes refer to matters not included in the theological record. Thus, in Gregory's *Histories* the Council of Mâcon in 585 was expected to deal with a quarrel between bishops Bertram of Bordeaux and Palladius of Saintes, and it did deal with the theology of a certain unnamed bishop who thought that the word *homo* in the Bible did not apply to women.[40] Fredegar, however, seems to have remembered this same council as being concerned with the foundation of the royal monastery of St Marcel at Chalon.[41] None of these matters appears in the canons which deal at length with a host of theological and ecclesiastical issues. This should alert us to the fact that the canons are incomplete records, and that they could even overlook matters of royal concern, like Guntram's foundation of the monastery of St Marcel. Nevertheless the evidence which we have is enough to show that the situation in Merovingian Francia may not have been so very different from Visigothic Spain, where kings are well known to have been closely involved in the major ecclesiastical councils of the kingdom.[42]

The range of legislation covered by the Merovingian capitularies is also impressive. Clovis's letter, which was sent in the aftermath of the battle of 'Vouillé', describes how he had decreed that no one was to harm the Church, those who had entered the religious life, those living with them, or slaves of the Church. Anyone belonging to these categories who had been taken captive was to be freed. Further, the power of the bishops to protect others was confirmed.[43] The fragmentary precept of Childebert I is likewise concerned with religious matters, with the destruction of idols, and sacrilegeous behaviour, including drunkenness, scurrility and singing at Easter and Christmas.[44] The edict of Guntram issued at Péronne, and appended to the canons of the Council of Mâcon of 585, continues royal involvement in ecclesiastical legislation, with an attack on Sunday work, and by backing the force of the canons with secular sanctions.[45] Also responding directly to the ecclesiastical council held in Paris in 614, Chlothar II's edict dealt with episcopal elections, clerical patronage, and the limits of the power of secular

37. Gregory, *Decem Libri Historiarum*, IX 39–43; X 15–17.
38. Gregory, *Decem Libri Historiarum*, X 19–20.
39. Fredegar, IV 24; the date is that of Pontal, *Die Synoden im Merowingerreich*, p. 152.
40. Gregory, *Decem Libri Historiarum*, VIII 20.
41. Fredegar, IV 1; like Pontal, *Die Synoden im Merowingerreich*, p. 164, I take this to be one and the same council.
42. For the councils of Toledo, see R. Collins, *Early Medieval Spain: Unity in Diversity, 400–1000*, pp. 72–3.
43. *Capitularia Merowingica*, 1.
44. *Capitularia Merowingica*, 2.
45. *Capitularia Merowingica*, 5.

judges over clerics, inheritance, freedom, the legal rights of Jews against Christians, and the punishment of nuns who married. Further, it addressed other secular matters relating specifically to the political situation following the fall of Brunhild.[46]

Secular legislation is more exclusively to the fore in the remaining Merovingian capitularies. The *Pactus pro tenore pacis* concerned itself largely with issues relating to theft; the crime itself and the tracking of the criminal by local officials called *centenarii*, even across the boundaries between the Merovingian kingdoms; it also dealt with trial by ordeal, punishment, and the right of sanctuary.[47] The edict of Chilperic I tackled a larger selection of issues, including inheritance, dowry and robbery, but above all it legislated on the whole process of bringing a slave to trial by ordeal; when he was to be handed over to trial, and what delays might be allowed before the king's legal officer, the *graphio*, and the local law-men, the *rachinburgi*, took action.[48] The edict in fact provides the fullest surviving account of the process of law outside the courts of the king or his agents.[49] The *Decretio Childeberti* from 594–6 is more wide-ranging still. At Andernach Childebert legislated on inheritance and incest, at Maastricht on ownership, rape, murder, the subversion of justice in court, and the death-penalty, and at Cologne he turned to the questions of the execution of thieves, the pursuit of criminals, and Sunday work.[50] The *Praeceptio* of Chlothar II similarly dealt with secular and religious legal matters.[51]

Childebert's legislation is remarkable not only for its range, but also for its clear dependence on Roman Law. In dealing with the question of possession it adopted the same time-limits as did the *Sentences* of Paul, as well as the thirty-year rule of late Roman Law.[52] In addition it followed Roman Law on rape.[53] These influences might partly be attributed to the official who authenticated the Cologne decree, Asclipiodus. He is usually identified with the *vir illustris* and *referendarius* Asclepiodatus, who delivered Guntram's instructions relating to the foundations of the queen and her daughters at Chalon-sur-Saône and Autun to the synod of Valence in 585.[54] He is also

46. *Capitularia Merowingica*, 9.

47. *Capitularia Merowingica*, 3; on *centenarii*, Murray, 'From Roman to Frankish Gaul: "Centenarii" and "Centenae" in the administration of the Frankish kingdom', pp. 59–100.

48. *Capitularia Merowingica*, 4.

49. Fouracre, '"Placita" and the settlement of disputes in later Merovingian Francia', pp. 39–41.

50. *Capitularia Merowingica*, 7.

51. *Capitularia Merowingica*, 8.

52. *Capitularia Merowingica*, 7; *Lex Romana Visigothorum*, V 2, 3–4; *interpretatio* V 5, 8; *Novella Valentiniani* III, 34. In general on this issue see I.N. Wood, 'The *Codex Theodosianus* in Merovingian Gaul', in J.D. Harries and I.N. Wood, eds, *The Theodosian Code* (forthcoming).

53. *Capitularia Merowingica*, 7; *Codex Theodosianus*, IX 24.

54. Council of Valence (585); the date is from Pontal, *Die Synoden im Merowingerreich*, pp. 143–4; on Asclepiodotus, see P. Wormald, 'The decline of the Roman Empire and the survival of its aristocracy', *Journal of Roman Studies* 66 (1976), p. 224.

thought to be the same as the Asclepiodatus who was *patricius* of Provence, and was the recipient of letters from Gregory the Great in 599 and 601.[55] With less reason he has been equated with the one-time *dux* Asclipius, who led Guntram's men against Chilperic's guards in Paris in 582.[56] Asclepiodatus can, therefore, be seen as beginning his career in the service of Guntram, for whom he acted as referendary, transferring to Childebert in 593, and then becoming *patricius* of Provence under Childebert's sons.

The identification of Guntram's referendary Asclepiodatus with Asclipiodus, the authenticator of the *Decretio Childeberti*, has obvious attractions. He could, for instance, have drawn many of the Roman elements in the *Decretio* from a Roman legal handbook compiled in the kingdom of the Burgundians, the *Lex Romana Burgundionum*.[57] Guntram had, after all, been king of Burgundy. Nevertheless it would be dangerous to assign laws to Asclepiodatus simply on the basis of his probable knowledge: the *praeceptio* of Chlothar II also shows signs of influence from Roman and Burgundian Law.[58] It is unlikely to have been the work of Asclepiodatus, who can scarcely have worked for Chlothar before 613, given his association with Childebert II, and is equally unlikely to have been active after that date. The legislation of Guntram, Childebert II and Chlothar II is indicative not of the work of one man, but of the style and practice of Merovingian law-giving in the late sixth and early seventh centuries. This casts doubt on the suggestion that Asclepiodatus was also responsible for the shorter prologue of *Lex Salica*.[59] The attribution, made on stylistic grounds alone, must be treated with caution. The evidence seems to point to a legal style which a number of royal servants were competent to use.

Lex Salica

The authorship of the shorter prologue to *Lex Salica* is a minor problem by comparison with the other conundra presented by the hornet's nest of Salic Law. The earliest written version of *Lex Salica* seems to have been made up of sixty-five titles. To these titles various laws were added during the Merovingian period, and indeed later. Under the Carolingians new recensions of the code were made.[60] To differentiate it from the Carolingian revisions

55. Gregory I, *Register*, IX 225; XI 43.

56. Gregory, *Decem Libri Historiarum*, VI 19

57. On the relations between the *Decretio Childeberti* and the *Lex Romana Burgundionum*, see Wood, 'The *Codex Theodosianus* in Merovingian Gaul'.

58. Wood, 'The *Codex Theodosianus* in Merovingian Gaul'.

59. P. Wormald, '*Lex Scripta* and *Verbum Regis*: legislation and Germanic kingship, from Euric to Cnut', in P.H. Sawyer and I.N. Wood, eds, *Early Medieval Kingship*, p. 126.

60. Wormald, '*Lex Scripta* and *Verbum Regis*: legislation and Germanic kingship, from Euric to Cnut', pp. 108; R. McKitterick, *The Carolingians and the Written Word*, pp. 40–1.

the Merovingian text has come to be called the *Pactus Legis Salicae*. The manuscript tradition seems to imply that the first sixty-five titles had no prologue, or at least there is none that survives.[61] As a result the *Pactus* is not clearly ascribed to any king or legislator. This lack of ascription was subsequently remedied by the shorter prologue, which survives in a limited number of manuscripts of the *Pactus*: apparently known to the author of the *Liber Historiae Francorum*,[62] the shorter prologue seems to date from the late seventh or early eighth century. It was incorporated into the longer Carolingian prologue.

The shorter prologue of *Lex Salica* states that

> With God's help it pleased the Franks and their nobility and they agreed that they ought to prohibit all escalations of quarrels for the preservation of enthusiasm for peace among themselves; and because they excelled other neighbouring peoples by force of arms, so they should excel them in legal authority, with the result that criminal cases might be concluded in a manner appropriate to the type of complaint. Therefore four men, chosen out of many among them, stood out: Their names were Wisogast, Arogast, Salegast and Widogast. They came from the *villae* of Bothem, Salehem and Widohem, beyond the Rhine. Coming together in three legal assemblies, and discussing the origins of all cases carefully, they made judgement on each case as follows.

Nothing else is known of these four lawmen, not even the period in which are supposed to have lived. They may well be legendary. What is particularly interesting, however, is the fact that the shorter prologue ascribes the *Pactus Legis Salicae* to the Franks, their nobility and these four individuals, and not to a king. Whoever wrote the prologue saw the compilation of a law-code, rightly or wrongly, not in the context of earlier Roman legislation, which culminated in the Theodosian Code, but in that of the pronouncement of law by the law-men of small communities. In this respect the first Merovingian code was at least perceived by men of the seventh century as being different from its Visigothic and Burgundian counterparts.

Effectively the shorter prologue to *Lex Salica* raises the question of the extent to which the law was royal and the extent to which it was customary. This problem may be related to a further question; that is the relationship between the code and Salic law in general. The *Pactus Legis Salicae* in fact did not contain all Salic law. There are general references within the *Pactus* to *Lex Salica*, which may not refer to any individual title.[63] Moreover, when the *Pactus pro tenore pacis* cites Salic law in detail, it is not an exact citation of any law contained within the sixty-five title text of the *Pactus Legis Salicae*.[64]

---

61. Wormald, '*Lex Scripta* and *Verbum Regis*: legislation and Germanic kingship, from Euric to Cnut,' p. 108.

62. *Liber Historiae Francorum*, 4.

63. e.g. *Pactus Legis Salicae*, 45, 2; 50, 2–3; 52, 1–2; 75, 2.

64. *Capitularia Merowingica*, 3; *Pactus Legis Salicae*, 82, 1; the closest parallel is 40, 8.

Further, on one occasion the *Pactus Legis Salicae* deals with those *rachinburgi*, or local law-men, who were unable to state the law in response to the demand, 'Tell us the Salic Law': *Dicite nobis legem Salicam*.[65] This suggests that there was unwritten law supposedly known by the *rachinburgi*, which was not contained in the *Pactus Legis Salicae*. That there is some discrepancy within the whole tradition of Salic Law is, therefore, not surprising.

Much of the law in the *Pactus Legis Salicae* probably did equate with that known by the *rachinburgi*, even if there was variation in detail. Nevertheless some of the law in the *Pactus* is likely to have had a royal origin. Those laws which deal with the king's authority could have originated in edicts;[66] the same could be true of laws concerned with Romans.[67] Equally, the complex legislation relating to slaves taken overseas, which involves registration of claims in foreign courts, is unlikely to have been traditional.[68] In origin such legislation is likely to have been similar to the *Pactus pro tenore pacis*, the edict of Chilperic I and the *Decretio Childeberti*, which were later attached to the *Pactus Legis Salicae*.

The inclusion of royal law within a law-code which is otherwise not directly ascribed to a king is more obviously apparent in another Merovingian law-book, associated with the east Frankish kingdom, the *Lex Ribvaria*, where the verb *iubere*, 'to order', is occasionally used. This is particularly true of the legislation concerning church freedmen, which includes a complex mixture of Roman and Frankish law.[69] Royal command is also apparent in the final clauses of the text, which warn officials against taking bribes, on pain of death, and against exacting fines too early in the legal process.[70] To some extent, therefore, the *Pactus Legis Salicae* and the *Lex Ribvaria* resemble the *Liber Constitutionum* of the Burgundians issued by Sigismund in 517, for without question this last text includes a number of royal edicts. In the Frankish codes such laws are included alongside other, plausibly customary, legislation. Moreover, just as there are general references to Salic law in the *Pactus Legis Salicae*, so too there are broad allusions to Ripuarian law in the *Lex Ribvaria*, suggesting once again that there was more to the law than what is contained in the code.[71] Like the *Pactus Legis Salicae*, the *Lex Ribvaria* is not directly attributed to any king,[72] but it bears the marks of royal involvement.

65. *Pactus Legis Salicae*, 57, 1.

66. e.g. *Pactus Legis Salicae*, 14, 4; 18; 41, 8; 56, 1, 4, 5.

67. *Pactus Legis Salicae*, 14, 2–3; 16, 5; 32, 3–4; 39, 5; 41, 8–10; 42, 4; on the extent to which Frankish law was influenced by Roman, see Wood, 'The *Codex Theodosianus* in Merovingian Gaul'.

68. *Pactus Legis Salicae*, 39, 2; on the possible Roman origins for this legislation, see Wood, 'The *Codex Theodosianus* in Merovingian Gaul'.

69. *Lex Ribvaria*, 61, 1, 7; see Wood, 'Administration, law and culture in Merovingian Gaul', p. 66.

70. *Lex Ribvaria* 91, 1, 2.

71. *Lex Ribvaria*, 32; 50, 1; 56; 73, 2.

72. Wormald, '*Lex Scripta* and *Verbum Regis*: legislation and Germanic kingship, from Euric to Cnut', p. 108.

A royal attribution for the *Pactus Legis Salicae* is first made in the so-called 'epilogue', which also provides a history for the early compilation of the text. This epilogue is included in still fewer manuscripts than the shorter prologue. In one manuscript the text runs as follows:

> The first king of the Franks established titles 1 to 62 [for 65?], and he set them out for judgement. After a little while he and his magnates added titles 63 [for 66?] to 78. Then indeed, after a long time, Childebert considered what ought to be added, and he instituted from 78 to 83, which he is known to have imposed worthily, and so he transmitted these writings to his brother Chlothar. Afterwards, when he [Chlothar] had gladly received these titles from his older brother [Childebert], he considered in his own kingdom what ought to be added there, and what further should be included, and he ordered clauses 84 to 63 [for 93?] to be fixed. And afterwards he sent the laws to his brother. And thus it was agreed between them that all this compilation should stand as it had done.

It can scarcely be claimed that this provides a much more authoritative or even revealing account of the composition of the *Pactus* than does the shorter prologue, but it is nevertheless worthy of some consideration.

Oddly enough, the author of the epilogue does not seem to have known the name of the king who first ordered the compilation. He is merely 'the first king of the Franks'. Usually, it is assumed that Clovis must be the monarch in question, but if so the failure to name him is peculiar: his reputation might have been expected to add lustre to the code. Either Merovech or Childeric would have had a better claim to being 'the first king' of the Franks. In all probability, the author did not know who was responsible for the original compilation: he merely assumed that legislation was an appropriate activity for the founder of a kingdom. For a modern historian to associate the *Pactus* with any individual among the early Merovingian kings on the basis of the epilogue is thus unwarranted. There is nothing in the epilogue to justify the attribution of the *Pactus Legis Salicae* to Clovis, or to any other other early Merovingian king.

Nevertheless the epilogue to the *Pactus* does provide a *terminus ante quem* for the compilation of the code. It talks in some detail about the additions made to the *Pactus* subsequent to those which 'the first king' had himself added. These additions it attributes to Childebert and to Chlothar. The epilogue claims that Childebert added six clauses and Chlothar ten. From this it is clear that the the additions which the author of the epilogue had in mind are what constitute the *Pactus pro tenore pacis* of Childebert and Chlothar. The clauses of the *Pactus pro tenore pacis* are divided between the two monarchs; if the prologue to the *Pactus* is counted as a separate clause, then Childebert is responsible for six and Chlothar ten. Further, the clauses of the *Pactus pro tenore pacis* appear as numbers 78 to 83 and 84 to 93 in some manuscripts of the *Pactus legis Salicae*, coinciding with the numbers which were perhaps intended by the author of the epilogue for the clauses issued by Childebert and Chlothar. The additions mentioned can be nothing more than the *Pactus pro tenore pacis* itself.

By assigning these additions to two brothers, the epilogue identifies the authors of the *Pactus pro tenore pacis* as Childebert I and Chlothar I. That it was correct in so doing is shown by the reference to brotherly love (*germanitatis caritas*) in the *Pactus pro tenore pacis* itself,[73] and by Chilperic I's citation of the legislation of his father and uncle.[74] If Childebert and Chlothar were indeed adding to the first sixty-five, or even the first seventy-eight, clauses of *Lex Salica*, then the first Merovingian code can be dated before 511. Certainly there are some odd discrepancies between the opening sixty-five clauses of the *Pactus Legis Salicae* and the legislation of Childebert and Chlothar, which should give cause for thought. In dealing with the matter of bringing a slave to the ordeal Childebert sets out the time-scale of the case, and states that his deadlines are as required in *Lex Salica*. In fact, Childebert sets out two periods of twenty days, but the appropriate clause in the first sixty-five titles of the *Pactus* apparently talks of two periods of seven days.[75] Perhaps this was a deliberate revision of earlier procedure. Despite such contradictions the unanimity of the manuscripts in the preservation of the first sixty-five titles makes it clear that these did constitute a code, and it seems probable that other surviving legislation postdates this compilation, and was, at times, intended to complement it. On balance, therefore, it is likely that the sixty-five title text of the *Pactus Legis Salicae* was compiled before 511.

Working from this hypothesis, it is possible to make one further deduction about the date of the original code. Clause 47 distinguishes the region between the Loire and the Charbonnière, the forest which came to divide the east and west Frankish kingdoms, from that beyond those two boundaries. During Clovis's reign these boundaries can have been significant only before the expansion of the Franks into Aquitaine as a result of 'Vouillé' and before Clovis destroyed the kingdoms of such rival kings as Sigibert the Lame. In other words it must belong to the period before 507. This means that the *Pactus Legis Salicae* antedates the *Liber Constitutionum* of the Burgundians by at least a decade. It probably also means that it was issued while Clovis was still a pagan. It is, therefore, not surprising that there are possible references to pagan practice within the code, most notably to sacrificial cattle.[76] Nor is it surprising that there is nothing that can be firmly attributed to Christian influence within the first sixty-five titles. Clovis's own edict on Church land, widows and orphans, issued in 507, is not included.

A legal code in Latin, among whose clauses are to be found royal edicts, can have been compiled only with the help of Roman lawyers. A parallel for this could well be found in the work of Sidonius's friend Syagrius, a 'Solon' active among the Burgundians by 470.[77] The Burgundians, however, were

73. *Pactus Legis Salicae*, 92.
74. *Pactus Legis Salicae*, 116.
75. Compare *Pactus Legis Salicae*, 40, 8 with 82, 1.
76. *Pactus Legis Salicae*, 2, 16.
77. Sidonius Apollinaris, ep. V 5, 3.

already Christian at the time of Syagrius's involvement in their legislation. The non-Christian, even pagan, nature of some of the clauses of the *Pactus Legis Salicae*, may make Roman involvement seem less likely. Here a useful parallel may be found not in law, but in Remigius's admonition addressed to Clovis at the start of his reign:[78] although the king was still pagan he was advised to listen to his bishops. Christian Romans were willing to collaborate with pagan Franks. In short, we may guess that the original recension of *Lex Salica*, a work which included traditional legal custom as well as royal edicts, was compiled for Clovis, perhaps by Frankish lawmen, but certainly with the help of Roman lawyers.

Revisions and ratifications of *Lex Salica*

The *Pactus pro tenore pacis* may well have been the first attempt to revise Clovis's legislation. It was certainly not the last. One insight into the process of revising the laws may be provided in the accounts of the martyrdom of the mid-seventh-century bishop of Autun, Leodegar. According to the first *Passio Leodegarii* 'all sought king Childeric (II), so that he might command throughout the three kingdoms which he had obtained, that judges should preserve the law and custom of each *patria*, as used to be the case'.[79] The date is 673, shortly after Childeric II had gained control of Neustria and Burgundy, as well as his original kingdom of Austrasia. The second *Passio* reveals what the bishop did in these circumstances: 'Having taken on the government of the kingdom, whatever laws he found to be useless, and in contradiction to the laws of the ancient kings and the greater nobility, he restored to their former state'.[80]

Some evidence that a legal reform was carried out by Leodegar may be found in one manuscript of the *Pactus Legis Salicae* where the epilogue is followed by a king-list.[81] The list consists of the names Theuderic, Clovis, Childebert, Dagobert, Chilperic, Theuderic and Childeric. It states the lengths of their reigns, and it also mentions an *interregnum* between the last two kings. From all this it is possible to identify the kings as Theuderic III (673, 675–90/1), Clovis III (690/1–694), Childebert III (694–711), Dagobert III (711–15/16), Chilperic II (715/16–21), Theuderic IV (721–37) and Childeric III (743–51/2). The list, therefore, includes most, although not all, Merovingian monarchs who reigned after 675. The addition of such a list to a law-book is not likely to have been fortuitous. In all probability the names began as an indication of royal ratification of the *Pactus Legis Salicae* by the monarchs in question, even though the reference to the *interregnum* of 737 to 743 suggests that by the end of the Merovingian period the list was indeed no

78. *Epistulae Austrasiacae*, 2.
79. *Passio Leudegarii I*, 7.
80. *Passio Leudegarii II*, 6.
81. *Pactus Legis Salicae*, MS A2. The juxtaposition is also found in the D/E manuscript tradition of the Carolingian 100-title text of *Lex Salica*.

more than a king-list. If the names did originally ratify the law-code, it is likely that much of the *Pactus* was in its present form by the reign of Theuderic III. Since Theuderic was the successor of Childeric II, under whom Leodegar is said to have effected a revision of the laws of the Frankish kingdoms, the king-list may have originated as ratification of the revised version of the *Pactus* prepared in Childeric's reign, and it may, therefore, support the argument for a Leodegarian recension of the text.[82]

If this is so, a further point may follow. The one name that is absent from the king-list is that of Chlothar IV (717–19). He was the puppet of Charles Martel, and only ever ruled in the east Frankish kingdom of Austrasia. His absence from the list may be important in the light of the fact that Leodegar's work was prompted by demands that the ancient laws and customs of each *patria*, that is each of the Merovingian kingdoms of Neustria, Austrasia and Burgundy, should be restored. The king-list may, therefore, suggest that by the time of Leodegar the *Pactus Legis Salicae* was not applicable to the whole Merovingian kingdom.

The *Pactus Legis Salicae* and the west Frankish kingdom

Although the *Pactus Legis Salicae* was probably directed at all the followers of Clovis, Leodegar's revision of the laws of each of the three Merovingian kingdoms suggests that by the mid-seventh century Austrasia, Neustria and Burgundy each had their own law-codes. Leaving aside for the time being the complex issue of the so-called 'personality of the law', that is the subjection of an individual to the law of his nation, rather than to that of the kingdom,[83] it is likely that the *Pactus Legis Salicae* had come to be regarded as the law of the Neustrians. One reason for the limitation of the *Pactus* to Neustria may lie in clause 47, which in dealing with property stolen from those living under *Lex Salica*, differentiates between possessions discovered between the Loire and the Charbonnière and any discovered beyond those boundaries. In the former case a summons had to be made within forty days, in the latter within eighty days. Although this clause would have made sense within the context of Clovis's kingdom before 507, thereafter it would have been relevant only to those living in Neustria. In this clause, at least, the *Pactus Legis Salicae* could be applicable only to the west Frankish kingdom. Since Chlothar I and Childebert I both ruled territory which was later to be included in Neustria, it is possible that what seems to have been their addition to the sixty-five title text of *Lex Salica*, the *Pactus pro tenore pacis*, helped to fix the notion that the *Pactus Legis Salicae* was west Frankish law.

82. It would follow that the Leodegarian text is represented by MS A2.
83. Wood, 'Ethnicity and the ethnogenesis of the Burgundians', p. 55.

The laws of the three kingdoms

While the *Pactus Legis Salicae* came to be associated with Neustria, it is likely that *Lex Ribvaria* was created for Austrasia and that the *Liber Constitutionum* came to be seen as the law-book for the kingdom of Burgundy. The process by which Austrasia and Burgundy came to have their own law is obscure. The Frankish conquest of Burgundy does not seem to have affected the authority of the *Liber Constitutionum* of the Burgundian kings. Gregory of Tours records a case of trial by battle involving Chundo, the chamberlain of king Guntram, and a forester.[84] The trial took place at Chalon-sur-Saône, in the heart of the kingdom of Burgundy, and the method of trial is one prescribed by the *Liber Constitutionum*,[85] indicating that this was the law in use in Guntram's *regnum*. The *Lex Gundobada*, as the Burgundian Code came to be known, was certainly in use in the ninth century.[86] In Aquitaine Roman Law, perhaps as preserved either in the Theodosian Code or in the *Breviary* of Alaric, is likely to have been in force.[87]

The use of separate codes in the different *patriae* of the Merovingian kingdom was, however, subject to one complication. The *Lex Ribvaria* states clearly that within a Ripuarian *pagus* a man was bound by the law of his own nation: thus it espouses the notion of 'the personality of the law'. It also defines it: 'However, we make this decree, that within a Ripuarian *pagus* a Frank, as well as a Burgundian, Alaman or man of whatever nation staying there, should be summoned to court according to the law of the place where he was born, and let him plead accordingly'.[88] A man was to be judged according to his race, but his race was defined by his place of birth. To some extent the laws of the *patria*, which seem to have been so significant in the time of Leodegar, had to give way before the law of the individual. How often they would conflict is a moot point. Most people would not have travelled far from their place of birth, and those who did would usually have been members of the royal family, the highest aristocracy, the senior clergy, or their agents. Cases involving such men would almost inevitably have reached the king.

Lex Ribvaria and the Laws of the Alamans and Bavarians

The *Lex Ribvaria*, which defines the 'personality of the law', is a complex text, like the *Pactus Legis Salicae*. It is made up of probably traditional lists of compensation, law from or equivalent to the *Pactus*, and royal edicts.[89] It also assumes the existence of Ripuarian law, which is not explicitly included in

84. Gregory, *Decem Libri Historiarum*, X 10.
85. *Liber Constitutionum*, 45.
86. Wood, 'Ethnicity and the ethnogenesis of the Burgundians', pp. 53–4.
87. Wood, 'The *Codex Theodosianus* in Merovingian Gaul'.
88. *Lex Ribvaria*, 35, 3.
89. Wood, 'Administration, law and culture in Merovingian Gaul', p. 66.

the code,[90] just as the *Pactus* assumes the existence of Salic law outside the code itself. Its dating is no more certain than that of the *Pactus*. It has no prologue and no epilogue. Some have argued that it is a Carolingian text, and one manuscript states that it was revised under Charlemagne.[91] Nevertheless, there is some reason for thinking that one or more recensions were made in the late sixth or early seventh century. There is an undoubted influence of Burgundian law,[92] which might suggest that it belongs to a period when Burgundy and the east Frankish kingdom were closely associated, as under Childebert II and his sons. It has even been argued that the *Decretio Childeberti* may have influenced some clauses in the *Lex Ribvaria*,[93] but this is doubtful. Equally uncertain is the suggestion that Chlothar II's Paris Edict of 614 had an impact on the Ripuarian code.[94] It is possible, however, to find a context for the issuing of *Lex Ribvaria* in the aftermath of Chlothar's take-over of Austrasia in 613, when he was concerned to secure support in his new territories, or ten years later when he set up an eastern sub-kingdom for his son Dagobert I.[95] Equally, Dagobert himself may have been responsible for the *Lex Ribvaria*. Childebert II, Chlothar II and Dagobert I are all potential candidates for the authorship of *Lex Ribvaria*.

A case for Dagobert's involvement can be derived from the prologue to the *Lex Baiwariorum*, or Law of the Bavarians. This prologue is made up of the short history of law-giving provided by Isidore of Seville in his *Etymologiae* and some additional information on Merovingian legislation.[96] The citation of Isidore effectively places Merovingian law-giving within a tradition of legislation beginning with Moses, and running through Egyptian, Greek and Roman law, culminating in the Theodosian Code. By the mid-eighth century at the very latest some writers were apparently setting the Merovingian law-codes within a long and honourable lineage. What the prologue to the *Lex Baiwariorum* has to say of Frankish legislation is as follows:

> Theuderic, king of the Franks, when he was at Châlons-sur-Marne, chose wise men who were well-versed in the ancient laws in his kingdom. In his own words he ordered them to write down the law of the Franks and the Alamans and Bavarians, for each people which was in his power, according to their custom, and he added what needed to be added, and he removed what was unsuitable and not properly arranged. And he altered those things which followed pagan custom to follow Christian law. And those things which king Theuderic could not emend on account of the extreme antiquity of the custom of the pagans,

90. *Lex Ribvaria*, 30; 50, 1; 56; 73, 2.
91. Wormald, '*Lex Scripta* and *Verbum Regis*: legislation and Germanic kingship, from Euric to Cnut', p. 108.
92. *Lex Ribvaria*, ed. F. Beyerle and R. Buchner, p. 17.
93. *Lex Ribvaria*, ed. Beyerle and Buchner, p. 16.
94. *Lex Ribvaria*, ed. Beyerle and Buchner, p. 17.
95. Fredegar, IV 43, 47.
96. *Lex Baiwariorum, prol.*; Isidore, *Etymologiae*, V 1.

king Childebert subsequently made a start on, but king Chlothar finished. All these the most glorious king Dagobert renewed with the help of the illustrious men Claudius, Chadoind, Magnus and Agilulf, and he transformed all the old things of the laws for the better, and gave to each people the writings which they preserve to this day.

Much of this, however, is likely to be the author's reconstruction of the history of Frankish law-giving rather than an account based on knowledge. The parallels with the epilogue to the *Pactus Legis Salicae* are too striking to be ignored. Theuderic takes the place of the *primus rex Francorum*, and his work is also revised by Childebert and Chlothar. The comment on Dagobert's involvement may depend on more certain tradition, but it may be significant that he is aided by four law-men, just as the *Pactus Legis Salicae* is attributed to four law-men in the shorter prologue.

More reliable than the information provided in its preface is the comment included in the first clause of the *Lex Baiwariorum*, which states that the law was decreed 'before the king and his leading men (*principes*) and before all the Christian people who live within the Merovingian kingdom'.[97] Subsequently the relationship between the Merovingians and the rulers of Bavaria is set out in legislation on rates of composition.[98] Five Bavarian families were always to receive twofold compensation, while members of the Agilolfing family, including the *dux*, were to receive fourfold compensation. 'And indeed the *dux* who is in charge of the people is always from the *gens* of the Agilolfings, and he ought to be, for thus the kings, our ancestors, conceded to them, so that they set up as *dux*, to rule the people, whoever is of their *gens* and faithful to the king, as well as prudent'. Clearly, the *Lex Baiwariorum* was Merovingian law, and the Agilolfings were the faithful agents of the Merovingian kings.

Perhaps more plausible than the prologue to the *Lex Baiwariorum* is that to be found in some manuscripts of the law of the Alamans. Here the *Lex Alamannorum* is attributed to Chlothar, 'together with his leading men (*principes*), that is thirty-three bishops, thirty-four *duces* and seventy-two *comites* together with the rest of the people'.[99] The evidence of the Ripuarian, Alaman and Bavarian law-codes suggests that the reigns of Chlothar II and Dagobert I constituted a remarkable period in the compilation and revision of legislation, but it has to be said that the evidence is of uncertain worth.

Legislation and the aristocracy

The attribution of the *Lex Alamannorum* to Chlothar II and his *principes* is also important because it places the promulgation of a law-code in the context of

97. *Lex Baiwariorum, titulus* 1.
98. *Lex Baiwariorum*, 3, 1.
99. *Lex Alamannorum*, Cod. B, *incipit*.

a gathering of laymen and ecclesiastics, not unlike that at which Chlothar issued his Paris edict of 614.[100] The issuing of law-codes, like the promulgation of edicts, took place at court. Chilperic I, Guntram and Childebert II all emphasized the consensual element in their legislation,[101] and a similar emphasis on consultation is apparent in the prefaces to the Laws of the Alamans and the Bavarians. Among the courtiers there would have been men like Asclepiodatus, learned in Roman law, the four men mentioned as assisting Dagobert in the prologue to the *Lex Bawariorum*, or Leodegar, whom Childeric II seems to have entrusted with a revision of all the laws of the kingdom. The *Pactus Legis Salicae* and *Lex Ribvaria* are likely to have been drawn up in similar ways.[102]

The Alaman Laws also reveal something of the limit of the fidelity of the regional nobility. While in some manuscripts the *Lex Alamannorum* is associated with Chlothar and his leading men, in others it is ascribed to Lantfrid, who was *dux* of the Alamans between 712 and 730.[103] Apparently, in the early eighth century Lantfrid usurped the right to issue a law-code. Earlier, however, law-giving had been one of the major activities of the Merovingian kings.

The *Pactus Legis Salicae* can reasonably be attributed to Clovis. Without doubt, the same king's letter to his bishops constitutes the earliest piece of datable Merovingian legislation. Clovis's sons and grandsons also issued a number of laws, and certainly kings were issuing law-codes in the early seventh centuries: the reigns of Childebert II, Chlothar II and Dagobert I seem to have been the great age of Merovingian legislation. After the reign of Dagobert there is less evidence for royal law-giving, yet under Childeric II Leodegar embarked on what appears to have been a massive revision of Merovingian law. In the early eighth century, however, the Alamannic *dux* Lantfrid usurped what seems previously to have been a royal prerogative.

Nevertheless the Merovingians did not entirely lose their legal functions; they continued to play an important role in the giving of judgments, even into the eighth century. The significance of a king and his court in the exercise of justice is nowhere more apparent than in Fredegar's description of Dagobert I's descent on Burgundy, shortly after Chlothar II's death.[104] His arrival caused alarm to the bishops and the magnates and joy to the poor. At St-Jean-de-Losne he dispensed what justice he could. He also ordered the murder of his brother's leading supporter, Brodulf, but since he is said to have done so 'while getting into the bath', it may be assumed that the order was delivered as a surreptitious aside. Although Fredegar provides very little detail

100. *Capitularia Merowingica*, 9.
101. *Capitularia Merowingica*, 4, 7; Gregory, *Decem Libri Historiarum* IX 20.
102. Wormald, '*Lex Scripta* and *Verbum Regis*: legislation and Germanic kingship, from Euric to Cnut', p. 126; Wood, 'Disputes in late fifth- and sixth-century Gaul: some problems', p. 22; Wood, 'The *Codex Theodosianus* in Merovingian Gaul'.
103. *Lex Alamannorum*, Cod. A, *incipit*; Wormald, '*Lex Scripta* and *Verbum Regis*: legislation and Germanic kingship, from Euric to Cnut', p. 109.
104. Fredegar, IV 58; Wallace-Hadrill, *The Long-Haired Kings*, p. 217.

on the justice dispensed by the king, its form can be deduced from the survival of Merovingian *placita*, that is the legal agreements or 'final accords', drawn up at the end of law suits.[105] Each begins with a reference to the king or his officer sitting at the seat of justice, and the plaintiff arriving and putting a case, which the defendant had then to answer or concede, before judgment was given. Most *placita* provide only the barest outline of the evidence brought to court, but they do show kings in action, exercising judicial authority. It was an authority they preserved until almost the end of the Merovingian period. Even Einhard's derision of the Merovingians travelling by ox-cart is, as we have seen, an indication of the surviving importance of royal justice.

105. Fouracre, '"Placita" and the settlement of disputes in later Merovingian Francia', pp. 23–7.

Chapter Eight

Royal Women: Fredegund, Brunhild and Radegund

There are a number of crucial periods in Merovingian history when women dominate events. Indeed, the political influence of women in Francia was arguably more important than in any other early medieval state. This may seem curious given the notorious role that the Salic Law was to play in royal succession in the later Middle Ages. In fact *Lex Salica* is not unusual among early law codes in privileging the inheritance of land by males. It did not prevent women from owning property. The influence of royal women, however, depended not so much on their land-holdings, although these could be important, but on the opportunities afforded by the structure of Merovingian politics.

Merovingian princesses

On the whole the daughters of the kings of the Franks attract scant attention in our sources. Royal blood gave them very little, except airs and graces, which did not always stand them in good stead in later life: the revolt of the nuns of Poitiers, which occupies a considerable proportion of Books Nine and Ten of Gregory's *Histories*, was caused at least in part by the pretensions of the nuns Basina and Chlothild, both princesses unhappy with their lot.[1] The best that a princess could hope for was a prestigious marriage, but the history of royal marriages between Merovingian women and the princes of neighbouring kingdoms was not a happy one. Clovis's daughter Chlothild had to be rescued from her husband, the Visigothic king Amalaric.[2] Rigunth, the daughter of Chilperic, was betrothed to the Visigothic prince Reccared. The wedding, however, was put off because of the death of her brother, and ultimately it was abandoned because of the murder of her father; the girl was

1. Gregory, *Decem Libri Historiarum*, IX 39–43; X 15–17.
2. Gregory, *Decem Libri Historiarum*, III 2, 10.

consigned to a lifetime of arguments with her mother and, according to Gregory, to sleeping with all and sundry.[3] Happier at first was the lot of her cousin Ingund, daughter of Brunhild, who was married to Reccared's brother, Hermenegild, but after her husband's rebellion she fell into the hands of the Byzantines. As a result she and her young son became the centre of diplomatic negotiations between Brunhild and the emperor Tiberius II. She died in Africa before these came to fruition.[4] Of all the Merovingian princesses the most fortunate was perhaps Bertha, who at the time of her marriage to the Kentish prince Æthelberht was little better than an orphan. Her husband was scarcely a king of great status in the eyes of the Merovingians, to whom he may well have been tributary, but, perhaps because of this, Bertha appears to have been a figure of some significance at the Kentish court: with the arrival of Augustine's mission, if not before, she was given the opportunity to play a role in the Christianization of England.[5] Few Merovingian princesses who married had careers of equivalent distinction, and of most princesses we know nothing, not even their names. Their activities were only of occasional interest to Gregory of Tours. Some may have contracted non-royal marriages, others certainly went into nunneries; for many of them appearance in the historical record was fleeting.

Merovingian queens

Names are sometimes almost the only thing known of the other group of royal women, the queens, and more generally, given the lifestyle of the Merovingians, the sleeping partners of the Frankish kings. However, there are a number of queens who figure prominently in the historical record. Some of them were the daughters of neighbouring kings, and were therefore of diplomatic importance. The Visigothic king Athanagild must have hoped to strengthen his relations with the Franks when he married his daughters Brunhild and Galswinth to Sigibert and Chilperic.[6] A foreign princess might hope that her position as a pawn in the diplomatic relations between kingdoms would protect her in times of difficulty. In the case of Chilperic's queen, Galswinth, however, neither wealth nor kin saved her when her husband decided to have her murdered.[7] Other royal partners may have gained from having Frankish kinsmen to protect them, but almost nothing is known of the family background of most of them, and some Merovingians

3. Gregory, *Decem Libri Historiarum*, VI 18, 34, 44; VII 9, 10, 15, 39; IX 34.

4. Gregory, *Decem Libri Historiarum*, V 38; VI 40; VIII 18, 21, 28; *Epistulae Austrasiacae*, 27, 28, 43, 44, 45.

5. Gregory, *Decem Libri Historiarum*, IV 26; IX 26; Gregory I, *Register*, VI 57; VIII 4; XI 48; also I.N. Wood, 'The mission of Augustine' (forthcoming).

6. Gregory, *Decem Libri Historiarum*, IV 27, 28; see J.L. Nelson, 'À propos des femmes royales dans les rapports entre le monde wisigothique et le monde franc à l'époque de Reccared', in *XIV Centenario Concilio III de Toledo 589–1989*, pp. 468–70.

7. Gregory, *Decem Libri Historiarum*, IV 28.

seem actively to have preferred women of low birth. Sigibert I deliberately chose not to follow the example of his brothers when he married the Visigothic princess Brunhild.[8] Usually the status of a queen or concubine depended almost entirely on the support of her husband. Nevertheless they could be very powerful indeed.

A queen's power depended on her relationship with her husband, her role as the bearer of his heirs, and on her control of wealth.[9] Some, if not all, queens took charge of their husband's treasuries. After Chilperic was murdered, Fredegund had in her control a considerable treasure, which included a golden salver which the king had commissioned.[10] Charibert's widow, Theudechild, and Brunhild also had plenty of treasure with them when their husbands died.[11] It is not clear how much of what they had was their own. Shortly after Chlothar II had established himself as sole ruler of the Merovingian kingdom in 613, bishop Leudemund told queen Berthetrude to send all the treasure she could to Sion, in expectation of her husband's death.[12] The bishop's intention was that she should marry Alethius, who would then succeed to the throne. Probably the treasure in question was not simply the queen's private wealth. What the story may also suggest is that a woman could carry a claim to the throne: unfortunately Fredegar's meaning at this point is obscure.

The treasure referred to in all these instances might have been that of the king, but queens had treasure of their own. Although the treasure which Fredegund had with her in 584 may have been Chilperic's, when her daughter Rigunth set out for Spain she conferred so much on her that the king was alarmed, and the queen had to explain that she had saved up from her own revenues and estates.[13] All queens would have received dowries, or rather *morgengaben*, from their husbands. Chilperic bestowed on Galswinth five cities.[14] This colossal gift may have been abnormal. Its size may have been determined by Chilperic's desire to eclipse his half-brother Sigibert, who had already married Brunhild. It may also have been intended to convince Galswinth's father Athanagild of the sincerity of Chilperic's commitment to the marriage. There is nothing to suggest that other *morgengaben* were on this scale.[15] Nevertheless, all queens had access to considerable wealth, and they were therefore powerful patrons. As such they were both courted and hated.

With the king's ear and control of his purse, a queen could establish herself as the most influential political figure in the kingdom, but her route to power began in the royal bedchamber. The first priority for any queen or concubine

8. Gregory, *Decem Libri Historiarum*, IV 27.
9. P. Stafford, *Queens, Concubines and Dowagers*, pp. 104–6.
10. Gregory, *Decem Libri Historiarum*, VII 4; see VI 2.
11. Gregory, *Decem Libri Historiarum*, IV 26; V 1.
12. Fredegar, IV 44.
13. Gregory, *Decem Libri Historiarum*, VI 45.
14. Gregory, *Decem Libri Historiarum*, IX 20.
15. Nelson, 'À propos des femmes royales dans les rapports entre le monde wisigothique et le monde franc à l'époque de Reccared', p. 469.

was to retain the affections of the king, who could all too easily discard a woman who no longer took his fancy. The problems of retaining a king's affections are apparent in the *Histories* of Gregory of Tours; Deuteria, who had left one husband for Theudebert I, realized that her daughter's beauty was a threat to her own position, and arranged to have her drowned at Verdun. Perhaps as a result of this Theudebert abandoned Deuteria and instead married the Lombard Wisigard, to whom he had been betrothed for some time.[16] Charibert's first wife Ingoberg tried to prevent her husband from falling for the daughters of a wool-worker by setting the father to work in the king's presence, but the plan backfired and Charibert dismissed Ingoberg.[17] More peculiar was the outcome of the wish of Chlothar I's wife, Ingund, to find her sister a suitable husband: once the king had seen the girl he decided to marry her himself, and thus became husband to both sisters in turn, or perhaps at once.[18] Against these tales of marital upsets the ability of Fredegund, Chilperic's second wife, to re-establish her position after the king's marriage to Galswinth, and thenceforth to become a driving force in her husband's kingdom, is truly remarkable.

Fredegund

Gregory's information on Fredegund hinges largely on her concern for her own offspring, and by extension with her desire to wipe out any conceivable challenge to her children's chance of succeeding to their father's kingdom. To this end she pursued her two stepsons, Clovis and Merovech, arranging the murder of the first and driving the second to suicide.[19] Nor did their supporters fare much better. Clovis's allies, Leudast and the two Riculfs, all suffered at her hands.[20] Merovech's baptismal sponsor, bishop Praetextatus of Rouen, who received the prince and Brunhild when they fled to Rouen to be married, faced trial, exile and ultimately murder.[21] Meanwhile the deaths of her own children prompted extravagant displays of grief. When Chlodobert and Dagobert were dying of dysentery, Fredegund concluded that this was divine punishment for unjust government and insisted on the incineration of her husband's new tax registers.[22] On the death of another son, Theuderic, she burned all his belongings and had a group of Parisian women tortured for supposed witchcraft.[23] Her concern for her family can also be seen in the quantity of gifts she made to her daughter, Rigunth, prior

---

16. Gregory, *Decem Libri Historiarum*, III 26, 27.
17. Gregory, *Decem Libri Historiarum*, IV 26.
18. Gregory, *Decem Libri Historiarum*, IV 3.
19. Gregory, *Decem Libri Historiarum*, V 18, 39.
20. Gregory, *Decem Libri Historiarum*, V 49.
21. Gregory, *Decem Libri Historiarum*, V 18; VIII 31.
22. Gregory, *Decem Libri Historiarum*, V 34; VI 34–5.
23. Gregory, *Decem Libri Historiarum*, VI 34–5.

to her departure for Spain.[24] In addition, protection of her husband and her children underpinned Fredegund's behaviour towards others. She was probably responsible for the murder of Sigibert, when he looked set to destroy the kingdom of her husband, Chilperic, and is said by Gregory to have been the evil genius behind assassination attempts on both Brunhild and Childebert, as well as Guntram.[25]

Thus far Fredegund might be seen as a model, if somewhat bloodthirsty, queen, whose chief concern was the protection of her immediate family. Gregory, however, also suggests that her actions were rather more self-centred. Although she lamented the deaths of Chlodobert, Dagobert and Theuderic, she rejected her newborn son Samson and wanted him to die, because she thought herself at death's door.[26] It was left to Chilperic to insist on his baptism. Similarly, although she endowed Rigunth with treasure for her journey to Spain, when the princess ended up as a spinster at court Fredegund tried to murder her.[27] The chief source of conflict between the two women, says Gregory, was the loose morals of Rigunth. Nevertheless Fredegund's morals were not above suspicion: Guntram doubted the parentage of Chlothar II,[28] and Gregory insists that the queen turned against Eberulf because he refused to become her lover.[29] The bishop of Tours had no liking for Fredegund, and it is possible that the picture of her which he presents is misleading. The eighth-century *Liber Historiae Francorum*, however, went further than Gregory, accusing the queen of the murder of her own husband, Chilperic, after he discovered that she was having an affair.[30] Fredegund's career cannot be reduced simply to that of a woman concerned only for the survival and inheritance of her children, but such concerns were crucial to her as to other Merovingian queens.

Royal widows

Fredegund's career as queen appears not to have been interrupted by Chilperic's murder. She continued her lethal brand of politics during the early years of Chlothar II's reign, and apparently died a natural death in 587.[31] Most royal women, however, seem to have left the political stage on the death of their husbands. Since a queen's power depended on her position as wife of the king and the mother of his sons, it is not surprising that most queens ceased to be significant figures in widowhood. Those royal women

24. Gregory, *Decem Libri Historiarum*, VI 45.
25. Gregory, *Decem Libri Historiarum*, IV 51; VII 20; VIII 29, 44; X 18.
26. Gregory, *Decem Libri Historiarum*, V 22.
27. Gregory, *Decem Libri Historiarum*, IX 34.
28. Gregory, *Decem Libri Historiarum*, VIII 9; see also Wood, 'The secret histories of Gregory of Tours'.
29. Gregory, *Decem Libri Historiarum*, VII 21, 22, 29.
30. *Liber Historiae Francorum*, 35.
31. Fredegar, IV 17; *Liber Historiae Francorum*, 37.

who remained important in secular politics after the death of their husbands were the mothers of princes who had not yet reached the age of majority. The problems of establishing a young prince on the throne and of organizing a regency provided royal widows with an opportunity to continue to hold on to power. Fredegund had a role to play in the establishment of Chlothar II as king;[32] Brunhild was to witness the minorities of her son Childebert II, her grandsons, Theudebert II and Theuderic II, and ultimately to see the failure of her great-grandson, Sigibert II.[33] In the seventh century Balthild, widow of Clovis II, acted in the regency for her son Chlothar III, and was probably also involved in the elevation of another son, Childeric II, to the throne of Austrasia.[34] In this action she appears to have acted together with her sister-in-law, Chimnechild, the widow of Sigibert III. The latter ensured the continuance of her own role at court, in extremely complex political circumstances, by arranging for the marriage of her daughter to Childeric.[35] The collusion of the two queens resulted in the only known case of Merovingian endogamy, a significant, but unique, variation in the pattern of royal succession. Closer to the traditional behaviour of Merovingian queens was the action taken by the widow of the ruling aristocrat Pippin II, Plectrude, in 714, when she tried to prevent her stepson Charles Martel from taking over her husband's power and treasure.[36] It is possible that Plectrude was deliberately acting as if she were a queen in this instance, but her behaviour might equally well indicate that aristocratic women in general were faced with the same problems and embarked upon the same strategies as their royal counterparts.

The precise weapons which queens and queen-mothers could use in such circumstances are nowhere clearly stated, but it is likely that most were dependent on a following built up by the distribution of patronage during their husband's lifetime. This could continue after the king's death. In his record of a meeting between Fredegund and two clerics, who were being sent to assassinate Childebert and Brunhild, Gregory puts into the queen's mouth a speech in which she promises either a lavish reward for the assassins or, should they die in the attempt, wealth and office for their relatives.[37] The wealth on which a queen or a queen-regent could draw would certainly have included her own personal treasure.

Many of the actions of royal women presented in the sources are seen as being underhand or stealthy. Chlothild is depicted as having harboured notions of vengeance for decades on end, before she found in Chlodomer a

32. Gregory, *Decem Libri Historiarum*, VIII 9; X 11.
33. Gregory, *Decem Libri Historiarum*, VIII 29; IX 9; Fredegar, IV 18, 19, 42.
34. Fredegar, cont. 1–2; *Liber Historiae Francorum*, 44–5; *Vita Balthildis*, 5; Nelson, 'Queens as Jezebels: Brunhild and Balthild in Merovingian history', pp. 19–21.
35. On the marriage of Childeric II and Bilichild, see *Vita Balthildis*, 5; *Passio Leudegarii* I, 8; on the continuing influence of Chimnechild, see *Passio Praeiecti*, 24.
36. Fredegar, cont. 8; *Liber Historiae Francorum*, 51.
37. Gregory, *Decem Libri Historiarum*, VIII 29.

champion to destroy her Burgundian relatives.[38] Time and again in Gregory's narrative Fredegund appears as the employer of assassins.[39] The bishop of Tours narrates her activities in graphic detail, although he must have been dependent on rumour and hearsay for much of his evidence. In the next century Brunhild would be the butt of similar accusations with fatal consequences.[40] The accusations levelled against both queens suggest that it was assumed that the employment of assassins was a mode of operation which they were likely to employ. Being women, they were unlikely to fight their own battles, although on occasion both did behave in manly fashion: Brunhild, for instance, intervened to prevent open war between the followers of Ursio and Berthefred on the one hand, and those of her favourite, Lupus, on the other:[41] Fredegund later tried to intervene in a bloodfeud, and when neither party listened to her she had the survivors killed at a banquet.[42]

Brunhild

The full range of difficulties and opportunities facing a queen are most clearly apparent in the career of Brunhild. At the same time the problems posed by the literary sources for the late sixth and early seventh centuries are particularly apparent in her history. Brunhild clearly impressed Gregory and also Venantius Fortunatus. The latter's poems written at the court of Sigibert have a notably classical flavour, being modelled on the works of Claudian and Sidonius Apollinaris.[43] They may well reflect the taste of the queen. The image of Brunhild offered by both Fortunatus and Gregory, however, needs to be treated with some care; it appears from Fortunatus that Brunhild played a role in the appointment of Gregory to Tours, something that the latter never mentions.[44] As for Fortunatus himself, in his early years in Francia he lived entirely on patronage, and much of the support he received in those early years came from the Austrasian court of Sigibert.[45] Both writers may have been biased in her favour. By contrast seventh-century sources, including Fredegar's *Chronicle* and the *Life of Columbanus* by Jonas of Bobbio, are consistently hostile to the queen. Their position seems to have been determined by the destruction of Brunhild and her dynasty by Chlothar II. Perhaps less liable to bias was pope Gregory the Great, who seems to have

38. Gregory, *Decem Libri Historiarum*, III 6.
39. Gregory, *Decem Libri Historiarum*, IV 51; V 39; VII 20; VIII 29, 31, 44; VIII 18; see Wood, 'The secret histories of Gregory of Tours'.
40. Fredegar, IV 42.
41. Gregory, *Decem Libri Historiarum*, VI 4.
42. Gregory, *Decem Libri Historiarum*, X 27.
43. Reydellet, *La Royauté dans la littérature latine de Sidoine Apollinaire à Isidore de Séville*, pp. 306–8.
44. Venantius Fortunatus, carm., V 3, 11. 15–15.
45. George, *Venatius Fortunatus: A Latin Poet in Merovingian Gaul*, pp. 27–9.

thought highly of Brunhild. But even his comments are suspect, because he depended on the queen for the implementation of Church reform in Francia.

Brunhild was the daughter of the Visigothic king Athanagild and his wife Goiswinth; she was sought in marriage by Sigibert, who was, says Gregory, particularly concerned to find a wife of noble birth, in contrast to his brothers who had up until that time married women of no status.[46] Little is known of her career during the lifetime of her husband, except that she abjured the arian creed of her parents. It would be wrong to assume from this, however, that she was of no importance; comments ascribed to Ursio and Berthefred by Gregory suggest that some members of the Austrasian aristocracy thought that she had too much influence over Sigibert.[47] Something of her influence is indicated by Fortunatus, when he reveals the involvement of Brunhild in the appointment of Gregory to Tours. It is likely that the queen exercised patronage to considerable effect.

What neither Fortunatus nor Gregory reveal is Brunhild's response to the death of her sister, Galswinth. According to the bishop of Tours, Chilperic's brothers were furious with him when he murdered Galswinth,[48] but no comment is passed here or later in the *Ten Books of Histories* on Brunhild's reaction. Certainly there is reference to animosity between Brunhild and Fredegund, but there is nothing in Gregory or in other sixth-century writers to suggest that Brunhild saw herself as the avenger in a bloodfeud. Nor, indeed, is there any indication that Fredegund was involved in Galswinth's murder, which is laid entirely at Chilperic's door. Equally, Fredegund's apparent involvement in the murder of Sigibert is not described by Gregory as instigating a feud. Brunhild may have been responsible for Chilperic's death, as Fredegar claimed. But Gregory makes no such suggestion, and the *Liber Historiae Francorum* held Fredegund responsible.[49] Since Gregory does describe Clovis's wife, Chlothild, as prosecuting a bloodfeud when dealing with the collapse of the Burgundian kingdom,[50] it is clear that he did not regard such a role as being inappropriate even for saintly queens; his failure to depict relations between Brunhild and Fredegund in terms of a vendetta either requires a detailed explanation, or it should be assumed that such a vendetta did not exist. Any murders which were committed by these queens were part of the politics of survival, not of the bloodfeud.

The murder of Sigibert brings Brunhild rather further to the fore in Gregory's narrative. Whatever her influence before Sigibert's death, her position was precarious in the following years. Her son, Childebert, was taken from her by the *dux* Gundovald, who arranged for the prince to be accepted by his father's followers. Brunhild herself was left to the mercy of Chilperic, who had her exiled to Rouen.[51] At this point her career became enmeshed

46. Gregory, *Decem Libri Historiarum*, IV 27.
47. Gregory, *Decem Libri Historiarum*, VI 4.
48. Gregory, *Decem Libri Historiarum*, IV 28.
49. Fredegar, IV 42; *Liber Historiae Francorum*, 35.
50. Gregory, *Decem Libri Historiarum*, III 5.
51. Gregory, *Decem Libri Historiarum*, V 1.

with that of Merovech, Chilperic's son by Audovera, who seized the opportunity to strengthen his position by marrying Sigibert's widow.[52] Chilperic separated the two, taking his son into custody and apparently allowing Brunhild to return to the eastern kingdom of Austrasia. There, after escaping from his father and taking sanctuary at St Martin's, Merovech followed her, only to be turned away by the Austrasians.[53]

What Merovech stood to gain from his marriage to Brunhild seems reasonably clear; he was strengthening his chance of becoming king, in opposition to any plans being laid by Fredegund.[54] Whether he saw his claim as centring on his father's kingdom or on that of Sigibert, which was now in the hands of a minor, is debatable. Brunhild's position is opaque. She had apparently been ignored by the Austrasians when Gundovald took over the protection of Childebert; Gregory, recounting the events of 587, says that Ursio and Berthefred wished then to humiliate the queen as they had done when she was first widowed.[55] As well as enhancing his own position, Merovech might, therefore, be seen as offering the queen some protection.

The events following the separation of Brunhild and Merovech raise further questions. Had the situation changed in her favour when she was received in Austrasia? And when Merovech tried to follow her, was he driven out with or without her connivance? Whatever the answers, Brunhild cannot have remained absolutely powerless for long, since in 581 she intervened to prevent Ursio and Berthefred from fighting her supporter, Lupus.[56] By that date she clearly had a following, and although her influence was not unopposed, she was a force to be reckoned with. That this was so three years later is clear from the fact that in 584 she was able to have Lupentius, abbot of Javols, tried for *lèse-majesté*. He was acquitted, but then murdered while travelling home.[57] A similar murder, that of bishop Desiderius of Vienne, in the early seventh century would be linked firmly with Brunhild;[58] it is presumably a mark of Gregory's personal bias that no shred of suspicion is raised against her in this instance. That she could make the charge against Lupentius, even if it did not stick, is a mark of her power. The same year saw the murder of Chilperic, which was later to be attributed to Brunhild, and also the escalation of Gundovald's revolt.

52. Gregory, *Decem Libri Historiarum*, V 2.
53. Gregory, *Decem Libri Historiarum*, V 14.
54. Nelson, 'Queens as Jezebels: Brunhild and Balthild in Merovingian history', pp. 10–12.
55. Gregory, *Decem Libri Historiarum*, IX 9.
56. Gregory, *Decem Libri Historiarum*, VI 4; Nelson, 'Queens as Jezebels: Brunhild and Balthild in Merovingian history', p. 12.
57. Gregory, *Decem Libri Historiarum*, VI 37.
58. Fredegar, IV 32; Sisebut, *Vita vel Passio sancti Desiderii*, 15–18; *Passio sancti Desiderii*, 9; on the propaganda in this material, see Wood, 'Forgery in Merovingian hagiography', pp. 373–5.

Brunhild seems to have had some contact with Gundovald and, later, with his sons.[59] She offered protection to his sometime supporter Waddo.[60] But, as we have seen, she was not a natural ally of the other Austrasians who were involved in the revolt. She was opposed to Guntram Boso, whose death Childebert ordered in 587.[61] In the same year she and Childebert were the intended victims of a plot led by Rauching, Ursio and Berthefred.[62] Also involved was bishop Egidius of Rheims, who seems to have been implicated in the Gundovald affair.[63] These men disliked Brunhild's influence over Childebert, who Guntram had recognized as being fit to rule in the last stages of Gundovald's revolt. The implication of all this is that Brunhild, although she was not powerless in the last years of Childebert's minority, had to cooperate with members of the aristocracy who were hostile to her. The period between her return to Austrasia in 575 and 585 seems, therefore, to have been one in which no single faction could maintain control over the king. It must have been a difficult time for Brunhild, who had to work with men who, according to Gregory, openly reviled her.

The mid-580s saw Brunhild's power considerably enhanced, above all because Childebert was able increasingly to establish his authority and with it that of his mother. He was first recognized as being fit to rule by Guntram in 584.[64] Not long afterwards his tutor, Wandelenus, died, and Brunhild was able to take over responsibility for her son.[65] She still faced opposition from among the aristocracy, as is apparent from her failure to gain any sympathy for her daughter, Ingund, who was currently languishing in Africa, having fallen into the hands of the Byzantines after the revolt of Hermenegild.[66] Concern for daughter and grandson was to lead to Brunhild appealing to the Byzantines in a series of notable diplomatic letters, but all to no avail.[67] In Austrasia, by contrast, she had more success. The years after 585 saw the gradual elimination of her enemies, Guntram Boso, and then Rauching, Ursio and Berthefred, who plotted to kill Childebert, take control of his sons, and humiliate his mother.[68] Finally Septimima and Sunnegisel were dealt with. They planned to kill Brunhild and Faileuba, Childebert's consort, and then either to govern through the king, or if he proved intractable, to kill him and replace him with his sons.[69] The discovery of this last plot also led to the exposure of Egidius of Rheims's role in earlier conspiracies, and to the

59. Gregory, *Decem Libri Historiarum*, VII 33, 34; IX 28, 32.
60. Gregory, *Decem Libri Historiarum*, VII 43.
61. Gregory, *Decem Libri Historiarum*, IX 8, 10.
62. Gregory, *Decem Libri Historiarum*, IX 9.
63. Gregory, *Decem Libri Historiarum*, X 19; see also chapter 6.
64. Gregory, *Decem Libri Historiarum*, VII 33.
65. Gregory, *Decem Libri Historiarum*, VIII 22; Nelson, 'Queens as Jezebels: Brunhild and Balthild in Merovingian history', pp. 12–13.
66. Gregory, *Decem Libri Historiarum*, VIII 21.
67. *Epistulae Austrasiacae*, 27, 28, 43, 44, 45.
68. Gregory, *Decem Libri Historiarum*, IX 8–10, 11.
69. Gregory, *Decem Libri Historiarum*, IX 38.

bishop's exile.[70] By 589 the opposition appears to have been crushed, but already two years previously Brunhild's position had been assured by the Treaty of Andelot between Childebert and Guntram, which recognized her right to protection, and also confirmed her claims to the *morgengab* of her murdered sister, Galswinth.[71]

Gregory's *Histories* end in 591, and thereafter evidence on Brunhild changes dramatically. In general the last decade of the sixth century is, in fact, very poorly represented in the historical record. In so far as there is a coherent narrative of the later stages of Brunhild's life it has to be drawn from Fredegar's extremely hostile account in his *Chronicle*, to which may be added the evidence of certain saints' *Lives*, together with a group of letters from Gregory the Great, which provide crucial information on the 590s. These years saw the death both of Guntram in 592 and of Childebert in 596.[72] Guntram's death resulted in Childebert's acquisition of Burgundy, a development which must have affected Brunhild's position. Fredegar, however, has nothing to say about the queen at this juncture, and her status has to be inferred from Gregory the Great's earliest letters to her, which make it quite clear that the pope regarded Brunhild as a dominant force, perhaps the dominant force, in the kingdom.[73] The death of Childebert tends to confirm this impression, since Brunhild seems to have acted as regent for both his sons, Theudebert II, who ruled in Austrasia, and Theuderic II, who took over Guntram's old kingdom of Burgundy.[74] Her supporters at this moment included men of Gallo-Roman background who had previously worked for both Guntram and Childebert.[75] As regent Brunhild asked the pope to grant the *pallium* to her favourite, Syagrius, bishop of Autun; Gregory agreed, although the request was unusual in that Autun was not a metropolitan diocese.[76] That he was concerned to please the queen is implied by his subsequent refusal to grant the *pallium* to the metropolitan of Vienne when he requested it.[77] The pope's aim in pandering to Brunhild was probably to secure the queen's support in his attempt to reform the Frankish church, which he had heard to be infected with simony.[78] He was also concerned to ensure the continuance of Frankish aid for Augustine's mission to Kent.[79] In turning to Brunhild he was not disappointed: she contributed, so he claimed, more to the success of the mission than anyone except God.[80] Gregory's

---

70. Gregory, *Decem Libri Historiarum*, X 19.
71. Gregory, *Decem Libri Historiarum*, IX 11, 20.
72. Fredegar, IV 14, 16.
73. Gregory I, *Register*, VI 5, 57; VIII 4; IX 213; XI 46, 48, 49.
74. Fredegar, IV 16.
75. Nelson, 'Queens as Jezebels: Brunhild and Balthild in Merovingian history', p. 14.
76. Gregory I, *Register*, VIII 4; IX 213, 222.
77. Gregory I, *Register*, IX 220; compare also his treatment of Lyons, *Register*, XI 40.
78. Gregory I, *Register*, IX 213; XI 49.
79. Gregory I, *Register*, VI 57; VIII 4; XI 48.
80. Gregory I, *Register*, XI 48; on the Frankish involvement in the christianization of the English, see Wood, 'The mission of Augustine'.

realization that the queen's support was worth having is a vital indication of the strength of her position after Childebert's death.

The pope's letters urging Brunhild to involve herself in reforming the Austrasian Church continue until 602.[81] Assuming that Gregory was reasonably well informed on Frankish politics, this must suggest that Brunhild held power in Austrasia until that year, despite the fact that Fredegar claims that she was driven out of the eastern kingdom in 599.[82] Quite apart from the chronological error, Fredegar's narrative at this point is open to question. He states that after Brunhild had been exiled from Austrasia, a poor man found her and took her to Theuderic: in recompense she had the pauper made bishop of Auxerre. It is highly unlikely that an exiled queen would have been left wandering alone, and the so-called pauper seems in any case to have been Desiderius, whom local Auxerre tradition remembered as being of royal blood.[83] Fredegar's account of this event is a precursor of his later full-scale denigration of the queen. Nevertheless it does seem that at the beginning of the seventh century members of the Austrasian aristocracy were able to drive Brunhild from Theudebert's court. It may be significant that they did so at about the time that the king reached the age of 15, by Merovingian standards the age of majority. While Brunhild had outfaced her opponents during the minority of Childebert and, more particularly at the moment that he took control of the kingdom, she failed to do so at the start of Theudebert's period of rule.[84] The Austrasian aristocracy, or at least a faction within it, had driven her out, and had secured the king for themselves.

The arrival of Brunhild at Theuderic's court marks the start of the final and most infamous stage of her life. The image of her in these years, much more compelling than anything in either Gregory of Tours or Venantius Fortunatus, is that of an evil old woman, 'a second Jezebel'. This image is most powerfully set out in the *Vita Columbani* of Jonas of Bobbio, where Brunhild emerges as the chief adversary of the holy Columbanus.[85] Jonas's account of the conflict between the queen and the saint is a narrative *tour de force*, but it should be remembered that it takes much from the Old Testament, and in doing so presents a deliberately deformed portrait of the queen. Despite this, the events recorded both by Jonas and by Fredegar, who for the most part follows the former's interpretation scrupulously, allow an interpretation of Brunhild's career in her last years which not only is compatible with what had gone before, but also actually clarifies her earlier concerns.

Although she was apparently welcomed at Theuderic's court, her influence was certainly not unopposed. Fredegar records the death of the patrician

81. Gregory I, *Register*, VIII 4; IX 213; XI 46, 49; XIII 7.
82. Fredegar, IV 19.
83. J.M. Wallace-Hadrill, *The Fourth Book of the Chronicle of Fredegar*, p. 13, n. 1.
84. Nelson, 'Queens as Jezebels: Brunhild and Balthild in Merovingian history', p. 15.
85. Jonas, *Vita Columbani*, I 18; it is copied by Fredegar, IV 36.

Aegyla at Brunhild's instigation, as well as the exile of bishop Desiderius of Vienne.[86] Having strengthened her position, the queen, supported by her favourite, Protadius, who was also her bedfellow according to Fredegar,[87] turned Theuderic against his brother Theudebert, claiming that he was in fact not Childebert's son, but the son of a gardener.[88] Although preparations were made to march against Theudebert, the Burgundian army had no wish to fight against the Austrasians: Protadius was killed, and Theuderic was forced to make peace. As yet Brunhild was not firmly enough established to pursue her chosen policy against Austrasia. Instead she directed her energies against those who had been responsible for Protadius's death.

This build-up of support and elimination of opposition is scarcely out of line with what can be seen in the reign of Childebert. More revealing are the events which followed. According to Fredegar a marriage was arranged between Theuderic and Ermenberga, the daughter of the Visigothic king Witteric, but it was not consummated because Brunhild and her granddaughter, Theudila, persuaded Theuderic against it.[89] Fredegar also tells us something omitted by Gregory, that the queen had previously prevented Childebert from marrying a Frankish lady, Theudelinda, who subsequently married a king of the Lombards.[90] Brunhild was apparently concerned to prevent her son and grandsons from taking wives who would challenge her position as queen. The marriage of Theudebert to Bilichild, who had once been a slave of Brunhild, and who now began to send her old mistress contemptuous messages,[91] was thus a double blow.

Against this concern to maintain her position as queen, the conflict between Brunhild and Columbanus falls into place. Jonas relates how the old queen once approached the saint, while he was visiting the royal court, and asked him to bless the children of Theuderic. This he refused to do on the grounds that they were bastards. Brunhild's request can be seen as a perfectly reasonable one in the light of Gregory of Tours's opinion that the sons of kings should automatically be recognized as such. Columbanus, however, clearly took the view that legitimacy was important, thus implying that if Theuderic wanted heirs he should take a wife rather than a concubine, an action which would inevitably call into question Brunhild's status as queen.[92] The saint's stand can also be set within Merovingian tradition. Germanus of Paris and Nicetius of Trier had both censured kings for their sex-lives.[93] Moreover Columbanus may not have been the first to have reprimanded Theuderic on this score.

86. Fredegar, IV 21, 24.
87. Fredegar, IV 24, 26, 27.
88. Fredegar, IV 27.
89. Fredegar, IV 30.
90. Fredegar, IV 34.
91. Fredegar, IV 35.
92. Nelson, 'Queens as Jezebels: Brunhild and Balthild in Merovingian history', p. 29.
93. Gregory, *Decem Libri Historiarum*, IV 26; *Liber Vitae Patrum*, 17, 2.

According to the anonymous *Passio* of Desiderius of Vienne the saint criticized Theuderic's marital status, and in so doing infuriated Brunhild.[94] Although this version of the *Life of Desiderius* is little regarded because it is in conflict with Fredegar's account of the saint's martyrdom, it was probably written shortly after 613, in response to the flourishing of the cult of Desiderius.[95] Brunhild's ultimate opponent and killer, Chlothar II seems deliberately to have promoted the memory of a martyr who had died at the hands of the queen's henchmen. The *Passio Desiderii* is, therefore, the earliest witness to the conflict between Brunhild and members of the clergy over whether Theuderic's children, being the offspring of concubines, were legitimate. Indeed, it seems to have been a source for Jonas's *Vita Columbani*. Columbanus was not the only one to challenge Brunhild's position as queen on moral grounds.

There is another respect in which the histories of Desiderius and Columbanus illuminate Brunhild's policies. Both the persecution of Desiderius and the attack on Columbanus show that the queen treated the Church much as she treated secular power structures. Desiderius challenged her and her son; he was therefore removed, in the first instance with the help of local factions in Vienne, and later by Brunhild's own agents, although it is not clear that she actually desired his martyrdom.[96] Similarly Columbanus was driven into exile because he presented a threat to the royal family.[97] That this policy was not a peculiar development of Brunhild's last years is suggested by the earlier charge brought against abbot Lupentius of Javols, and his subsequent death in circumstances remarkably similar to those of Desiderius's martyrdom.[98]

Alongside this hostility towards clerics who criticized the regime, it is important to note Brunhild's concern with the appointment of bishops of her own choice. Venantius Fortunatus reveals that she was behind the appointment of Gregory of Tours,[99] and Fredegar ascribes the elevation of Desiderius of Auxerre to her.[100] Domnulus, the replacement for Desiderius at Vienne, is likely to have been Brunhild's appointee.[101] That bishops could play a crucial role in the factional politics of the period is clear from the activities of Egidius of Rheims: to create a reliable bench of bishops was thus politically astute, and, to judge from the episcopal attack on Columbanus, Brunhild's choice of bishops was successful. It is no wonder that Gregory the Great regarded the Frankish Church as being stained with simony.[102] In

94. *Passio sancti Desiderii*, 8; see I.N. Wood, 'The Irish and social subversion in the early Middle Ages', in *Irland, Gesellschaft und Kultur*, pp. 263–70.

95. Wood, 'Forgery in Merovingian hagiography', pp. 373–4.

96. Compare *Passio sancti Desiderii*, 8–9, with Sisebut, *Vita vel Passio sancti Desiderii*, 16.

97. Jonas, *Vita Columbani*, I 19–20.

98. Gregory, *Decem Libri Historiarum*, VI 37.

99. Venantius Fortunatus, carm. V 3, 11. 15–16.

100. Fredegar, IV 19.

101. Nelson, 'Queens as Jezebels: Brunhild and Balthild in Merovingian history', p. 25.

102. Gregory I, *Register*, IX 213; XI 49.

turning to the queen to help reform the abuses, he was appealing to the person most implicated in episcopal appointments. Nevertheless, despite all this Brunhild was a lady of notable piety; the pope recognized her as such, and probably not just to secure her support for his policies of reform. She was, after all, a major benefactor of the Church in Autun, where she and the bishop, Syagrius, collaborated in a series of notable foundations, with papal support.[103] Although it is possible to see Brunhild's treatment of the Church as an exact counterpart to her treatment of the aristocracy, it would be wrong to see her as no more than a cynical manipulator of ecclesiastical power.

By 612 Brunhild had established a seemingly unchallengeable position in Theuderic's kingdom. There is no trace of aristocratic opposition. Ecclesiastical criticism had been silenced: Desiderius was dead and Columbanus had been driven out of Burgundy. Moreover the queen was finally in a position to eliminate her opponents in Austrasia. Theuderic marched against his brother, captured and killed him, and had his young son killed as well. Next, he threatened Chlothar. Had Brunhild been involved in a bloodfeud against Fredegund, the destruction of Chlothar would have been the final act of vengeance. But in any case the plans of Brunhild and Theuderic were suddenly brought to nothing by the king's death from dysentery. As in earlier crises the queen acted to secure her own position; disregarding all but the eldest of Theuderic's sons, she had Sigibert II elevated to the throne. In terms of Merovingian succession this was a novel act, but it may well have seemed the best way of ensuring the survival of her family at a time when Chlothar looked set to attack. Meanwhile she also sent Sigibert and the *maior* Warnachar to gather forces in the east. Not content with this, however, she also tried to use this mission as the occasion for having Warnachar murdered. Once again, it seems, she was faced with aristocrats whom she did not trust. As it so happened the plot was discovered; the aristocracy deserted to Chlothar; Brunhild, Sigibert and his brothers were captured and killed, the queen in a particularly public and barbarous fashion – having been exhibited on the back of a camel, she was torn apart by wild horses.[104]

According to Fredegar, when Brunhild was brought before Chlothar, he accused her of killing ten kings, including her first husband, Sigibert, together with her grandchildren, Theudebert, Theuderic and their offspring, as well as Merovech, her second husband, and his father, Chilperic.[105] Of these deaths those of Theudebert and his son could reasonably be held against her. It is possible that she was implicated in the murder of Chilperic, although Fredegund was held responsible by the *Liber Historiae Francorum*.[106] Since she depended on her husband Sigibert for her position, she is unlikely to have been responsible for his death, which Gregory ascribed to Fredegund.[107] Such

103. Gregory I, *Register*, XIII 7, 11, 12, 13.
104. Fredegar, IV 37–42.
105. Fredegar, IV 42.
106. *Liber Historiae Francorum*, 35.
107. Gregory, *Decem Libri Historiarum*, IV 51.

accusations, however, were not uncommon; Guntram thought that Brunhild wanted to murder him and that Theodore of Marseilles had killed Chilperic.[108] Allegations of this sort are best not taken at face value. They were political. What Chlothar was concerned to do was to find a scapegoat for the royal murders of the previous half-century, and this he did, with a vengeance. The conflicts between Sigibert and Chilperic, Theudebert, Theuderic and himself could now all be forgotten; they were the work of an outsider in the kin-group. At the same time all suspicion against Fredegund could be dropped. Chlothar's accusations may have been bad history, but they served to mark the reunification of the kingdom. For the modern historian they also symbolize the fear which successful queens could arouse and indicate that their power was seen as being centred in the seedier side of politics, particularly in assassination.

Fredegar saw Brunhild in much the same way as Gregory saw Fredegund. The similarities between the two women extended beyond their supposed propensity for assassination. Both depended on their husbands and their children, and both did their best to protect their descendants. Brunhild's concern can be seen at first hand in her letters relating to her daughter Ingund, and to her grandson, Athanagild. One other possible testimony to her affection for her husband and her children is a list inscribed on the back of a sixth-century Byzantine ivory, known as the Barberini diptych. This list was probably commemorative, for use in the liturgy. It includes many names, including those of Heldberti, Theudeberti, Theuderici, Clothari, Sygisberti, Childeberti, Athanagildi, Fachilevvae and Ingundae.[109] Traditionally the list has been ascribed to the mid-seventh century.[110] However, Sigibert is the name of Brunhild's husband, Childebert of her son, Ingund of her daughter and Theuderic, Theudebert and Athanagild those of her grandsons. Chlothar was the name of Sigibert's father and Faileuba that of Childebert's wife. If the ordering of names is significant the first three might be taken as referring to Merovingians of previous generations, all of them, however, with names also given to Brunhild's son and grandsons; the last six could then refer to Brunhild's immediate family. The diptych, which bears the image of an emperor on horseback, could have been sent from the Byzantine court to that of the Merovingians almost any time in the sixth century. It might even have been brought to Francia during the ultimately fruitless negotiations relating to Ingund and Athanagild, whose names are inscribed on it.

Despite her fondness for her family, Brunhild, like Fredegund, was constrained by her concern for her own power and safety. She questioned the legitimacy of Theudebert, after she had been driven from Austrasia. Her attitude towards the wives of her son and of her grandchildren was apparently

108. Gregory, *Decem Libri Historiarum*, VIII 4, 5.
109. J. Vezin, 'Une nouvelle lecture de la liste des noms copiée au dos de l'ivoire Barberini', *Bulletin archéologique du Comité des travaux historiques et scientifiques* 7 (1971), pp. 19–56.
110. Gerberding, *The Rise of the Carolingians and the Liber Historiae Francorum*, pp. 55–6.

determined by the possibility that they might usurp her place at court. Childebert was prevented from marrying Theudelinda. Theuderic was turned against his wife Ermenberga by his mother and his sister Theudila. Both may have been worried by the threat to their own positions. One result was the absence of legitimate princes. Theudebert's wife, Bilichild, who had once been a slave of Brunhild, seems to have been one of the foci of Austrasian opposition to the royal grandmother. Finally, Brunhild was prepared to act against the norms of the Merovingian succession in having only one of Theuderic's sons elevated in 613, again, possibly to ensure the continuance of her power.

In many respects the most remarkable aspect of Brunhild's career is its length. There is nothing to suggest that she was a woman of great political vision or that she saw her role in a different light from other queens. Essentially all her actions can be seen in terms of her desire to hold on to power; she did this by supporting Sigibert I, Childebert II, Theuderic II and Sigibert II, by preventing her son and grandson taking a wife who might challenge her position as queen, and by using every weapon at hand to counter, or better eliminate, opposing factions among the aristocracy and within the Church. Looked at in this way her career sheds light on the problems facing all queens, as well as the possibilities open to them. On the other hand, because she was successful for so long, and died, so to speak, in harness, albeit at the hands of her enemies, her career did not encompass a period of holy retirement, and in this respect it differed from that of many queens.

Holy retirement: Radegund

The tradition of retirement to the religious life was established by Clovis's wife Chlothild, who, according to Gregory, served as a religious at Tours after her husband's death.[111] Some queens were forced into a monastic retirement: Guntram packed Theudechild, widow of his brother Charibert, off to a nunnery in Arles, but kept her treasure for himself. She later tried to escape, but was prevented from doing so.[112] Nor was it only royal widows who found the religious life irksome: Charibert's supposed daughter, Chlothild, together with Chilperic's daughter, Basina, found life in Radegund's convent of the Holy Cross so intolerable under the regime of the abbess Leubovera, that they led a revolt against her, which in Gregory's narrative became a *cause célèbre*.[113] Monastic retirement, however, did not necessarily mean that a queen ceased to be of significance. Some time after Clovis's death Chlothild moved to Paris, and according to Gregory she was

111. Gregory, *Decem Libri Historiarum*, II 43.
112. Gregory, *Decem Libri Historiarum*, IV 26.
113. Gregory, *Decem Libri Historiarum*, IX 39–43; X 15–17.

the moving force behind Chlodomer's Burgundian war.[114] Later she was called upon by Childebert and Chlothar to decide the fate of Chlodomer's sons.[115] She is also credited with preventing civil war by her prayers.[116] The religious life at Tours had certainly not taken her entirely out of the limelight of Merovingian politics.

Similar continuity of influence can be seen in the case of Radegund. She was the daughter of the Thuringian king Berthar. When Theuderic I and Chlothar I destroyed the kingdom of her uncle Hermanfrid in 531 she was taken back to Francia as booty. Subsequently Chlothar married her.[117] As queen she behaved like a nun, although the extent of her almsgiving could scarcely have been matched by anyone without access to the royal treasury.[118] Eventually she left Chlothar and was consecrated to the religious life by bishop Medard of Soissons.[119] Her two hagiographers, Venantius Fortunatus and the nun Baudonivia, differ in their interpretations of the king's attitude towards her decision to become a nun. Fortunatus relates that the king sent her to Medard, after the murder of her brother, suggesting that there was a political context to her retirement from the queenship.[120] Baudonivia, however, claims that the king tried to take her back as his queen, even after he had founded a nunnery for her at Poitiers.[121] Radegund subjected her community of the Holy Cross in Poitiers to the *Rule* of St Caesarius of Arles,[122] and tried to behave as a relatively normal inmate, appointing Agnes as abbess over her.[123]

Although Radegund deliberately tried to present herself as no different from the other nuns in her community, her position was never ordinary. As a queen who had apparently left her husband and voluntarily embraced the religious life, she had stepped outside the normal behaviour of Merovingian women. By subordinating herself to Agnes she emphasized the abnormality of that behaviour. The extremity of her mortification of the flesh, some of it physically repulsive,[124] confirmed the depth of her self-abasement, but it also showed her determination to be outstanding in her chosen life. Eventually she had herself immured, effectively living out her last years as a hermit within her own foundation.[125] At the same time she did not deny herself the advantages of her royal status. She kept up her contacts with the world

114. Gregory, *Decem Libri Historiarum*, III 6.
115. Gregory, *Decem Libri Historiarum*, III 18.
116. Gregory, *Decem Libri Historiarum*, III 28.
117. Gregory, *Decem Libri Historiarum*, III 7.
118. Venantius Fortunatus, *Vita Radegundis*, 3, 9, 13, 14; Baudonivia, *Vita Radegundis*, 1. 45.
119. Venantius Fortunatus, *Vita Radegundis*, 12.
120. Venantius Fortunatus, *Vita Radegundis*, 12.
121. Baudonivia, *Vita Radegundis*, 4, 6, 7.
122. Gregory, *Decem Libri Historiarum*, IX 40; Venantius Fortunatus, *Vita Radegundis*, 24.
123. Gregory, *Decem Libri Historiarum*, IX 40; Baudonivia, *Vita Radegundis*, 8.
124. Venantius Fortunatus, *Vita Radegundis*, 25, 26.
125. Venantius Fortunatus, *Vita Radegundis*, 21.

outside. While a nun she developed a close friendship with Venantius Fortunatus,[126] something which would have been impossible for the average inmate of a community governed by the *Rule* of Caesarius. Fortunatus would become one of her chief apologists. Another was Gregory of Tours. And she had other contacts among the episcopate. She had been able to write to bishop Germanus of Paris, to prevent Chlothar from reclaiming her as queen.[127]

Her position and her contacts made her a figure of some political authority. When there was a possibility that Reccared would marry Chilperic's daughter Basina, who was already a nun at Poitiers, Radegund scotched the idea quickly.[128] Rigunth was betrothed to the Visigothic prince instead. Gundovald may have thought that her word carried weight in Merovingian circles: according to Gregory he told those who doubted his claim to be a son of Chlothar to ask Radegund, as well as Ingitrude, a religious of Tours who may well have been another member of the royal family.[129] Confinement within the walls of a nunnery was not automatically the end of the influence of a Merovingian queen.

The most striking indication of Radegund's importance comes from her collection of relics. She sent to Jerusalem for relics of St Mammes,[130] and, with the permission of Sigibert, she wrote to the emperor Justin in Constantinople asking for a fragment of the True Cross. The emperor sent her the relics which she had requested, and also Gospels studded with gold and gems.[131] The involvement of Sigibert may imply that there was a diplomatic context to Justin's gift. Between 565 and 574 Sigibert sent ambassadors to Justin to negotiate peace.[132] Since Radegund's request for and reception of the relics is not dated, it is impossible to say whether they were bound up with these particular negotiations. Whether they were or not, Radegund herself had some international status.

Although the emperor sent a fragment of the True Cross, Radegund was nearly prevented from having it installed in her own nunnery. The bishop of Poitiers refused to install it, and it was initially housed in another of Radegund's foundations at Tours.[133] From the bishop of Poitiers's point of view, the convent of the Holy Cross presented a threat to his own authority, and he did what he could to limit the prestige of the nunnery. For similar reasons bishop Maroveus was later to refuse to be present at Radegund's burial, and Gregory of Tours had to preside in his place.[134] Over the

---

126. George, *Venantius Fortunatus: A Latin Poet in Merovingian Gaul*, pp. 161–78.

127. Baudonivia, *Vita Radegundis*, 7.

128. Gregory, *Decem Libri Historiarum*, VI 34.

129. Gregory, *Decem Libri Historiarum*, VII 36.

130. Baudonivia, *Vita Radegundis*, 14.

131. Baudonivia, *Vita Radegundis*, 16; A. Cameron, 'The early religious policies of Justin II', in D. Baker, ed., *The Orthodox Churches and the West, Studies in Church History* 13 (1976), pp. 54–62.

132. Gregory, *Decem Libri Historiarum*, IV 40.

133. Baudonivia, *Vita Radegundis*, 16.

134. Baudonivia, *Vita Radegundis*, 23; Gregory, *Liber in Gloria Confessorum*, 104.

question of the installation of the relic of the True Cross, Radegund was able to exploit her family connections: she wrote to Sigibert, who instructed bishop Eufronius of Tours to install the relic in the convent of the Holy Cross.[135] However much Radegund wished to appear as an ordinary member of her foundation, she did not relinquish the power which went with her association with the Merovingian family. Nor did the other Merovingian princesses, Basina and Chlothild, who later disrupted the nunnery, and who appealed to Guntram to support them.[136]

Radegund as ascetic and Brunhild as Jezebel may seem to represent the two extremes of Merovingian queenship. These images, however, are to some extent the creation of writers; of Fortunatus and Baudonivia on the one hand, and the author of the *Passio Desiderii*, Jonas and Fredegar on the other. Nor were the extremes necessarily incompatible. Both Radegund and Brunhild used the resources of a Merovingian queen, her wealth and her contacts; the one to safeguard her position and her community, the other to protect her family and her power. Moreover, the most influential queen of the seventh century, Balthild, was perceived both as Jezebel and as an ascetic in the mould of Radegund, though not, of course, in the same source.[137]

135. Baudonivia, *Vita Radegundis*, 16; Gregory, *Decem Libri Historiarum*, IX 40.
136. Gregory, *Decem Libri Historiarum*, IX 39, 40.
137. *Vita Balthildis*, 18; Stephanus, *Vita Wilfridi*, 6.

Chapter Nine

Redefining the Kingdom:
Chlothar II, Dagobert I, Sigibert III
and Clovis II

With the death of Brunhild in 613 the whole of the Merovingian kingdom fell, once again, to one man: Chlothar II, the son of Fredegund and heir of Chilperic II. For the next two generations there was, remarkably, to be little or no civil war in the Merovingian kingdom. Not that the kingdom was permanently united under one monarch during that period. Chlothar created a sub-kingdom for his son Dagobert I in 623,[1] and in so doing established what was to become a more or less standard division between the west Frankish kingdom of a combined Neustria and Burgundy and the east Frankish kingdom of Austrasia. Despite the peace and despite the crystallization of Francia into two standard political entities, there is little to suggest that the structure of politics changed. The evidence of Fredegar, although not as full as that provided by Gregory, continues to illuminate the shifting relations between the king, the aristocracy and the Church. Indeed, despite the relatively terse nature of Fredegar's account, he provides important evidence on factional conflict, and on the involvement of a number of families who make their first clear appearance in the written record during this·period. Within this conflict the importance of the royal court and the dominance of the Merovingians is clearly visible in Fredegar's *Chronicle*, as in various saints' *Lives* and the letters of Desiderius of Cahors. Despite the importance of faction, the reigns of Chlothar II (584–629) and Dagobert I (623/29–39) can be seen as marking the apogee of Merovingian power, both at home and abroad.

The emergence of Chlothar II

According to Jonas of Bobbio, the Irish saint Columbanus prophesied Chlothar's ultimate triumph,[2] but at the time of Chilperic's murder in 584 it

1. Fredegar, IV 47.
2. Jonas, *Vita Columbani*, I 20, 24.

was certainly no foregone conclusion. In the aftermath of his father's death the prince's immediate survival depended on the actions taken by Ansoald,[3] one of Chilperic's leading supporters. During the months that followed, Guntram expressed open doubt about Chlothar's legitimacy; Gregory of Tours seems to have harboured similar suspicions. To dispel the king's doubts Fredegund called upon the oaths of three bishops and three hundred magnates.[4] Thereafter Guntram helped ensure the survival of his nephew, but at various points over the next quarter of a century Chlothar found himself and his kingdom under considerable threat. In the early 590s, according to Fredegar, he repulsed one attack,[5] and although in the middle of the decade he took Paris,[6] in 600 his territory was reduced to twelve *pagi*, counties, between the Seine, the Oise and the sea.[7] Pressure on him was relieved only by tensions elsewhere. When Theuderic II repudiated his wife, the daughter of the Visigothic king Witteric, her father formed an alliance with Chlothar and Theudebert II,[8] and when Theuderic and Theudebert fell out subsequently, Theuderic made overtures to Chlothar, to keep him neutral.[9] As a result of the civil war between Brunhild's two grandsons, Chlothar took advantage of Theudebert's defeat and seized the *ducatus* of the Dentelin, which lay on the border between Neustria and Austrasia.[10] Theuderic's death left Chlothar without any serious rivals.

Although Brunhild did try to put her great-grandson, Sigibert II, on the throne, her own unpopularity led the magnates of Austrasia and Burgundy to transfer their allegiance to Chlothar. Arnulf, bishop of Metz, and Pippin I, the first notable representative of what was to become the Carolingian family, incited him to enter the former kingdom. At the same time Brunhild's plot to kill Sigibert II's *maior domus*, Warnachar, provoked a number of Burgundian magnates into handing her and her family over to the Neustrian king. Her trial and gruesome execution followed. As a result of these events, by the end of 613 Chlothar ruled a kingdom which included most of France, Belgium, the Rhineland and the lands to the north and north-west of the Alps.[11] A year later he was able to call a council at Paris, which was attended by bishops from throughout Neustria, Austrasia, Burgundy and Aquitaine, as well as by Justus, bishop of Rochester, and Peter, abbot of Dover.[12] Clearly, from the very beginning of his reign over the united kingdom, Chlothar's authority was considerable. That it was so extensive at such an early date must redound

3. Gregory, *Decem Libri Historiarum*, VII 7.
4. Gregory, *Decem Libri Historiarum*, VIII 9; Wood, 'The secret histories of Gregory of Tours'.
5. Fredegar, IV 14.
6. Fredegar, IV 17.
7. Fredegar, IV 20.
8. Fredegar, IV 30–1.
9. Fredegar, IV 37.
10. Fredegar, IV 38.
11. Fredegar, IV 40–2.
12. Council of Paris (614), subscriptions.

in some measure to the credit of Brunhild, and to her grandchildren, Theudebert and Theuderic, who had themselves been powerful rulers, with considerable influence both within their own domains and further afield; even in Kent, if Gregory the Great is to be believed[13] – and the presence of Peter and Justus at Paris in 614 lends some weight to the pope's statement.

For the years which followed the only substantial account is that by Fredegar, and even he scarcely offers a coherent narrative of the reigns of Chlothar II and his son Dagobert I. He is particularly uninformative about the period from 613 to 622. Instead he provides a series of vignettes, several of which deal with the history of the neighbours of the Franks, rather than that of the Franks themselves. Leaving aside, for the moment, the matter of Merovingian foreign policy, the historian may add to Fredegar's Chronicle two other sources, the anonymous *Passio* of bishop Desiderius of Vienne, and the royal edict which followed the acts of the ecclesiastical Council of Paris of 614, in order to gain a fuller understanding of the period.

Desiderius of Vienne was murdered in *c.* 611, at approximately the time that Theuderic II and Brunhild drove the Irish saint Columbanus out of Luxeuil.[14] Both saints seem to have fallen foul of the king and his grandmother over the question of the royal succession. At Chalaronne, where the bishop was martyred, miraculous cures were reported.[15] After Brunhild's execution Chlothar was approached for permission to move the martyr's body, and with royal approval it was publicly translated to St Peter's at Vienne.[16] Although the anonymous *Passio* has been condemned as a forgery, there is no reason to doubt that it was written shortly after 613: it seems to have been consulted by Jonas of Bobbio when he wrote the *Life of Columbanus* in *c.* 643.[17] The *Passio* suggests that Chlothar promoted the saint cult in order to denigrate the previous regime.[18] Further evidence of Chlothar's attempt to make use of the victims of Brunhild and Theuderic comes from the overtures he made to Columbanus, to persuade him to return to Francia.[19] The appeal was in vain, but the king did protect Luxeuil, as Columbanus requested. To judge by Jonas's depiction of Brunhild and Theuderic II he secured Luxeuil as a further base for propaganda in so doing. Chlothar profited much from the *damnatio memoriae* of the old queen and her progeny.

Another indication of Chlothar's attack on the previous regime can be found in his edict of 614, where over the matter of tolls, and apparently over the issue of ecclesiastical immunities, the king reaffirmed the legislation of

13. Gregory I, *Register*, VI 49; I.N. Wood, 'Frankish hegemony in England', in M. Carver, ed., *The Age of Sutton Hoo*, p. 235.

14. On the chronological problem, see Wood, 'Forgery in Merovingian hagiography', pp. 373–4.

15. *Passio sancti Desiderii*, 10; also 11–13.

16. *Passio sancti Desiderii*, 15–19.

17. Wood, 'Forgery in Merovingian hagiography', p. 374.

18. Wood, 'Forgery in Merovingian hagiography', p. 374–5.

19. Jonas, *Vita Columbani*, I 30.

Guntram, Chilperic and Sigibert, but not that of the descendants of Brunhild.[20] Childebert II, Theudebert II and Theuderic II were to be forgotten. Nevertheless the realities of the previous decades had also to be faced. Restitution was to be made to those *fideles* and *leudes* who had lost property in the service of their legitimate lords during the *interregna*:[21] precisely what Chlothar understood by the *interregna* is not made clear. More generally Chlothar legislated 'that with Christ's help there might be peace and order in our kingdom, and that the rebel and the insolence of evil men should be most severely curbed'.[22] One of the chief concerns of the edict appears to be the restoration of peace and justice to the whole kingdom. The transformation of Brunhild, Childebert and Theuderic into scapegoats was useful here as in so many other contexts. At the same time those who had suffered during the period of conflict, whoever their lord, were to receive some compensation. Chlothar could not afford to alienate the one-time followers of Theudebert and Theuderic; they included the majority of the political nation. The Edict of Paris was an astute response to the problems following the destruction of Childebert's heirs.

Other aspects of the edict, however, are more problematic. In particular, Chlothar seems to have been concerned with questions concerning the enforcement of justice. 'And may no legal official from one province or region be installed in another, so that, if he commits any crime of any sort, that which he wrongly took should be made good according to the law from his own property'.[23] Parallel to this is another clause requiring that 'bishops or magnates who have property in other regions, should not set up legal officials or itinerant agents other than men from the locality, to observe justice and render it to others'.[24] These clauses have been seen as concessions by Chlothar, which strengthened the power of the aristocracy against that of the king. The agents of bishops and magnates, however, were no less constrained by the legislation than were the officials of Chlothar himself. What was at issue was not royal, aristocratic or ecclesiastical power, but the answerability of the personnel involved in its enforcement.[25]

In the aftermath of Brunhild's fall Chlothar was certainly aware of the need not to alienate local and regional interests, and that meant supporting the established aristocracy. Fortunately for him, although the leading families of Burgundy and Austrasia had been closely associated with the regimes of Theuderic II and Theudebert II, Brunhild had lost their support in 613.

20. *Capitularia Merowingica*, 9, 9, 14.
21. *Capitularia Merowingica*, 9, 17.
22. *Capitularia Merowingica*, 9, 11.
23. *Capitularia Merowingica*, 9, 12.
24. *Capitularia Merowingica*, 9, 19.
25. Wallace-Hadrill, *The Long-Haired Kings*, pp. 214–16. In a lecture delivered at Kalamazoo on 9 May 1992, 'Immunity, nobility and the Edict of Paris', A.C. Murray convincingly placed Chlothar's Edict within an imperial tradition of legislation employing distraint, and totally destroyed the case for seeing it as a concession to the nobility.

There were very few who remained loyal to the memory of Childebert's heirs. The *Lives* of Lupus of Sens and Rusticula of Arles are unusual in describing hostility to Chlothar. That of Rusticula states that the saint was accused of harbouring a king, presumably one of Theuderic's sons.[26] As a result of the general hostility to Brunhild and her descendants there could be continuity with the past; indeed Chlothar could not avoid coming to terms with the established magnates.

Burgundy and Austrasia

When the Burgundian aristocracy handed Brunhild and her great-grandchildren to Chlothar, Warnachar retained the office of *maior domus* on the understanding that he should not be removed from that position during his lifetime.[27] That this was a personal concession to Warnachar, rather than a recognition of regional independence, however, is suggested by the events which followed Warnachar's death in 626. When Chlothar asked the Burgundian magnates at Troyes whether they wanted the office to be filled, they unanimously rejected the offer,[28] and it was not until the reign of Clovis II (639–57) that another *maior* was appointed in the kingdom of Burgundy.[29] Apparently the Burgundians wanted direct access to the king's court, rather than having to deal with a regional official. In retrospect Warnachar's appointment looks like the reward demanded by an individual aristocrat for his part in the overthrow of Brunhild. It is the political stance of individuals, and not any regional sentiment, which seems to dominate the politics of Chlothar's Burgundy.

Other events in Burgundy, however, reveal the aristocracy in a rather more complex light. Apart from confirming Warnachar as *maior*, Chlothar also established as *dux*, in the district east of the Jura, Herpo, who is described as a Frank,[30] which may suggest that he had not been born in Burgundy. This was an unpopular appointment, and Herpo was killed by the inhabitants of his duchy at the instigation of the patrician Alethius and Leudemund, bishop of Sion. According to Fredegar, the bishop then tried to persuade queen Berthetrude to send him all her treasure, asserting that Chlothar would die within the year. Leudemund hoped that Berthetrude would marry Alethius, who was to rule in Chlothar's place. The plot failed, because the queen refused to comply.[31]

---

26. *Vita Rusticulae*, 9; *Vita Lupi episcopi Senonici*, 9, 11.

27. Fredegar, IV 42; On the office of *major* in the seventh century, see P. Fouracre, 'Merovingians, mayors of the palace and the notion of a "low-born" Ebroin', *Bulletin of the Institute of Historical Research* 57 (1984), pp. 1–14.

28. Fredegar, IV 54.

29. Fredegar, IV 89.

30. Fredegar, IV 43.

31. Fredegar, IV 44.

The episode is both revealing and problematic. Antipathy towards Herpo may have resulted from some long-standing rivalry, or it may have been caused by simple jealousy at his appointment to the Transjuran duchy. The fact that he is specifically said to have been a Frank, and not a Burgundian, may be of relevance here, not least since the whole affair must have taken place close in time to the Council of Paris, and to Chlothar's edict recognizing the need to appoint locals to judicial office. But the conflict between Herpo and Alethius, both of whom had deserted Brunhild,[32] should also be seen in the context of the distribution of offices in the wake of Chlothar's take-over. It was a matter of political infighting. The second stage of the affair, however, is rather more complex. According to Fredegar, the planned succession of Alethius depended on the fact that either he, or perhaps Berthetrude, was a member of the Burgundian royal family. Unfortunately Fredegar's Latin makes it impossible to tell which of them had royal blood. But there are more general problems: for instance, what is meant by Burgundian?[33] And why was Burgundian royal blood relevant to the Merovingian succession? One thing that is clear is that the plot was not an entirely separatist move. The idea was to supplant Chlothar, but to involve his queen in the usurpation.

Chlothar's relations with the east Frankish kingdom, now known as Austrasia, almost inevitably fell into a different pattern. Although there had been occasions when a single Merovingian had ruled over the whole of the Frankish kingdom, and although Burgundy had been united with the eastern kingdom under Childebert II, since 511 the history of the kingdom of Theuderic I and his successors had usually differed from that of the rest of the Merovingian realm. In fact, while Fredegar provides little detail on Austrasian reactions to Chlothar's victory, there is good reason to think that the established aristocracy were confirmed in power. Then in 622 Chlothar created a sub-kingdom for his eldest son, Dagobert, who was set over a reduced Austrasia, which excluded lands lying to the west of the Vosges.[34] This attempt to redraw the Austrasian frontier was to lead to conflict between father and son in later years.[35] The creation of a sub-kingdom for a prince was not a complete novelty: in 589 Childebert had established Theudebert II in Soissons and Meaux at the request of the leading citizens.[36] The implications of this earlier event are obscure, although it cannot be irrelevant that Soissons had been Chilperic I's capital. The creation of an Austrasian sub-kingdom for Dagobert in 622, and Dagobert's own revival of a sub-kingdom for his son Sigibert III ten years later,[37] have more important long-term implications for the general structure of Merovingian Francia.

32. Fredegar, IV 40, 42.
33. Wood, 'Ethnicity and the ethnogenesis of the Burgundians', pp. 54–5.
34. Fredegar, IV 47.
35. Fredegar, IV 53.
36. Gregory, *Decem Libri Historiarum*, IX 36.
37. Fredegar, IV 75.

During the sixth century, although the kingdom of the Franks had been divided on numerous occasions, each of the divisions had been *ad hoc*, determined by the number of sons claiming the throne on their fathers' deaths. Admittedly certain regions had already emerged as identifiable political units by the end of the sixth century, most notably the eastern kingdom, later to become Austrasia, and also Burgundy, as it developed under Guntram. Nevertheless, it was not until Chlothar's reign that Neustria, centred on the Seine and Oise, Austrasia, based on the Rhine and Meuse, and Burgundy, were fixed as the basic territorial blocks of the Merovingian kingdom. From 622 onwards Francia was usually divided into two units, a combined Neustro-Burgundy, that is essentially the kingdom which Chlothar kept for himself, and Austrasia, or the lands set aside as a sub-kingdom for Dagobert. Aquitaine continued to be treated separately, with particular cities being associated with one or other of the northern kingdoms. There were some variations: the frontier between Neustria and Austrasia had a chequered history, and when Dagobert created a kingdom for his half-brother Charibert, he carved it out of Aquitaine.[38] But the division of Neustro-Burgundy and Austrasia was to be the norm.

Royal politics, 622–30

Chlothar's institution of a sub-kingdom of Austrasia in 622 might be seen as a concession to regional forces, and an admission that the Merovingian kingdom could never be truly united. Alongside this interpretation, however, it is important to stress the fact that the Merovingian family remained central to the political structures of Francia. After the fall of Theudebert II, his aristocratic following may have had no wish to serve Brunhild and Theuderic, but they certainly did not think in terms of rejecting the Merovingians. Instead they seem to have transferred their loyalty to Chlothar II. After Theuderic's death, his Burgundian followers, including Warnachar, deserted Brunhild, but they did so because she presented a threat to them, and they merely switched allegiance to Chlothar.

Although the evidence for Austrasia between 613 and 622 is slight, Fredegar is more informative about the rivalries which emerged after Chlothar had established Dagobert as sub-king. In 623 two of Dagobert's chief advisers, Arnulf and Pippin, who had earlier betrayed Brunhild, turned the young king against Chrodoald, on the grounds of what appear in Fredegar as the most generalized of accusations.[39] As in the conflict between Alethius and Herpo it seems best to envisage a background of political rivalry. For Chrodoald, however, we have one additional piece of information of significance, since he is stated as being a member of the noble *gens* of the Agilulfings.

38. Fredegar, IV 57.
39. Fredegar, IV 40, 52

This family group is unusual in that early medieval sources identify it by name; for the most part membership of a particular lineage has to be inferred from what is known of an individual's relatives. Clearly the Agilulfings were a family of immense standing, particularly in the eastern fringes of the Merovingian kingdom; they provided Merovingian Bavaria with a notable line of *duces*, and are singled out in the Bavarian law-code of the eighth century as the only family from which the *dux* could come.[40] In part this status stemmed from the fact that the Agilulfings were connected with the ruling families of both Francia and Lombard Italy. Nevertheless, the Agilulfings who lived in Austrasia were not above the rivalries of the royal court. Dagobert's attack on Chrodoald, instigated as it was by Arnulf and Pippin, looks to be a matter of conflict between powerful Austrasian families. Nor were such rivalries confined to a single generation. Chrodoald's son, Fara, was later to join the revolt of Radulf of Thuringia against Sigibert III,[41] one of whose leading councillors was Grimoald, son of Pippin.

For the most part Pippin and his allies seem to have been the beneficiaries of the political conflicts of this period, but Fredegar's account of events after Chlothar's death may indicate that Dagobert was not entirely deaf to Pippin's opponents. While his father was alive it appears that Dagobert was very much under the influence of Pippin, who had been appointed *maior* of the Austrasian palace, presumably by Chlothar.[42] According to Fredegar, Dagobert ruled well at this time, but when, after his father's death, he took over Neustria there was a marked decline, apparent in his debauchery and his greed, which was directed against the property of the Church and of his followers: in Fredegar's word, his *leudes*. On hearing their complaints Pippin reprimanded the king. The Austrasians, however, took advantage of this, hoping that it would lead to the death of Pippin.[43] What appears at first sight to be an account of a major change in Dagobert's behaviour, looks on closer inspection to be no more than a shift away from Pippin's dominance, and the assertion of alternative views by an opposition group not only in Neustria, but also in Austrasia itself. Fredegar's implicit bias is perhaps not surprising, given the fact that the continuations which were added to his chronicle in the eighth century were commissioned by descendants of Pippin.[44] This later connection might imply that Fredegar himself was associated with earlier generations of the Pippinid family.

Politics in the time of Chlothar and Dagobert, therefore, were apparently dominated by the rivalries of leading magnates and their families. Far from directing attention away from the court, or even from offering a challenge to Merovingian power, these rivalries were intimately connected with central politics. Alethius's actions were directed first against a royal appointee, and

40. *Lex Baiwariorum*, 3, 1.
41. Fredegar, IV 87.
42. Fredegar, IV 52.
43. Fredegar, IV 60–1.
44. Fredegar, cont. 34.

second towards gaining the throne itself, but even then he was concerned to ensure continuity of regime, by marrying the queen. Nor were the kings themselves above the factionalism of their courts. The Chrodoald affair came to the attention of Chlothar, who intervened with his son on Chrodoald's behalf, although in the end Dagobert had him killed none the less.[45] The Carolingian *Gesta Dagoberti I*, admittedly a highly unreliable text, has a further story about Dagobert's hostility towards a member of the aristocracy, Sadregisel, who caused some conflict between Chlothar and his son, and who was finally killed after the death of the former.[46]

Kings did not just preside over the rivalries of aristocratic families, they were actually involved in them. The most significant illustration of this point comes not from any study of the Merovingian aristocracy, but from consideration of the royal family itself. According to the *Gesta Dagoberti I* the king's mother was Berthetrude.[47] As we have seen, she may have been descended from Burgundian royalty.[48] In any case, her family was probably aristocratic, and she was popular with the aristocracy on account of her generosity.[49] If she were indeed Dagobert's mother,[50] one of her relatives, Erchinoald, later became *maior* to Clovis II,[51] but this may say more about the status of her family after it had become associated with royalty, than about any earlier dignity. After Berthetrude's death, however, Chlothar married again, this time a lady called Sichild, by whom he seems to have had another son, Charibert.[52] Subsequently Sichild's sister, Gomatrude, married Dagobert in circumstances which seem to have been dictated by Chlothar.[53] These two marriages suggest that the king was deliberately aligning himself with one particular family. When Chlothar died, a bid for the throne was made on behalf of Charibert by the prince's uncle, Brodulf, probably Sichild's brother, who had already been involved in political conflicts in Chlothar's last years.[54] Although this bid for power failed, Dagobert did assign Aquitaine to his half-brother.[55] Shortly after, however, he arranged the assassination of

45. Fredegar, IV 52.
46. *Gesta Dagoberti I*, 6, 35.
47. *Gesta Dagoberti I*, 5.
48. Fredegar, IV 44.
49. Fredegar, IV 46.
50. On the problems of this identification see the entries under 'Berthetrude', 'Charibert II', 'Dagobert I' and 'Sichild' in the 'Prosopography of the Merovingian Family', below. Unlike E. Ewig, 'Die Namengebung bei den ältesten Frankenkönigen und im merowingischen Königshaus', *Francia* 18, 1 (1991), p. 64, I am inclined to think that the *Gesta Dagoberti I*, which may have originated at St Denis, a monastery richly endowed by Dagobert, would have recorded the name of the mother of that monastery's greatest benefactor accurately. Its information is not biologically impossible, and it is, in any case, possible that the related evidence in Fredegar is misleading.
51. Fredegar, IV 84.
52. *Gesta Dagoberti I*, 5.
53. Fredegar, IV 53.
54. Fredegar, IV 55, 56; *Gesta Dagoberti I*, 16.
55. Fredegar, IV 57.

Brodulf, and within weeks of so doing, he discarded Gomatrude and took Nantechild as his queen.[56] It looks as if Dagobert spent the opening months of his reign disentangling himself from the family ties which Chlothar had forced on him. In all probability this was a necessary precursor to the death of Charibert. Nevertheless, even in 628 Dagobert could not entirely break with the past. A year later, Pippin, who had only recently reprimanded the king, took Dagobert's son Sigibert to see Charibert, who subsequently stood as godfather to the prince.[57] By 632, however, Dagobert was in a stronger position. In that year Charibert died in mysterious circumstances: some held that Dagobert's followers had killed him.[58] Even if it were Haldetrude who was the mother of Dagobert and Berthetrude who was the mother of Charibert,[59] the general observation holds true: seventh-century kings were not above the factional politics of their subjects. Indeed, on certain occasions members of the aristocracy intervened to end conflicts between Chlothar and Dagobert.[60]

Desiderius of Cahors and the Merovingian court

There is another line of approach to the politics of the early seventh century. As we have seen, a number of letter-collections survive from later Roman Gaul and early medieval Francia; of these the latest is a collection of correspondence written by and to Desiderius, bishop of Cahors.[61] In its current form it is made up of thirty-six letters, but more were available to the author of the *Life of Desiderius*, writing in the Carolingian period, who inserted several which are not included in the collection into his text.[62] The letters of Desiderius deal with a number of matters relating to episcopal administration, to law-suits and simply to the exercise of *amicitia*, or friendship. This last category of letters in particular looks back to the tradition of letter-writing which had been prominent in the times of Sidonius Apollinaris, Avitus of Vienne and later Venantius Fortunatus, and it is an indication of the remarkable continuity in social and political life from the Later Roman Empire through to the seventh century. The cultivation of *amicitia* to facilitate social and political action clearly had an uninterrupted history. In this respect the general impression conveyed by the Desiderius collection is far more important than any of the detail included within the letters. Desiderius and his friends exchanged greetings to ensure that whenever

56. Fredegar, IV 58.
57. Fredegar, IV 61.
58. Fredegar, IV 67.
59. As suggested by Ewig, 'Die Namengebung bei den ältesten Frankenkönigen und im merowingischen Königshaus', p. 64.
60. Fredegar, IV 53.
61. See chapter 2.
62. *Vita Desiderii*, 9, 10, 11, 13, 14.

they should have any need to call on each other for help, the lines of communication were properly oiled.[63]

The literary and social continuity implied by the letters of Desiderius, however, is only one aspect of the importance of the collection. For understanding the reigns of Chlothar II, Dagobert I and of his two sons, Sigibert III (632–c. 656) and Clovis II (639–57), the correspondents themselves are of equal importance. One letter in particular highlights this; writing to Audoin, bishop of Rouen, Desiderius reminisces about old times at the court of Chlothar, where the two of them, together with Eligius of Noyon, Paul of Verdun and Sulpicius of Bourges, had all been companions together.[64] As bishops these men were figures of importance; Audoin and Eligius were arguably the most influential churchmen in Francia during the seventh century. From Desiderius's correspondence it is clear that even after their elevation to the episcopate they kept in contact with each other. Not that the royal court was the only nursery of talent; Columbanus's monastery of Luxeuil provided education for a very notable group of bishops.[65] Nevertheless Chlothar's household seems to have been of particular importance in determining who was to be of political importance for the next two reigns.

Consideration of Desiderius's correspondents also casts light on the function of Chlothar's court within the structure of the kingdom. Fortunately some of the men in question were the subject of saints' *Lives*, and hence something may be said about their origins. Of the bishops referred to in Desiderius's letter to Audoin two are the subject of surviving *Vitae*. The *Life of Sulpicius* is a forgery of the Carolingian period, and is uninformative about the saint's early life. Eligius's biography was originally written by Audoin, and although only a Carolingian recension of the text survives, it is an important source for seventh-century Francia.[66] Eligius himself was born in the Limousin; not much is said about the social status of his family, although his father apprenticed him to the goldsmith Abbo, a moneyer in Limoges.[67] Apprenticeship to Abbo, however, was the stepping stone to greater things, for having learnt his trade Eligius went to Neustria where he was noticed by Chlothar's treasurer, Bobo, and subsequently received commissions from the king, of which the most important was for a golden throne.[68] To everybody's

63. Wood, 'Administration, law and culture in Merovingian Gaul', pp. 68–71.
64. Desiderius, ep. I 10.
65. Jonas, *Vita Columbani*, II 8.
66. P. Fouracre, 'The work of Audoenus of Rouen and Eligius of Noyon in extending episcopal influence from the town to the countryside in seventh-century Neustria', in D. Baker, ed., *The Church in Town and Countryside, Studies in Church History* 16, p. 78, n. 5; Gerberding, *The Rise of the Carolingians and the Liber Historiae Francorum*, p. 86, n. 96.
67. *Vita Eligii*, I 3.
68. *Vita Eligii*, I 4–5; on Eligius's metalwork, see H. Vierck, 'L'œuvre de saint Eloi, orfèvre, et son rayonnement', in P. Périn and L-C. Feffer, *La Neustrie: Les pays au nord de la Loire, de Dagobert à Charles le Chauve (VIIe–IXe siècles)*, pp. 403–9.

astonishment he made two thrones out of the metal set aside for one. As a highly favoured goldsmith he had an entrée to the court, and thus fell in with the group of pious aristocrats which included Audoin and Desiderius. At the same time he was entrusted with a variety of political and diplomatic tasks, including the negotiation of a truce between Dagobert and the Bretons.[69] Under Clovis II he became bishop of Noyon in 641.[70] Throughout his time at court he continued to work as a goldsmith, while acting as a royal adviser, so we are told, and a diplomat. Eligius's origins and career provide an admirable illustration of the accessibility of Chlothar's court to regional talent, and of the social mobility open to the talented.

In addition to the *Lives* of Sulpicius and Eligius themselves, *Vitae* also survive for Audoin and for Desiderius. The *Life of Audoin* is among the few hagiographical works that can be assigned with almost total certainty to the Merovingian period. It is a text, however, that is more concerned with the saint's virtues than with his career. Nevertheless it does tell of the birth of three sons, Ado, Dado (Audoin) and Rado to Audechar and Aega, at Soissons; of their education and their attracting the notice of the king.[71] Rado subsequently became treasurer. In 641, the year that Eligius was appointed to the see of Noyon, Audoin became bishop of Rouen.[72] A little more is known about Audoin's family background from the *Life of Columbanus*, by Jonas of Bobbio. After being sent into exile by Theuderic and Brunhild, Columbanus visited a number of followers of Theudebert, including Autharius (Audechar) and Aega, and he blessed their sons, Ado and Dado.[73] The former, says Jonas, was the founder of Jouarre, and the latter, the founder of Rebais. From Jonas, therefore, it appears that Audoin came from a landed family which probably supported Theudebert, and subsequently transferred its allegiance to Chlothar. At least two of Audechar's sons joined the royal court. Further, the family was deeply involved in the monastic movement associated with Columbanus, as indeed was Eligius.[74] Like the latter, Audoin spent a long time at court before he became a bishop.

Of greater interest still for an understanding of the political importance of Chlothar's court is the evidence contained in the *Vita Desiderii*. Desiderius was born in Aquitaine, in Obrège. He had two brothers: Rusticus, who was archdeacon of Rodez and subsequently became an abbot and finally bishop of Cahors, and Syagrius, who, after a time at court, was appointed count of Albi, and later *iudicarius* of Marseilles.[75] Desiderius himself was well educated, particularly in Roman Law.[76] He went to court and became treasurer under

69. *Vita Eligii*, I 13.
70. *Vita Eligii*, II 2.
71. *Vita Audoini*, 1.
72. *Vita Audoini*, 4, 7; *Vita Eligii*, II 2.
73. Jonas, *Vita Columbani*, I 26.
74. Wallace-Hadrill, *The Frankish Church*, pp. 68–9.
75. *Vita Desiderii*, 1.
76. *Vita Desiderii, 1*; Wood, 'Administration, law and culture in Merovingian Gaul', p. 67.

Chlothar. Subsequently, when Syagrius died, he became *iudicarius* in his place.[77] Shortly afterwards his other brother, Rusticus, was killed.[78] The people of Cahors elected Desiderius as bishop in his place, and Dagobert ratified the appointment.[79] Thereafter Desiderius's career was concerned with his episcopal city, which he endowed massively with new and restored buildings.[80]

The history of this southern family, and above all of Desiderius himself, with his period at court, and his continuing friendship with Audoin, Eligius and their like, is a further indication of the centrality of the Merovingian palace for the whole of their kingdom.[81] Although Desiderius and his brothers all held office, both secular and ecclesiastical, in the south, they had strong contacts with the north, and two of them had spent some time there. Dagobert sent Desiderius to replace Syagrius at Marseilles, and was apparently much concerned at Rusticus's murder. Doubtless he was only too pleased to confirm the election of Desiderius as bishop of Cahors, despite the latter's regret at his separation from his friends at court.

There is one further point which is well illustrated by the *Life of Desiderius*. While on the one hand the court was in a sense a clearing-house for talent, and while it provided the focus for national politics, there was another more local political level, exemplified by the murder of Rusticus.[82] The *Vita* also refers to other problems faced by the bishop, even to criticisms of him made by clergy.[83] Such local antagonisms are known from elsewhere: they are very much apparent in sixth-century Clermont,[84] and similar conflicts are known from Eligius's Noyon as well.[85] In the last quarter of the seventh century, episcopal, national and local politics coincided with increasing frequency, to cause difficulties for bishops, as at Autun and in the Auvergne, to which we shall return,[86] and at Maastricht.[87] Local rivalries and conflicts were ever present, but, at least in the sixth and seventh centuries, they were not a challenge to the central position of the royal court.

The court in action

Since the court of Chlothar and later of Dagobert provided the chief focus for the kingdom, it is necessary to be more specific about its structure, and its

77. *Vita Desiderii*, 2, 7.
78. *Vita Desiderii*, 8.
79. *Vita Desiderii*, 12.
80. *Vita Desiderii*, 16.
81. Wood, 'Administration, law and culture in Merovingian Gaul', pp. 74–5.
82. *Vita Desiderii*, 8.
83. *Vita Desiderii*, 39, 40.
84. See chapter 5.
85. *Vita Eligii*, II 6.
86. See chapter 13.
87. *Vita Landiberti episcopi Traiectensis vetustissima*, 5, 11–17.

importance. Throughout the Merovingian period it was a peripatetic institution: although some kings had favourite palaces and shrines, there was no fixed centre. The court was the royal household on the move. It was staffed by several officials, of whom the *maior domus*, or 'greater man of the royal household (palace)' was becoming increasingly significant. There were also a treasurer, various treasury officials, a *comes palatii*, or count of the palace, and a host of household officers, including notaries and scribes. When it comes to defining their duties, however, it is often very difficult to apportion specific tasks to particular servants. The *maior* and the *comes palatii* clearly had important administrative and, particularly, legal functions at court, but they could be employed elsewhere, and *comites* from other parts of the kingdom could subscribe to documents at the royal palace. The treasurer and various officials connected with the treasury tended to be involved in aspects of royal finance and the collection of dues; at the same time they could be employed in other ways, for instance on diplomatic missions. There are some writing-officers who appear to have been responsible for a number of royal documents, but there are others who appear only once, and who may have been drafted in for a single occasion. All in all the picture is one of fluidity, with the court being able to draw on a pool of competent servants, and assign them a range of tasks; title perhaps being a better guide to status than to the exact sphere of activity of any single individual.

Most royal officials would have had to read and write, and these skills seem to have been reasonably widespread among the political classes, and among the abler servants: although Merovingian Latin was not classically correct, there is nothing to suggest that illiteracy was the norm in the upper levels of society in the seventh century.[88] The kings of the Merovingian period were unquestionably literate, which is more than can be said for many later medieval rulers. In describing the childhood of Chlothar I's supposed son Gundovald, Gregory states that he was brought up in the manner of the Merovingians, and was educated: *litteris eruditus*.[89] Exactly how learned this would have left a young prince is open to question, but Chilperic I, who may well have been Gundovald's half-brother, could write poetry of a sort and indulge in theology.[90] For the kings of the seventh and eighth centuries we are less well informed, but they could write, and their signatures survive at the foot of many charters.[91]. The charters also reveal that the major court scribes had a mastery of a very complicated form of shorthand, known as Tironian notes, after Cicero's secretary Tiro. These provided one of the chief means of authenticating documents.[92] For others a knowledge of law would have been more useful. The author of the *Vita Desiderii* commented on his

88. Wood, 'Adminstration, law and culture in Merovingian Gaul', pp. 66–7.

89. Gregory, *Decem Libri Historiarum*, VI 24.

90. Gregory, *Decem Libri Historiarum*, V 44; Chilperic, *Ymnus in sollemnitate s. Medardi*.

91. Wood, 'Administration, law and culture in Merovingian Gaul', pp. 67.

92. D. Ganz, 'Bureaucratic shorthand and Merovingian learning', in P. Wormald, ed., *Ideal and Reality in Frankish and Anglo-Saxon Society*, pp. 61–2.

subject's competence in Roman law,[93] and similar comments are made about Bonitus, who held several offices under Dagobert's son, Sigibert III, first at court and later in Provence, before returning to his native town of Clermont as bishop.[94]

Chlothar II, Dagobert I and the Church

The *Lives* of saints such as Eligius, Audoin and Desiderius shed light on the royal court under Chlothar II and Dagobert I. Their careers emphasize the dovetailing of Church and State in the Merovingian kingdom. This is equally apparent in the evidence of Church councils. The ecclesiastical Council of Paris of 614, which immediately preceded the promulgation of Chlothar's edict, was among the most imposing held in Merovingian Francia. It was attended by twelve metropolitans and fifty-six Frankish bishops, together with two clerics from Kent. It was held within months of the overthrow of Brunhild and should almost certainly be seen as a council assembled to mark Chlothar's acquisition of the whole kingdom. Like many other Merovingian Church councils, it was summoned by the king and it met, significantly enough, in the basilica of St Peter, in Paris, that is the church of the Holy Apostles, which had been founded by Clovis, perhaps in imitation of Constantine, and which served as his mausoleum.[95] A sizeable number of the Church canons are concerned with matters of interest to secular officials; clergy are not to seek secular help against their bishops;[96] judges are not to condemn clerics without their bishop's knowledge,[97] and so forth. There are also several canons concerned with Church property; in particular no bishop or layman was to take advantage of the division of the kingdom to seize the possessions of another bishop or a church.[98] The more overtly ecclesiastical legislation was also of concern to the king. There is even some tension implied between what the bishops had to say about episcopal appointments, and what the king ordered in his edict eight days later. The synod insisted that bishops be elected by the metropolitan, together with the clergy and people of the diocese.[99] The king's edict reserved the right of veto, and envisaged the election of members of the palace staff.[100]

Thirteen or fourteen years later Chlothar summoned another Church council, this time to the basilica of St Mary on the royal estate of Clichy. Again there are clauses of secular significance; in particular no one subject to

93. *Vita Desiderii*, 1; Wood, 'Administration, law and culture in Merovingian Gaul', p. 67.
94. *Vita Boniti*, 2, 3.
95. Council of Paris (614), *titulus;* Gregory, *Decem Libri Historiarum*, II 43.
96. Council of Paris (614), 5.
97. Council of Paris (614), 6.
98. Council of Paris (614), 11.
99. Council of Paris (614), 2.
100. *Capitularia Merowingica*, 9, 1.

the *census* was to enter the religious life without the permission of the king or a judge.[101] The bishops also legislated on a matter directly related to judicial inquiry; no slave or man of low birth could make an accusation, and anyone who had brought forward one accusation that had failed was barred from making any more.[102] Although there is no royal edict associated with this second council, it is possible that it too was a major gathering of bishops and laymen. Fredegar records just such a gathering at Clichy, which he dates a year later than the date given in the canons.[103] According to Fredegar, Chlothar summoned the bishops and magnates of Neustria and Burgundy *pro utilitate regia et salute patriae*. The absence of any reference to Austrasians may be significant, since bishops from Austrasia did attend the synod whose canons survive. The gathering recorded by Fredegar was marred by an outbreak of violence in which an official of Charibert's household was killed, with the result that the prince's uncle, Brodulf, gathered a force to attack the killers.

Chlothar II and Dagobert I depended on their bishops for their advice and support. They also relied on the shrines of the saints; Dagobert was especially devoted to the shrine of St Denis just outside Paris. A church had been built to house the remains of the saint by the virgin Genovefa in the late fifth century, but it was not until Dagobert's reign that the cult received the full backing of the Frankish monarchy.[104] According to the late and unreliable *Gesta Dagoberti I* the prince was indebted to the martyr and his companions for protecting him against his father's anger; as a result Dagobert rebuilt the church and richly endowed it as a monastic foundation with treasure and land.[105] That he was responsible for promoting the cult and enriching the martyr's shrine is not in doubt, whatever the cause of his generosity.[106] As a result St Denis became the saint most closely associated with the Merovingian dynasty.[107]

Sigibert III and Clovis II

In 639 Dagobert died and was buried in St Denis. He left two sons: Sigibert III, who had already been set over the sub-kingdom of Austrasia for six years,[108] and Clovis II, who was still a minor.[109] Shortly after the birth of Clovis, at the request of the Neustrians, Dagobert had arranged with Sigibert and the Austrasians that the new prince should inherit Neustro-Burgundy: the division between Neustro-Burgundy and Austrasia was, therefore,

101. Council of Clichy (626/7), 8.
102. Council of Clichy (626/7), 17.
103. Fredegar, IV 55.
104. Wallace-Hadrill, *The Frankish Church*, pp. 126–9.
105. *Gesta Dagoberti I*, 7–11.
106. Fredegar, IV 79; Wallace-Hadrill, *The Frankish Church*, pp. 126–9.
107. Wallace-Hadrill, *The Long-Haired Kings*, pp. 224–5.
108. Fredegar, IV 75.
109. Fredegar, IV 79.

perpetuated.[110] This is probably best not interpreted as a sign of separatism within the kingdom, although it might well be indicative of the power of different political factions. Sigibert, the son of Ragnetrude,[111] and his supporters were already established in power in Austrasia. Clovis's mother, Nantechild, and her supporters, therefore, were dependent on their prince succeeding to the Neustrian throne.

The dominant figures of the early years of Sigibert and Clovis were to a large extent those who had come to the fore under Dagobert and even Chlothar. In Neustria the office of *maior* was held by Aega, who had been Dagobert's chief adviser.[112] From Fredegar he receives a good press, but Jonas refers to him as a persecutor of the nunnery of Faremoutiers.[113] Otherwise he remains obscure. After his death, Erchinoald, a relative of Dagobert's mother, was appointed in his place.[114] Perhaps more important than either of these two men was Nantechild, the queen-mother. Once again a royal minority provided an opportunity for a royal woman to exert her authority. Shortly before Aega's death his son-in-law was responsible for a murder at court, and it was apparently Nantechild who authorized the exacting of revenge.[115] It was she, too, who persuaded the Burgundians to agree to the renewal of the office of *maior*, and who appointed Flaochad to the position.[116] The appointment, however, very quickly led to conflict, particularly between Flaochad and the Burgundian magnate Willebad, and after the death of Nantechild the conflict escalated into a pitched battle in which Willebad was killed. Flaochad died a few days later, of fever.[117] It may be that Willebad's opposition to the *maior* was prompted by the fact that the latter was a Frank and not a Burgundian, as Herpo had been thirty years before. But since the two of them had often sworn friendship together, it may well be that political jealousy was the sole cause of the conflict.

With the deaths of Willehad and Flaochad Fredegar's *Chronicle* ends, and despite the *Liber Historiae Francorum*, and the continuations to Fredegar which are based on it, there is no single narrative source of any stature for the second half of the seventh century. Nevertheless, other types of evidence, notably saints' *Lives* and charters, provide plenty of information for Neustria in the 660s and later. The two decades that fall between, that is the period of Clovis II's adult rule, are unfortunately badly served. Even so, the little that can be said about the policies of Clovis provides an important bridge between our knowledge of early- and late-seventh-century Francia.

110. Fredegar, IV 76.
111. Fredegar, IV 59.
112. Fredegar, IV 62, 79, 80, 83.
113. Jonas, *Vita Columbani*, II 17. Both Fredegar, IV 80, and *Gesta Dagoberti I,* 45, however, comment on his avarice.
114. Fredegar, IV 84.
115. Fredegar, IV 83.
116. Fredegar, IV 89.
117. Fredegar, IV 90.

To the author of the *Liber Historiae Francorum* Clovis was profligate and avaricious. Among his evil deeds his attempt to seize the arm of St Denis is singled out for special opprobrium.[118] According to the *Gesta Dagoberti I*, his taking of the relic drove Clovis mad.[119] Set in the context of the relationship between the crown and the cult of St Denis the escapade makes some sense. Clovis was intent on securing part of the martyr for himself. Although the monks may have seen the act as spoliation, Clovis was by no means hostile to the cult which his father had revered. He took relics of the martyr, an act which should be seen as a mark of his devotion to the saint, and of his desire to associate the dynasty more closely with his cult, however it was interpreted by the monks. Equally damaging for his relations with the community of St Denis may have been the fact that he took large quantities of silver, which Dagobert had given to decorate the apse of the monastic church, in order to relieve the poor.[120] Yet at the same time Clovis conferred estates on the monastery and, more important, he persuaded Landeric, bishop of Paris, to grant the community a privilege of immunity from episcopal interference.[121] This and other immunities of Clovis's reign established a pattern which was continued by the king's widow, Balthild, after his death in 657. In this respect, while continuing his father's interest in the cult of St Denis, Clovis laid the foundations of some of the ecclesiastical developments of the middle of the century.

The evidence for the reign of Dagobert's other son, Sigibert III, is rather poorer. According to Fredegar, Sigibert's chief advisers in Austrasia were Pippin, who had been Dagobert's *maior* during Chlothar's lifetime, and Chunibert, bishop of Cologne, who had taken over the political importance of Arnulf, when the latter retired to live the religious life.[122] Fredegar's narrative also reveals that the faction-fighting which had been a marked feature of politics twenty years earlier again became a matter of importance after Pippin's death in the late 630s. Otto, the son of Sigibert's tutor, took over as *maior*, much to the fury of Pippin's son, Grimoald; it was not until 643 that Grimoald could engineer his murder and take over the office for himself.[123] And there may be further evidence of hostility to Pippin's family: in 639 Fara, the son of Pippin's old opponent, Chrodoald, joined the rebellion of Radulf, *dux* of Thuringia.[124]

Radulf's revolt was successful: Sigibert, still a minor, was defeated and had to be hurried away ignominiously. As a result Radulf declared himself king of an independent Thuringia.[125] The defeat of Sigibert III has been seen as a

118. *Liber Historiae Francorum*, 44.
119. *Gesta Dagoberti I*, 52.
120. *Gesta Dagoberti I*, 50.
121. *Gesta Dagoberti I*, 50, 51.
122. Fredegar, IV 85.
123. Fredegar, IV 86, 88.
124. Fredegar, IV 52, 87.
125. Fredegar, IV 87.

crucial moment in the decline of Merovingian power.[126] To see it in this light runs the risk of ignoring the significance of some of the kings of the next two generations. Nevertheless, as we shall see, the set-back in Thuringia did have important implications for the relations between the Merovingians and the peoples east of the Rhine, which had been a major area of Frankish influence for well over a century.

126. Wallace-Hadrill, *The Long-Haired Kings*, p. 234.

Chapter Ten

The Merovingians and their Neighbours

Although the political and governmental history of the Merovingians centres around the activities of the royal court and its agents in Neustria, Austrasia, Burgundy and Aquitaine, the influence of the Frankish kings was very much more widespread. Indeed relations with the neighbouring peoples provide perhaps the best indication of the real extent of Merovingian power. Dealings with the Ostrogoths, Visigoths and Lombards show what prestige the Merovingians had in the other courts of Europe, while nearer to home the greatest kings were able to dominate the Bretons, Thuringians, Bavarians and Saxons; the ability to control the peoples east of the Rhine and other immediate neighbours of the Franks was almost a barometer of Frankish power at any given moment.

Brittany

It is difficult to determine the exact status of Brittany within the Merovingian kingdom. When Chramn fell foul of his father, Chlothar I, he fled to Brittany, where he clearly thought that he was out of his father's reach.[1] Equally indicative of the independence of the Bretons are their recurrent raids against the people of the lower Loire, which prompted retaliatory expeditions by Chilperic I and Guntram, a war with Childebert II and threats from Dagobert I.[2] After each retaliation or threat the Bretons sued for peace. This submissive aspect of Breton politics, is apparent in Gregory of Tours's descriptions of the rulers of Brittany as if they were local Frankish officials, *comites*.[3] The balance of submission and independence is also apparent at the

---

1. Gregory, *Decem Libri Historiarum*, IV 20.
2. Gregory, *Decem Libri Historiarum*, V 26; X 9; Fredegar, IV 15, 78.
3. Gregory, *Decem Libri Historiarum*, IV 4.

time of Guntram's punitive raid against Brittany in 590, when Fredegund sent a force of Saxons to help the Bretons against the invading army of Guntram.[4]

Gregory's diocese was close to the border with the Bretons, and he kept a professional eye on the activities of his western neighbours. Tours indeed claimed metropolitan status over the Breton Church.[5] Further, the bishops of those dioceses which bordered on Brittany could play an influential role in Breton politics: in his account of the conflict between *comes* Chanao and his brother Macliaw, Gregory relates the success of Felix, bishop of Nantes, in freeing Macliaw.[6] In addition clerics from Brittany can be found within Francia at this time; Bishop Samson, who came to be associated with the diocese of Dol, attended the Council of Paris in 561/2,[7] and he had connections with the court of Childebert I.[8]

Unfortunately, but inevitably, evidence for relations between Franks and Bretons becomes much less good after the death of Gregory. The *Vita Eligii* records a diplomatic mission which concluded with the saint negotiating peace with the Breton *princeps*, whom he brought back to Dagobert's court.[9] Presumably it is to the same events that Fredegar refers in recording Dagobert's threatened campaign against the Bretons, which prompted the submission of their *rex* Judicael. The account of this in Fredegar says much about Breton fear of Dagobert, but even more about the religious reputation of his then referendary, Audoin, with whom Judicael dined.[10] This episode in relations between Bretons and the seventh-century Merovingians is unusual in appearing in more than one source. Thereafter there is a dearth of evidence until the compilation of the so-called *Annales Mettenses Priores*, or Prior Metz Annals, compiled probably at St Denis in 806 or thereabouts.[11] They list the Bretons among a number of peoples supposedly subdued by Pippin II in 691.[12] Whether this is a reliable statement is open to question: glorification of the Carolingians was one of the purposes of the *Annales Mettenses Priores*.[13]

Frisia and the lands to the east of the Rhine

There are similar problems when it comes to determining the status of much of the area to the east of the Rhine. Gregory's account of Hygelac's raid, and

4. Gregory, *Decem Libri Historiarum*, X 9.
5. Council of Tours (567), 9.
6. Gregory, *Decem Libri Historiarum*, IV 4.
7. Council of Paris (561/2), subscriptions; the date is from Pontal, *Die Synoden im Merowingerreich*, p. 122; see also the subscriptions for the Councils of Orléans (511) and Tours (567) for bishops of Rennes and Vannes.
8. *Vita Samsonis*, I 53; see Wood, 'Forgery in Merovingian hagiography', pp. 381–2.
9. *Vita Eligii*, I 13.
10. Fredegar, IV 78.
11. Wallace-Hadrill, *The Frankish Church*, p. 141.
12. *Annales Mettenses Priores*, s.a. 691.
13. R. McKitterick, *The Frankish Kingdoms under the Carolingians, 751–987*, pp. 7, 24.

its defeat at the hands of Theudebert I,[14] seems to suggest that the Merovingians already controlled the lower Rhine in the second or third decades of the sixth century. Indeed there is little evidence for an independent Frisia in the early Merovingian period, other than a coin issue with the inscriptions AVDVLFVS FRISIA and VICTVRIA AVDVLFO, assigned to the sixth century.[15] This has to be set against the poems of Venantius Fortunatus, where Chilperic terrorizes the Frisians.[16] Nevertheless, the history of mission implies that the Franks paid little attention to the area before the reign of Dagobert I, who established a missionary outpost at Utrecht.[17] The later problems faced by Willibrord and Boniface show that Dagobert's policies were of only temporary value.[18]

To the south, Clovis seems to have taken over territories of the Alamans after his victory in *c.* 506.[19] The region, nevertheless, retained its own identity, with its own *duces*,[20] and its own law-code, perhaps issued by Chlothar II.[21] By the early eighth century, however, the laws are indicative of independence from Merovingian rule, since they were reissued by the *dux*, Lantfrid.[22] The religious history of the upper Rhine adds a little more detail. In the early seventh century Theudebert II supported the activities of Columbanus in the region of Bregenz.[23] Eighth-century traditions about Columbanus's pupil, Gallus, however, depict the Bodensee as being on the fringe of Merovingian authority,[24] and this may imply that the secular and religious authorities of the area were left largely to their own devices.

Further to the east Bavaria presents particular problems of interpretation. Although there are a number of references to the region in Merovingian and Carolingian sources, a good proportion of the evidence comes from the pen of the Lombard, Paul the Deacon, writing at the end of the eighth century. He rated the authority of the local rulers very much higher than did other writers. Thus, according to Gregory of Tours, Chlothar I conferred Theudebald's widow, Wuldetrada, on the *dux* Garivald.[25] To Paul, Garivald was king of the Bavarians.[26] Subsequently Paul also records that Childebert II made Tassilo king,[27] affirming the royal nature of Agilolfing power, as well as Merovingian involvement in its institution. Garivald and Tassilo were both

14. Gregory, *Decem Libri Historiarum*, III 3.

15. Grierson and Blackburn, *Medieval European Coinage*, 1, *The Early Middle Ages (5th–10th Centuries)*, p. 137.

16. Venantius Fortunatus, carm. IX 1, ll. 75–6.

17. Boniface, ep. 109.

18. See chapter 18.

19. Gregory, *Decem Libri Historiarum*, II 30.

20. Fredegar, IV 8, 68, 88.

21. *Lex Alamannorum*, Cod. B, *incipit*; see also chapter 7.

22. *Lex Alamannorum*, Cod. A, *incipit*.

23. Jonas, *Vita Columbani*, I 27.

24. *Vitae Galli vetustissimae fragmentum.*

25. Gregory, *Decem Libri Historiarum*, IV 9; Paul, *Historia Langobardorum*, I 21.

26. Paul, *Historia Langobardorum*, III 10, 30.

27. Paul, *Historia Langobardorum*, IV 7.

members of the Agilolfing dynasty, and through Theudelinda, daughter of Garivald, they were related to a number of Lombard kings.[28] Paul may have misrepresented the status of Garivald and Tassilo because of this relationship. Alternatively Gregory may have oversimplified matters in reducing Garivald to the status of *dux*. That the Merovingians did dominate Bavaria, at least in the early seventh century, is, however, clear from Merovingian involvement in the compilation of the *Lex Baiwariorum*.[29] Dagobert, moreover, was able to exercise some authority in the region: according to Fredegar he settled a group of Bulgarians in Bavaria and then ordered their execution.[30]

The balance between subordination to central Frankish power and independent authority to be found in the Agilolfing position shifted during the seventh century. Bavaria became something of a haven for opponents of the Pippinid faction which came to dominate the royal court after 687: the secular power of the Agilolfing family was clearly substantial enough to offer protection against the Pippinids. Thus, bishop Rupert of Salzburg fled from Francia, probably out of hostility to Pippin II.[31] By the early eighth century Bavaria seems to have had closer links with Lombard Italy than with Merovingian Francia: at least that is what is suggested by the *Life of Corbinian*, composed at the end of the century by Arbeo of Freising.[32] The evidence, therefore, suggests that at some point after Dagobert's reign Bavaria moved out of the Frankish sphere of influence.

The unstable nature of Frankish dominance is further illustrated by the history of Thuringia, north of Bavaria. After it had been crushed by Theuderic I and Chlothar I in the 520s Thuringia seems to have been subordinated to the east Frankish kingdom.[33] That there was some resentment against Frankish rule is indicated by the fact that the Thuringians supported a Saxon revolt against Chlothar in the mid-550s.[34] There was a subsequent rebellion against Childebert II forty years later,[35] but both Saxons and Thuringians fought for Theudebert II against Theuderic II in the civil war of 612.[36] In the reign of Dagobert I, Thuringia was subject to a number of attacks by the Wends, which were repulsed by the *dux* Radulf.[37] According to Fredegar, Radulf's military success was one of the factors which prompted his revolt against Sigibert III, as a result of which he called himself king of Thuringia.[38]

---

28. Fredegar, IV 34.
29. See chapter 7.
30. Fredegar, IV 72.
31. *Vita Hrodberti episcopi Salisburgensis*, 1–4; P. Geary, *Before France and Germany*, p. 210; Wallace-Hadrill, *The Frankish Church*, p. 147.
32. Arbeo, *Vita Corbiniani*, 16, 21.
33. Gregory, *Decem Libri Historiarum*, III 7.
34. Gregory, *Decem Libri Historiarum*, IV 10.
35. Fredegar, IV 15 (where the Thuringians are referred to as Warni).
36. Fredegar, IV 38.
37. Fredegar, IV 68, 74, 75, 77.
38. Fredegar, IV 87.

East of the Rhine Radulf's uprising does seem to have had a long-term impact on Merovingian authority. Although evidence for the region falters after 639, the ninth-century *Passio Kiliani* implies a period of independence under Radulf's successors, Hetan I, and his son Gozbert, who was said to have been converted by the seventh-century missionary Kilian.[39] The paganism of Gozbert may be a further indication of independence from Merovingian power, but his son, Hetan II, was unquestionably a Christian and a supporter of Willibrord.[40] Despite this, he seems to have fallen foul of the Carolingians, since he was driven from his *regnum* by the East Franks according to the *Passio Kiliani*.[41] Thereafter Boniface worked in Thuringia with Carolingian approval.[42] When Charles Martel divided his power between his two sons in 740 he assigned Austrasia, Alamannia and Thuringia to Carloman.[43] Thuringia was clearly back under Frankish control.

Less accessible to the Merovingians, Saxony was nevertheless subject to their influence. Gregory of Tours implies that the Saxons became a subject people in the time of Theuderic I,[44] and he clearly regarded them as rebels in the mid-550s when they defeated Chlothar I.[45] Although Gregory has no more to say about Saxony, it appears that before Chlothar died he re-established Frankish overlordship and forced the Saxons to pay a tribute of five hundred cows each year. According to Fredegar this arrangement continued until the time of Dagobert I, when the Saxons offered to provide military protection of the eastern frontier against the Wends instead.[46] In fact it is debatable whether tribute was paid annually from the time of Chlothar I through to that of Dagobert I, since there is a reference in the *Liber Historiae Francorum* to Chilperic I and Sigibert I campaigning against the Saxons,[47] which may find some support in the poems of Venantius Fortunatus.[48] The *Liber Historiae Francorum* describes a further Saxon rebellion directed against Dagobert I when he was sub-king in Austrasia.[49] Chlothar II's intervention to save Dagobert became the subject of verse, and in the ninth century women were said to have sung about the campaign.[50] As in the case of other subject peoples, the Saxons fade from the record in the late seventh century, only to reappear in the eighth, when they joined the coalition which opposed Charles

39. *Passio Kiliani*, 2, 7.
40. See his charters for Willibrord, in 704, 716; Willibald, *Vita Bonifatii*, ed. R. Rau, p. 495, n.11.
41. *Passio Kiliani*, 14.
42. Boniface, ep. 48.
43. Fredegar, cont. 23.
44. Gregory, *Decem Libri Historiarum*, IV 10.
45. Gregory, *Decem Libri Historiarum*, IV 14, 16.
46. Fredegar, IV 74; I.N. Wood, *The Merovingian North Sea*, pp. 9–10.
47. *Liber Historiae Francorum*, 31.
48. Venantius Fortunatus, carm., VI 1a, ll. 7–18; VII 7, ll. 49–60; VII 16, l. 47; IX 1, ll. 73–6; Wood, *The Merovingian North Sea*, p. 10; George, *Venantius Fortunatus: A Latin Poet in Merovingian Gaul*, pp. 40–1, 79, 81.
49. *Liber Historiae Francorum*, 41; *Gesta Dagoberti I*, 14.
50. *Vita Faronis*, 78.

Martel.[51] Charles and his sons Carloman and Pippin III all fought campaigns against them,[52] although a third son, Gripho, was actually supported by Saxons.[53] Pippin III eventually reinstituted the tribute that had been imposed by Chlothar I.[54] Under Charlemagne Saxony was finally integrated into the Carolingian state, and only then was paganism, which had become a key element in Saxon independence under Widukind, crushed.[55]

The relationship between the Merovingians and their eastern neighbours was a crucial aspect of Frankish power and politics. The tribute owed by the Saxons was substantial. Of equal importance were the military resources which could be drawn upon by powerful Austrasian kings. Sigibert I, Theudebert II and Sigibert II are all known to have drawn on the peoples across the Rhine for help in their civil wars.[56] On the other hand Childebert I and Chramn both timed an attack on Chlothar I to coincide with problems in the East.[57] In this respect the eastern frontier was an ambivalent factor in Merovingian politics. It presented considerable problems in the shape of Saxon and Thuringian rebellions and of Hunnic or Wendish invasions, but at the same time it offered enormous potential for the more successful Merovingian kings. Anyone who could harness the power of the eastern peoples could genuinely be regarded as exercising overlordship, such as that envisaged by Venatius Fortunatus, or the author of the *Annales Mettenses Priores*. Effectively, the greatest of the Merovingians had hegemonial influence east of the Rhine: it was neither firmly institutionalized nor constant, depending rather on military prowess and prestige, but it could be very considerable. It seems not to have lasted beyond Radulf's rebellion in 639, and in this respect the reign of Sigibert III may mark a decline in Merovingian power.

Italy

Relations with Italy in the days of Theodoric the Great were different in kind. The Ostrogoths were never the inferiors of the Franks. Theodoric unquestionably saw himself as the arbiter of western Europe, and tried in vain to lecture Clovis on how to behave.[58] It was also he who provided the defeated Alamans with a refuge,[59] and who set himself up to avenge the defeat of the Visigoths at 'Vouillé'.[60] The Burgundians, however, rather than

51. Fredegar, cont., 11.
52. Fredegar, cont., 19, 27, 31, 35.
53. *Annales Mettenses Priores*, s.a. 748, 749.
54. Fredegar, cont., 31, 35.
55. McKitterick, *The Frankish Kingdoms under the Carolingians, 751–987*, pp. 61–3.
56. Gregory, *Decem Libri Historiarum*, IV 49, 50; Fredegar, IV 38, 40.
57. Gregory, *Decem Libri Historiarum*, IV 16.
58. Cassiodorus, *Variae*, II 41; III 4.
59. Cassiodorus, Variae, II 41; Ennodius, *Panegyric*, 72–3; Wolfram *History of the Goths*, p. 314.
60. Wolfram, *History of the Goths*, pp. 243–6.

the Franks, suffered from Theodoric's incursions across the Alps.[61] Meanwhile, in 508, the emperor Anastasius honoured Clovis with some kind of consular office,[62] apparently with the intention of raising his status above that of the Ostrogothic king. When Clovis died, however, it seems to have been the Burgundian kings, Gundobad and his son Sigismund, who were rewarded by the emperor with the title of *magister militum*.[63] By 519 the Ostrogoths were firmly back in imperial favour with Theodoric's son-in-law, Eutharic, receiving the consulship.[64] The shifting interests of imperial diplomacy may not tell us much about the realities of power within Gaul, although the second decade of the sixth century does seem to have been a fallow period in terms of Frankish military success, except perhaps for Theuderic I in the Rhineland.

Later involvement in Ostrogothic Italy came only in the wake of Justinian's invasion, when first Theudebert I and later Theudebald sent expeditions against the Ostrogoths. Unfortunately the evidence for these expeditions is far from satisfactory, although the contemporary histories by Gregory of Tours, Procopius and Agathias provide many fragments of detail. For the Byzantine historians, the involvement of the Franks was a side-issue, despite the apparent Frankish annexation of territory in Italy at this time,[65] and despite the alarm caused in Constantinople by Theudebert's policies.[66] For Gregory, the Ostrogothic campaigns of Theudebert and Theudebald were simply confusing, as can be seen from his account of Buccelin's expedition, which he wrongly assigned to the reign of Theudebert, and which he saw as an achievement of heroic proportions.[67] His account in this instance is closer to legend than history. Nevertheless the Italian wars of the successors of Theuderic I were important in so far as they marked the beginning of Frankish military interest in Italy, which was to continue throughout the wars of Justinian against the Ostrogoths and beyond the arrival of the Lombards in Italy in 568. They were also significant in that they affected relations between the Franks and the Byzantines, who tried by diplomatic means to harness the Merovingian armies to imperial policy.

The Lombard occupation of northern Italy did not just mean the substitution of one neighbour for another, because relations between the Franks and the Lombards were already well established long before the latter had migrated across the Alps. In certain respects for the fifty years before 568 the Lombards need to be seen in the context of other peoples who lived to the east of the Rhine. Thus Chlodoswintha, daughter of Chlothar I, married

61. Wolfram, *History of the Goths*, pp. 311–13.
62. Gregory, *Decem Libri Historiarum*, II 38; McCormick, *Eternal Victory*, pp. 335–7.
63. Avitus, epp. 93–4.
64. Wolfram, *History of the Goths*, p. 328.
65. Procopius, *Wars*, VII 33, 7; VIII 14, 4, 6–8; Wolfram, *History of the Goths*, pp. 347–8, 355.
66. Agathias, I 4, 1–4; see also chapter 4.
67. Gregory, *Decem Libri Historiarum*, III 32; IV 9.

the Lombard king Alboin.[68] Nicetius, bishop of Trier, hoped in vain that the marriage would lead the king to convert to catholicism.[69] Theudebert I married Wisigard, daughter of the Lombard king Waccho,[70] and his son Theudebald later married another of Waccho's daughters, Wuldetrada (see Figure 1).[71] On Theudebald's death Chlothar took over his widow, but was

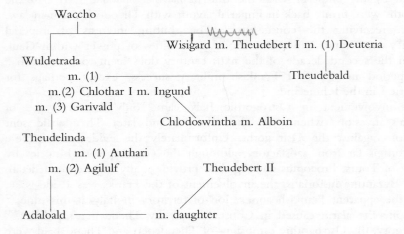

Figure 1   Merovingian – Lombard marriages

forced to give her up; he then handed her on to Garivald of Bavaria.[72] This marriage was to be of great importance, since the daughter of Wuldetrada and Garivald, Theudelinda, could claim to be descended from Lombard royalty. She was betrothed to Childebert II, but he rejected her on Brunhild's advice. She later married the Lombard king Authari.[73] He had previously negotiated to marry Childebert's sister, Chlodosind, but was passed over in favour of the Visigothic king Reccared. In the event the marriage of Chlodosind did not take place.[74] It was, nevertheless, Theudelinda who became queen of the Lombards. Moreover, on Authari's death in 590 she married Agilulf, remaining queen and ensuring his succession.[75] As Agilulf's queen she held a key position in pope Gregory the Great's policies towards the Lombards, who presented a constant threat to Rome.[76] Equally important was the status conferred on her paternal (Bavarian) relatives through her association with the Lombard crown.

68. Gregory, *Decem Libri Historiarum*, IV 3, 41.
69. *Epistulae Austrasiacae*, 8.
70. Gregory, *Decem Libri Historiarum*, III 20, 27; Paul, *Historia Langobardorum*, I 21.
71. Gregory, *Decem Libri Historiarum*, IV 9; Paul, *Historia Langobardorum*, I 21.
72. Gregory, *Decem Libri Historiarum*, IV 9.
73. Fredegar, IV 34.
74. Gregory, *Decem Libri Historiarum*, IX 16, 20, 25, 28.
75. Paul, *Historia Langobardorum*, III 30, 35; Fredegar, IV 34, is confused.
76. Gregory I, *Register*, IV 4; IX 67; XIV 12.

About the year 600 Agilulf's son Adaloald married a daughter of Theudebert II.[77] No further marriage alliances between the Franks and the Lombards are recorded, and in this respect there is a marked difference between the relations of the two peoples in the seventh century and those of the later sixth. Nevertheless the Merovingians appear to have regarded Theudelinda's daughter, Gundeperga, as a relative. According to Fredegar she married the Lombard king, Arioald, who later imprisoned her, until a deputation from Chlothar II led to her reinstatement.[78] Later she married Rothari, forcing him to set aside his wife, in return for her support in making him king.[79] The parallel between her behaviour on the death of Arioald and that of her mother, Theudelinda, on the death of Authari, is an important indication of the role which royal widows could play in the Lombard succession. Nevertheless, despite her importance, Rothari, like Arioald, locked Gundeperga away, but was frightened into releasing her by an envoy of Clovis II, or so Fredegar relates.[80] Paul the Deacon's version of events is rather different. In his account Gundeperga married not Rothari but his successor, Rodoald, and it was he who set her aside.[81] In this account her reinstatement owed nothing to the Merovingians. Chronologically Fredegar's version is more likely to be accurate, and it may well be right to emphasize Merovingian interest in the family affairs of the Lombard kings. Where Paul's emphasis is valuable is in Gundeperga's building activities at Pavia, in imitation of what her mother had done at Monza, which shed valuable light on the practice of queenship among the Lombards.[82]

Marriage alliances were only one aspect of relations between the Franks and the Lombards. For the half century following 568 military conflict was a recurrent theme. Already in the early 570s Lombard armies were crossing the Alps into Francia, presumably in search of plunder. After the murder of Alboin in 572 and that of Cleph in 573 the raids escalated,[83] perhaps partly because there was no king to control the Lombard military leadership. The threat presented to Burgundy gave several Merovingian generals the opportunity to distinguish themselves, and to rise to positions of considerable power, the most notable being Guntram's *dux*, Mummolus.[84] At the same time the Franks began to shift the war zone into Italy, at first simply in retaliation, but later in collaboration with the Byzantines, whose hopes of reconquering parts of the west were on the increase. In 584, 585 and 590 the emperor Maurice sent quantities of gold to Childebert II, to involve him in his Lombard campaigns. On each occasion Childebert sent an expedition into

77. Paul, *Historia Langobardorum*, IV 30.
78. Fredegar, IV 34, 51.
79. Fredegar, IV 70.
80. Fredegar, IV 71.
81. Paul, *Historia Langobardorum*, IV 47.
82. Paul, *Historia Langobardorum*, IV 47.
83. Gregory, *Decem Libri Historiarum*, IV 42; Paul, *Historia Langobardorum*, III 1–4, 8–9.
84. Gregory, *Decem Libri Historiarum*, IV 42; Paul, *Historia Langobardorum*, III 8.

Italy. In 584 the Lombards quickly came to terms, and the Franks withdrew, much to the fury of the Byzantines.[85] In 585 Childebert again complied with Maurice's demands, in part because his sister was said to be in Constantinople. His generals, however, were at loggerheads one with another, and achieved nothing.[86] In 589 he was no more successful.[87] A year later, despite Frankish military successes, the planned collaboration of Frankish and Byzantine armies failed, and dysentery forced Childebert's generals to withdraw.[88] It was apparently between Reccared's betrothal to Chlodosind in 588 and the 590 campaign, that Authari took Theudelinda as his wife. This suggests that the Lombards were using marriage alliances to keep the Franks at bay, first by seeking a Merovingian queen, and then by drawing the Bavarians into a defensive alliance against the Franks.

The majority of the evidence for these wars is preserved by Gregory, and copied with some differences by Paul. The rather different information relating to this period, which is recorded by Fredegar, needs to be seen in the light of Gregory's information. According to Fredegar the Lombards agreed in the early 580s to pay a substantial annual tribute of twelve thousand *solidi*, and in addition they offered Guntram Aosta and Susa. Shortly after, Guntram and Childebert II agreed to the elevation of Authari as king. The tribute was apparently paid throughout the reign of Authari, into that of Agilulf, when Chlothar II was given a lump sum of thirty-six thousand *solidi*, and some of his leading advisers were suitably bribed to accept the deal.[89] Fredegar's account with its emphasis on tribute and cooperation certainly sits awkwardly with that of Gregory, which emphasizes war. Moreover, there are reasons for thinking that he was wrong to see the Lombards, rather than the Byzantines as being in possession of Susa.[90] On the other hand Susa was certainly in Frankish hands in the early eighth century.[91] It is possible, however, that Fredegar does offer genuine information about relations between Authari and Guntram, who throughout the 580s pursued a different foreign policy from that of his nephew Childebert. Contemporary Merovingian kings in fact often developed rival foreign policies: they competed outside Francia almost as much as they did inside the *regnum Francorum*.[92] But although the rulers of Burgundy sometimes dealt separately with the Lombards, it was usually the kings of Austrasia who pursued the dominant Italian policy in any given period. This is true not only of Childebert II, but also of his son Theudebert II, whose daughter married Adaloald, and whose agents attended the elevation of the prince, during Agilulf's lifetime.[93]

85. Gregory, *Decem Libri Historiarum*, VI 42; Paul, *Historia Langobardorum*, III 17.
86. Gregory, *Decem Libri Historiarum*, VIII 18; Paul, *Historia Langobardorum*, III 23.
87. Gregory, *Decem Libri Historiarum*, IX 25; Paul, *Historia Langobardorum*, III 28–9.
88. Gregory, *Decem Libri Historiarum*, X 3; Paul, *Historia Langobardorum*, III 31.
89. Fredegar, IV 45; C. Wickham, *Early Medieval Italy: Central Power and Local Society 400–1000*, pp. 32–3.
90. Wallace-Hadrill, *The Fourth Book of the Chronicle of Fredegar*, p. 38, n. 1.
91. P. Geary, *Aristocracy in Provence*, p. 33.
92. Wood, 'Frankish hegemony in England', pp. 237–8.
93. Paul, *Historia Langobardorum*, IV 30.

Following the civil war between Theuderic II and Theudebert II information about Merovingian involvement in Italy drops noticeably. This is largely a result of the cessation of Gregory's *Histories*, but it may also be a reflection of the ending of military conflict. After 614 the Lombards seem to have become increasingly self-confident in their dealings with the Franks. In the late sixth century the tribute paid to Guntram suggests Lombard inferiority, as does the agreement of Guntram and Childebert to Authari's election, and the same might be said of the presence of Theudebert II's agents at the elevation of Adaloald. But Chlothar's agreement to waive the tribute owed by the Lombards may be an indication of a decline in Frankish influence. Moreover, after Theudebert II's death the Lombard kings are not seen to draw their wives from the Merovingian family.

Nevertheless there is evidence of continuing contact between the Franks and the Lombards which suggests that Frankish influence in Italy did not end either with the reign of Chlothar, or even with that of Dagobert I. The *Life of Eligius of Noyon* refers to Lombard ambassadors in Francia,[94] and the late and extremely unreliable *Gesta Dagoberti I* does suggest that Dagobert I retained some influence over the Lombards, when it records their involvement in his wars against the Wends.[95] Further, if Fredegar is right to associate Clovis II with Gundeperga's reinstatement as queen, the Franks continued to involve themselves in Lombard politics. In addition Paul refers to one otherwise unattested Frankish invasion of Italy, which apparently took place in the 660s,[96] at the same time as the Lombard king Perctarit fled to Francia for fear of the usurper Grimoald.[97] Paul's goes on to relate how Perctarit planned to flee from Francia to England, because Grimoald made an alliance with the Frankish king Dagobert II (676–9).[98] Unfortunately Grimoald died in 671, five years before Dagobert was restored to the throne of Austrasia: as it stands Paul's narrative is, therefore, untenable. Whatever the underlying reality, Grimoald's death and that of his son Garibald shortly afterwards paved the way for Perctarit's return to Italy.[99]

The Visigoths

Turning to Merovingian relations with the Visigoths, marriage once again appears to have been a crucial factor. After Clovis's death Amalaric, son of Alaric II, asked to marry his daughter Chlothild, but according to Gregory he maltreated her because of her catholicism. Her brother Childebert decided to avenge the insults heaped on her, and invaded Spain. During the invasion

94. *Vita Eligii*, I 10.
95. *Gesta Dagoberti I*, 27.
96. Paul, *Historia Langobardorum*, V 5.
97. Paul, *Historia Langobardorum*, V 2–4.
98. Paul, *Historia Langobardorum*, V 32.
99. Paul, *Historia Langobardorum*, V 33.

Amalaric was killed, but Chlothild also died while returning to Paris.[100] Subsequently Childebert attacked Spain again, with his brother Chlothar. The campaign was chiefly notable for the Frankish failure to capture the city of Saragossa, which was protected by relics of St Vincent.[101]

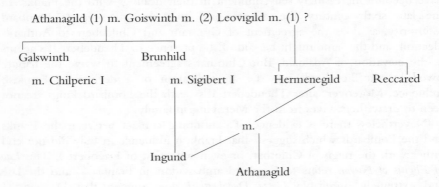

Figure 2 Merovingian–Visigothic marriages

In the middle of the sixth century marriage again became a prominent issue, when first Sigibert I and then Chilperic I took a Visigothic princess as wife (see Figure 2). The repercussions of these marriages within the Frankish kingdom have already concerned us, but they were also to dominate Merovingian foreign policy in the south-east for fifty years. Gregory of Tours portrays Chilperic's decision to take as his wife Galswinth, the sister of Brunhild, whom Sigibert had married, as an act of fraternal rivalry.[102] The circumstances of the marriages and the scale of the *morgengab* given by Chilperic to Galswinth, however, suggest that something more complex was involved. Galswinth and Brunhild were the daughters of the Visigothic king and queen Athanagild and Goiswinth. Athanagild had no sons. By marrying two daughters to Frankish kings he may have intended to involve the Merovingians in the Visigothic succession.[103] Perhaps he hoped that the marriages would produce grandsons who could succeed him. His death in 567, however, altered the situation. Galswinth's murder at the hands of Chilperic probably followed soon after.[104]

Venantius Fortunatus records that Goiswinth was particularly aggrieved by her daughter's murder.[105] In the aftermath of Athanagild's death she may well have hoped to have her own position bolstered by her Merovingian connections. Nevertheless, she was a woman of some importance, and she

100. Gregory, *Decem Libri Historiarum*, III 10.
101. Gregory, *Decem Libri Historiarum*, III 29.
102. Gregory, *Decem Libri Historiarum*, IV 27.
103. Nelson, 'À propos des femmes royales dans les rapports entre le monde wisigothique et le monde franc à l'époque de Reccared', p. 469.
104. Gregory, *Decem Libri Historiarum*, IV 28.
105. Venantius Fortunatus, carm., VI 5, ll. 321–46; George, *Venantius Fortunatus: A Latin Poet in Merovingian Gaul*, pp. 96–101.

was able to restore her position when she married Leovigild, who became co-ruler with Athanagild's successor, Liuva, and subsequently succeeded to the throne himself.[106] Leovigild already had two sons, Hermenegild and Reccared, who were to complicate relations with the Merovingians by seeking Frankish wives.[107] The former married Ingund, daughter of Sigibert and Brunhild. In so doing he may have bolstered Goiswinth's position further, since the girl was her granddaughter. The marriage of Hermenegild and Ingund also complicated relations between the Franks and the Visigoths.

The crux of the problem lay in Hermenegild's rebellion against his father. The evidence for this is remarkably full, in that it is recorded by Spanish, Italian and Frankish writers, but unfortunately the accounts are contradictory.[108] Gregory of Tours, who naturally provides the fullest information on those aspects of the rebellion which most concerned the Merovingians, is arguably the least reliable of the sources, because he allowed his religious bias to determine his interpretation of events. According to him, soon after her arrival in Spain Ingund met with persecution at the hands of her mother-in-law, Goiswinth. She nevertheless converted her husband to catholicism, but this conversion led to conflict between Hermenegild and Leovigild, and ultimately to open rebellion.[109] Other sources make Leander of Seville the author of Hermenegild's conversion, which seems to have taken place some time after the start of the rebellion, and they suggest that Goiswinth, far from being an evil influence in affairs, actually favoured Hermenegild.[110] This is perhaps less surprising when it is remembered that Goiswinth was not only Ingund's mother-in-law, but also her grandmother.

Leovigild was clearly worried about the repercussions of Hermenegild's revolt on his relations with the Merovingians, for even though Sigibert I was dead, his son, Childebert II, the brother of Ingund, were taking an interest in events.[111] To counteract any Frankish support for the rebels, the Gothic king now pressed ahead with negotiations for the marriage of Reccared and Chilperic's daughter, Rigunth.[112] Chilperic's death, however, forestalled Rigunth's entry into Spain, and rendered the marriage diplomatically useless from Leovigild's point of view.[113] Nor did the collapse of the revolt and

106. Gregory, *Decem Libri Historiarum*, V 38; Nelson, 'À propos des femmes royales dans les rapports entre le monde wisigothique et le monde franc à l'époque de Reccared', p. 469.

107. Gregory, *Decem Libri Historiarum*, IV 38; IX 16; Nelson, 'À propos des femmes royales dans les rapports entre le monde wisigothique et le monde franc à l'époque de Reccared', p. 470–4.

108. Collins, *Early Medieval Spain: Unity in Diversity, 400–1000*, pp. 45–9; Wood, 'Gregory of Tours and Clovis', pp. 259–61.

109. Gregory, *Decem Libri Historiarum*, V 38.

110. John of Biclarum, s.a. 579 (Tiberius, 3 [3]).

111. Gregory, *Decem Libri Historiarum*, VI 40.

112. Gregory, *Decem Libri Historiarum*, VI 34.

113. Gregory, *Decem Libri Historiarum*, VI 46; VII 9; Nelson, 'À propos des femmes royales dans les rapports entre le monde wisigothique et le monde franc à l'époque de Reccared', p. 473.

Hermenegild's capture and execution remove the threat of a major conflict with the Franks, since Guntram was committed to the cause of Ingund, and invaded Septimania.[114] Meanwhile a letter was found, purporting to have been sent from Leovigild to Fredegund, instructing her to assassinate Brunhild and Childebert, and to make peace with Guntram.[115] The latter continued his campaigns against Septimania, rejecting all peace negotiations initiated by Leovigild.[116]

In all this there was one further complication: the fate of Ingund. She had not been captured with Hermengild, but had fallen into Byzantine hands, where first she and then her young son became pawns in the emperor's diplomacy to draw Childebert into the Italian wars.[117] The attempts of Brunhild to secure the return of her grandson, after Ingund's death in Africa, form part of a remarkable group of letters preserved in the *Epistulae Austrasiacae*, which are the key source for the diplomatic history of the late sixth century. The letters of Brunhild and Childebert II concerning Ingund's son, Athanagild, are only a selection of those addressed to the emperor and empress, the patriarch of Constantinople, the *apochrysiarius*, the bishop of Malta, the quaestor John, the *curator* Megatas as well as Ingund's son and the exarch, Smaragdus.[118] The *Epistulae Austrasiacae* are, thus, important not only for the social and cultural history of the Merovingian kingdom, but also for the insight they provide into the continuing complexity of international politics in the western Mediterranean.

Childebert's willingness to come to terms with the Visigoths after Leovigild's death is not easily explained. His grandmother Goiswinth may have played a part, since Gregory records that Reccared made peace with her, and received her as his mother.[119] The Visigothic king then sent ambassadors to Guntram and Childebert; the former rejected their overtures, while the latter accepted them.[120] For a while it seemed as if Guntram had taken the treatment of Ingund more to heart than had her mother or brother. Ultimately, however, he gave his permission for another daughter of Brunhild, Chlodosind, to marry Reccared.[121] Nevertheless he remained suspicious of Austrasian links with Spain, and sent yet another army against Septimania.[122] As for the marriage of Reccared and Chlodosind, had it taken place it would have further strengthened the position of Goiswinth,

114. Gregory, *Decem Libri Historiarum*, VIII 28.
115. Gregory, *Decem Libri Historiarum*, VIII 28.
116. Gregory, *Decem Libri Historiarum*, VIII 30.
117. Gregory, *Decem Libri Historiarum*, VIII 28.
118. *Epistulae Austrasiacae*, 29–47; Goubert, *Byzance avant l'Islam*, 2, *Byzance et l'Occident*.
119. Gregory, *Decem Libri Historiarum*, IX 1; Nelson, 'À propos des femmes royales dans les rapports entre le monde wisigothique et le monde franc à l'époque de Reccared', p. 474.
120. Gregory, *Decem Libri Historiarum*, IX 16.
121. Gregory, *Decem Libri Historiarum*, IX 20.
122. Gregory, *Decem Libri Historiarum*, IX 31–2.

Chlodosind's grandmother. In the event it came to nothing, and Reccared took another wife, a Gothic lady called Baddo.[123] Soon afterwards Goiswinth, now only the stepmother of the king, died.[124]

Although Goiswinth gets a bad press from Gregory, as a result of her arianism, and perhaps because of her position as Ingund's mother-in-law,[125] she is one of the more remarkable figures in late-sixth-century Europe. Like Theudelinda and Gundeperga she was queen to two kings, providing some stability in the royal succession. Like Brunhild, she tried to hold on to power even after she had lost the queenship. More than any of these fellow queens she saw the possibility of exploiting international marriage alliances to strengthen her own position. Her daughters married Merovingian kings; one Merovingian granddaughter married a Visigothic king; another was betrothed to one. As a result she retained her influence until the failure of this final marriage.[126]

Goiswinth's death did not mark the end of connections between the Visigoths and the family of Brunhild. Fredegar records a further marriage in the early seventh century, between Theuderic and Ermenberga, daughter of the Visigothic king Witteric. Brunhild and her granddaughter Theudila, however, persuaded Theuderic to send his wife back to Spain:[127] perhaps they saw her as a threat to their own influence at court. Witteric then formed a coalition with Chlothar and Theudebert to exact vengeance, but it came to nothing.[128] More intriguing is the interest in Francia shown by one of Witteric's successors as king; Sisebut composed an account of the martyrdom of Brunhild's opponent Desiderius of Vienne, shortly after the old queen's execution. Although much of the text is a generalized attack on the government of Theuderic and Brunhild, rather than an informative work of history, it is important in that it reveals continuing hostility towards their regime, even after the deaths of Brunhild and Witteric, and presumably suggests a willingness to get on with Chlothar and his advisers.[129] It is likely that Fredegar had access to Sisebut's work, not least because the Burgundian historian inserts a surprisingly laudatory account of Sisebut's reign, after referring to the martyrdom of Desiderius. In particular he provides an account of the king's conquest of Cantabria, which had previously paid tribute to the Merovingians.[130]

---

123. Nelson, 'À propos des femmes royales dans les rapports entre le monde wisigothique et le monde franc à l'époque de Reccared', p. 474.

124. John of Biclarum, s.a. 589 (Maurice, 7 [1]).

125. Gregory, *Decem Libri Historiarum*, V 38; Wood, 'Gregory of Tours and Clovis', pp. 259–61.

126. Nelson, 'À propos des femmes royales dans les rapports entre le monde wisigothique et le monde franc à l'époque de Reccared', p. 474.

127. Fredegar, IV 30.

128. Fredegar, IV 31.

129. Sisebut, *Vita vel Passio sancti Desiderii*; J. Fontaine, 'King Sisebut's Vita Desiderii and the political function of Visigothic hagiography', in E. James, ed., *Visigothic Spain: New Approaches*, pp. 93–129.

130. Fredegar IV, 33; Wood, 'Forgery in Merovingian hagiography', p. 375.

The half century following Brunhild's marriage to Sigibert makes particularly clear the complexity of foreign relations in this period. Numerous factors were involved. There was the queen's own background, her family in Spain and Francia. In addition there were the vicissitudes of politics both within the Visigothic kingdom, with its lack of a stable dynastic succession, and within the *regnum Francorum*, where a single but divided dynasty presided over a changeable political scene, and was capable of pursuing two or more conflicting policies at once. Finally there was the complicating matter of Byzantine diplomacy.[131] The interrelation of the whole range of factors render explicable some of the apparent oddities of Brunhild's own attitudes towards the Visigothic kingdom, and they stand as a reminder that Merovingian foreign policy might look very different if the evidence was as consistently full as it is for the late sixth century.

After Brunhild's death the information is slight in the extreme. In 631, in return for military aid against the Visigothic king Swinthila, the rebel Sisenand offered Dagobert I the great dish or *missorium* which Aëtius had given to Thorismund in the mid-fifth century. After he had gained the crown, he had to pay Dagobert 200,000 *solidi* instead, because the Goths would not countenance the loss of the dish.[132] The sum stated was a huge amount, and the improvement in the metal content of the Merovingian coinage in the 630s has even been linked to this windfall.[133] In 673 another rebel, Paul, who tried to set himself up in a Septimanian kingdom in opposition to the Visigothic king Wamba, called on the Franks for support, and the Aquitanian *dux*, Lupus, took advantage of the rebellion to attack Béziers.[134] It seems as though the Franks kept a careful eye on Visigothic politics for much of the seventh century, and intervened when they could. In the south-east there is not the same evidence for a collapse in Merovingian influence as there is to the east of the Rhine.

The evidence for Lupus's involvement in the rebellion of Paul is contained in the *Historia Wambae* of Julian of Toledo, a text which has much to say about the Visigothic succession[135] and also about the Visigothic province of Septimania, which, albeit east of the Pyrenees, did not fall into Frankish hands until the mid-eighth century.[136] Indeed, Septimania seems to have had little contact with Francia, despite its geographical position; archaeological and numismatic evidence suggests that there was an effective border between the Visigothic province and the Frankish kingdom.[137] Perhaps not surprisingly

131. Goubert, *Byzance avant l'Islam*, 2, *Byzance et l'Occident*.

132. Fredegar, IV 73.

133. J.P.C. Kent, 'The coins and the date of the burial', in R. Bruce Mitford, ed., *The Sutton Hoo Ship Burial*, 1, p. 600.

134. Julian, *Historia Wambae Regis*, 28.

135. R. Collins, 'Julian of Toledo and the royal succession in late seventh-century Spain', in P.H. Sawyer and I.N. Wood, eds, *Early Medieval Kingship*, pp. 30–49.

136. See chapter 16.

137. E. James, 'Septimania and its frontier: an archaeological approach', in James, ed., *Visigothic Spain: New Approaches*, pp. 223–41.

the *Historia Wambae* has little to say about relations between the Visigoths and Franks, but it does suggest that the former were extremely wary of the latter even in the 670s: Wamba was careful to treat well the Frankish troops who were captured during the rebellion.[138]

Gascony

In addition to calling for Frankish help, Paul also turned to the Gascons. These people, who lived in the Pyrenees, had long posed a problem for the Visigoths and for the Franks.[139] Gregory of Tours occasionally mentions them. Chilperic I sent a general to overawe the Gascons in the early 580s,[140] and in 587 they made a raid on the lowlands.[141] Fifteen years later Theudebert II and Theuderic II sent an army against them, and set Genialis up as their *dux*,[142] which shows that they were a people that were sometimes brought firmly under control. Two bishops of Eauze were accused of having incited them to rebellion in the days of Chlothar II,[143] but when Charibert II was given a kingdom in Aquitaine by his brother Dagobert I, he extended his authority by conquering them.[144] After his death there was a major Gascon rebellion, but Dagobert sent an army and the Gascons retreated to their mountain fastnesses.[145] Nevertheless they submitted to the Franks, although, to judge by Fredegar's comment, not for long.

Until the late 630s those Gascons who lived on the northern side of the Pyrenees appear, therefore, to have been a group not unlike the Bretons. Sometimes they were firmly subjected to Merovingian rule, but at other times they asserted their independence. For the most part they are associated with the mountains, although occasionally they encroached on the plain to the south of the Garonne. Thereafter the evidence becomes less easy to interpret. For instance, Ebroin's opponents are described as fleeing across the Loire to Gascony in 675.[146] Nor were they the last to flee to the Gascons for safety: Gripho, the half-brother of Pippin III and Carloman, did so to escape their clutches.[147] The flight of Ebroin's opponents might imply that the Gascons extended their territory far to the north. Certainly they seem to have become an increasingly significant military power. The Gascons provided a number of armies which fought against Charles Martel and his sons.[148] On the other

---

138. Julian, *Historia Wambae Regis*, 27.
139. R. Collins, *The Basques*, pp. 82–98.
140. Gregory, *Decem Libri Historiarum*, VI 12.
141. Gregory, *Decem Libri Historiarum*, IX 7.
142. Fredegar, IV 21.
143. Fredegar, IV 54.
144. Fredegar, IV 57.
145. Fredegar, IV 67, 78.
146. Fredegar, cont. 2; *Passio Leudegarii II*, 12, where they appear as *Vaccaei*; Collins, *The Basques*, pp. 96–7.
147. *Annales Mettenses Priores*, s.a. 749, 753.
148. Fredegar, cont. 10, 25, 28.

hand it is possible that northern sources on occasion found it convenient to label the Aquitanians with the less complimentary name of Gascon. The duchy of Aquitaine still survived throughout this period, and under such *duces* as Lupus, and later Eudo, it was a force to be reckoned with. It may well be that in eighth-century sources there is not always a clear line to be drawn between Gascony and Gascons on the one hand and Aquitaine and Aquitanians on the other.

The English

There remain the neighbours who lived to the north of Frankish Gaul, in southern and eastern Britain. Unlike the other peoples who surrounded the Merovingian kingdom they presented no threat, although there was certainly some raiding across the Channel. Nevertheless, according to Bede, the Neustrian *maior* Ebroin regarded abbot Hadrian and Theodore as imperial spies when the latter was sent as archbishop to Canterbury.[149] Despite the presence of the emperor Constans II in Sicily at this time,[150] this is perhaps best seen as an indication of Ebroin's paranoia. There is, however, a case for seeing Frankish influence on England as being substantial until the mid-seventh century. Indeed Merovingian interests in England in the late sixth and early seventh century seem to have much in common with the hegemonic authority which the Franks exercised across the Rhine.

It is clear from Procopius that the Merovingians were claiming overlordship in southern England in the 550s, when an embassy sent to Constantinople declared that the Franks ruled over *Brittia*, which must be some part of the British Isles.[151] References in the panegyrics of Venantius Fortunatus may suggest that such claims continued into the days of Sigibert I and Chilperic I.[152] Gregory the Great seems to have thought that Theudebert I and Theuderic I exercised some authority in England, presumably in the kingdom of Kent.[153] The marriage of king Æthelberht to Charibert I's daughter, Bertha, needs to be set against this background.[154] Whereas other Merovingian princesses married kings of considerable status, Bertha appears to have married 'down', but since, as we have seen, her father was almost certainly dead by the time of her marriage, she can hardly be compared with those Merovingians who married Visigothic royalty. A more apt comparison might be with Wuldetrada, who was bestowed on Garivald of Bavaria. Just as the kings of the Franks appear to have involved themselves in the fate of

149. Bede, *Historia Ecclesiastica*, IV 1.
150. *Liber Pontificalis, Vita Vitaliani*.
151. Procopius, *Wars*, VIII 20, 8–10.
152. Venantius Fortunatus, carm. IX 1, 11. 73–5; Wood, *The Merovingian North Sea*, pp. 10–11.
153. Gregory I, *Register*, VI 49.
154. Gregory, *Decem Libri Historiarum* IV 26; IX 26; Wood, *The Merovingian North Sea*, pp. 15–17.

Wuldetrada's granddaughter Gundeperga, so too they seem to have retained an interest in Bertha and her descendants. Bertha's daughter Ethelberga felt able to send her children to Dagobert I for protection after the death of her husband, Edwin.[155]

In addition to taking an interest in Æthelberht's daughter and her children, the Franks also took an interest in Æthelberht's son, Eadbald. It is not clear whether he was the son or stepson of Bertha. But he did marry a Frankish woman, Emma, who appears to have been the daughter of Erchinoald, the Neustrian *maior*.[156] Although the evidence for this is late, the names of Eadbald's son, Earconberht, and granddaughter, Earcongota, offers some confirmation. If Eadbald's wife was indeed the daughter of Erchinoald, then Æthelberht's successor married a lady from the Merovingian aristocracy, and not from the royal dynasty. This must have had considerable implications for the relative status of the kings of Francia and Kent, and of the *maior* of Neustria.

Nor was Æthelberht's the only English family to have had connections with Francia. Just as Ethelberga's children sought refuge in Francia, so too did Sigbert of East Anglia, when he fled from his father, or stepfather, Redwald.[157] Given the fact that Sigbert is the same name as Sigibert, it is possible that he too had Merovingian blood in his veins.[158] A further indication of connections between the Merovingians and the East Anglian royal dynasty may be found in the treasure buried at Sutton Hoo. Most remarkable are the thirty-seven coins all drawn from different mints. It is scarcely possible that such a collection was made in England, and if it was made on the continent the likelihood is that it should be assigned to a period when all the mints were in the hands of one ruler. That would date the collection either to the period of Chlothar II's sole rule, that is 613–22, or to the years between the death of Charibert II and the election of Sigibert III as sub-king of Austrasia, in other words 630–33. If the most recent of the coins postdate 622, which is possible, though not certain,[159] it may be significant that Sigbert was in exile in Francia before 630. It may be that the Sutton Hoo coins are the remnants of treasure given to the East Anglian prince to help restore him to the throne.[160]

Although the action of Ethelberga in sending her children to Dagobert presupposes a Merovingian interest in English politics, there is little to indicate the nature of that interest, beyond a concern for the safety of individuals

155. Bede, *Historia Ecclesiastica*, II 20.
156. Wood, 'Frankish hegemony in England', p. 240.
157. Bede, *Historia Ecclesiastica*, III 18.
158. I.N. Wood, 'The Franks and Sutton Hoo', in I.N. Wood and N. Lund, eds, *People and Places in Northern Europe*, 500–1600, p. 9.
159. A.M. Stahl, 'The nature of the Sutton Hoo coin parcel', in C.B. Kendall and P.S. Wells, eds, *Voyage to the Other World: The Legacy of Sutton Hoo*, pp. 3–14, raises significant doubts about the chronology of the coins and about the oddity of the selection.
160. Wood, 'The Franks and Sutton Hoo', pp. 10–11.

related to the Frankish royal house. The coins at Sutton Hoo may indicate that Merovingian involvement in Anglo-Saxon England could be active as well as passive. More remarkable, perhaps, is the presence of Justus of Rochester and Peter of Dover at the Council of Paris in 614.[161] There is also the possibility that the *Pactus Legis Salicae* had some influence on Æthelberht's code.[162] That Frankish law did have some impact on England is further suggested by a clause in the *Pactus* relating to the retrieval of slaves who had been taken across the sea.[163] All in all the evidence, though slight, is consistent with the idea that the Merovingians looked upon their northern neighbours as inferiors who were worth keeping an eye on, not least because of their position on the Channel, which would have allowed some surveillance of maritime activity.

There is one other aspect to Merovingian relations with England, and that is religion. It is probable that Bertha and her entourage played a role in arousing Æthelberht's interest in Christianity, which had certainly been stimulated before Augustine's arrival in 597, as Gregory the Great reveals in a letter to Theudebert II and Theuderic II.[164] Indeed, Æthelberht himself may have been converted before 597: Bede seems to date the conversion to 595, despite depicting the king as a pagan at the time of his first meeting with Augustine.[165] Gregory's letter to Theudebert and Theuderic appears to be requesting the help of Frankish clergy in Augustine's mission. By the standards of the sixth century this was as much as could be expected by way of missionary activity. Brunhild, however, more than fulfilled Gregory I's expectations.[166]

Attitudes towards mission seem to have changed in the early seventh century. Previously there had been no great missionary fervour in the Church: thereafter there is a flurry of activity. This change is often associated with the presence of Irish monks on the continent, but by far the most impressive figure was the Aquitanian Amandus. He is said to have preached to the Slavs and the Gascons,[167] but his chief field of evangelization lay in present-day Belgium and in the diocese of Maastricht, to which he was appointed by Dagobert I. Although there is no reason for linking him with England, contemporaries of his did cross the Channel: the Burgundian Felix went to East Anglia,[168] Agilbert went to Wessex,[169] and Richarius is said to

161. Council of Paris (614), signatories.

162. J.M. Wallace-Hadrill, *Early Germanic Kingship in England and on the Continent*, pp. 36–9.

163. *Pactus Legis Salicae*, 39 2; Wood, *The Merovingian North Sea*, pp. 12–13.

164. Gregory I, *Register*, VI 49.

165. Bede, *Historia Ecclesiastica*, II 5, states that the king had been Christian for twenty-one years before his death (in 616).

166. Gregory I, *Register*, XI 48; see Wood; 'The mission of Augustine'.

167. *Vita Amandi*, 16, 20.

168. Bede, *Historia Ecclesiastica*, II 15; III 18.

169. Bede, *Historia Ecclesiastica*, III 7.

have worked in England.[170] From the days of Dagobert, therefore, it is necessary to see Frankish clergy as being closely involved in the English Church. In all probability it was Brunhild's response to the Augustinian mission which instigated this tradition of involvement.

Frankish influence on the early English Church was not confined to mission. Bede recorded that a number of Anglo-Saxon princesses entered nunneries in Francia. In particular there was Sæthryth, stepdaughter, and Æthelburh, daughter of Anna, king of the East Angles, both of whom became abbesses at Faremoutiers in the diocese of Meaux.[171] The presence of Anglo-Saxon royal women in Frankish nunneries must have had some diplomatic repercussions; certainly the nunneries had an impact on English monasticism. So too did Frankish monasteries, which were closely observed by Benedict Biscop and Wilfrid.[172]

The nunneries of the Paris basin were among the few Merovingian institutions that impressed Bede, who for the most part was not impressed by or not interested in the Franks. If he had been, the evidence for English relations with the continent before the late seventh century might have been rather more plentiful. As it is, the material that survives is slight and patchy. For the most part, the same is true of the evidence for relations between the Merovingians and all their neighbours, despite occasional pools of light like that associated with Ingund. A plausible image can, however, be reconstructed out of this fragmentary material.

The greatest of the peoples whose territory bordered that of the Franks were unquestionably the Ostrogoths and the Visigoths, although in time the Lombards achieved considerable political significance and status. For the most part these peoples were treated by the Merovingians as equals. The more distant empire in the east had a status entirely of its own. It still retained something of the authority of the Roman Empire. It was a constant factor in the diplomatic life of western Europe, even if its emperors attracted the attention of Frankish historians only occasionally.[173] Both Gregory of Tours and Fredegar included excursus on individual emperors in their histories, and Gregory in particular used the emperor Tiberius II as an example of a good ruler.[174] At the beginning of the sixth century, the emperor Anastasius had granted some consular title to Clovis,[175] and in the middle Theudebert I found a need to justify his titles to the emperor Justinian.[176] Byzantine

---

170. *Vita Richarii sacerdotis Centulensis primigenia*, 7; Alcuin, *Vita Richarii*, 8, changes the place of his mission from England to Britain.

171. Bede, *Historia Ecclesiastica*, III 8.

172. P. Wormald, 'Bede and Benedict Biscop', in G. Bonner, ed., *Famulus Christi*, pp. 141–69; I.N. Wood, 'Ripon, Francia and the Franks Casket in the early Middle Ages', *Northern History* 26 (1990), pp. 8–17.

173. E. Chrysos, 'Byzantine diplomacy, A.D. 300–800: means and ends', in J. Shepard and S. Franklin, eds, *Byzantine Diplomacy*, p. 32.

174. Gregory, *Decem Libri Historiarum*, IV 40; V 19.

175. Gregory, *Decem Libri Historiarum*, II 38.

176. *Epistulae Austrasiacae*, 20.

diplomacy lay at the heart of Childebert II's Lombard policies.[177] And it is likely that Byzantine intrigue was involved in the early stages of the Gundovald affair.[178] Later Ebroin was to fear imperial contacts with England, and he kept abbot Hadrian under arrest on the grounds that he was a spy.[179] The shadow of Byzantium was a considerable one, however slight its direct influence on the Frankish kingdom.

But Byzantium was far away. Although the Visigoths, Ostrogoths and Lombards were often the equals of the Franks, the majority of their other neighbours were inferiors, whose subjection to Frankish dominance depended on the prestige of individual Merovingian monarchs and on internal politics in Francia and elsewhere. Naturally some of the most powerful Merovingians were those who were the sole rulers of Francia, but it was possible for a king to achieve extraordinary prestige even when rule of the Frankish kingdom was divided, as in the time of Theudebert I. Among later kings Chlothar II and Dagobert I appear to have exercised particularly extensive authority. After them there seems to have been a period of decline in Merovingian authority east of the Rhine, indicated by Radulf's victory over Sigibert III. It is, however, dangerous to put too much emphasis on this as an indication of the growing weakness of the Frankish kingdom. On the whole the evidence for foreign relations in the period after Dagobert's death cannot compare with that for what had gone before, but even in the information that we have there are references to campaigns against the Visigoths and the Lombards in the second half of the seventh century. Nevertheless, it should be remembered that the kingdoms with which the Franks were in contact had themselves evolved; the Lombards under Rothari and the Northumbrians under Oswiu cannot easily be compared with their counterparts of fifty years earlier. This evolution necessarily affected the relative status of the Merovingian kingdom.

177. Goubert, *Byzance avant l'Islam 2, Byzance et l'Occident*, pp. 71–202.
178. Goffart, 'Byzantine policy in the west under Tiberius II and Maurice: the pretenders Hermenegild and Gundovald'.
179. Bede, *Historia Ecclesiastica*, IV 1.

Chapter Eleven

The Place of the Monasteries: Politics and the Religious Life, 613–64

The religious policies of Clovis II revolved around the shrine and the community of St Denis. After the king's death his widow, Balthild, who acted as regent for their eldest son, Chlothar III (657–73), had even greater monastic interests. As a result the history of monasticism is a central feature of Merovingian history in the seventh century. That is not to say that it had previously been insignificant. The endowment of communities of ascetics had long been a mark of piety, which it was hoped would bring divine support to a benefactor and to the benefactor's family. As for the monasteries themselves, the majority were probably communities either of monks or of nuns, but in the sixth and seventh centuries there were a number of double monasteries, where a single abbess ruled over separate, but associated, male and female houses.[1] The ascetics lived according to a *Rule*, chosen by the monastic founder or by the current abbot or abbess. Although the *Rule* of St Benedict was known in seventh-century Francia, it was only one *Rule* among many, most of which were of greater antiquity. And even where it was used, it was blended with the legislation of other monastic founders.

The development of a monastic tradition

Monasticism was already established in Gaul before the fifth century. The first major foundations were those of St Martin at Ligugé and Marmoutier. Equally if not more important was the island monastery of Lérins, founded by Honoratus shortly after 400.[2] Here numbers of Gallo-Roman aristocrats sought refuge during the period of barbarian invasion and settlement, and from here was drawn a significant proportion of the saintly bishops who oversaw the transition from Roman to sub-Roman Gaul. When they left the

1. C.H. Lawrence, *Medieval Monasticism*, pp. 51–3; F. Prinz, *Frühes Mönchtum im Frankenreich*, pp. 658–63.
2. See chapter 2.

island monastery they took with them its ideals and promoted its traditions in their own dioceses, thus helping to spread its reputation. By the end of the century it was a centre to which many aspiring monks and monastic founders turned for at least a period of their ascetic training.

All this is clear from contemporary or near-contemporary texts. In the sixth century, however, there is an apparent decline in the quantity and quality of evidence for monasticism, which has sometimes been taken to imply a decline in monasticism itself. To some extent this interpretation may be supported by the canons of Church councils, which have much to say about monastic discipline, and which were not infrequently concerned to broadcast the subjection of abbots and their houses to the jurisdiction of the episcopate.[3] In other respects the case for monastic decline in the sixth century is less easy to substantiate: there is a danger in expecting the same sort of evidence from a period of consolidation as from one of innovation. Moreover, although Gregory of Tours has little to say about monasteries, with the exception of that of the Holy Cross at Poitiers, which achieved notoriety because of the revolt of some inmates against their abbess, his silence may say more about his own, rather different, concerns than about any general failure of asceticism. Equally, while Venantius Fortunatus seems more preoccupied with the holiness of bishops than with that of monastic saints, his most important inspiration came from Radegund, the founder and chief inmate of the same convent of the Holy Cross. Writers in the Carolingian period looked back at the sixth century as a great age of piety, particularly in such cities of the Rhône valley as Vienne,[4] and while it would be wrong to accept their comments without question, to dismiss them out of hand may be even more wrong-headed, not least because there is some contemporary evidence to support the notion of a continuing period of monastic expansion.

Lérins itself continued to be a source of inspiration. At the end of the fifth century Caesarius became a monk there, and after his move to Arles, and subsequently to episcopal office, he acted as a champion of the monastic ideal. In particular he founded a nunnery, for which he composed a *Rule*. He also wrote a second rule which he circulated to monastic communities.[5] His reputation as a legislator was such that Radegund asked Caesaria, who was abbess of the nunnery in Arles, for a copy of the nuns' *Rule*.[6] Caesarius's successor, Aurelian, was himself a monastic founder and legislator.[7] Here then was one tradition that continued unabated into the late sixth century.

Also inspired in part by Lérins were the Jura monasteries founded by

3. Council of Orléans (511), 19; Council of Epaon (517), 19; Council of Orléans (533), 21; Council of Orléans (538), 26; Council of Orléans (541), 11; see also chapter 5.

4. Ado, *Vita Theudarii* 7; I.N. Wood, 'A prelude to Columbanus: the monastic achievement in the Burgundian territories', in H.B. Clarke and M. Brennan, eds, *Columbanus and Merovingian Monasticism*, p. 19.

5. Lawrence, *Medieval Monasticism*, pp. 22–3.

6. Gregory, *Decem Libri Historiarum*, IX 39, 40.

7. Aurelian, *Regulae PL* 68, col 385–406.

Romanus and Lupicinus in the mid-fifth century. Although there is evidence of problems within these communities in the early sixth century, they had at least one successor of note in Eugendus. The lives of all three abbots were written up in the second decade of the sixth century for two ascetics who had established themselves at Agaune, the cult site of saint Maurice and the Theban legion, and the resulting work, the *Vita Patrum Iurensium* is among the most valuable documents for the history of monasticism in the fifth- and sixth-century West.[8]

Agaune itself was to become a monastic centre, albeit not because of the ascetics for whom the *Life of the Jura Fathers* had been written. In 515 the Burgundian prince Sigismund, advised by Maximus of Geneva, and with the backing of Avitus of Vienne and other bishops of his father's kingdom, founded a monastery at the burial place of St Maurice.[9] It was later also to house the body of Sigismund himself, the first martyr king of the Middle Ages.[10] The most noteworthy aspect of Agaune was its division of the monks into a number of groups who took it in turns to sing the liturgy, which could thus be carried on without interruption day and night.[11] This liturgical arrangement, known as the *laus perennis* or 'perpetual chant', although never widespread, attracted the attention of other founders, in particular kings, who may have seen in Agaune a model for a specifically royal monasticism. Most notable among the houses which instituted the perpetual chant were Guntram's St Marcel at Chalon and Dagobert's St Denis,[12] and there is also evidence for the liturgy being used at the monastery of Remiremont, as well as other non-royal centres.[13]

Royal monasteries

About Arles and Agaune we are well informed. The same cannot be said for other sixth-century foundations, with the exception of the community of nuns established in Poitiers by Radegund, whose religious retirement we have seen as providing one model for queenship. The two *Lives* devoted to the saint, one by Venantius Fortunatus and the other by the nun Baudonivia, concentrate on her piety, which often drove Radegund to physically repulsive extremes,[14] rather than on her monastery, although they offer plenty of

8. Wood, 'A prelude to Columbanus: the monastic achievement in the Burgundian territories', pp. 4–8.
9. Avitus, hom. 25; *Vita Abbatum Acaunensium absque epitaphiis*, 3.
10. Gregory, *Liber in Gloria Martyrum*, 74; *Passio Sigismundi Regis*, 10–11.
11. F. Masai, 'La *Vita patrum iurensium* et les débuts du monachisme à Saint-Maurice d'Agaune', in *Festschrift Bernhard Bischoff zu seinem 65. Geburtstag*, pp. 66–9; Wood, 'A prelude to Columbanus: the monastic achievement in the Burgundian territories', p. 16.
12. Fredegar, IV 1; *Gesta Dagoberti I*, 35.
13. *Vita Amati*, 10; Prinz, *Frühes Mönchtum im Frankenreich*, pp. 102–12.
14. See chapter 8.

insights in passing. In his *Histories* Gregory, who became involved in sorting out the troubles which hit the convent of the Holy Cross after Radegund's death, was primarily concerned with the tensions generated when royal princesses were placed under the authority of their social inferiors, but he also gathered together information relating to Radegund's intentions in founding the nunnery,[15] because they were relevant to the settlement of the troubles. Thus it is he who cites Radegund's letter referring to Caesarius's *Rule*.

One of the most significant aspects of the convent of the Holy Cross was its association with royalty. It was founded by Radegund, a queen, albeit one who was determined to leave secular life, with the help of her husband, Chlothar I, bishop Pientius and *dux* Austrapius.[16] It can reasonably be called a royal monastery. Royal involvement is a marked feature of sixth-century monastic history.[17] Among Clovis's sons, Childebert I was especially involved in religious foundations; he and his wife built a *xenodochium* in Lyons,[18] and there is some reason to associate him with the foundation of St Calais, in the diocese of Le Mans.[19] St Pierre-le-Vif in Sens was probably founded by a daughter of Theuderic I and hence a granddaughter of the Burgundian king and martyr Sigismund.[20] In later generations, apart from Guntram, Brunhild stands out, not only as being responsible for the foundation of a monastery and a hospital in Autun, but also for taking care to secure letters from Gregory the Great which ensured that the abbot or priest in charge could be replaced only by the monarch acting in concert with the monks.[21]

Later sources suggest that there was yet more royal involvement in sixth-century monasticism, but it is not always easy to know how much reliance can be placed on them. As it is, there is enough material to show that kings and their consorts were involved in founding monasteries as well as other religious institutions, like hospitals or basilicas established at major shrines, of which the most famous was that of St Medard at Soissons, patronized by Chlothar I and his son Sigibert.[22] What is more difficult to assess is the proportional significance of royal activity within the whole spectrum of early Merovingian asceticism. The patchy nature of our information renders any estimate suspect.

'Columbanian' monasticism

Another question affected by the vagaries of the evidence is that of the geographical distribution of monasteries. The majority of those mentioned for

15. Gregory, *Decem Libri Historiarum*, IX 39.
16. Baudonivia, *Vita Radegundis*, 5.
17. Prinz, *Frühes Mönchtum im Frankenreich*, pp. 152–63.
18. Council of Orléans (549), 15.
19. G.H. Pertz, *Diplomata* 2; the document is unquestionably forged, but it might well have been based on a genuine tradition of royal endowment.
20. J.M. Pardessus, *Diplomata*, 335.
21. Gregory I, *Register*, XIII 7, 11, 12, 13.
22. Gregory, *Decem Libri Historiarum*, IV 19.

the sixth century lie in Provence, Aquitaine and Burgundy, and most of them are urban rather than rural. This is likely to reflect the actual distribution of religious houses. At the same time what northern monasticism there may have been might be underrepresented in the historical record, since our surviving sources for the early Merovingian period tend to be less informative about the north and north-east of Francia than about other areas. This caveat should perhaps be kept in mind when it comes to considering the developments in monasticism which began around the turn of the seventh century.

Sometime around the year 590 an Irishman from Leinster, called Columbanus, settled in Burgundy, where he founded a number of monasteries, of which the most important was that of Luxeuil.[23] In Carolingian and modern historical writing his impact on the spiritual life of Francia is regarded as seminal, and certainly there was a dramatic increase in the number of monasteries founded in north-eastern and northern Francia, many of which can be shown to have been influenced in some way or other by Columbanus's foundations.[24] The best evidence for this influence comes from a number of saints' *Lives*, of which some were written in the Merovingian period, while others which were composed in later centuries seem to have had access to some reliable traditions. Of these *Lives* the most important is the *Vita Columbani* written by Jonas of Bobbio probably between 639 and 643.[25] Apart from describing Columbanus's own foundations of Luxeuil and Bobbio, this *Life* also deals with the saint's relations with a number of aristocratic families who were to champion the 'Columbanian' monastic tradition. Among those who visited Columbanus were Waldelenus and his wife Flavia: their eldest son Donatus was to become bishop of Besançon, where he founded a monastery; his mother founded a nunnery in the same city, and his younger brother founded a monastery in the Jura.[26] Jonas also records a visit by Columbanus to the house of Chagneric at Meaux, where the holy man blessed his host's daughter Burgundofara.[27] The saint's successor at Luxeuil, Eustasius, was later involved in helping with the nunnery founded at Faremoutiers for Burgundofara.[28] A good proportion of Book Two of the *Vita Columbani* is concerned with miraculous occurrences at Faremoutiers, which seems to have become a model for nunneries in the Seine basin, and later in England.[29] Burgundofaro, or Faro, perhaps

---

23. Jonas, *Vita Columbani*, I 6, 10.
24. P. Riché, 'Columbanus, his followers and the Merovingian Church', in H.B. Clarke and M. Brennan, eds *Columbanus and Merovingian Monasticism*, pp. 59–72; F. Prinz, 'Columbanus, the Frankish nobility and the territories east of the Rhine', ibid., pp. 73–87.
25. I.N. Wood, 'The *Vita Columbani* and Merovingian hagiography', *Peritia* I (1982), p. 63.
26. Jonas, *Vita Columbani*, I 14.
27. Jonas, *Vita Columbani*, I 26.
28. Jonas, *Vita Columbani*, II 7.
29. Jonas, *Vita Columbani*, II 11–22; Wood, 'The *Vita Columbani* and Merovingian hagiography', pp. 68–9.

monastic
immunities
from
secular
power

Burgundofara's brother, was to become bishop of Meaux,[30] and was to play an important role in the development of monastic immunities from episcopal power.[31] A third family visited by Columbanus was that of Autharius and Aega, two of whose sons are described by Jonas as monastic founders: he names Dado as founder of Rebais and Ado as founder of Jouarre.[32] Dado, who is better known as Audoin, or in modern French as Ouen, was, of course, one of the leading figures of the courts of Chlothar and Dagobert.

Jonas was writing too early to record the full range of Audoin/Dado's career, for he became bishop of Rouen only in 641. Thereafter he presided over a further expansion of 'Columbanian' monasticism, particularly at *Fontanella* (St Wandrille) and Jumièges. The foundation of the former is recorded in the seventh-century *Vita Wandregisili*, which tells how Wandregisil became an ascetic and joined the community first of Bobbio and later of Romainmôtier, before building his own monastery on land, which had previously belonged to the royal fisc, on the banks of the lower Seine.[33] Not far away at Jumièges the Aquitanian Filibert built another monastery also on royal land. Filibert had become acquainted with Audoin at the court of Dagobert and had subsequently gained first-hand experience of Luxeuil tradition at his mentor's foundation of Rebais.[34]

Audoin's friends in fact played a major role in the spread of 'Columbanian' monasticism. Eligius, whose *Vita* was originally written by Audoin, was another member of the royal court, as we have seen. His most significant monastic foundation was at Solignac in Aquitaine, also built on royal land.[35] One of the earliest inmates at Solignac was Remaclus, who was later to be the first abbot of the double house of Stablo-Malmédy, which was founded jointly by Sigibert III and his *maior* Grimoald, Pippin I's son.[36] Among Audoin's other friends yet one more Aquitanian, Desiderius of Cahors, whose letters are crucial for understanding the court, was responsible for a number of monastic foundations in his diocese.[37] In addition queen Balthild, who seems to have been much influenced by Audoin, appointed as the first abbot of her foundation of Corbie an inmate of Luxeuil, Theudefred.[38]

Also directly linked with Luxeuil were several monasteries in northern Burgundy and Austrasia. The first abbot of the double monastery of Remiremont founded by Romaric was Amatus, who had trained under Eustasius, although he was later to take sides against his old master in a

30. Jonas, *Vita Columbani*, II 21; Jonas is not explicit about any family relationship.
31. Pardessus, *Diplomata.*, 275; E. Ewig, 'Das Formular von Rebais und die Bischofsprivilegien der Merowingerzeit', in Ewig, *Spätantikes und fränkisches Gallien*, 2, pp. 456–84.
32. Jonas, *Vita Columbani*, I 26.
33. *Vita Wandregisili*, 9, 10, 14.
34. *Vita Filiberti*, 1, 2, 6.
35. *Vita Eligii*, I 15.
36. *Vita Remacli*, 1, 4.
37. See chapter 9.
38. *Vita Balthildis*, 5, 7; D. Ganz, *Corbie in the Carolingian Renaissance*, pp. 14–15.

religious dispute caused by another Luxeuil product, Agrestius.[39] After Amatus's death, Romaric, who had himself joined the community at Luxeuil, took over control of his own foundation.[40] The chief evidence for the early history of Remiremont comes in the *Lives* of Amatus and Romaric, which are unfortunately of disputed date.[41] There is no reason, however, to doubt that the two saints had spent some time at Columbanus's foundation. They certainly attracted attention within the circle of Luxeuil, since their brief hostility to Eustasius is recorded in the *Vita Columbani*.[42] It seems to have been through Romaric that Arnulf of Metz was introduced to the ascetic life.[43]

Two of the first inmates at Remiremont were the brothers Germanus and Numerian.[44] They later went to Luxeuil where they lived under Eustasius's successor Waldebert.[45] Subsequently Germanus founded the monastery of Grandval, where he was murdered in somewhat obscure circumstances. His life and death are recorded in a near contemporary *Vita*. Numerian, who became bishop of Trier, apparently built another Luxeuil-influenced house at St Dié.[46] Also attached to the Luxeuil–Remiremont nexus was Sadalberga. Her *Vita* was written probably in the Carolingian period, and is, at least in its detail, of uncertain worth: it records how, after an early encounter between her and Eustasius, she wished to join Remiremont, and how she was prevented; she subsequently married and had children, but then, after a meeting with Eustasius's successor, Waldebert, she persuaded her husband to allow her to enter the monastic life. With Waldebert's help she built a nunnery at Langres: later, also on his advice, she moved to Laon.[47]

Another indication of the spread of the 'Columbanian' tradition can be found in the career of Jonas himself. He became a monk in Columbanus's Italian monastery of Bobbio during the abbatiate of Athala.[48] He promised the latter's successor, Bertulf, a relative of Arnulf of Metz,[49] that he would write the *Life* of the abbey's founder, but the work was not written until after Bertulf's death, by which time Jonas had spent three years working with Amandus on the Scheldt.[50] Amandus was certainly deeply involved with the spread of 'Columbanian' monasticism, as can be seen from the foundation charter for Barisis-du-Bois.[51] Doubtless his other foundations, Elno (St

39. *Vita Amati*, 7; *Vita Romarici*, 4, 5.
40. *Vita Romarici*, 6.
41. Wood, 'Forgery in Merovingian hagiography', pp. 370–1.
42. Jonas, *Vita Columbani*, II 10.
43. *Vita Arnulfi*, 6, 19, 22; *Vita Romarici*, 11.
44. Bobolenus, *Vita Germani Grandivallensis*, 1, 5.
45. Bobolenus, *Vita Germani Grandivallensis* 6.
46. Pardessus, *Diplomata*, 360.
47. *Vita Sadalbergae*, 4–6, 9–14.
48. Jonas, *Vita Columbani*, II 5.
49. Jonas, *Vita Columbani*, II 23.
50. Jonas, *Vita Columbani*, ep. to Waldebert and Bobolenus.
51. Pardessus, *Diplomata*, 350; see also Pertz, *Diplomata*, 25.

Amand)[52] and Nant[53] also followed 'Columbanian' tradition. Jonas himself may have become abbot of Marchiennes, another foundation associated with Amandus.[54] In 659, long after his work on the Scheldt, he was summoned to the royal court, and on the way he stopped at the monastery of Réomé, whose abbot had been trained at Luxeuil. He was persuaded to write a biography of the house's sixth-century founder, John.[55] A third work ascribed to Jonas is the *Life* of Clovis's contemporary, Vedast, bishop of Arras, and it may be no coincidence that the monastery of St Vaast is associated with bishop Autbert of Cambrai, who had been a monk at Luxeuil.[56]

To the biographical evidence relating to founders and abbots may be added other material which points to connections with Luxeuil; in particular the use of Columbanus's monastic *Rule* is a valuable indication of the extent of his influence. Not that the *Rule* was much used in its original form; in all probability even at Luxeuil it was soon modified by being combined with the *Rules* of other monastic legislators.[57] Since it was the norm for *Rules* to be adapted or combined in a way that suited a particular abbot or abbess, this is how it would have been known to most seventh- and eighth-century monks and nuns. The classic description of this comes in the *Vita Filiberti*, where the saint is described as behaving like a bee, drawing nectar from the flowers of earlier legislators, in particular Basil, Macarius, Benedict and Columbanus.[58] Nor was this attitude towards monastic legislation new. Aurelian in Arles had drawn on Caesarius's *Rule*,[59] and Ferreolus borrowed from both of them.[60] Of the surviving rules that draw on Columbanus, one is anonymous and cannot be linked to a particular place or person,[61] but two can be tied down very precisely. There is Waldebert's *Rule* for the nuns of Faremoutiers, which draws on Benedict and Columbanus,[62] and Donatus's *Rule* for the nunnery he founded in Besançon, which also used the nun's *Rule* of Caesarius.[63] From the *Passio Praeiecti* we learn that the same mixture was used at the Auvergnat nunnery of Chamalières.[64] Apart from the existence of the *Rules* themselves

52. *Vita Amandi*, 22; *Testamentum Amandi*.

53. *Vita Amandi*, 23.

54. Wood, 'The *Vita Columbani* and Merovingian hagiography', p. 63, n. 2.

55. Jonas, *Vita Iohannis, incipit*; Wood, 'A prelude to Columbanus: the monastic achievement in the Burgundian territories', p. 3.

56. Prinz, *Frühes Mönchtum im Frankenreich*, p. 179.

57. Prinz, *Frühes Mönchtum im Frankenreich*, pp. 286–9.

58. *Vita Filiberti*, 5; Wormald, 'Bede and Benedict Biscop', p. 143.

59. A. De Vogüé, *Les Règles monastiques anciennes (400–700)*, pp. 53–4; Prinz, *Frühes Mönchtum im Frankenreich*, p. 80.

60. De Vogüé, *Les Règles monastiques anciennes (400–700)*, p. 56; Prinz, *Frühes Mönchtum im Frankenreich*, pp. 264–6.

61. *Regula Cuiusdam Patris*; De Vogüé, *Les Règles monastiques anciennes (400–700)*, p. 56.

62. *Regula Waldeberti*; De Vogüé, *Les Règles monastiques anciennes (400–700)*, pp. 59–60.

63. *Regula Donati*; De Vogüé, *Les Règles monastiques anciennes (400–700)*, p. 56.

64. *Passio Praeiecti*, 15.

there are some references in charters to indicate what regular practice was followed in particular communities. The most important of these is the charter of Burgundofaro for Rebais,[65] but there are others including those of Amandus for Barisis,[66] and of Waldelenus's parents, Amalgar and Aquilina, for Bèze.[67]

There is, therefore, narrative, regular and diplomatic evidence for the spread of 'Columbanian' monasticism. It is, however, important to note various stages of development within this 'Columbanian' tradition. The impact of the saint himself was by no means as widespread as that of Eustasius and the next generation of ascetics connected with Luxeuil, nor was direct contact with Columbanus's main foundation necessarily the same as indirect influence stemming from access to his *Rule*. Even less indicative of a direct 'Columbanian' connection was a claim to have the same privileged status as Luxeuil. Certainly the legal rights of Luxeuil, alongside those of Agaune, Lérins and St Marcel at Chalon, did become a model for other monasteries,[68] but the model they presented was no more than possession of a certain type of legal privilege. Thus the reference to the rights of Lérins, Agaune and Luxeuil in the *Formulary* of Marculf does not imply that such rights were obtained only by monasteries which had spiritual connections with those three houses.[69]

It is important to stress the variation within 'Columbanian' influence, because otherwise it is only too easy to see seventh-century monasticism in Francia as being dominated by one man. It is equally important to remember that earlier monastic traditions still flourished. Although Lérins was corrupt by this time, and Aigulf left the 'Columbanian' house of Fleury[70] to reform it,[71] there were southern traditions which continued to be influential, not least those associated with Caesarius, whose *Rule* remained particularly significant for communities of nuns. Nor were 'Columbanian' foundations hostile to other monastic traditions: the early history of the dissemination of the *Rule* of St Benedict is very closely associated with houses influenced by Luxeuil.[72]

Fursey, Foilan and the Pippinids

Columbanus was not the only figure to bring new influences to bear on Merovingian monasticism. Even in terms of Irish influence he did not have a monopoly. Among other Irishman living in Francia one of the most notable

65. Pardessus, *Diplomata*, 275.
66. Pardessus, *Diplomata*, 350.
67. Pardessus, *Diplomata*, 351.
68. Pardessus, *Diplomata*, 275; Ewig, 'Das Formular von Rebais und die Bischofsprivilegien der Merowingerzeit', p. 462.
69. Marculf, *Formulary*, I 1.
70. Pardessus, *Diplomata*, 358; Prinz, *Frühes Mönchtum im Frankenreich*, pp. 177–8.
71. *Vita Aigulfi I*, 1, 7; Prinz, *Frühes Mönchtum im Frankenreich*, pp. 276–7.
72. Prinz, *Frühes Mönchtum im Frankenreich*, pp. 263–92.

was Fursey. Unlike his compatriot he appears to have come from Ulster, or at least from a part of Ireland where the cult of Patrick was predominant.[73] He spent some time in East Anglia, where he must have come across the Burgundian missionary, Felix, but eventually he moved to Francia, where he founded the monastery of Lagny.[74] After his death, the *maior* Erchinoald had him buried at Péronne.[75] There his brother Foilan established himself, but in time he fell foul of Erchinoald, and was driven out. He then went to see Idoberg (Itta) and Gertrude, the widow and daughter of Pippin I, at Nivelles, and was set in charge of the monastery of Fosses. He was murdered while travelling back there after paying a visit to his benefactors.[76]

Pippin's family and friends had been influenced by 'Columbanian' monasticism. His son Grimoald was involved in the foundation of Stablo, which took its first abbot from Eligius's foundation of Solignac.[77] In addition, Pippin's great ally, Arnulf of Metz, was in close contact with the founder of Remiremont, Romaric.[78] Moreover, Gertrude was inspired by Amandus.[79] Foilan and his brother Ultan, however, provided another Irish influence, and they brought with them their own cults, in particular that of Patrick, who was ready, according to Ultan, to receive Gertrude in heaven.[80]

Gertrude's mother, Itta, founded a monastery for Foilan at Fosses.[81] It was remembered as a peculiarly Irish monastery, as a *monasterium Scottorum*.[82] In this it was like Péronne, where Fursey was buried, which was long thought of as being especially Irish; it was called *Peronna Scottorum*.[83] Luxeuil never received such an epithet, a fact which tends to confirm the idea that Columbanus's Frankish successors were, in many ways, more influential than he was. This distinction between the two Irish traditions also suggests that, rather than heap all the different elements of seventh-century monastic history into one single movement, it is better to think in terms of a diversity of influences. Columbanus, although the most outstanding individual in seventh-century monastic history, did not represent the only form of Irish asceticism to be found. Nor did he play the major role in the spread of Luxeuil's influence. That took place after his death, at the hands of Franks rather than Irishmen, by which time even Luxeuil had modified its founder's legislation.

73. On the cult of Patrick in this circle, see *Vita Geretrudis*, 7.
74. *Vita Fursei*, 6, 9.
75. *Vita Fursei*, 10.
76. *Additamentum Nivialense de Fuilano*.
77. *Vita Remacli*, 4; Pertz, *Diplomata*, 22; *Diplomata Arnulforum*, 1; Prinz, *Frühes Mönchtum im Frankenreich*, p. 169.
78. *Vita Arnulfi*, 6, 19, 22; *Vita Romarici*, 11.
79. *Vita Geretrudis*, 2.
80. *Vita Geretrudis*, 7.
81. *Additamentum Nivialense de Fuilano*.
82. Prinz, *Frühes Mönchtum im Frankenreich*, p. 186.
83. Prinz, *Frühes Mönchtum im Frankenreich*, p. 128–9.

The impact of Luxeuil: evangelization and reform

The results of the monastic developments which occurred in Francia in the first half of the seventh century were of varying significance. In the south, Aquitaine and Burgundy, new monasteries were founded as a result of the influence of Luxeuil, and old ones were reformed, but the impact on the religious landscape was not enormous. In the north matters were different. The number of foundations in Neustria, particularly in the basins of the Seine and the Somme, and also in western Austrasia, seem to have increased dramatically during the seventh century, and they included a significant number of nunneries. For the most part these new foundations were rural; the majority of southern foundations of the sixth century had probably been urban. One side-effect of this was the role played by some of these monastic houses in the Christianization of the countryside, which, although nominally Christian, still retained much that was pagan.

This promotion of Christianity within the environs or on the estates of monasteries needs to be distinguished from full-blown missionary activity, although that too can be associated with some seventh-century foundations. Columbanus himself intended to undertake missionary work, although it is doubtful whether he ever did much.[84] More important, once again, was the activity of the next generation of Luxeuil monks, under Eustasius, who is known to have led a mission to Bavaria.[85] The greatest evangelist of the period, however, was Amandus, whose chief field of activity lay in present-day Belgium, where he was helped by Columbanus's biographer, Jonas.[86] According to his *Vita* Amandus also worked among the Slavs and among the Gascons, or Basques.[87]

In addition to their contribution to the evangelization of rural Francia, and of neighbouring areas, the new foundations had an impact on the Church itself. Jonas saw Columbanus as a great reformer, especially as regards the enforcement of penance,[88] and modern scholars have gone somewhat further in seeing Columbanus not just as a reformer, but even as an innovator, within the context of the continental Church. Certainly he was important in spreading the notion of private penance, prescribed by handbooks of penitentials. This insular penitential practice was unquestionably different from the traditional notion of public penance which could be performed only once in a lifetime. But it is likely that even in Francia public penance had in practice already evolved a long way towards the Irish penitential system.[89] Less open to debate is the role of the 'Columbanian' houses in the transmission of the *Rule of St Benedict*, whose early history has largely to be

---

84. Columbanus, ep. 3, 3; Wood, 'The *Vita Columbani* and Merovingian hagiography', p. 75.
85. Jonas, *Vita Columbani*, II 8.
86. Jonas, *Vita Columbani*, ep. to Waldebert and Bobolenus.
87. *Vita Amandi*, 16, 20.
88. Jonas, *Vita Columbani*, 15, 10, 12.
89. Wood, 'The *Vita Columbani* and Merovingian hagiography', pp. 72–4.

reconstructed from its combination with the *Rules* of Columbanus and Caesarius, and its consequent use in such houses as Faremoutiers and Besançon.[90]

Monasticism and the royal court in the seventh century

Above all the impact of Columbanus needs to be set within a very specific social and political framework. This is clear even from a cursory glance at the supporters of 'Columbanian' monasticism. To begin with Burgundy and Neustria, Jonas has little to say about the political affiliations of the three aristocratic families who appear most prominently in the *Vita Columbani*, although he does reveal that Burgundofara's father Chagneric was a follower of Theudebert II,[91] and it is possible to show that the family of Waldelenus was among the best established in Burgundy.[92] About Autharius and his sons Ado and Dado/Audoin Jonas has less to say,[93] but the *Vita Audoini* compensates for this reticence in revealing the family's close links with the court of Chlothar II, where a third brother, Rado, is said to have become treasurer.[94] The importance of the court is borne out by the *Life of Eligius*, and above all by the letter-collection of Desiderius of Cahors, which shows how closely connected were Audoin, Eligius and other second-generation champions of the traditions of Luxeuil. Not mentioned by Desiderius, but also to be associated with this group is Filibert, whose father sent him to the court of Dagobert, where he became one of Audoin's companions.[95] Another significant, although less well-defined group of individuals influenced by the traditions of Luxeuil can be found in Austrasia. The family of Romaric had been supporters of Theudebert II, and had suffered greatly at Theuderic's hands.[96] In addition Arnulf of Metz must have been numbered among Theudebert's men.[97] Later, under Dagobert I and then Sigibert III, both Wandregisel and Germanus of Grandval had connections with the Austrasian court.[98]

In view of the association of so many leading families with Luxeuil, it is hardly surprising that the descendants of Chlothar II were extremely lavish in their support for monasteries founded on the lines of Columbanus's houses. Apart from their own foundations, such as Clovis II's St Maur-des-Fossés[99]

90. Wallace-Hadrill, *The Frankish Church*, pp. 69–70.

91. Jonas, *Vita Columbani*, I 26.

92. Jonas, *Vita Columbani*, I 14; Geary, *Aristocracy in Provence*, pp. 103–4, 107, 112, 114, 115, 120, 123.

93. Jonas, *Vita Columbani*, I 26.

94. *Vita Audoini*, 1.

95. *Vita Filiberti.*, 2–3.

96. *Vita Romarici*, 3.

97. *Vita Arnulfi*, 3, 4, 6.

98. *Vita Wandregisili*, 3, 7; Bobolenus, *Vita Germani Grandivallensis*, 1.

99. Pardessus, *Diplomata*, 291; Prinz, *Frühes Mönchtum im Frankenreich*, p. 173.

and Balthild's Chelles and Corbie,[100] several houses were established on land given to a would-be monastic founder by a monarch expressly for the purpose of establishing a monastery. Dagobert gave Solignac to Eligius,[101] Elno to Amandus,[102] and Rebais to Audoin.[103] Clovis II provided the land for Montier-la-Celle,[104] and either he or his widow, Balthild, seems to have granted *Fontanella* to the *maior* Erchinoald so he could endow Wandregisel.[105] The *maior*'s foundation of Péronne might equally have been built on fiscal land;[106] the estate was apparently in royal hands during the reign of Guntram.[107] Sigibert III provided Remaclus with land for the foundation of Cugnon,[108] and he acted in concert with Grimoald in setting up Stablo-Malmédy.[109] Childeric II provided Amandus with Nant,[110] and, together with his mother-in-law Chimnechild, he endowed the same saint with an estate at Barisis.[111] Chlothar III provided Leodebodus with the land for Fleury.[112] On top of these major endowments, there were numerous other grants of land and income. The seventh-century Merovingians seem to have been even more generous towards monasteries than their predecessors had been, and none of them is said to have complained that they were being impoverished by the Church, as did Chilperic I, according to Gregory of Tours.[113]

In one particular respect the seventh-century Merovingians certainly did more for monastic communities than had been done before: they were involved in the development of charters granting exemption from episcopal and secular intervention. Privileges as such were not new, as can be seen from those acquired from Gregory the Great by Brunhild's foundations at Autun,[114] but the mid-seventh century saw a crystallization of the concessions that were granted. Essentially they concerned the exclusion or limitation of episcopal or secular power from an abbey and its holdings. The privilege granted by Landeric of Paris to the monastery of St Denis openly states that it had been requested by Clovis II,[115] and it may be inferred from the *Vita*

100. Pertz, *Diplomata*, 38; *Vita Balthildis*, 7, 18.

101. *Vita Eligii*, I 15.

102. *Testamentum Amandi*; Prinz, *Frühes Mönchtum im Frankenreich*, pp. 164–5.

103. Pertz, *Diplomata*, 15.

104. Adso, *Vita Frodberti*, 11–12.

105. *Vita Wandregisili*, 14; F. Lot, 'Études critiques sur l'Abbaye de Saint-Wandrille', *Bibliothèque de l'École des Hautes Études* 204 (1913), pp. iii–xii.

106. *Vita Fursei*, 10.

107. *Capitularia Merowingica*, 5.

108. Pertz, *Diplomata*, 21.

109. *Vita Remacli*, 4.

110. *Vita Amandi*, 23.

111. Pertz, *Diplomata*, 25.

112. T. Head, *Hagiography and the Cult of Saints: The Diocese of Orléans, 800–1200*, p. 22.

113. Gregory, *Decem Libri Historiarum*, VI 46.

114. Gregory I, *Register*, XIII 7, 11, 12, 13.

115. Pertz, *Diplomata*, 19.

Balthildis that this was by no means the only time that members of the royal family were instrumental in persuading bishops to grant privileges to monastic foundations within their dioceses. Balthild herself is said to have insisted that the basilicas of St Denis, St Germain, St Medard, St Aignan and St Martin should live under a monastic *Rule*, in return for which they were to receive ecclesiastical privileges and secular immunities.[116] Other foundations for which documents of immunity have survived, in particular Balthild's Corbie,[117] were closely associated with the monarchy, and many of them are known to have had attachments to Luxeuil.

Inevitably this commitment to monasticism, shown both by the Merovingians themselves and by their aristocracy, had its political implications. At the most fundamental level the investment was expected to be repaid by prayers for the benefactor and for the State, ensuring peace on earth and after death. Naturally enough the fates of benefactors, their kin and their foundations all became entangled, and it is not surprising to find monasteries being affected by politics. The Pippinid foundation of Nivelles, for instance, faced problems in the time of abbess Wulfetrude, probably after the fall of her father Grimoald.[118] Burgundofara's Faremoutiers is known to have suffered while Aega was *maior*,[119] and Sadalberga's foundations were much affected by the civil wars of 675.[120] Politics must have provided the background for the martyrdom of abbot Germanus of Grandval,[121] and possibly for the murder of Foilan.[122]

Piety, theology and politics: the *Vita Columbani*

The interrelation between spirituality and politics can be clearly demonstrated by consideration of the *Vita Columbani*. On the face of it Jonas's work is concerned primarily with the ascetic standards of Columbanus and his followers, in particular Athala, Eustasius, Burgundofara and Bertulf.[123] In Book One the chief distraction from this spiritual emphasis relates to Theuderic II and Brunhild, their attempt to get the saint to bless his children and, having failed in this, their persecution of him.[124] In the second book further distractions are caused by the wayward monk, Agrestius, who tries to

116. *Vita Balthildis*, 9; Nelson, 'Queens as Jezebels: Brunhild and Balthild in Merovingian history', pp. 38–41.

117. Pertz, *Diplomata*, 38.

118. *Vita Geretrudis*, 6.

119. Jonas, *Vita Columbani*, II 17.

120. *Vita Sadalbergae*, 13.

121. Bobolenus, *Vita Germani Grandivallensis*, 10–12.

122. *Additamentum Nivialense de Fuilano*; Gerberding, *The Rise of the Carolingians and the Liber Historiae Francorum*, pp. 59–61; J.-M. Picard, 'Church and politics in the seventh century: the Irish exile of King Dagobert II', in Picard, ed., *Ireland and Northern France, AD 600–850*, pp. 31–8.

123. Wood, 'The *Vita Columbani* and Merovingian hagiography', p. 80.

124. Jonas, *Vita Columbani*, I 18–23.

engineer the condemnation of Eustasius and Luxeuil;[125] by Probus, bishop of Tortona, who is intent on making Bobbio subject to his jurisdiction,[126] and by Arioald, the arian king of the Lombards.[127]

Before considering these sections of Jonas's narrative, it is important to note some earlier problems presented by the *Vita Columbani*. Among several puzzling errors and silences, Jonas's confusions over the saint's arrival in Francia and the foundation of Luxeuil stand out. Jonas states that Columbanus landed in Gaul during the reign of Sigibert I (561–75),[128] and that when the saint first went to Luxeuil it was a wilderness;[129] by implication Columbanus needed no benefactor for his foundation. The reality behind these stories can only be guessed at, but in the light of the saint's own writings his arrival should be dated to the reign of Childebert II (575–96).[130] Further, given the role of the Merovingian kings in founding other monastic houses in forest or wilderness, it is more than likely that Luxeuil was a royal foundation, in which case its founder will have been Childebert or his son Theuderic II, supposedly Columbanus's persecutor. If this was the case, it is not difficult to sympathize with Theuderic and Brunhild, who must have backed Columbanus in order to have a spiritual supporter for their regime, only to find that he was not prepared to follow their demands.

From Jonas's viewpoint, however, the regime that deserved Columbanus's support was that of Chlothar II, who had become the major patron of Luxeuil after the death of Theuderic, and who may well have granted an immunity to the monastery.[131] Indeed under Chlothar and his successors the monastery clearly emerges as being under royal control, not least in the way it was to become a prison for notable political figures like Ebroin and Leodegar of Autun.[132] Already other royal monasteries had served as prisons: St Calais for Merovech,[133] and St Marcel for Sagittarius and Salonius.[134] At the very time that Ebroin and Leodegar were incarcerated at Luxeuil, Theuderic III was sent to St Denis.[135] Stablo would hold Lambert, bishop of Maastricht.[136]

Given Luxeuil's close association with Chlothar and his descendants, it is not surprising that, according to Jonas, on three occasions Columbanus predicted the king's ultimate success.[137] In this way, while Luxeuil ought to have been a foundation which upheld the reputation of its founder, Theuderic II, it actually came to function as a propagandist centre for

125. Jonas, *Vita Columbani*, II 9–10.
126. Jonas, *Vita Columbani*, II 23.
127. Jonas, *Vita Columbani*, II 24.
128. Jonas, *Vita Columbani*, I 6.
129. Jonas, *Vita Columbani*, I 10.
130. Columbanus, ep. 2, 6.
131. Jonas, *Vita Columbani*, I 30.
132. *Passio Leudegarii I*, 12, 13; *Passio Leudegarii II*, 4, 7.
133. Gregory, *Decem Libri Historiarum*, V 14.
134. Gregory, *Decem Libri Historiarum*, V 27.
135. *Passio Leudegarii I*, 6.
136. *Vita Landiberti episcopi Traeiectensis vetustissima*, 5.
137. Jonas, *Vita Columbani*, I 20, 24, 29.

Chlothar. This point may also explain Jonas's error over the date of Columbanus's arrival in Francia. To bring Columbanus to Francia in the time of Sigibert was probably one more aspect of Jonas's careful recreation of late-sixth- and early-seventh-century politics. Jonas was therefore involved in an exercise similar to that of the author of the *Passio* of Desiderius of Vienne, who was involved in the elevation of another opponent of Theuderic and Brunhild, almost certainly with Chlothar's approval.[138] Both hagiographical works reflect the *damnatio memoriae* already apparent in the Edict of Paris, where Chlothar recognized the legislation of Sigibert, but not that of Childebert, who as Brunhild's son and Theuderic's father was to be forgotten.[139]

[margin handwritten note: Spiritual text which took in political developments after 613]

In writing the *Vita Columbani*, therefore, Jonas was writing a spiritual text, which took into account the political developments of the period after 613. He was also influenced by other changes, theological and regular, which had occurred since Columbanus's death. In Book Two of the *Vita Columbani* the two greatest threats to the saint's foundations came from the monk Agrestius and from bishop Probus of Tortona. The description of the Agrestius affair is anything but clear.[140] Two major issues were certainly at stake: one was theological, and here Jonas was faced with a specific problem. In 544 the Byzantine emperor Justinian issued an edict condemning the so-called Three Chapters, or the writings of the fifth-century theologians Theodore of Mopsuestia, Theodoret of Cyrrhus and Ibas of Edessa. In this he was opposed by the papacy and the western Church. The reconquest of Italy by Justinian, however, enabled him to force a public condemnation of the Three Chapters out of pope Vigilius in 548. As a result the north Italian Church broke with the papacy – the split is known as the Aquileian schism.[141] Columbanus himself seems to have backed the north Italian Church,[142] as did Agrestius.[143] By contrast Eustasius, Columbanus's successor at Luxeuil, followed the ultimate papal line. In this respect, therefore, it was Agrestius and not Eustasius who was the true disciple of Columbanus. This is obscured by Jonas, who was concerned to support Eustasius, without impugning Columbanus himself.

According to Jonas, Agrestius raised a second matter in opposition to Eustasius, when he attacked him together with the *Rule* of Columbanus. Here there is an additional difficulty for the historian. At some point quite substantial modifications were made to the monastic life as practised at Luxeuil. Unfortunately it is unclear whether these changes were made before Agrestius's onslaught or after.[144] In either case Jonas was faced with the need apparently to defend the monastic lifestyle instituted by Columbanus,

138. Wood, 'Forgery in Merovingian hagiography', pp. 374–5.
139. *Capitularia Merowingica*, 9, 9, 14; see also chapter 9.
140. Jonas, *Vita Columbani*, II 9–10.
141. J. Herrin, *The Formation of Christendom*, pp. 119–27.
142. Columbanus, ep. 5.
143. Jonas, *Vita Columbani* II 9.
144. J. Laporte, *Le Pénitentiel de saint Colomban*, pp. 44–5.

although it had been changed before he put pen to paper. His account of the Agrestius affair is arguably a deliberate piece of obfuscation.

In another respect Jonas makes capital out of Agrestius's criticisms and the subsequent council held at Mâcon by royal command to investigate them. During the crisis leading up to and including the Council of Mâcon, at least in Jonas's version of events, the enemies of Luxeuil were the *maior* Warnachar, who got his just deserts by dying before the council, and a number of misguided bishops.[145] A similar question of episcopal behaviour is crucial in the conflict between abbot Bertulf of Bobbio and bishop Probus of Tortona, who wished to subject Bobbio to his jurisdiction. The Lombard king Arioald, for once behaving virtuously, refused to intervene, and the matter went before pope Honorius, who granted what was to become the model privilege exempting a monastery from episcopal control.[146] Clearly the behaviour of bishops and the question of immunity from episcopal jurisdiction were matters of considerable concern to Jonas.

Jonas himself had not met Columbanus. He was primarily a pupil of Athala and Bertulf, and he had been involved in securing Honorius's privilege.[147] He was also a companion of Amandus, and he was certainly acquainted with Balthild and Chlothar III.[148] That is, he belonged to the second generation of 'Columbanian' monasticism and he voiced its concerns. He has plenty to say about spirituality, but what he describes may reflect the mid-seventh century rather than the late sixth. Arguably it is the monasticism of Eustasius, Bertulf and Athala which he describes rather than that of Columbanus. He certainly sets the spirituality of 'Columbanian' monasticism in a legal context which relates to the period of Honorius's exemption for Bobbio and the Merovingian privileges of the reigns of Dagobert, Clovis II and Balthild. As for the political context, it is that of Chlothar and his successors and the *damnatio memoriae* of Brunhild and her offspring. In short, the *Vita Columbani*, which seems at first sight to be an account of the piety of one saint and his followers, is a document full of the tensions and assumptions which underlay the monastic developments of the mid-seventh century.

Balthild and monastic immunity

Jonas's concern with exemption from episcopal interference takes on a particular interest when his work is set against the precise background of the reigns of Clovis II (639–57) and Chlothar III (657–73), for it was in this period that royal use of immunities effectively became the central element in Merovingian Church policy. The earliest surviving episcopal privilege is that of Faro, Burgundofara's brother, for Audoin's Rebais, given in 637,[149] and

145. Jonas, *Vita Columbani*, II 9.
146. Jonas, *Vita Columbani*, II 23.
147. Jonas, *Vita Columbani*, II 23.
148. Jonas, *Vita Iohannis*, *incipit*.
149. Pardessus, *Diplomata*, 275.

there are a number of others from the seventh century, including one for Corbie.[150] Most important, however, is the reference in the *Life of Balthild* to the queen granting privileges and immunities to a handful of major basilicas, which were to be subjected to a monastic rule.[151] This policy involved the transfer of major shrines out of the control of the bishops into that of newly appointed abbots, who were answerable only to the crown. Although the policy, like other aspects of Church reform,[152] seems to have begun under Clovis II, the person with whom it is chiefly associated is his queen, Balthild.

The chief source for understanding Balthild's career is her *Life*. The first version of this text was written shortly after the saint's death, probably at Chelles, where she lived from the moment of her enforced retirement, and where she was buried.[153] It is almost exclusively concerned with monastic matters; apart from providing the basic outline of her career, it concentrates on her monastic gifts and foundations and on her life at Chelles, and even when not dealing with her involvement in ecclesiastical matters the author's criteria are those of a nun or monk; from the start humility is seen as the dominating feature of her personality. Nor does the author try to disguise a debt to earlier models in so depicting her. Reference to Chlothild, Ultrogotha and Radegund is overt.[154] Despite all this, the text is of vital importance because it draws the whole of Balthild's ecclesiastical policy together, providing the only coherent account of her treatment of monasteries and of the shrines of the Neustrian saints. In so doing the author gives a hint of the political steel underlying this apparent paragon of humility.

Balthild's career was an extraordinary one. An Anglo–Saxon slave in the household of Erchinoald, according to her biographer she managed to hold off her master's advances, and eventually caught the eye of the king, Clovis II, instead.[155] During his lifetime she seems not to have played a particularly notable role, but after his death in 657, she became regent for her son, Chlothar III, and as such she ruled Neustro-Burgundy for around seven years,[156] during which time her prestige was further increased, since the Austrasians chose as their king her second son, Childeric II (662–75), who ruled under the tutelage of Sigibert III's widow, whose daughter he

---

150. Pardessus, *Diplomata*, 345; E. Ewig, 'Das Privileg des Bischofs Berthefrid von Amiens für Corbie von 664 und die Klosterpolitik der Königin Balthild', in Ewig, *Spätantikes und fränkisches Gallien*, 2, pp. 538–83.

151. *Vita Balthildis*, 9.

152. Council of Chalon-sur-Saône (647/53); see Pontal, *Die Synoden im Merowingerreich*, p. 195, on its novelties.

153. *Vita Balthildis*, 15–16; Nelson, 'Queens as Jezebels: Brunhild and Balthild in Merovingian history', p. 17.

154. *Vita Balthildis*, 18.

155. *Vita Balthildis*, 3.

156. *Vita Balthildis*, 5–9; *Liber Historiae Francorum*, 44; Nelson, 'Queens as Jezebels: Brunhild and Balthild in Merovingian history', pp. 16–23.

married.[157] At the end of that time Balthild was ousted in a palace coup, which probably coincided with Chlothar III's coming of age.[158]

Since saints' *Lives* provide all the significant narrative accounts of her period of rule, it is not surprising that the only aspects of her policies that can be reconstructed are ecclesiastical. The appointment of bishops was a keystone of Balthild's ecclesiastical policy, as in that of any early medieval ruler.[159] She seems to have been influential in the appointment of Erembert to Toulouse.[160] Genesius, who became bishop of Lyons apparently in 660, had previously been put in charge of the queen's almsgiving by Clovis II, and he took over the see in the aftermath of the death of Aunemundus, who was said to have been martyred at Balthild's instigation.[161] She was also responsible for the appointment of Leodegar as bishop of Autun[162] and of Sigobrand as bishop of Paris.[163] In many respects Balthild's relations with the episcopate are similar to those of Brunhild, even down to their supposed involvement in the deaths of leading clerics: Lupentius, abbot of Javols, and Desiderius of Vienne, in the case of Brunhild, and Aunemundus of Lyons, as well as eight unnamed bishops, in that of Balthild.[164] The two queens differed, however, in one crucial respect: Brunhild's episcopal policy was perceived by contemporaries as being based on simony,[165] whereas Balthild, like her husband, was noted for her opposition to simoniac practices.[166] Balthild seems also to have involved her bishops more directly in government than her predecessor had done. When Clovis died the two chief figures of the regency, apart from the queen and her mayor of the palace, Ebroin, were the bishops of Rouen and Paris, Audoin and Chrodobert.[167]

In addition to her involvement with the episcopate, Balthild was also noted for her interest in the shrines of the saints. This commitment needs to be set in the context of Merovingian devotion. The writings of Gregory of Tours provide a very substantial insight into the importance of cult-sites in the sixth century. Arguably their importance had increased in the seventh. The *Life of Eligius* relates that the saint redecorated numerous shrines, especially those of Martin, Brictius (Brice) and Denis.[168] The same *Life* shows the importance of

---

157. *Vita Balthildis*, 5; Nelson, 'Queens as Jezebels: Brunhild and Balthild in Merovingian history', p. 20.
158. *Vita Balthildis*, 10; Nelson, 'Queens as Jezebels: Brunhild and Balthild in Merovingian history', p. 22.
159. Nelson, 'Queens as Jezebels: Brunhild and Balthild in Merovingian history', pp. 31–8.
160. *Vita Eremberti*, 1.
161. *Vita Balthildis*, 4; on Aunemundus, see Stephanus, *Vita Wilfridi*, 6; Nelson, 'Queens as Jezebels: Brunhild and Balthild in Merovingian history', pp. 35–8.
162. *Passio Leudegarii* I, 2.
163. *Vita Balthildis*, 10.
164. Stephanus, *Vita Wilfridi*, 6.
165. Gregory I, *Register*, IX 23; XI 49; see also chapter 8.
166. *Vita Balthildis*, 6.
167. *Vita Balthildis*, 5.
168. *Vita Eligii*, I 32.

discovering and acquiring the bodies of saints; Eligius himself was involved in the invention and translation of several holy corpses,[169] and when he died Balthild attempted to secure his body for her own foundation at Chelles.[170]

Concern to acquire relics for one's own foundations could, however, be more than a matter of piety. We have seen that the monks of St Denis resented the fact that Clovis II had taken an arm of their patron saint, even though he was one of their major benefactors, and they attributed his subsequent madness to divine vengeance.[171] Since in other ways Balthild seems to have been following her husband's religious policy, it is likely that she was deliberately expanding the royal relic-collection at the expense of the interests of others. She seems to have met with opposition when she tried to secure the body of Eligius: she may well have had problems elsewhere.

More significant was Balthild's decision to institute monasticism at the 'senior basilicas of the saints', that is the shrines of Denis, Germanus at Paris, Medard at Soissons, Peter (perhaps St-Pierre-le-Vif at Sens), Aignan at Orléans and Martin at Tours, and to have them granted immunity from episcopal intervention.[172] Her avowed intention was that these great shrines should concentrate on prayers for the king and the kingdom. The policy of exemption must have affected the authority of bishops. Clovis II's confirmation of the privilege granted by bishop Landeric of Paris to St Denis survives to show something of what was at stake: the bishop and his successors were prohibited from taking anything which had been given to the community.[173] Other privileges concede jurisdiction.[174] Certainly in granting a privilege, a bishop could hope to gain the favour of the saint and the prayers of the community which benefited: a grant was intended to reward the benefactor as well as the beneficiary. Nevertheless, in removing the great cults of the kingdom from episcopal control Balthild may have angered some members of the episcopate. Nor was it only for the 'senior basilicas' that Balthild sought episcopal immunities. From bishop Berthefred of Amiens she extracted a privilege for her foundation of Corbie in 662.[175] In it the bishop allowed the election of the abbot without episcopal intervention, and conceded to the monastery the right to retain offerings. In addition he bound himself and his successors to bless altars, to provide chrism and to consecrate priests, all without charge. The grant of an immunity could amount to the alienation of substantial revenues. Bishops may not have always have made such concessions with a good grace.

169. *Vita Eligii*, II 6, 7.

170. *Vita Eligii* II 37

171. *Gesta Dagoberti I*, 52; *Liber Historiae Francorum*, 44; see also chapter 9.

172. *Vita Balthildis*, 9; Nelson, 'Queens as Jezebels: Brunhild and Balthild in Merovingian history', pp. 38–41.

173. Pertz, *Diplomata*, 19. Landeric's privilege survives, but in altered form: Pardessus, *Diplomata*, 320.

174. Pardessus, *Diplomata*, 345.

175. Pardessus, *Diplomata*, 345; Ewig, 'Das Privileg des Bischofs Berthefrid von Amiens für Corbie von 664 und die Klosterpolitik der Königin Balthild'.

That Balthild did alienate some members of the Church is suggested by her supposed involvement in the deaths of nine bishops, including Aunemundus of Lyons.[176] Nevertheless, it would be wrong to see Balthild's policy in too political a light. Stephanus, the author of the *Vita Wilfridi*, which contains the earliest account of Aunemundus's martyrdom, unquestionably set out a confused account of the death of Aunemundus, whom he calls Dalphinus; he may even have elided Brunhild and Balthild.[177] Since Balthild was apparently much influenced by Audoin and Eligius, and since some of the bishops appointed at this period were her protégés, as for example Genesius of Lyons, her policy cannot have been intended as a simple attack on the episcopate. On the other hand, any reform of the episcopate, and its control over monasticism, would have meant a challenge to vested interests.

Balthild's religious policy was doubtless a genuine attempt at a reform of the Merovingian Church. To the many bishops who had been affected by the monastic developments of the seventh century, the reorganization of the cult-sites of Francia can scarcely have seemed improper. At the same time Balthild's institution of monasticism, probably modelled on that of Luxeuil, at the great shrines of the kingdom had significant political implications for the episcopate. Some bishops may, therefore, have seen the reform of the monasteries and the episcopate as a challenge to the established order. The elevation as bishops of reformers associated with Balthild could have been a further challenge to families who had been used to dominating local episcopal politics. Yet the queen's monastic policy seems to have had considerable episcopal backing, to judge by the signatures appended to the privileges granted during this period.[178]

When she was removed from power in 664/5 Balthild retired to her nunnery of Chelles,[179] which in its own way was to serve as a prison for her. There she lived a life which her biographer thought was directly comparable to that of Radegund, shut away in Poitiers almost a century before. Indeed sizeable passages of the *Vita Balthildis* are derived directly from Venantius Fortunatus's account of the earlier queen. Others thought that Balthild was more like Brunhild, of whose personal piety there can be no doubt, despite the later attempts to blacken her name. As for Clovis II, whose policies she seems to have been continuing, he was to be regarded by later traditions, especially those associated with St Denis, as a madman. Such was the possible range of interpretations of royal piety.

For the period between Dagobert's death in 639 and Balthild's retirement twenty-five years later it is only the history of the Church which can be studied in reasonable detail. This may in itself be significant. Certainly churchmen played an important part at court, and certainly monasteries were

176. Stephanus, *Vita Wilfridi*, 6.
177. Nelson, 'Queens as Jezebels: Brunhild and Balthild in Merovingian history', pp. 35–8; Wood, 'Ripon, Francia and the Franks Casket in the early Middle Ages', p. 13.
178. Pontal, *Die Synoden im Merowingerreich.*, pp. 204–12.
179. *Vita Balthildis*, 10.

a focus of royal and aristocratic attention. Such attention was not new. Monasticism had a long and dignified history in late Roman Gaul and in sixth-century Francia. Nevertheless the early seventh century saw important developments in monasticism. In particular the period was rich in the foundation of new monasteries, especially in the north east of the Merovingian kingdom. Inevitably there were political repercussions, but there is no reason to doubt the piety of those involved.

Chapter Twelve

Land, Wealth and the Economy

Because the endowment of the new monasteries and decoration of their shrines and churches involved considerable alienation of land and wealth, the growth of monasticism in the seventh century necessarily had an impact on the economy of the Merovingian kingdom. From the historian's point of view the increase in monastic foundations is not only a significant development in itself, but also has important evidential ramifications. This is not because new methods of conveyancing were developed in order to transfer land to the monasteries, although such was to be the case in Anglo-Saxon England; the seventh-century Merovingian charter probably descends more or less directly from Roman prototypes.[1] Rather, it is a matter of preservation: like most powerful individuals and institutions in the early Middle Ages, monasteries were concerned to keep a record of their possessions and their rights, but whereas no public or private secular archive has survived at all, some holdings of monastic archives, especially from that of St Denis, have come down to us, largely because they were preserved in their original institutions until the French Revolution. Among these holdings were charters, detailing and confirming the alienation of land, grants of immunity, which circumscribed and even prevented the activities of royal officials on the exempt ecclesiastical land, and wills. In addition to such official documentation, there are the writings of hagiographers, who took a keen interest in the treasures offered to the shrines of the saints. Thus, while the seventh century may well have seen an escalation of the alienation of land to the Church, and almost certainly saw a radical extension of the granting of rights of immunity over land, it also provides material from which to make an assessment of land-holding throughout the Merovingian period. Further, while describing the wealth of the shrines of seventh-century saints, the

1. P. Classen, 'Fortleben und Wandel spätrömischen Urkundenwesens im frühen Mittelalter', in Classen, ed., *Recht und Schrift im Mittelalter, Vorträge und Forschungen* 23 (1977), pp. 13–54.

hagiographers also provide useful information to add to what else is known about treasure in the Merovingian kingdom.

Charters and immunities

The surviving charters of the Merovingian period are concerned primarily with two types of grants: land and immunity from certain dues. Although no authentic charters survive from the sixth century, it is clear that this is an accident of survival. Individuals and institutions were endowed with land, and legal confirmations of rights show that immunities were also conceded from at least the time of Chlothar I. Thus the *Edict* of Chlothar II confirms immunities from public duties which had been granted to churches and clergy by the king's father and grandfather.[2] Despite this confirmation, the earliest authentic immunity of standard Merovingian form dates only from 635.[3] A normal grant of this kind exempted monastic estates from intervention by royal officials who were no longer allowed to hear lawsuits, claim the fines due as a result of the exercise of justice, expect rights of hospitality or demand sureties. This list of concessions gives an idea of the dues which a monarch could expect from land which was not immune, that is from most, if not all, land held by laymen, and perhaps a sizeable proportion of that held by the Church. The alienation of these dues did not just restrict the activity of the king's agents; it also involved the transfer of sources of income into the hands of the immunist. The extent to which the Merovingians alienated these sources of income during the seventh and eighth centuries is open to question, since the relevant evidence relates only to a handful of important monasteries, which may always have been exceptional.

At least in the sixth century not only were charters written to be preserved by the beneficiary as a record, but also their contents were entered into the local archives, the *gesta municipalia*.[4] Grants were supposedly perpetual, and charters and the *gesta municipalia* were there to ensure that they were respected. Nevertheless, it is clear that the beneficiaries had doubts about their security of possession, and as a result some sought for confirmation. This desire to have past grants ratified casts an interesting light on Merovingian land-holding. Thus, in a charter of 716 Chilperic II (715/6–21) confirmed the gifts and the immunities made by six predecessors to St Wandrille.[5] The implications of such confirmations is that royal grants should not be regarded as absolutely irrevocable: the alienation of land by the king did not necessarily mean a permanent diminution of resources, though such may often have been the effect in practice. Kings could, and did, replenish their landholdings,

2. *Capitularia Merowingica*, 9, 14
3. Pertz, *Diplomata*, 15
4. Wood, 'Disputes in late fifth- and sixth-century Gaul: some problems', pp. 12–14.
5. Pertz, *Diplomata*, 85.

through the reversion of estates to the crown and through confiscation. This is most clearly apparent in a charter dealing with land which had once been held by laymen. In 688 Theuderic III (673, 675–90/1) granted to St Denis an estate which had reverted to the crown, after being held by the *maiores* Ebroin, Waratto and Ghislemar.[6] Eleven years earlier Theuderic had allowed the deposed bishop Chramlinus to dispose of his lands as he wished, but it is clear that his crimes might have resulted in the confiscation of his property.[7]

From the landowner's point of view, a change in royal policy was not the only threat to possession. There were plenty of competitors for land, and they resorted to force as well as law to seize property. The absence of estates, known to have been granted to the monastery of St Germain in Paris during the Merovingian and early Carolingian period, in the *Polyptych*, or land register, compiled by abbot Irmino between 802 and 829,[8] may illustrate the difficulties in retaining land during the eighth century.

Chilperic II's confirmation of 716 involves immunities as well as land-grants. There are many other documents to confirm the importance assigned to the ratification of such rights. Thus, among the surviving charters of St Denis there is one of Clovis III (690/1–4) in 692 confirming toll rights which had been granted by Dagobert I and confirmed by Sigibert III (632–*c.* 656), Chlothar III (657–73), Childeric II (662–75) and Theuderic III.[9] A later charter of Chilperic II confirms the gifts and immunities of Theuderic III, Clovis III, Childebert III (694–711) and Dagobert III (711–15/16).[10] Similar confirmations are known from other monasteries; for St Bertin (Sithiu), Chilperic II reiterated the immunities conferred by half a dozen kings,[11] while for St Calais, Dagobert III confirmed the immunity from royal intervention given by no fewer than eight previous rulers.[12] It was clearly necessary to have grants recognized regularly.

The more privileged monasteries might hope to gain grants of immunity on their estates, but like any other landowner they relied on rents or services. The most significant evidence for the payment of renders, the twenty-eight fragmentary records of payments from tenants to St Martin's at Tours, dating from around 700, may in fact concern yields which were to be commuted into tax payments.[13] Ordinary charters, however, in their descriptions of the types of land being granted, suggest that a landowner could expect considerable renders both from estates cultivated by slaves or serfs, and also from those leased out. Land was a great source of revenue.

6. Pertz, *Diplomata*, 57.
7. Pertz, *Diplomata*, 48.
8. McKitterick, *The Frankish Kingdoms under the Carolingians, 751–987*, p. 19.
9. Pertz, *Diplomata*, 61.
10. Pertz, *Diplomata*, 84.
11. Pertz, *Diplomata*, 90.
12. Pertz, *Diplomata*, 80.
13. P. Gasnault, 'Documents comptables du VIIe siècle provenant de Saint-Martin de Tours', *Francia* 2 (1974), pp. 1–18; W. Goffart, 'Merovingian polyptychs: reflections on two recent publications', in Goffart, *Rome's Fall and After*, pp. 241–6.

Merovingian wills

Although the transfer of land and rights is apparent from the surviving charters, no Merovingian archive has survived in its entirety. It is, therefore, not possible to use charters to reconstruct the complete land-holdings of a single individual or institution. For this it is necessary to turn to the wills of the Merovingian period. There are twelve which are accepted as being largely authentic;[14] this may be a slight underestimate, and some related documents, like the *donatio* of Ansemundus of Vienne, may include authentic material even if they have been doctored at some later date.[15] Nevertheless, the twelve recognized texts provide a useful fund of information on which to draw. Among them there are four episcopal wills, of Remigius of Rheims (pre-533),[16] Caesarius of Arles (pre-542),[17] Bertram of Le Mans (616)[18] and his successor Hadoindus (645),[19] as well as that of the deacon Adalgisel Grimo (634).[20] Then there are the wills of abbot Aridius of Limoges, acting with his mother Pelagia (572),[21] of abbot Widerad of Flavigny (722)[22] and of abbess Burgundofara of Faremoutiers (633/4).[23] In addition, there is the will of Abbo, *patricius* of Provence and founder of Novalesa (739),[24] and those of Ermintrude (probably from the early seventh century),[25] Irmina of Oeren (697/8),[26] and finally of the unnamed son of Idda (*c.* 690).[27]

As a group they cover the whole of the Merovingian period, and they are also geographically scattered. There is a north-eastern group, comprising the wills of Remigius, Adalgisel Grimo, who was deacon at Verdun, and Irmina, who provided Willibrord with the estate on which he founded Echternach. Those of Burgundofara, Ermintrude and Idda's son relate to the Ile de France

14. U. Nonn, 'Merowingische Testamente: Studien zum Fortleben einer römischen Urkundenform im Frankenreich', *Archiv für Diplomatik* 18 (1972), 1–129; see also P. Geary, *Aristocracy in Provence*.

15. On the text, see P. Amory, 'The textual transmission of the *Donatio Ansemundi*' (forthcoming).

16. Remigius, *Testamentum*, ed. B. Krusch, *MGH, SRM* III, pp. 336–47; A.H.M. Jones, P. Grierson and J.A. Crook, 'The authenticity of the Testamentum S. Remigii', *Revue Belge de Philologie et d'Histoire* 35 (1957), pp. 356–73.

17. G. Morin, 'Le testament de saint Césaire d'Arles et la critique de M. Bruno Krusch', *Revue Bénédictine* 16 (1899), pp. 97–112.

18. *Actus Pontificum Cenomannis in urbe degentium*, ed. G. Busson and A. Ledru, pp. 102–41.

19. *Actus Pontificum Cenomannis in urbe degentium*, ed. Busson and Ledru, pp. 157–62.

20. W. Levison, 'Das Testament des Diakons Aldgisel-Grimo von J. 634', in Levison, *Aus rheinische und fränkische Frühzeit*, pp. 118–38.

21. Pardessus, *Diplomata*, 180.

22. Pardessus, *Diplomata*, 514.

23. J. Guerot, 'Le testament de Ste. Fare: matériaux pour l'étude et l'édition critique de ce document', *Revue d'Histoire ecclésiastique* 60 (1965), pp. 761–821.

24. Geary, *Aristocracy in Provence*.

25. Pardessus, *Diplomata*, 452.

26. Pardessus, *Diplomata*, 449.

27. Pardessus, *Diplomata*, 413.

and the lower Seine, while Bertram and Hadoindus were bishops of Le Mans. From Burgundy there is the will of Widerad, from Aquitaine that of Aridius and Pelagia, and from Provence those of Caesarius and Abbo. All the dispositors must have been people of high social rank; Remigius belonged to the senatorial aristocracy of the fifth century,[28] Burgundofara to the nobility of Neustria,[29] and Abbo to that of Provence.[30] Noteworthy is the high proportion of women in the list; three of the wills are those of women, one is of Aridius and his mother, and, because of the fragmentary nature of the text, Idda's son is identified only by his mother and his wife, Chamnethrude. It may be that the surviving wills are unusual, since they tend to relate to instances when the testators had no direct biological heir, and, therefore, may have had more freedom of disposal. Nevertheless they provide a clear indication that some non-royal women were major land-holders.

Bertram of Le Mans

For the most part the documents are concerned with the disposition of estates concentrated in a relatively compact area, but there are exceptions to this pattern, in particular in the will of Bertram, bishop of Le Mans from 586 to 616.[31] At the time of his election Le Mans was in the hands of Guntram, who was safeguarding the rights of his young nephew Chlothar II, after the murder of Chilperic.[32] When Guntram died in 592 Bertram transferred his allegiance to Chlothar. The latter's cousin, Childebert II, however, seized Le Mans, drove out the bishop, and appointed Berthegisel instead. The estates of the church and of Bertram himself were taken over.[33] When Childebert died three years later Chlothar regained the city and reinstated Bertram, but in 600 Theuderic II and Theudebert II recaptured it, restored Berthegisel, and once more transferred the estates of the church and its bishop to him. In 604 the city returned to Chlothar, who again reinstated Bertram to the see.[34] Thereafter Le Mans remained in Chlothar's hands, and over the next twelve years the king rewarded Bertram for his loyalty, ensuring compensation for the vicissitudes to which he and his estates had been subjected.[35] On 27 March 616 Bertram drew up his final, though certainly not his first, testament.[36]

28. Hincmar, *Vita Remigii,* 1.

29. Jonas, *Vita Columbani,* I 26; II 7.

30. Geary, *Aristocracy in Provence,* pp. 101–5.

31. H. Leclercq, 'L'épiscopat de saint Bertrand', in F. Cabrol and H. Leclercq, *Dictionnaire d'Archéologie Chrétienne et de Liturgie,* 10, cols 1490–522.

32. Gregory, *Decem Libri Historiarum,* VIII 39.

33. Lerclercq, 'L'épiscopat de saint Bertrand', col 1492: Bertram, *Testamentum,* in *Actus Pontificum Cenomannis in urbe degentium,* ed. Busson and Ledru, pp. 110, 114–15.

34. Lerclercq, 'L'épiscopat de saint Bertrand', col 1492: Bertram, *Testamentum,* ed. Busson and Ledru, pp. 114–15.

35. Bertram, *Testamentum,* 107, 109, 110, 111, 115, 116, 128, 129.

36. Bertram, *Testamentum,* pp. 102, 128.

Bertram's father had left him estates in the Seine valley.[37] From his mother he received land in the Bordelais and Saintonge.[38] He seems, therefore, to have been attached to landowning families in both Neustria and Aquitaine. The Neustrian link can be followed through his contacts with Gundolandus, *maior domus* under both Chlothar II and Dagobert I.[39] Along with Gundolandus he received lands from Avitus, son of Felix.[40] If, as seems likely, Felix had been bishop of Bourges and Avitus bishop of the Auvergne, further light is shed on his connections with the Aquitainian aristocracy. But Bertram also had Austrasian connections: he appears to have been close to Arnulf of Metz, with whom he was involved in various land transactions, as a result of which he was remembered in the *Liber Vitae*, or confraternity book, of the church of Metz.[41] Clearly, then, Bertram was well connected throughout the Merovingian kingdom. Even so the scale of his will is astonishing.

The document is long and rambling. There is no obvious logic in its arrangement, and on occasion it records the disposition of estates which the bishop had almost forgotten.[42] Despite this, there are references to legal documents (*diplomata*) including deeds of sale (*cartae venditionis*), some of which had been deliberately burned by Bertram's rival, Berthegisel.[43] There are also references to the archives of the cathedral of Le Mans, and above all to the municipal records (the *gesta municipalia*), in which the archdeacon was to register Bertram's own will.[44] The will itself was witnessed as Roman Law required, by seven witnesses,[45] suggesting that late Roman bureaucratic traditions were still continuing in Le Mans.

Bertram disposed of lands as far apart as the Seine valley, Lorraine, Burgundy, Provence, the Pyrenees and Bordeaux.[46] It has been estimated that 135 units of land are mentioned in the will, including 62 *villae*, 13 groups of *villae*, and other smaller properties, perhaps amounting to some 300,000 hectares.[47] In addition, the bishop had treasure to bequeath, despite the ravages of the civil wars.[48] All in all the will of Bertram constitutes the largest document relating to Merovingian land-holding to have survived.

Some of Bertram's wealth came from his parents, but he lists only a few estates as being inherited from them.[49] He may have already disposed of

37. Lerclercq, 'L'épiscopat de saint Bertrand', col 1490.
38. Lerclercq, 'L'épiscopat de saint Bertrand', col 1490–1.
39. Bertram, *Testamentum*, p. 129; Fredegar, IV 45; *Liber Historiae Francorum*, 40, 42.
40. Bertram, *Testamentum*, p. 129.
41. Bertram, *Testamentum*, pp. 129, 131–2.
42. Bertram, *Testamentum*, p. 139.
43. Bertram, *Testamentum*, pp. 109, 115.
44. Bertram, *Testamentum*, p. 141.
45. Bertram, *Testamentum*, pp. 140–1; *Codex Theodosianus*, IV 4, 1.
46. Leclercq, 'L'épiscopat de saint Bertrand', col 1495.
47. Leclercq, 'L'épiscopat de saint Bertrand', col 1495.
48. Bertram, *Testamentum*, p. 123.
49. e.g. Bertam, *Testamentum*, pp. 111–12, 117, 121.

others; he may even have lost some in 593 and 600 when he was dispossessed. Certainly Chlothar restored estates to him, while he himself bought others back. Nor was he the first member of the family to have been deprived of property; at least two estates had been taken from his mother when she was orphaned.[50] In any event, family land does not constitute the majority of the property covered by Bertam's will. Far more significant was land conferred on him, either directly or indirectly, by the king. Apart from estates which Chlothar restored to him, there were others which the bishop received by royal command as compensation for the devastation of his lands and those of the church of Le Mans.[51] In addition the king gave Bertram a number of estates, including land described as coming from the royal fisc.[52]

Of the land received from the king not all was Bertram's to dispose of freely. The will expressly mentions royal permission for the disposition of some estates,[53] while at Chlothar's insistence, one estate, granted as compensation for the seizure and maltreatment of property, had to be given to St Stephen's, Metz.[54] In other words, although the king was Bertram's greatest benefactor, he himself retained some say in the subsequent transmission of his benefactions. Further, in some cases the king granted land to Bertram together with two or three other beneficiaries.[55]

In addition to granting property, Chlothar also gave Bertram money with which to purchase land. The bishop mentions four estates as being bought with money given by the king.[56] Other estates were also acquired through purchase. Some fifty-eight purchases of property are mentioned explicitly by Bertram, and there may have been others. Prices paid range from 60 to 300 *solidi* in those instances where the text is clear. Obviously there was a market for land, and Bertram had considerable quantities of moveable wealth which he could put into property. Bertram ascribes his wealth to God, the king and friends, but his own estate management should also be noted, since the will refers on occasion to the improvement of land and labour.[57]

With regard to his tenants and slaves, Bertram's will, although scarcely detailed, is also of interest. Only one tenant, the poor deacon Domnegisel who built huts (*casellae*) on his estate, is mentioned.[58] Probably Bertram had few free tenants. More important were the tied-labourers and slaves. Bertram refers to farm-houses (*colonicae*) on nine occasions, and to peasant tenants (*coloni*) once. There are eighteen references to slaves (*mancipia*), who are to be found in one instance on a *colonica*, and in another on Domnegisel's estate.[59]

50. Bertram, *Testamentum*, p. 121.
51. Bertram, *Testamentum*, pp. 109, 111, 115, 129, 130.
52. Bertram, *Testamentum*, p. 106.
53. Bertram, *Testamentum*, pp. 104–5, 107, 110.
54. Bertram, *Testamentum*, p. 129.
55. Bertram, *Testamentum*, p. 132.
56. Bertram, *Testamentum*, p. 109.
57. Bertram, *Testamentum*, pp. 112, 127–8.
58. Bertram, *Testamentum*, p. 140.
59. Bertram, *Testamentum*, p. 140.

Bertram himself introduced them on two estates. There are several other references to servile tenants, including a group of former captives whom Bertram had ransomed, but who had then become his slaves, presumably because they were unable to repay him.[60] In addition the will mentions a group of pitchmakers who were tied to their estate at Braesetum, and who owed an annual render of pitch to the church of SS Peter and Paul at Le Mans.[61] Servile tenure seems to have been the norm on Bertram's estates, and it is no wonder that at the end of his life he was greatly concerned with the manumission of slaves, both Roman and barbarian.

Abbo of Provence

Almost a century and a quarter later, on 5 May 739, the second most substantial of the Merovingian wills was drawn up, for Abbo, *patricius* of Provence and founder of the monastery of Novalesa.[62] The document has survived only in a somewhat suspect context, but its core is unquestionably authentic. Like Bertram, Abbo weathered a period of civil war, and benefited from its outcome. In all probability he was a man of an important family in south-east Gaul, whose ancestors had been closely involved in supporting Columbanus.[63] By 726, when Abbo founded Novalesa, he was governor, or *rector*, of Maurienne and Susa. It is likely that he had already thrown his weight behind Charles Martel, and that he was active on Charles's behalf as *rector*. During the civil wars of the 730s he appears to have remained a staunch supporter of Charles against Maurontus, and his appointment as *patricius* is likely to have been his reward.[64]

Although the scale of Abbo's land-holdings cannot compare with those of Bertram, they still stretched from the Mâconnais in Burgundy to the Mediterranean and from the Rhône valley into present-day Piedmont.[65] Unlike Bertram, Abbo had acquired the majority of his lands from his family. From his father, Felix, he had inherited estates in the area to the south-east of Vienne, and from his mother, Rustica, he had inherited further properties in the same region, together with land on the Mediterranean, in the vicinity of Marseilles.[66] Other estates in the Alpes Maritimes had come to him from identifiable relatives and from four other individuals, three of them women, who are also likely to have been related to him. From them he purchased or otherwise acquired property which had previously belonged to his maternal

---

60. Bertram, *Testamentum*, p. 139.
61. Bertram, *Testamentum*, p. 123.
62. Geary, *Aristocracy in Provence*, pp. 33–5.
63. I.N. Wood, review of P. Geary, *Aristocracy in Provence*, *French History* 1 (1987), pp. 118–19.
64. Geary, *Aristocracy in Provence*, pp. 125–31.
65. Geary, *Aristocracy in Provence*, pp. 81–90.
66. Geary, *Aristocracy in Provence*, p. 116.

grandparents.[67] Although Abbo did receive estates from Charles Martel, most notably those of the 'rebel' Riculf, these constituted a very small proportion of his whole estate.[68]

Whereas, despite his family connections, Bertram seems to have depended for his wealth on the support of Chlothar II, Abbo's wealth was quite clearly inherited: he had gained little from Charles Martel, although by being on the winning side in the civil wars of the 730s he was at least able to retain and build up his family estates. Further comparisons between the land-holdings of Bertram and those of Abbo are, however, of uncertain worth. Whether the distinction between Bertram, with his grants from the king, and Abbo, with his family lands, is indicative of general developments in aristocratic land-holding is open to question: Bertram's landed wealth was extraordinary for the Merovingian period: it may reflect the precise circumstances of Chlothar's supporters after 613. Further, it is possible that the chief distinction between Bertram and Abbo is one of geography rather than chronology. Despite the broad distribution of Bertram's estates, the centre of his holdings was the north and the west: Abbo's lands lay almost exclusively in the south-east. There may always have been a difference between the aristocrats whose power base was centred in Provence and those whose estates lay chiefly in Neustria, Austrasia or Burgundy.

Labour

In fact, for all the richness of the Merovingian wills, they cast little light on the economic development of the early medieval countryside. In the ninth-century *polyptychs* there is evidence for what has been described as a manorial economy, or, more precisely, there is evidence for a combination of demesne farming with a system of rents and renders, some of which seem to have their origins in dues owed to the Roman state. In general, however, the Roman origins of the Carolingian manor, are unclear, not least because knowledge of the realities of the villa economy of Late Roman Gaul is limited. There is nothing to suggest that *latifundia*, that is estates cultivated by large numbers of slaves kept in special quarters, which used to be regarded as a hallmark of the Roman villa economy, were ever common in the region. It is scarcely surprising, then, that even in the earliest of the Merovingian wills there is no clear indication of large-scale slavery. On the sixteen estates listed in the early-sixth-century will of Remigius bishop of Rheims, himself a member of the senatorial aristocracy of the later Empire, more than seventy-eight individuals are mentioned, almost all by name, including winegrowers, a swineherd and a cook. Of these, ten are said explicitly to have been slaves, *servi*, and an eleventh was a freed slave; twelve were *coloni*, of whom one was freed and transferred to the *familia* of the bishop's nephew;

67. Geary, *Aristocracy in Provence*, p. 117.
68. Geary, *Aristocracy in Provence*, p. 129.

thirty-one others were also freed, and two were free, *ingenuus*, anyway.[69] Thus there were free and unfree peasants as well as slaves on Remigius's estates. At times the bishop seems to have made a clear distinction between *servi* and *coloni*, although both groups were servile. It is possible, but not certain, that some groups were subject to heavier labour services than others. On the other hand, Remigius is vague about the status of more than nineteen individuals, some of whom are mentioned as being transferred to the *dominium* of the beneficiary. This vagueness may suggest that, for all Remigius's precision elsewhere in the will, distinctions between the various servile classes were not always of significance.

The picture provided by Abbo's will, at the other end of the Merovingian period, is not vastly different. Again the tenants on the estates are essentially servile or tied, whether they are described as *servi*, *mancipia*, *coloni* or *liberti*.[70] The free status of one group of *liberti* is, in fact, explicitly said to depend on their continuing to pay the proper dues to Abbo's heir, in this instance to Novalesa.[71] Among dependants of all classes only Tersia, the daughter of Abbo's freedwoman Honoria, seems to have received land without any obligations on it.[72] The other Merovingian wills convey a similar impression, although their references to *mancipia* are usually formulaic.

The wills do, however, throw some further light on the general problem of slavery and servile status. For the most part servility was hereditary. There is no indication here of a slave trade, although there is a little elsewhere. By contrast there are references in the wills of both Remigius and Bertram to captives who had been ransomed, but who had been subsequently enslaved presumably because they could not repay the bishop[73] – an observation which casts unpleasant light on the ecclesiastical tradition of ransoming prisoners, so lauded in saint's *Lives*. In the *formulae* there is also evidence of freemen entering into servile relationships voluntarily, doubtless in return for protection, perhaps even as a result of pressure, although the motive is sometimes said to be piety.[74] At the same time, both in the *formulae* and in the wills, there is considerable evidence for manumission, which could result in a shift from slavery to tied tenancy or, on occasion, complete liberty. Thus, even for slaves, there was the possibility of social mobility in the Merovingian period. Gregory of Tours tells of the slave Andarchius, who succeeded in dispossessing a citizen of Clermont and marrying the man's daughter, before being killed by his infuriated servants.[75] More spectacular, but different in kind, was the case of the female slave Balthild, who married Clovis II:[76] since

69. See also Jones, Grierson and Crook, 'The authenticity of the Testamentum S. Remigii', pp. 372–3.

70. Geary, *Aristocracy in Provence*, pp. 90–7.

71. Abbo, *Testamentum*, 45.

72. Abbo, *Testamentum*, 53.

73. Hincmar, *Vita Remigii,* 32; Bertram, *Testamentum* p. 139.

74. e.g. Marculf, *Formulary*, II 28.

75. Gregory, *Decem Libri Historiarum*, IV 46.

76. *Vita Balthildis*, 2–4.

she was a captive, her enslaved condition need not imply that she was of low birth. Thus, despite a clear distinction in the laws, the dividing line betwen slavery and free status could be a blurred one in the Merovingian period; certainly it is not always possible to distinguish between slaves, tied tenants and even free peasants. As for the treatment of slaves, here the wills have nothing to offer, and other evidence is scarce. Gregory of Tours was horrified by Rauching's burying two slaves alive. Such action was probably exceptional: Rauching is known from other anecdotes in Gregory's *Histories* to have been a sadist.[77]

The issue of slavery also overlaps with other major aspects of the Merovingian economy. The evidence which survives relates almost exclusively to the estates of great landowners; the existence of a free peasantry can be assumed, but in no way quantified. Even on the great estates there were free tenants. With regard to the estates themselves, there is no indication of the extent of cultivation. It is likely that there was a labour shortage in Merovingian Francia; there had been a considerable problem of *agri deserti*, that is of land left uncultivated as a result of declining population, in late Roman Gaul;[78] the civil wars and barbarian invasions of the fifth century, as well as the plagues of the mid-sixth century probably kept population levels lower than they had been in Roman times. Labour shortages may be reflected in the donation of large areas of forest land to the monasteries such as Corbie in the seventh century.[79] In theory, declining manpower ought also to have improved the lot of the peasantry and of the slaves, as was the case for the serfs of the fourteenth century. Unfortunately, however, the evidence is too slight for any interpretation to be detailed or certain. Material relating to the living conditions of the lower classes is no more satisfactory, and for the most part must be deduced from the excavations of village sites. Unfortunately the discoveries from the best known site, that of the village of Brebières, are open to wide variety of interpretations: crucial information was not forthcoming from the upper soil layers.[80]

St Wandrille

The will of Remigius can be seen as indicative of the holdings of some members of the late Roman aristocracy: those of Bertram and Abbo of the property of Merovingian magnates. Equally these wills provide some insight into the possessions of the major ecclesiatical institutions of Merovingian

77. Gregory, *Decem Libri Historiarum*, V 3.
78. C.E.V. Nixon, 'Relations between Visigoths and Romans in fifth-century Gaul', in J. Drinkwater and H. Elton, eds, *Fifth-Century Gaul: A Crisis of Identity?*, pp. 70–1.
79. Pertz, *Diplomata*, 40.
80. J.M. Wallace-Hadrill, *Early Medieval History*, p. 2; James, *The Franks*, pp. 212–14.

Gaul. The chief, although not the only, heir of Bertram was the church of Le Mans, that of Abbo was his monastic foundation of Novalesa. Unfortunately the absence of any complete Merovingian cartulary or estate register comparable to the Carolingian *polyptychs* means that the full extent of the holdings of a Merovingian church or monastery can only be guessed.

Some approach to this question, however, may be made through the histories of various churches compiled in the Carolingian period. Of these perhaps the most striking is the *Gesta abbatum Fontanellensium*, or 'Deeds of the abbots of *Fontanella*'.[81] Founded by Wandregisil in 649, *Fontanella*, or St Wandrille as it came to be known, has not left a large collection of early charters, but the hagiographic and historical writings of the monastery, including the *Gesta*, contains numerous references to such material. Indeed Ferdinand Lot estimated that there was information on sixty-three grants of the Merovingian period to be found in these sources.[82] More striking still is the statement in the *Gesta* that in 787 the monastery held 4,264 properties (*mansus*), although only 1,582 of them had not been granted out as benefices or alienated on other terms.[83] Since the majority of endowments for St Wandrille belonged to the Merovingian period, and since the early Carolingian period was one of alienation of the monastery's estates, rather than acquisition, this figure must indicate something of the scale of the holdings of a leading Merovingian abbey. Although for the most part these holdings lay in the region of the lower Seine and more generally in the area between the Cotentin peninsula and Boulogne, St Wandrille also held several estates further south, including some on the Loire, and others further afield in the Saintonge, Burgundy and Provence.[84] Thus its holdings, like the estates of Bertram, were scattered through much of Gaul, and the likelihood is that most other major Merovingian monasteries and churches were similarly endowed.

The Merovingian economy

In all probability, the scatter of possessions over a wide area, incorporating a variety of agricultural land, was deliberate. Bertram owned corn-producing land, pasture, vineyards, forest, *salinae* (salt-works), as well as an estate producing pitch. Similarly Abbo's estates included pasture, both Alpine and low-lying, vineyards, forest, and nearer the Mediterranean olive-groves and salt-pans.[85] From the *Constitutio* of Ansegisus, which organized the economy of St Wandrille in 829, it is clear that the monastery could rely on a similar range of products from a handful of its estates, most of which had probably

---

81. I.N. Wood, 'Saint-Wandrille and its hagiography', pp. 1–14.
82. Lot, 'Études critiques sur l'Abbaye de Saint-Wandrille', pp. 3–20.
83. *Gesta abbatum Fontanellensium,* ed. F. Lohier and J. Laporte, 11, 3.
84. Lot, 'Études critiques sur l'Abbaye de Saint-Wandrille', pp. xiii–xxix.
85. Geary, *Aristocracy in Provence*, p. 82.

been granted in the Merovingian period.[86] Not every monastery could hope to cover all its requirements from its own estates; there are numerous grants and immunities intended to yield money to pay for the lights of a monastery,[87] that is presumably, the oil needed to fill its lamps. Nevertheless, the implication of these vast holdings is likely to be that a major landowner, whether an individual or an institution, would exploit his, her or its own resources as much as possible; some goods would have been transported between several estate centres, while other produce would have been sold off to purchase items and materials which had to be acquired from elsewhere.

This suggests that freedom from toll must have been of considerable value for those few monasteries known to have been exempt. Thus in 660 Chlothar III exempted the monks of Corbie and their agents from payment of *teloneum*, *pontaticum*, *rotaticum*, *ceterasque redhibitiones*, that is tolls, bridge-dues, a wheel-tax and other levies.[88] In his charter, or perhaps confirmation, for St Denis, Theuderic III was either more generous or more explicit. He granted exemptions for the monastery's boats and carts from *pontaticum*, *portaticum* (portage), *pulviraticum* (labour-dues), *rodacum*, *salutaticum* (hospitality), *cispetaticum* and other dues, wherever they were levied in Neustria, Austrasia and Burgundy, in *civitates* and fortified centres (*castella*). The money saved by the monastery was to help fund its lighting.[89] The list of dues mentioned in the charter is close to one included in a *formula* added to Marculf's *Formulary*,[90] and it may, therefore, be formulaic in nature. Nevertheless an indication of the value of such concessions can be seen in the 651 grant to the monastery of Stablo-Malmédy by Sigibert III of income from tolls collected on the rivers round Liège and on the Loire and its environs.[91] Again, the money was to go towards lighting the church, as well as to the upkeep of the monks. Additional indications of the importance of toll may come from two charters relating to rights granted to St Denis: these show that for a while the monastery received a hundred *solidi*, perhaps in coin or in provisions, every year from the public fisc at Marseilles,[92] and it is likely from the documentation that this was drawn largely from tolls collected by the king's agents at the port.

Of course it was not simply produce of their own estates which were transported to the great monasteries of the Merovingian kingdom. The list of items on which Chilperic II confirmed toll concessions for Corbie in 716 gives an indication of the range of goods involved. It included quantities of oil, fish, pepper, cumin, cloves, cinnamon, nard, bitter root (?), dates, figs, almonds, pistachios, olives, *hidrio* (water-pots?), chick-peas, rice, gold pigment, skins, including skins from Cordova, parchment, horses carrying wine, beer,

86. *Gesta abbatum Fontanellensium*, 13, 8.
87. e.g. Pertz, *Diplomata*, 86.
88. Pertz, *Diplomata*, 38.
89. Pertz, *Diplomata*, 51.
90. *Additamenta e codicibus Marculfi*, 3.
91. Pertz, *Diplomata*, 23.
92. Pertz, *Diplomata*, 67, 82.

meat, spices, fish, a goat, chickens, eggs, oil, fish sauce, salt, vinegar and wood.[93] Some of these commodities could have been produced on the monastery's estates, but it is likely that the spices were foreign imports, and other material, like the Cordovan skins, will have been imported as well.

Tolls, and the exemptions from them, raise the question not only of the transfer of goods between estates, but also of trade. Literary evidence for trade in Merovingian Francia is slight. Gregory of Tours does shed a little light on the economy of some cities, including Verdun, which profited from a loan secured by the bishop from Theudebert I, and was able to set itself up as a business centre.[94] Elsewhere Gregory refers to merchants, including one Syrian, Eufronius who owned relics of St Sergius,[95] and another, Eusebius, who became bishop of Paris in 591.[96] In all probability these men were involved in long-distance trade. Gregory also refers to markets, some of which may have been local. At times these markets are apparently associated with religious festivals, or at least they take place in the vicinity of shrines. Thus markets provide contexts for a handful of miracles relating to perjury, deceit and meanness.[97] The association of market, fair and shrine is also be be found in Childebert III's judgement of 710 in favour of St Denis, which granted to the monastery all the tolls from St Denis's fair, despite the fair's removal from monastic land to Paris.[98] By the early eighth century it was obviously a long-standing institution.

The economic importance of shrines may also have been one of the factors causing changes in the urban landscape of Gaul during the Merovingian period. Generalization is not easy here, because the fate and development of individual cities varied enormously. Many of those of the north-east were irrevocably affected by the disasters of the fifth century, and in the south even a city as important as Marseilles seems to have shrunk dramatically in size. Elsewhere churches came to provide the main *foci* of the urban area. Lyons and Vienne appear to have been dominated by their churches, and it has been suggested that the former became little more than a clerical city, although, granted the number of churches and clergy, there may well have been a very substantial service population,[99] and this would have increased on the great ecclesiastical feasts. A better case for total ecclesiastical dominance can be made out for Tours, where the church, and above all the shrine of St Martin, was almost the only significant focus. Despite its religious importance, Tours does not seem to have become an economic centre, whereas some Aquitanian cities, like Poitiers and Limoges, apparently fared better. At

93. Pertz, *Diplomata*, 86.
94. Gregory, *Decem Libri Historiarum,* III 34.
95. Gregory, *Decem Libri Historiarum,* VII 31.
96. Gregory, *Decem Libri Historiarum,* X 26.
97. e.g. Gregory, *Liber in Gloria Martyrum,* 57; *Liber in Gloria Confessorum,* 109; see also Gregory, *Liber de Virtutibus sancti Martini,* IV 29.
98. Pertz, *Diplomata,* 77.
99. c.f. the figures for seventh-century Vienne, in Wood, 'A prelude to Columbanus: the monastic achievement in the Burgundian territories', p. 9.

Limoges the town came ultimately to cluster round the shrine of St Martial, rather than the cathedral, and it is possible that the cult of Martial was already becoming the chief focus of economic activity in the Merovingian period.

Coinage

Although the literary references to Merovingian trade are few, they presuppose merchants and systems of exchange. So too does the coinage, despite the numerous difficulties of interpretation which it presents.[100] First there is the question of dating. The early Merovingian coinage is gold, and is modelled on imperial types, which provide the chief clue to their date. From around 570, however, the coins bear the name of a mint, a moneyer and sometimes a king, a saint, or a church. The chronology of some coins can be established by dating the periods of activity of individual moneyers, as in the case of Eligius, later bishop of Noyon. For the most part, however, those coins which bear only the name of moneyer and mint have to be dated by a metrological comparison with the few coins bearing the name of the king. In general the gold coinage was steadily debased with silver. It continued until the 660s or thereabouts, when a new silver *denarius* was introduced, possibly authorized by the *maior* Ebroin.[101] In addition to these gold and silver issues 'small change' was also minted in the Rhône valley during the sixth century.[102] This 'small change' can scarcely have been used for anything except local purchases. In Frisia and in the north Frankish port of Quentovic a silver coinage, known as *sceattas*, although better described as pennies, developed in the late seventh century. These *sceattas*, whose main function must have been mercantile, will be considered in the context of the growth of the northern emporia in the late Merovingian period.[103]

The main Frankish coinage is rather more difficult to interpret. There are, however, two literary references which may be of significance. The first, which we have already met in the context of ecclesiastical power, comes in the *Visio Baronti*, a text of the late seventh century. Here the author has a vision in which he is told to pay as penance twelve *solidi*, each weighed and signed by the hand of a priest. This might suggest that the coins with the names of churches are in fact part of an ecclesiastical coinage used for acts of penance and charity.[104] The second and more famous passage, from the *Life of Eligius*, relates how a treasury official who was collecting tax for the king, was having the gold melted down before paying it into the royal coffers; the

---

100. Grierson and Blackburn, *Medieval European Coinage*, 1, *The Early Middle Ages (5th–10th Centuries)*, pp. 81–154.

101. Grierson and Blackburn, *Medieval European Coinage*, 1, *The Early Middle Ages (5th–10th Centuries)*, p. 94.

102. Grierson and Blackburn, *Medieval European Coinage*, 1, *The Early Middle Ages (5th–10th Centuries)*, p. 102.

103. See chapter 17.

104. *Visio Baronti*, 13.

gold, however, remained solid until the arrival of Eligius.[105] The melting-down of gold sounds like part of a fixed procedure for tax collection, while the involvement of Eligius, who at this stage in his life was still a gold–smith, and who is known from coins to have been a moneyer,[106] might suggest that the process being described involved recoining before payment into the treasury. If this were the case, the royal coinage of the Merovingians might have been related in some way to taxation: in other words it might, in the first instance, have been a fiscal coinage.

This, however, leaves the abundant non-royal issues of the Merovingian kingdom unexplained. To judge by the weight and metrology of the coins as well as the system of moneyers, these coins may well have been produced under government aegis. As for their function, it is difficult to avoid the conclusion that they were used for mercantile transactions, despite the fact that, up until the late seventh century, they were extremely valuable, being in gold, and minted only in the two denominations of the *solidus* and the third of a *solidus* or *triens*. They also suggest that the numerous references to *solidi* in the charters, wills and even in the hagiography are not simply to units of account.

The new silver coinage introduced in the late seventh century, being of lower value, could have been used in a wider range of transactions. This might, indeed, be one of the reasons for the change, although other factors could certainly have been relevant.[107] It is possible that gold was in short supply. Much of that present in Francia could have been taken out of circulation as monasteries were endowed with treasure. At the same time external sources of gold may have dried up; plunder of neighbouring peoples becomes less significant during the seventh century, and the Franks had little to export in exchange for eastern gold. Certainly the rise of Islam was inimical to the westward movement of bullion. Also relevant is the greater availability of silver, which could have been mined at Melle in Aquitaine, where there was certainly a Carolingian mint which produced *denarii*, or pennies.[108]

While it is probable that a monetary economy operated within Merovingian Gaul, at least for the more costly exchanges, there must also have been a non-monetary economy, particularly at a local level, where even the *triens*, or later the silver *denarius* would have been an impossibly valuable denomination. At the same time, within the great estate systems of the aristocracy there would have been little need for coin. Moreover, at least in the early Merovingian period, the eastern frontiers of the kingdom appear to have relied on bullion rather than coin. Indeed, there is a clear archaeological

105. *Vita Eligii*, I 15

106. Grierson and Blackburn, *Medieval European Coinage, 1, The Early Middle Ages (5th–10th Centuries)*, pp. 98–9, 128–30.

107. Grierson and Blackburn, *Medieval European Coinage, 1, The Early Middle Ages (5th–10th Centuries)*, pp. 95–7.

108. Grierson and Blackburn, *Medieval European Coinage, 1, The Early Middle Ages (5th–10th Centuries)*, pp. 81–154.

divide between western regions, where coin appears, and eastern ones, where grave-finds sometimes include scales, presumably used for weighing bullion.[109]

Treasure

Even in the west, however, treasure and jewellery were of great significance, both as an indication of wealth, and also of status. Gregory of Tours occasionally comments on the wealth of individuals, usually as a means of commentating on their rapacity. Thus Mark, tax collector and referendary of Chilperic, had vast stores of gold, silver and precious objects.[110] So too did Mummolus: when his treasure was seized after his death in 585 it included two hundred and fifty talents of silver and thirty of gold.[111] When Rauching was murdered in 587 he had a large quantity of gold on him. At the same moment his wife was parading around the streets of Soissons bedecked with jewels, gems and gold. And when Childebert II's agents discovered Rauching's hidden wealth, it was found to amount to more than might be expected in the royal treasury.[112] It is perhaps relevant that Rauching claimed to be a son of Chlothar I. Finally, when Egidius of Rheims was put on trial in 590 his coffers were full of gold and silver.[113]

In the case of Rauching wealth and status were clearly intended to go hand in hand. Although Gregory apparently frowned on such display it was probably accepted behaviour. Thus, in the next century, it was a mark of the sanctity of Eligius that he took off his gold arm-bands to give to the poor.[114] As his biographer commented, 'he used at first to wear gold and gems and had belts made out of gold and gems and also bejewelled purses; his undergarment shone with real metal; the front of his tunic was covered with gold and he had other very precious garments, a number of which were of silk'. After his conversion 'you might often have seen him going around with rope for a belt and dressed in vile garments, whom before you saw covered with radiance of gold and a heap of gems. Indeed once when the king saw him denuded on account of devotion and love of Christ, snatching his own belt and tunic he gave them to him for he said that it was not right for those who fought worldly battles to go around in finery, whilst those who undertook tasks for Christ were shabby'.

Display was, of course, equally important for members of the royal family. The treasure sent with Rigunth as she set out to marry Reccared was said to have filled fifty carts. Some of it came from the king; some the princess's

---

109. See K.F. Werner's map of mint-sites and balances, reproduced in James, *The Franks*, p. 201.
110. Gregory, *Decem Libri Historiarum*, VI 28.
111. Gregory, *Decem Libri Historiarum*, VII 40.
112. Gregory, *Decem Libri Historiarum*, IX 9.
113. Gregory, *Decem Libri Historiarum*, X 19.
114. *Vita Eligii*, I 10.

mother Fredegund provided from her own estates.[115] Nor were ascetic members of the royal family any less ostentatious in giving up their wealth than was Eligius. Radegund and Balthild are said to have distributed their ornaments and jewellery in acts of piety and charity. In both cases their hagiographers single out the distribution of a precious belt, which might be seen as a symbol of their queenship.[116] Balthild, however, seems to have retained some of her appreciation of opulence. According to the *Life of Eligius*, the bishop, when admonishing her in a vision, allowed her to keep her arm-bands.[117] Moreover, a garment associated with her, which is preserved at Chelles, has a design imitating a Byzantine-style necklace embroidered on it.[118]

Display was thought of as a necessary means of marking the glory of a people[119] and the status of an individual. Nevertheless wealth was also thought of as something which could be usefully employed, particularly in acts of charity, which included the endowment of churches. The charters specifically see ecclesiastical benefactions as being useful; they talk of the *utilitas regni*. Apart from records of donations of land, there are accounts of the gifts of treasure to the shrines of saints. In addition to making two gold thrones Eligius decorated the tombs of Germanus, Severinus, Piato, Quentin, Lucius, Genovefa, Columba, Maximian, Lolian, Julian, Martin and Brice.[120] In the vision which Balthild had of him after his death, apart from inducing the queen to relinquish her jewellery, he persuaded her to make a cross for his tomb. The tomb was covered with gold and jewels, including whole brooches (*fibulae*). It was so bright that it was veiled during Lent, when it was said to sweat.[121]

Less spectacular, but perhaps more reliable, are some of the accounts of treasure in later monastic and ecclesiastical histories. In his account of the church of Auxerre the ninth-century writer Heiric describes gifts of plate, which had their donor's name inscribed on them.[122] Inscriptions, commemorating generous gifts of plate made by Desiderius of Cahors, were also carefully recorded by his hagiographer.[123] Acts of generosity were, of course, intended to be recorded, to the glory of benefactor as well as beneficiary. Wealth, status and piety were closely connected in the Merovingian period, and they add a peculiar twist to the history of the economy.

115. Gregory, *Decem Libri Historiarum*, VI 45.
116. Venantius Fortunatus, *Vita Radegundis*, 13; *Vita Balthildis*, 8.
117. *Vita Eligii*, II 41.
118. H. Vierck, 'La "chemise" de sainte Balthilde et l'influence byzantine sur l'art de cour mérovingienne au VIIe siècle', *Centenaire de l'abbé Cochet, Actes du Colloque International d'Archéologie*, pp. 521–64.
119. Gregory, *Decem Libri Historiarum*, VI 2.
120. *Vita Eligii*, II 32.
121. *Vita Eligii*, II 41.
122. Hericus, *Miracula s. Germani, PL* 124, IV 39.
123. *Vita Desiderii*, 54.

Chapter Thirteen

The Failure of Consensus: Merovingian Politics, 656–80

The reigns of Clovis II and Sigibert III suggest that developments within the Merovingian kingdom after Dagobert's death did not all point in the same direction. While the revolt of Radulf marked a set-back for the Merovingians east of the Rhine, the ecclesiastical policies of Clovis II and Balthild reveal the ability of the monarchy to extend its authority in new ways. The history of the kings of the next generation seems to suggest yet more new developments. Sigibert III's son, Dagobert II, was exiled, and although he subsequently succeeded to his father's throne (676), he was murdered three years later. His cousin Childeric II (662–75) was also murdered. Childeric's brother Theuderic III was deposed (673), but subsequently reinstated (675–690/1). Certainly they were not the first Merovingians to face exclusion from the throne or murder. Nevertheless they differ from their predecessors in that those who engineered their exclusion from the throne and their murders were members of the aristocracy, not fellow Merovingians. The nature of politics had, therefore, changed.

This is not to say that power had shifted irrevocably out of the hands of the royal family into those of the magnates: the Merovingian family was still central to the kingdom. And even though the kings of the period were more obviously subject to the influence of aristocratic factions than their predecessors had been, such influence was nothing new to Merovingian politics. Aristocratic rivalries had long been a feature of the court: they had flourished in the days of Brunhild and in the reign of Dagobert I. Nor did the reigns of Chlothar III, Childeric II and Dagobert II see any noble family establish permanent political dominance. The most successful of the magnates of this period, Ebroin, appears not to have come from an established political dynasty, and he apparently had no heirs. The family which was to prove most successful in the long-run, the descendants of Pippin I, spent a quarter of a century in the political wilderness, and was lucky to survive. Although the twenty-five years from 656 to 680 saw some important developments in the political structure of the Merovingian kingdom, the changes were by no means clear-cut.

Nor are they easy to trace. Merovingian history in the second half of the seventh century is a minefield. The evidence is sketchy, and at times contradictory. As a result, even the basic outline of events is open to question. On the other hand, there are some moments, or rather crises, within the period for which there is considerable information. The best documented of these are those associated with Childeric II's brief rule, between 673 and 675, over a reunited kingdom. Perhaps as important, but infinitely harder to reconstruct are the two crises involving Dagobert II; his exclusion from the throne and his later rule. It is these crises which make it possible to analyse the politics of the Merovingian kingdom in the generation of the grandsons of Dagobert I.

The Grimoald coup and its aftermath

The first crisis of the period is neither well-evidenced, nor is it even clearly dated. When Sigibert III died, probably in 656,[1] he was succeeded not by his son Dagobert, but by the son of Grimoald, son of Pippin I, and *maior* of the Austrasian palace after the fall of Otto in 641.[2] Dagobert was taken into exile in Ireland by bishop Dido of Poitiers.[3] The exile of the young prince Dagobert is unquestionably an oddity: so too is the accession of the son of Grimoald, a child bearing the Merovingian name of Childebert. According to a somewhat later tradition Sigibert had adopted him,[4] which is peculiar, given the existence of his own son Dagobert. Childebert the Adopted, as he is known to historians, was king for at least five years, thus ruling until 662.[5] What happened to him is unknown. By 657, however, the Neustrians, angry at the turn of events in Austrasia, had captured Grimoald, and sent him to Paris, where their king Clovis II had him tortured and executed.[6] The survival of Childebert, despite his father's execution, is surprising to say the least. He may have been saved by Clovis II's death in 657, and by the succession of Chlothar III (657–73), who was only a minor.

1. Picard, 'Church and politics in the seventh century: the Irish exile of King Dagobert II', pp. 31–2; the suggestion of 651 by Gerberding, *The Rise of the Carolingians and the Liber Historiae Francorum*, pp. 47–53 is, nevertheless, not impossible.
2. *Liber Historiae Francorum*, 43; Fredegar, IV 88.
3. *Liber Historiae Francorum*, 43; Picard, 'Church and politics in the seventh century: the Irish exile of King Dagobert II', pp. 38–41.
4. Gerberding, *The Rise of the Carolingians and the Liber Historiae Francorum*, pp. 48–9.
5. Geberding, *The Rise of the Carolingians and the Liber Historiae Francorum*, p. 54; Grierson and Blackburn, *Medieval European Coinage, 1, The Early Middle Ages (5th–10th Centuries)*, p. 88.
6. *Liber Historiae Francorum*, 43; on *Franci* as Neustrians, see Gerberding, *The Rise of the Carolingians and the Liber Historiae Francorum*, pp. 76–7, 85, 89.

When Childebert's reign ended, Balthild and the Austrasians agreed on the elevation of her second son, Childeric II (662–75), as king in Austrasia. A marriage was arranged between the new king and his cousin, Bilichild, the daughter of Sigibert III and his queen Chimnechild.[7] In a sense the throne of Austrasia had passed through the female line. Chimnechild seems to have acted as regent, together with Wulfoald, who became *maior* of the Austrasian palace.[8]

Some of these events are recorded only in the *Liber Historiae Francorum*, a work written in Neustria, probably in Soissons, in 727.[9] A slightly earlier work, the *Life of Wilfrid*, bishop of York, by Stephanus, confirms the exile of Dagobert to Ireland.[10] Other texts may add relevant details: the *Additamentum Nivialense de Fuilano*, a text from the middle of the seventh century, records the presence of two of the men who sent Dagobert into exile, Dido of Poitiers and Grimoald, at the Pippinid monastery of Nivelles seventy-seven days after Foilan's murder. Foilan, who was the brother of the Irish monk Fursey, came to Francia in 649, staying briefly at Lagny, before being driven out, and moving on to found the monastery of Fosses in Austrasia.[11] The most likely date for his murder is 655, and the combined presence of Grimoald and Dido at Nivelles could have been related to the coup against Dagobert II.[12] Details associated with the fall of Grimoald are also preserved in the *Life* of his sister Gertrude, which records the persecution of his daughter Wulfetrude, abbess of Nivelles.[13] The general silence of the sources, however, even those written in the Carolingian period, concerning Grimoald's coup and fall, suggests that the episode was one over which Merovingians and Carolingians both wished to draw a veil.

The power of the dowager queen, Balthild, following the death of Clovis II recalls that of Brunhild, half a century earlier. Although the evidence for Chimnechild is slighter, there is a case for thinking that she too had considerable influence in Austrasia, certainly during the reign of Childeric II,[14] and perhaps earlier. This suggests that any interpretation of the exile of the child Dagobert should take Sigibert III's widow into account. It is likely that Dagobert was not Chimnechild's son, otherwise she would doubtless have pressed his claims to the throne, either on the death of Sigibert or at the fall of Grimoald. As it is, the sources are silent about his mother, and indeed

7. *Vita Balthildis*, 5.

8. Chimnechild signs Pertz, *Diplomata*, 29, second after her son; on Wulfoald, see Fredegar, cont. 2.

9. Gerberding, *The Rise of the Carolingians and the Liber Historiae Francorum*, pp. 1, 146–59.

10. Stephanus, *Vita Wilfridi*, 28.

11. *Additamentum Nivialense de Fuilano*; Picard, 'Church and politics in the seventh century: the Irish exile of King Dagobert II', pp. 31–2; A. Dierkens, *Abbayes et Chapitres entre Sambre et Meuse (VIIe–XIe siècles)*, pp. 70–6.

12. Picard, 'Church and politics in the seventh century: the Irish exile of King Dagobert II', pp. 35–7.

13. *Vita Geretrudis*, 6.

14. Pertz, *Diplomata*, 29; *Passio Praeiecti*, 24.

his claim to the throne was apparently not well-known to the Franks. That Chimnechild was keen to keep the crown within her own direct family is clear from the marriage of Bilichild to Childeric,[15] in defiance of the Church canons on consanguineous marriage, as bishop Leodegar of Autun would later point out, to his cost.[16] A neat solution to the whole problem might be to suggest that Chimnechild, lacking a son, but determined to keep control of the throne after Sigibert III's death, arranged for her daughter to marry Grimoald's son Childebert, and that this essentially was the adoption involved. With Bilichild and Childebert on the throne she no longer needed Grimoald's support, and thus abandoned him to the Neustrians and the wrath of Clovis II. When her position was undermined by the death of Childebert she threw in her lot with Balthild and the Neustrians. Such a history is not so very different from that of Goiswinth, also determined to keep control of the throne, despite a lack of sons, and attempting to do so by marrying first Hermenegild and then Reccared to her Merovingian granddaughters.[17]

Chlothar III, Childeric II and the western kingdom, 664–75

Although Clovis II was involved in the overthrow of Grimoald, and although Balthild was partly responsible for the elevation of Childeric II as king of Austrasia, most of the evidence relating to Neustria during this period relates to the Church, and in particular to the monastic policy associated with the queen. As we have seen, this policy had its political ramifications. Balthild was supposedly responsible for the death of nine bishops.[18] It is unlikely that she was so bloodthirsty in her pursuit of ecclesiastical reform. Nevertheless, her involvement in Church affairs undoubtedly created antagonisms. Indeed her ecclesiastical policies may have been related to her fall from power. In a rather cryptic passage the *Vita Balthildis* links the murder of the queen's appointee, Sigobrand of Paris, caused by his pride, with her enforced retirement.[19] The date, around 664–5, seems to have coincided with the coming of age of Balthild's son, Chlothar III.[20] Whatever the cause, she was allowed to retire to her foundation of Chelles, where interestingly enough she seems at first to have been somewhat unpopular. According to her biographer, however, she managed to win over her detractors, with the help of various bishops.[21] Her closing years were marked by displays of patience and humility, which set her in the tradition of earlier saint-queens, particularly Chlothild, Ultrogotha and Radegund.[22]

15. *Vita Balthildis*, 5.
16. *Passio Leudegarii I*, 8.
17. See chapter 10.
18. Stephanus, *Vita Wilfridi*, 6.
19. *Vita Balthildis*, 10.
20. Nelson 'Queens as Jezebels: Brunhild and Balthild in Merovingian history', p. 22.
21. *Vita Balthildis*, 10.
22. *Vita Balthildis*, 18.

The retirement of Balthild left Ebroin as the dominant figure at court. He had already made his mark during the lifetime of Clovis II, and subsequently, after the death of Erchinoald in about 659, he became *maior* of the Neustrian palace, presumably with Balthild's approval.[23] Nevertheless, he must have been involved in the coup against her. Loyalty to those who helped him was not to be one of the hallmarks of his ensuing career. As for the Neustrian king Chlothar III, he is among the most faceless of the seventh-century Merovingians. Even his charters, which constitute a major source for his reign, come, when they can be dated, with one exception, from the period of his minority.[24] His death in 673, however, initiated one of the most dramatic periods in Merovingian history: the ensuing reign of Childeric II over the whole Merovingian kingdom (673–5) and its aftermath involved civil war, the assassination of a king and his queen, and the martyrdom of two bishops.

Fortunately the years between 673 and 675, and in particular the events which took place at Easter in the latter year, are unusually well documented in Merovingian sources. The period is briefly, if crucially, covered by the *Liber Historiae Francorum*,[25] but it is a group of *Passiones* or martyr acts which make the years from 673 to 675 particularly vivid, and historiographically important. Three major saints' *Lives*, all of considerable evidential value, deal with the deaths of clerics involved in the crisis of Childeric II's reign.[26] Of these the earliest in date is the *Passio* of Praeiectus, bishop of Clermont, who was martyred after returning to his diocese from Childeric's Easter court, which was held in Autun in 675.[27] The *Passio* was written while the instigators of the bishop's martyrdom were still alive, by someone who seems not to have known the city of Clermont well,[28] but who had very good knowledge of the saint's shrine at Volvic, which suggests that he was writing for the community there. Indeed, the chief interest for the hagiographer was Praeiectus's career within the Auvergne. The *Passio* is, in fact, as remarkable for the light it sheds on the Auvergnat church as for the detailed evidence it provides for the origins of the crisis of 675. As a result it illuminates the relationship between events at court and those in this region.

The other two *Passiones* are both accounts of bishop Leodegar of Autun, who was exiled in 675, restored to his diocese later in the same year, but then deposed and mutilated, before being martyred in 679. Since the saint was one of the leading advisers of Childeric, and since Autun was the scene of the 675 Easter court, diocesan and national events are to a large extent indistinguishable in these two texts. Nevertheless the first *Passio* of Leodegar has a very strong local focus. It was written for Herminarius, who was abbot

---

23. *Liber Historiae Francorum*, 45.
24. Pertz, *Diplomata*, 32–43.
25. *Liber Historiae Francorum*, 45.
26. On these texts, see P. Fouracre, 'Merovingian history and Merovingian hagiography', *Past and Present* 127 (1990), pp. 3–38.
27. *Passio Praeiecti*, 24, 30.
28. Wood, 'The *Vita Columbani* and Merovingian hagiography', p. 68.

of St Symphorian at Autun during Leodegar's lifetime, and who was his successor but one to the bishopric.[29] Since the work was commissioned by Herminarius as bishop it must date to the period between 683 and 692. It hints darkly at a local background to the problems faced by Leodegar. The saint was appointed bishop in the aftermath of some unspecified local violence.[30] Moreover, during Leodegar's episcopate there seems to have been conflict within the ecclesiastical power-structure of Autun. Although Leodegar was responsible for the translation of the body of Symphorian, one of his opponents was a monk of the monastery which housed the saint's body.[31] This was also the monastery where Childeric and Bilichild celebrated the Easter vigil prior to exiling Leodegar.[32] Such details raise the suspicion that Herminarius, himself abbot of St Symphorian, was among Leodegar's opponents, despite the author's claim that he interceded on the saint's behalf.[33] More suspicious is the direct statement that Herminarius had not been canvassing for the see of Autun for himself.[34] Against this background the commissioning of the *Passio* by Herminarius in the 680s appears as an attempt both to expiate the opposition which had been shown to Leodegar by the community of St Symphorian and to procure the martyr's body at a time when his cult was proving embarrassingly popular. In the event the corpse of the martyr was not secured by Autun.

As it survives, this first *Passio* of Leodegar lacks its original conclusion, which might have shed more light on its purpose. Instead, its closing chapters are worked up from a second, and somewhat later, text. The second *Passio* claims to have been written by Ursinus for Ansoald, bishop of Poitiers, who was a contemporary of Leodegar.[35] According to Bruno Krusch, the text's editor, however, there are a number of details which are either suspect or wrong in this second version of the *Life*, and since the author draws on both the first *Passio* and also the early eighth-century continuator of Fredegar's chronicle, his work appears to be 'forgery' of the eighth or ninth centuries. Despite these criticisms, the second *Life* of Leodegar does contain important information, and also a distinctive view of events. This view suggests that the author was indeed writing in Poitiers. The text also provides a partial explanation for its particular perspective, since it states that Leodegar's uncle was Dido, the bishop of Poitiers (whom we have already met taking prince Dagobert into exile), and that it was he who was responsible for the saint's education.[36] Further, Leodegar's body was taken ultimately to St Maixent,

29. *Passio Leudegarii I, prologus*; Fouracre, 'Merovingian history and Merovingian hagiography', pp. 14–15.

30. *Passio Leudegarii I*, 2.

31. *Passio Leudegarii I*, 2, 10.

32. *Passio Leudegarii I*, 10.

33. *Passio Leudegarii I*, 12.

34. *Passio Leudegarii I*, 12.

35. *Passio Leudegarii II, praef*; Fouracre, 'Merovingian history and Merovingian hagiography', p. 14.

36. *Passio Leudegarii II*, 1–3.

near Poitiers, where it was interred by bishop Ansoald, the supposed dedicatee of the second *Passio*.[37] Thus, although it is suspect in certain respects, this later *Passio* of Leodegar is important in that it provides evidence of family interest and also of the development of the saint's cult in the diocese of Poitiers, at the hands of the bishop.

According to the first *Passio* of Leodegar, on Chlothar III's death in 673 Ebroin chose as his successor Theuderic III, the third son of Clovis and Balthild. This he appears to have done on his own initiative; nor did he summon the magnates to the formal elevation of the prince. Indeed he even prevented them from approaching the new king. As a result they offered the throne to Childeric II, who was already ruling in Austrasia, and then overthrew Ebroin and his nominee. Theuderic was tonsured and sent to St Denis. As for Ebroin, after the intervention of a number of bishops, most notably Leodegar of Autun, his life was spared, and he too was tonsured, and sent to Luxeuil. Childeric then confirmed for each part of the kingdom its own law and customs.[38] It was at this moment that Leodegar undertook the revision of Merovingian law.[39] In effect Childeric seems to have rejected the less open style of government implied by Ebroin's actions in preventing access to Theuderic.

This arrangement, however, did not last long. From his charters it appears that Childeric had only one *maior* for the whole kingdom: Wulfoald, who had been his *dux* in Austrasia.[40] Moreover, although Leodegar continued to be present at court, and indeed was blamed for Childeric's policies, he seems to have become increasingly critical of the king, attacking his failure to preserve the customs which he had undertaken to preserve when he became king in Neustria and Burgundy, and also condemning his marriage to his cousin Bilichild as uncanonical.[41] Growing hostility between Childeric, Bilichild and Wulfoald on the one side and Leodegar on the other finally came to a head at the Easter court held at Autun in 675.

According to the *Passio* of Praeiectus the crisis was provoked by a dispute involving the lands of a certain Claudia, who had dedicated herself to God, and, before her death, had given her land to the bishop of Clermont, Praeiectus. When she died she left a daughter, who was abducted by the *patricius* of Marseilles, Hector. The two of them then accused the bishop of appropriating Claudia's lands, and went to Childeric to make the accusation.[42] Thus far the dispute may have been of only minor importance; at court, however, Hector was supported by Leodegar. Praeiectus was summoned, but refused to plead because it was the Easter vigil, and thus one of the holy days on which Roman Law forbade the prosecution of legal

---

37. *Passio Leudegarii II*, 25–32.
38. *Passio Leudegarii I*, 5–6.
39. See chapter 7.
40. Pertz, *Diplomata*, 25–31; *Liber Historiae Francorum*, 45; *Passio Leudegarii I*, 9; *Passio Praeiecti*, 25.
41. *Passio Leudegarii I*, 8.
42. *Passio Praeiecti*, 23.

actions.[43] Instead Praeiectus commended his cause to the queen-mother, Chimnechild. Meanwhile the king and queen, Childeric and Bilichild, fearing that Hector and Leodegar were plotting against them, withdrew to the monastery of St Symphorian. That events were running in favour of Praeiectus became apparent when he was asked to say the mass for the king and the peace of the Church in the cathedral.[44] In all probability the *maior* Wulfoald, who was hostile to Leodegar, was the key figure in this development. With his involvement each bishop was allied to a leading layman: Leodegar was backed by Hector and Praeiectus by Wulfoald. Hector and Leodegar, realizing the danger they were in, fled from the court. Hector, however, was captured and executed, while Leodegar was sent into exile at Luxeuil, where he joined Ebroin.[45] This was not the end of the affair. Shortly after, Praeiectus was murdered in the Auvergne, possibly in revenge for the death of Hector.[46]

More important was the assassination of Childeric and Bilichild. According to the *Liber Historiae Francorum* the oppressive behaviour of Childeric alienated the Franks. The height of the king's tyranny came when he ordered the illegal binding and beating of Bodilo. As a result a number of Frankish magnates plotted against the king, and Bodilo and others ambushed him and his queen, killing the two of them. The queen was pregnant at the time. Wulfoald just managed to escape, and fled to Austrasia.[47] The continuator of Fredegar adds the detail that the assassinations took place in the forest of Livry.[48]

At first sight the author of the *Liber Historiae Francorum* seems to interpret Childeric's murder as being the result of his bad government. He was frivolous, *levis*, and acted rashly, *incaute*. His treatment of Bodilo was illegal – because Franks should not be bound or beaten. At the same time the use of the term Frank in the *Liber Historiae Francorum* carries additional overtones: the author of this Neustrian chronicle tends to use the word Frank to refer to members of the Neustrian aristocracy.[49] In all probability Childeric's court was dominated by Austrasians; that is by Chimnechild and Wulfoald. Childeric had, after all, been king of Austrasia for eleven years before he had been called in to rule Neustria and Burgundy. Reliance on Austrasians may well have been a cause of complaint: Wulfoald's flight to Austrasia could certainly support an interpretation of the crisis of 675 which put some emphasis on Childeric's association with Austrasian magnates. Moreover, since Clermont was one of the Austrasian cities in Aquitaine, Praeiectus can be seen as belonging to this Austrasian nexus. This may explain why the *Passio*

43. *Passio Praeiecti*, 24; *Codex Theodosianus*, II 8, 19, 21; IX 35, 4–5, 7.
44. *Passio Praeiecti*, 24–5.
45. *Passio Praeiecti*, 25–6; *Passio Leudegarii I*, 9–12.
46. *Passio Praeiecti*, 30; Fouracre, 'Merovingian history and Merovingian hagiography', p. 22.
47. *Liber Historiae Francorum*, 45.
48. Fredegar, cont. 2.
49. Gerberding, *The Rise of the Carolingians and the Liber Historiae Francorum*, pp. 76–7, 85, 89.

Praeiecti, along with the *Life* of the Austrasian bishop Lambert of Maastricht, is one of the few sources that is not hostile to Childeric.[50] Certainly the accusation of frivolity should not detract from a recognition of the power of the king, or his achievements. The brutality of his murder is a mark of the fear, rather than contempt, in which he was held by his opponents. Moreover the murder of Bilichild is also significant. At the time of her death she was pregnant: in killing her, therefore, her murderers intended to prevent the subsequent accession of any descendant of Childeric. His son, or at least a someone who is thought to have been his son, Daniel, and who we shall meet later as Chilperic II, may have been tonsured at this time.[51] The assassination of Childeric and Bilichild also ensured the destruction of the power of Chimnechild, widow of Sigibert III and queen dowager, who had earlier secured the continuance of her own power by the marriage of her daughter to Balthild's son.

The crises of Childeric's reign in Neustria and Burgundy had their counterpart in Aquitaine. Under Chlothar III the region had been governed by Felix, apparently a supporter of Ebroin:[52] its leading bishop was Chlothar's appointee, Erembert of Toulouse.[53] When Chlothar died, Erembert retired to the monastery of St Wandrille.[54] Felix's post fell to Lupus, with whom he had previously been in conflict.[55] Lupus was responsible for summoning a Church council at Bordeaux (St-Pierre-de-Granon), where he acted as Childeric's agent, essentially enforcing the legislation which had already been enacted at the Council of St-Jean-de-Losne.[56] Both councils suggest that Childeric II was a monarch of some importance and that he was continuing the ecclesiastical policies of his predecessors. Lupus was also involved in the revolt of Septimania against the Visigothic king Wamba in 673,[57] although this may have been an act of political opportunism rather than the execution of any Merovingian policy. After Childeric's murder Lupus seems to have claimed to be king of Aquitaine.[58] Not surprisingly Childeric's successor, Theuderic III (673, 675–90/1), confiscated his lands in the Orleannais, and donated them to the monastery of Fleury.[59] Before 675, however, Lupus's actions were those of a faithful agent of Childeric, and are thus an indication of that king's authority south of the Loire.

50. *Passio Praeiecti*, 20, 22, 23, 24, 25; *Vita Landiberti episcopi Traeiectensis vetustissima*, 4, 5.

51. *Liber Historiae Francorum*, 52; Fredegar, cont. 9.

52. *Miracula Martialis*, II 3; M. Rouche, *L'Aquitaine des Wisigoths aux Arabes*, pp. 98–103.

53. *Vita Eremberti*, 1.

54. *Vita Eremberti*, 5.

55. *Miracula Martialis*, II 3.

56. Council of St-Pierre-de-Granon (673/5), *prol.*, 4.

57. Julian, *Historiae Wambae Regis*, 27.

58. *Miracula Martialis*, II 3; Geary, *Before France and Germany*, p. 203; H. Wolfram, 'The shaping of the early medieval principality as a type of non-royal rulership', *Viator* 2 (1971), pp. 39–40.

59. Rouche, *L'Aquitaine des Wisigoths aux Arabes*, p. 102, with n. 105.

The return of Ebroin

The murder of Childeric marked the start of a new phase in the politics of the period. Again the events are covered in the *Passiones* of Leodegar. On the king's death Wulfoald immediately fled to Austrasia, and the exiles of the previous reign returned. Among them were Ebroin and Leodegar. Although they had been together at Luxeuil, their old differences soon resurfaced. In the ensuing confusion Leodegar and his followers gained the upper hand, and supervised the elevation of the last of Clovis II's sons, Theuderic III, to the throne at Noyon. Ebroin now gathered a following in Austrasia, and put forward his own nominee as king: a supposed son of Chlothar III called Clovis. Having overcome his opponents, however, he transferred his support to Theuderic III, whom he had, after all supported two years previously, in the last succession crisis.[60] He then embarked on a ruthless policy of exterminating the opposition. Leudesius, the son of Clovis II's *maior* Erchinoald, who had himself been made *maior* of Neustria after Childeric's murder, was killed;[61] Leodegar's brother, Gaerinus, *comes* of Paris was executed;[62] and Leodegar was arrested and mutilated, having his eyes, lips and tongue cut out, before being moved from one place of custody to another, and finally martyred in 678 or 679.[63]

The capture and death of Leodegar removed Ebroin's chief political rival. The actual treatment meted out to the bishop, however, may well have done Ebroin more harm than good. Admittedly the *Passiones* of the saint are biased witnesses when they record reactions to his mutilations and martyrdom. Nevertheless it does seem that there was considerable shock at what took place. Much to the embarrassment of Ebroin's regime miracles were ascribed to the saint's body and a martyr cult was quickly established.[64] Herminarius of Autun had to exculpate himself by commissioning the first *Passio*. The production of the text must itself have sharpened the problem. Almost all later writers, whether hostile or favourable to Ebroin, had to steer a course round his treatment of Leodegar.[65]

It was not just the immediate circle of Leodegar which suffered in the witch-hunt following Ebroin's return to power. Many are said to have fled, some of them joining Lupus south of the Loire.[66] This may be something of a hyperbole. Nevertheless a number of churchmen are known to have been deposed and imprisoned at this time, including Filibert, abbot of Jumièges,[67] Amatus, bishop of Sion,[68] and Chramnelenus, bishop of Embrun.[69] Further

60. *Passio Leudegarii I*, 13–18: c.f. 6.
61. *Passio Leudegarii I*, 18; *Liber Historiae Francorum*, 45; Fredegar, cont. 2.
62. *Passio Leudegarii I*, 29; *Liber Historiae Francorum*, 45; Fredegar, cont. 2.
63. *Passio Leudegarii I*, 29–35.
64. *Passio Leudegarii I*, 36–9.
65. Fouracre, 'Merovingian history and Merovingian hagiography', p. 16.
66. Fredegar, cont. 2.
67. *Vita Filiberti*, 25.
68. Hucbald, *Vita Rictrudis*, II 24.
69. Pertz, *Diplomata*, 48.

north bishop Lambert of Maastricht, like Praeiectus a supporter of Childeric II, was also deposed, although perhaps not by Ebroin.[70]

From the moment that he seized control of Theuderic III, Ebroin was careful to protect his followers by legislating that no claims could be made over any losses sustained during the crisis.[71] Meanwhile, Waimer, the *dux* of Champagne, Dido, bishop of Chalon-sur-Saône, and Bobo, who had previously been deposed from the bishopric of Valence, extracted a vast ransom of 5,000 *solidi* from Leodegar's cathedral city of Autun.[72] Dido and Bobo then joined the Austrasian *dux* Adalric Eticho, in a campaign against Lyons. There, however, the people put up a successful resistance, and saved their bishop, Genesius, from certain execution.[73] Despite this set-back Adalric hoped to gain further promotion and to become *patricius* of Provence in Hector's place, but he failed in his objective, and deserted Theuderic for his Austrasian enemies. The king confiscated the lands which he had held in the district of Langres, and gave them to the monastery of Bèze.[74]

Dagobert II and Austrasia

On deserting Theuderic, Adalric threw in his lot with those Austrasians who had chosen not to join Ebroin and his king, but had instead looked for a ruler of their own. The new king chosen by the Austrasians was none other than Dagobert, the son of Sigibert III, who had been sent into exile in Ireland. With the help of Wilfrid, bishop of York, he returned to Austrasia and was established on the throne.[75] The evidence for Dagobert II's reign (676–9) is pitifully slight. This absence of evidence, and the ignorance concerning Dagobert himself may be significant: he seems to have had no apologist or kinsman to perpetuate his memory. His murder in 679, further, suggests that he had powerful opponents who had no desire to see his memory preserved.[76]

Dagobert is not mentioned by the *Liber Historiae Francorum* or the continuators of Fredegar. The sole narrative references to the reign which have some claim to being reliable come in the *Life of Wilfrid* of York, written by the Ripon monk Stephanus in the second decade of the eighth century. Stephanus relates that Dagobert's friends and kinsmen asked Wilfrid to invite the exile to return from *Scottia et Hibernia*, which he did.[77] Subsequently,

70. *Vita Landiberti episcopi Traeiectensis vetustissima*, 5.
71. *Passio Leudegarii I*, 28.
72. *Passio Leudegarii I*, 25.
73. *Passio Leudegarii I*, 26.
74. Pertz, *Diplomata*, 46.
75. Stephanus, *Vita Wilfridi*, 28
76. The evidence for his murder is contained in the curious, and late, *Gesta Dagoberti III regis Francorum*, 13–14, which combines Dagobert II and III into a single creation.
77. Stephanus, *Vita Wilfridi*, 28; on Dagobert's exile, at Slane in Ireland, and his return, Picard, 'Church and politics in the seventh century: the Irish exile of King Dagobert II', pp. 41–6, 49–50.

when Wilfrid was passing through Austrasia en route for Rome in 679, Dagobert offered him the see of Strasbourg out of gratitude. Wilfrid declined the offer, and continued on his journey. On his return a year later, Wilfrid was intercepted by supporters of Ebroin, who revealed that Dagobert had been murdered because of his oppressive government: Wilfrid himself was held responsible for the tyrant's rule, and was nearly killed as a result.[78] There is only one further piece of information of unquestionable relevance to Dagobert's reign, a charter of confirmation for the monastery of Stablo-Malmédy.[79]

According to Stephanus it was the king's friends and relatives, *amici et proximi*, who were responsible for his return. Unfortunately nothing is known of Dagobert's mother's family: had it been aristocratic it would have presented a constant challenge to Chimnechild, during the reign of her son-in-law and daughter; they would have been waiting in the wings on Childeric II's death. As for the friends of Dagobert, one possible member of this group is Wulfoald, who had fled east after Childeric's murder.[80] On the other hand the *Liber Historiae Francorum* may imply that Pippin II and Martin seized power in Austrasia after Childeric's murder, in which case they could have been instrumental in recalling Dagobert. According to the *Liber Historiae Francorum* they came to dominance (*dominabantur*) after the death of Wulfoald and the deaths of kings (*decedentibus regibus*), possibly of Chlothar III and Childeric II.[81] Thus they may already have been established before Dagobert's return. Certainly they would have been well placed to recall the prince. Fursey's brother Ultan was still abbot of the Pippinid foundation of Fosses, and he would have had the connections to arrange for Dagobert's return from the monastery of Slane.[82]

There are, however, a number of reasons for remaining cautious in identifying Pippin and Martin among Dagobert's 'friends'. First, they would scarcely have needed the help of Wilfrid in contacting Dagobert, given their connections with Ultan. Second, Dagobert's one authentic charter is for Stablo-Malmédy. In it he refers to his father's benefactions, but he makes nothing of Grimoald's joint involvement in the monastery's foundation.[83] Of course Dagobert's silence about Grimoald is scarcely surprising, for Grimoald had been responsible for his original exile. This same responsibility would not have made Dagobert an entirely satisfactory candidate for the throne in the

---

78. Stephanus, *Vita Wilfridi*, 28, 33.

79. Pertz, *Diplomata*, 45; Pertz, *Diplomata*, 44, was actually issued by Dagobert III; Gerberding, *The Rise of the Carolingians and the Liber Historiae Francorum*, pp. 81–2.

80. *Liber Historiae Francorum*, 46; for the objections to Wulfoald being among Dagobert's friends, see Gerberding, *The Rise of the Carolingians and the Liber Historiae Francorum*, pp. 80–1.

81. *Liber Historiae Francorum*, 46; Gerberding, *The Rise of the Carolingians and the Liber Historiae Francorum*, p. 81.

82. Picard, 'Church and politics in the seventh century: the Irish exile of King Dagobert II', pp. 43–6.

83. Pertz, *Diplomata*, 45.

eyes of Pippin II. That Dagobert was not primarily dependent on the Pippinids is further suggested by the actions of the Alsatian *dux* Adalric Eticho, who deserted Theuderic III for the Austrasians in Dagobert's reign,[84] and who seems to have been opposed to the Pippinid family.

The evidence for Adalric Eticho's hostility to the Pippinids comes in another account of a saint's martyrdom, the *Vita* of Germanus abbot of Grandval. The work was written by the priest Bobolenus for three men, including Ingofrid abbot of Luxeuil,[85] whose predecessor, Waldebert, had been instrumental in the foundation of the monastery of Grandval by Germanus.[86] This connection with Luxeuil partly explains the commission, and sheds some light on the purpose of the *Vita*. Bobolenus's concern was with the spiritual life of the founder and the origins of his monastery. Germanus, he tells us, had been ordained by Arnulf, bishop of Metz.[87] More important for an understanding of the politics of the 670s is the revelation that the man responsible for the martyrdom of Germanus was Adalric Eticho.[88] It is not clear from the text whether the crime dates from the period in which Adalric was supporting Theuderic III, or after he had returned to the Austrasians. In either case he was taking advantage of events to plunder and to settle scores with old rivals. Since Adalric seems to have been opposed to associates of Arnulf of Metz and Pippin I, and since he also seems to have deserted Theuderic III for Dagobert II, it might be thought unlikely that the latter numbered the Pippinids among his close friends.

That these friends of Dagobert are so elusive suggests that there were a number of rival groups within Austrasia, and that as yet the Pippinids had not achieved dominance in the region, despite the words of the *Liber Historiae Francorum*. *Dominabantur* can scarcely mean that they ruled Austrasia. They had unquestionably suffered a considerable set-back with the fall of Grimoald, and the rise of Wulfoald. Moreover, the subsequent history of Rupert of Salzburg suggests that an anti-Pippinid party still existed in Austrasia in the 690s.[89]

One thing that is certain is Ebroin's hostility to the new regime in the east.[90] Inevitably war broke out between Theuderic and Dagobert. To judge by the evidence of the *Life of Sadalberga*, which tells how the abbess moved her nunnery from the suburbs of Langres to the safety of the city of Laon,[91] the war was waged well inside Burgundian territory. This suggests that for a while Dagobert held the upper hand. In 679, however, he was murdered at the instigation of unnamed *duces* and with the consent of equally anonymous bishops.[92] Ebroin may have been involved. He had supporters in Austrasia

84. Pertz, *Diplomata*, 46.
85. Bobolenus, *Vita Germani abbatis Grandivallensis, praef.*
86. Bobolenus, *Vita Germani abbatis Grandivallensis*, 7–8.
87. Bobolenus, *Vita Germani abbatis Grandivallensis*, 4.
88. Bobolenus, *Vita Germani abbatis Grandivallensis*, 10.
89. Wallace-Hadrill, *The Frankish Church*, p. 147.
90. Stephanus, *Vita Wilfridi*, 33.
91. *Vita Sadalbergae*, 14.
92. Stephanus, *Vita Wilfridi*, 33.

who had aided him in setting up a young prince called Clovis in opposition to Theuderic III in 675.[93] He certainly benefited from Dagobert's death, since Stephanus implies that he subsequently controlled Austrasia – it was into the hands of his followers that Wilfrid of York fell when he returned from Rome to what had been Dagobert's kingdom in 680.[94]

The involvement of groups favourable to Ebroin in the murder of Dagobert does help to limit the number of possible interpretations of the *Liber Historiae Francorum* at this point. As we have seen, the text refers to Martin and Pippin coming to power after the deaths of Wulfoald and of unnamed kings.[95] These unnamed kings might have included Dagobert II as well as Chlothar III and Childeric II, in which case Martin and Pippin might both have been implicated in Dagobert's murder. Since, however, the king was apparently killed by a group favourable to Ebroin, and since Martin and Pippin were at war with Ebroin within a year, the chances are that they belonged to a separate faction. They may at least be absolved of regicide.

The narrative of the *Liber Historiae Francorum* makes no mention of Dagobert II, his return or his murder. It speaks only of Wulfoald's death and the emergence of the *duces*, Martin and Pippin II, nephew of the Pippinid *maior* Grimoald, and their defeat by Ebroin at Lucofao, or the Bois-du-Fays. After the battle Martin retreated to Laon. From there he was persuaded by Ebroin to go to the nearby villa of Ecry, where he was murdered.[96] Ebroin's success, however, was short-lived. Back in Neustria a Frank called Ermenfred, thinking that his estates were under threat from Ebroin, gathered together a band of followers and killed him.[97] The assassin then went to Pippin in Austrasia, with gifts, which suggests that he was not in his pay. Nevertheless, Ebroin's death was certainly a boon for Pippin.

The Merovingians and aristocratic faction in the age of Ebroin

There is much about the period of Ebroin's political dominance which is uncertain. Nevertheless, it is possible to make some observations about the nature of political structures in the third quarter of the seventh century. What the nobles wanted was a ruler of Merovingian blood to whom they had access. Thus in 673 Ebroin's opponents turned to Childeric II,[98] and two years later, when they backed Theuderic III, Ebroin briefly discovered Clovis, an otherwise unknown son of Chlothar III.[99] In Austrasia, an equivalent hunt for a Merovingian led to the recall of Dagobert II from exile.[100] What these

93. *Passio Leudegarii* I, 19.
94. Stephanus, *Vita Wilfridi*, 33.
95. *Liber Historiae Francorum*, 46.
96. *Liber Historiae Francorum*, 46.
97. *Liber Historiae Francorum*, 47; Fredegar, cont. 4; *Vita Filiberti*, 27.
98. *Passio Leudegarii* I, 5.
99. *Passio Leudegarii* I, 19.
100. Stephanus, *Vita Wilfridi*, 28.

complicated manoeuvres also show is that any suggestion of a division of the kingdom between all the Merovingian princes was even less inevitable in the seventh century than it had been before. There was no clear succession pattern and no rigid adherence to a single Merovingian line in either of the two Frankish kingdoms. The elevation of Childebert the Adopted is further proof of the complexity of the system of royal inheritance.

Despite the promotion of the claims of individual princes by rival aristocratic groups, it is important to realize that Merovingian kings could still wield considerable power. Chlothar III may have been a cipher, but neither Childeric II nor Dagobert II was weak. Their murders are indications both of their strength and of opposition to what they were doing. In the case of Dagobert it is not easy to go much further; the only source to provide detail calls him a 'destroyer of cities, despising the counsels of the magnates (*seniores*), reducing the people with taxation, like Rehoboam, son of Solomon, being contemptuous of God's churches and their bishops'.[101] Much of this might have been said about other powerful Merovingian kings. In particular, rejection of magnate advice, in one way or another, comes close to the heart of the political problems of the whole period.

It is a recurrent complaint in the first *Passio* of Leodegar. Here, after the fall of Balthild, Ebroin is said to have deprived the Burgundians of access to court.[102] Matters became worse still after the death of Chlothar III:

But when Ebroin ought, having summoned the magnates, as is the custom, to have solemnly elevated his brother called Theuderic to the kingship, swollen with the spirit of pride he did not wish to call them. Therefore they began to fear greatly that while he might nominally maintain the king, whom he should have raised publicly to the glory of the state, he would be able boldly to inflict evil on whomsoever he wished.[103]

These fears can reasonably be linked to Childeric's concessions that every part of the Merovingian kingdom should be allowed its own laws, customs and officials.[104] Equally, Childeric's increasing reliance on Wulfoald should be seen as one aspect of his failure to fulfil his promises. Once these matters are set together they can be seen as relating to a series of complaints and concessions which are apparent from the reign of Chlothar II onwards.

The best known of these is Chlothar's own *Edict* of 614, in which he promised that the judges of each district should be appointed from the region.[105] It is likely that similar concessions were made to the Burgundians two years later, after the attempted usurpation by Alethius.[106] Later, after the

101. Stephanus, *Vita Wilfridi*, 33.
102. *Passio Leudegarii I*, 3.
103. *Passio Leudegarii I*, 5.
104. *Passio Leudegarii I*, 7.
105. *Capitularia Merowingica*, 9, 12.
106. Fredegar IV, 44.

death of their *maior*, Warnachar, the Burgundian leaders made an even more radical request: they asked that there should not be another *maior*, because they wanted direct access to the royal court.[107] In fact this concession was broken during the minority of Clovis II when his mother, Nantechild, persuaded the Burgundians to accept Flaochad as *maior*.[108]

This provides a background to the actions of Ebroin, in particular to his prevention of Burgundians from approaching Chlothar III.[109] Fortunately the wealth of evidence relating to the protagonists in the crisis of 673 further elucidates what was at stake in Ebroin's day. First, it is important to recognize that mention of Burgundy and Burgundians does not necessarily imply a regionally defined or coherent group. The leader of the Burgundians was unquestionably Leodegar,[110] who had been brought up, on Chlothar II's orders, by Dido of Poitiers;[111] in other words he was brought up in Aquitaine by an uncle from Neustria, who had close political ties with Austrasia, as can be seen in the fact that it was he who took the young Dagobert into exile in Ireland. Moreover, Leodegar was appointed to the Burgundian bishopric of Autun by Balthild;[112] his was a court appointment, and, unlike Genesius at Lyons, he appears not to have enjoyed overwhelming local support.[113] Of his known supporters, Leudesius was the son of Erchinoald, and was thus of Neustrian family,[114] while Leodegar's own brother, Gaerinus, was *comes* of Paris.[115] In short, the leader of the Burgundian group, opposed by Ebroin, was a bishop who seems to have been of Neustrian extraction, and who brought up in Aquitaine by an uncle with Neustrian and Austrasian connections. To complicate matters, Ebroin himself was a Neustrian, probably from the Soissons area,[116] and he was *conpater*, that is related as a godparent, to Leudesius, a fellow Neustrian, whom he killed.[117] Thus an interpretation of the crisis of 673 to 675 in terms of Burgundian regionalism is not acceptable.

There may be more of a case for interpreting relations between Neustro-Burgundy and either Austrasia or Aquitaine in regional terms. After all Childeric II's court seems to have been dominated by a recognizably Austrasian group. Nevertheless it would be unwise to push this example of regionalism too far. Earlier Grimoald had exiled the young Dagobert with the

107. Fredegar IV, 54.
108. Fredegar IV, 89.
109. *Passio Leudegarii I*, 3.
110. *Passio Leudegarii I*, 3.
111. *Passio Leudegarii II*, 1; on Dido's family, see Picard, 'Church and politics in the seventh century: the Irish exile of King Dagobert II', p. 39.
112. *Passio Leudegarii I*, 2.
113. Compare *Passio Leudegarii I*, 2, 10, with 26.
114. *Liber Historiae Francorum*, 45
115. Pertz, *Diplomata*, 77.
116. Fouracre, 'Merovingians, mayors of the palace and the notion of a "low-born" Ebroin', p. 14.
117. Fredegar, cont. 2.

help of Dido of Poitiers.[118] Subsequently Ebroin regained power after the death of Childeric II by calling in Austrasians.[119] Among his supporters at the time was the Alsatian *dux* Adalric Eticho. When Adalric failed to obtain the patriciate in Provence he abandoned Ebroin and Theuderic and rejoined the Austrasians, which seems to have meant that he threw his weight behind Dagobert II.[120]

Turning to Provence, Hector, the *patricius* of Marseilles, was in league with Leodegar, and he fell foul of Praeiectus of Clermont, over a matter of land in the Auvergne.[121] As for the rulers of Aquitaine, Felix was apparently a supporter of Ebroin;[122] his successor, Lupus, was Childeric's man. Despite the Austrasian origins of Childeric's rule, Lupus had estates in the Orleannais, well to the west of Austrasia.[123] All in all the evidence portrays an aristocracy whose political interests were supra-regional, as might have been expected from the pattern of land-holdings which we have observed from a study of the Merovingian wills.[124] Thus, although this aristocracy was politically divided, the division was based on something other than geography. The precise reason for the association between individuals can rarely be detected, but what is likely to be at issue is the formation of interest groups, or, as the first *Passio* of Leodegar calls them, *factiones*.[125] The complaint against Ebroin was thus a complaint against one faction monopolizing access to the king, and therefore controlling all royal favours.

A recognition of factionalism also helps explain the divergence of attitude towards different individuals in the sources, for the sources themselves often represented factional positions. Opinions expressed about Ebroin are particularly revealing. He is depicted as a wicked and bloodthirsty figure by the first *Passio* of Leodegar, which is hardly surprising, given the author's subject and his desire to exonerate Herminarius from any blame.[126] The second *Passio* is perhaps not quite as extreme in its language, although in some respects it is more single-minded in its attack on Ebroin himself.[127] The *Life* of another cleric to suffer at Ebroin's hands, Filibert, founder of the Neustrian monastery of Jumièges, is equally ill-disposed to Ebroin.[128] The same is not true of the *Passio Praeiecti*, although this last work is critical of his brutal treatment of Leodegar.[129] More favourable are the *Life* of Eligius[130]

118. *Liber Historiae Francorum*, 43.
119. *Passio Leudegarii I*, 18.
120. *Passio Leudegarii I*, 26; Pertz, *Diplomata*, 46.
121. *Passio Praeiecti*, 23.
122. *Miracula Martialis*, II 3.
123. Rouche, *L'Aquitaine des Wisigoths aux Arabes*, p. 102, with n. 105.
124. See chapter 12.
125. *Passio Leudegarii I*, 15, 28.
126. Fouracre, 'Merovingian history and Merovingian hagiography', p. 16.
127. Fouracre, 'Merovingian history and Merovingian hagiography', p. 20.
128. *Vita Filiberti*, 24, 25, 27.
129. *Passio Praeiecti*, 26.
130. *Vita Eligii*, II 56; but see II 9.

and, above all, the *Miracula Martialis* from Limoges.[131] Most interesting, however, is the silence of the *Life* of Audoin of Rouen, since it is known from elsewhere that the saint was a supporter of Ebroin,[132] and indeed he was the original author of the *Vita Eligii*. Here it looks as if Audoin's hagiographer found the image presented by the supporters of the cult of Leodegar too strong to challenge, but whereas the author of the *Passio Praeiecti* depicted Ebroin's treatment of the bishop of Autun as an aberration, the biographer of the bishop of Rouen dealt with the problem by silence. The manipulation of a martyr-cult could interfere with the record of events and the subsequent reputation of the protagonists. The conclusion of the first *Passio* of Leodegar shows clearly how important it was for Ebroin to prevent the cult of a martyr from forming, and the silence of the *Life* of Audoin shows how complete was Ebroin's failure in doing this, even though he had managed to dominate the court more ruthlessly than his predecessors.

The *Life* of Audoin, the *Passio* of Praeiectus and the *Miracles* of Martial provide a salutary reminder that Ebroin had a considerable and respectable following. Nevertheless it is the works which are hostile to Ebroin which are, arguably, more revealing of the significance of the twenty-five years from 656 to 680. As the *Passiones* of Leodegar reveal, Ebroin had demonstrated that it was possible for a single faction to exclude other factions from court. He may not have been the first to do so: Grimoald had already managed to seize control of the throne, if only for a year. Nor did Ebroin succeed without considerable opposition. However, in so doing, he undermined the central position of the court in the Merovingian kingdom. Hitherto, whatever the quality of an individual king, the court had been the chief political, and indeed social, focus of the *regnum Francorum*. As a result the kingdom had remained unified, despite the divisions between Austrasia, Neustria, Burgundy and Aquitaine, and despite the recurrent civil wars, which had so disturbed Gregory of Tours. The creation of a monopoly of influence at court in the late seventh century seems to have weakened the centripetal forces which had held the Merovingian kingdom together.

In so far as access to the royal court had created a political consensus in Merovingian Francia, the actions of Grimoald and Ebroin undermined that consensus. In their own day, however, court and country were still closely related. Thus a law-suit over land in the Auvergne precipitated a political crisis at court and the subsequent assassination of Praeiectus. Local rivalries in Autun between the monastery of St Symphorian and Leodegar contributed to the saint's downfall. And in the countryside the martyrdom of Germanus of Grandval was apparently part of the fall-out of political rivalry. As yet the kingdom held together. But, although the Merovingians themselves were not yet a spent force, the power-structures on which the dynasty had depended were under threat.

131. *Miracula Martialis*, II 3.
132. *Liber Historiae Francorum*, 45; *Vita Filiberti*, 25.

Chapter Fourteen

The Culture of Churchmen: Education, Theology and Book-Production in the Later Seventh Century

The fates of Praeiectus, Germanus of Grandval and, above all, Leodegar cast a particularly gruesome light over the history of the late-seventh-century Church in Francia, and by extension call into question the state of the Merovingian Church at the time. Yet there was nothing new about the murder of ecclesiastics. In the sixth century Praextextatus of Rouen had fallen to Fredegund's assassins,[1] and Lupentius, abbot of Javols, seems to have been one of Brunhild's victims.[2] Another, in the early seventh century, was Desiderius of Vienne.[3] Thereafter there was Rusticus of Cahors,[4] and Foilan, the brother of Fursey.[5] Then, in the days of Balthild's regency, Aunemundus of Lyons was executed, as perhaps were eight other bishops.[6] One who is known to have died in violent circumstances at this time was Leodegar's own predecessor at Autun.[7] Nor did the 670s see the last of the Merovingian martyrdoms. In about the year 700 Lambert of Maastricht was murdered, according to later sources, at the hands of the supporters of Pippin II's bigamous wife, Alpaida.[8] Against this background the bloodshed of the 670s seems less remarkable. What was unusual about the martyrdom of Leodegar was the mutilation which preceded his death, and it was probably this which shocked some of Ebroin's own supporters. Essentially, because bishops and abbots were important political figures, they shared the same dangers as any Frankish magnate.

Writing in the mid-eighth century the Anglo-Saxon missionary, Boniface, denounced the religious standards of the Merovingian Church of his own

---

1. Gregory, *Decem Libri Historiarum*, VIII 31.
2. Gregory, *Decem Libri Historiarum*, VI 37.
3. *Passio sancti Desiderii episcopi et martyris,* 9.
4. *Vita Desiderii,* 8.
5. *Additamentum Nivialense de Fuilano.*
6. Stephanus, *Vita Wilfridi,* 6.
7. *Passio Leudegarii I,* 2.
8. *Vita Landiberti episcopi Traeiectensis vetustissima* 17; Sigebert, *Vita Landiberti episcopi Traeiectensis,* 18–20.

day,[9] and it is all too easy to see the clergy of the late seventh century through his eyes as well. Nevertheless there was more to men like Leodegar than is revealed by the political narrative. They were among the leading exponents of the frequently underestimated Christian culture of seventh-century Francia. As such they played a role in the transmission of Roman culture within western Europe, which is often overlooked.

The knowledge of administrators

According to the first *Passio* of Leodegar, the saint was educated by his uncle, Dido, bishop of Poitiers, and became especially learned in secular and canon law.[10] The second *Passio* adds some important details, which are particularly noteworthy since the work was apparently written in Poitiers, and might therefore reflect local traditions about the schooling arranged by the bishop. Here Leodegar is handed over to Chlothar II for his education, and it is the king who sends him to Dido, who in turn hands him over to a learned priest. In addition to a knowledge of law, both secular and ecclesiastical, the Poitevin author refers to the saint's knowledge of the scriptures.[11]

Just as Leodegar's martyrdom can be paralleled in the hagiography of other saints, so too can his education. Audoin, for instance, was educated by members of the aristocracy, seemingly with royal approval.[12] From the same generation Arnulf of Metz, Desiderius of Cahors and Filibert of Jumièges all went to court after they had received their education.[13] Filibert was taught in a local, perhaps episcopal, school at Aire, in the south-west of Aquitaine,[14] while Praeiectus was educated at Issoire, the centre of the cult of the Auvergnat saint Stremonius.[15] Like Leodegar, Desiderius is known to have been trained in Roman Law.[16]

From the *Lex Ribvaria* it is clear that Roman Law was associated with the Church:[17] some indication of its importance may be seen in the surprising number of manuscripts of the *Codex Theodosianus* and the *Breviary* of Alaric to have survived from the Merovingian period.[18] In addition churchmen had to know the canons of the Church. Here the manuscript known as the *Collectio Corbeiensis*, which contains the decrees of various Church councils, including

9. Boniface, epp. 50, 60.
10. *Passio Leudegarii I*, 1.
11. *Passio Leudegarii II*, 1.
12. *Vita Audoini*, 1.
13. *Vita Arnulfi*, 3; *Vita Desiderii*, 1; *Vita Filiberti*, 1; Wood, 'Administration, law and culture in Merovingian Gaul', pp. 74–5.
14. *Vita Filiberti*, 1.
15. *Passio Praeiecti*, 2.
16. *Vita Desiderii* 1; Wood, 'Administration, law and culture in Merovingian Gaul', p. 67.
17. *Lex Ribvaria*, 61, 1.
18. Wood, 'The *Codex Theodosianus* in Merovingian Gaul'.

the 573 Council of Paris, as well as letters of Childebert I and Chlothar I, may provide an insight into Leodegar's knowledge of the canons.[19] If the manuscript was indeed used, as has been suggested, at the Council of Clichy in 626–7 and subsequently by Leodegar himself, it sheds direct light on the saint's knowledge of canon law, so vaunted by his hagiographers. The *Passiones* of Leodegar further imply that he was learned in Frankish law, since Childeric II is said to have entrusted him with revising the laws of his three kingdoms.[20] As we have seen there may be traces of this revision in *Lex Salica*.

Leodegar's expertise in law may have been outstanding, but a knowledge of law was useful for any bishop in the administration of his see, and particularly in the protection of the rights of his Church. It was, significantly, a bishop, Landeric of Paris, who commissioned the most substantial Merovingian collection of legal *formulae*, that of Marculf, in the late seventh or early eighth century.[21] Such legal knowledge was crucial for any holder of administrative office, and, as the hagiographers reveal, education was not just the preserve of those intending to enter the church. Indeed many Merovingian saints opted for the religious life only in their maturity. Desiderius of Cahors had a significant career at court and in Provence before becoming bishop.[22] Equivalent careers are known for Arnulf of Metz, Eligius of Noyon and Audoin of Rouen, whose brothers Ado and Rado had a similar education, but never entered the Church.[23] In so literate a kingdom it is not surprising that every Merovingian king seems to have been able to read and write.[24]

Bishops and their writings

This picture of well-educated aristocrats is presented by the hagiographers, and in a sense, therefore, the information relating to the learning of the aristocracy comes from biased sources, and is second-hand. It can, however, be filled out a little by the few surviving writings of the saints themselves. For the first generation of bishops to be influenced by Luxeuil there are the letters of Desiderius of Cahors, which, as we have seen, demonstrate continuing mastery of the social and literary traditions of Late Antique letter-writing at the courts of Chlothar II and Dagobert I. Although the Latin of Desiderius is no longer that of Sidonius, he and his contemporaries who are represented in the collection still display an ability to use a florid style intended to foster

---

19. D. Ganz, 'The Merovingian Library of Corbie', in H. B. Clarke and M. Brennan, eds, *Columbanus and Merovingian Monasticism*, p. 163.
20. *Passio Leudegarii I*, 7; *Passio Leudegarii II*, 6; see also chapter 7.
21. Marculf, *Formulary, praef.*
22. *Vita Desiderii*, 2, 3, 7, 8.
23. *Vita Arnulfi*, 4, 7; *Vita Eligii*, I; Jonas, *Vita Columbani*, I 26; *Vita Audoini*, 1, 2.
24. Wood, 'Administration, law and culture in Merovingian Gaul', p. 67.

social contact and, by extension, religious and political cooperation.[25] Equally rooted in the past – although they may actually be later compilations – are the sermons attributed to Eligius, which are little more than a *florilegium* of biblical quotations, with a leavening of theology taken from Caesarius of Arles.[26] Among other clerics of this generation to have left literary or theological works is Theudefred, first abbot of Corbie, who had been a monk at Luxeuil, and who is thought to have composed a poem on the seven ages of the world.[27]

Perhaps more impressive than any of these is Audoin, who wrote a *Life* of his friend and contemporary Eligius, which unfortunately survives only in a later, revised version. If the scale of the original was anything like that of the surviving text, then the bishop of Rouen's hagiographical undertaking was a very substantial one. Nor was Audoin the only bishop of the period to write a saint's *Life*. Praeiectus is said to have written a *libellus* on the martyrs Cassius, Victorinus and Antolianus, as well as the *gesta* of Stremonius, in appropriate style (*digno sermone*), while he was still a deacon,[28] but none of these works is known to have survived.

For Leodegar the evidence is slighter than that for Desiderius, Eligius or Audoin, but more intriguing. There is a letter of consolation supposedly sent from the saint to his mother, Sigrada, after the death of his brother Gaerinus.[29] Sigrada herself was, by this time, an inmate of the monastery of St Mary in Soissons. Since this was a foundation of Ebroin it is possible that she was there as a prisoner.[30] If the letter was indeed written by Leodegar, and this may be thought unlikely since he is said to have been blinded before his brother's death, it is both a demonstration of his biblical knowledge and a remarkable example of Christian stoicism.

As regards the literary skills of the bishops of the next generation the direct evidence is slighter. Ansbert, who had been referendary under Chlothar III, before becoming a monk and later abbot at St Wandrille, succeeded Audoin as bishop of Rouen in 684.[31] While the latter was still alive, Ansbert addressed an acrostic poem to him, which survives.[32] Like all acrostic poems it is ingenious, albeit written in somewhat barbarous Latin. Ansbert is also said to have written works for the monastery of St Wandrille, which were still thought to be useful in the Carolingian period.[33] One of these may have been the now lost *Quaestiones ad Siwinum reclausum*, recorded in the *Gesta abbatum Fontanellensium*.[34] Nor is Ansbert the only bishop of the period known to have written works of piety or theology.

25. See chapters 2 and 9.
26. Eligius, *Praedicationes*, 1; 2.
27. Ganz, 'The Merovingian Library of Corbie', p. 154.
28. *Passio Praeiecti*, 9.
29. *Epistolae Aevi Merowingici Collectae*, 17.
30. Pardessus, *Diplomata*, 355.
31. *Vita Ansberti*, 15.
32. *Ymnus de sancto Ansberto episcopo*, MGH SRM 5, p. 641.
33. *Vita Ansberti*, 22.
34. *Gesta abbatum Fontanellensium*, 12, 3.

Merovingian theology and Rome: Bonitus and Amandus

Bonitus of Clermont is said by his biographer to have been the son of noble parents, Theodatus and Siagria. As a result of his schooling he was well versed in the Theodosian Code, and thereafter he was sent to the court of Sigibert III, where, in time, he became referendary, before being appointed as prefect of Provence.[35] Meanwhile his brother, Avitus, bishop of Clermont, died (*c.* 690), but not before naming him as his successor. As bishop, Bonitus lived a pious and ascetic life, until worry over the uncanonical nature of his appointment led him to resign the see and enter the monastery of Manglieu in the Auvergne.[36] Subsequently he determined to visit Rome. This he did, after a long and fascinating journey, during which he became involved in political crises in Lyons[37] and in Lombardy.[38] He then returned to Lyons, where he remained for two years, until his death (*c.* 705).[39] Sometime later his body was translated to Clermont.[40]

In many respects the *Vita Boniti*, which was apparently written soon after the saint's translation, is an extraordinarily valuable text. It sheds light on the Merovingian episcopate in the closing years of the seventh century, as well as the royal court, and its information stretches from the Auvergne to Lyons, Lombardy and Rome. Bonitus's resignation of his see provides an indication that the long-standing Merovingian concern about simony and episcopal appointments continued throughout the seventh century. His pilgrimage to Rome similarly marks the continuance of direct connections with the papal see. In the first half of the seventh century Amandus had made two visits to Rome,[41] and in 675, at the moment of the political crisis at the end of Childeric II's reign, Audoin had also made the pilgrimage;[42] the timing of his journey may have been important, since the bishop had a reputation as a peace-maker.[43]

The *Life of Bonitus* also provides some surprising, if not downright odd, information about a letter of the saint directed against an upsurge of Novatian and Jovinian heresy in the Auvergne.[44] It is unlikely that these heresies, which were of Late Antique origin, did actually resurface in late-seventh-century Clermont. Probably Bonitus merely borrowed labels from Jerome and Isidore to denounce certain theological positions of which he disapproved. Nevertheless, the fact that he wrote a letter against these heresies is in itself an indication of some intellectual liveliness in the Church of Clermont. Taken together with his pilgrimage to Rome it indicates wider

35. *Vita Boniti*, 1, 2.
36. *Vita Boniti*, 9, 16.
37. *Vita Boniti*, 19.
38. *Vita Boniti*, 23.
39. *Vita Boniti*, 29.
40. *Vita Boniti*, 34–42.
41. *Vita Amandi*, 6–7, 10.
42. *Vita Audoini*, 10.
43. *Vita Audoini*, 12.
44. *Vita Boniti*, 17.

horizons for the late Merovingian Church than those of court and diocesan politics, whether secular or ecclesiastical.

Although Bonitus is one of the last Merovingian bishops known to have shown a concern about heresy, the interest was by no means unique to him. The Merovingian Church was generally concerned with the question of doctrinal orthodoxy. In 549, at the Council of Orléans, the bishops had considered the theological conflicts arising from problem of the Three Chapters, that is, from the emperor Justinian's condemnation as heretical of the writings of three bishops, who had signed the Council of Chalcedon in 451. At Orléans the clergy came down in favour of the papal line, condemning the eastern heresies of Nestorius and Eutyches.[45] The same issue was to crop up again years later, at Mâcon in 626–7, after the monk Agrestius became involved in the development of the Three Chapters controversy known as the Aquileian schism.[46] By this time the papacy and the Frankish Church had changed their positions and now accepted that of the Byzantine emperor. There may be a further hint of concern over this conflict in the *Life of Amatus* of Remiremont, where the saint has the letter of pope Leo to Flavian read to him on his deathbed.[47] The letter in question was the doctrinal statement known as the 'Tome of Leo', the orthodoxy of which the western Church had been determined to uphold during the conflict over the Three Chapters. Since Amatus had once supported Agrestius during the schism, it looks as if his final concern was to impress everyone with his orthodoxy.

Nor was the TriCapitoline schism the only matter to draw the Frankish Church and the papacy into contact during the late sixth and early seventh centuries. Columbanus, in his disagreements with the Merovingian episcopate, wrote to Gregory the Great and to his successor Boniface IV on a number of occasions.[48] In 603 he appealed to Gregory over the question of the date of Easter, which he was computing according to the old Irish cycle, while the Frankish Church was probably following that of Victorius of Aquitaine.[49] Moreover, in his appeals to the papacy, Columbanus set precedents for his successors, particularly for Bertulf, abbot of his Italian foundation of Bobbio, who sought papal immunity against bishop Probus of Tortona.[50] In so doing Bertulf established the basic *formula* for all immunities from episcopal intervention granted by the papacy to monastic houses, including those of Merovingian Francia.[51]

While the argument over the Three Chapters provided the chief focus of doctrinal conflict between east and west in the sixth century, that over the

45. Council of Orléans (549), 1.
46. Jonas, *Vita Columbani*, II 9.
47. *Vita Amati*, 12.
48. Columbanus, epp. 1; 3; 5.
49. Columbanus, ep. 1
50. Jonas, *Vita Columbani*, II 23.
51. *Codice Diplomatico del Monasterio di S. Colombano di Bobbio,* ed. C. Cipolla, *Fonti per la Storia d'Italia* 52, 10; *Liber Diurnus*, 77.

Monothelete doctrine of the emperor Heraclius, who insisted that there should be no discussion of Christ's nature, but only a recognition of His single will, was central to the theological disputes of the seventh.[52] Yet again the Merovingian Church followed the papal line, even if it cannot be said to have been in the forefront of the theological debate. Here the most valuable information is contained in the ninth-century additions made by Milo to the Merovingian *Vita Amandi*.

Amandus himself has some claim to being the most important of all the Merovingian saints. According to his earliest biographer he was born in Aquitaine and entered the monastic life on the Ile de Yeu.[53] Later he went to Tours and then to Bourges, before making his first pilgrimage to Rome. He returned to Francia in order to preach, and was forced to become a missionary bishop by Chlothar II.[54] Once again he visited Rome, returning to continue his work of evangelization in the northern part of the Merovingian kingdom, before turning his attention to the Danubian Slavs.[55] Subsequently he fell out with Dagobert I over the king's morals, but was finally persuaded to become godfather to prince Sigibert.[56] Dagobert forcibly installed him as bishop of Maastricht, and he continued his missionary work in the Low Countries, before turning unsuccessfully to the pagan Basques.[57] He returned to Francia, but then established the monastery of Nant in the Aveyron, with the help of Childeric II.[58] When he died (*c.* 676) he was buried in his foundation of Elno, which he had established long before, with the help of Dagobert I.[59]

Such is the late Merovingian picture of Amandus: an ascetic missionary bishop and wonderworker, prepared to stand up to the kings of his day. This portrait is, however, incomplete. Despite its references to two journeys to Rome, it neglects the importance both of theology and of the papacy for the saint. Here the additional material provided by Milo in his ninth-century reworking of the *Vita Amandi* is of crucial importance. In particular Milo records contacts between Amandus and pope Martin I, who sent the bishop, among other things, a volume of synodal decrees from the papal council of 649, which dealt with the Monothelete heresy.[60] Milo transcribed in full Martin's accompanying letter, which responded to the saint's concerns about the standards of the Frankish Church, encouraging him to continue with his attempts to improve those standards, as well as informing him about the current Monothelete crisis.[61] A century earlier communication with Vigilius

52. Herrin, *The Formation of Christendom*, pp. 250–9.
53. *Vita Amandi*, 1.
54. *Vita Amandi*, 8.
55. *Vita Amandi*, 16.
56. *Vita Amandi*, 17.
57. *Vita Amandi*, 20.
58. *Vita Amandi*, 23.
59. *Vita Amandi*, 22, 25.
60. Milo, *Vita Amandi*, 1.
61. Milo, *Vita Amandi*, 2.

may well have prompted the Council of Orléans's pronouncement on the Three Chapters controversy in 549.[62] At the end of the sixth century Gregory the Great had critizised ecclesiastical standards in Francia and urged Brunhild to embark on a policy of reform.[63] Now Martin was both looking for backing in his conflict with the Byzantine east, and exhorting a favourable bishop to persevere in reforming the Church.

It is not easy to determine the extent to which Martin's appeal was heeded. The *Vita Eligii* describes a council which had already been held, between 639 and 641, in response to a papal letter; at the council an otherwise unknown bishop Salvius dealt with a foreigner who was preaching Monothelete heresy in Autun.[64] At about the same time Wandregisel visited Rome, according to the second *Vita* of the saint:[65] his visit may have had a theological as well as a spiritual purpose. The *Gesta abbatum Fontanellensium* also refers to a mission of Wandregisel's nephew, Godo, to pope Vitalian to obtain relics for *Fontanella*. The mission was a success: not only did Godo bring back the relics, but also he brought biblical texts and works of Gregory the Great.[66] Clearly the papacy and its theology impinged on Francia in the middle of the seventh century. And Martin's letter to Amandus may not have been the last time that members of the Merovingian clergy would hear of the Monothelete heresy, since Frankish clerics may have been present at the papal synod of 679, when it was condemned once again.[67] Although the Franks, unlike the Anglo-Saxons, claimed no special relationship with Rome, there were strong contacts between the Merovingian Church and the papacy.

Hagiographic and historical writing in the seventh century

Information on the learning and culture of individual bishops of later-seventh-century Francia has to be pieced together from their few surviving works and from their *Vitae*. More generally, the culture of the Merovingian Church in this period can be explored through a consideration of the hagiography composed at the time. Whereas the hagiography of the sixth century is dominated by the writings of Gregory of Tours and Venantius Fortunatus, and that of the middle years of the seventh century by Jonas of Bobbio, biographer of Columbanus and his disciples, as well as of John of Réomé and Vedast, the saints' *Lives* of the late seventh and early eighth centuries are, for the most part, anonymous. Nevertheless, this group of texts constitutes a formidable body of material, made up of roughly a dozen *Vitae*,

62. Council of Orléans (549), 1; for Vigilius's contact with Childebert I, see Gregory I, *Register*, IX 216.
63. Gregory I, *Register*, IX 213; XI 49.
64. *Vita Eligii*, I 33–5.
65. *Vita Wandregisili II*, 10, 11.
66. *Gesta abbatum Fontanellensium*, I, 6.
67. Bishop Deodatus acted as Wilfrid's guide to the papacy in that year: Stephanus, *Vita Wilfridi*, 28–32.

most of which can be assigned to the three decades between 670 and 700. They come from a wide area of Merovingian Francia, and they include the *Lives* of Gertrude of Nivelles, Audoin of Rouen, Wandregisel, Bonitus and Balthild, the *Passiones* of Germanus of Grandval, Praeiectus and Leodegar and the *Visio* Baronti. Of these only the *Passio* of Germanus has a named author, Bobolenus.

The range of subject matter and intention within this group of texts is considerable. There are martyrs and confessors, bishops, monks and nuns. Alongside *Vitae* and *Passiones*, there are also the visionary texts of Fursey and Barontus. The *Lives* set out episcopal and monastic standards for the improvement of the reader, and the *Visio Baronti* deals in considerable detail with the spiritual and liturgical failings of the community of St Cyran in Berry.[68] At the same time this hagiography is concerned with the promotion of the cult of individual saints, and on occasion, if not always, such promotion had its significance for the world of secular politics. The *Passiones*, above all, must have been intended to have a political impact, both on the kingdom as a whole, in their treatment of such figures as Ebroin and Adalric Eticho, and also on the local politics of the cities of Autun and Clermont. In short, these are not simple, credulous works, but complex texts exploring the potential of a religious and literary tradition.

One of the distinguishing features of the hagiography of this period for its greatest editor, Bruno Krusch, was the barbarous nature of its Latin. Certainly Merovingian grammar was far removed from that of Cicero, and like Merovingian orthography it was infinitely less regular than the written language of the Ancient World. Nevertheless, the prefaces of these texts show an awareness of appropriate literary form, even if they are not written grammmatically. That is, the passages in which hagiographers acknowledged their patrons, their literary debts and their intellectual unworthiness to carry out the task of writing, were usually written in a more florid style than the subsequent narratives.[69] Such variation in style was traditional.[70] The narratives themselves are often well constructed according to the conventions of hagiography. Indeed they quote directly from earlier texts, sometimes with acknowledgement in the preface and sometimes without.

One model which influenced late Merovingian hagiographers was Jonas's *Vita Columbani*. Its influence is clear in the *Passiones* of Germanus of Grandval and of Praeiectus, as well as the *Life* of Wandregisel, and may be present in that of Bonitus.[71] Although this is not a large group,[72] it does bear witness to the distribution, within a limited circle, of Jonas's great work, which itself had been composed only between 639 and 643. Since Wandregisel had trained at Columbanus's foundation of Bobbio the influence of Jonas in the *Vita*

---

68. *Visio Baronti*, 10, 14, 15.
69. Wood, 'Administration, law and culture in Merovingian Gaul', pp. 72–3.
70. A. Loyen, *Sidoine Apollinaire et l'espirit précieux en Gaule*, pp. xiii–xvi.
71. Wood, 'The *Vita Columbani* and Merovingian hagiography', p. 68.
72. Wood, 'The *Vita Columbani* and Merovingian hagiography', p. 69.

Wandregisili is only to be expected;[73] equally Germanus of Grandval was much influenced by Waldebert, abbot of Luxeuil, and his *Passio* was dedicated by its author, Bobolenus, to Waldebert's successor, Ingofrid, as well as to two otherwise unknown clerics.[74] The *Vita Columbani* had a considerable impact, but only within a very well defined circle.

The relatively limited influence of the *Vita Columbani* and the ascertainable links between Bobbio and Luxeuil, on the one hand, and St Wandrille and Grandval, on the other, casts significant light on to the *Chronicle* of Fredegar, a very substantial passage of which is borrowed directly from the *Vita Columbani*.[75] The first version of the chronicle is an extraordinary compilation. It tacks together various earlier writings on the history of the world, before exerpting the first six books of Gregory of Tours's *Histories*, whose narrative is then extended to 642, when it breaks off.[76] Although it has been suggested that this compilation was made in two stages, the first around 613/14 and the second around 660, the fact that the author's account of the opening years of the seventh century is dominated by Jonas's writing, to which is added material from the *Passio Desiderii* by the Visigothic king Sisebut, indicates that it cannot have reached its present form before the composition of the *Vita Columbani*, that is before the early 640s. Other indications suggest a date of composition in or after 658.[77] Equally as important as the implications of textual dependence on Jonas for dating Fredegar's work are those which help to assign the chronicler to a specific milieu. Although for the most part his own narrative is remarkably secular in tone, the fact that he knew of the *Vita Columbani* within a short time of its being written suggests that Fredegar himself should be placed firmly within the nexus of Luxeuil, which dovetails nicely with the emphasis on Burgundian matters within the narrative. Thus it is reasonable to see his *Chronicle*, with its early sections taken from the *Liber Generationis* of Hippolytus, from Jerome, Hydatius, Gregory of Tours and Isidore, as an indication of the material available to a historian working within a 'Columbanian' milieu. Further, the supposed secularity of Fredegar's *Chronicle*, with its mythical origin legend for the Franks and its legends relating to Theodoric the Great and to the emperor Justinian, should be taken as an indication of the range of culture available within the orbit of 'Columbanian' monasticism.

Despite its importance for Fredegar and for the authors of the *Passiones* of Praeiectus and Germanus, and of the *Life* of Wandregisel, Jonas's *Vita Columbani* is not the text which most widely influenced late-seventh-century Merovingian writers. More influential were the writings of Gregory the

73. *Vita Wandregisili*, 9.
74. Bobolenus, *Vita Germani Grandivallensis, praef.,* 6, 7, 8, 9.
75. Fredegar, IV 36; Jonas, *Vita Columbani*, I 18–20.
76. J.M. Wallace-Hadrill 'Fredegar and the history of France', in Wallace-Hadrill, *The Long-Haired Kings*, pp. 71–94.
77. Goffart, 'The Fredegar problem reconsidered', p. 354.

Great, especially the *Dialogues*. These provided the model for the *Visio Baronti*,[78] and they were known by the authors of the *Lives* of Fursey, Praeiectus and Bonitus.[79] In addition the *Passio Praeiecti* and the *Vita Wandregisili* borrow from the *Moralia* of Gregory,[80] while the *Visio Baronti* was also indebted to the pope's *Homilia in Evangelium*.[81] Since Godo had returned to St Wandrille from Rome with works by Gregory,[82] the influence of the pope's writings on the *Vita Wandregisili* is perhaps to be expected. Nevertheless it is clear that Frankish hagiographers of the late seventh century in general were not without biblical, theological or hagiographical knowledge, despite their poor grammar and unclassical orthography.

Merovingian books

Awareness of the Church Fathers in seventh-century Francia can also be shown from a consideration of the manuscripts known to have been available. There are problems in using manuscripts as an indication of the library of any individual Merovingian Church or monastery, since books were transferred from one place to another in the course of time, and there is not the same weight of paleographical evidence for Late Antique and Merovingian manuscripts as there is for those of the Carolingian period, to help locate books in specific scriptoria. Nevertheless it is possible to assign some Late Antique and Merovingian manuscripts to Lyons on historical and paleographical grounds. Paleography has also allowed the ascription of a number of manuscripts to Luxeuil and Corbie, and, less certainly, to the nunnery at Chelles. For the most part the texts in question are patristic, although there are also some important legal works. Notable among the manuscripts assigned to Lyons are various works of St Augustine, but there is also the earliest copy of the *Codex Theodosianus*, and, less certainly, a *Lex Romana Visigothorum*.[83]

The texts thought to have been transcribed at Luxeuil are in many ways the sorts of works which one might expect from a monastery: a lectionary, missals, the *Cura Pastoralis* of Gregory the Great, and other patristic works.[84] The list may seem uninteresting; indeed a classicist might say that 'Columbanian' monks erased works of greater interest than they transcribed, since they reused parchment, scraping off earlier texts and writing over them. On the other hand the paleographical importance of Luxeuil cannot be

78. *Visio Baronti, passim.*
79. *Vita Fursei,* 1; *Passio Praeiecti;* 36; *Vita Boniti,* 4, 30.
80. *Passio Praeiecti, prologus; Vita Wandregisili,* 1.
81. *Visio Baronti,* 6, 16, 22.
82. *Gesta Abbatum Fontanellensium,* 1, 6.
83. R. McKitterick, 'The scriptoria of Merovingian Gaul: a survey of the evidence', in H.B. Clarke and M. Brennan,, eds, *Columbanus and Merovingian Monasticism,* pp. 177–82.
84. McKitterick, 'The scriptoria of Merovingian Gaul: a survey of the evidence', pp. 184–92.

doubted. From the middle of the seventh century onwards the scribes of Luxeuil experimented with several scripts, evolving a distinctive calligraphic minuscule, an individual style of decorated initials and a notion of a hierarchy of scripts, which is to be found in a number of theological and liturgical manuscripts attributable to the monastery.[85] This development continued unabated through the late seventh and into the early decades of the eighth century.[86]

Doubtless some of the books at Corbie were brought from Luxeuil by Theudefred when he was first appointed as abbot of the new foundation between 657 and 661.[87] By the end of the century Corbie had a particularly fine collection of monastic *Rules*, as well, it seems, as the manuscript of canon law known as the *Collectio Corbeiensis*: from these were compiled a major handbook of canon law, the *Vetus Gallica*, in the days of abbot Grimo (694–747).[88] But Corbie was also a centre of paleographical importance: there the script of Luxeuil was developed into a forerunner of Carolingian minuscule.[89] In this and other ways late Merovingian Corbie was a harbinger of the Carolingian Renaissance.

In the late Merovingian period, therefore, it was possible for a monastery to build up a significant library. This can be demonstrated paleographically for Corbie. It can also be argued for St Wandrille, which was handsomely enriched in the eighth century by abbot Wando (747–54), according to the *Gesta abbatum Fontanellensium*.[90] The manuscripts given by Wando were gospels, monastic rules, a martyrology, and a copy of the canons of the Council of Nicaea, together with copies of religious works by Clement, Arnobius, Athanasius, Rufinus, Augustine, Jerome, Gennadius, Sedulius, Leo I, Leo of Nola, Gregory the Great, Isidore, and Bede, together with the *Getica* of Jordanes and the *History of Apollonius of Tyre*. It was not an insignificant gift.

The state of the Merovingian Church in the late seventh century

The seventh-century Merovingian Church, as it appears in contemporary sources, is more impressive than the picture of the Frankish Church of his own day presented by Boniface in 742. In a letter addressed to pope Zacharias, the archbishop of Mainz claimed that the Church had been ignored for sixty or seventy years, and that no ecclesiastical councils had been held for

85. McKitterick, 'The scriptoria of Merovingian Gaul: a survey of the evidence', p. 189.
86. McKitterick, 'The scriptoria of Merovingian Gaul: a survey of the evidence', p. 188.
87. Ganz, 'The Merovingian Library of Corbie', p. 154.
88. Ganz, 'The Merovingian Library of Corbie', p. 163.
89. D. Ganz, 'The preconditions for caroline minuscule', *Viator* 18 (1987), pp. 23–44.
90. *Gesta abbatum Fontanellensium*, 12, 2.

eighty.[91] This last claim can be directly refuted. From the *Vetus Gallica* it appears that at some point between 663 and 675 Leodegar summoned a diocesan synod in Autun.[92] Further, there are surviving canons from councils held at St-Jean-de-Losne under Childeric II (673–5) and at St-Pierre-de-Granon, Bordeaux, summoned for Childeric by Lupus of Aquitaine. St-Jean-de-Losne in particular dealt with major issues of doctrine and ecclesiastical organization. Subsequently Chramnelenus of Embrun was deposed by a gathering of bishops at Mâlay in 677,[93] as was Leodegar at a royal villa during the same period.[94] In addition the *Vita Ansberti* records a council held in Rouen in 688/9, which granted a privilege to the monastery of St Wandrille.[95] Charters also provide evidence of clerical gatherings, for instance in 683,[96] 692[97] and 695/6.[98] Some of these councils, like those which deposed Chramnelenus and Leodegar, may have been summoned for purely political reasons, but others clearly addressed ecclesiastical matters. The councils thus confirm the evidence provided by the saints' *Lives*, and in particular by the *Vita Boniti*: despite Boniface's opinions the Merovingian Church was still active at the end of the seventh century.

Certainly there were some clerics of dubious reputation. Most obvious among these are Leodegar's opponents, Dido of Chalon and Bobo of Valence.[99] It is possible that the authors of the *Passiones Leudegarii* have deliberately blackened these men, but the actions recorded of them suggest that they were primarily political figures, acting in much the same way as other bishops would later act in the days of Charles Martel. Nor were they the first clerics to bring discredit to the episcopate. Already in the days of Guntram Sagittarius of Gap and Salonius of Embrun had behaved more like warriors than ecclesiastics.[100] The behaviour of a few individuals, however, should not overshadow the standards of the Church as a whole.

One further saint's *Life* confirms the continuity of standards among some ecclesiastics up to the very last years of the seventh century. According to the *Vita* of Lambert, which probably dates from the mid-eighth century, the saint was born in Maastricht, where he was handed over to bishop Theodard for theological and monastic education. He was also apparently educated at court.[101] When Theodard was killed Lambert was elected bishop in his place, and the election was approved by Childeric II.[102] He became a leading figure

91. Boniface, ep. 50.
92. Pontal, *Die Synoden im Merowingerreich*, pp. 197–8.
93. Pertz, *Diplomata*, 48.
94. *Passio Leudegarii I*, 33; *Passio Leudegarii II*, 16–17.
95. *Vita Ansberti*, 18.
96. Pardessus, *Diplomata*, 401, 451.
97. Pardessus, *Diplomata*, 423.
98. Pardessus, *Diplomata*, 435; see Pontal, *Die Synoden im Merowingerreich*, pp. 204–12.
99. *Passio Leudegarii I*, 26; *Passio Leudegarii II*, 16.
100. Gregory, *Decem Libri Historiarum*, IV 42; V 20, 27; VII 28, 38–9.
101. *Vita Landiberti episcopi Traeiectensis vetustissima*, 2–3.
102. *Vita Landiberti episcopi Traeiectensis vetustissima*, 4.

in Childeric's court, perhaps becoming an Austrasian equivalent to Leodegar in Burgundy. His importance can be gauged by the fact that he was exiled to Stablo-Malmédy when Childeric was murdered in 675 and Pharamund took his place.[103] After seven years he was restored to his see by Pippin II, but was martyred sometime before 701.[104]

In many respects his career can be paralleled in the *Lives* of earlier saints. In particular his education and his connections with the Merovingian court are not dissimilar from those of the majority of seventh-century bishops whose *Lives* survive. Lambert does, however, seem to have been the last saint whose *Vita* looked back to the days of Childeric II and the crisis of 675. Moreover his reinstatement at Maastricht and the circumstances of his martyrdom are associated with a new group of political figures, of whom the most important was Pippin II.

The comments of Boniface, therefore, are not a reliable guide to the late seventh-century Merovingian Church. Moreover, when considering the Church of the early eighth century it is important to remember that Boniface's view was not an objective one, and that some of the criteria which he used came from the Anglo-Saxon Church and were alien to Frankish tradition. Even if there was a decline in ecclesiastical standards after the end of the seventh century, it was not absolute; there were still some notable Frankish, as opposed to Anglo-Saxon, ecclesiastics in Francia in the early eighth century; in particular there were a number of distinguished abbots and abbesses, among them Wando of St Wandrille and Grimo of Corbie. As we shall see, there were also some significant missionary bishops, like Corbinian of Freising, whom Boniface, or his hagiographer, seems deliberately to have ignored.

Northumbria and Merovingian Church culture

There is another Anglo-Saxon view of the Merovingian Church to set against that of Boniface. It is the view of Wilfrid, Benedict Biscop and their hagiographers. Both Wilfrid and Biscop drew on the monastic tradition of Merovingian Francia, when creating their own monasteries in the 660s, 670s and 680s.[105] But they took more from Francia than its monastic tradition. It was in Vienne that Biscop acquired manuscripts for his new foundations[106] – confirming the importance of the Rhône valley as a repository of books in the seventh century.

Biscop also used Gallic masons and glaziers to provide his monasteries with

103. *Vita Landiberti episcopi Traeiectensis vetustissima*, 5.
104. *Vita Landiberti episcopi Traeiectensis vetustissima*, 7, 17.
105. Wormald, 'Bede and Benedict Biscop', pp. 142–3; Wood, 'Ripon, Francia and the Franks Casket in the early Middle Ages', pp. 8–17.
106. Bede, *Historia Abbatum*, 4.

stone buildings.[107] It is probable that Wilfrid did so too.[108] Indeed there is a strong case for seeing the surviving remains at Monkwearmouth, Jarrow and Hexham, as illustrating a Merovingian tradition of architecture, which is known best from the excavation of the monastic church at Nivelles.[109] The possibility that Frankish, rather than Roman, architecture inspired the buildings of Benedict Biscop and Wilfrid in Northumbria, suggests that there may have been real originality in some of the great ecclesiastical buildings of Francia. Although little Merovingian architecture survives above ground, descriptions of buildings in Merovingian texts confirm that this was the case. Thus the *Vita Boniti*, which is apparently of eighth-century date, describes the church of St Mary in the monastery of Manglieu as having a pentagonal tower on a quadrangular base, while the church of the Apostles at the same monastery was a triangular building, with carved columns, perhaps reused from the Roman period.[110]

Although Merovingian architecture has to be studied largely through descriptions, some sculpture does survive. There is the decoration from the *Hypogée des Dunes* at Poitiers built by abbot Mellobaudes around the year 700. The work is provincial,[111] and its iconography is theologically suspect: it represents angels, invocations to whom were condemned as heretical at the Roman synod of 745.[112] Nevertheless the representation of the angels belongs in the mainstream of early Medieval art, and looks directly to the angels on the coffin of St Cuthbert. Much more impressive is the work from Jouarre, a monastery founded by Audoin's brother Ado,[113] and closely associated with Agilbert, missionary bishop to the West Saxons, patron of Wilfrid and finally bishop of Paris.[114] Jouarre was very much at the centre of Merovingian religious and political life in the middle of the seventh century. The *sarcophagi* preserved there, some of which seem to date from that period, imply a fine school of carving, and the iconography of the tomb of Agilbert, with its figures awaiting the last judgement, and its depiction of Christ and the symbols of the apostles, is genuinely impressive. From further east in the Merovingian kingdom, there is the extraordinary tomb portrait of Chrodoara, dating from the second quarter of the eighth century, at Amay in Belgium.[115] The architecture and sculpture of late-seventh- and early-eighth-century Francia is not likely to have been greatly inferior to that which has survived from the Northumbria of Wilfrid and Biscop.

Considered on its own merits the Frankish Church of the late seventh century cannot be regarded as a particularly creative institution, although the

107. Bede, *Historia Abbatum*, 5.

108. Stephanus, *Vita Wilfridi*, 22; Wood, 'Ripon, Francia and the Franks Casket in the early Middle Ages', p. 10.

109. E. Fernie, *The Architecture of the Anglo-Saxons*, p. 57.

110. *Vita Boniti*, 16.

111. James, *The Franks*, p. 149.

112. Boniface, ep. 59.

113. Jonas, *Vita Columbani*, I 26.

114. Wormald, 'Bede and Benedict Biscop', pp. 145–6.

115. Personal communication from Alain Dierkens.

achievements of its hagiographers should not be underestimated. For the most part it was not a centre for original thought. It is almost symptomatic of Merovingian culture that the main work of theology to have survived from this period, the *Liber Scintillarum* of Defensor of Ligugé, is a *florilegium* of material from the Bible and from patristic sources. But the *Liber Scintillarum* is more than a heap of quotations; it is a systematic collection, presenting a synthesis of its own, and its own manuscript tradition suggests that it achieved some popularity.[116] Nevertheless, despite its intellectual limitations, the Frankish kingdom was still a repository of manuscripts in the seventh century. Both points are important when assessing the contribution of Merovingian Francia to the culture of western Europe: the Franks of the seventh and eighth centuries produced no Bede, but Bede's scholarship would have been impossible without the books purchased by Biscop in Vienne.

Boniface's view was much more negative. Of course the opening years of the eighth century saw political developments which affected the Merovingian Church for the worse. Their impact, as we shall see, may not have been as disastrous as Boniface's correspondence would imply. In one respect, however, the Merovingian Church was unquestionably poorer in the mid eighth century than it had been fifty years previously. When the Carolingians came to look back on the seventh century in the Rhône valley in particular, they acknowledged the wealth of learning which had been available.[117] The onslaught of the Arabs, and the counterattacks of Charles Martel, around 732 seem to have been devastating to Vienne, whose bishop, Willicarius, fled to the monastery of Agaune in that year.[118] External factors played a considerable part in transforming the Merovingian Church of the seventh century into that of the eighth.

116. Wallace-Hadrill, *The Frankish Church*, p. 77.
117. e.g. Ado, *Vita Theudarii*, 7.
118. Ado, *Chronicon, PL* 123, col 122.

Chapter Fifteen

The Checks on Ambition: Merovingian Politics, 680–721

The years between Ebroin's murder and the death of Pippin II in 714 are traditionally seen as years of Pippinid dominance: the Merovingians are supposed already to have been in their dotage, their *fainéance*. What opposition there was to Pippinid power is thought to have been based largely in the periphery of the Frankish world. The basic narrative of the period, however, suggests that this is not an entirely accurate reading of the situation.

The age of Pippin II

After the defeat of the Austrasians at Lucofao, and the subsequent murder of Martin, Ebroin's success was complete. His rule, however, came to an abrupt end in *c.* 680 when he was murdered by Ermenfred, a Frank against whom he was plotting.[1] His assassin fled to Pippin in Austrasia. After careful consideration the Neustrian aristocracy appointed Waratto as *maior*.[2] He appears to have been a *graphio* already in 659, and was apparently a landowner in the Paris region.[3] His policy was one of conciliation with various parties, including the Austrasians under Pippin II, who gave him hostages, and made peace. His son, Ghislemar, however, was less conciliatory, and overthrew his father, establishing himself in his place, only to die of natural causes.[4] Waratto was then re-established in office for a short period of time until his own death, in *c.* 686. After a period of indecision the Neustrians appointed Waratto's son-in-law, Berchar, as *maior*, but the appointment was not a good one.[5] Conflict arose in the western kingdom; Berchar alienated numerous

1. *Liber Historiae Francorum*, 47; Fredegar, cont. 4.
2. *Liber Historiae Francorum*, 47; Fredegar, cont. 4.
3. Pertz, *Diplomata*, 37; *Vita Filiberti*, 31; Gerberding, *The Rise of the Carolingians and the Liber Historiae Francorum*, pp. 89–90.
4. *Liber Historiae Francorum*, 47; Fredegar, cont. 4.
5. *Liber Historiae Francorum*, 48; Fredegar, cont. 5.

members of the western aristocracy, including Reolus, the bishop of Rhiems. Civil war erupted between the Neustrians and the Austrasians: it culminated in Pippin's victory at Tertry in 687. This battle, however, did not resolve the crisis, and it was left to Waratto's widow, Ansfled, to organize the assassination of her own son-in-law a year later. With the murder of Berchar, the way was open for Pippin to establish himself in Neustrian politics. He became *maior*, and took over the treasury, but then returned to Austrasia, leaving Nordebert to act in his place.[6] At about the same time Drogo, the elder of Pippin's two sons by his wife Plectrude, married Berchar's widow, Adaltrude,[7] and was established in the *ducatus* of Champagne.[8]

In 690/1 the Merovingian who had held the throne since the crisis of 675, Theuderic III, died, to be followed by his son Clovis III. Neither of them made much of an impression, but when Clovis died in 695 he was succeeded by a brother, Childebert III (694–711), who was much more highly regarded by contemporaries.[9] A year or so later Nordebert died, and Pippin's second son Grimoald took over the office of *maior* in Neustria.[10] For the next decade and more there was a period of calm within the kingdom, although Pippin campaigned against the Frisians and the Sweves.[11] Even the Frisians were drawn into the peace when Grimoald married Theudesinda, the daughter of their leader, Radbod.[12] In 711, however, Childebert III died, to be succeeded by the child Dagobert III (711–15/16).[13] Three years later Pippin himself died, but not before Grimoald had been murdered while praying at the shrine of St Lambert at Liège.[14] Drogo was already dead. In order to preserve her family's dominance Plectrude appointed Grimoald's son Theudoald as *maior*.[15] Theudoald, however, was a minor. His appointment was the signal for renewed civil war between Neustrians and Austrasians.

6. *Liber Historiae Francorum*, 48.

7. *Annales Mettenses Priores*, s.a. 693 (where she is called Anstrudis); *Gesta abbatum Fontanellensium*, 4, 1; Gerberding, *The Rise of the Carolingians and the Liber Historiae Francorum*, pp. 93–4.

8. *Liber Historiae Francorum*, 48; Fredegar, cont. 6.

9. *Liber Historiae Francorum*, 49; Fredegar, cont. 6; Gerberding, *The Rise of the Carolingians and the Liber Historiae Francorum*, pp. 158–9, 162.

10. *Liber Historiae Francorum*, 49.

11. *Liber Historiae Francorum*, 49; Fredegar, cont. 6; *Annales Mettenses Priores*, s.a. 697 (there is no reason to accept the marginal date of *c.* 689 given by the editor B. von Simson).

12. *Liber Historiae Francorum*, 50; Fredegar, cont. 7.

13. *Liber Historiae Francorum*, 50.

14. *Liber Historiae Francorum*, 50; Fredegar, cont. 7; *Annales Mettenses Priores*, s.a. 714; Sigebert, *Vita Landiberti episcopi Traeiectensis*, 27.

15. *Liber Historiae Francorum*, 51; Fredegar, cont. 8; *Annales Mettenses Priores*, s.a. 714.

The *Liber Historiae Francorum*, the continuations of Fredegar and the *Annales Mettenses Priores*

This, at least, is the narrative supplied by the *Liber Historiae Francorum*, filled out with one or two details from other sources. The *Liber Historiae Francorum* is the earliest narrative to cover the whole of this period. Written in 727, probably in Soissons, it provides a near-contemporary account of the closing years of the seventh century and the early years of the eighth. Further, although its author takes a clear political stance, that stance is one which itself sheds light on the period in question. The account is effectively history seen through the eyes of a member of the Neustrian aristocracy, or to be more precise, of the aristocracy of the Paris basin.[16] What was important for the author in political terms during the period up until 714 was not the victory of Pippin at Tertry, or the rise of the Carolingians in general, but rather the relationship of the king, or his court, to the Neustrian aristocracy. When the king consulted his magnates, that is his Neustrian magnates rather than those from the whole of Francia, then the kingdom could still function well, as it did under Childebert III (694–711). When such consultation failed, as it did during the periods in which Ebroin and Ghislemar were dominant, then there was oppression, resentment and the makings of civil war. Such was a Neustrian reading of the period up until 714.

The other major narratives dealing with the period are dependent on the *Liber Historiae Francorum*, directly or indirectly, but they present a different interpretation of events, betraying a growing Carolingian bias, which reflects attitudes and propaganda appropriate to the later eighth and ninth centuries, but not to the earlier period.[17] The *Liber Historiae Francorum* itself was known to the continuator of Fredegar, working for Childebrand in *c.* 751.[18] Since Childebrand himself was the half-brother of Charles Martel, it is not surprising that the Fredegar continuator added to the information contained in the *Liber Historiae Francorum* material largely concerned with Austrasia and the family of Pippin II. The additional information alters the focus of events by providing extra detail on Austrasia and on Frisia, but it does not destroy the interpretation put forward by the *Liber Historiae Francorum*. That task was left to an early ninth-century chronicler, writing probably in St Denis in about the year 806.[19] In his account the picture is changed radically.

The *Annales Mettenses Priores*, as they are known, begin with Pippin II taking over a *principatus* in 688;[20] probably the reference is to his dominance

16. Gerberding, *The Rise of the Carolingians and the Liber Historiae Francorum*, pp. 146–72.

17. P.J. Fouracre, 'Observations on the outgrowth of Pippinid influence in the "Regnum Francorum" after the Battle of Tertry (687–715)', *Medieval Prosopography* 5 (1984), p. 12.

18. Fredegar, cont 34; Wallace-Hadrill, *The Fourth Book of the Chronicle of Fredegar*, p. xiii.

19. Wallace-Hadrill, *The Frankish Church.*, p. 141.

20. *Annales Mettenses Priores*, s.a. 688.

of Austrasia after the murder of Ebroin. They allude to the power held by previous members of the family, especially by Pippin I. They also allude to Pippin I's relationship to Arnulf, bishop of Metz, although they do not specify the nature of that relationship. In addition they make much of Pippin II's grandmother, Itta, and his aunt, Gertrude. From the start, therefore, the *Annales Mettenses Priores* announce their intention of turning the history of the late seventh and eighth centuries into a history of the Pippinids, or the Carolingians as they were to become. After an account of campaigns against peoples east of the Rhine, the chronicler recaps the histories of Leodegar, Ebroin and Waratto, allocating, where possible, a role to Pippin II, before turning to the outbreak of war between Pippin and Berchar in 686/7, which is linked with a request for restitution for loss and damage caused by Ebroin.[21] Berchar's highhanded rejection of the request leads Pippin to summon his followers, and to march to Tertry, where final negotiations with the Merovingian king Theuderic fail. In the ensuing battle Berthar flees and Pippin is victorious.[22] As a result he takes over the *principatus* of all the Franks.[23] He then turns his mind to Radbod of Frisia, who becomes tributary. Thereafter Pippin holds annual councils on the first of March, and he also receives numerous foreign legations.[24] When Theuderic III dies, Pippin, says the chronicler, appoints the dead king's son Clovis III in his stead, and four years later he appoints Childebert III.[25] Meanwhile, Drogo, Pippin's eldest son, is married to Anstrude (Adaltrude), and she gives birth to a child, Hugo. His second son, Grimoald, becomes Childebert's *maior*. From Austrasia Pippin continues his wars against the Frisians[26] and he later fights the Alamans.[27] He also appoints Dagobert III as king when Childebert dies in 711.[28] Three years later, however, he falls ill and subsequently dies, but not before Grimoald has been murdered.[29]

For the period up until 714, therefore, the *Annales Mettenses Priores* produce a substantially different account of events from that offered by the *Liber Historiae Francorum*, making Pippin the centre of attention, and conferring on him complete power from the battle of Tertry onwards. As a reading of history the so-called *Prior Metz Annals* have been extremely influential, providing the most popular interpretation of the late Merovingian period. Nevertheless, they show the Pippinids and Merovingian history as the Carolingians wished to see them. In order to understand the late seventh and early eighth centuries on their own terms it is necessary to use the narrative framework of the *Liber Historiae Francorum*, together with other early evidence

---

21. *Annales Mettenses Priores*, s.a. 689.
22. *Annales Mettenses Priores*, s.a. 690.
23. *Annales Mettenses Priores*, s.a. 691.
24. *Annales Mettenses Priores*, s.a. 692.
25. *Annales Mettenses Priores*, s.a. 693.
26. *Annales Mettenses Priores*, s.a. 697.
27. *Annales Mettenses Priores*, s.a. 709, 710, 712.
28. *Annales Mettenses Priores*, s.a. 711.
29. *Annales Mettenses Priores*, s.a. 714.

in the first instance. Some later records are certainly of value, and even some details in the *Annales Mettenses Priores*, as for example those relating to Pippin's request for restitution of property and possessions in the period before Tertry,[30] are worthy of attention. But they cannot be used to determine the overall interpretation of the period.

Warattonids and Pippinids

All the accounts agree that the chain of events leading up to the battle of Tertry originated in the policies pursued by the family of Waratto. Three members of this family in turn, Waratto, Ghislemar and Berchar, secured the office of *maior* in Neustria. This post was the most important in the Merovingian kingdom. For most of the seventh century Neustria had been the dominant partner in the Merovingian state: Dagobert I had moved there from Austrasia after his father's death in 629.[31] Although Sigibert III was the elder of Dagobert's two sons, Clovis II was his child by his queen Nantechild, and it was he who became king of the West Frankish kingdom in 638.[32] Further, it was the Neustrian court that had ended Grimoald's usurpation of the Austrasian throne on behalf of his son Childebert the Adopted.[33] Moreover, during the seventh century there had been a long line of powerful Neustrian *maiores*, including Erchinoald and Ebroin.[34] When Waratto was chosen by the Frankish aristocracy as Ebroin's successor he was being appointed to what was unquestionably the most important secular position in the Merovingian kingdom. When his son Ghislemar seized the office from him, and later, when Berchar was appointed in Waratto's place, albeit with some misgiving, the Warattonids must have seemed to be the most important of all the magnate families in Francia.

The family of Pippin was not yet better established than that of Waratto. Certainly Pippin I had been *maior* in Austrasia, as had his son Grimoald, but the latter had blotted the family's copybook badly. The other asset which the family was to develop, its sanctity, was beginning to be realized only in the last decades of the seventh century. Although Arnulf of Metz is thought to have been Pippin II's grandfather, the evidence for this is not early, and even the *Annales Mettenses Priores* were uncertain about the nature of the relationship between Arnulf and the Pippinids.[35] Nor is it clear that the *Vita Arnulfi*, which is a remarkably uninformative text, was written in the seventh

---

30. *Annales Mettenses Priores*, s.a. 789.
31. Fredegar, IV 60.
32. Fredegar, IV 76, 79.
33. *Liber Historiae Francorum*, 43.
34. Fouracre, 'Merovingians, mayors of the palace and the notion of a "low-born" Ebroin'.
35. Paul the Deacon, in the *Gesta episcoporum Mettensium*, is the first to link Arnulf and Pippin I through the marriage of their children: there is no reason to accept his assertion.

century.[36] The other major saint claimed by the Pippinids, Gertrude of Nivelles, certainly was an aunt of Pippin II. She died in 659, and her sanctity was unquestionably promoted by the family in the late seventh century: her *Vita* was compiled in *c.* 670. The reputation of Gertrude and Nivelles had not, however, helped Grimoald, or his daughter against Clovis II.[37]

The power of the Warattonids, even so, was also limited. Waratto himself had been chosen as *maior* by the Neustrian nobility.[38] His authority depended on election, and given the hostility which had been engendered by Ebroin's highhanded activities, it is likely that he had been chosen in the hopes that he would not behave like his predecessor. All the sources are favourably disposed towards him, emphasizing his nobility and the legitimacy of his claim to office, as well as his role in restoring peace with Pippin. Yet although he was the appointee of the Franks, his son was nevertheless powerful enough to depose him, and was independent-minded enough to embark on what appears to have been a more aggressive period of government. So too Waratto's son-in-law and successor, Berchar, adopted a forceful style of rule. It was this which prompted the crisis of 686/7.[39]

Despite his defeat at Tertry, it was not the battle which ended Berchar's rule, but his mother-in-law. Ansfled, Waratto's widow, is described as being noble and intelligent in the sources.[40] She was certainly ruthless. After Berchar's murder, she is likely to have been involved in the appointment of Pippin as *maior* in Neustria. She ensured the continuance of her own influence when her daughter, Adaltrude, married Pippin's son, Drogo.[41] Later she took charge of the upbringing of her grandchild, Hugo, the son of Drogo and Adaltrude.[42] In many respects she appears to have behaved more like a Merovingian queen than a member of the aristocracy, but this may reflect the increasing attention paid to members of the aristocracy by the sources.

The importance of noble women during the seventh century casts some light on the gradual emergence of the Pippinid family. Ansfled collaborated with Pippin in Neustria, and the marriage of Drogo to Adaltrude must have been intended to help strengthen Carolingian influence in the western kingdom. Nor was this the first marriage to have extended Carolingian power, which was built up through a series of marriage alliances, each bringing estates and influence in different regions of the Austrasian kingdom. Thus, to judge by the disposition of land to monasteries, which provides the clearest indication of the whereabouts of a family's property, Pippin I's wife, Itta, came from a family whose lands lay around Nivelles and the *Silva*

36. Wood, 'Forgery in Merovingian hagiography', pp. 370–1.
37. *Vita Geretrudis*, 6.
38. *Liber Historiae Francorum*, 47; Fredegar, cont. 4.
39. *Liber Historiae Francorum*, 48; Fredegar, cont. 5.
40. *Liber Historiae Francorum*, 48; Fredegar, cont. 5.
41. *Annales Mettenses Priores*, s.a. 693; *Gesta abbatum Fontanellensium*, 4, 1; Gerberding, *The Rise of the Carolingians and the Liber Historiae Francorum*, pp. 93–4.
42. *Gesta abbatum Fontanellensium*, 4, 1.

Carbonnaria;[43] Pippin II married into a family well-established in the region around the monastery of Echternach, which was founded on land given by Irmina, mother of Plectrude.[44] The family of his second wife, or concubine, Alpaida, held estates in the valley of the Meuse.[45] The marriage of Drogo to Adaltrude was merely a continuation, this time in Neustria, of a pattern of political alliance and acquisition of land. Nor was the male side of the family the only side to profit from this policy. After all, the Pippinids themselves were descended from Pippin I through his daughter, Begga, and not through his son Grimoald. In working together with Pippin II, Ansfled was breaking the power of the family of Berchar, in order to preserve that of her daughter, the direct decendant of Waratto. And she was successful: Adaltrude's son Hugo seems to have been thought of as being a descendant of Ansfled rather than the grandson of Pippin II.[46] Such political manoeuvring was infinitely more important than Tertry in bringing the Pippinids into Neustrian politics.

The evidence of the charters, 675–711

For the *Annales Mettenses Priores* Tertry led to the establishment of Pippinid rule in Neustria. The outcome of the battle was in reality nowhere near so clear-cut, neither was the change of political control. Admittedly the evidence for government during this period is slight; essentially it has to be pieced together from a study of royal charters and their witness lists. For the reigns of Theuderic III (675–90/1), Clovis III (690/1–4) and Childebert III (694–711) Pertz published thirty-four such documents, twelve for Theuderic, nine for Clovis, and thirteen for Childebert.[47] Together they amount to over one-third of the royal charters published by Pertz for the Merovingian period. Among them are twenty which survive in their original manuscripts, and one in a near-contemporary copy. Such documents are not necessarily a sign of royal power. For the most part they concern the alienation or confirmation of land, income or immunity to churches. This was once taken as a sign of weakness. In fact the alienation of individual estates, even of estates which had once been highly favoured by kings, like the villa at Clichy,[48] is no criterion for assessing the strength or weakness of a monarch, since property could be acquired almost as quickly by a powerful monarch as it could be alienated, and the granting of land was one of the chief ways of ensuring a loyal

---

43. Gerberding, *The Rise of the Carolingians and the Liber Historiae Francorum*, p. 121.
44. Gerberding, *The Rise of the Carolingians and the Liber Historiae Francorum*, p. 101.
45. Gerberding, *The Rise of the Carolingians and the Liber Historiae Francorum*, pp. 119–20.
46. *Gesta abbatum Fontanellensium*, 4, 1; Wood, 'Saint-Wandrille and its hagiography', p. 11.
47. Pertz, *Diplomata*, 46–57, 58–66, 67–78.
48. Pertz, *Diplomata Amulforum*, 14.

following. When a king was a minor, as was Clovis III, such grants would have redounded to the credit of the *maior*, and would have help to strengthen his position. When the king was of mature age, as was Childebert III, at least after the opening years of his reign, gifts of land would have secured support for him.

While the grants recorded by charters do not in themselves serve as a guide to royal authority, the names of the witnesses provide an indication of who was present at the court at a given moment. In a period when consensus between a king and his magnates was the foundation of good government, at least in the mind of the author of the *Liber Historiae Francorum*,[49] these lists are a sensitive indicator of the continuation of that consensus. As long as the body of witnesses was made up largely of independent members of the aristocracy, the Pippinids did not have complete control of government. Further, although grants and confirmations do not give any indication of the strength or weakness of the king, one further group of documents within the charters, that is the *placita*, or records of the settlement of disputes, provide better evidence, for they show that individuals or communities were prepared to bring their law-suits to the royal court. The judicial function of the Merovingian kings remained a crucial aspect of their office. We have already seen that their famed mode of transport, the ox-cart, had its origins in that of Late Roman governors, who travelled by just such means, so that petitioners should be able to approach them even when they were on the move.[50]

Among the charters for the period from 675 to 711 are twelve *placita*, one for Theuderic III, four for Clovis III and seven for Childebert III.[51] Clearly cases were being brought to the royal court during these three reigns, and judgment was being given by the king and his officers, even when the *maior* was not present. The scale of some of the court gatherings can be seen in a *placitum* held before Clovis at Valenciennes in 693.[52] The case concerned the lands of an orphan, Ingramn, who appears to have been a ward of the *maior* Nordebert. His plea was upheld, and the *placitum* was signed by no fewer than twelve bishops, including those of Aix, Auxerre, Beauvais, Lyons, Metz, Paris and Rouen, twelve *viri inlustres*, that is nobles of the highest class, including Nordebert, nine *comites*, four *grafiones*, four *referendarii*, two seneschals and the *comes palatii*. The gathering was clearly one of significance.

More interesting as a case was that dealt with four years later by Childebert III at Compiègne.[53] Here the king was holding court with a large body of leading figures, including, this time, Pippin himself. On this occasion Magnoald, abbot of the monastery of Tussonval, accused Pippin's son, Drogo, of seizing an estate which had been granted to the monastery by Theuderic III.

49. Gerberding, *The Rise of the Carolingians and the Liber Historiae Francorum*, p. 162.
50. See chapter 7.
51. Pertz, *Diplomata*, 49, 59, 60, 64, 66, 68, 70, 73, 76, 77, 78, 79.
52. Pertz, *Diplomata*, 66.
53. Pertz, *Diplomata*, 70.

Drogo in reply claimed that the estate had belonged to his father-in-law Berchar, and hence to his wife Adaltrude, but he was unable to produce any documentation to prove that this was so. The case went against him, and the *placitum* was signed by six bishops, including those of Amiens, Auxerre, Beauvais and Paris, Pippin II, four *optimates* (nobles), three *domestici*, two seneschals and the *comes palatii*.

This extraordinary case seems to show the king and the nobility sitting in judgment on Pippin's son, and finding against him, even in his father's presence. So strange is the case that it has been seen as a fictive dispute, that is one in which there was no real conflict, but where the process of a court case was used to ratify an agreed claim to property ownership.[54] The witness list to the judgment of 697 may, however, suggest that this was no fictive process. Among the signatories are at least two men who would later emerge as firm opponents of the Pippinids. There is Savaric, bishop of Auxerre, whose family was later driven from that city by Charles Martel,[55] and there is Antenor, *patricius* of Marseilles, who was to seize power in Provence in the early eighth century.[56]

Two other *placita* add to this picture of support for the Merovingian court, but reservation towards the sons of Pippin. In 709/10 the agents of Dalphinus, abbot of St Denis, approached Childebert and his nobles at the royal estate of Maumaques.[57] There they rehearsed the grants of tolls from St Denis's fair, which had been made to them by Clovis II, Childeric II, Theuderic III and Chlothar III. Then they accused Grimoald of taking half the income. The *comes palatii*, Sigofred, testified on the monastery's behalf, and Grimoald conceded that the tolls should be restored. Again, in the same year, agents of Dalfinus approached the king at Maumaques to complain about Grimoald's men taking over a mill at Chailly: once more the case was judged in favour of St Denis.[58] Thus, at the end of the first decade of the eighth century the monastery of St Denis could challenge Pippin's son, Grimoald, himself *maior* in Neustria, and win the case. No wonder the monastery still supported the Merovingian family. Out of the seven *placita* from Childebert III's reign, three uphold the claims of institutions bringing cases against the sons of Pippin. *The Liber Historiae Francorum*'s assessment of Childebert as *bonae memoriae gloriosus domnus Childebertus rex iustus* (just and glorious king . . . of revered memory) was not wide of the mark.[59]

54. Gerberding, *The Rise of the Carolingians and the Liber Historiae Francorum*, pp. 103–4.

55. *Vita Eucherii*, 4, 9; *Gesta episcoporum Autissiodorensium*, 27–8; Fouracre, 'Observations on the outgrowth of Pippinid influence in the "Regnum Francorum" after the Battle of Tertry (687–715)', p. 8.

56. Fouracre, 'Observations on the outgrowth of Pippinid influence in the "Regnum Francorum" after the Battle of Tertry (687–715)', p. 8.

57. Pertz, *Diplomata*, 77.

58. Pertz, *Diplomata*, 78.

59. *Liber Historiae Francorum*, 50.

Pippin II and the Merovingian Church

Although most later sources present a picture of Pippin II's period of dominance in terms similar to that in the *Annales Mettenses Priores*, some Carolingian texts offer a very much more nuanced reconstruction of the period. A substantial number of hagiographical works were composed at the monastery of St Wandrille in the first half of the ninth century. Unlike the *Annales Mettenses Priores* these texts interpret history in a manner critical of the Pippinids, not least because the family's policy of granting ecclesiastical land in precarial tenure to its followers had led to the abbey sustaining considerable property losses.[60] The resulting narratives are, therefore, as much creations of the Carolingian period as are the *Annales Mettenses Priores*. Nevertheless it is clear that the authors had access to very considerable quantities of evidence, particularly with regard to the estates of the monastery.[61]

The St Wandrille texts also have much to say about Pippinid treatment of individual ecclesiastics. Of particular interest here is the *Life of Ansbert*, abbot of St Wandrille and later bishop of Rouen. Ansbert came from the Vexin. After a career at court as referendary under Theuderic III, he joined Wandregisil's monastery, where he became abbot in succession to Lantbert, when the latter was appointed as bishop of Lyons.[62] Subsequently he himself was elected to the see of Rouen, but within a short space of time he had fallen foul of Pippin, who had him imprisoned in the monastery of Hautmont, installing Gripho as bishop in his place.[63] Although Pippin later decided to release him, the saint died while still in exile.[64] According to the hagiographer, the return of Ansbert's body to St Wandrille, was marked by processions and a number of miraculous cures.[65] This can scarcely have been welcome to the Pippinid regime.[66]

The exile of Ansbert provides the clearest case both of conflict between Pippin and the Neustrian Church and of his meddling in ecclesiastical affairs. Other evidence, however, backs up this impression. In the diocese of Rouen, for instance, Pippin not only interfered with the episcopate, but also appointed Bainus as abbot of St Wandrille, and he later set him over his new foundation of Fleury as well.[67] The appointment of Godinus as abbot of Jumièges is equally likely to reflect Pippin's influence.[68] Such clerical appointments in the region of the lower Seine were the ecclesiastical equivalent to the secular involvement brought by the marriage of Drogo to Adaltrude.

---

60. *Gesta abbatum Fontanellensium*, 6, 1; Wood, 'Saint-Wandrille and its hagiography', pp. 9–10, 12.
61. See chapter 12.
62. *Vita Ansberti*, 13.
63. *Vita Ansberti*, 15, 21.
64. *Vita Ansberti*, 22, 24.
65. *Vita Ansberti*, 25–36.
66. Wood, 'Saint-Wandrille and its hagiography', pp. 11–12.
67. *Gesta abbatum Fontanellensium*, 2, 1–2.
68. Gerberding, *The Rise of the Carolingians and the Liber Historiae Francorum*, p. 98.

It is possible that a similar policy was attempted in the Champagne, where Drogo was made *dux*.[69] Already before Tertry, Reolus, bishop of Rheims, had deserted Berchar and joined Pippin.[70] When Reolus died Pippin ensured that the bishopric remained in the hands of a supporter, appointing Rigobert as bishop.[71] Further, since Ansbert was imprisoned in Hautmont,[72] that monastery is likely to have been a house loyal to Pippin, who was also involved in endowing the neighbouring foundation of Montier-en-Der.[73]

The majority of places where Pippin can be seen to have pursued some sort of ecclesiatical policy, however, were closer to the centres of his family's estates. That is to say they lay in the vicinity of Nivelles, Metz and Echternach. South of Nivelles lay Lobbes, two of whose abbots, Ursmar and Ermino, were certainly backed by Pippin.[74] To the church of St Arnulf in Metz[75] and to the monastery of Stablo-Malmédy, which had been founded by Sigibert III and Grimoald, he granted immunities.[76] Echternach itself was founded for Willibrord by Pippin's mother-in-law Itta in 698, and Pippin and Plectrude were keen supporters of the abbey.[77]

Despite the potential of the king as an independent agent, Pippin was consolidating his own position and that of his family, especially through his dealings with certain churches and monasteries. The evidence for Pippin's involvement in the Church is impressive. Yet when taken altogether, it does not amount to a monastic or an ecclesiastical policy comparable to that pursued by Balthild fifty years earlier: for the most part Pippin's actions were those open to any magnate, even though they were pursued on a larger scale; the endowment of monasteries and churches had always been a way of promoting the interests of a family. Essentially Pippin's ecclesiastical interventions were limited to those foundations to which circumstances and family connections gave him access.

The opposition to Pippin II

Juxtaposition of the activities of Pippin II and Childebert III shows just how delicate was the political balance between the traditional power of the Merovingian court and the expanding influence of the Pippinid family. The

69. *Liber Historiae Francorum*, 48; Fredegar, cont. 6.

70. Fredegar, cont. 5.

71. *Vita Rigoberti*, 2, 4, 8.

72. *Vita Ansberti*, 21.

73. Pardessus, *Diplomata*, 423.

74. Anso, *Vita Ursmari*, 2; Anso, *Vita Erminonis*, 3; Gerberding, *The Rise of the Carolingians and the Liber Historiae Francorum*, pp. 98–9; Dierkens, *Abbayes et Chapitres entre Sambre et Meuse (VIIe–XIe siècles)*, pp. 95–8, 103–4, 321–5.

75. Pertz, *Diplomata Arnulforum*, 2.

76. Pertz, *Diplomata Spuria*, 77; Gerberding, *The Rise of the Carolingians and the Liber Historiae Francorum*, p. 100, n. 55.

77. Gerberding, *The Rise of the Carolingians and the Liber Historiae Francorum*, p. 101.

difficulties in maintaining such a balance, however, were considerable. Already in the days of Ebroin and Berchar the Merovingian aristocracy had shown their hostility to the emergence of an overpowerful individual within the political structure of the kingdom, and in Pippin's day things were no different. Indications of opposition may be found in the exile of Ansbert to Hautmont. More obscure is the first part of the career of Hrodbert, better known as Rupert, bishop of Salzburg. His *Vita*, which dates from the early Carolingian period, states that he was originally bishop of Worms, and that he moved to Bavaria at the request of the *dux* Theoto.[78] If he did abandon the see of Worms it may well have been in the mid-690s, in opposition to Pippin.[79] In addition, the move to Bavaria might well be taken as an indication of the growing alienation and independence of the peripheral regions of the Merovingian state.

Despite Hrodbert's move to Salzburg, the Merovingian kingdom appears to have held together during the lifetime of Childebert. The witness lists for the royal charters certainly suggests that the court was still providing a focus for more than just the followers of Pippin. When Childebert died in 711, however, matters may have changed. He was succeeded by his young son, Dagobert III, but the elevation of a minor may have led members of the aristocracy to doubt the ability of the court to maintain a balance of power. It is perhaps in this period that Antenor asserted his independence in Provence.[80] That he had been loyal to Merovingians is indicated by his presence at the dispute at Compiègne over the lands of Tussonval in 697.[81] His opposition to the Pippinids in shown in Charles Martel's confiscation of his lands.[82] His revolt is, therefore, likely to be an indication of hostility to Pippin. Similarly the presence of bishop Savaric among the witnesses to the placita of 693 and 697 suggests that he too was loyal to Childebert, and began to build up an independent enclave in the Auxerre region only after that king's death.[83] These men were opponents not of the Merovingians, but of the Pippinids.

78. *Vita Hrodberti*, 1, 3.

79. Geary, *Before France and Germany*, p. 210; Wallace-Hadrill, *The Frankish Church*, p. 147.

80. Antenor's revolt is known only from later charter evidence: *Chartularium sancti Victoris*, 31; Geary, *Before France and Germany*, p. 126; Fouracre, 'Observations on the outgrowth of Pippinid influence in the "Regnum Francorum" after the Battle of Tertry (687–715)', pp. 8–9. The coin evidence is irrelevant: Grierson and Blackburn, *Medieval European Coinage, 1, The Early Middle Ages (5th–10th Centuries)*, p. 88.

81. Pertz, *Diplomata*, 70.

82. *Chartularium sancti Victoris*, 31.

83. *Vita Eucherii*, 4, 9; *Gesta episcoporum Autissiodorensium*, 27–8; Fouracre, 'Observations on the outgrowth of Pippinid influence in the "Regnum Francorum" after the Battle of Tertry (687–715)', p. 8.

The crisis of 714–17

Although problems are likely to have escalated with Childebert's death, worse was to follow. In 714 Pippin fell ill.[84] Drogo, his eldest son by his wife Plectrude, had already died.[85] Plectrude's second son, Grimoald, was murdered while praying at the shrine of St Lambert of Maastricht at Liège, before he could visit his father.[86] Plectrude, however, was determined that the office of *maior* of the Neustrian palace should remain with her descendants. Grimoald's son, Theudoald, was therefore appointed *maior* in his father's place. Pippin then died, leaving Plectrude to rule with her grandsons (*nepotibus suis*), that is Theudoald, and presumably the sons of Drogo. Of these Arnulf may have been of mature age: he seems to have assumed some power in Austrasia.[87]

This was the signal for those hostile to Pippinid dominance to unite. The Neustrians defeated Theudoald and his followers at the Forêt de Cuise, near Compiègne, and then appointed the Neustrian Ragamfred as *maior*. Next they advanced to the Meuse, allying themselves with Radbod, the leader of the Frisians. Plectrude, meanwhile, was faced with opposition from within the Pippinid family. She therefore imprisoned Charles, Pippin's son by Alpaida, but he promptly escaped from custody.[88] Then in 715 Dagobert III died, and the Neustrians elevated as his successor a monk called Daniel, who took the name of Chilperic II (715/16–21). Subsequently the new king and his followers marched against Charles, as did the Frisians, who defeated him. Thereafter Chilperic II and Ragamfred attacked Cologne, and seized treasure from Plectrude, but Charles defeated them at Amblève, as they withdrew.[89] He defeated them again at Vinchy in 717, when they fled, leaving him to turn against Plectrude, from whom he took his father's treasure. With this behind him he appointed his own Merovingian king, Chlothar IV (717–19), perhaps the son of Theuderic III.[90]

The elevation first of Daniel as Chilperic II by Ragamfred, and then of Chlothar IV by Charles, is an indication of how necessary a monarch of Merovingian blood remained. Just as Ebroin and Leodegar had appointed kings to legitimize their own power in the 670s, so too Ragamfred and Charles promoted their candidates in 715–17. Ragamfred's choice was a

---

84. *Liber Historiae Francorum*, 51; Fredegar, cont. 8.
85. *Liber Historiae Francorum*, 49; Fredegar, cont. 7.
86. *Liber Historiae Francorum*, 50; Fredegar, cont. 8.
87. Pertz, *Diplomata Arnulforum*, 7, implies that he was of age in 715/16.
88. *Liber Historiae Francorum*, 51; Fredegar, cont, 8; *Annales Mettenses Priores*, s.a. 714.
89. *Liber Historiae Francorum*, 52; Fredegar, cont. 9; *Annales Mettenses Priores*, s.a. 716.
90. *Liber Historiae Francorum*, 53; Fredegar, cont. 10; *Annales Mettenses Priores*, s.a. 717.

particularly interesting one: Daniel was a cleric. He may have been the son of Childeric II, whose murder had prompted the crisis of 675. If so he cannot have been younger than 40 in 715. Unlike many of the later Merovingians he seems to have come to the throne as a man of mature age.

Chilperic II and his allies

The basic narrative of the period between 714 and 721 is again that of the *Liber Historiae Francorum*. As for the previous years the Fredegar continuator essentially transcribes this text with slight additions. The *Annales Mettenses Priores* add yet more information, largely in order to glorify Charles, and to portray him as the rightful heir to Pippin II.[91] For information without a Pippinid gloss it is necessary to return to the charters. Pertz published ten royal charters for Chilperic II's reign, five of them in their original manuscripts, all dating from *c.* 716–18.[92] Even allowing for the vagaries of charter survival this represents an exceptional number of grants. The majority of the charters are in favour of such Neustrian houses as St Denis,[93] St Wandrille,[94] Corbie,[95] St Maur-des-Fossés[96] and Sithiu.[97] Less expected, however, is a grant to the church of St Arnulf at Metz, made in 717, apparently after Charles's victory at Vinchy.[98] Chilperic was, it seems, bidding for the support of a church which had been endowed by Pippin II, and which was to become firmly associated with the Pippinids, although there may as yet have been no clear claim of descent from the saint. Although Charles had gained the upper hand by the end of 717, Chilperic and Ragamfred were not yet out of the political running.

Within the Frankish evidence it is only the charters which illuminate the strength of Chilperic's position. All the narratives date from after the failure of his reign and are, therefore, affected by the distortions of hindsight. Fortunately another view is preserved in Anglo-Saxon sources. In 717 abbot Ceolfrith of Monkwearmouth/Jarrow decided to go on pilgrimage to Rome, and to do so he sought permission from Chilperic II, through whose lands he had to travel. As a result a Monkwearmouth/Jarrow writer mentions the king, and he describes him as a powerful monarch.[99] Further, in the *Liber Vitae* of Durham, the confraternity book, probably of Lindisfarne, but possibly of Jarrow, Chilperic's name is recorded, the only Merovingian name to appear.[100] He was clearly a force to be reckoned with. Since Childebert III

91. *Annales Mettenses Priores*, s.a. 714.
92. Pertz, *Diplomata*, 81–90.
93. Pertz, *Diplomata*, 81–4, 87.
94. Pertz, *Diplomata*, 85.
95. Pertz, *Diplomata*, 86.
96. Pertz, *Diplomata*, 88.
97. Pertz, *Diplomata*, 90.
98. Pertz, *Diplomata*, 89.
99. *Historia Abbatum auctore anonymo*, 32.
100. *Liber Vitae Ecclesiae Dunelmensis*, fol, 12v, ed. J. Stevenson, p. 1.

seems to have managed to achieve some authority in the years before 711, it is perhaps not surprising that Chilperic II could also impress his contemporaries. Ragamfred's choice of monarch seems to have been inspired.

Nor should the power of the Neustrian aristocracy be overlooked. Ragamfred was clearly a figure of considerable importance. He already appears as a *domesticus* during the reign of Clovis III, in the *placitum* dealing with Ingramn's estates in 693.[101] In Chilperic's charters he can be seen advising the king over grants to St Denis and St Maur-des-Fossés.[102] Among the advisers appearing in Chiperic's charters is the *comes palatii* Warno, who had also been active at the court of Clovis:[103] others had served under Childebert III.[104] Between them these men had built up considerable experience, and they probably formed the kernel of the anti-Pippinid party. They may have been joined by Hrodbert/Rupert, who is said to have returned home from Salzburg at the end of his life.[105]

Of yet greater significance was Radbod, the Frisian ally of Chilperic and Ragamfred. In the early Merovingian period the area around and to the north-east of the Rhine delta does not appear in the sources as an independent territory. Gregory of Tours's account of the raid of Hygelac, for instance, suggests that the lower Rhine was subject to Theuderic I.[106] Given the peculiar geographical and economic circumstances it is likely that the region was politically fragmented, and that it was overshadowed by its powerful neighbour. The development of Frankish society to the south and the growing importance of Frisia itself for trade, however, will doubtless have had an impact on the political structure of the territories of the Rhine delta. By 678 the area could boast a ruler, Aldgisl, described as a king by Stephanus in the *Vita Wilfridi*. Moreover, Aldgisl appears as a pagan with a policy quite independent of Ebroin.[107] Frisian independence is equally apparent under Radbod. He was among the *principes* against whom Pippin fought at the turn of the eighth century.[108] Presumably he came to terms with the Franks, for his daughter, Theudesinda, married Pippin's son Grimoald:[109] to judge by his name, Grimoald's son Theudoald must have been Radbod's grandson.

If Theudoald was the grandson of Radbod, it is likely that the Frisian king supported Plectrude in her attempt to establish the child as *maior* in 714. If he was present at the Forêt de Cuise he must, therefore, have been opposed to

101. Pertz, *Diplomata*, 66.

102. Pertz, *Diplomata*, 87, 88; Fouracre, 'Observations on the outgrowth of Pippinid influence in the "Regnum Francorum" after the Battle of Tertry (687–715)', p. 10.

103. Pertz, *Diplomata*, 60, 83.

104. Fouracre, 'Observations on the outgrowth of Pippinid influence in the "Regnum Francorum" after the Battle of Tertry (687–715)', pp. 9–11.

105. *Conversio Bagoariorum et Carantanorum*, 1.

106. Gregory, *Decem Libri Historiarum*, III 3; see also chapter 10.

107. Stephanus, *Vita Wilfridi*, 26–7.

108. *Liber Historiae Francorum*, 49; Fredegar, cont. 6; *Annales Mettenses Priores*, s.a. 692, 697.

109. *Liber Historiae Francorum*, 50; Fredegar, cont. 7; *Annales Mettenses Priores*, s.a. 711.

the Neustrians. By the end of the year, however, he had come to terms with Ragamfred. Such a *volte face* could be explained only by the threat to Frisia posed by Charles, whose mother's family seems to have been well endowed with land in the lower valley of the Meuse, close to the Frisian frontier.[110] By joining Ragamfred, Radbod faced Charles with a war on two fronts: the middle Rhine and the border region between Neustria and Austrasia.

The emergence of Charles Martel

There was a further problem facing Charles, and that was the split within Pippin's own family. As the son of Alpaida, Charles was opposed by Plectrude and her supporters. It is possible that the rivalry between Alpaida and Plectrude was already well established by 714. In the oldest version of the *Life* of Lambert of Maastricht the saint was murdered by Pippin's *domesticus*, Dodo, as a result of an outbreak of violence involving the latter's kin.[111] Subsequent versions of the text add the information that Lambert had criticized Pippin for his liaison with Alpaida, who is said to have been Dodo's sister.[112] Although this information is included only in texts dating to the late Carolingian period and beyond, it could have some basis in fact.[113] Consonant with these secondary narratives is the interest in the cult of St Lambert taken by Plectrude's son, Grimoald, who was murdered at the martyr's shrine at Liège in 714.[114] Certainly Plectrude herself showed no liking for Charles, imprisoning him after Pippin's death, and keeping his father's treasure from him until forced to give it up.[115] Nor was Plectrude's position an impossible one in 714. Although both her sons were dead, and her grandson, Theudoald, who was *maior* in Neustria, was only a minor, another grandson, Arnulf, apparently became *maior* in Austrasia, and was old enough to make an independent grant to his great-grandmother's foundation of Echternach in 715/16.[116] In addition Plectrude will have had the backing of her own kin, and perhaps even that of Radbod in 714.

In fact it is not easy to see how Charles did gain the upper hand in Austrasia. Crucial must have been his victory in 716 over Ragamfred and Chilperic. The battle was fought at Amblève, near Liège, as they returned

110. Gerberding, *The Rise of the Carolingians and the Liber Historiae Francorum*, pp. 119–20.

111. *Vita Landiberti episcopi Traeiectensis vetustissima*, 11, 13–17.

112. Sigebert, *Vita Landiberti episcopi Traeiectensis*, 16–20.

113. The opposite stance is taken by Gerberding, *The Rise of the Carolingians and the Liber Historiae Francorum*, p.117–19.

114. *Liber Historiae Francorum*, 50; Fredegar, cont. 7; *Annales Mettenses Priores*, s.a. 714.

115. *Liber Historiae Francorum*, 51, 53; Fredegar, cont. 8, 10; *Annales Mettenses priores*, s.a. 714, 717.

116. Pertz, *Diplomata Arnulforum*, 7.

from harrying the region around Cologne. Probably Charles was on mother's home territory, and probably he was dependent on her kin and the, dependants. The battle itself seems to have brought him increased support within Austrasia. Thereafter Willibrord, who owed the foundation of Echternach to Plectrude and her family, and who may well have been their agent in the region of the lower Meuse, is to be found baptizing Charles's son, Pippin (III).[117] It is possible that the saint had prudently switched his political allegiance. It is equally possible that, at the time, Charles was attempting some reconciliation with Plectrude and her supporters. The body of St Lambert was translated to a new shrine in Liège, presumably with Charles's approval, under the supervision of bishop Hubert,[118] who was a relative of Plectrude.[119] If his policy was one of conciliating other branches of the family, and if Charles had indeed united the whole of the Pippinid faction by the end of 716, this could help to explain his forward policy towards the Neustrians in the following year. It was he who was the aggressor at Vinchy, way over to the west, in the vicinity of Cambrai, and not the Neustrians.

Even if Charles did embark upon a policy of reconciliation within Austrasia after Amblève, he took advantage of his victory at Vinchy to secure his power by crushing Plectrude, for it was then that he forced her to hand over his father's treasure.[120] Francia outside the regions of the Meuse and the Rhine, however, was still firmly under the control of Ragamfred and Chilperic. The charters for 717 reveal them as being active in the Paris basin, and even as far into Austrasia as Metz, for the grant to St Arnulf's apparently post-dates Vinchy. The Neustrian cause, in other words, was still far from lost. Indeed, it may have become apparent that Charles intended to increase his challenge to Chilperic and Ragamfred only when he appointed a rival claimant, Chlothar IV, to the throne. In response to this action Ragamfred and his king turned to Eudo, *dux* of Aquitaine. Charles, however, defeated their combined forces in 719, and pursued Eudo as far as Orléans.[121] Then he asked that Chilperic be handed over to him: Eudo complied. According to the author of the *Annales Mettenses Priores* Charles acted *misericorditer*, conceding a *sedes regalis*, subject to his own authority, to Chilperic.[122] Chlothar IV was already dead, and Chilperic died at Noyon in 721.[123] He was the last of the Merovingians to be anything other than a puppet of the Pippinids, and with Ragamfred he had offered a substantial challenge to the

117. Alcuin, *Vita Willibrordi*, 23; Gerberding, *The Rise of the Carolingians and the Liber Historiae Francorum*, p. 134.

118. *Vita Landiberti episcopi Traeiectensis vetustissima*, 25–7.

119. Gerberding, *The Rise of the Carolingians and the Liber Historiae Francorum*, p. 129.

120. *Liber Historiae Francorum*, 53; Fredegar, cont. 10; *Annales Mettenses Priores*, s.a. 717.

121. *Liber Historiae Francorum*, 53; Fredegar, cont. 10; *Annales Mettenses Priores*, s.a. 717–18.

122. *Annales Mettenses Priores*, s.a. 718.

123. *Liber Historiae Francorum*, 53; Fredegar, cont. 10.

heirs of Pippin II. Charles appointed Theuderic IV (721–37), son of Dagobert III, in his place. Theuderic is described as having been brought up at Chelles: he may have been a monk, but he may have been little more than a child. With his elevation the *Liber Historiae Francorum* ends. Charles's problems, however, were not over. What had begun as a competition over the succession to Pippin II's authority, fought out between members of the Neustrian and Austrasian aristocracy, had become a crisis enveloping the whole of the Merovingian kingdom.

Chapter Sixteen

Towards Reunification: Wars and Politics, 721–51

With the appointment of Theuderic IV and the conclusion of the *Liber Historiae Francorum*, the first continuator of Fredegar began his own original account of events. Since he was working for Charles Martel's half-brother, the *comes* Childebrand, by the year 752, his account is contemporary.[1] Essentially it is a list of campaigns, and inevitably it is favourable to Charles and his sons, Pippin III and Carloman. It conveys the impression of the steady establishment of Carolingian authority throughout the Frankish world, despite the recalcitrance of certain hostile groups in the outlying parts and on the fringes of the kingdom. Clearly the continuator's account lacks depth, but there are also reasons for doubting the accuracy of what he records. The last years of the Merovingian kingdom were very much more complex than the continuator suggests. Exposing the issues, however, is not always straightforward.

'Carolingian' sources and Charles Martel

The events as recorded by the continuator of Fredegar run roughly as follows. After the elevation of Theuderic, Charles attacked Ragamfred, whom he beseiged in Nantes, before turning his attention (in 724) to the Saxons, who are described as rebels.[2] A year later he marched against the Alamans, the Sweves and the Bavarians, and he brought back with him Pilitrude, the widow of Grimoald, *dux* of Bavaria, and her niece, Sunnichild.[3] Eudo of Aquitaine then rose in revolt, and Charles moved against him. Eudo, according to the continuator, called for the assistance of the Saracens under Abd ar-Rahman, who marched to Poitiers. Before he could move on to Tours he was defeated by Charles; the traditional date for the battle is 732,

1. Fredegar, cont. 34.
2. Fredegar, cont. 11.
3. Fredegar, cont. 12.

although as we shall see this is certainly one, if not two, years too early.[4] In the following year Charles marched into Burgundy, and settled members of his own following there to ensure loyalty.[5] Then (in 735) Eudo died, and Charles took over Aquitaine.[6]

Burgundy's loyalty, however, was still suspect, and (apparently in 736) Charles again subjugated it, this time as far as the Mediterranean.[7] Nevertheless a rebellion led by Maurontus, who had Saracen backing, broke out in Provence in *c.* 737/8, and Childebrand, the patron of the Fredegar continuator, was sent to beseige Avignon. Charles himself attacked Narbonne, and defeated the Saracens at the river Berre. After the victory his followers plundered the south, before he joined Childebrand in the war against Maurontus. This was to be the last of Charles's campaigns.[8] In 739 the pope, Gregory III, asked for his help, but he was already ill. He divided the Frankish kingdoms between his two sons, placing Carloman over Austrasia and the territories to the east of the Rhine, and Pippin over Neustria, Burgundy and Provence. The latter, in the company of Childebrand, set off for Burgundy with an army, but Charles died at Quierzy, and was buried in St Denis.[9] The year was 741: there had been no Merovingian monarch for four years.

To the continuator's account the *Annales Mettenses Priores* and other early Carolingian annals add some detail. For the most part, however, the outline of the period from the death of Chilperic II to that of Charles seems reasonably straightforward: with the defeat of Ragamfred in *c.* 723 Neustrian opposition to Charles was broken: Aquitaine, the Rhône valley and Provence continued to offer opposition, but the intervention of the Muslims provided Charles with an opportunity to intervene in the south. At the same time he was able to deal with threats from the peoples east of the Rhine.

On the whole the Carolingian sources do not call into question the narrative of the Fredegar continuator, although as we shall see there are other sources that do. For the time being more problematic than the establishment of a narrative is the question of interpretation, not least because Carolingian writers made considerable play with the history of this period for propagandist purposes. They did so in two quite separate ways. On the one hand, Charles was remembered as an ancestor of the Carolingian dynasty, and his life was promoted to enhance the family's prestige. On the other he was portrayed as the archetype of the ruler who secularized Church lands, distributing them to his followers. This latter picture was largely developed in the ninth century by Hincmar, the archbishop of Rheims, and his contemporaries, who were objecting to the enforced alienation of ecclesiatical property, caused by the

---

4. Fredegar, cont. 13.
5. Fredegar, cont. 14.
6. Fredegar, cont. 15.
7. Fredegar, cont. 18.
8. Fredegar, cont. 20–1.
9. Fredegar, cont. 22–4.

need to build up secular fighting forces in a period of Viking raids. By contrast with the Carolingian monarchs, who regarded the secularization of property as a solution to the problem of defence, Hincmar and many of his colleagues saw the policy as a cause of the Norse invasions, which were a divine punishment for the royal treatment of the Church's estates.[10] Charles Martel was, therefore, depicted as especially sinful in alienating land, and he was said to have burned in hell as a punishment. A forged text, the *Visio Eucherii*, described his sufferings in detail.[11] It was a warning to the sons of Louis the Pious.

In the accounts of Charles written in the Carolingian period it is difficult to separate genuine tradition from political propaganda. The emphasis on him as one of the ancestors of the imperial family, propagated early in the period, is not of great interpretative significance; it merely adds to the narratives a level of bias which is easily recognised. The depiction of Charles as a seculariser of Church property is a different matter. Indeed any interpretation of him based on those sources dating from Hincmar's time and later is radically different from one deriving primarily from eighth-century evidence. That is not to say that the Carolingian reading of Charles is completely wrong, but merely that it is not how he was seen by contemporaries, and it is the contemporary view of him which should provide the starting point, when trying to understand him within his late Merovingian context.

The heirs of Savaric: Eucherius of Orléans and Ainmar of Auxerre

Among the earliest and most interesting works of hagiography to provide information on Charles's rule is the *Vita Eucherii*, written by someone who had contact with the saint's sisters, and therefore in the mid- or late eighth century.[12] Born of noble parents, Eucherius was handed over to be educated at the age of 7, and having learned the Church canons he entered the monastery of Jumièges.[13] Some while later his uncle, Savaric, who was bishop of Orléans (among other places), died and the people of Orléans asked Charles to appoint Eucherius in his place. He agreed, and the saint proved a worthy and popular bishop.[14] At the time of the Saracen invasion of Aquitaine, however, supporters of Charles suggested that he should exile Eucherius and his family and redistribute their offices. Again Charles agreed, sending the saint and his relatives into exile at Cologne.[15] Afraid of the backlash, he handed Eucherius secretly over to a man called Chrodebert.

---

10. Wallace-Hadrill, *The Frankish Church*, p. 134; McKitterick, *The Frankish Kingdoms under the Carolingians, 751–987*, p. 41.
11. *Vita Rigoberti*, 13; also Council of Quierzy (858), 7.
12. *Vita Eucherii*, 1.
13. *Vita Eucherii*, 3.
14. *Vita Eucherii*, 4.
15. *Vita Eucherii*, 7–9.

Subsequently the gaoler, following the advice of his prisoner, endowed the monastery of St Trond, where Eucherius died and was buried in 738.[16]

The context of Eucherius's episcopal career is a complicated one. The diocese of Orléans itself provides the backdrop. At the time of his election the city was probably dominated by the saint's family; his predecessor was his uncle. Moreover in 732 the leading offices in the diocese are said to have been held by his relatives.[17] Nevertheless his exile was more than a matter of local politics. The bishop's opponents seem to have been followers of Charles, and in all probability were not from Orléans. Certainly Eucherius's own family was of considerable standing within the Frankish kingdom. His parents are described as noble, and he himself had trained at the monastery of Jumièges. More important, however, was his uncle, Savaric. He was one of the great ecclesiastics of the previous generation. Originally he appears to have been bishop of Auxerre, and it was perhaps as such that he witnessed the *placita* of 693 and 697 which we have already considered.[18] In the ninth-century *Gesta episcoporum Autissiodorensium* he is said to have taken over Orléans, Nevers, Tonnerre, Avallon and Troyes by force.[19] Presumably this usurpation of power dates to the period after the death of Childebert III in 711. Savaric died when invading the diocese of Lyons.[20] His successor in Auxerre, Ainmar, may well have been a relative. Ainmar continued his predecessor's policy, eventually gaining control of almost the whole *ducatus* of Burgundy.[21]

The position of Savaric must in part explain the election of Eucherius to the see of Orléans. According to the *Vita Eucherii* the election was approved by Charles.[22] If this was so, it casts interesting light on Charles's position, because Savaric and his family can scarcely be seen as friends of Pippin II or of his successor. It looks as if Charles had to acquiesce in the appointments of both Eucherius and Ainmar, which suggests that in the opening years of his rule he was treading carefully in his dealings with the nobility. By the early 730s, however, he was in a very different position. He had already been established in Austrasia and Neustria for over ten years. Moreover he had followers who were themselves hungry for office and land. The Saracen invasion of Aquitaine provided a context for the overthrow of Eucherius and his family in Orléans, and for the redistribution of their positions. The fall of Ainmar was slightly delayed; he seems to have fought for Charles against the Saracens in 737, but was later deposed and imprisoned after letting Eudo slip through his hands. He was killed while trying to escape.[23]

16. *Vita Eucherii*, 9–10.
17. *Vita Eucherii*, 7.
18. Pertz, *Diplomata*, 66, 70; Fouracre, 'Observations on the outgrowth of Pippinid influence in the "Regnum Francorum" after the Battle of Tertry (687–715)', p. 8; see also chapter 15.
19. *Gesta episcoporum Autissiodorensium*, 26.
20. *Gesta episcoporum Autissiodorensium*, 26.
21. *Gesta episcoporum Autissiodorensium*, 27.
22. *Vita Eucherii*, 4.
23. *Gesta episcoporum Autissiodorensium*, 27.

There is much in the *Life* of Eucherius which can be paralleled in other, usually later, works relating to Charles's period of rule, and it can, therefore be used to provide something of a key to interpretation. Although in 719 Charles was in no position to overthrow Eucherius in Orléans, he was, it seems, able to deal with unreliable or hostile clerics nearer to the centres of his own power. The first bishop to suffer at his hands was Rigobert of Rheims. In the *Vita Rigoberti*, which was written between 888 and 895, the author records how the saint, who had earlier baptized Charles,[24] refused to open the gates of his city to him as he marched against Ragamfred. As a result Charles subsequently deprived him of the see.[25] Although the text comes from Rheims, and dates to the period after Hincmar's death, and although the account of the confrontation between Rigobert and Charles is followed by a discussion of two suspect texts, the *Visio Eucherii*[26] and the forged, or rather interpolated, letter of pope Hadrian to Tilpin,[27] it is possible that Rigobert did indeed refuse to commit himself to Charles in 718, and that he was deposed as a result. His diocese was put into the hands of Milo, who also had charge of a number of other ecclesiastical offices, including the bishopric of Trier.[28]

The abbots of St Wandrille

Similar political issues can be detected in the *Gesta abbatum Fontanellensium*. In 716, for unstated reasons, abbot Benignus was deposed by Ragamfred, and Wando was appointed in his place. The new abbot accompanied Ragamfred and Chilperic to Vinchy, and indeed it was on his horse that Ragamfred made his escape. It was not long before Charles was in a position to restore Benignus, and to send Wando into exile at Maastricht.[29] Clearly Charles dealt with those clerics whom he distrusted as and when he could. Rigobert and Wando suffered early in his period of rule, Eucherius and Ainmar fell later, as he expanded his control into the Loire valley and northern Burgundy.

The *Gesta abbatum Fontanellensium* has more to say about Charles's treatment of a monastery than does any other text. The earliest surviving version of the *Gesta* dates from around 840, and like other texts of the period it is concerned about the alienation of monastic property and about the Vikings.[30] Nevertheless it has been seen as pro-Carolingian in outlook. This is to underestimate the subtlety of the work, which is dominated by a

24. *Vita Rigoberti*, 8.
25. *Vita Rigoberti*, 9, 12.
26. *Vita Rigoberti*, 13.
27. *Vita Rigoberti*, 14.
28. *Gesta Treverorum*, 24; the classic study is E. Ewig, 'Milo et eiusmodi similes', in Ewig, *Spätantikes und fränkishes Gallien*, 2, pp. 189–219; see also Wallace-Hadrill, *The Frankish Church*. p. 137.
29. *Gesta abbatum Fontanellensium*, 3, 1.
30. Wood, 'Saint-Wandrille and its hagiography', pp. 4–5.

smouldering resentment of the treatment meted out to the monastery by Charles and his successors.[31] The chief source of irritation was the standard of the abbots appointed by Charles and his son Pippin.

Oddly enough the abbot most obviously associated with the Pippinids was in certain respects the least representative of their appointees. Hugo was a man of great political importance. Like Milo, he was a notorious pluralist, holding the sees of Rouen, Bayeux and Paris, as well as the monasteries of St Wandrille and Jumièges.[32] More significant, he was relative of Charles, being, as we have seen, the son of Drogo and Adaltrude, and thus the grandson of Pippin II. The author of the *Gesta*, however, makes much more of his descent from the Neustrian *maior* Waratto and, above all, Ansfled, who was responsible for his upbringing.[33] In fact, although Hugo was related to Charles, his promotion at his uncle's hand is best seen as a concession to the families of Ansfled and Waratto, and perhaps of Plectrude, rather than the elevation of a relative who could be relied on. Hugo was his own man: even after Vinchy he made a grant to Ragamfred's appointee at St Wandrille, Wando.[34] In later years, after he became abbot, the monastery continued to do well by him.

It is the successors of Hugo who stand as a condemnation of the policies of Charles and Pippin III. Worst was Hugo's successor but one, Teutsind,[35] but he was followed by another relative of Charles, Wido, a pluralist, uneducated and a huntsman. He was eventually accused of treason and executed at Noyon.[36] After him Ragamfred, archbishop of Rouen, took over the running of the abbey.[37] Like Wido, and like his predecessor in the see of Rouen, Grimo, he was lacking in education. Eventually the monks appealed to Pippin, and had him removed from his position as abbot. The man appointed in his place is an indication of the monastery's hostility to those abbots chosen by Charles, and also of Pippin's awareness of the need to conciliate the monks; he was the same Wando who had been sent into exile twenty years before, after the defeat of Ragamfred and Chilperic II. He was received back in scenes resembling a triumph.[38]

Not all of Charles's appointees in the Frankish Church were of poor standard. Nevertheless, the chief exception, Boniface, was blistering in his condemnation of the bishops appointed by Charles. Among those he singled out for particular criticism were Rigobert's successor at Rheims, the pluralist Milo, and the adulterous Gewilib of Mainz.[39] Milo does not perhaps deserve

---

31. Wood, 'Saint-Wandrille and its hagiography', pp. 10–12.
32. *Gesta abbatum Fontanellensium*, 4, 1.
33. *Gesta abbatum Fontanellensium*, 4, 1; see also chapter 15.
34. *Gesta abbatum Fontanellensium*, 4, 2.
35. *Gesta abbatum Fontanellensium*, 6.
36. *Gesta abbatum Fontanellensium*, 7.
37. *Gesta abbatum Fontanellensium*, 8.
38. *Gesta abbatum Fontanellensium*, 9, 1; Wood, 'Saint-Wandrille and its hagiography', p. 12.
39. Boniface, epp. 60. 87.

all the opprobrium to which he has been subjected. He was appointed in succession to his father, Liutwin, doubtless because Charles needed men in Austrasia on whom he could rely. He did protect the church of Trier and St Maximin and he even founded a monastery at Mettlach, but like other clerics of the period he used the Church for his own profit and security, and for that of Charles.[40]

This was not unlike the crime of Teutsind at St Wandrille. Teutsind was responsible for a decline in monastic standards; the *Gesta* claim that it was in his time that St Wandrille ceased to follow the *Rule* of St Benedict,[41] although it may be doubted whether the monastery had ever followed anything other than a mixed rule instituted by Wandregisel. More important, however, from the point of view of the author of the *Gesta* was Teutsind's alienation of the abbey's estates as *precaria*, or tenancies.[42] Up to one-third of the lands of St Wandrille are said to have been lost during his abbacy. The *Gesta* indeed provide detailed evidence culled from charters on the establishment of *precaria*, especially those established for the *comes* Ratharius.[43] Moreover, the author explains that to begin with Ratharius did pay a rent of sixty *solidi* a year, but that this lapsed during the abbacy of Witlaic. Such documentation earns for the *Gesta* more respect than other texts of the Carolingian period deserve. In fact, at times the work reads like nothing so much as a list of grants, and it may well be that its chief *raison d'être* was precisely to catalogue the abbey's main land-holdings and their loss.

Charles and the lands of the Church

Although the *Gesta* is a text of the mid-ninth century, it is one of the first documents to produce detailed information on the alienation of Church property in the time of Charles Martel. There is earlier information in terms of *placita* held while Pippin III was *maior*, dealing with specific estates or sources of revenue, particularly those of St Denis,[44] but it is unclear whether Charles was personally involved in the alienations. Such *placita*, moreover, are no different from those of earlier generations. In the light of this it is an open question as to whether the account of Teutsind in the *Gesta abbatum Fontanellensium* provides evidence of the actions of an individual abbot, or of the policy of the ruler of the Merovingian kingdom. An interpretation which maximized the importance of *ad hoc* responses and of individual greed would be perfectly compatible with the account of the dispossession of Eucherius and his family, at the suggestion of Charles's jealous followers, reported in the *Vita Eucherii*.

40. *Gesta Treverorum*, 24; Wallace-Hadrill, *The Frankish Church*, p. 137.
41. *Gesta abbatum Fontanellensium*, 6, 1.
42. *Gesta abbatum Fontanellensium*, 6, 1–3.
43. *Gesta abbatum Fontanellensium*, 6, 2.
44. Pertz, *Diplomata Arnulforum.*, 18, 21, 22, 23.

There are, however, two texts with some claim to be contemporary, which may imply that a more general policy was involved. The more critical, and more questionable, of the two is a letter of Boniface, addressed to king Æthelbald of Mercia, which recounts that 'Charles, *princeps* of the Franks, destroyer of many monasteries, and embezzler of Church revenues for his own use, was consumed in a long period of agony and a fearful death'. Unfortunately the passage survives only in a single group of manuscripts associated with England, none of them early. Nevertheless, it does seem likely that, even though the passage is not Boniface's own, it was inserted during the eighth century, perhaps by his contemporary, Egbert, archbishop of York.[45] Thus the sentence could have some significance for an understanding of Charles's policy. Less explicit, although unquestionable as a contemporary record, is a passage in the continuation of Fredegar. After the invasion of Burgundy in 733, the author relates that the Lyonnais was handed over to Charles's *fideles*.[46] This may imply that Burgundy was treated more harshly that other areas of the Merovingian kingdom, and that Charles reallocated land there. Such interpretation is compatible with the narratives of other Carolingian chronicles, most notably the *Gesta episcoporum Autissiodorensium*, which relate that the lands of the Church of Auxerre were reduced to a hundred *manses* through secularization by the time of Aidulf, whose episcopate lasted from the time of Charles into that of Pippin III.[47] Although the account is late, it may be accurate: it is not out of line with the comments of the continuator of Fredegar. It is certainly possible to argue that Charles was more ruthless in his treatment of Burgundy and Aquitaine than in that of Austrasia and Neustria. Nevertheless, even the seizure of land at Auxerre is best placed in a specific context; it is less likely to have happened at the time of Charles's first attack on Burgundy than after the deposition of bishop Ainmar for his part in Eudo's escape.

Provence: Abbo of Novalesa and Maurontus

The best contemporary evidence for the south implies that Charles worked there within the existing political framework as best he could, and that the pattern there was not greatly different from that in the north. Crucial is the information contained in the will of Abbo, founder of the Alpine monastery of Novalesa. Although this document is preserved only in a later, contaminated version, it apparently provides crucial information relating not only to the economy of southern Burgundy and Provence, but also to the politics of the region during Charles's day.[48] To judge by names, Abbo came

45. Boniface, ep. 73.
46. Fredegar, cont. 14.
47. *Gesta episcoporum Autissiodorensium*, 32; Wallace-Hadrill, *The Frankish Church*, p. 135.
48. Geary, *Aristocracy in Provence*; see also chapter 12.

from a noble family long established in Burgundy, indeed from a ¦
which had provided some of Columbanus's earliest Frankish supporters.·
726 he himself had become *rector* of the region around Maurienne and Su;
He may already have been a supporter of Charles by that date, though th¦
questionable: but he certainly was in 739, when his will was compiled.[51] In
all probability he played a significant role in opposition to the 'rebellion' of
Maurontus in Provence; among the estates listed in his will are several gained
as a result of the suppression of the revolts of the period from 733–8.[52] Thus
the estates in the *pagus* of Embrun, Die, Gap and Grenoble, given to Abbo at
the command of Theuderic IV and Charles, had once been held by one
Riculf, who had committed treason by joining the Saracens against the
kingdom of the Franks.

In the case of Abbo, Charles was rewarding a member of the southern
aristocracy who had supported him against the 'rebel' Maurontus. He must
have behaved in like manner with many a northern magnate. As for
Maurontus, despite the fact that the Fredegar continuator states that his
rebellion in the 730s depended on cooperation with and reliance on the
Saracens, he appears to have been related to northern aristocratic families,
perhaps even to that of Erchinoald and Leudesius.[53] That is, he needs to be
understood in the context of Merovingian politics as a whole, and not simply
in terms of Provençal separatism. As we have seen, a generation earlier
Antenor had begun his career attending court, and he had witnessed a royal
placitum in 697, but subsequently had led a revolt, probably directed against
Pippin II rather than against any Merovingian.[54] Now Maurontus, himself
arguably a member of one of the leading families of Neustria, was in arms
against Pippin's son and those southern aristocrats who were prepared to
support Charles. What was new in Maurontus's case was his involvement
with the Saracens. This, however, is best considered in the light of the
evidence for Aquitaine.

Eudo, the Saracens and Aquitaine

If the growing independence of Burgundy and Provence was a development
of the early eighth century, caused by the increased power of the Pippinids,
that of Aquitaine is likely to have been of longer standing. Ever since the days
of Clovis I the region had been treated differently from the other parts of the
Merovingian *regna*, being allocated to individual kings city by city, rather than
in the same manner as the regions to the north and the east. Its cultural

---

49. Wood, review of Geary, *Aristocracy in Provence*, *French History 1* (1987), pp.
118–19.
50. *Monumenta novaliciensia vetustiria*, 1; Geary, *Aristocracy in Provence*, p. 33.
51. Geary, *Aristocracy in Provence*, p. 33.
52. Abbo, *Testamentum*, 16, 25, 55, 56.
53. Geary, *Aristocracy in Provence*, pp. 131–8.
54. Pertz, *Diplomata*, 70; see also chapter 15.

identity, like that of Provence, also remained distinct from the northern heartlands of the Frankish kings. Nevertheless, despite political rivalries within Aquitaine, it had remained firmly within the Merovingian kingdom until the late seventh century. We have already noted that the crisis years of the 670s had an impact on relations between the Merovingian court and Aquitaine. First there was rivalry between Felix, Ebroin's appointee as *dux*, and Lupus, who was a loyal supporter of Childeric II. Then, after Childeric's murder, Lupus appears to have tried to assert his independence of the new regime under Ebroin.[55] He was acting in a manner not unlike that of Antenor and Maurontus in Provence in the next century.

Thereafter, little is known about the history of Aquitaine, outside the Auvergne, until the days of Eudo. He is presented by the continuator of Fredegar as the leader of an army of Gascons or Basques (*Vasconi*), unable to defeat Charles, and forced to call in Saracen help.[56] The following of Eudo presents an interesting problem, which we have already touched on.[57] In the early part of the seventh century the pagan Gascons had been a threat to the southern border of Aquitaine, although they had been incorporated into a kingdom for Chlothar II's younger son Charibert.[58] Later, according to the Fredegar continuator, but not the *Liber Historiae Francorum*, the opponents of Ebroin fled across the Loire to the Gascons.[59] The author of the second *Passio* of Leodegar follows the Fredegar continuator, saying essentially the same, but calling them Basques, *Vaccaei*.[60] What is difficult to assess is the extent to which the Gascons had expanded into the area north of the Garonne, and to what extent outside observers were merely conflating them with the Aquitanians to denigrate the latter. If Aquitaine was indeed becoming Gascon, then its growing independence had an ethnic as well as a political context. As we have seen the truth probably lies somewhere between the two extremes.

Because of the failure of the alliance between Ragamfred, Chilperic II and Eudo, and because of the successes of both Charles and the Saracens in Aquitaine it is easy to underestimate the importance of Eudo and his army of Gascons. One victory which the *Liber Historiae Francorum*, the continuator of Fredegar and the *Annales Mettenses Priores* overlook is that of Eudo over a Saracen force outside Toulouse in 721. The battle is, however, recorded in the Mozarabic *Chronicle of 754*, a work of considerable importance for understanding the history of the Arab conquest of Spain, and apparently written in the mid-eighth century.[61] The Mozarabic chronicler records that the Muslim leader As-Samh, having ruled in Spain for three years (from 718), took over Narbonne, and from there he attacked the Franks, until Eudo

55. *Miracula Martialis*, II 3; see also chapter 13.
56. Fredegar, cont. 10, 13.
57. See chapter 10.
58. Fredegar, IV 57.
59. Fredegar, cont. 2; *Liber Historiae Francorum*, 45.
60. *Passio Leudegarii II*, 12.
61. R. Collins, *The Arab Conquest of Spain*, pp. 26–30.

defeated him at Toulouse.[62] The *Chronicle of 754* is not alone in referring to these events: Eudo's victory is given considerable prominence in the *Liber Pontificalis*, which also reveals that Gregory II and Eudo corresponded before and after the battle.[63]

The *Chronicle of 754* also provides crucial information on the background to Charles Martel's victory at 'Poitiers'. In 731 Abd ar-Rahman came to power in Spain. Shortly after, a Berber leader in Spain known as Munnuza rebelled against him, setting himself up in Cerdaña, in the eastern Pyrenees. He allied himself with the Franks, taking Eudo's daughter as his wife. Abd ar-Rahman beseiged Cerdaña, but Munnuza escaped; subsequently, however, he committed suicide. Thereafter Abd ar-Rahman crossed the Pyrenees, defeating Eudo to the north of the Garonne. He marched to Tours, where he was defeated and killed by Charles. The Franks, nevertheless, failed to take advantage of their victory and let the Saracens slip away overnight.[64] In many respects the account of the Mozarabic chronicle has important information on the events leading up to Charles's victory. In crucial respects it differs from other sources. It gives Abd ar-Rahman a three-year period of rule, thus placing his death in 733/4, and it locates the battle not at Poitiers, but at Tours.

The account of the Fredegar continuator is rather different. It begins with Eudo breaking a treaty with Charles in approximately the year 725. Charles therefore crossed the Loire and plundered Aquitaine. When he saw that he had been beaten Eudo called in the Saracens to help him. Abd ar-Rahman crossed the Garonne, sacked Bordeaux and Poitiers, but was prevented from marching on Tours by Charles, who defeated and killed him.[65] Although the continuator's narrative is generally thought to place the battle at Poitiers, and to date it to 732, in fact its indication of location is vague, and apparently places the battle the year before Eudo's death which is usually dated 735. In these respects the account of the Fredegar continuator may be reconciled with that of the Mozarabic chronicler and the battle of Poitiers may be placed at Tours and dated to 733 or 734.[66]

Such agreement is not possible with respect to the accounts of relations between Eudo and the Muslims. According to the *Chronicle of 754* Eudo had been allied to Munnuza, but he was consistently opposed to Abd ar-Rahman. The Fredegar continuator makes Eudo ally with Abd ar-Rahman, after he had been defeated by Charles. In all probability either the continuator or Charles hoped to make propagandist gains by eliding Munnuza and Abd ar-Rahman, and turning Eudo into a coward who had to call in the Saracens to protect him against Charles. The dissemination of this corrupt reading of events obviously raises doubts about the accuracy of the continuator elsewhere.

62. *Chronicle of 754*, 69.
63. *Liber Pontificalis, Vita Gregorii II*, 11; see also the confused account in Paul, *Historia Langobardorum*, 6, 46; Collins, *The Arab Conquest of Spain*, p. 87.
64. *Chronicle of 754*, 79, 80.
65. Fredegar, cont. 13.
66. Collins, *The Arab Conquest of Spain*, pp. 90–1.

The Fredegar continuator portrays Maurontus as working together with the Saracens in the 730s.[67] In the light of the accusations made against Eudo, the account of Maurontus might be equally seen as equally suspect. There are, however, reasons for thinking that the continuator's account might be more accurate in this case. First, the will of Abbo refers to Riculf as being in league with the Saracens.[68] Unless the will itself repeats propaganda there is, therefore, evidence that Provençal magnates did work with the Muslim invaders. Second, the history of Munnuza, as recounted by the *Chronicle of 754*, shows that even Eudo allied with some Muslims when it suited him. For Maurontus, then, the Saracens may have been a convenient ally against the current power in the north. At the same time the involvement of the Saracens did allow Charles to depict the uprising of Provence as the result of collaboration between traitors and the descendants of the Ishmaelites.

Fortunately the evidence for Aquitaine is not confined to Eudo's relations with the Saracens. The text which has by far the most to say about Eudo's period of rule in Aquitaine is the *Liber Miraculorum* of bishop Austregisil of Bourges.[69] Unfortunately it is an eleventh-century work, and it consistently confuses Charles with Pippin. Although it may contain some authentic information about the impact of war on the diocese of Bourges, it can scarcely be used as evidence. More worthy of attention is the late-eighth-century *Vita Pardulfi*. Pardulf was abbot of Guéret, to the north-east of Limoges, and for the most part his *Life* is concerned with his asceticism and his miracles. The wider world, however, does occasionally impinge on the author's narrative. For instance there is an account of the plundering committed by the Saracens, in the aftermath of their defeat at 'Poitiers'.[70] More important is the evidence on Chunoald, Eudo's son, who is called *princeps* and is also described as legate of Charles.[71] Although he subjugated Aquitaine after Eudo's death in 735, Charles nevertheless found it politic to appoint his old rival's son as ruler in his place. As the *Annales Mettenses Priores* comments, he acted with *pietas*,[72] which probably means that political circumstances forced him to be conciliatory. After Charles's death, however, Chunoald rebelled against Carloman and Pippin III,[73] but even then he managed to maintain his office, although he entered the monastic life, supposedly voluntarily, soon after murdering his brother in *c.* 744.[74] Nevertheless, he was able to leave his post to his son Waifar. Charles and his sons did not have things all their own way south of the Loire, even after 734.

67. Fredegar, cont. 20.
68. Abbo, *Testamentum*, 56.
69. *Miracula Austregisili*, 5–8.
70. *Vita Pardulfi*, 15.
71. *Vita Pardulfi*, 17, 21.
72. *Annales Mettenses Priores*, s.a. 735.
73. Fredegar, cont. 25; *Annales Mettenses Priores*, s.a. 742.
74. *Annales Mettenses Priores*, s.a. 744.

The peoples to the east of the Rhine

Aquitaine had been part of the Merovingian kingdom since the days of Clovis and his sons. The regions to the east of the Rhine, however, had always been more peripheral to the Frankish state. To some extent they were a barometer of the power of a king. As the author of the *Annales Mettenses Priores* commented in the context of Pippin II's wars against the Sweves, Bavarians and Saxons, 'on account of the sloth of kings and civil wars, which had broken out in many parts of the divided kingdom, they had deserted their rightful domination, each seeking to defend their freedom by force on their own soil'.[75] The same, from a Pippinid point of view, was true in Charles's day.

Although Radbod had been the earliest of Ragamfred's allies, the Frisians appear to have posed little of a threat between 715 and 734, when Charles campaigned against their pagan leader, the *dux* Bubo.[76] But while they presented no great danger, they were also a difficult people to subdue, largely because of the watery landscape of the Rhine delta and the lands to the north-east. As a result of the failure of any political settlement the missionaries in Frisia found their work hard going. The Saxons presented equal problems. They did not have the same geographical advantages as the Frisians, but their lands lay further to the east. They suffered at Charles's hands in 724, and became tributary in 738,[77] but they did not give up their pagan religion. Neither of these peoples, however, challenged the authority of the Charles in the way that the Alamans and the Bavarians did.

The Alamans had been subject to the Franks since the reign of Clovis. Occasionally their leaders had proved disloyal, and had taken advantage of the conflicts within the royal family, but they are not known to have reasserted their independence before the days of Pippin II and Charles. Relating to the lifetime of the latter there is a precious piece of information preserved in the ninth-century *Breviary of Erchanbert*: 'At that time Gotefrid, *dux* of the Alamans, and the other *duces* round about him, refused to obey the *duces* of the Franks, because they were no longer able to serve the Merovingian kings as they had been accustomed to do before. So each of them kept to himself'.[78] Some of the implications of this are made clear by the recension of the *Lex Alamannorum* which claims to be the work of Gotefrid's son, Lantfrid, and probably dates from the 720s.[79] There could be no clearer way for a *dux* to assert independence than that he should issue his own version of his people's lawcode.

The Bavarians may have followed suit: the *Lex Baiwariorum* seems to survive in a recension of the early 740s.[80] Bavarian independence, however,

75. *Annales Mettenses Priores*, s.a. 688.
76. Fredegar, cont. 17.
77. Fredegar, cont. 11, 19; see also *Annales Mettenses Priores*, s.a. 716, 719, 736, 738.
78. Erchanbert, *Breviarium Regum Francorum*.
79. *Lex Alamannorum, incipit*, cod. A; see also chapter 7.
80. R. Buchner, *Die Rechtsquellen*, Wattenbach-Levison, *Deutschlands Geschichtsquellen im Mittelalter*, pp. 26–9.

was not new in the mid-eighth century. Although the Agilolfings were apparently of Frankish extraction, and had been promoted by the Merovingian kings, they had for a long while developed their own policies. In part, these policies involved the exploitation of local Bavarian governmental structures. Agilolfing policy also exploited connections with Italy. These were in part the result of geography, but, as we have seen, they were also the result of marriage, particularly of that of Theudelinda, sister of *dux* Grimoald and Gundoald, to the Lombard king Agilulf, in the early seventh century. At the same time Gundoald married a Lombard noblewoman.[81] It is not, therefore, surprising to find the Bavarians taking an increasingly independent line from the time of Pippin II onwards. Indeed, the Agilolfing court seems to have been a refuge for Hrodbert/Rupert, the anti-Pippinid bishop of Worms.[82] In 716, *dux* Theoto turned to Rome, rather than Francia, for help with ecclesiastical organization.[83] Nine years later Charles invaded and seized Pilitrude, the widow of Theoto's recently murdered son, Grimoald, and her niece, Sunnichild.[84] The latter he married, and by her he had a son, Gripho, who was to cause considerable trouble for his half-brothers, Carloman and Pippin. Nor did Charles solve the problem of the relations between the Franks and the Bavarians in 725 or later.

The achievement of Charles Martel

Considered within the context of the early eighth century, and, as far as possible from the viewpoint of early sources, Charles does not look like the hero or the villain of later historiographical tradition. Victor at 'Poitiers' he certainly was, but that was not the first Frankish victory against the Saracens, which had been won by Eudo in 721, and had been recognized by the pope. Nor did 734 mark the end of the Saracen threat. Maurontus was still to ally with the Muslims, and his alliance suggests that there were some in the south who preferred Islamic friends to Pippinid lordship. Even in 739 the Saracens may have seemed dangerous enough for Charles to have needed Lombard assistance, and therefore to have refused to help the pope against his Italian neighbours.[85] But for Charles the Arab threat did provide the opportunity to invade Aquitaine, Burgundy and Provence. If he was the saviour of Christendom, that was a by-product of actions dealing with less elevated political concerns.

81. Fredegar, IV 34; see also chapter 10.
82. See chapter 15.
83. *Liber Pontificalis, Vita Gregorii II*, 4; T.F.X. Noble, *The Republic of St Peter: The Birth of the Papal State 680–825*, pp. 26–7.
84. Fredegar, cont. 12; Arbeo, *Vita Corbiniani*, 24, 31.
85. Paul, *Historia Langobardorum*, VI 54; Fredegar, cont. 22; *Annales Mettenses Priores*, s.a. 741; *Liber Pontificalis, Vita Gregorii III*, 14; *Vita Stephani II*, 15; Noble, *The Republic of St Peter: The Birth of the Papal State 680–825*, pp. 44–8.

At the same time, the evidence does not support the ninth-century depiction of Charles as the great secularizer of Church property. Some estates were confiscated and others granted out as *precaria*, but there was no overall policy of secularization. Essentially, Charles was doing what any ruler did with the lands of his opponents. The uniqueness of his position derived simply from the number of his enemies, and the fact that he defeated many of them in battle. He was not, as has been claimed, the architect of a new type of state, arranged round the need for cavalry. There is no evidence to support the view that Charles was a man who developed a new type of mounted military force, and who initiated a revolution in land-tenure in order to provide for his horsemen.

The overriding impression of Charles is of a successful man working within very specific limitations. He removed opponents when circumstances permitted, but otherwise left them in peace. Thus Plectrude was tolerated in 716 but not in 717. Eudo, and later Chunoald, were left in office. Eucherius of Orléans and Ainmar of Auxerre were removed when the time was ripe but not before. This is best read as the *realpolitik* of a man who could not afford to alienate or alarm too many people at once. His sense of what would wash is seen as clearly in his dealings with royalty as anywhere else. He did not depose Chilperic II, but, in the word of the *Annales Mettenses Priores*, *misericorditer* allowed him a palace.[86] Then, when Chilperic died, he appointed another king, Theuderic IV.[87] The latter was certainly his puppet, but he was not quite a cipher. He still made grants, and his court still dealt with law-suits.[88] But already in Austrasia Charles was behaving like a king, as in the *placitum* he issued in favour of Stablo in *c.* 719.[89] It seems that he knew that the Neustrian aristocracy would not condone the abolition of Merovingian kingship. And in 737, on the death of Theuderic, Charles chose not to usurp. When he himself died four years later there were still problems to be resolved before a Carolingian could sit on the Frankish throne.

Carloman and Pippin III

Before his death Charles divided the Frankish kingdom between his two sons: Carloman was set over the eastern part of the kingdom and Pippin III over the western.[90] When he died in 741, however, pandemonium broke out. First, the Fredegar continuator records the flight of the dead man's daughter, Chiltrude, to Odilo of Bavaria, on the advice of her stepmother, Sunnichild, herself a member of the Agilolfing dynasty. Odilo then married Chiltrude.[91]

---

86. *Annales Mettenses Priores.*, s.a. 718.
87. Fredegar, cont. 10.
88. Pertz, *Diplomata* 91–5.
89. Pertz, *Diplomata Arnulforum*, 10.
90. Fredegar, cont. 23; *Annales Mettenses Priores.*, s.a. 741.
91. Fredegar, cont. 25.

The sequence of events was long remembered as a *cause célèbre*. Meanwhile, Chunoald had revolted in Aquitaine, and Carloman and Pippin III attacked Bourges and Loches.[92] Next these two sons of Charles had to turn on the Alamans. Then, in 743, the Bavarians rebelled, and they had to lead an army against Odilo, whom they defeated at the river Lech.[93] The following year Carloman attacked the Saxons, while Pippin attacked Godefred, who had rebelled in Alamannia.[94] The year 745 saw Carloman and Pippin march on the Gascons of Aquitaine, and then Carloman had to turn his mind to the Alamans again.[95] His victory was followed by mass executions. The following year, however, he decided to enter the monastic life in Italy, leaving his son, Drogo, and his *regnum* in Pippin's hands.[96] Thereafter the latter had to deal with a revolt among the Saxons, who agreed to pay tribute.[97] Then in 749 the Bavarians rebelled at the instigation of Gripho, son of Charles and Sunnichild.[98] Again Pippin defeated them. Finally he turned his mind to the kingship, and, with papal sanction, became king of the Franks.[99]

Gripho and Bavaria

Such is the narrative of the continuator of Fredegar. It is again a record of wars, and to a large extent the wars are resurgences, encouraged by the death of Charles, of the conflicts of the previous two decades. The *Annales Mettenses Priores* repeat most of this narrative, but with crucial additions relating to Gripho and to Bavaria.[100] What the annalist shows in general in these additions is the united nature of the hostility of the peripheral regions to the sons of Charles. For instance, Odilo is backed by the Saxons, Alamans and Slavs, and he in turn supports the revolts of the Alamans.[101] Nor was his position regarded as unjustified: the papal legate, Sergius, is said to have attempted to prevent Pippin's invasion of Bavaria in 743.[102] Equally important, in the same year, Odilo persuaded Chunoald of Aquitaine to attack Neustria, and to burn Chartres.[103] From the narrative of the continuator of Fredegar such collusion is implied simply by the chronology of events, the annalist provides the detail to support these implications.

It is over Gripho, however, that the *Annales Mettenses Priores* have most to offer. They reveal that before Charles's death Sunnichild persuaded her

92. Fredegar, cont. 25; *Annales Mettenses Priores*, s.a. 742.
93. Fredegar, cont. 26; *Annales Mettenses Priores*, s.a. 743.
94. Fredegar, cont. 27; *Annales Mettenses Priores*, s.a. 744.
95. Fredegar, cont. 28, 29; *Annales Mettenses Priores*, s.a. 746.
96. Fredegar, cont. 30; *Annales Mettenses Priores*, s.a. 747.
97. Fredegar, cont. 31.
98. Fredegar, cont. 32; *Annales Mettenses Priores*, s.a. 749.
99. Fredegar, cont. 33; *Annales Mettenses Priores*, s.a. 750.
100. *Annales Mettenses Priores*, s.a. 743, 746, 748–51.
101. *Annales Mettenses Priores*, s.a. 743.
102. *Annales Mettenses Priores*, s.a. 743.
103. *Annales Mettenses Priores*, s.a. 743.

husband to create a middle kingdom for her son Gripho.[104] The Franks took exception to her intervention, as they were later to do over the similar influence of Judith, second wife of Louis the Pious,[105] and when Charles died Carloman and Pippin turned on Sunnichild and her son, who fled to Laon. There they came to terms, and Gripho was sent into custody at Neuf-Château, while his mother was placed in the nunnery of Chelles.[106]

Subsequently the significance of Sunnichild's advice to her stepdaughter, Chiltrude, that she should flee from her brothers to Odilo, became apparent. Gripho remained in custody until the retirement of Carloman to Rome and later to Montecassino. Then Pippin freed him and gave him a *comitatus*, or county.[107] Nevertheless, Gripho took advantage of a synod held at Düren to escape to Saxony,[108] and when Pippin followed him there he moved on to Bavaria. There his uncle, Odilo, had recently died. Taking advantage of this, Gripho dispossessed his cousin, Tassilo, and seized the *ducatus* for himself. Pippin promptly intervened, restoring Tassilo, but setting Gripho up with twelve *comitatus* in Le Mans. From there Gripho escaped to Chunoald in Aquitaine.[109] Pippin, who had been anointed king, maybe by Boniface, then demanded that Chunoald should hand over his guest.[110] He refused, but Gripho, realizing that he was not safe from his half-brother in Aquitaine, set out for Lombardy, and the protection of king Aistulf. On the way he was killed, by a group of Frankish nobles.[111]

Gripho's career is important in a number of respects. It reveals the standard problems surrounding a son by a second marriage. His mother would be well placed to advance his claims during his father's lifetime, but thereafter the son would be at the mercy of other factions, surrounding older brothers. The problem is apparent as early as 561, when Chilperic quarrelled with his half-brothers.[112] In the early seventh century Charibert had suffered in similar manner,[113] and Charles the Bald would be hard pressed in the ninth.[114] Gripho's case also sheds particularly valuable light on the role of maternal kin in such a situation. Because Sunnichild was an Agilolfing, the impact of Gripho's own problems extended into Bavaria, where briefly he held the office of *dux*.

More important still, the career of Gripho provides a reminder that there was no inexorable path to a single Carolingian kingship in 751. Gripho was a

104. *Annales Mettenses Priores*, s.a. 741.
105. McKitterick, *The Frankish Kingdoms under the Carolingians, 751–987*, p. 169.
106. *Annales Mettenses Priores*, s.a. 741.
107. *Annales Mettenses Priores*, s.a. 747.
108. *Annales Mettenses Priores*, s.a. 748.
109. *Annales Mettenses Priores*, s.a. 749.
110. *Annales Mettenses Priores*, s.a. 750.
111. *Annales Mettenses Priores*, s.a. 751.
112. Gregory, *Decem Libri Historiarum*, IV 22.
113. Fredegar, IV 57.
114. McKitterick, *The Frankish Kingdoms under the Carolingians, 751–987*, pp. 169–72.

son of Charles, with a genuine claim to part of his father's estate, and Pippin seems actually to have recognized that his half-brother had some justice on his side and some support, otherwise he would scarcely have tried to appease him with *comitatus* on two occasions. That the support was of some consequence is indicated by the annals, which record that before his flight to Saxony, Gripho had bound many nobles to him 'with the pride of a tyrant'.[115]

Pippin III and the deposition of Childeric III

Carloman and Pippin thus found their authority questioned on a variety of fronts. The peripheral regions were as hostile as they had been under Charles, and in the person of Gripho they had a focus for opposition within the Carolingian family: the Pippinids were no more united in the 740s than they had been thirty years earlier. The extent of the reserve shown towards the two brothers may be reflected in their decision to appoint another Merovingian, Childeric III, as king in 743, after an *interregnum* of six years.[116] It has been suggested that Carloman was the chief figure behind the elevation of Childeric, and this may have been so. Certainly it is Carloman who is named in Childeric's last surviving charter,[117] but this would have been dictated by geographical reasons rather than any other. The elevation of Childeric III was almost certainly an attempt to appease certain elements in the Frankish kingdom and on its borders, and those elements are likely to have included all the opponents of Carloman and Pippin, as well as waverers, such as those from whom Gripho would later draw support. The creation of a new Merovingian king need not shed any light on relations between Carloman and Pippin.

In fact it is not easy to draw distinctions between Pippin and Carloman before the latter's retreat to Rome and Montecassino. Thereafter Carloman certainly appears as an opponent of his brother, lobbying the papal court against him and on behalf of the Lombard king Aistulf in 754.[118] Beforehand, it is just possible to detect a difference between the two brothers in their enthusiasm for Boniface's reforms.[119] If, however, there had been any great conflict between them it is difficult to understand Carloman leaving his son and his *regnum* in Pippin's hands in 747. Nevertheless, Carloman's pious retirement brought the possibility of the throne closer to Pippin. Most likely

115. *Annales Mettenses Priores*, s.a. 748.
116. *Pactus Legis Salicae*, king-list, MS A2; Pertz, *Diplomata*, 97, 98; Council of Soissons (744), *praef.*
117. Pertz, *Diplomata*, 97.
118. *Liber Pontificalis, Vita Stephani II*, 30.
119. The case depends on there being earlier references to Carloman than Pippin in Boniface's correspondence, Boniface, ep. 50, 51, and the chronological priority of the *Concilium Germanicum* (742) over the Council of Soissons (744), though this chronology may be affected by geographical rather than spiritual issues; see also Wallace-Hadrill, *The Frankish Church*, p. 139, 156.

it was the latter's usurpation and its implications for his brother's family which led to Carloman's hostility. The precise context in which the usurpation took place, however, was created by circumstances in Italy, rather than the Frankish kingdom.

The most immediate problem for the papacy in the early eighth century was the threat posed by the Lombard kings of northern Italy, notably by Liudprand and then by Aistulf.[120] Although Rome was subject to Byzantium, the emperor was too preoccupied with the threats posed by the Arabs and by the Avars in the east to be able to offer protection against the Lombards. Further, the emperor Leo III's policies against the Arabs had led to the official promulgation of the doctrine of iconoclasm, that is the condemnation of the cult of icons, and at the same time to a dramatic increase in the taxes demanded from Italy, and in particular from the papal estates.[121] The papacy regarded iconoclasm as a heresy, and the added burden of taxation it found equally unwelcome. All these factors led popes to consider the possibility of securing protection against the Lombards from western rulers rather than from the Byzantine emperor. By the middle decades of the century, the Franks under Charles and his sons were increasingly attractive as allies. In part this is an indication of the prestige of the Pippinids, and in part it is the result of the growing ties between the Roman and Frankish Churches, developed by the Anglo-Saxon missionaries working on the continent. Nevertheless, such an alliance must have seemed less attractive before the 730s, not least because the fate of the Merovingian kingdom was still unclear. Not surprisingly, there are indications that the Pippinids were not the only leaders whose support was being canvassed before 751. Gregory II's approach to Eudo before and after his victory over the Saracens in 721 can certainly be seen in this light.[122] Even in 739 when Gregory II sent two embassies to Charles, with major gifts of relics, offering, according to the Fredegar continuator, to desert the emperor,[123] an alliance between the papacy and the Pippinids was not practicable. Charles was ill, but equally important, he may have needed Lombard support against the Saracens:[124] besides his own son Pippin had been adopted by Liudprand, and had been sent to the Lombard court as part of his upbringing.[125] The presence of the papal legate, Sergius, in the Bavarian camp in 743 may suggest that Zacharias was also looking for help from that quarter.[126]

120. Noble, *The Republic of St Peter: The Birth of the Papal State 680–825*, pp. 40–57.

121. D.H. Miller, 'The Roman revolution of the eighth century: a study of the ideological background of the Papal separation from Byzantium and alliance with the Franks', *Medieval Studies* 36 (1974), pp. 79–133.

122. *Liber Pontificalis, Vita Gregorii II*, 11.

123. Fredegar, cont. 22.

124. Paul, *Historia Langobardorum*, VI 54.

125. Paul, *Historia Langobardorum*, VI 53.

126. *Annales Mettenses Priores*, s.a. 743.

By 750, however, the political situation in the Frankish *regnum* was clearer. Since his brother's retirement Pippin's campaigns had been successful, and problems in Bavaria, Saxony and Alamannia had been solved momentarily. After 749 the continuator of Fredegar was able to claim that there were two years of peace. In this context Pippin was able to send Burghard, bishop of Würzburg, and Fulrad, abbot of St Denis, to ask for papal approval of the deposition of Childeric III and the elevation of Pippin to the Frankish kingship.[127] It was a convenient moment for pope Zacharias as well, because the Lombard king Aistulf was casting increasingly covetous eyes on the Byzantine holdings in Italy, including Rome. In 751/2 the last Merovingian king was deposed, and Pippin III was anointed in his place, perhaps by Boniface.[128] The usurpation allowed the Carolingians to begin their steady downgrading of the last century and a half of what had been, at least until 719, a remarkably hardy form of government.

127. *Annales Regni Francorum*, s.a. 749.
128. *Annales Regni Francorum*, s.a. 750; *Annales Mettenses Priores*, s.a. 750.

Chapter Seventeen

The Northern Emporia:
Quentovic, Dorestad and the
'Sceatta' Economy

The late seventh and eighth centuries saw considerable changes in the political structure of the Merovingian kingdom. There were economic changes as well. These were most notable in the north, particularly in the region of the lower Rhine and on the North Sea and Channel coast, where a number of major trading centres emerged. This development has often been set alongside the rise of the Pippinids.[1] Since, however, the authority of the Pippinids seems not to have been established as early as is assumed by many historians, following the account in the *Annales Mettenses Priores*, it is necessary to be cautious about attributing to Pippin II and Charles Martel a prime role in the developments of the seventh and early eighth centuries. Given the long and interrupted nature of the rise of the Pippinids to political dominance, it is unlikely that they will have had a significant impact on the economy of the Merovingian kingdom. There can be no *a priori* case for assuming that the development of emporia in Neustria and even on the fringes of Austrasia and Frisia was dependent on Pippinid influence.

Quentovic and Dorestad under the Carolingians

Two northern emporia stand out as being of particular significance to seventh-century Francia: Quentovic and Dorestad, the former lying close to the modern town of Étaples, on the river Canche, in Neustria,[2] the latter on the old course of the Rhine, to the south of Utrecht, on the boundary between Austrasia and Frisia.[3] A third, at Domburg on the Frisian island of Walcheren, seems to have been a major economic centre in the Merovingian

1. R. Hodges, *Dark Age Economics: The Origins of Towns and Trade, AD 400–1000*, p. 39.
2. P. Leman, 'Contribution à la localisation du Quentovic ou la relance d'un vieux débat', *Revue du Nord* 63 (1981), pp. 935–45.
3. S. Lebecq, *Marchands et navigateurs frisons du haut moyen âge,* 1, pp. 149–63.

period, but it is known only from poor archaeological evidence obtained in the face of marine erosion.[4] Even Quentovic and Dorestad are poorly documented in the seventh and early eighth centuries, although they were already centres for minting coin.[5] In the early Carolingian period, by contrast, both are relatively well attested, in the written sources as well as numismatically. Their mints were producing coin in quantities.[6] By chance each featured in hagiography. Moreover their vicissitudes in the Viking period are recorded in various chronicles.

The *Gesta Abbatum Fontanellensium* reveals that Gervold, who was abbot of St Wandrille from 789 to 807, was set up by Charlemagne as *procurator* for the trade of the Frankish kingdom, and that as a result he was responsible for levying tolls (*tributa atque vectigalia*), especially in Quentovic. Perhaps because of these duties he also played a leading role in Charlemagne's dealings with Offa, king of Mercia.[7] A charter of Charlemagne granting exemptions to the community of St Germain-des-Prés from various tolls in 779 confirms the economic importance of the emporium.[8] Later the place came to have a particular significance for the community of St Wandrille. After the Viking attacks on the Seine in 839 the relics of Wandregisel and Ansbert were taken first to Bloville and then to the church of St Peter, outside Quentovic.[9] As a result a notable cult of Wandregisel and Ansbert grew up in the region. The cures effected at the shrines of the saints, and recorded in the ninth-century *Miracula Wandregisili*, provide a remarkable insight, if not into the trading-centre itself, at least into the ailments of some of the townspeople and other inhabitants of the region. The cures can be dated to the second half of the ninth century, when Quentovic was supposedly in decline, largely as a result of the Viking onslaught: the evidence of the *Miracula* may imply that the decline of Quentovic was less marked than has been supposed.

Dorestad is also mentioned in Charlemagne's exemption for St Germain-des-Prés.[10] Similarly, it is well known from a text relating to the Viking period. In the *Life of Anskar*, written between 865 and 876 by Rimbert, his successor as archbishop of Hamburg-Bremen, there is a long excursus on the almsgiving carried out at Dorestad by Catla, who had come from the Swedish emporium of Birka to give alms in memory of her mother.[11] To Rimbert, Dorestad was a place of many churches, priests and paupers; it was also a place of holy sites and religious women. The

4. Lebecq, *Marchands et navigateurs frisons du haut moyen âge*, 1, pp. 142–5.
5. Grierson and Blackburn, *Medieval European Coinage*, 1, *The Early Middle Ages (5th–10th Centuries)*, pp. 134–5, 137.
6. Grierson and Blackburn, *Medieval European Coinage*, 1, *The Early Middle Ages (5th–10th Centuries)*, p. 197.
7. *Gesta abbatum Fontanellensium*, 12, 2.
8. *Recueil des chartes de Saint-Germain-des-Prés*, 19.
9. *Miracula Wandregisili*, I 10–11; II 12–22; III 23–31; IV 32–41; V 42–3.
10. *Recueil des chartes de Saint-Germain-des-Prés*, 19.
11. Rimbert, *Vita Anskarii*, 20; see also 7, 24, 27.

hagiography of the ninth century, thus, puts a little human flesh on the bones of coin-inscriptions, charter references and annal entries relating to Dorestad and to Quentovic. The same is not the case for the Merovingian period.

Merovingian Quentovic

What appears at first sight to be the earliest text to mention Quentovic, a charter of Dagobert I concerned with merchants travelling to the fair of St Denis via Quentovic or Rouen, is unfortunately a forgery of the late ninth century.[12] The earliest written references in fact come in Anglo-Saxon literary texts, Stephanus's *Life of Wilfrid* and Bede's *Ecclesiastical History*. The latter states that Raedfrid was sent by Egbert king of Kent to accompany archbishop Theodore from the Frankish kingdom to England in 668. He is said to have received permission from the *maior* Ebroin, and to have taken the new archbishop to Quentovic, where Theodore had to stop to recuperate from some illness.[13] Stephanus also associates Ebroin with Quentovic. When in 678 Wilfrid determined to appeal to Rome against the division of his diocese, his opponents sent gifts to Theuderic III and Ebroin, to persuade them to drive the bishop into exile, or even to kill him. It was decided to intercept him at Quentovic, but, according to Stephanus, Wilfrid crossed the Channel to Frisia, and bishop Winfrid of Lichfield was seized by mistake.[14] Bearing in mind the fact that the two anecdotes relating to the port of Quentovic in the seventh century both involve Ebroin, and the exercise of his authority, it may be significant that Quentovic, or *Wic in Pontio*, is relatively close to the royal villa of Crécy-in-Ponthieu. In the 660s and 670s Quentovic seems to have been under the eye of the Neustrian *maior,* and it was well placed to be so. Whether the emporium was still tightly supervised in 718, when Boniface landed at the port, is not revealed by his biographer, Willibald.[15] The fact that Ceolfrith, abbot of Monkwearmouth/Jarrow, needed letters of introduction for his journey though Francia in 716 may indicate that there was still close supervision of the chief points of entry into the kingdom at that time.[16]

To the literary evidence for Quentovic may be added the evidence of the coinage. The mint of Quentovic was already producing gold *trientes*, bearing an image of a royal bust, and also the moneyer's name, in the first half of the seventh century.[17] There is a coin of Quentovic in the treasure from Mound One at Sutton Hoo.[18] More important, a high proportion of the Frankish

---

12. Lebecq, *Marchands et navigateurs frisons du haut moyen âge*, 2, pp. 400–1.
13. Bede, *Historia Ecclesiastica*, IV 2.
14. Stephanus, *Vita Wilfridi*, 25.
15. Willibald, *Vita Bonifatii*, 5.
16. *Historia Abbatum auctore anonymo*, 32.
17. Grierson and Blackburn, *Medieval European Coinage*, 1 *The Early Middle Ages (5th–10th Centuries)*, nos 471–4.
18. Kent, 'The coins and the date of burial', in *The Sutton Hoo Ship Burial*, 1, p. 632.

coins in the Crondall hoard, dated to the mid-seventh century, were minted at Quentovic.[19] The discovery in England of a substantial number of gold *trientes* from the Quentovic mint may well suggest that the port played a particularly significant role in relations between Merovingian Francia and Anglo-Saxon England:[20] this would be in keeping with the literary evidence relating to Theodore, Wilfrid, Boniface, and later abbot Gervold. Perhaps equally indicative of Quentovic's position in communications with England is the fact that one of the moneyers was actually called Anglus.[21]

There is, however, a difficulty in combining the evidence of Bede, Stephanus and Willibald on the one hand and that of the coins on the other. The literary references are concerned with the period from 668 to 718; Merovingian gold coinage such as that produced at Quentovic was minted until *c.* 670.[22] It was followed by a coinage of silver deniers or pennies. Curiously the Quentovic mint does not seem to have been active in the production of these deniers,[23] despite its importance earlier in the production of gold *trientes* and later in that of the silver coinage of the Carolingians.[24] There is a further puzzle, in that there is a case for attributing the introduction of the silver denier currency to Ebroin,[25] the *maior* who was able to keep close political control over Quentovic. If he was responsible for the introduction of the silver denier, it is curious that the emporium produced none of the new coins.

Dorestad in the Merovingian period

The early history of Quentovic is tantalizing. So too is that of Dorestad. Again the information for the Merovingian period is slight. The earliest literary reference to survive comes from the *Ravenna Cosmographer*, writing in around the year 670. He describes Dorestad as being in the Frisian part of Germany, and he states that the Rhine enters the Ocean below Dorestad, the *patria* of the Frisians.[26] The second reference is to be found in the additions made to the chronicle of Fredegar by 751. Here Pippin II is said to have

19. Grierson and Blackburn, *Medieval European Coinage*, 1, *The Early Middle Ages (5th–10th Centuries)*, pp. 126–7.

20. Grierson and Blackburn, *Medieval European Coinage*, 1, *The Early Middle Ages (5th–10th Centuries)*, pp. 134–5.

21. S. Lebecq, *Les Origines franques, Ve–IXe siècle*, p. 150.

22. Grierson and Blackburn, *Medieval European Coinage*, 1, *The Early Middle Ages (5th–10th Centuries)*, pp. 93–5.

23. Grierson and Blackburn, *Medieval European Coinage*, 1, *The Early Middle Ages (5th–10th Centuries)*, pp. 145–6.

24. Grierson and Blackburn, *Medieval European Coinage*, 1, *The Early Middle Ages (5th–10th Centuries)*, p. 197.

25. Grierson and Blackburn, *Medieval European Coinage*, 1, *The Early Middle Ages (5th–10th Centuries)*, p. 94.

26. Lebecq, *Marchands et navigateurs frisons du haut moyen âge*, 2, p. 208.

defeated the *dux* of the Frisians, Radbod, at the fortress of Dorestad, *castro Duristate*, in about 695.[27] By that date Dorestad seems to have been in the hands of Radbod, who was clearly opposed to Pippin. Control of the port may have passed to the Austrasians as a result of the battle. Whether it did so or not, relations between Radbod and Pippin must have improved by the time of the marriage of Radbod's daughter Theudesinda to Pippin's son Grimoald.[28] With Pippin's death, however, hostility between the Frisian leader and the family of Pippin resurfaced.[29] Boniface arrived at Dorestad from London on his first visit to the continent in 716. He then proceeded to Utrecht to speak to Radbod, but he returned to England shortly after, having ascertained that the time was not favourable for missionary work.[30] As Radbod was to be found in Utrecht in 716 it is likely that the Frisians had control of Dorestad during this stage of their wars with the Pippinids, since Dorestad and Utrecht seem to have been closely associated: the late-eighth-century *Life* of Boniface's disciple Gregory of Utrecht talks of the saint illuminating the old *civitas* of Utrecht and the famous *vicus* of Dorestad,[31] as if the two places were associated. They are unquestionably geographically close. If Radbod lost Dorestad and Utrecht to Pippin in the 690s, he had regained them by 716. After the death of Radbod in 719, Utrecht seems to have passed firmly into the control of Charles Martel.

Unlike Quentovic, whose site is now known, but has not yet been extensively excavated, Dorestad has been the object of a major excavation programme.[32] As a result archaeological evidence can be added to that of the written sources. The site of Dorestad covers a vast area of some two hundred and forty hectares. The most striking features of the excavations were the jetties, which were gradually extended to compensate for the steady shift of the river. At the landward end of the jetties were wooden buildings, presumably built by the traders who used the jetties. In addition there were small farm complexes, and the whole site was served by around eighty wells.

The first major phase of development seems to have begun in *c.* 675, at roughly the time that the *Ravenna Cosmographer* was writing. In terms of Frankish politics this can be correlated with the reign of Childeric II, or with that of Dagobert II, and certainly before the re-emergence of the Pippinid family after the débâcle of Grimoald's coup. Since, however, the *Ravenna Cosmographer* stresses the Frisian nature of Dorestad, it may be misleading to emphasize the Frankish political context. At this time Frisia seems to have been independent. The situation in Frisia is illuminated by Stephanus, who states that Wilfrid was welcomed by Aldgisl when he avoided Ebroin by sailing to Frisia rather than Quentovic in 678.[33] Aldgisl is the first ruler of the

27. Fredegar, cont. 6
28. *Liber Historiae Francorum*, 50; Fredegar, cont. 7; see also chapter 15.
29. *Liber Historiae Francorum*, 51; Fredegar, cont. 8
30. Willibald, *Vita Bonifatii*, 4.
31. Liudger, *Vita Gregorii*, 5.
32. Lebecq, *Marchands et navigateurs frisons du haut moyen âge,* 1, pp. 149–63.
33. Stephanus, *Vita Wilfridi*, 26–7.

Frisians to be described as king in a source. Even the Audulf who minted coins in the sixth century seems not to have claimed such a title.[34] It is possible that Aldgisl was claiming greater independence from the Franks than had previous Frisian rulers. In Aquitaine, Lupus seems to have claimed the royal title in the aftermath of Childeric II's murder;[35] Aldgisl may have acted likewise. Moreover, since Dagobert II had only recently returned from exile in Ireland, he may not have been strongly placed to oppose such a move. Encouragement for a trading centre on the borders of Frisia and Austrasia might have been part of the expression of Aldgisl's new royal power. That Dorestad remained in Frisian hands during the ensuing decade, in which Pippin II did finally come to prominence, is suggested by the battle at Dorestad between Pippin II and Aldgisl's successor, Radbod.

The literary and archaeological evidence, therefore, points to a Frisian development of the site of Dorestad in the 670s. The evidence of the coinage, however, complicates this history. The earliest coins for Dorestad, like those for Quentovic, are Merovingian gold *trientes*.[36] They must belong to the period before the transfer to the silver denier in *c.* 670; indeed, they are reckoned on numismatic grounds to date to the first half of the seventh century. Merovingian gold coins were thus being minted at Dorestad before the major development of the site as evidenced in the archaeology. Further, these gold *trientes* were minted by moneyers called Rimoaldus and Madelinus. Both are known to have minted coins at Maastricht, which may imply that they were moved from a well-established mint to a new one.[37] The Dorestad mint may even have been subordinate to that at Maastricht.

The development of Dorestad revealed by the coinage thus implies a different, Frankish, context for the original development of the *vicus* than that which saw its expansion in the 670s. Some insight into this original context may be found in a letter of 753 where Boniface told pope Stephen II that king Dagobert had given the bishop of Cologne the *castellum* of Utrecht as a base for the evangelization of the Frisians.[38] In all probability the Dagobert in question was Dagobert I. His interest in the evangelization of the region of the lower Rhine is otherwise attested by his support for Amandus.[39] The establishment of a missionary centre at Utrecht between 623 and 639 could coincide with the date for the Rimoaldus and Madelinus coinage. There was, therefore, a Merovingian development of the site of Dorestad in the first half

34. Grierson and Blackburn, *Medieval European Coinage*, 1, *The Early Middle Ages (5th–10th Centuries)*, p. 137

35. See chapter 13.

36. Grierson and Blackburn, *Medieval European Coinage*, 1, *The Early Middle Ages (5th–10th Centuries)*, p. 137; Lebecq, *Marchands et navigateurs frisons du haut moyen âge*, 1 pp. 50–4.

37. Grierson and Blackburn, *Medieval European Coinage*, 1, *The Early Middle Ages (5th–10th Centuries)*, p. 100; p. 137; Lebecq, *Marchands et navigateurs frisons du haut moyen âge*, 1 pp. 50–4.

38. Boniface, ep. 109.

39. *Vita Amandi*, 13, 18.

of the seventh century, known only from the coinage, and a Frisian development, attested archaeologically and in the literary sources, in the second half.

The chronology of the 'sceattas'

Madelinus continued to mint coins in Dorestad until approximately 650.[40] Thereafter no new Merovingian moneyer seems to have been established on the site. Moreover, there are no Merovingian silver deniers of the type introduced in *c.* 670 which can be assigned to the mint at Dorestad, just as none can be assigned to Quentovic. Since the archaeological evidence for Dorestad provides incontrovertible evidence that the site not only survived but also was massively expanded, the apparent collapse of the Dorestad mint needs careful consideration. Fortunately there is numismatic evidence which may well relate to Dorestad in this period, even if the origins and the chronology of the coins are the subject of debate.

Although there is no evidence that Merovingian silver deniers were minted at Dorestad, and although Madelinus seems to have left the *vicus* in *c.* 650, coins of the 'Madelinus' type, bearing the same inscription, were minted, not necessarily at Dorestad itself, in the second half of the seventh century. What distinguishes them from the official Merovingian issues is the fact that they were minted in silver and not gold.[41] They are among the earliest Frisian 'sceattas', or more correctly silver pennies. 'Sceattas' were minted in a variety of styles, and there is nothing to suggest that they were a royal coinage. Nevertheless, they are usually of high standard, in terms both of their technical and also their silver content. While there is little firm evidence to indicate where 'sceattas' were minted, patterns of distribution point to Frisia, possibly north Francia, as well as England and later Denmark.[42]

Despite the difficulty of provenancing these coins, some 'sceatta' issues have been assigned to Dorestad. Imitations of the Madelinus *trientes* are likely to have been minted there, although some specimens in the series were almost certainly struck elsewhere.[43] A second type of 'sceatta', known as the 'Maastricht' type, has also been partially assigned to Dorestad, on the grounds of the relatively large numbers of examples which have been discovered

40. Lebecq, *Marchands et navigateurs frisons du haut moyen âge*, 1, pp. 52–4.

41. Grierson and Blackburn, *Medieval European Coinage*, 1, *The Early Middle Ages (5th–10th Centuries)*, p. 151.

42. Lebecq, *Marchands et navigateurs frisons du haut moyuen âge*, 1, pp. 54–60; Grierson and Blackburn, *Medieval European Coinage*, 1, *The Early Middle Ages (5th–10th Centuries)*, pp. 149–54, 164–89; D.M. Metcalf, 'A note on sceattas as a measure of international trade, and on the earliest Danish coinage', in D. Hill and D.M. Metcalf, eds, *Sceattas in England and on the Continent*, pp. 159–64.

43. Grierson and Blackburn, *Medieval European Coinage*, 1, *The Early Middle Ages (5th–10th Centuries)*, p. 151.

there.[44] A further type which might have been minted at Dorestad is known as 'Continental Runic', although other suggested centres of production have included Quentovic and Domburg.[45]

The probable minting of 'sceattas' in Dorestad in the second half of the seventh century goes some way to explaining the absence of a Merovingian mint in the *vicus* at that time. If some 'sceattas' were to be ascribed to Quentovic this might also explain the absence of silver deniers from the Neustrian emporium. Nevertheless with regard to the history of Dorestad difficulties remain. These difficulties are largely associated with the problem of determining the chronology of the 'sceattas'. The detailed chronology of the 'sceatta' coinage is difficult to establish, depending largely on the archaeological dating of finds, particularly of hoards.[46] Very few of the 'sceattas' found at Dorestad belong to the primary series of issues, that is to those issues which were thought to have been minted in the period between 690 and 725: later issues from the so-called secondary series of 'sceattas' are considerably more numerous.[47] Following this dating of the coins, there would appear to have been a recession in Dorestad between *c.* 690 and *c.* 725, that is almost exactly the period in which Radbod ruled as king in Frisia. This supposed recession has understandably been linked with Radbod's wars against the Pippinids.[48]

As we have seen, however, the narrative sources do not support the idea of constant war between Franks and Frisians in Radbod's day.[49] At the same time, the archaeological evidence of the jetties at Dorestad suggests that the half century preceding 725 was a period of development, even if it did not compare in intensity with the subsequent activity on the site.[50] If these chronologies for the archaeology and the 'sceattas' are correct, the two types of material provide conflicting evidence for the development of the emporia, with the archaeology indicating the development of Dorestad as a trading centre at a time when the coinage suggests decline.

This apparent conflict between the evidence of the timber remains and of the coin finds at Dorestad might be explained by the continuing problems involved in dating the coinage. The so-called secondary series of 'sceattas', which was thought to have begun *c.* 725, is now seen by Grierson as

44. W. op den Velde, W.J. de Boone and A. Pol, 'A survey of sceatta finds from the Low Countries', in D. Hill and D.M. Metcalf eds, *Sceattas in England and on the Continent*, p. 138.

45. Grierson and Blackburn, *Medieval European Coinage*, 1, *The Early Middle Ages (5th–10th Centuries)*, pp. 152–3.

46. Grierson and Blackburn, *Medieval European Coinage*, 1, *The Early Middle Ages (5th–10th Centuries)*, pp. 151–2

47. op den Velde, de Boone and Pol, 'A survey of sceatta finds from the Low Countries', p. 135.

48. op den Velde, de Boone and Pol, 'A survey of sceatta finds from the Low Countries', p. 136.

49. See chapters 10 and 15.

50. Lebecq, *Marchands et navigateurs frisons du haut moyen âge, 1*, pp. 154–7.

beginning some ten to fifteen years earlier.[51] The primary series, therefore, should be seen as belonging to a shorter period than was previously envisaged. The numismatic argument for a significant Frisian recession between *c.* 690 and *c.* 725, based on the paucity of finds of coins of the primary series,[52] as a result becomes less convincing, and the archaeological and numismatic evidence appears to be more compatible. Radbod's reign was not a period of economic decline.

The 'sceatta' economy and the early medieval state

The relationship between the fortunes of Dorestad and the political history of the Merovingian kingdom was, therefore, a complex one. Certainly the early development of the site, in the days of Dagobert I, is likely to have been as a result of royal intervention, or so the presence of moneyers who had previously worked at Maastricht would suggest. Equally, it is unlikely that the site of Dorestad would have developed in the 670s without the support of the ruler, in all probability Aldgisl. Nor is Radbod likely to have been hostile to continuing activity at the emporium. By extension, if the development of Dorestad between the 670s and the 720s owed something to the newly established kings of Frisia, then it is likely to have owed little to the Merovingians and nothing whatsoever to the Pippinids in that period.

On the other hand, while the Franks seem not to have played a vital role in the development of Dorestad in the period after 670, there is still a danger of assigning too much importance to the kings of Frisia. Just as the 'sceatta' coinage was not an official Frankish coinage, so too it may not have been an official coinage of the kingdom of Frisia either. Here the fact that 'sceattas' were produced in more than one kingdom is significant.[53] Indeed, there is debate over the provenance of certain series of 'sceattas': thus the majority of the 'Porcupine' series may be Frisian, but some issues may be English, and the origins of the 'Woden/monster' type is still in doubt.[54] The 'sceatta' coinage, in short, looks like the coinage of a trading nexus, which spread from Frisia and north Francia, to England and Denmark.[55] Unlike the royal Merovingian coinage it is unlikely to have had any fiscal function. Nevertheless, despite the apparent absence of royal control, the coinage of this northern trading nexus was of remarkably high and consistent quality.

51. Grierson and Blackburn, *Medieval European Coinage, 1, The Early Middle Ages (5th–10th Centuries)*, pp. 186–7.

52. op den Velde, de Boone and Pol, 'A survey of sceatta finds from the Low Countries', pp. 135–6.

53. Grierson and Blackburn, *Medieval European Coinage, 1, The Early Middle Ages (5th–10th Centuries)*, p. 149–50.

54. Grierson and Blackburn, *Medieval European Coinage, 1, The Early Middle Ages (5th–10th Centuries)*, p. 153–4.

55. Metcalf, 'A note on sceattas as a measure of international trade, and on the earliest Danish coinage', pp. 159–64.

This trading nexus certainly incorporated the great emporia of the Merovingian kingdom and Frisia, but it also stretched across the English Channel to take in such Anglo-Saxon ports as London, Hamwic and Ipswich.[56] For all three of these sites literary evidence is lacking, and thus the interpretation of their origins must be questionable. The concentration of centres of the East Anglian kingdom in the coastal and riverine regions immediately to the north of Ipswich could suggest that trade in that region developed under the aegis of the kings of East Anglia.[57] The development of Hamwic, in *c.* 690, might be related to the power either of Caedwalla (686–8), who attacked Sussex and seized the Isle of Wight, or of Ine (688–725/6), who also harassed the South Saxons, and who was responsible for the earliest West Saxon law-code.[58] Neither in Ipswich, nor in Hamwic, however, is there clear evidence of royal involvement in the development of the sites as emporia. The same is even more true of London, which was not consistently associated with any one Anglo-Saxon kingdom.[59] Certainly kings will have wished to establish tolls at such emporia, but there is nothing to suggest that they attempted to encourage trade in this period, nor do they seem to have established a royal coinage as the main medium of mercantile exchange before the mid-eighth century. Thus, while the emporia of the north, English as well as Frankish and Frisian, may have been established with royal support, the subsequent development of trade seems not to have been determined by the kings of Francia, Frisia or England. As in the case of the trade of the great cities of the High Middle Ages, that of the Merovingian period seems to have flourished most in the interstices between the centres of royal power.

The economic connections between England and the continent were no less important for being outside the immediate purview of the Anglo-Saxon and Merovingian kings. Moreover the impact of those connections was more than economic. Some of the English who went to work on the continent as missionaries in the late seventh and eighth centuries claimed to do so because of an awareness that they were ethnically related to the pagans who lived to the east of the Rhine.[60] The chronological correlation between the development of the emporia and the arrival of the missionaries is such as to suggest that this perception of ethnic similarity was encouraged by the growing importance of trading contacts. Although Quentovic was of significance long before Wilfrid arrived there in 678, the decision first of Ecgbert and then of Willibrord to work in Frisia came within a generation of

56. Hodges, *Dark Age Economics: The Origins of Towns and Trade, AD 400–1000*, pp. 43–5.

57. Hodges, *Dark Age Economics: The Origins of Towns and Trade, AD 400–1000*, pp. 70–3.

58. Hodges, *Dark Age Economics: The Origins of Towns and Trade, AD 400–1000*, p. 44.

59. C.N.L. Brooke and G. Keir, *London 800–1216: The Shaping of a City*, pp. 16–18.

60. Bede, *Historia Ecclesiastica*, V 9; compare Boniface, ep. 46.

the development of Dorestad.[61] Similarly, Willibrord is known to have visited Denmark with a view to missionary work.[62] Archaeology now places the origins of the Danish emporium of Ribe in *c.* 710, which must be approximately the date of Willibrord's visit.[63] The patterns of trade and mission were to continue to overlap. Gregory of Utrecht's pupil Liudger went to study in York with Alcuin, but had to leave when a Frisian merchant killed the son of a *comes* of the *provincia*.[64] Later still, the Christians of the Swedish emporium of Birka looked to Dorestad.[65] Christianization, like trade, could be particularly important on the fringes of the Merovingian kingdom.

61. Bede, *Historia Ecclesiastica*, V 9; Alcuin, *Vita Willibrordi*, 5.

62. Alcuin, *Vita Willibrordi*, 9.

63. K. Bendixen, 'Sceattas and other coin finds', in M. Bencard, ed., *Ribe Excavations 1970–76*, 1, pp. 76–7; S. Jensen, *The Vikings of Ribe*, pp. 5–11.

64. Altfrid, *Vita Liudgeri*, 11.

65. Rimbert, *Vita Anskarii*, 20.

Chapter Eighteen

Mission Accomplished: The Merovingian Church East of the Rhine

It is possible that it was Boniface who anointed Pippin king in 751/2.[1] Certainly he had played an increasingly important part in the Frankish Church during the 740s. As the Carolingians established their control over the kingdom, and were able to depose such ecclesiastical families as that of Savaric of Auxerre, and also to reduce their own dependence on clerics like Milo of Trier and Gewilib of Mainz, so too were they increasingly able to patronize ecclesiastical reform. In 742, the year after Charles Martel's death, Carloman supported the so-called *Concilium Germanicum*.[2] A year later an Austrasian synod was held at Estinnes,[3] and Pippin summoned its western counterpart to Soissons in 744.[4] The three synods dealt with clerical standards and provision, calling for annual councils; they subjected monks to the *Rule of St Benedict*, and they dealt with the surviving remnants of paganism. Two further councils were certainly held, in 745 and 747.[5] At the former it seems that Gewilib was deposed. As a result Boniface, who had been an archbishop without a see since 732, was given the diocese of Mainz.[6] The reform of the late Merovingian Church was well under way, and its future assured. Already, in 742, Chrodegang, who was to some extent a pupil of Boniface, had been appointed bishop of Metz.[7] In 754, the year of Boniface's martyrdom, Chrodegang was elevated to the archiepiscopate;[8] he was to be the dominant force in the continuation of ecclesiastical reform during Pippin's reign.

1. *Annales Regni Francorum*, s.a. 750.
2. *Concilium Germanicum, MGH, Concilia* 2. (742), *praef.*
3. Council of Estinnes, *MGH, Concilia* 2. (743).
4. Council of Soissons, *MGH, Concilia* 2. (744), *praef.*
5. Boniface, epp. 60, 78.
6. Willibald, *Vita Bonifatii*, 8.
7. E. Ewig, 'Saint Chrodegang et la réforme de l'église franque', in Ewig, *Spätantikes und fränkisches Gallien*, 2, pp. 233–4; Wallace-Hadrill, *The Frankish Church*, pp. 174–6.
8. Ewig, 'Saint Chrodegang et la réforme de l'église franque', p. 238.

In the 740s Boniface was concerned primarily with the reform of the Frankish Church, and in many respects the reform was one of his major achievements, but he had originally come to the continent to Christianize the lands east of the Rhine, and it was for this that he died a martyr. Similarly, it was largely as a missionary in Frisia, Germany and Bavaria that his earliest biographer, Willibald, chose to depict him. Although Willibald's narrative does not provide the only basis for interpreting the Church east of the Rhine, it, together with a collection of letters relating to Boniface and his pupil Lull, has been given rather more credit than other sources. The credit may not be justified, but the evidence of Willibald provides a convenient point of departure for assessing the career of Boniface.

The *Life* of Boniface

Willibald's narrative runs roughly as follows: Boniface, or rather Winfrith as he was originally called, was born in the English West Country, and at an early age entered a monastery at Exeter.[9] From there he transferred to Nursling, near Southampton, where he completed his education, and became a teacher of some note.[10] While at Nursling he served on at least one embassy sent by king Ine to the archbishop of Canterbury.[11] But rather than continue a career in England, he determined to leave for the continent, crossing to Dorestad, in Frisia. He arrived in 716, at the height of the war between Charles Martel and Radbod, and so returned to Nursling.[12] Two years later his abbot died, and Winfrith was elected in his place, but he determined to leave again for the continent, travelling to Rome, where in 719 he received backing from pope Gregory II for missionary work.[13] It was at this time that he was given the name Bonifatius, although Willibald assigns the change of name to his next visit to Rome.[14] Thereafter, having left Italy and crossed Bavaria and Thuringia, he joined another Englishman, Willibrord, who was then re-establishing his mission in Frisia, after the death of Radbod. He worked with Willibrord between 719 and 721. But when the latter tried to persuade him to become his coadjutor, Boniface argued that his papal commission did not permit this, and left, establishing himself instead at Amöneburg, in Hesse.[15]

After working in Hesse, he returned in 722 to Rome, where he submitted a profession of faith to the pope, and was consecrated bishop. He was then given letters of introduction to Charles Martel.[16] The letters to Charles do

9. Willibald, *Vita Bonifatii*, 1.
10. Willibald, *Vita Bonifatii*, 2.
11. Willibald, *Vita Bonifatii*, 4.
12. Willibald, *Vita Bonifatii*, 4.
13. Willibald, *Vita Bonifatii*, 5.
14. Boniface, ep. 12; Willibald, *Vita Bonifatii*, 5, 6.
15. Willibald, *Vita Bonifatii*, 5.
16. Willibald, *Vita Bonifatii*, 6; Boniface, epp. 16, 18.

not survive, but Gregory's letters to the religious and secular leaders of Germany, to the magnates of Thuringia and to the Old Saxons do.[17] The letters to Charles he delivered, before returning to Hesse, where he destroyed a sacred oak tree at Geismar. Subsequently he founded monasteries at Ohrdruf, Fritzlar, and at the site of his original mission in the region, Amöneburg.[18] While he was involved in this work pope Gregory II died. His successor and namesake sent Boniface the *pallium*, elevating him to the archiepiscopate in 732.[19] Thereafter, Boniface moved to Bavaria, before visiting Rome once again in 736.[20] On leaving Rome, he returned to Bavaria, this time to reorganize the Bavarian Church into four dioceses, Salzburg, Regensburg, Passau and Freising.[21] The following years were taken up with the reforming councils of the early 740s, and with the creation of dioceses at Eichstätt and Würzburg, as well as Büraburg and Erfurt in 741.[22] But Boniface was determined to return to the missionary work for which he had originally left England. To achieve this he had his pupil, Lull, consecrated bishop in his place, and in 754 he set out for Frisia, where he was martyred.[23]

Willibald's masterly narrative, especially his chilling account of Boniface's death, and the survival of numerous letters by the saint and his successor, Lull, have ensured that Boniface has been seen as the central figure in the process of Christianization east of the Rhine. Certainly Willibald's *Life of Boniface* was composed soon after his subject's death. One of the two dedicatees of the work was Megingoz, who was bishop of Würzburg from 763 to 769.[24] The *Vita Bonifatii* is, therefore, one of the earliest of a group of saints' *Lives* which deal with ecclesiastical activity, undertaken largely by Englishmen, in Germany in the eighth century. Nevertheless, it is important to recognize the limitations of Willibald's work; much in the *Vita Bonifatii* is vague, and a precise chronology is lacking. At times this vagueness may well be deliberate. For instance, other sources, in particular Eigil's *Life* of Boniface's pupil Sturm, emphasize the significance to Boniface of his monastic foundation of Fulda, where the saint wished to be buried.[25] Willibald makes only four references to the monastery, and two of these are oblique, the last so oblique indeed that the casual reader might think that Boniface was buried in Mainz.[26] Since the bishop of Mainz, Lull, was the first dedicatee of the *Vita Bonifatii*, and since relations between him and Fulda were not always of the best,[27] it is possible that the comparative absence of explicit references to the monastery was deliberate on Willibald's part.

17. Boniface, epp. 17, 19, 20.
18. Willibald, *Vita Bonifatii*, 6.
19. Willibald, *Vita Bonifatii*, 6; Boniface, ep. 28.
20. Willibald, *Vita Bonifatii*, 7.
21. Willibald, *Vita Bonifatii*, 7; Boniface, ep. 45.
22. Willibald, *Vita Bonifatii*, 8; Boniface, epp. 50, 51.
23. Willibald, *Vita Bonifatii*, 8.
24. Willibald, *Vita Bonifatii*, praef.
25. Eigil, *Vita Sturmi*, 5, and passim.
26. Willibald, *Vita Bonifatii*, 8.
27. Eigil, *Vita Sturmi*, 15, 16.

Arbeo of Freising and the Bavarian Church

There are other reasons for questioning the accuracy of Willibald's depiction of Boniface's work in Germany. In around 769 Arbeo, bishop of Freising, wrote a *Life* of the Bavarian saint Corbinian,[28] which he addressed to Virgil, bishop of Salzburg. He related how Corbinian, a native of Melun, travelled to Rome in the days of Gregory II, who consecrated him bishop and gave him the *pallium*.[29] He returned to Francia, and to Pippin, but then withdrew from the world for seven years. Thereafter he travelled east, coming into contact with the Agilolfing rulers of Bavaria, Theoto and his son Grimoald.[30] After a second visit to Rome, he returned to Bavaria, where he stayed, despite being in conflict with Grimoald over the latter's marriage to his brother's widow, Pilitrude, and over his reliance on witchcraft to cure his son.[31] Soon after Grimoald was killed, and Charles Martel overran Bavaria, capturing Pilitrude – an event which can be dated to 725.[32] Corbinian made his peace with Hugbert, who succeeded as *dux*, but died while on a visit to Italy.[33] His body was later moved, first to Mais, where the saint had wished to be buried, and then, in 765, to Freising.[34]

In 772 Arbeo wrote a second *Life* of a Bavarian saint, this time the seventh-century martyr Emmeram of Regensburg.[35] He came from Poitiers, and having preached throughout Gaul, determined to evangelize the Avars in Pannonia. He approached Theoto, the *dux* of Bavaria in Regensburg, and announced his intention of working among the Avars, but was prevented because the Bavarians were currently at war with them. Instead, Theoto offered him the see of Regensburg, which he accepted, settling down to evangelize the locals for the next three years.[36] Subsequently, however, Emmeram was killed as a result of some suspicion that he was responsible for the pregnancy of Theoto's daughter.[37] After his death, and a number of miraculous occurrences, he was recognized as a martyr, and eventually his body was moved to Regensburg.[38]

Arbeo's two hagiographical works have not been thought to have the same value as Willibald's *Vita Bonifatii* for the historian of the German Church, but they do suggest that already in the 760s and 770s there were alternative views of the process of the establishment of the Church in certain areas. From the *Life* of Emmeram it is clear that Arbeo and his contemporaries thought that

28. Arbeo, *Vita Corbiniani, prologus*; H. Wolfram, *Die Geburt Mitteleuropas*, p. 136.
29. Arbeo, *Vita Corbiniani*, 6–9.
30. Arbeo, *Vita Corbiniani*, 10, 14, 15.
31. Arbeo, *Vita Corbiniani*, 20, 23–4, 29.
32. Arbeo, *Vita Corbiniani*, 31; Fredegar, cont. 12; *Annales Mettenses Priores*, s.a. 719; Wolfram, *Die Geburt Mitteleuropas*, p. 97.
33. Arbeo, *Vita Corbiniani*, 32–4.
34. Arbeo, *Vita Corbiniani*, 37–9, 41–6.
35. Arbeo, *Vita Haimhramni*, ed. B. Krusch, *MGH, SRM* 4, pp. 455–6.
36. Arbeo, *Vita Haimhramni*, 3–5.
37. Arbeo, *Vita Haimhramni*, 7–20.
38. Arbeo, *Vita Haimhramni*, 22–34.

Bavaria was largely Christianized in the seventh century, even though there were still some paganism and much that the Church found unorthodox: the *Life of Corbinian* talks of witchcraft and of uncanonical marriage within the ruling dynasty.[39] A similar picture of Christianity and dubious moral practice emerges from the ninth-century *Life* of the seventh-century Irish missionary Kilian, who was said to have established himself at Würzburg, converting the *dux*, Gozbert, and his people, before achieving martyrdom as a result of his criticisms of the marriage of Gozbert to his brother's widow.[40]

Arbeo seems deliberately to describe Corbinian as a figure of similar stature to Boniface; the saint goes to Rome, where he is elevated to the episcopate by Gregory II and receives the *pallium*.[41] Further, by writing about the early history of the churches of Freising and Regensburg Arbeo seems to have been concerned to undermine the significance of Willibald's claims that Boniface divided Bavaria into four dioceses, appointing John to Salzburg, and Erembert to Regensburg.[42] Given the date of the composition of Arbeo's hagiography, immediately after that of the *Life of Boniface*, there is some reason for thinking that it was intended as a deliberate refutation of Willibald's work.

In addition, Salzburg had its own view of the history of the conversion of Bavaria; the ninth-century compilation of the *Conversio Bagoariorum et Carantanorum* also began its narrative in Theoto's day, with the anti-Pippinid saint, Hrodbert/Rupert.[43] His cult was clearly being developed at precisely the time that Arbeo was writing, since his relics were brought from Worms to Salzburg in 774,[44] presumably under the aegis of Virgil, the dedicatee of the *Life of Corbinian*, as well as one of the heroes of the *Conversio*,[45] and an opponent of Boniface in the 740s.

Nor should we assume that Willibald had a monopoly of the truth; he suppressed evidence for the earlier appointment of Vivilo to the see of Passau, by Gregory III.[46] In drawing a veil over the earlier history of the Bavarian Church Willibald may even have taken a harsher line than did Boniface and his disciples. Erembert, the bishop of Freising appointed by Boniface, was probably Corbinian's brother.[47] Further, according to Arbeo, Boniface's appointee to the see of Regensburg, Garivald, was responsible for the translation of Emmeram.[48] Similarly, Burghard, Boniface's choice as bishop of Würzburg, translated the body of Kilian, with the approval of pope Zacharias and of Boniface himself.[49] That Willibald should have taken a more extreme

39. Arbeo, *Vita Corbiniani*, 24, 29.
40. *Passio Kiliani*, 8–10.
41. Arbeo, *Vita Corbiniani*, 8–9.
42. Willibald, *Vita Bonifatii*, 7.
43. *Conversio Bagoariorum et Carantanorum*, 1.
44. *Annales Iuvavenses maximi*, s.a. 774; Wolfram, *Die Geburt Mitteleuropas*, pp. 136–7.
45. *Conversio Bagoariorum et Carantanorum*, 2, 5.
46. Willibald, *Vita Bonifatii*. 7; Boniface, ep. 44, 45.
47. Willibald, *Vita Bonifatii*, 7; Arbeo, *Vita Corbiniani*, 30.
48. Arbeo, *Vita Haimhramni*, 35; Willibald, *Vita Bonifatii*, 7.
49. *Passio Kiliani*, 15.

line over the Bavarian Church than did others may be explained in part by the political situation. Between 725 and 740/1 the Agilolfings seem to have accepted Charles Martel's dominance.[50] It was during this period that Boniface was able to work in Bavaria.[51] After Charles's death, however, there was a series of crises, as we have seen, involving the Agilolfings and Charles's son Gripho.[52] During this period Boniface would scarcely have been welcome to the Bavarians, who were clearly cultivating non-Frankish ecclesiastical links. The presence of the papal legate Sergius in the Bavarian army in 743 may have been significant here.[53] Certainly the appearance of Virgil of Salzburg in 746/7 is indicative of the decline in Boniface's influence.[54] Hostility between the Agilolfings and the Carolingians was to continue until 788.[55] It therefore provided a background not only for the problems faced by Boniface in the 740s, but also for the compositions of Willibald and Arbeo. Although both hagiographers had axes to grind, since Garivald of Regensburg, Erembert of Freising and Burghard of Würzburg all seem to have seen their work as lying within an established tradition, it is possible that the *Life of Corbinian* presents a more accurate picture of the Bavarian Church in the first half of the eighth century, than that implied in the *Life of Boniface*.

Paganism, heresy and Church reform

It is not just with regard to the history of Bavaria that the *Life of Boniface* is questionable. According to Willibald, Dettic and Deorulf, who ruled in Hesse, worshipped idols in the name of christianity. Other Hessans worshipped springs, as well as the oak at Geismar and consulted auguries.[56] In Thuringia, under Theobald and Hetan, whom Willibald depicts as tyrants, Christian religion is said to have came to an end, and heretical sects are said to have become established.[57] The nature cults and auguries which are said to have been popular in Hesse are well attested in numerous documents, including the Bonifacian *Indiculus Superstitionum*.[58] Unfortunately, however, Willibald is our only source for the semi-paganism of Dettic and Deorulf.

---

50. Fredegar records no hostility between 725 (cont. 12) and 742 (cont. 25), nor do the *Annales Mettenses Priores*; see also Wolfram, *Die Geburt Mitteleuropas*, pp. 97–98.
51. Wolfram, *Die Geburt Mitteleuropas*, p. 98.
52. See chapter 16.
53. *Annales Mettenses Priores*, s.a. 743.
54. H. Wolfram, 'Virgil of St Peter's at Salzburg', in P. Ní Chatháin and M. Richter, eds, *Irland und die Christenheit*, p. 146.
55. Wolfram, *Die Geburt Mitteleuropas*, pp. 98–106.
56. Willibald, *Vita Bonifatii*, 6.
57. Willibald, *Vita Bonifatii*, 6.
58. A. Dierkins, 'Superstitions, christianisme et paganisme à la fin de l'époque mérovingienne', in H. Hasquin, ed., *Magie, sorcellerie, parapsychologie*, pp. 9–26; J.T. McNeill and H.M. Gamer, *Medieval Handbooks of Penance: A Translation of the Principal Libri Poenitentiales*, pp. 419–21.

This silence is troubling because other evidence casts doubt on Willibald's claims. Thus, Hetan is also known as a benefactor of Willibrord's foundation of Echternach.[59] He is also known to have fallen foul of Charles Martel, which might explain the bad press he received from Willibald.[60] In addition Theobald is known to have been a founder of churches.[61]

That Boniface himself was capable of labelling people as heretics with excessive zeal is known from a letter of pope Zacharias, condemning him for ordering rebaptism because a priest in Bavaria had baptized ungrammatically: complaints on the matter had come from Virgil of Salzburg and Sidonius of Passau.[62] Zacharias also found himself embarrassed by Boniface's criticisms of New Year festivities in Rome, although he agreed with the criticism.[63] In other words, Boniface had a more stringent view of Christianity than did many others: this is likely to have meant that for him and his closest followers, evangelization was a more rigorous concept than it was for other missionaries.

Nevertheless, Boniface himself does not seem to have confused the semi-Christianity of Hesse, Thuringia, and Bavaria with the paganism of the Frisians or Saxons. Few of his letters are concerned with the conversion of pagans. Those that do tend to date from very particular points in his life. One of the most important letters in the Boniface collection, Daniel of Winchester's advice on how to convert the heathen, dates from early in Boniface's continental career.[64] A letter of Boniface himself, asking for the prayers of the English in support of the Christianization of the Saxons, dates to *c.* 738.[65] That was a year in which Charles Martel inflicted a crushing defeat on the Saxons,[66] which may explain why Boniface felt that a mission was possible. For the most part, however, Boniface's correspondence is concerned with improving the Church, its standards, its organization and its cult. Hence the importance in Hesse and Thuringia of the building and restoration of chapels and churches, and also of the foundation of monasteries.[67] The significance of local church-foundation is equally clear from the Bavarian *Conversio Bagoariorum et Carantanorum*.[68] Such buildings and their clergy, however, needed to be inspected regularly, to prevent apostasy or lapse into heresy: hence the need for an episcopal organization. In this way mission merged naturally with the concerns of the Church reform.

59. Willibald, *Vita Bonifatii*, ed. R. Rau, p. 495, n. 11.
60. *Passio Kiliani*, 14.
61. Willibald, *vita Bonifatii*, ed. R. Rau, p. 495, n. 11.
62. Boniface, ep. 68.
63. Boniface, epp. 50, 51.
64. Boniface, ep. 23.
65. Boniface, ep. 46.
66. Fredegar, cont. 19; *Annales Mettenses Priores*, s.a. 738.
67. Willibald, *Vita Bonifatii*, 7.
68. *Conversio Bagoariorum et Carantanorum*, 5.

Christianization in the Merovingian kingdom

The ecclesiastical history of Hesse, Thuringia and Bavaria suggests that Boniface's work in Germany was not that of a missionary, but rather that of an organizer and reformer. It was, therefore, the culmination of an earlier tradition, rather than the beginning of a new phase in the religious history of Germany. Although Boniface and his English predecessors, Wilfrid and Willibrord, have been regarded as a new force in the history of the Merovingian Church, they were dependent on and influenced by the work of previous generations.

The Christianization of the Merovingian kingdom had its roots in the establishment of the Church in Late Roman Gaul, and in the winning of the Visigoths, Burgundians and Franks for Christianity. It is possible also that the Thuringians had been christianized by the early years of the sixth century; the sixth-century *Lives* of the Thuringian princess Radegund suggest no conversion from paganism on her part.[69] After Clovis's baptism, however, there is little evidence for mission within Frankish and Burgundian Gaul until the end of the century, despite the fact that Avitus of Vienne envisaged the king's conversion as being the start of a period of evangelization.[70] In fact Avitus was unusual among early-sixth-century theologians in talking about mission to barbarian peoples. In so far as there was an influential missionary ideal, it was that of Caesarius of Arles, concerned with raising local religious standards and Christianizing people within Gaul. In the Merovingian kingdom, as in Italy, the question of evangelizing the heathen was generally of little significance before the end of the sixth century.

The sending of Augustine's mission to the English by Gregory I provides the clearest indication of ideological change in papal circles. In Francia the shift towards a missionary ideology is most frequently associated with the arrival of Columbanus at the court of Childebert II, and the subsequent establishment of the monasteries of Annegray and Luxeuil. There are, however, problems in attributing a clear concept of mission to Columbanus. While it is true that he was involved in the Christianization of the area round Luxeuil,[71] and thought of working among the Thuringian Slavs,[72] the depth of his commitment to Christianizing the pagans is questionable. He himself admitted that he lost interest in evangelizing the Bavarians when he was at Bregenz.[73] His career is best seen not as that of a missionary but of an Irish *peregrinus pro Christo*, of a man who abandoned his native land for the sake of Christ.[74] If he was responsible for evangelizing people in the vicinity of his foundations, this was a byproduct of his life as a *peregrinus*, and not his prime concern.

69. Venantius Fortunatus, *Vita Radegundis*; Baudonivia, *Vita Radegundis*.
70. Avitus, ep 46.
71. Jonas, *Vita Columbani*, I 10.
72. Jonas, *Vita Columbani*, I 27.
73. Columbanus, ep. 4, 5.
74. T.M. Charles-Edwards, 'The social background to Irish peregrinatio', *Celtica* 11 (1976), pp. 43–59.

Nevertheless one of his disciples unquestionably developed an interest in Christianization. Eustasius, the second abbot of Luxeuil, did organize missions to the Bavarians.[75] Of these little is known, beyond the involvement of the monk Agrestius, who was to cause considerable problems for the 'Columbanian' foundations. Another disciple of Columbanus who may well have played a significant role in Christianizing the region to the south of the Bodensee was Gallus, but the evidence for him is not contemporary with his life.[76] Indeed, what evidence there is for the establishment and survival of the Church in Swabia, Bavaria and Rhaetia during the seventh and early eighth centuries is consistently difficult to interpret. In Augsburg and Chur Christianity seems to have survived from the Roman period.[77] Elsewhere, the careers of individual saints shed some light on the religious affiliations of the aristocracy. The Agilofing *duces* of Bavaria, with their close links to both the Merovingian and the Lombard royal dynasties, were Christian, but the work of Rupert of Salzburg in the early eighth century suggests that many of their subjects had not been Christianized, and that the churches of Bavaria were in need of restoration and repair.[78] In Würzburg, although Kilian managed to convert the pagan *dux*, Gozbert, he was martyred when he tried to force Gozbert to accept the Church canons on marriage.[79] A further indicator of Christian affiliations among the aristocracy is to be found in the history of monasticism. Thus, the foundation of monasteries by Pirmin and his disciples in the first half of the eighth century provides crucial information on the Church in Alsace, Swabia and even Bavaria. The most important of these monasteries, Reichenau, on the Bodensee, and Murbach and Hornbach in Alsace, seem to look back to the tradition of *peregrinatio* espoused by Columbanus, and suggest that the monastic ideals of Luxeuil, at least, were being spread by Pirmin.[80]

The history of Christianization in the north-east of Francia is rather better documented. Columbanus's biographer, Jonas, tells us in the preface to the *Vita Columbani* that he was involved in evangelizing the countryside round the river Scheldt, where he worked with the great missionary bishop Amandus.[81] Although Jonas was probably not a major figure in the Christianization of the region, his writings do shed some precious evidence on the attitudes of missionaries in the mid-seventh century. Despite his own involvement in mission, he made little attempt to portray Columbanus as a missionary, which is not surprising given the saint's own comments. In so far

75. Jonas, *Vita Columbani*, II 8.

76. Even the *Vitae Galli vetustissimae fragmentum* is assigned to the late eighth century.

77. Wolfram, *Die Geburt Mitteleuropas*, p. 109; Wallace-Hadrill, *The Frankish Church*, p. 341.

78. *Conversio Bagoariorum et Carantanorum*, 1; *Vita Hrodberti* 5, 6, 7.

79. *Passio Kiliani*, 7–8.

80. A. Angenendt, *Monachi Peregrini: Studien zu Pirmin und den monastischen Vorstellungen des frühen Mittelalter*; Wallace-Hadrill, *The Frankish Church*, pp. 148–9.

81. Jonas, *Vita Columbani*, ep. to Waldebert and Bobolenus.

as he wrote any *Life* of a missionary saint, it was that of Clovis's contemporary, Vedast, bishop of Arras.[82] Jonas and those for whom he wrote seem to have found a model missionary bishop in Vedast, and to have looked back to the Church of the previous century without recognizing the divide which modern historians see as having been introduced by the arrival of Columbanus. Jonas may have interpreted the lives of bishop Vedast and his third subject, the sixth-century monastic founder John of Réomé, to make them relevant to his readers, just as he presented the career of Columbanus in a manner appropriate to his own generation, but he does provide a warning against seeing too sharp a break between the supposedly quiescent Church of the sixth century and the missionary fervour of the mid-seventh.

Nevertheless, the career of Jonas's contemporary Amandus is quite unlike any recorded for the early Merovingian period. We have already considered the evidence of the second *Life of Amandus*, by Milo, with its important additions on relations between Amandus and pope Martin:[83] for the saint's missionary activity the first *Life*, which may date from the early eighth century,[84] contains all the crucial information. After a first visit to Rome Amandus began to preach in Gaul, where his activities attracted the attention of Chlothar II, and he was compelled to join the episcopate.[85] As bishop he ransomed captives, arranging for them to be taught and placed in monasteries.[86] After a second visit to Rome he returned to Ghent, evangelizing the people who had lapsed into paganism. With the backing of Dagobert I he resorted to forcible conversion.[87] He followed up his missionary work by founding, and encouraging the foundation of numerous monasteries in the region.[88] Despite his close association with what is now part of Belgium, he refused a fixed see, until Maastricht was forced on him.[89] Nevertheless he subsequently undertook an extensive missionary expedition among the Basques, as he had earlier done among the Slavs.[90] In so doing he set a precedent for preaching to pagans outside the lands which had once been part of the Roman Empire. In this respect he seems to have gone beyond the two traditions, Gregorian and Columbanian, which are likely to have inspired him. That he had links with Luxeuil and the pupils of Columbanus is clear from Jonas's involvement in missionary activity in the region of the Scheldt, and from his own monastic interests. That he was influenced by the ideals of Gregory I is probable, given his two visits to Rome, and his correspondence with pope Martin I. In his own preaching,

---

82. Jonas, *Vita Vedastis*.
83. See chapter 14.
84. J.N. Hillgarth, *Christianity and Paganism, 350–750: The Conversion of Western Europe*, p. 138.
85. *Vita Amandi*, 6–8.
86. *Vita Amandi*, 9.
87. *Vita Amandi*, 10–13.
88. *Vita Amandi*, 15.
89. *Vita Amandi*, 18.
90. *Vita Amandi*, 16, 20.

inside and outside the Merovingian kingdom, in his educating ransomed captives, and in his use of monasticism, he seems to have drawn on the ideals of Gregory and Eustasius. By combining this with forcible conversion, and with an interest in the pagans beyond the frontiers of the Merovingian kingdom, he appears to have created a new model for missionary activity.[91] Nor was he without followers; in his time Dagobert I apparently gave bishop Chunibert of Cologne the fort of Utrecht as a base for evangelizing Frisia,[92] while in the next generation bishops like Eligius of Noyon continued his work of evangelization in the north-east of the Merovingian kingdom.[93]

The influences which weighed on Amandus were not far different from those which affected the first missionaries to work in England. Gregory the Great put his missionary ideals into practice in sending Augustine to Kent, and the Church established in Canterbury was responsible for further activity in East Anglia and Northumbria. In addition the Irish played a crucial role from the great religious foundation of Iona. But the Frankish monarchy and Church were also of importance in evangelizing the English. Having been disappointed by the lack of support given by Theuderic and Theudebert to the people of Kent in their search for Christianity in 596,[94] Gregory the Great regarded Brunhild as having contributed more than any other human being to the success of the mission by 600.[95] We know of no Frank actually involved in the mission of Augustine himself, but it may well be that we should attribute to Brunhild and her court clergy a real revolution in missionary thinking in the last years of the sixth century.

For the next generation we are better informed about Frankish involvement in the English Church. The leading ecclesiastic in the evangelization of East Anglia was the Burgundian, Felix, who may well have had links with Luxeuil.[96] In addition, the earliest bishop of the West Saxons was the Frank, Agilbert, whose family came from the Ile de France, and whose later career shows him to have been intimately involved in the 'Columbanian' monasticism of the Paris basin.[97] Nor was he the only Neustrian to be involved in the Christianization of the English; the monastic founder Richarius is said by his first biographer to have worked in England,[98] although Alcuin later broadened the identification of his field of work to

---

91. W.H. Fritze, '*Universalis Gentium Confessio*. Formeln, Träger und Wege universalmissionarischen Denkens im 7. Jahrhundert', *Frühmittelalterliche Studien* 3 (1969), pp. 78–130.

92. Boniface, ep. 109.

93. *Vita Eligii*, II 16, 20; Fouracre, 'The work of Audoenus of Rouen and Eligius of Noyon in extending episcopal influence from the town to the county in seventh-century Neustria'.

94. Gregory I, *Register*, VI 49.

95. Gregory I, *Register*, XI 48.

96. Bede, *Historia Ecclesiastica*, II 15, 18; in general see J. Campbell, 'The first century of Christianity in England', in Campbell, *Essays in Anglo-Saxon History*, p.55.

97. Wormald, 'Bede and Benedict Biscop', pp. 145–6.

98. *Vita Richarii*, 7.

Britain.[99] Perhaps significantly the involvement of men such as Felix, Agilbert and Richarius in the Christianization of England coincides with Amandus's mission in Belgium, backed by Dagobert. The establishment of the Church in England, therefore, has much in common with ecclesiastical developments in Francia in the late sixth and early seventh centuries, and the common features are more than coincidental.

Wilfrid and the disciples of Ecgbert

The Franks themselves achieved much east of the Rhine before the arrival of the Anglo-Saxon missionaries. The fact that the Merovingians and their clergy had also played a vital role in the development of the English Church further indicates that the English did not constitute a completely new force in the history of the German mission. This suggestion receives strong support from what is known of the earliest of the Englishmen to work in Frisia, the Northumbrian bishop, Wilfrid. Wilfrid himself was a protégé of Agilbert, for whom he is said to have spoken at the so-called Synod of Whitby in 664.[100] That his early connections with Agilbert were of enduring significance is suggested by Wilfrid's later visit to Meaux, a city with which Agilbert's family had close contacts, and where he recuperated from an illness.[101] Nor was Agilbert the only member of the Frankish Church with whom Wilfrid was associated. He spent a considerable period of time in Lyons with bishop Aunemundus, who seems to have had links with the abbot of Luxeuil.[102] Further, as we have seen, Wilfrid was involved in the restitution of Dagobert II to the kingdom of Austrasia, and the king offered him the diocese of Strasbourg.[103] All in all, the Frankish Church was a major influence on Wilfrid, and it is hardly surprising, therefore, that the *Vita Wilfridi* is closer to Merovingian hagiography than is any other eighth-century Anglo-Saxon saint's *Life*.[104]

Wilfrid's mission to Frisia was not central to his career. Moreover the later strength of paganism in the area suggest that his meeting with Aldgisl and his preaching cannot have had the dramatic impact on the Frisian people which is claimed by Stephanus and Bede.[105] Nevertheless, Wilfrid did set a precedent for English ecclesiastics to work on the continent, and particularly for them to work in Frisia. Among the earliest to follow this precedent was Swithbert.

99. Alcuin, *Vita Richarii*, 8.

100. Bede, *Historia Ecclesiastica*, III 25; Stephanus, *Vita Wilfridi*, 10.

101. Stephanus, *Vita Wilfridi*, 56; Wood, 'Ripon, Francia and the Franks Casket in the early Middle Ages', 13.

102. Stephanus, *Vita Wilfridi*, 4, 6; Wood, 'Ripon, Francia and the Franks Casket in the early Middle Ages'. p. 11.

103. Stephanus, *Vita Wilfridi*, 28.

104. Wood, 'Ripon, Francia and the Franks Casket in the Middle Ages', pp. 13–16.

105. Stephanus, *Vita Wilfridi*, 26–7; Bede, *Historia Ecclesiastica*, V 19.

Although he seems to have been consecrated as a bishop for Frisia by Wilfrid, he left the region to Willibrord, and instead concerned himself with the Christianization of the *Bructeri*, who inhabited Westfalia. When his mission to the *Bructeri* failed, he retired to the monastery of Kaiserwerth, which had been given to him by Pippin II's wife, Plectrude.[106] Her family seems to have been strongly committed to helping the Anglo-Saxon missionaries, for it was her mother, Irmina, who gave Willibrord the site of Echternach.[107]

Also influential in the Anglo-Saxon missions to the continent was the Northumbrian Ecgbert, himself a *peregrinus pro Christo*, living in a foreign land, albeit Ireland rather than Germany.[108] Unfortunately there is little that can be said about Ecgbert's early life. As a result it is not possible to identify the influences which weighed on him. Nor is it possible to discover the origins of the missionary ideology attributed to him by Bede, who relates that he wished to evangelize the 'Garmans' on the continent. The 'Garmans' included a number of peoples, among whom were the Saxons and the *Bructeri*, with whom Swithbert worked.[109] Bede's account of Ecgbert's ideology appears to be the first indication of the notion that the English ought to act as missionaries to the continental Germans, because they were related. It was a notion which Boniface was later to adopt in the context of an intended Saxon mission.[110]

Although Ecgbert determined to leave Ireland himself, to become a missionary on the continent, he was prevented, in Bede's account, by a vision, and instead sent his pupil, Wihtbert, to Frisia.[111] Wihtbert, however, was discouraged by his failure to make headway in Radbod's territories, and returned. In his place Ecgbert sent others, including two brothers, known as the White and Black Hewalds. Their attempt to evangelize the Saxons ended in martyrdom at the hands of *vicani*, who were determined to prevent them from reaching the local chieftain, for fear that they might well succeed in winning him over to the new faith.[112] The story is interesting for the insight it gives into the varying forces for and against Christianization among the pagans: members of the aristocracy were thought to be more likely to succumb to the religion of the neighbouring Franks, than were less elevated Saxons.[113] Further, the murders were brutally avenged, and the bodies of the martyrs taken to Cologne, suggesting a considerable degree of support for the Hewalds within the Frankish State and Church.

106. Bede, *Historia Ecclesiastica*, V 11.
107. Gerberding, *The Rise of the Carolingians and the Liber Historiae Francorum*, p. 102.
108. Bede, *Historia Ecclesiastica*, III 27; V 9.
109. Bede, *Historia Ecclesiastica*, V 9.
110. Boniface, ep. 46.
111. Bede, *Historia Ecclesiastica*, V 9.
112. Bede, *Historia Ecclesiastica*, V 10.
113. I. N. Wood, 'Pagans and holy men, 600–800', in P. Ní Chatháin and M. Richter, eds, *Irland und die Christenheit*, p. 352.

Willibrord

The most important of Ecgbert's pupils was Willibrord. Ecgbert's influence on Willibrord is referred to by Bede,[114] and by Alcuin, who also talks of Wihtbert as the saint's teacher.[115] In addition the influence of Ecgbert's monastery of Rathmelsigi is apparent in a number of manuscripts associated with Willibrord.[116] Nevertheless, Willibrord had originally been a monk at Ripon, and a pupil of Wilfrid, as Stephanus emphasizes.[117] He is unlikely to have forgotten his original training at Ripon. Moreover, although Ecgbert and Ireland undoubtedly provided the immediate background to Willibrord's mission, it appears that his connections with Northumbria were revived and strengthened once he was on the continent. Bede mentions a meeting between Wilfrid, Acca and Willibrord in Frisia.[118] In addition one of Willibrord's monks is known to have visited Northumbria.[119] Further, the manuscripts associated with his monastery of Echternach seem to imply increasing Anglo–Saxon influence.[120]

For Willibrord the evidence is richer than it is for Swithbert or for the other pupils of Ecgbert. Nevertheless the evidence is still patchy. It consists largely of Alcuin's *Vita Willibrordi*, together with the charters and manuscripts of the monastery of Echternach, in particular its gospels and the remarkable liturgical calendar, some of whose additional entries were undoubtedly written in Willibrord's own hand.[121] Despite this material, any narrative reconstruction of Willibrord's life is necessarily slight.

After relating the saint's birth, his entry into monastic life at Ripon, his transfer to Rathmelsigi, and his arrival in Frisia, Alcuin recounts Willibrord's visit to Rome, made, so he claims, on the advice of Pippin II.[122] In fact Alcuin amalgamates two visits to Rome, combining an original journey seeking papal approval, which took place in 690, with a second journey in 695, when he received the name Clemens and was consecrated bishop.[123] Further, his emphasis on Pippin's role in sending Willibrord to Rome may well be an anachronistic reconstruction on his part, dependent on an

---

114. Bede, *Historia Ecclesiastica*, V 10.
115. Alcuin, *Vita Willibrordi*, 4.
116. D. O Cróinín, 'Is the Augsburg Gospel Codex a Northumbrian manuscript?', in G. Bonner, D. Rollason and C. Stancliffe, eds, *St Cuthbert, his Cult and his Community to AD 1200*, pp. 189–201; N. Netzer, 'Willibrord's Scriptorium at Echternach and its relationship to Ireland and Lindisfarne', in Bonner, Rollason and Stancliffe, eds, *St Cuthbert, his Cult and his Community to AD 1200*, pp. 203–7.
117. Stephanus, *Vita Wilfridi*, 26; Alcuin, *Vita Willibrordi*, 3.
118. Bede, *Historia Ecclesiastica*, III 13.
119. *Vita Cuthberti Auctore Anonymo*, IV 16; Bede, *Vita Cuthberti*, 44.
120. Netzer, 'Willibrord's Scriptorium at Echternach and its relationship to Ireland and Lindisfarne', pp. 207–12.
121. O Cróinín, 'Is the Augsberg Gospel Codex a Northumbrian Manuscript?', p. 192.
122. Alcuin, *Vita Willibrordi*, 6, 7.
123. For the second journey, see Willibrord, *Calendar*, 21 November.

assumption of cooperation between the Carolingians and the papacy. Throughout the *Vita Willibrordi*, Alcuin simplifies the political situation, making Pippin and Charles Martel kings and obscuring the opposition to them, despite the fact that it was to the family of Plectrude, one of Charles's most bitter opponents, that Willibrord owed the monastery of Echternach.[124]

The conflict between Charles and Plectrude may be relevant to Alcuin's almost complete silence over Echternach. This silence is all the more peculiar given that the dedicatee of the *Life of Willibrord* was Beornrade, archbishop of Sens, and perhaps more importantly, one-time abbot of Willibrord's monastery. He was also, like Alcuin, a relative of the saint.[125] As in the *Life of Boniface* the saint's greatest monastic foundation is scarcely mentioned by the hagiographer. But Alcuin and Beornrade had good reason to approve Willibrord's foundation, while Willibald and Lull may have had reason to pass over Fulda in near silence. Whatever the explanation, Alcuin chose to emphasize Willibrord's pastoral and missionary work, rather than his significance as a monastic founder.

It is possible to keep some check on Alcuin's manipulation of Merovingian politics: it is more difficult to evaluate his account of Willibrord's work among the pagans of Frisia and Denmark. First, Alcuin describes Willibrord's failure to convert Radbod.[126] Despite his intransigence, the Frisian ruler is not portrayed as an aggressively hostile figure, but rather as a stubborn one, who none the less did not prevent Willibrord from attempting to evangelize his people. The portrait of Radbod is not as favourable as that in the *Life* of Wulfram of Sens, written in response to Alcuin's work. In the later text, Radbod comes close to being baptized, going so far as to put one foot in the font.[127] The story can scarcely be true since Wulfram died long before the event could have taken place,[128] but the image of Radbod presented is interesting, since it is far removed from the normal denunciation of the king to be found in annalistic texts. Moreover, despite the anachronisms in the *Vita Vulframni*, the monastery of St Wandrille, where the *Life* was written, may well have had access to reliable traditions about Radbod. One of the abbots of the community, Wando, was apparently exiled to Maastricht by Charles Martel after the battle of Vinchy, and he remained there until he was reinstated in the middle of the century.[129] In exile he is likely to have heard much about Radbod, and about Willibrord. Indeed he may even have had direct contact with the Englishman: the *Gesta Abbatum Fontanellensium* actually states that Wando was sent to Utrecht. The *Vita Willibrordi*, without going so far as the *Life of Wulfram*, seems to share in the notion that Radbod was not

124. For Willibrord's own shift of allegiance, see Gerberding, *The Rise of the Carolingians and the Liber Historiae Francorum*, pp. 134–6.
125. Alcuin, *Vita Willibrordi, praefatio*, 1, 31.
126. Alcuin, *Vita Willibrordi*, 9–11, 13.
127. *Vita Vulframni*, 9; Wood, 'Saint-Wandrille and its hagiography', pp. 13–14.
128. Wood, 'Saint-Wandrille and its hagiography', p. 13.
129. *Gesta abbatum Fontanellensium*, 3, 1; VIII, 1; IX, 1; Wood, 'Saint-Wandrille and its hagiography', pp. 12–14.

entirely hostile,[130] and this presentation makes sense in the light of the marriage between the Frisian's daughter and Pippin's son, Grimoald,[131] and of his later support for Chilperic II and Ragamfred, who were no less Christian than their opponent, Charles Martel.[132] If Frisia really was impossible territory for missionary work, it can have been so only for a brief period when Radbod was in open war with the Carolingians. At that moment Willibrord and his followers, who had benefited directly from Pippin and his wife Plectrude, could scarcely have been welcome.

After the failure of Willibrord to Christianize Frisia, Alcuin records a further mission to the Danes and their king, Ongendus.[133] Here the saint was even less successful than among the Frisians, but Alcuin does relate that Willibrord brought back thirty Danish boys, and baptized them. It was a policy that had already been developed by Gregory the Great as a preliminary to the English mission,[134] and has something in common with the purchase of captives by Amandus.[135] More dramatic was an incident on the return journey. According to Alcuin, Willibrord and his companions landed on the island of Fosite, where there were temples and a sacred well. This the saint used to perform three baptisms, and in so doing he broke a taboo. The pagans were astonished that those involved in the sacrilege were not instantly struck down, but they did nothing except report the event to their king, who cast lots to see if the Christians should be killed. The death of one only was called for. Then the king sent Willibrord and his followers back to Pippin.[136] The casting of lots can be paralleled from other sources,[137] and the story may well be based on a genuine episode in the saint's life.

The descriptions of Willibrord's encounters with the pagans are, therefore, less obviously affected by bias than are Alcuin's comments on his subject's relations with Pippin II, Charles Martel and the papacy. Nevertheless, the general context in which he was writing may well have affected his presentation of the pagans. From 772 Charlemagne was involved in trying to subdue and Christianize the Saxons.[138] In that year he destroyed the sacred Irminsul, and in 776 and 777 many Saxons were baptized as a result of Frankish victories. In reaction the Saxon leader, Widukind, adopted an overtly pagan stance from 780. Charlemagne responded with brutal anti-pagan legislation in the *Capitulare de partibus Saxoniae*, and in 785 he forced Widukind to accept baptism. In the ensuing period the *capitulare* was

130. Alcuin, *Vita Willibrordi.*, 9–11.
131. *Liber Historiae Francorum*, 50; Fredegar, cont. 7; see also chapter 15.
132. *Liber Historiae Francorum*, 9; Fredegar, cont. 52; *Annales Mettenses Priores*, s.a. 714, 716.
133. Alcuin, *Vita Willibrordi*, 9.
134. Gregory I, *Register*, VI 10.
135. *Vita Amandi*, 9.
136. Alcuin, *Vita Willibrordi*, 11.
137. Wood, 'Pagans and holy men, 600–800', p. 356.
138. McKitterick, *The Frankish Kingdoms under the Carolingians, 751–987*, pp. 61–3; P.D. King, *Charlemagne*, pp. 8–12, 15–18, 23–6.

ruthlessly enforced, to Alcuin's horror: he thought the brutality counterproductive,[139] and he was right. There was a further Saxon uprising in 793 and the next three years saw renewed campaigns, and in 797 more legislation.[140] Against this background, Alcuin's remarkably imprecise account of Willibrord, which anachronistically depicts Pippin II and Charles Martel as monarchs, could contain a blueprint for a less aggressive Carolingian missionary policy: the *Vita Willibrordi* was written between 785 and 797.[141]

Alcuin's chronological narrative effectively comes to an end half way through the *Vita Willibrordi*; thereafter the work becomes a collection of miracle stories. Immediately before the change Alcuin records the death of Pippin, Charles Martel's acquisition of Frisia, and his concession of Utrecht to the saint as the centre of his episcopal see.[142] That Utrecht was a place of some political importance is suggested by Willibald's statement that Boniface met Radbod there on his first, abortive, stay on the continent.[143] The history of Utrecht as a centre for missionary activity is covered by a letter of Boniface to pope Stephen, written in 753.[144] As we have seen, the fortress had been given by king Dagobert to the bishop of Cologne as a missionary centre. If the king in question was Dagobert I and the bishop Cunibert, then the grant was made during the period of evangelization led by Amandus. Thereafter the church fell into disrepair, until Willibrord made it the seat of his diocese. After Willibrord's death Boniface himself consecrated a new bishop to the diocese, but the bishop of Cologne, Hildegar laid claim to it on account of Dagobert's original grant. Boniface's letter is revealing in that it draws attention to recurrent features as well as discontinuities in the history of mission in the Merovingian period. Utrecht was identified as a centre of potential importance in the time of Dagobert; this was recognized in Willibrord's day, when it became the centre of a diocese. Boniface confirmed the importance of the place when he consecrated a successor for Willibrord. At the same time the Church of Cologne, having been in possession of Utrecht, had no wish to see it in anyone else's hands, once its importance was realized. It is possible that Boniface's final journey to Willibrord's missionfield of Frisia was an attempt to strengthen his case against the see of Cologne. More generally the evidence for Utrecht as a mission station reveals that missionary traditions and territorial interests had long histories in the Merovingian period.

To take Boniface's career as Willibald presents it is to ignore the complexities of the mid-eighth century, and also to ignore what had already been achieved by the Merovingian Church. Nor are Boniface's own

139. Alcuin, epp. 107, 110; McKitterick, *The Frankish Kingdoms under the Carolingians, 751–987*, p. 62.
140. McKitterick, *The Frankish Kingdoms under the Carolingians, 751–987*, pp. 62–3.
141. H.-J. Reischmann, *Willibrord – Apostel der Friesen*, p. 14.
142. Alcuin, *Vita Willibrord*, 13.
143. Willibald, *Vita Bonifatii*, 4.
144. Boniface, ep. 109.

comments a completely trustworthy guide to the ecclesiastical standards of his own day. The great Anglo-Saxon was doubtless correct to see some of Frankish clergy as corrupt and in need of reform. Nevertheless his criteria were more stringent than those of other bishops and missionaries, who were remembered as saints; on some issues his criteria were even more stringent than those of the papacy. It is important to remember this when assessing his view that the Merovingian Church had been in decline for sixty or seventy years. What decline there was coincided with the rise of the Carolingians themselves, and it was scarcely universal. Only a generation earlier, Wilfrid and Benedict Biscop had learned much from the Merovingian Church; the former, in particular, appears to have recognized the achievements of the churchmen influenced by Luxeuil and its daughter houses. And in Boniface's own day Willibrord seems to have been able to cooperate with most secular and ecclesiastical leaders. As for the world of mission, Rupert, Emmeram and Kilian had achieved much in the seventh century, as did Pirmin and Corbinian in the early eighth. And among Boniface's younger contemporaries his rival Virgil of Salzburg arguably achieved more than he did.[145] Boniface's achievement in reforming the Church in Francia and organizing that east of the Rhine was important, but it belonged in a well-established context.

145. Wolfram, 'Virgil of St Peter's at Salzburg', p. 420.

Conclusion: The Merovingian Achievement

At the time of Childeric III's deposition the Merovingians were the longest established ruling dynasty in western Europe. From 719, admittedly, their authority was insignificant, although the Carolingians seem to have thought that a Merovingian was still necessary to give their own power legitimacy, and to limit aristocratic opposition. Before Eudo handed Chilperic II over to Charles Martel, however, matters had been very different. That the Merovingians had been powerful from the reign of Clovis I until that of Dagobert I is generally accepted. But even after that there were strong monarchs. Clovis II was a figure to be reckoned with, as was his son Childeric II. So too was Dagobert II, to judge by the hostility he engendered. In the next generation Childebert III operated successfully in collaboration with the aristocracy, or so the *Liber Historiae Francorum* implies.[1] And even Chilperic II was a significant figure before the failure of his allies, Ragamfred and Eudo. Few dynasties had been so powerful for so long.

Nor was their power confined to the Merovingian kingdom. The peoples to the east of the Rhine were usually subject to Merovingian influence, at least until the defeat of Sigibert III at the hands of the Thuringian *dux*, Radulf, in 639. Nor does that seem to have been the last date at which the Merovingians intervened outside their own kingdom. Paul the Deacon records some Frankish intervention in Italy in the 660s,[2] and the *dux* of Aquitaine, Lupus, was involved in the revolt of Septimania against the Visigothic king Wamba in the following decade.[3] Earlier, however, Merovingian influence outside their own kingdom could be considerable. Theudebert II was involved in the elevation of Adaloald as king of the Lombards in 604,[4] and Dagobert I helped to place Sisenand on the Visigothic

1. Gerberding, *The Rise of the Carolingians and the Liber Historiae Francorum*, pp. 171–2.
2. Paul, *Historia Langobardorum*, V 5.
3. Julian, *Historia Wambae Regis*, 27.
4. Paul, *Historia Langobardorum*, IV 30.

throne in 631.[5] No other kingdom in the early medieval west exercised such influence so regularly.

Despite the criticisms of Gregory of Tours and Fredegar, the descendants of Clovis I were powerful, and despite the fantasies of the *Annales Mettenses Priores* they exercised their power for a considerable period of time. Merovingian history, therefore, provides a focus for understanding the political history of western Europe in the two and a half centuries following the deposition of Romulus Augustulus. It also sheds light on the structure of that political history, which depended upon military aggression, family ties and aristocratic faction.

That the early Merovingians were of some importance in the political history of western Europe is well enough known: the chief points of debate have been the chronology and the extent of that influence. The cultural significance of the Merovingian period has been less well appreciated. Gregory of Tours's assessment of his own literary merits has been taken at face value, while the importance of the writing of letters in the Merovingian kingdom has been largely ignored, as has the achievement of the hagiographers. Moreover, the production of manuscripts by such monasteries as Luxeuil and Corbie has been considered more in terms of the origins of the Carolingian Renaissance than as an aspect of Merovingian culture. In fact, although it lacked a scholar of the stature of Bede, the Merovingian kingdom had a significant role to play in the transmission of culture from the late Roman through to the Carolingian period. There were cultural continuities within the Frankish world. Moreover the Rhône valley acted as a storehouse of manuscripts, without which Benedict Biscop could never have equipped his great monastery of Monkwearmouth/Jarrow. The English contribution to the Carolingian Renaissance depended on Merovingian resources.

The Merovingian Church, however, was more than a book-store for the Anglo-Saxons. It had a distinguished tradition in ecclesiastical legislation in the sixth and seventh centuries: it witnessed a flowering of the monastic tradition which was crucial to the development of monasticism in the west: and it boasted a long line of saints and martyrs. It was not a wholly passive organization. Certainly its achievement was greater than the critical remarks made by Boniface in 742 might suggest. Admittedly it was an institution which was deeply involved in politics, as was the Church in any early medieval state. It may also be true that there was a falling off of standards in the very last years of the seventh century and the beginning of the eighth, although there were notable exceptions even then. More important, however, was the fact that the Merovingian period had seen considerable missionary work east of the Rhine, even if the result did not conform to the high standards set by Boniface.

Just as Pippin's usurpation marks the end of Merovingian political history, so too Boniface's death at Dokkum can be seen as the last chapter in the Merovingian Church. Yet Francia is usually seen as being a Carolingian state

5. Fredegar, IV 73.

long before 751, and the Bonifatian Church is likewise thought of in terms of the future rather than the past. In some respects these observations on the early eighth century are valid, but they depend on downgrading the last century of the Merovingian Church and State, and on ignoring the continuities of Merovingian history. To a considerable extent such a perspective is forced on the student of the period by the sources, many of which are *parti pris* and deliberately seek to create the impression of a caesura between the great days of the early Merovingians and the obscure times of their successors. Such were the intentions of Fredegar and his continuators and the author of the *Annales Mettenses Priores*; Boniface and Alcuin provided support for the reading from their own vantage points. Yet to accept such a reading is to oversimplify Merovingian history, and to ignore the complexities. Worse, it allows for a reading of the Dark Ages which concentrates only on a perceived transmission of culture running from Italy in the sixth century, to the British Isles in the seventh and then to Carolingian Francia in the eighth. To accept such a reading is to fail to understand the potential and the limitations of the Franks in the Merovingian period, and by extension to misunderstand the achievements of their contemporaries. The Merovingian kingdom boasted no counterpart to Gregory the Great, Isidore, Bede or Boniface. Nevertheless no other state equalled the overall achievement of the Franks in the sixth, seventh and eighth centuries.

Bibliography

In writing this book I have addressed two separate audiences: the first is that of students whose first, and perhaps only, language is English, the second is that of fellow researchers. The footnotes reflect this. I have simply directed the researcher to primary sources. Citations of secondary material are aimed largely at students; as a result this material in usually in English; only occasionally, when there is no English alternative or where the work in question is fundamental, have I referred to works in French and German. My citations of secondary material, therefore, provide no guide to recent scholarship. Short, but useful, bibliographical essays are to be found in E. James, *The Origins of France* (London, 1982) and P. Geary, *Before France and Germany* (New York, 1988). S. Lebecq, *Les Origines franques Ve–IXe siècle* (Paris, 1990); E. Ewig, *Die Merowinger und das Frankenreich* (Stuttgart, 1988) and (from the former DDR) W. Bleiber, *Das Frankenreich der Merowinger* (Berlin, 1988), provide valuable introductions to French and German scholarship.

Abbreviations

AASS	*Acta Sanctorum.*
CSEL	*Corpus Scriptorum Ecclesiasticorum Latinorum (Vienna).*
MGH	*Monumenta Germaniae Historica*
AA	*Auctores Antiquissimi* (Berlin, 1877–1919).
Epistolae	(Berlin, 1887–).
Formulae	*Formulae Merowingici et Karolini Aevi* (Hannover, 1886).
Leges	*Leges Nationum Germanicarum* (Hannover/Leipzig, 1892–).

SRG in usum scholarum	*Scriptores Rerum Germanicarum in usum scholarum seperatim editi* (Hannover/Leipzig, 1871–).
SRM	*Scriptores Rerum Merowingicarum* (Hannover/Leipzig, 1885–1951).
SS	*Scriptores* (Hannover/Leipzig, 1826–1934).
Pardessus, *Diplomata*	J.M. Pardessus, *Diplomata, Chartae, Epistolae, Leges ad res Gallo-Francicas spectantia* (Paris, 1843–9).
Pertz, *Diplomata*	G.H. Pertz, *Diplomata regum Francorum e stirpe Merowingica,* MGH, *Diplomatum Imperii 1* (Hannover, 1872).
Pertz, *Diplomata Spuria*	G.H. Pertz, *Diplomata regum Francorum e stirpe Merowingica, MGH, Diplomatum Imperii 1* (Hannover, 1872).
Pertz, *Diplomata Arnulforum*	G.H. Pertz, *Diplomata maiorum domus e stirpe Arnulforum,* MGH, *Diplomatum Imperii 1* (Hannover, 1872).
PL	Patrologia Latina.

Primary sources

Abbo, *Testamentum*, ed., Geary, P., *Aristocracy in Provence.* (Stuttgart, 1985).
Actus Pontificum Cenomannis in urbe degentium, ed. G. Busson and G. Ledru (Le Mans, 1901–2).
Additamenta e codicibus Marculfi, ed., K. Zeumer, MGH, *Formulae.*
Additamentum Nivialense de Fuilano, ed., B. Krusch, MGH, *SRM* 4.
Ado, *Chronicon*, PL 123, cols 23–138.
Ado, *Vita Theudarii*, PL 123, cols 443–50.
Adso, *Vita Frodberti*, ed., W. Levison, MGH, *SRM* 5.
Agathias, ed. and trans. in A. Cameron, 'Agathias on the early Merovingians', *Annali della Scuola normale superiore di Pisa* 37 (1968), pp. 95–140.
Alcuin, *Epistulae*, ed., E. Dümmler, MGH, *Epistolae* 4, *Karolini Aevi* 2.
Alcuin, *Vita Richarii*, ed., B. Krusch, MGH, *SRM* 4.
Alcuin, *Vita Willibrordi*, ed., H.-J. Reischmann, *Willibrord – Apostel der Friesen* (Sigmaringendorf, 1989); trans., C.H. Talbot, *The Anglo-Saxon Missionaries in Germany* (London, 1954).
Altfrid, *Vita Liudgeri*, ed., W. Diekamp, *Die Geschichtsquellen des Bisthums Münster* 4 (Münster, 1881).
Ammianus Marcellinus, ed., J.C. Rolfe (Cambridge, Mass., 1935–9).
Annales Iuvavenses maximi, ed., G.H. Pertz, MGH, *SS* 1.

Annales Mettenses Priores, ed., B. von Simson, *MGH, SRG in usum scholarum* 10.

Annales Regni Francorum, ed., F. Kurze, *MGH, SRG in usum scholarum* 6.

Anonymi Valesiani Pars Posterior, in Ammianus Marcellinus, 3, ed. J.C. Rolfe (Cambridge, Mass., 1939).

Ansbert, *Hymnus de sancto Ansberto episcopo*, ed. W. Levison, *MGH, SRM* 5.

Anso, *Vita Erminonis*, ed., W. Levison, *MGH, SRM* 6.

Anso, *Vita Ursmari*, ed., W. Levison, *MGH, SRM* 6.

Arbeo, *Vita Corbiniani*, ed., B. Krusch, *MGH, SRM* 6.

Arbeo, *Vita Haimhramni*, ed., B. Krusch, *MGH, SRM* 4.

Auctarium Havniense, ed., T. Mommsen, *Chronica Minora* 1, *MGH, AA* 9: trans., S. Muhlberger, 'The Copenhagen continuation of Prosper: a translation', *Florilegium* 6 (1984), pp. 50–70.

Aurelian, *Regulae*, *PL* 68, cols 385–406.

Avitus, ed., R. Peiper, *MGH, AA* 6, 2.

Baudonivia, *Vita Radegundis*, ed., B. Krusch, *MGH, SRM* 2.

Bede, *Historia Abbatum*, ed., C. Plummer, *Venerabilis Baedae Opera Historica* (Oxford, 1896).

Bede, *Historia Ecclesiastica*, ed., C. Plummer, *Venerabilis Baedae Opera Historica* (Oxford, 1896).

Bede, *Vita Cuthberti*, ed., B. Colgrave, *Two Lives of Saint Cuthbert* (Cambridge, 1940).

Bertram, *Testamentum*, see *Actus Pontificum Cenomannis in urbe degentium*.

Bobolenus, *Vita Germani Grandivallensis*, ed., B. Krusch, *MGH, SRM* 5.

Boniface, *Epistolae*, ed., M. Tangl, *MGH, Epistolae Selectae* 1 (Berlin, 1916); trans., E. Emerson, *The Letters of St Boniface* (New York, 1940); partial trans., C.H. Talbot, *The Anglo-Saxon Missionaries in Germany* (London, 1954).

Caesarius, ed., M.-J. Delage, *Césaire d'Arles: sermons au peuple* 1, *Sources Chrétiennes* 175 (Paris, 1971).

Capitularia Merowingica, ed., A. Boretius, *MGH, Capitularia regum Francorum* 1 (Hannover, 1883).

Cassiodorus, *Chronicle*, ed., T. Mommsen, *Chronica Minora* 2, *MGH, AA* 11.

Cassiodorus, *Variae*, ed., T. Mommsen, *MGH, AA* 12; partial trans., T. Hodgkin, *The Letters of Cassiodorus* (London, 1886); also S.J.B. Barnish, *Cassiodorus: Variae* (Liverpool, 1992).

Chartularium sancti Victoris, ed., M. Guérard (Paris, 1857).

Chilperic I, *Ymnus in sollemnitate s. Medardi*, ed., K. Strecker, *MGH Poetae* 4, 2 (Berlin, 1923), pp. 455–8.

Chronicle of Saragossa (*Chronica Caesaraugustana*), ed., T. Mommsen, *Chronica Minora* 2, *MGH, AA* 11.

Chronicle of 452, ed., T. Mommsen, *Chronica Minora* 1, *MGH, AA* 9.

Chronicle of 511, ed., T. Mommsen, *Chronica Minora* 1, *MGH, AA* 9.

Chronicle of 754, ed., E. López Pereira, *Crónica mozárabe de 754: edición crítica y traducción* (Zaragossa, 1980); trans., K.B. Wolf, *Conquerors and Chroniclers of Early Medieval Spain* (Liverpool, 1990).

Chronologica Regum Francorum Stirpis Merowingicae, Catalogi, computationes annorum vetustatae cum commentariis, ed., B. Krusch, *MGH, SRM* 7.

Codex Theodosianus, ed., T. Mommsen and P. Meyer (Berlin, 1905); trans. C. Pharr, *The Theodosian Code* (Princeton, NJ, 1952).

Codice Diplomatico del Monasterio di S. Colombano di Bobbio, ed. C. Cipolla, *Fonti per la Storia d'Italia* 52 (Rome, 1918).

Columbanus, ed., G.S.M. Walker, *Scriptores Latini Hiberniae* 2 (Dublin, 1970).

Concilia Galliae A.511–695, ed., C. de Clercq, *Corpus Christanorum Series Latina* 148A (Turnhout, Belgium, 1963).

Concilia, MGH, Concilia 1, ed., F. Maasen (Hannover, 1893).

Concilia, MGH, Concilia 2, ed., A. Werminghoff (Hannover, 1906–8).

Constantius, *Vita Germani*, ed., R. Borius, *Constance de Lyon, Vie de saint Germain d'Auxerre, Sources Chrétiennes* 112 (Paris, 1965); trans., F.H. Hoare, *The Western Fathers* (London, 1954).

Conversio Bagoariorum et Carantanorum, ed., H. Wolfram (Vienna, 1979).

Councils. See *Concilia Galliae A.511–695* and *Concilia, MGH*.

Desiderius of Cahors, ed., W. Arndt, *MGH, Epistolae* 3, *Merowingici et Karolini Aevi* 1.

Eigil, *Vita Sturmi*, ed., G.H. Pertz, *MGH, SS* 2; trans., C.H. Talbot, *The Anglo-Saxon Missionaries in Germany* (London, 1954).

Einhard, *Vita Caroli Magni*, ed., O. Holder-Egger, *MGH, SRG in usum scholarum* 25.

Eligius, *Praedicationes*, ed., B. Krusch, *MGH, SRM* 4.

Ennodius, ed., F. Vogel, *MGH, AA* 7.

Epistulae Aevi Merowingici Collectae, ed., W. Gundlach, *MGH, Epistolae* 3, *Merowingici et Karolini Aevi* 1.

Epistulae Austrasiacae, ed., W. Gundlach, *MGH, Epistolae* 3, *Merowingici et Karolini Aevi* 1.

Erchanbert, *Breviarium Regum Francorum*, ed., G.H. Pertz, *MGH, SS* 2.

Fasti Vindobonenses Priores, ed., T. Mommsen, *Chronica Minora* 1, *MGH, AA* 9.

Flodoard, *Historia Remensis Ecclesiae*, ed., J. Heller and G. Waitz, *MGH, SS* 13.

Formulae Arvernenses, ed., K. Zeumer, *MGH, Formulae*.

Fredegar, ed., B. Krusch, *MGH, SRM* 2; also J.M. Wallace-Hadrill, *The Fourth Book of the Chronicle of Fredegar* (London, 1960).

Gesta abbatum Fontanellensium, ed., F. Lohier and J. Laporte, *Gesta ss. patrum Fontanellensis coenobii* (Rouen, 1936).

Gesta Dagoberti I, ed., B. Krusch, *MGH, SRM* 2.

Gesta Dagoberti III regis Francorum, ed., B. Krusch, *MGH, SRM* 2.

Gesta episcoporum Autissiodorensium, ed., P. Labbe, *Bibliotheca nova manuscriptorum* 1 (Paris, 1657); also, ed., G.H. Pertz, *MGH, SS* 13.

Gesta Treverorum, ed., G.H. Pertz, *MGH, SS* 7.

Gregory I, *Register*, ed., P. Ewald and L.M. Hartmann, *MGH, Epistolae* 1 and 2.

Gregory of Tours, *Decem Libri Historiarum*, ed., B. Krusch and W. Levison, *MGH, SRM* 1, 1; trans. L. Thorpe, *Gregory of Tours: The History of the Franks* (Harmondsworth, 1974).

Gregory of Tours, *Liber de Virtutibus sancti Martini*, ed., B. Krusch, *MGH, SRM*, 1, 2; partial trans., E. Peters, *Monks, Bishops and Pagans: Christian Culture in Gaul and Italy, 500–700* (Philadelphia, 1975).

Gregory of Tours, *Liber in Gloria Confessorum*, ed., B. Krusch, *MGH, SRM* 1, 2; trans. R. Van Dam, *Gregory of Tours: Glory of the Confessors* (Liverpool, 1988).

Gregory of Tours, *Liber in Gloria Martyrum*, ed., B. Krusch, *MGH, SRM* 1, 2; trans. R. Van Dam, *Gregory of Tours: Glory of the Martyrs* (Liverpool, 1988).

Gregory of Tours, *Liber Vitae Patrum*, ed., B. Krusch, *MGH, SRM* 1, 2; trans, E. James, *Gregory of Tours: Life of the Fathers* (Liverpool, 1985).

Hericus, *Miracula s. Germani*, *PL* 124, cols 1207–70.

Hincmar, *Vita Remigii*, ed., B. Krusch, *MGH, SRM* 3.

Historia Abbatum auctore anonymo, ed. C. Plummer, *Venerabilis Baedae Opera Historica* (Oxford, 1896).

Hucbald, *Vita Rictrudis*, ed., W. Levison, *MGH, SRM* 6.

Hydatius, *Chronicle*, ed., T. Mommsen, *Chronica Minora* 2, *MGH, AA* 11.

Indiculus Superstitionum, ed. A. Dierkens, 'Superstitions, christianisme et paganisme à la fin de l'époque mérovingienne', in H. Hasquin, ed., *Magie, sorcellerie, parapsychologie* (Brussels, 1985), pp. 9–26; trans., J.T. McNeill and H.M. Gamer, *Medieval Handbooks of Penance: A Translation of the Principal Libri Poenitentiales* (New York, 1938), pp. 419–21.

Isidore, *Etymologiae*, ed., W.M. Lindsay (Oxford, 1910).

John of Antioch, trans. in C.D. Gordon, *The Age of Attila* (Ann Arbor, Mich., 1960).

John of Biclarum, *Chronicle*, ed., J. Campos, *Juan de Biclaro, obispo de Gerona, su vida y obra* (Madrid, 1960); trans., K.B. Wolf, *Conquerors and Chroniclers of Early Medieval Spain* (Liverpool, 1990).

Jonas, *Vita Columbani*, ed., B. Krusch, *MGH, SRM* 4; partial trans., E. Peters, *Monks, Bishops and Pagans: Christian Culture in Gaul and Italy, 500–700* (Philadelphia, 1975).

Jonas, *Vita Iohannis*, ed., B. Krusch, *MGH, SRM* 3.

Jonas, *Vita Vedastis*, ed., B. Krusch, *MGH, SRM* 3.

Jordanes, *Getica*, ed., T. Mommsen, *MGH, AA* 5, 1; trans., C.C. Mierow, *The Gothic History of Jordanes* (Princeton, NJ, 1915).

Julian of Toledo, *Historia Wambae Regis*, ed., W. Levison, *MGH, SRM* 5.

Lex Alamannorum, ed., K. Lehmann, *MGH, Leges* 5, 1; trans., T.J. Rivers, *Laws of the Alamans and Bavarians* (Philadelphia, 1977).

Lex Baiwariorum, ed., E. von Schwind, *MGH, Leges* 5, 2; trans., T.J. Rivers, *Laws of the Alamans and Bavarians* (Philadelphia, 1977).

Lex Ribvaria, ed., F. Beyerle and R. Buchner, *MGH, Leges* 3, 2; trans., T.J. Rivers, *Laws of the Salian and Ripuarian Franks* (New York, 1986).

Lex Romana Visigothorum, ed., G. Haenel (Berlin, 1849).

Liber Constitutionum, ed., L.R. von Salis, *Leges Burgundionum*, MGH, *Leges* 2, 1; trans., K.F. Drew, *The Burgundian Code* (Philadelphia, 1949).

Liber Diurnus, ed., H. Foerster, *Liber Diurnus Romanorum Pontificum* (Bern, 1958).

Liber Historiae Francorum, ed., B. Krusch, *MGH, SRM* 2; trans, B. Bachrach (Lawrence, Kansas, 1973).

Liber Pontificalis, ed., L. Duchesne, *Le Liber Pontificalis, Texte, introduction et commentaire*, 2 vols (Paris, 1886–92): trans., R. Davis, *The Book of the Pontiffs* (Liverpool, 1989), and id., *The Lives of the Eighth-Century Popes* (Liverpool, 1992).

Liber Vitae Ecclesiae Dunelmensis, ed., J. Stevenson, *Publications of the Surtees Society* 13 (1841); ed., A.H. Thompson, *Publications of the Surtees Society* 136 (1923).

Liudger, *Vita Gregorii*, ed., O. Holder-Egger, *MGH, SS* 15.

Marcellinus Comes, *Chronicle*, ed., T. Mommsen, *Chronica Minora* 2, *MGH, AA* 11.

Marculf, *Formulary*, ed., K. Zeumer, *MGH, Formulae*.

Marius of Avenches, *Chronicle*, ed. J. Favrod, *La Chronique de Marius d'Avenches (455–581)* (Lausanne, 1991).

Milo, *Vita Amandi*, ed., B. Krusch, *MGH, SRM* 5.

Miracula Austregisili, ed., B. Krusch, *MGH, SRM* 4.

Miracula Martialis, ed., O. Holder-Egger, *MGH, SS* 15.

Miracula Wandregisili, *AASS*, 5 July, pp. 281–90.

Monumenta novaliciensia vetustioria, ed., C. Cipolla, *Fonti per la Storia d'Italia* 31 (Rome, 1898).

Novellae Valentiniani, ed., T. Mommsen and P. Meyer (Berlin, 1905); trans. C. Pharr, *The Theodosian Code* (Princeton, NJ, 1952).

Olympiodorus, in R. Blockley, *The Fragmentary Classicising Historians of the Late Roman Empire: Eutropius, Olympiodorus, Priscus, Malchus* (Liverpool, 1981): trans. in C.D. Gordon, *The Age of Attila* (Ann Arbor, Mich., 1960).

Orosius, *Historia Adversos Paganos*, ed., C. Zangemeister, *CSEL* 5 (Vienna, 1882).

Pactus Legis Salicae, ed., K.A. Eckhardt, *MGH, Leges* 4, 1; trans., T.J. Rivers, *Laws of the Salian and Ripuarian Franks* (New York, 1986); also, K.F. Drew, *The Laws of the Salian Franks* (Philadelphia, 1991).

Panegyrici Latini, ed., R.A.B. Mynors (Oxford, 1964).

Pardessus, J.M., *Diplomata, Chartae, Epistolae, Leges ad res Gallo-Francicas spectantia* (Paris, 1843–9).

Passiones Leudegarii, ed., B. Krusch, *MGH, SRM* 5.

Passio Kiliani, ed., W. Levison, *MGH, SRM* 5.

Passio Praeiecti, ed., B. Krusch, *MGH, SRM* 5.

Passio sancti Desiderii episcopi et martyris, ed., B. Krusch, *MGH, SRM* 3.

Passio Sigismundi Regis, ed., B. Krusch, *MGH, SRM* 2.

Paul the Deacon, *Historia Langobardorum*, ed., G. Waitz, *MGH, SRG in usum scholarum*; trans., W. D. Foulke, *Paul the Deacon, History of the Langobards* (Philadelphia, 1907).

Paul the Deacon, *Gesta episcoporum Mettensium*, ed., G.H. Pertz, *MGH, SS* 2.

Paulinus of Pella, *Eucharisticon*, ed., H.G.E. White, *Ausonius* 2 (Cambridge, Mass., 1921).

Pertz, G.H., *Diplomata regum Francorum e stirpe Merowingica, MGH, Diplomatum Imperii* 1 (Hannover, 1872).

Priscus, in R. Blockley, *The Fragmentary Classicising Historians of the Late Roman Empire: Eutropius, Olympiodorus, Priscus, Malchus* (Liverpool, 1981); trans. in C.D. Gordon, *The Age of Attila* (Ann Arbor, Mich., 1960).

Procopius, *Wars*, ed., H.B. Dewing, *Procopius* 1–5 (Cambridge, Mass., 1914–28).

Prosper, *Chronicle*, ed., T. Mommsen, *Chronica Minora* 1, *MGH, SRM* 9.

Ravenna Annals, ed., B. Bischoff and W. Koehler, 'Eine illustrierte Ausgabe der spätantiken Ravennater Annalen', in W.R.W. Koehler, ed., *Studies in Memory of A. Kingsley Porter* (Cambridge, Mass., 1939), pp. 125–38.

Recueil des chartes de Saint-Germain-des-Prés, ed., R. Poupardin (Paris, 1909–32).

Regula Cuiusdam Patris, PL 66, cols 987–94.

Regula Donati, ed., A. de Vogüé, 'La Règle de Donat pour l'abbesse Gauthstrude: texte critique et synopse des sources', *Benedictina* 25 (1978), pp. 219–313.

Regula Waldeberti, PL 88, cols 1053–70.

Remigius, *Testamentum*, ed., B. Krusch, *MGH, SRM* 3.

Rimbert, *Vita Anskarii*, ed., W. Trillmich, *Quellen des 9. und 11 Jahrhunderts zur Geschichte der Hamburgishen Kirche und des Reiches* (Darmstadt, 1961).

Ruricius, ed., B. Krusch, *MGH, AA* 8.

Salvian, *De Gubernatione Dei*, ed., F. Pauly, *CSEL* 8 (Vienna, 1883).

Sidonius Apollinaris, ed., W.B. Anderson (Cambridge, Mass., 1936–65).

Sigebert, *Vita Landiberti episcopi Traeiectensis*, ed., B. Krusch, *MGH, SRM* 6.

Sisebut, *Vita vel Passio sancti Desiderii*, ed., B. Krusch, *MGH, SRM* 3.

Stephanus, *Vita Wilfridi*, ed., B. Colgrave, *The Life of Bishop Wilfrid by Eddius Stephanus* (Cambridge, 1927).

Testamentum Amandi, ed., B. Krusch, *MGH, SRM* 5; trans., J.N. Hillgarth, *Christianity and Paganism, 350–750: The Conversion of Western Europe* (Philadelphia, 1986).

Venantius Fortunatus, *Opera Poetica*, ed., F. Leo, *MGH, AA* 4, 1.

Venantius Fortunatus, *Opera Pedestria*, ed., B. Krusch, *MGH, AA* 4, 2.

Visio Baronti, ed., W. Levison, MGH, SRM 5; trans., J.N. Hillgarth, *Christianity and Paganism, 350–750: The Conversion of Western Europe* (Philadelphia, 1986).

Vita Abbatum Acaunensium absque epitaphiis, ed., B. Krusch, *MGH, SRM* 7.

Vita Aigulfi I, *AASS*, 1 September, pp. 743–7.

Vita Amandi, ed., B. Krusch, *MGH, SRM* 5: trans., J.N. Hillgarth, *Christianity and Paganism, 350–750: The Conversion of Western Europe* (Philadelphia, 1986).

Vita Amati, ed., B. Krusch, *MGH, SRM* 4.

Vita Ansberti, ed., W. Levison, *MGH, SRM* 5.

Vita Apollinaris, ed., B. Krusch, *MGH, SRM* 3.

Vita Arnulfi, ed., B. Krusch, *MGH, SRM* 2.

Vita Audoini, ed., W. Levison, *MGH, SRM* 5.

Vita II Audoini, AASS, 4 August, pp. 810–19.

Vita Balthildis, ed., B. Krusch, *MGH, SRM* 2.

Vita Boniti, ed., B. Krusch, *MGH, SRM* 6.

Vitae Caesarii episcopi Arelatensis libri duo auctoribus Cypriano, Firmino Viventio episcopis, Messiano presbytero, Stephano diacono, ed., B. Krusch, *MGH, SRM* 3.

Vita Cuthberti Auctore Anonymo, ed. B. Colgrave, *Two Lives of Saint Cuthbert* (Cambridge, 1940).

Vita Desiderii Cadurcensis, ed., B. Krusch, *MGH, SRM* 4.

Vita Eligii, ed., B. Krusch, *MGH, SRM* 4.

Vita Eremberti, ed., W. Levison, *MGH, SRM* 5.

Vita Eucherii, ed., W. Levison, *MGH, SRM* 7.

Vita Faronis, ed., B. Krusch, *MGH, SRM* 5.

Vita Filiberti, ed., B. Krusch, *MGH, SRM* 5.

Vita Fursei, ed., B. Krusch, *MGH, SRM* 4.

Vitae Galli vetustissimae fragmentum, ed., B. Krusch, *MGH, SRM* 4.

Vita Geretrudis, ed., B. Krusch, *MGH, SRM* 2.

Vita Hrodberti episcopi Salisburgensis, ed., W. Levison, *MGH, SRM* 6.

Vita Landiberti episcopi Traeiectensis vetustissima, ed., B. Krusch, *MGH, SRM* 6.

Vita Lantberti Fontanellensis, ed., W. Levison, *MGH, SRM* 5.

Vita Lupi episcopi Senonici, ed., B. Krusch, *MGH, SRM* 4.

Vita Marcelli Deiensis, ed. F. Dolbeau, 'La Vie en prose de saint Marcel, évêque de Die', *Francia* 11 (1983), pp. 97–130.

Vita Pardulfi, ed., W. Levison, *MGH, SRM* 7.

Vita Patrum Iurensium, ed., F. Martine, *Vie des Pères du Jura, Sources Chrétiennes* 142 (Paris, 1968).

Vita Remacli, ed., B. Krusch, *MGH, SRM* 5.

Vita Richarii sacerdotis Centulensis primigenia, ed., B. Krusch, *MGH, SRM* 7.

Vita Rigoberti, ed., W. Levison, *MGH, SRM* 7.

Vita Romarici, ed., B. Krusch, *MGH, SRM* 4.

Vita Rusticulae, ed., B. Krusch, *MGH, SRM* 4.

Vita Sadalbergae, ed., B. Krusch, *MGH, SRM* 5.

Vita Samsonis, ed., R. Fawtier, *La Vie de saint Samson: Essai de critique hagiographique, Bibliothèque de l'École pratique des Hautes Études* 197 (Paris, 1912).

Vita Sulpicii episcopi Biturgi, ed., B. Krusch, *MGH, SRM* 4.

Vita Vulframni, ed., W. Levison, *MGH, SRM* 5.

Vita Wandregisili, ed., B. Krusch, *MGH, SRM* 5.

Vita Wandregisili II, ed., *AASS*, 5 July, pp. 272–81.

Willibald, *Vita Bonifatii*, ed., W. Levison, *MGH, SRG in usum scholarum* 57; ed., R. Rau, *Briefe des Bonifatius: Willibalds Leben des Bonifatius* (Darmstadt, 1968); trans., C.H. Talbot, *The Anglo-Saxon Missionaries in Germany* (London, 1954).

Willibrord, *Calendar*, ed., H.A. Wilson, *Henry Bradshaw Society* 55 (1918).

Secondary works

Amory, P., 'The textual transmission of the *Donatio Ansemundi'*, (forthcoming).

Angenendt, A., *Monachi Peregrini: Studien zu Pirmin und den monastischen Vorstellungen des frühen Mittelalter* (Munich, 1972).

Bachrach, B., *Merovingian Military Organisation 481–751* (Minneapolis, 1972).

Barnwell, P., ' "Epistula Hieronimi de Gradus Romanorum": an English school book', *Historical Research* 64 (1991), pp. 77–86.

Bendixen, K., 'Sceattas and other coin finds', in M. Bencard, ed., *Ribe Excavations 1970–76*, 1 (Esbjerg, 1981), pp. 63–101.

Brennan, B., 'The conversion of the Jews of Clermont in AD 576', *Journal of Theological Studies* 36 (1985), pp. 321–37.

Brooke, C.N.L. and Keir, G., *London 800–1216: The Shaping of a City* (London, 1975).

Brown, P.R.L., *Relics and Social Status in the Age of Gregory of Tours*, Stenton Lecture 1976.

Brulet, R., Ghenne-Dubois, M.-J. and Coulon, G., 'Le quartier Saint-Brice de Tournai à l'époque mérovingienne', *Revue du Nord* 69 (1986), pp. 361–9.

Brunhölzl, F., *Histoire de la littérature latine du Moyen Age*, I/1, *L'époque mérovingienne* (Louvain, 1990).

Buchner, R., *Die Rechtsquellen*, *Wattenbach-Levison*, *Deutschlands Geschichtsquellen im Mittelalter* (Weimar, 1953).

Cameron, A., 'Agathias on the early Merovingians', *Annali della Scuola normale superiore di Pisa* 37 (1968), pp. 95–140.

Cameron, A., 'The early religious policies of Justin II', in D. Baker, ed., *The Orthodox Churches and the West, Studies in Church History* 13 (1976), pp. 51–67.

Campbell, J., 'The first century of Christianity in England', in Campbell, *Essays in Anglo-Saxon History* (London, 1986).

Chadwick, O., *John Cassian*, 2nd edn (Cambridge, 1968).

Charles-Edwards, T.M., 'The social background to Irish peregrinatio', *Celtica* 11 (1976), pp. 43–59.

Chrysos, E., 'Byzantine diplomacy, A.D. 300–800: means and ends', in J. Shepard and S. Franklin, eds, *Byzantine Diplomacy: Papers from the Twenty-Fourth Spring Symposium of Byzantine Studies, Cambridge, March 1990* (London, 1992), pp. 25–39.

Classen, P., 'Fortleben und Wandel spätrömischen Urkundenwesens im frühen Mittelalter', in Classen, ed., *Recht und Schrift im Mittelalter, Vortäge und Forschungen* 23 (1977), pp. 13–54.

Collins, R., 'Julian of Toledo and the royal succession in late seventh-century Spain', in P.H. Sawyer and I.N. Wood, eds, *Early Medieval Kingship* (Leeds, 1977), pp. 30– 49.

Collins, R., 'Theodebert I, "Rex Magnus Francorum" ', in P. Wormald, ed., *Ideal and Reality in Frankish and Anglo-Saxon Society* (Oxford, 1983), pp. 7–33.

Collins, R., *Early Medieval Spain: Unity in Diversity, 400–1000* (London, 1983).

Collins, R. *The Basques* (Oxford, 1986).

Collins, R., *The Arab Conquest of Spain* (Oxford, 1989).

Dawson, C., *The Making of Europe* (London, 1932).

Delage, M.-J., *Césaire d'Arles: sermons au peuple*, 1, *Sources Chrétiennes* 175 (Paris, 1971).

de Nie, G., *Views from a Many-Windowed Tower* (Amsterdam, 1987).

De Vogüé, A., *Les Règles monastiques anciennes (400–700), Typologie des Sources du Moyen Age occidental* 46 (Turnhout, Belgium, 1985).

Dierkens, A., 'Superstitions, christianisme et paganisme à la fin de l'époque mérovingienne', in H. Hasquin, ed., *Magie, sorcellerie, parapsychologie* (Brussels, 1985), pp. 9–26.

Dierkens, A., *Abbayes et Chapitres entre Sambre et Meuse (VIIe–XIe siècles)* (Sigmaringen, 1985).

Duchesne, L., *Fastes épiscopaux de l'ancienne Gaule* (Paris, 1894–1915).

Duparc, P., 'La Sapaudia', *Comptes rendus de l'Academie des Inscriptions et Belles Lettres* (1958), pp. 371–83.

Durliat, J., 'Les attributions civiles des évêques mérovingiens: l'exemple de Didier, évêque de Cahors (630–655)', *Annales du Midi* 91 (1979), pp. 237–54.

Ewig, E., *Spätantikes und fränkisches Gallien*, 1 and 2 (Munich, 1976–9).

Ewig, E., 'Die fränkishen Teilungen und Teilreiche (511–613), in Ewig, *Spätantikes und fränkisches Gallien*, 1.

Ewig, E., 'Die fränkischen Teilreiche im 7. Jahrhundert (613–714), in Ewig, *Spätantikes und fränkisches Gallien*, 1.

Ewig, E., 'Milo et eiusmodi similes', in Ewig, *Spätantikes und fränkisches Gallien*, 2.

Ewig, E., 'Saint Chrodegang et la réforme de l'église franque', in Ewig, *Spätantikes und fränkisches Gallien*, 2.

Ewig, E., 'Das Formular von Rebais und die Bischofsprivilegien der Merowingerzeit', in Ewig, *Spätantikes und fränkisches Gallien*, 2.

Ewig, E., 'Das Privileg des Bischofs Berthefred von Amiens für Corbie von 664 und die Klosterpolitik der Königin Balthild', in Ewig, *Spätantikes und fränkisches Gallien*, 2.

Ewig, E., 'Die Namengebung bei den ältesten Frankenkönigen und im merowingischen Königshaus', *Francia* 18, 1 (1991), pp. 21–69.

Favrod, J., *La Chronique de Marius d'Avenches (455–581)* (Lausanne, 1991).

Fernie, E., *The Architecture of the Anglo-Saxons* (London, 1983).

Fontaine, J., 'King Sisebut's Vita Desiderii and the political function of Visigothic hagiography', in E. James, ed., *Visigothic Spain: New Approaches* (Oxford, 1980), pp. 93–129.

Fouracre, P., 'The work of Audoenus of Rouen and Eligius of Noyon in extending episcopal influence from the town to the countryside in seventh-century Neustria', in D. Baker, ed., *The Church in Town and Countryside, Studies in Church History* 16 (1979), pp. 77–91.

Fouracre, P., 'Merovingians, mayors of the palace and the notion of a "low-born Ebroin" ', *Bulletin of the Institute of Historical Research* 57 (1984), pp. 1–14.

Fouracre, P., 'Observations on the outgrowth of Pippinid influence in the "Regnum Francorum" after the Battle of Tertry (687–715)', *Medieval Prosopography* 5 (1984), pp. 1–31.

Fouracre, P., ' "Placita" and the settlement of disputes in later Merovingian Francia', in W. Davies and P. Fouracre, eds, *The Settlement of Disputes in Early Medieval Europe* (Cambridge, 1986), pp. 23–43.

Fouracre, P., 'Merovingian history and Merovingian hagiography', *Past and Present* 127 (1990), pp. 3–38.

Fritze, W.H., '*Universalis Gentium Confessio*. Formeln, Träger und Wege universalmissionarischen Denkens im 7. Jahrhundert', *Frühmittelalterliche Studien* 3 (1969), pp. 78–130.

Ganz, D., 'The Merovingian Library of Corbie', in H.B. Clarke and M. Brennan, eds, *Columbanus and Merovingian Monasticism, BAR International Series* 113 (Oxford, 1981), pp. 153–72.

Ganz, D., 'Bureaucratic shorthand and Merovingian learning', in P. Wormald, ed., *Ideal and Reality in Frankish and Anglo-Saxon Society* (Oxford, 1983), pp. 58–75.

Ganz, D., 'The preconditions for caroline minuscule', *Viator* 18 (1987), pp. 23–44.

Ganz, D., *Corbie in the Carolingian Renaissance* (Sigmaringen, 1990).

Gasnault, P., 'Documents comptables du VIIe siècle provenant de Saint-Martin de Tours', *Francia* 2 (1974), pp. 1–18.

Gaudemet, J., *L'Église dans l'Empire Romain* (Paris, 1958).

Geary, P., *Aristocracy in Provence* (Stuttgart, 1985).

Geary, P., *Before France and Germany* (New York, 1988).

George, J., 'Poet as politician: Venantius Fortunatus' panegyric to King Chilperic', *Journal of Medieval History* 15 (1989), pp. 5–18.

George, J., *Venantius Fortunatus: A Latin Poet in Merovingian Gaul* (Oxford, 1992).

Gerberding, R.A., *The Rise of the Carolingians and the Liber Historiae Francorum* (Oxford, 1987).

Goffart, W., 'Byzantine policy in the west under Tiberius II and Maurice: the pretenders Hermenegild and Gundovald', *Traditio* 13 (1957), pp. 85–118.

Goffart, W., *Barbarians and Romans: Techniques of Accommodation, AD 418–584* (Princeton, NJ, 1980).

Goffart, W., *The Narrators of Barbarian History* (Princeton, NJ, 1988).

Goffart, W., *Rome's Fall and After* (London, 1989).

Goffart, W., 'The Fredegar problem reconsidered', in Goffart, *Rome's Fall and After*.

Goffart, W., 'Old and new in Merovingian taxation', in Goffart, *Rome's Fall and After*.

Goffart, W., 'Merovingian polyptychs: reflections on two recent publications', in Goffart, *Rome's Fall and After*.

Goffart, W., 'The Conversions of Avitus of Clermont and similar passages in Gregory of Tours', in Goffart, *Rome's Fall and After.*

Goffart, W., 'From *Historiae* to *Historia Francorum* and back again: aspects of the textual history of Gregory of Tours', in Goffart, *Rome's Fall and After.*

Gordon, C.D., *The Age of Attila* (Ann Arbor, Mich., 1960).

Goubert, P., *Byzance avant l'Islam, 2, Byzance et l'Occident sous les successeurs de Justinien; 1, Byzance et les Francs* (Paris, 1956).

Grierson, P. and Blackburn, M., *Medieval European Coinage 1, The Early Middle Ages (5th–10th Centuries)* (Cambridge, 1986).

Guerot, J., 'Le testament de Ste. Fare: matériaux pour l'étude et l'édition critique de ce document', *Revue d'Histoire ecclésiastique* 60 (1965), pp. 761–821.

Harries, J.D., 'Sidonius Apollinaris, Rome and the barbarians: a climate of treason?', in J. Drinkwater and H. Elton, eds, *Fifth-Century Gaul: A Crisis of Identity* (Cambridge, 1992), pp. 298–308.

Head, T., *Hagiography and the Cult of Saints: The Diocese of Orléans, 800–1200* (Cambridge, 1990).

Heather, P., *Goths and Romans 332–489* (Oxford, 1991).

Heinemeyer, K., *Das Erzbistum Mainz in römischer und fränkisher Zeit* (Marburg, 1979).

Heinzelmann, M., *Bischofsherrschaft in Gallien* (Munich, 1976).

Heinzelmann, M. and Poulin, J.-C., *Les Vies anciennes de sainte Geneviève de Paris: Étude critique* (Paris, 1986).

Herrin, J., *The Formation of Christendom* (Princeton, NJ, 1987).

Hillgarth, J.N., *Christianity and Paganism, 350–750: The Conversion of Western Europe* (Philadelphia, 1986).

Hodges, R., *Dark Age Economics: The Origins of Towns and Trade, AD 400–1000* (London, 1982).

James, E., 'Septimania and its frontier: an archaeological approach', in James, ed., *Visigothic Spain: New Approaches* (Oxford, 1980), pp. 223–41.

James, E., *The Origins of France* (London, 1982).

James, E., 'Beati pacifici: bishops and the law in sixth-century Gaul', in J. Bossy, ed., *Disputes and Settlements: Law and Human Relations in the West* (Cambridge, 1983), pp. 25–46.

James, E., *The Franks* (Oxford, 1988).

Jensen, S., *The Vikings in Ribe* (Ribe, 1991).

Jones, A.H.M., Grierson, P., and Crook, J.A., 'The authenticity of the Testamentum S. Remigii', *Revue Belge de Philologie et d'Histoire* 35 (1957), pp. 356–73.

Kent, J., 'The coins and the date of the burial', in R. Bruce Mitford, ed., *The Sutton Hoo Ship Burial*, 1 (London, 1975).

King, P.D., *Charlemagne* (London, 1986).

Laporte, J., *Le Pénitentiel de saint Colomban* (Tournai, 1958).

Lawrence, C.H., *Medieval Monasticism* (London, 1989).

Lebecq, S., *Marchands et navigateurs frisons du haut moyen âge* (Lille, 1983).

Lebecq, S., *Les Origines franques, Ve–IXe siècle* (Paris, 1990).

Leclercq, H., 'L'épiscopat de saint Bertrand', in F. Cabrol and H. Leclercq, *Dictionnaire d'Archéologie Chrétienne et de Liturgie*, 10, cols 1490–522.

Leman, P., 'Contribution à la localisation du Quentovic ou la relance d'un vieux débat', *Revue du Nord* 63 (1981), pp. 935–45.

Levison, W., 'Das Testament des Diakons Aldgisel-Grimo von J. 634', in Levison, *Aus rheinische und fränkische Frühzeit* (Düsseldorf, 1948), pp. 118–38.

Lewis, A.R., 'The dukes of the *Regnum Francorum*, A.D. 550–751', *Speculum* 51 (1976), pp. 381–410.

Liebeschuetz, J.H.W.G., *Barbarians and Bishops: Army, Church and State in the Age of Arcadius and Chrysostom* (Oxford, 1990).

Lot, F., 'Études critiques sur l'Abbaye de Saint-Wandrille', *Bibliothèque de l'École des Hautes Études* 204 (1913).

Loyen, A., *Sidoine Apollinaire et l'espirit précieux en Gaule* (Paris, 1943).

McCormack, S., *Art and Ceremony in Late Antiquity* (Berkeley, Calif, 1981).

McCormick, M., *Eternal Victory: Triumphal Rulership in Late Antiquity, Byzantium and the Early Medieval West* (Cambridge, 1986).

McCormick, M., 'Clovis at Tours, Byzantine public ritual and the origins of medieval ruler symbolism', in E.K. Chrysos and A. Schwarcz, eds, *Das Reich und die Barbaren* (Vienna, 1989), pp. 155–80.

McKitterick, R., 'The scriptoria of Merovingian Gaul: a survey of the evidence', in H.B. Clarke and M. Brennan, eds, *Columbanus and Merovingian Monasticism*, BAR International Series 113 (Oxford, 1981), pp. 173–207.

McKitterick, R., *The Frankish Kingdoms under the Carolingians 751–987* (London, 1983).

McKitterick, R., *The Carolingians and the Written Word* (Cambridge, 1989).

McNeill, J.T. and Garner, H.M. *Medieval Handbooks of Penance: A Translation of the Principal Libri Poenitentiales* (New York, 1938).

Markus, R., *The End of Ancient Christianity* (Cambridge, 1990).

Masai, F., 'La *Vita patrum iurensium* et les débuts du monachisme à Saint-Maurice d'Agaune', in *Festschrift Bernhard Bischoff zu seinem 65. Geburtstag* (Stuttgart, 1971), pp. 43–69.

Mathisen, R.W., 'Epistolography, literary circles and family ties in Late Roman Gaul', *Transactions of the American Philological Association* 111 (1981), pp. 95–109.

Mathisen, R.W., 'The family of Georgius Florentius Gregorius and the Bishops of Tours', *Medievalia et Humanistica* 12 (1984), pp. 83–95.

Mathisen, R.W., *Ecclesiastical Factionalism and Religious Controversy in Fifth-Century Gaul* (Washington, DC, 1989).

Matthews, J.F., *Western Aristocracies and Imperial Court A.D. 364–425* (Oxford, 1975).

Metcalf, D.M., 'A note on sceattas as a measure of international trade, and on the earliest Danish coinage', in D. Hill and D.M. Metcalf, eds, *Sceattas in England and on the Continent*, BAR British Series 128 (Oxford, 1984), pp. 159–64.

Miller, D.H., 'The Roman revolution of the eighth century: a study of the ideological background of the Papal separation from Byzantium and alliance with the Franks', *Medieval Studies* 36 (1974), pp. 79–133.

Moisl, H., 'Anglo-Saxon royal genealogies and Germanic oral tradition', *Journal of Medieval History* 7 (1981), pp. 215–48.

Morin, G., 'Le testament de saint Césaire d'Arles et la critique de M. Bruno Krusch', *Revue Bénédictine* 16 (1899), pp. 97–112.

Muhlberger, S., *The Fifth-Century Chroniclers, Prosper, Hydatius and the Gallic Chronicler of 452* (Leeds, 1990).

Murray, A.C., 'The position of the *grafio* in the constitutional history of Merovingian Gaul', *Speculum* 64 (1986), pp. 787–805.

Murray, A.C., 'From Roman to Frankish Gaul: "Centenarii" and "Centenae" in the administration of the Frankish kingdom', *Traditio* 44 (1988), pp. 59–100.

Murray, A.C., 'Immunity, nobility and the Edict of Paris', 27th International Congress on Medieval Studies, Kalamazoo, May 7–10, 1992.

Nelson, J.L., *Politics and Ritual in Early Medieval Europe* (London, 1986).

Nelson, J.L., 'Queens as Jezebels: Brunhild and Balthild in Merovingian history', in Nelson, *Politics and Ritual in Early Medieval Europe*.

Nelson, J.L., 'À propos des femmes royales dans les rapports entre le monde wisigothique et le monde franc à l'époque de Reccared', in *XIV Centenario Concilio III de Toledo 589–1989* (Madrid, 1991).

Netzer, N., 'Willibrord's Scriptorium at Echternach and its relationship to Ireland and Lindisfarne', in G. Bonner, D. Rollason and C. Stancliffe, eds, *St Cuthbert, his Cult and his Community to AD 1200* (Woodbridge, 1989), pp. 203–12.

Nixon, C.E.V., 'Relations between Visigoths and Romans in fifth-century Gaul', in J. Drinkwater and H. Elton, eds, *Fifth-Century Gaul: A Crisis of Identity*? (Cambridge, 1992), pp. 64–74.

Noble, T.F.X., *The Republic of St Peter: The Birth of the Papal State 680–825* (Philadelphia, 1984).

Nonn, U., 'Merowingische Testamente: Studien zum Fortleben einer römischen Urkundenform im Frankenreich', *Archiv für Diplomatik* 18 (1972), pp. 1–129.

O Cróinín, D., 'Is the Augsburg Gospel Codex a Northumbrian manuscript?', in G. Bonner, D. Rollason and C. Stancliffe, eds, *St Cuthbert, his Cult and his Community to AD 1200* (Woodbridge, 1989), pp. 189–201.

op den Velde, W., de Boone, W.J. and Pol, A., 'A survey of sceatta finds from the Low Countries', in D. Hill and D.M. Metcalf, eds, *Sceattas in England and on the Continent, BAR British Series* 128 (Oxford, 1984), pp. 117–45.

Pauly-Wissowa, *Real-Encyclopädie der classischen Altertumswissenschaft*.

Paxton, F.S., *Christianizing Death* (Ithaca, NY, 1990).

Picard, J.-M., 'Church and politics in the seventh century: the Irish exile of King Dagobert II', in Picard, ed., *Ireland and Northern France, AD 600–850* (Dublin, 1991), pp. 27–52.

Pontal, O., *Die Synoden im Merowingerreich* (Paderborn, 1986).

Prinz, F., 'Columbanus, the Frankish nobility and the territories east of the Rhine', in H.B. Clarke and M. Brennan, eds, *Columbanus and Merovingian Monasticism*, BAR International Series 113 (Oxford, 1981), pp. 73–87.

Prinz, F., *Frühes Mönchtum im Frankenreich*, 2nd edn (Munich, 1988).

Reischmann, H.-J.,*Willibrord – Apostel der Friesen* (Sigmaringendorf, 1989).

Reydellet, M., *La Royauté dans la littérature latine de Sidoine Apollinaire à Isidore de Seville* (Rome, 1981).

Riché, P, 'Columbanus, his followers and the Merovingian Church', in H.B. Clarke and M. Brennan, eds, *Columbanus and Merovingian Monasticism*, BAR International Series 113 (Oxford, 1981), pp. 59–72.

Rouche, M., *L'Aquitaine des Wisigoths aux Arabes* (Paris, 1979).

Rousseau, P., *Ascetics, Authority and the Church* (Oxford, 1978).

Salway, P., *Roman Britain* (Oxford, 1981).

Scheibelreiter, G., *Der Bischof in merowingischer Zeit* (Vienna, 1983).

Stafford, P., *Queens, Concubines and Dowagers* (London, 1983).

Stahl, A.M., 'The nature of the Sutton Hoo coin parcel', in C.B. Kendall and P.S. Wells, eds, *Voyage to the Other World: The Legacy of Sutton Hoo* (Minneapolis, 1992), pp. 3–14.

Stancliffe, C., *St. Martin and his Hagiographer: History and Miracle in Sulpicius Severus* (Oxford, 1983).

Stevens, C.E., *Sidonius Apollinaris and his Time* (Oxford, 1933).

Strohecker, K.F., *Der senatorische Adel im spätantiken Gallien* (Tübingen, 1948).

Teitler, H.C., 'Un-Roman activities in late antique Gaul: the cases of Arvandus and Seronatus', in J. Drinkwater and H. Elton, eds, *Fifth-Century Gaul: A Crisis of Identity* (Cambridge, 1992), pp. 309–17.

Thompson, E.A., 'The settlement of the barbarians in southern Gaul', *Journal of Roman Studies* 46 (1956), pp. 65–75.

Thompson, E.A., *Romans and Barbarians: The Decline of the Western Empire* (Madison, 1982).

van de Vyver, A., 'La victoire contre les Alamans et la conversion de Clovis', *Revue Belge de Philologie et d'Histoire* 15 (1936), pp. 859–914; 16 (1937), pp. 35–94.

van de Vyver, A., 'L'unique victoire contre les Alamans et la conversion de Clovis en 506', *Revue Belge de Philologie et d'Histoire* 17 (1938), pp. 793–813.

Verdon, J., *Grégoire de Tours* (Le Coteau, 1989).

Vezin, J., 'Une nouvelle lecture de la liste des noms copiée au dos de l'ivoire Barberini', *Bulletin archéologique du Comité des travaux historiques et scientifiques* 7 (1971), pp. 19–56.

Vierck, H., 'La "chemise" de sainte Balthilde et l'influence byzantine sur l'art de cour mérovingienne au VIIe siècle', *Centenaire de l'abbé Cochet, Actes du Colloque International d'Archéologie* 3 (Rouen, 1975), pp. 521–64.

Vierck, H., 'L'œuvre de saint Eloi, orfèvre, et son rayonnement', in P. Périn and L.-C. Feffer, *La Neustrie: Les pays au nord de la Loire, de Dagobert à Charles le Chauve (VIIe–IXe siècles)* (Créteil, 1985), pp. 403–9.

Wallace-Hadrill, J.M., 'Fredegar and the history of France', in Wallace-Hadrill, *The Long-Haired Kings*.

Wallace-Hadrill, J.M., *The Fourth Book of the Chronicle of Fredegar* (London, 1960).

Wallace-Hadrill, J.M., *The Long-Haired Kings* (London, 1962).

Wallace-Hadrill, J.M., review of A.H.M. Jones, *The Later Roman Empire*, in *English Historical Review* 80 (1965), pp. 785–90.

Wallace-Hadrill, J.M., *Early Germanic Kingship in England and on the Continent* (Oxford, 1971).

Wallace-Hadrill, J.M., *Early Medieval History* (Oxford, 1975).

Wallace-Hadrill, J.M., *The Frankish Church* (Oxford, 1983).

Wickham, C., *Early Medieval Italy: Central Power and Local Society 400–1000* (London).

Wolfram, H., 'The shaping of the early medieval principality as a type of non-royal rulership', *Viator* 2 (1972), pp. 33–51.

Wolfram, H., 'Virgil of St Peter's at Salzburg', in P. Ní Chatháin and M. Richter, eds, *Irland und die Christenheit* (Stuttgart, 1987), pp. 415–20.

Wolfram, H., *History of the Goths* (Berkeley, Calif., 1988).

Wolfram, H., *Die Geburt Mitteleuropas* (Vienna, 1987).

Wood, I.N., 'Kings, kingdoms and consent', in P.H. Sawyer and I.N. Wood, eds, *Early Medieval Kingship* (Leeds, 1977), pp. 6–29.

Wood, I.N., 'Early Merovingian devotion in town and country', in D. Baker, ed., *The Church in Town and Countryside, Studies in Church History* 16 (Oxford, 1979), pp. 61–76.

Wood, I.N., 'A prelude to Columbanus: the monastic achievement in the Burgundian territories', in H.B. Clarke and M. Brennan, eds, *Columbanus and Merovingian Monasticism, BAR International Series* 113 (Oxford, 1981), pp. 3–32.

Wood, I.N., 'The *Vita Columbani* and Merovingian hagiography', *Peritia* 1 (1982), pp. 63–80.

Wood, I.N., *The Merovingian North Sea* (Alingsås, 1983).

Wood, I.N., 'The ecclesiastical politics of Merovingian Clermont', in P. Wormald, ed., *Ideal and Reality in Frankish and Anglo-Saxon Society* (Oxford, 1983), pp. 34–57.

Wood, I.N., 'Gregory of Tours and Clovis', *Revue Belge de Philologie et d'Histoire* 63 (1985), pp. 249–72.

Wood, I.N., 'Disputes in late fifth- and sixth-century Gaul: some problems', in W. Davies and P. Fouracre, eds, *The Settlement of Disputes in Early Medieval Europe* (Cambridge, 1986), pp. 7–22.

Wood, I.N., 'Pagans and holy men, 600–800', in P. Ní Chatháin and M. Richter, eds, *Irland und die Christenheit* (Stuttgart, 1987), pp. 347–61.

Wood, I.N., review of P. Geary, *Aristocracy in Provence*, *French History* 1 (1987), pp. 118–19.

Wood, I.N., 'Forgery in Merovingian hagiography', in *MGH Schriften* 33, *Fälschungen im Mittelalter* V (Hannover, 1988), pp. 369–85.

Wood, I.N., 'Clermont and Burgundy: 511–534', *Nottingham Medieval Studies* 32 (1988), pp. 119–25.

Wood, I.N., 'The Irish and social subversion in the early Middle Ages', in *Irland, Gesellschaft und Kultur, Kongress und Tagungsberichte der Martin-Luther-Universität Halle-Wittenberg* (Halle, 1989), pp. 263–70.

Wood, I.N., 'Ethnicity and the ethnogenesis of the Burgundians', in H. Wolfram and W. Pohl, eds, *Typen der Ethnogenese unter besonderer Berücksichtigung der Bayern*, I (Vienna, 1990), pp. 53–69.

Wood, I.N., 'Administration, law and culture in Merovingian Gaul', in R. McKitterick, ed., *The Uses of Literacy in Early Medieval Europe* (Cambridge, 1990), pp. 63–81.

Wood, I.N., 'The Channel from the fourth to the seventh centuries AD', in S. McGrail, ed., *Maritime Celts, Frisians and Saxons*, CBA Research Report 71 (London, 1990), pp. 93–7.

Wood, I.N., 'Ripon, Francia and the Franks Casket in the early Middle Ages', *Northern History* 26 (1990), pp. 1–19.

Wood, I.N., 'The Franks and Sutton Hoo', in I.N. Wood and N. Lund, eds, *People and Places in Northern Europe, 500–1600: Essays in Honour of Peter Sawyer* (Woodbridge, 1991), pp. 1–14.

Wood, I.N., 'Saint-Wandrille and its hagiography', in I.N. Wood and G.A. Loud, eds, *Church and Chronicle in the Middle Ages: Essays presented to John Taylor* (London, 1991), pp. 1–14.

Wood, I.N., 'Continuity or calamity?: the constraints of literary models', in J. Drinkwater and H. Elton, eds, *Fifth-Century Gaul: A Crisis of Identity?* (Cambridge, 1992), pp. 9–18.

Wood, I.N., 'Frankish hegemony in England', in M. Carver, ed., *The Age of Sutton Hoo* (Woodbridge, 1992), pp. 235–41.

Wood, I.N., 'The secret histories of Gregory of Tours', *Revue Belge de Philologie et d'Histoire* (forthcoming).

Wood, I.N., 'The *Codex Theodosianus* in Merovingian Gaul', in J.D. Harries and I.N. Wood, eds, *The Theodosian Code* (forthcoming).

Wood, I.N., 'The mission of Augustine' (forthcoming).

Wormald, P., 'Bede and Benedict Biscop', in G. Bonner, ed., *Famulus Christi* (London, 1976), pp. 141–69.

Wormald, P., 'The decline of the Roman Empire and the survival of its aristocracy', *Journal of Roman Studies* 66 (1976), pp. 217–26.

Wormald, P., '*Lex Scripta* and *Verbum Regis*: legislation and Germanic kingship from Euric to Cnut', in P.H. Sawyer and I.N. Wood, eds, *Early Medieval Kingship* (Leeds, 1977), pp. 105–38.

Zöllner, E., *Geschichte der Franken bis zum Mitte des sechsten Jahrhunderts* (Munich, 1970).

Genealogies of the Merovingian Family

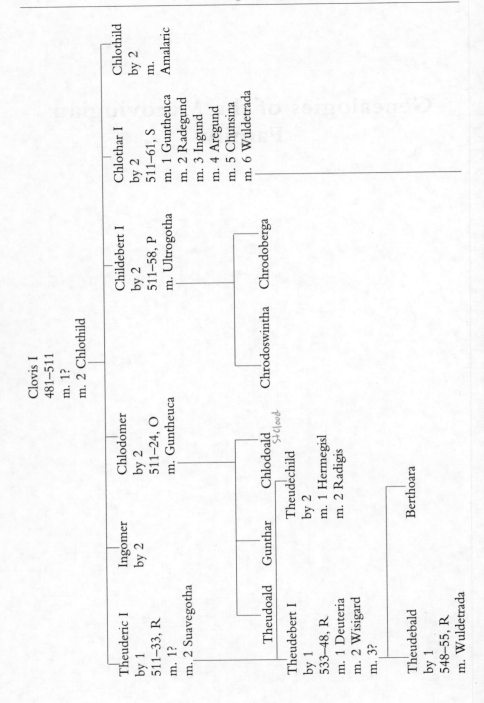

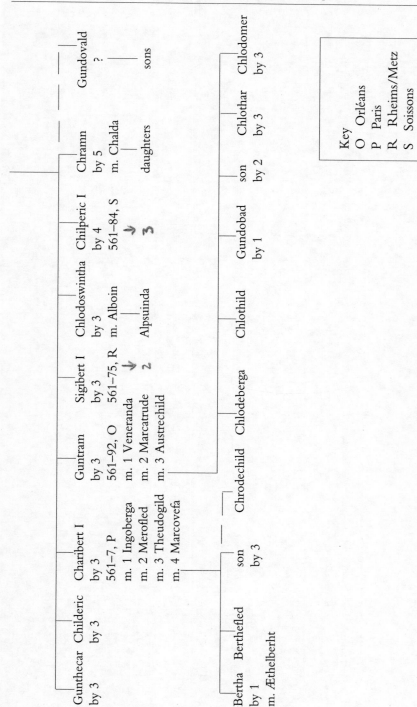

Genealogy of the Merovingian Family 1

Key
O Orléans
P Paris
R Rheims/Metz
S Soissons

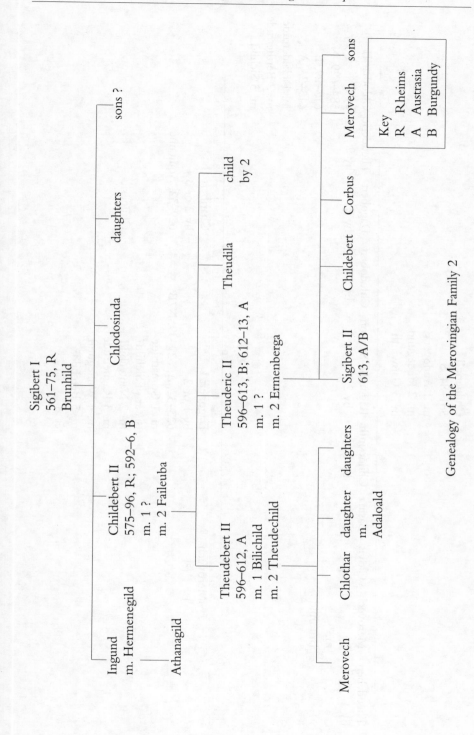

Genealogy of the Merovingian Family 2

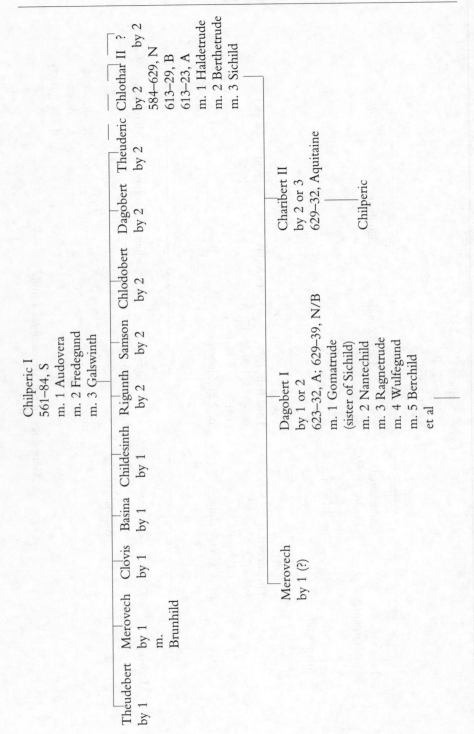

Chilperic I
561–84, S
m. 1 Audovera
m. 2 Fredegund
m. 3 Galswinth

Theudebert
by 1

Merovech
by 1
m.
Brunhild

Clovis
by 1

Basina
by 1

Childesinth
by 1

Rigunth
by 2

Samson
by 2

Chlodobert
by 2

Dagobert
by 2

Theuderic
by 2

Chlothar II ?
by 2   by 2
584–629, N
613–29, B
613–23, A
m. 1 Haldetrude
m. 2 Berthetrude
m. 3 Sichild

Merovech
by 1 (?)

Dagobert I
by 1 or 2
623–32, A; 629–39, N/B
m. 1 Gomatrude
(sister of Sichild)
m. 2 Nantechild
m. 3 Ragnetrude
m. 4 Wulfegund
m. 5 Berchild
et al

Charibert II
by 2 or 3
629–32, Aquitaine

Chilperic

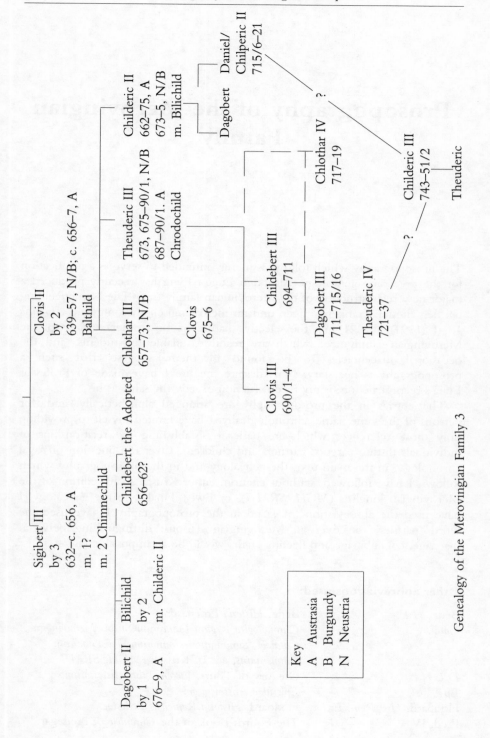

Genealogy of the Merovingian Family 3

Prosopography of the Merovingian Family

The prosopography which follows is merely intended to serve as a justification for the preceding genealogy. Although Eugen Ewig has recently produced a major new reconstruction of the Merovingian family tree ('Die Namengebung bei den ältesten Frankenkönigen und im merowingischen Königshaus', *Francia* 18, 1 (1991), pp. 21–69), the selective nature of most other versions of the Merovingian family tree which are readily available to students, and the occasional inaccuracies to be found in them, suggests that such a prosopography is necessary. Nor, despite the use I have made of Professor Ewig's reconstruction, is my reconstruction exactly the same as his.

The entries in the prosopography are arranged alphabetically, and, for persons of the same name, chronologically. I have limited myself to providing only those references which are basic to establishing the relationships of individuals (listing parents, partners and children). Over the question of royal chronology, in the main text, the genealogy and in the prosopography which follows, I have followed, without citation, either Krusch in his edition of the Merovingian kinglists (*MGH*, *SRM* 7), or Ewig. Finally, in the genealogy, I have used the abbreviation 'm.', and in the prosopography I have used the word 'partner' to cover all Merovingian liaisons: distinguishing between marriage, concubinage and fleeting affairs would be an impossible task.

Other abbreviations used:

Bede, *H.E.*	Bede, *Historia Ecclesiastica*.
Catal.	*Chronologica Regum Francorum Stirpis Merowingicae, Catalogi, computationes annorum vetustatae cum commentariis*, ed. B. Krusch, *MGH*, *SRM* 7.
D.L.H.	Gregory of Tours, *Decem Libri Historiarum*.
Ep. Aust.	*Epistulae Austrasiacae*.
Flodoard, *Hist Rem. Eccl.*	Flodoard, *Historia Remensis Ecclesiae*.
Fred. IV	The Fourth Book of the *Chronicle* of Fredegar.

Fred. cont.   Continuations of the *Chronicle* of Fredegar.
G.A.F.   *Gesta Abbatum Fontanellensium.*
L.H.F.   *Liber Historiae Francorum.*
Pass. Leud. I   *Passio Leudegarii I.*
Paul, *H.L.*   Paul the Deacon, *Historia Langobardorum.*
Pardessus, *Diplomata*   J.M. Pardessus, *Diplomata, Chartae, Leges ad res Gallo-Francicas spectantia.*
Pertz, *Diplomata*   G.H. Pertz, *Diplomata regum Francorum e stirpe Merowingica.*
Vit. Balt.   *Vita Balthildis.*
Vit. Lant.   *Vita Lantberti Fontenallensis.*
Vit. Wilf.   Stephanus, *Vita Wilfridi.*
V.F.   Venantius Fortunatus.

Adaloald   parents: Agilulf/Theudelinda, Fred. IV 34; Paul, *H.L.* IV 25.
parents: daughter of Theudebert II; Paul, *H.L.* IV 30.
d. 626.

Æthelberht   partner: Bertha, *D.L.H.* IV 26; IX 26.

Alboin   partners: Chlodoswintha, Rosamund, *D.L.H.* IV 3, 41; *Ep. Aust.* 8; Paul, *H. L.* I 27.
daughter: Alpsuinda, Paul, *H.L.* I 27.

Alpsuinda   parents: Alboin/Chlodoswintha, Paul, *H.L.* I 27.

Amalaric   parent: Alaric II, *D.L.H.* II 37.
partner: Chlothild, *D.L.H.* III 1.
d. 531, *D.L.H.* III 10

Aregund   sister: Ingund, *D.L.H.* IV 3.
partner: Chlothar I, *D.L.H.* IV 3.
son: Chilperic I, *D.L.H.* IV 3.

Athanagild   parents: Hermegild/Ingund, *Ep. Aust.* 27, 28, 43, 44, 45, 47; *D.L.H.* VIII 28.

Audovera   partner: Chilperic I, *D.L.H.* IV 28.
sons: Theudobert, Merovech, Clovis, *D.L.H.* IV 28.
daughter: Basina, *D.L.H.* V 39; VI 60.

Austrechild   partner: Guntram, *D.L.H.* IV 25.
sons: Chlothar, Chlodomer, *D.L.H.* IV 25.
d. 580, *D.L.H.* V 35.

Balthild	partner: Clovis III, *L.H.F.* 43; Fred. cont. 1; *Vit. Balt.* 3. sons: Chlothar III, Childeric II, Theuderic III, *L.H.F.* 44; Fred. cont. 1; *Vit. Balt.* 3, 5; *Pass. Leud. I*, 2. d. 680.
Basina	parents: Chilperic I/Audovera, *D.L.H.* V 39; VI 34. (? = Childesind in *L.H.F.* 31).
Berchild	partner: Dagobert I, Fred. IV 60.
Bertha	parents: Charibert I/Ingoberga, *D.L.H.* IV 26; IX 26. partner: Æthelberht, *D.L.H.* IV 26; IX 26; Bede, *H.E.* I 25.
Berthefled	parent: Charibert I, *D.L.H.* IX 33.
Berthetrude	? of Burgundian royal blood, Fred. IV 44. partner: Chlothar II, Fred. IV 43. sons: Dagobert I (?), *Gesta Dagoberti I*, 5; Charibert (?), suggested by E. Ewig, 'Die Namengebung bei den ältesten Frankenkönigen und im merowingischen Königshaus', p. 64. d. 618/19, Fred. IV 46.
Berthoara	parent: Theudebert I, V.F. carm. II 11.
Bilichild	partner: Theudebert II, Fred. IV 35. d. 609/10, Fred. IV 37.
Bilichild	parents: Sigibert III/Chimnechild, *Passio Praeiecti*, 24; *Pass. Leud. I*, 10. partner: Childeric II, *L.H.F.* 45; Fred. cont. 2; Pertz, *Diplomata*, 29. d. 675, *L.H.F.* 45; Fred. cont. 2.
Brunhild	parents: Athanagild/Goiswinth, *D.L.H.* IV 27. sister: Galswinth, *D.L.H.* IV 28. partners: Sigibert I, Merovech, *D.L.H.* IV 27; V 2. sons: Childebert II, sons (?), *D.L.H.* IV 51, V 1. daughters: Ingund, Chlodosinda, daughters, *D.L.H.* V 1, 38; VIII 21; IX 10, 16, 20, 25, 28. d. 613, Fred. IV 42.
Chalda	parent: Wilichar, *D.L.H.* IV 20; *L.H.F.* 28. partner: Chramn, *D.L.H.* IV 20; *L.H.F.* 28. daughters: *L.H.* IV 20. d. 560, *D.L.H.* IV 20.

Charibert I

parents: Chlothar I/Ingund, *D.L.H.* IV 3.
partners: Ingoberga, Merofled, Theudogild,
Marcovefa, *D.L.H.* IV 26.
son: *D.L.H.* IV 26.
daughters: Bertha, Berthefled, Chrodechild (?),
D.L.H. IV 26; IX 26, 33, 39.
kingdom: Paris, *D.L.H.* IV 22.
d. 567, *D.L.H.* IV 26.

Charibert II

parents: Chlothar II/Berthetrude or Sichild,
Fred. IV, 55; *Gesta Dagoberti I*, 5 identifies
Sichild as the mother; Ewig, 'Die Namengebung
bei den ältesten Frankenkönigen und im
merowingischen Königshaus', p. 64 argues, in
favour of Berthetrude. Since Chlothar married
Sichild after 618, while Charibert had a son by
632, Berthetrude may seem a more likely
mother, but Sichild is not biologically impossible.
uncle: Brodulf, Fred. IV 55.
son: Chilperic, Fred. IV 67.
kingdom: Aquitaine, Fred. IV 57.
d. 631/2, Fred. IV 67.

Childebert I

parents: Clovis I/Chlothild, *D.L.H.* III 1, 18.
partner: Ultrogotha, *D.L.H.* IV 20; V.F. carm.
VI 6.
daughters: Chrodoswinth, Chrodoberga, *D.L.H.*
IV 20; V.F., *Vita Germani*, 61; Pardessus,
Diplomata, 172.
kingdom: Paris, *D.L.H.* IV 22.
d. 558, *D.L.H.* IV 45.

Childebert II

parents: Sigibert I/Brunhild, *D.L.H.* IV 51; V 1.
partner: Faileuba, *D.L.H.* IX 20.
sons: Theudebert II, Theuderic II, *D.L.H.* VIII
37; IX 4.
daughter: Theudila, Fred. IV 30, 42.
child: *D.L.H.* IX 38.
kingdoms: Rheims, *D.L.H.* V 1; Burgundy,
Fred. IV 14.
d. 596, Fred. IV 16.

Childebert

parents: Theuderic II/concubine, Fred. IV 24.

Childebert

parent: Grimoald; adoptive parent: Sigibert III,
L.H.F. 43; *Catal.* 3.
d. *c.* 662.

Childebert III
parent: Theuderic III, *L.H.F.* 49; Fred. cont. 6.
son: Dagobert III, *L.H.F.* 50; Fred. cont. 7.
d. 711, *L.H.F.* 50; Fred. cont. 7.

Childeric
parents: Chlothar I/Ingund; *D.L.H.* IV 3.

Childeric II
parents: Clovis II/Balthild, *L.H.F.* 44; Fred.
cont. 1; *Vit. Balt.* 5.
partner: Bilichild (daughter of Sigibert III and
Chimnechild), Fred. cont 2.
sons: Dagobert, *L.H.F.* 43: *Vit. Lant.* 4; *Vita II
Audoini*, 41; Daniel/Chilperic II (?).
kingdoms: Austrasia, Neustria, Burgundy, *L.H.F.*
45; Fred. cont. 2; *Pass. Leud. I*, 5–7.
d. 675, *L.H.F.* 45; Fred. cont. 2.

Childeric III
parent: Theuderic IV (?), *G.A.F.* 8; Pertz,
Diplomata, 96; Ewig, 'Die Namengebung bei
den ältesten Frankenkönigen und im
merowingischen Königshaus', p. 68, argues in
favour of Chilperic II being Childeric's father on
the grounds of his name.
son: Theuderic (?), Ewig, 'Die Namengebung
bei den ältesten Frankenkönigen und im
merowingischen Königshaus', p. 69.

Childesinth
parents: Chilperic I/Audovera, *L.H.F.* 31 (? =
Basina).

Chilperic I
parents: Chlothar I/Aregund, *D.L.H.* IV 3.
partners: Audovera, Fredegund, Galswinth,
D.L.H. IV 28.
sons: Theudobert, Merovech, Clovis, Samson,
Chlodobert, Dagobert, Theuderic, Chlothar II
(?), *D.L.H.* IV 28; V 34, 42; VI 23, 27, 41; VII
5; VIII 9; *V.F. carm.* IX, 2–3.
daughters: Basina (? = Childesinth in *L.H.F.* 31),
Rigunth, *D.L.H.* IV 38; V 38, 49; VI 34.
child (?): *D.L.H.* VII 7.
kingdom: Soissons, *D.L.H.* IV 22.
d. 584, *D.L.H.* VI 46.

Chilperic
parent: Charibert, Fred. IV 67.
d. 631/2, Fred. IV 67.

Chilperic II
see Daniel.

Chimnechild
partner: Sigibert III, *Passio Praeiecti*, 24; *Pass.
Leud. I* 10.

	daughter: Bilichild, *Passio Praeiecti*, 24; *Pass. Leud. I*, 24; Pertz, *Diplomata*, 29.
Chlodeberga	parent: Guntram, Council of Valence, 585.
Chlodoald	parent: Chlodomer, *D.L.H.* III 6, 18.
Chlodobert	parents: Chilperic/Fredegund, *D.L.H.* V 34; V.F. carm. IX 4. d. 580, *D.L.H.* V 34.
Chlodomer	parents: Clovis I/Chlothild, *D.L.H.* II 29. partner: Guntheuca, *D.L.H.* III 6. sons: Theudoald, Gunthar, Chlodoald, *D.L.H.* III 6. kingdom: Orléans, *D.L.H.* IV 22. d. 524, *D.L.H.* III 6.
Chlodomer	parents: Guntram/Austrechild, *D.L.H.* IV 25. d. 577, *D.L.H.* V 17.
Chlodosinda	parents: Sigibert I/Brunhild, *D.L.H.* IX 16, 20.
Chlodoswintha	parents: Chlothar/Ingund, *D.L.H.* IV 3. partner: Alboin, *D.L.H.* IV 41; *Ep. Aust.* 8; Paul, *H.L.* I 27. daughter: Alpsuinda, Paul, *H.L.* I 27.
Chlothar I	parents: Clovis I/Chlothild, *D.L.H.* III 1. partners: Guntheuca, Radegund, Ingund, Aregund, Chunsina, Wuldetrada, *D.L.H.* III 6, 7; IV 3, 9. sons: Gunthecar, Childeric, Charibert, Guntram, Sigibert I, Chilperic I, Chramn, Gundovald (?), *D.L.H.* IV 3; VI 24. daughter: Chlodoswintha, *D.L.H.* IV 3. kingdom: Soissons, *D.L.H.* IV 22. d. 561, *D.L.H.* IV 21.
Chlothar	parents: Guntram/Austrechild, *D.L.H.* IV 25. d. 577, *D.L.H.* V 17.
Chlothar II	parents: Chilperic I/Fredegund (?), *D.L.H.* VI 41; VII 7; VII 9. partners: Haldetrude, Berthetrude, Sichild, *Vita II Audoini*, 41; Fred. IV 42, 53; *Gesta Dagoberti I*, 5. sons: Merovech, Dagobert I, Charibert, Fred. IV 25, 26, 47, 55. kingdom: Neustria, *D.L.H.* VII 7; Francia, Fred. IV 43. d. 629, Fred. IV 56.

Chlothar	parent: Theudebert II, Fred. IV 42.
Chlothar III	parents: Clovis II/Balthild, *L.H.F.* 44; Fred. cont. 1; *Vit. Balt.* 5. son: Clovis (?), *Pass. Leud. I*, 19. kingdom: Neustria, Burgundy, *L.H.F.* 44. d. 673.
Chlothar IV	parent: unnamed. kingdom: Austrasia, *L.H.F.* 53; Fred. cont. 10. d. 719, *L.H.F.* 53; Fred. cont. 10.
Chlothild	parent: Chilperic II of Burgundy, *D.L.H.* II 28. partner: Clovis I, *D.L.H.* II 28. sons: Ingomer, Chlodomer, Childebert I, Chlothar I, *D.L.H.* II 29; III 1, 6, 18. daughter: Chlothild, *D.L.H.* III 3, 10. d. 544, *D.L.H.* V 1.
Chlothild	parents: Clovis I/Chlothild, *D.L.H.* III 3, 10. partner: Amalaric, *D.L.H.* III 3, 10. d. 531, *D.L.H.* III 10.
Chlothild	parent: Guntram, Council of Valence, 585; *D.L.H.* IX 20.
Chramn	parents: Chlothar I/Chunsina, *D.L.H.* IV 3. partner: Chalda, *D.L.H.* IV 20; *L.H.F.* 28. daughters: *D.L.H.* IV 20. d. 560, *D.L.H.* IV 20.
Chrodechild	parent: Charibert I (?), *D.L.H.* IX 39.
Chrodoberga	sister: Chrodoswinth, Pardessus, *Diplomata*, 172. parents: Childebert I/Ultrogotha, *D.L.H.* 20; Pardessus, *Diplomata*, 172.
Chrodochild	partner: Theuderic III, *L.H.F.* 49; *Vita Audoini*, 14. sons: Clovis III, Childebert III (?), *L.H.F.* 49; Fred. cont. 6.
Chrodoswintha	sister: Chrodoberga, Pardessus, *Diplomata*, 172. parents: Childebert I/Ultrogotha, D.L.H. 20; V.F. *Vita Germani*, 61; Pardessus, *Diplomata*, 172.
Chunsina	partner: Chlothar I, *D.L.H.* IV 3. son, Chramn, *D.L.H.* IV 3.
Clovis I	parents: Childeric/Basina, *D.L.H.* II 12. partners: ?, Chlothild, *D.L.H.* II 28. sons: Theuderic, Ingomer, Chlodomer,

	Childebert I, Chlothar I, *D.L.H.* II 28, 29; III 1, 6, 18. daughter: Chlothild, *D.L.H.* III 3, 10. d. 511, *D.L.H.* II 43.
Clovis	parents: Chilperic I/Audovera, *D.L.H.* II 28. d. 584, *D.L.H.* V 39.
Clovis II	parents: Dagobert I/Nantechild, Fred. IV 76; *L.H.F.* 42. partner: Balthild, *L.H.F.* 43, 44; Fred. cont. 1; *Vit. Balt.* 3. sons: Chlothar III, Theuderic III, Childeric II, *L.H.F.* 44; Fred. cont. 1; *Vit. Balt.* 5. kingdoms: Neustria, Burgundy, *L.H.F.* 43; Fred. cont. 1. d. 657, Fred. cont. 1; *L.H.F.* 44.
Clovis	parent: Chlothar III (?), *Pass. Leud. I*, 19.
Clovis III	parents: Theuderic III/Chrodochild, *L.H.F.* 49; Fred. cont. 6. d. 694, Fred. cont. 6: *L.H.F.* 49.
Corbus	parents: Theuderic II/concubine, Fred. IV 24. d. 613, Fred. IV 42.
Dagobert	parents: Chilperic I/Fredegund, *D.L.H.* V 34; *V.F.* carm. IX 5. d. 580, *D.L.H.* V 34.
Dagobert I	parents: Chlothar II/Haldetrude or Berthetrude, Fred. IV, 47; *Gesta Dagoberti I*, 5 identifies Berthetrude as the mother; Ewig, 'Die Namengebung bei den ältesten Frankenkönigen und im merowingischen Königshaus', p. 64, argues in favour of Haldetrude, who appears in *Vita II Audoini*, 41, although not as Dagobert's mother. The problem is a chronological one, caused by Fredegar's comments on Berthetrude and Sichild. See above, under 'Charibert II'. partners: Gomatrude, Nantechild, Ragnetrude, Wulfegund, Berchild, et al., Fred. IV 53, 58, 59, 60. sons: Sigibert III, Clovis II, sons, Fred. IV 59; *L.H.F.* 43. kingdoms: Austrasia, Fred. IV 47; Neustria, Burgundy, Fred. IV 57; Aquitaine, Fred. IV 67. d. 639, Fred. IV 79.

Dagobert II   parent: Sigibert III, *L.H.F.* 43.
exiled, 656, Fred. IV 43.
kingdom: Austrasia, *Vit. Wilf.* 28, 33.
d. 679, *Vit. Wilf.* 33.

Dagobert   parents: Childeric II/Bilichild, *L.H.F.* 43; *Vit. Lant.* 4; *Vita II Audoini*, 41.

Dagobert III   parent: Childebert III, *L.H.F.* 50; Fred. cont. 7.
son: Theuderic IV, *L.H.F.* 53.
d. 715, *L.H.F.* 52: Fred. cont. 9.

Daniel
= Chilperic II   parent: Childeric II (?)
kingdom: Neustria, Burgundy, *L.H.F.* 52; Fred. cont. 9–10.
d. 721, *L.H.F.* 53: Fred. cont. 10.

Deuteria   partners: man of Beziers, Theudebert I, *D.L.H.* III 22.
son: Theudebald, *D.L.H.* III 27.
daughter: (by man of Beziers ?), *D.L.H.* III 26.

Ermenberga   parent: Witteric, Fred. IV 30.
partner: Theuderic II, Fred. IV 30.

Faileuba   partner: Childebert II, *D.L.H.* IX 20.
child: *D.L.H.* IX 38.

Fredegund   partner: Chilperic I, *D.L.H.* IV 28.
sons: Samson, Chlodobert, Dagobert, Theuderic, Chlothar II, *D.L.H.* V 22, 34; VI 23, 27, 41; *V.F. carm.* IX 4, 5.
daughter: Rigunth, *D.L.H.* VI 45.
child (?): *D.L.H.* VII 7.
d. 596–7, Fred. IV 17.

Galswinth   parents: Athanagild/Goiswinth, *D.L.H.* IV 27–8.
sister: Brunhild, *D.L.H.* IV 28.
partner: Chilperic I, *D.L.H.* IV 28.

Gomatrude   siblings: Sichild, Brodulf (?), Fred. IV 53, 55.
partner: Dagobert I, Fred. IV 53.

Gundobad   parents: Guntram/Veneranda, *D.L.H.* IV 25.

Gundovald   parent: Chlothar I (?), *D.L.H.* VI 24.
sons: *D.L.H.* IX 28.
d. 585, *D.L.H.* VII 38.

Gunthar   parent: Chlodomer, *D.L.H.* III 6.

Gunthecar   parents: Chlothar I/Ingund, *D.L.H.* III 21; IV 3.

Guntheuca   partners: Chlodomer, Chlothar I, *D.L.H.* III 6.

Guntram   parents, Chlothar I/Ingund, *D.L.H.* IV 3.
partners: Veneranda, Marcatrude, Austrechild, *D.L.H.* IV 25.
sons: Gundobad, son, Chlothar, Chlodomer, *D.L.H.* IV 25.
daughters: Chlodeberga, Chlothild, Council of Valence, 585: *D.L.H.* IX 20.
kingdom: Orléans, *D.L.H.* IV 22.
d. 593, Fred. IV 14.

Haldetrude   partner: Chlothar II, *Vita II Audoini*, 41.
sons: Merovech (?), Dagobert I (?).

Hermegisl   partners: ?, daughter of Theuderic I = Theudechild (?), Procopius, *Wars*, VIII 20.
son: Radigis, Procopius, *Wars*, VIII 20.

Hermenegild   parent: Leovigild, *D.L.H.* IV 38.
partner: Ingund, *D.L.H.* IV 38; V 38.
son: Athanagild, *Ep. Aust.* 27, 28, 43, 44, 45, 47; *D.L.H.* VIII 28.

Ingoberga   partner: Charibert, *D.L.H.* IV 26.
daughter: *D.L.H.* IV 26; IX 26; Bede, *H.E.* I 25.

Ingomer   parents: Clovis I/Chlothild, *D.L.H.* II 29.

Ingund   sister: Aregund, *D.L.H.* IV 3.
partner: Chlothar I, *D.L.H.* IV 3.
sons: Gunthecar, Childeric, Charibert I, Guntram, Sigibert I, *D.L.H.* IV 3.
daughter: Chlodoswintha, *D.L.H.* IV 3.

Ingund   parents: Sigibert I/Brunhild, *D.L.H.* V 38; VIII 21.
partner: Hermenegild, *D.L.H.* V 38.
son: Athanagild, *Ep. Aust.* 27, 28, 43, 44, 45, 47: *D.L.H.* VIII 28.

Marcatrude   parent: Magnachar, *D.L.H.* IV 25.
partner: Guntram, *D.L.H.* IV 25.
son: *D.L.H.* IV 25.

Marcovefa   parent: wool-worker, *D.L.H.* IV 26.
sister: Merofled, *D.L.H.* IV 26.
partner: Charibert, *D.L.H.* IV 26.

Merofled   parent: wool-worker, *D.L.H.* IV 26.
sister: Marcovefa, *D.L.H.* IV 26.
partner: Charibert, *D.L.H.* IV 26.

Merovech   parents: Chilperic I/Audovera, *D.L.H.* IV 28.
partner: Brunhild, *D.L.H.* V 2.
d. 578, *D.L.H.* V 18.

Merovech   parent: Chlothar II, Fred. IV 25.

Merovech   parent: Theudebert II, Fred. IV 38.
d. 613, Fred. IV 38.

Merovech   parent: Theuderic II, Fred. IV 29.
d. 613, Fred. IV 40.

Nantechild   parent: a Saxon, *L.H.F.* 42.
partner: Dagobert I, Fred. IV 58, 60; *L.H.F.* 42.
son: Clovis II, Fred. IV 76 (Clovis II and
Sigibert III, *L.H.F.* 42).
d. 641/2, Fred. IV 90.

Radegund   parent: Berthacar, *D.L.H.* III 7.
partner, Chlothar I, *D.L.H.* III 7.
d. 587, *D.L.H.* IX 2.

Radigis   parent: Hermegisl, Procopius, *Wars*, VIII 20.
partner: daughter of Theuderic I = Theudechild
(?), Procopius, *Wars*, VIII 20.

Ragnetrude   partner: Dagobert I, Fred. IV 59.
son: Sigibert III, Fred. IV 59.

Rigunth   parents: Chilperic I/Fredegund, *D.L.H.* VI 45.
betrothed to Reccared, *D.L.H.* VI 34.

Samson   parents: Chilperic/Fredegund, *D.L.H.* V 22.
d. 578, *D.L.H.* V 22.

Sichild   siblings: Gomatrude, Brodulf (?), Fred. IV 53, 55.
son: Charibert (?), *Gesta Dagoberti I*, 5. See
above, under 'Charibert II'.

Sigibert I   parents: Chlothar I/Ingund, *D.L.H.* IV 3.
partner: Brunhild, D.L.H. IV 27.
sons: Childebert II, sons (?), *D.L.H.* IV 51; V 1.
daughters: Ingund, Chlodosinda, daughters,
D.L.H. V 1, 38; VIII 21; IX 10, 16, 20, 25, 28.
kingdom: Rheims, *D.L.H.* IV 22
d. 675, *D.L.H.* VI 46.

Sigibert II   parents: Theuderic II/concubine, Fred. IV 21.
kingdom: Austrasia, Burgundy, Fred. IV 40.
d. 613, Fred. IV 42.

Sigibert III

parents: Dagobert I/Ragnetrude, Fred. IV 59 (Nantechild, *L.H.F.* 42).
partner: Chimnechild, *Passio Praeiecti* 24; *Pass. Leud. I* 10.
son: Dagobert II, *L.H.F.* 43.
adopted son: Childebert, *L.H.F.* 43; *Catal.* 3.
daughter: Bilichild, *Passio Praeiecti*, 24; *Pass. Leud. I*, 10; Pertz, *Diplomata*, 29.
kingdom: Austrasia, Fred. IV 75.
d. 656 (?).

Suavegotha

parents: Sigismund/Ostrogotha (?), *D.L.H.* III 5: Flodoard, *Hist. Rem. Eccl.* II 1.
partner: Theuderic I, *D.L.H.* III 5.
daughter: Theudechild, Flodoard, *Hist. Rem. Eccl.* II 1.

Theudebald

parents: Theudebert I/Deuteria, *D.L.H.* III 27.
partner: Wuldetrada, *D.L.H.* IV 9.
kingdom: Rheims, *D.L.H.* III 37.
d. 555, *D.L.H.* IV 9.

Theudebert I

parent: Theuderic I, *D.L.H.* III 1.
partners: Deuteria, Wisigard, ?, *D.L.H.* III 20, 22, 27.
son: Theudebald, *D.L.H.* III 27.
daughter: Berthoara, V.F. carm. II 11.
kingdom: Rheims, *D.L.H.* III 23.
d. 548, *D.L.H.* III 36.

Theudebert

parents: Chilperic/Audovera, *D.L.H.* IV 23, 28.
d. 575, *D.L.H.* IV 50.

Theudebert II

parent: Childebert II (?), *D.L.H.* VIII 37; Fred. IV 5, 27.
partners: Bilichild, Theudechild, Fred. IV 35, 37.
sons: Merovech, Chlothar, Fred. IV 38, 42
daughters: Paul, *H.L.* IV 30; *L.H.F.* 38, 39.
kingdoms: Soissons/Meaux, *D.L.H.* IX 32, 36: Austrasia, Fred. IV 16.
d. 612, Fred. IV 38.

Theudechild

parents: Theuderic I/Suavegotha (?), Flodoard, *Hist. Rem. Eccl.* II 1; V.F. IV 25.
partners: Hermegisl (?), Radigis (?), Procopius, *Wars*, VIII 20.

Theudechild

partner: Theudebert II, Fred. IV 37.

Theuderic I	parent: Clovis I, *D.L.H.* II 28. partners: ?, Suavegotha, *D.L.H.* III 5; Flodoard, *Hist. Rem. Eccl.* II 1. son: Theudebert I, *D.L.H.* III 1. daughters: Theudechild, ?, V.F. carm. IV 25: Flodoard, *Hist. Rem. Eccl.* II 1; Procopius, *Wars*, VIII 20. kingdom: Rheims, *D.L.H.* IV 22. d. 533, *D.L.H.* III 23.
Theuderic	parents: Chilperic I/Fredegund, *D.L.H.* VI 23, 27. d. 584, *D.L.H.* VI 34.
Theuderic II	parent: Childebert II, *D.L.H.* IX 4: Fred. IV 7. partners: ?, Ermenberga, Fred. IV 21, 24, 29, 30. sons: Sigibert II, Childebert, Corbus, Merovech, sons (?), Fred. IV 21, 24, 29, 36. kingdoms: Burgundy, Fred. IV 16; Austrasia, Fred. IV 38. d. 613, Fred. IV 39.
Theuderic III	parents: Clovis II/Balthild, *L.H.F.* 44; Fred. cont. 1. partner: Chrodochild, *L.H.F.* 49. sons: Clovis III, Childebert III, Chlothar IV (?), *L.H.F.* 49, Fred. cont. 6. kingdoms: Neustria/Burgundy, *L.H.F.* 45; Fred. cont 2, 3; Austrasia, *L.H.F.* 46. d. 690/1, *L.H.F.* 49; Fred. cont. 6.
Theuderic IV	parent: Dagobert III, *L.H.F.* 53; Fred. cont. 10. d. 737.
Theuderic	parent: Childeric III, G.A.F. X 4.
Theudila	parent: Childebert II, Fred. IV 30, 42.
Theudoald	parent: Chlodomer, *D.L.H.* III 6.
Theudogild	parent: a shepherd, *D.L.H.* IV 26. partner: Charibert I, *D.L.H.* IV 26.
Ultrogotha	partner: Childebert I, *D.L.H.* IV 20; V.F. carm. VI 6. daughters: Chrodoswinth, Chrodoberga, *D.L.H.* IV 20; V.F., *Vita Germani* 61; Pardessus, *Diplomata*, 172.
Veneranda	partner: Guntram, *D.L.H.* IV 25. son: Gundobad, *D.L.H.* IV 25.

Wisigard

parents: Waccho/Austrigusa, Paul, *H.L.* I 21.
sister: Wuldetrada, Paul, *H.L.* I 21.
partner: Theudebert I, *D.L.H.* III 20, Paul, *H.L.* I 21.

Wuldetrada

parents: Waccho/Austrigusa, Paul, *H.L.* I 21.
sister: Wisigard, Paul, *H.L.* I 21.
partners: Theudebald, Chlothar I, Garibald, *D.L.H.* IV 9: Paul, *H.L.* I 21.

Wulfegund

partner: Dagobert I, Fred. IV 60.

Maps

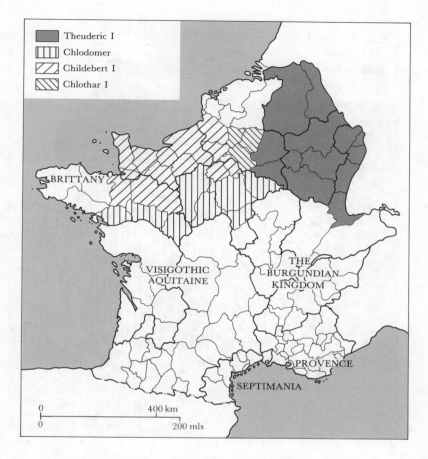

Map 1. The division of the Merovingian Kingdom in 511
[Maps 1–3 show the three most important divisions of the Merovingian
kindom in the sixth century. They are based on E. Ewig, *Die fränkischen
Teilungen und Teilreiche*. It is not possible to assign every *civitas* to a king with
any degree of certainty. I have, therefore, left some *civitates* unassigned. For
the division of 561, however, I have assumed that Guntram's Burgundian
territories in 561 included all that he is known to have held in that region
after 567. I have not, on the other hand, assigned the northern part of *Belgica
Secunda* to Chlothar I in 511 or to Chilperic I in either 561 or 567, which
may lead to a substantial underestimate of their lands.]

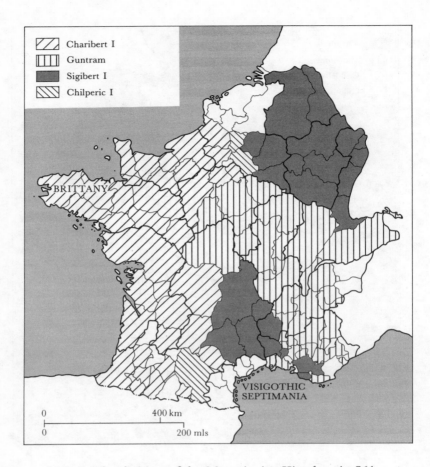

Map 2. The division of the Merovingian Kingdom in 561

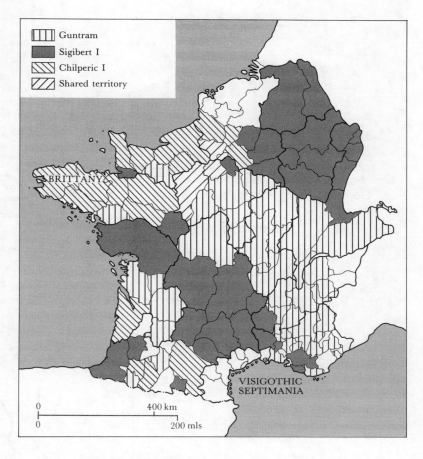

Map 3. The division of the Merovingian kingdom in 567

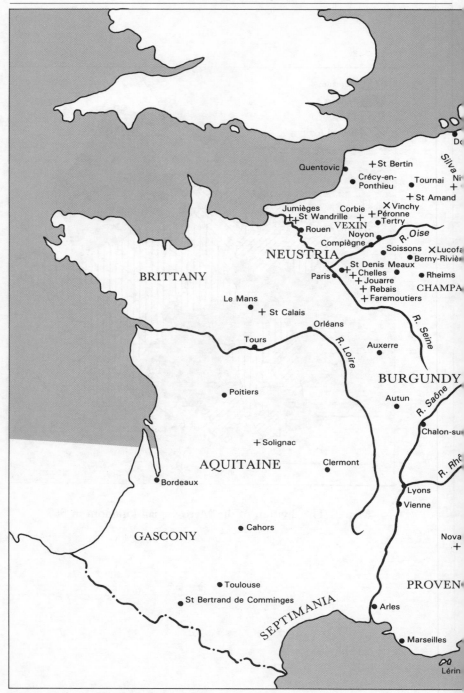

Map 4. Francia and the territories to the east of the Rhine

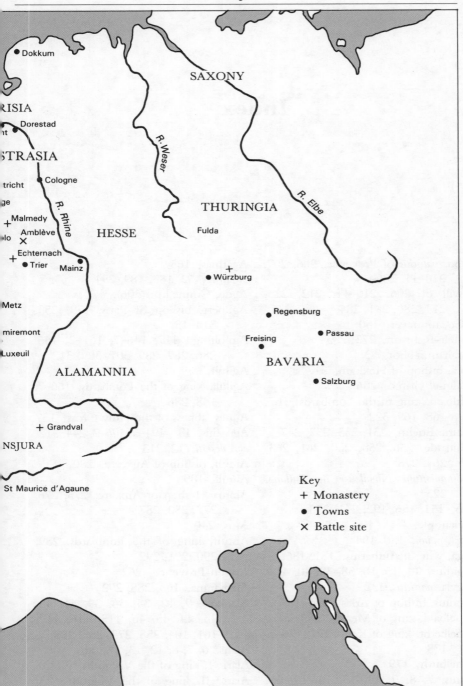

Dokkum

SAXONY

RISIA

Dorestad

nt

STRASIA

R. Weser

tricht

Cologne

ge

R. Rhine

+ Malmedy

R. Elbe

lo

Amblève

THURINGIA

HESSE

×

Echternach

Fulda

+

Trier

Mainz

+

Würzburg

Metz

Regensburg

miremont

Passau

Freising

Luxeuil

BAVARIA

ALAMANNIA

Salzburg

+ Grandval

NSJURA

Key

+ Monastery

St Maurice d'Agaune

• Towns

× Battle site

Index